T0395907

Religious Ways of Experiencing Life

Religious Ways of Experiencing Life: A Global and Narrative Approach surveys world religions, using the narratives and discourses of each tradition to describe it in its own terms. Carl Olson examines each tradition's practices, teachings, material culture, roles of women, and path to salvation, as well as the experiences of its followers. The exploration of lived experience draws out and emphasizes the plural nature of religious traditions. The volume includes chapters on all current major world religions, as well as material on ancient religions of the Mediterranean, indigenous North American and African spiritual traditions, and New Age and new religious movements. Featuring timelines and suggestions for further reading, this text will be of interest to undergraduate students seeking a broad introduction to World Religion or Lived Religion.

Carl Olson is Professor of Religious Studies at Allegheny College. He is the author of 18 books, including *Indian Asceticism: Power, Violence, and Play* (2015), *The Allure of Decadent Thinking: Religious Studies and the Challenge of Postmodernism* (2013), and *Religious Studies: The Key Concepts* (Routledge 2011).

Religious Ways of Experiencing Life

A Global and Narrative Approach

Carl Olson

Routledge
Taylor & Francis Group

NEW YORK AND LONDON

First published 2016
by Routledge
711 Third Avenue, New York, NY 10017

and by Routledge
2 Park Square, Milton Park, Abingdon, Oxon, OX14 4RN

Routledge is an imprint of the Taylor & Francis Group, an informa business

Library of Congress Cataloging-in-Publication Data
Olson, Carl.
   Religious ways of experiencing life : a global and narrative approach /
Carl Olson. — 1st ed.
      pages cm
   1. Religions. I. Title.
   BL80.3.O47 2016
   200—dc23
   2015031605

ISBN: 978-0-415-70660-5 (hbk)
ISBN: 978-0-415-70661-2 (pbk)
ISBN: 978-1-315-88737-1 (ebk)

Typeset in Goudy
by Apex CoVantage, LLC

This book is dedicated to my longtime colleague and friend Glenn Holland, a man of many talents and good cheer. Hollywood lost out on his talents, but Gatorland was the winner when he joined the college on the hill.

Contents

Preface

This textbook exhibits less of a general thesis than a particular approach that distinguishes it from previous texts of this genre. The approach of this book to its subject (various religious traditions around the globe) is embodied in the proposed title. A religious way of experiencing life stands in sharp contrast to a secular way of doing the same thing because religion is a quest for spiritual experience, meaning, and power. This does not make religion necessarily unique, but it does suggest that it is different than a secular approach to life. The term "experience" must be grasped as plural within both a global context and within particular religious traditions and understood as integral to all religions, even though the experiences are very different within a tradition and in comparison to other traditions. Within a particular religious tradition, there are often many ways to experience religion that include cognitive, emotional, sexual, and aesthetic forms of perception and feelings. Some of these ways of experiencing religion stand in tension or even conflict with each other. For many religious traditions around the globe, there is little or no distinction between life and religion because they are synthesized into a seamless culture. In fact, some traditions do not even have a term that is equivalent to the Western notion of "religion." In accordance with these remarks, this textbook stresses the plurality of particular religious traditions around the world, such as Hinduism, Buddhism, Islam, or Christianity, and their differences with contrary traditions. Moreover, particular religious traditions manifest rich differences within its particular tradition.

The first chapter of this textbook is intended to provide students with an introduction to the nature of religion and a discussion of the definition of the subject, its roots, the problem of otherness, the problematic nature of "world religions," an example of how certain features of religion are intertwined with narrative, power, violence, and play, the wide variety of methodological approaches to the study of religion, the nature of religious experience, the global nature of religion, and the role of comparison. The chapter ends with a discussion of pluralism and secularism. The overall intention of this chapter is to introduce students to the discipline of religious studies, its terminology and problems.

The second chapter includes a selection of three religions of the past that have become museum artifacts. These selected dead religions of the past are Egyptian, Greek, and Roman. These Mediterranean religions provide historical context for the later discussions of Judaism and Christianity. Other ancient religions such as Gnosticism and Manichaeism are discussed briefly within the context of early Christianity. The remaining chapters are focused on currently living religious traditions still being practiced somewhere around the globe.

The third and fourth chapters are devoted respectively to selections of Native American and African religious traditions. The inclusion of these mostly oral traditions provides balance in comparison to more technologically developed and textual cultures discussed later in the book. It also affords readers an opportunity to learn more about the language and concepts of religious studies, such as divine beings, cultural heroes, ritual process, sacrifice, rites of passage (cf. initiation and death), sacred persons, cult organizations, sexuality, spirituality, ecology, and millenarianism.

The remaining chapters cover religions around the globe that are identified in the table of contents. These chapters will include a discussion of some of the following topics as they pertain to each tradition: worldview, history, basic teachings, ritual practice, spiritual experience, social aspects, material and artistic expressions of the religions, and eschatology (teaching of last things). These topics will be covered within a narrative context in order to invite students into the various religions and help them comprehend these traditions. By way of confession and honesty, the various chapters of this book do not include extensive historical data for each religious tradition because the importance of time and history is built into its narrative approach. Moreover, the major religious cultures are accompanied by a concise historical chronology. There is also more emphasis on the formative periods of a particular religious tradition. The individual chapters will also highlight the religious lives of ordinary people and women usually neglected by other textbooks in favor of the mainline tradition. This will provide a more balanced presentation of the particular traditions because the prevailing tradition is usually developed and presented from a masculine and elitist viewpoint in the major texts.

The concluding chapter of the book examines new religious movements such as Baha'i, Scientology, Krishna consciousness, and several others. To understand these new religious movements, I will provide some historical context for them by initially discussing esotericism in the West and New Age movements. This chapter also includes a discussion of some black religious movements.

There are some scholars of religion who are opposed to teaching theology within the context of a college or university religious studies department. These scholars think that theology belongs to a seminary setting and not a secular situation where religion can be studied critically by scholars and students. I do not completely agree with that position. However, I do not give very much attention to theology in this text, although I do discuss the belief systems of various religions. In some religious traditions, one may or may not be able to distinguish between theology and philosophy within a given tradition, a point that is especially germane to Eastern cultures.

I want to thank the folks at Routledge for their patience. A medical leave from teaching enabled me to complete this book in a shorter time span. Nurse Peggy diligently worked to restore my health. When well, it is a pleasure to work with colleagues who are the best folks with whom one can hope to work. Over the years, the teaching and course needs of the department challenged me to stretch my research and teaching responsibilities, making the college on the hill a stimulating and great place to work. In a sense, this book is the culmination of a long teaching career that has also enabled me to learn more about different religious traditions, enabling my career to be a wonderful adventure in foreign lands.

1   Introduction

A basic presupposition of this book is that religion is an elusive subject because of its complexity and its tendency to not readily reveal its secrets and its interconnections with other features of a particular culture. For the purposes of coming to grips with the nature of religion, we can imagine culture as a huge spider web, while religion represents a thread in the web, a single strand among many other threads that are interconnected in a culture. We can also imagine a spider as the creator of the web, a position occupied non-metaphorically during life by human actors and their experiences. Conceiving of this situation in the plural, it is important to be aware that this situation suggests the communal or collective nature of creating culture and the fact that humans are social creatures, creating elements of culture together with others. Within the created spider web, there are gaps that observers can see that represent the blank or invisible points of culture that invite others to fill them. In other words, for those agents either inside or outside of the web, there are additional spaces that can be filled in or developed in the future. Thus, a culture is always a work in progress, with its development never truly ending despite periods of stagnation, decline, or spontaneous bursts of creativity. The spider web metaphor also indicates that religion is part of a larger web that also includes language, spiritual experiences of various kinds, social system, laws, legal system, symbols, games, dance, song, narratives, and customs connected to dress, diet, and ordinary habits.

Culture is derived from the Latin term *colere*, which suggests an original sense of cultivating crops and animals. As it evolved, culture expanded to include cultivating human beings before becoming an abstract condition of achieved development. In more recent times, culture is attached to a description of educated people capable of creating a body of artistic products. Culture and religion are so intertwined, as the web metaphor suggests, that it can be safely asserted that there is no religion outside of culture. The entire web of culture is inundated with meaning because it is created by humans seeking, struggling with, and purposively finding and creating meaning. It is the duty of the student of religion to discern the meaningful messages, which will differ from one cultural complex to another.

From a cross-cultural perspective, it is often difficult to separate a culture from its religion because they are so intertwined that it is difficult to differentiate between them. From this same perspective, a student must admit that there is no such thing as religion, but there are only religions and their cultures, just as there are many threads that constitute a spider web. Our spider metaphor also suggests the central place occupied by the spider, which represents the indispensable part played by a human creature and her experiences. The metaphorical spider web thus points to the creative abilities of human agents, who create cultural elements such as religion. This implies that humans, who are seekers of meaning and power, are constructors of culture and religion by means of a social/historical process.

If truth(s) is constructed by humans within a socio-cultural context and process, humans can interpret and understand the messages of truth embodied within a religious culture. What religion contributes to a culture is a web of meaning and value, which are ways of life that are transmitted from one generation to the following one. Thus, culture and religion constitute a system of meanings. It thus behooves a student of religion to place each aspect of a religion being studied into its cultural context. Many cultures, however, deny their religions are created by their subjects but rather give the credit to a god or several deities and/or cultural heroes, even if the creative handiwork of humans is just under the surface of the tradition's narratives.

The central place of religion in a particular culture is proven by an inability for any student to answer the following question: Is there any culture around the globe—past or present—that does not have some type of religion or actions that can be interpreted as religious behavior? The point of such a question is to indicate how difficult it can be to differentiate religion from culture. But this does not mean that culture and religion can be equated.

The Role of Experience

The one constant that all religious traditions share cross-culturally is experience of some kind, although it is pushing it too far to claim that experience is the essence of religion. These religious experiences can include conversion, dreams, a vague felt presence of something greater and more powerful than oneself, hallucinations, mystical experiences of different kinds, an experience of the numinous, out of body experiences, trance states, feeling possessed, and visions. The seventeenth century Zen master Hakuin refers, for example, to an enlightenment experience triggered by a *kōan* (an enigmatic statement used for meditation purposes) that he invented about the sound made by a single hand clapping. When this sound enters your ear all minds are revealed, not a single bit of ignorance remains, birth and death no longer exist because "[a]ll is vast perfection, all is vast emptiness." Placing this type of experience within its cultural context is important for a reader in order to grasp its significance and meaning within a particular culture.

The phenomenon of experience can be traced back to an Indo-European verbal root (*per*) meaning to attempt, venture, or risk. In Middle English and Old French, we get from Latin *experiential*, denoting trial, proof, or experiment. In German, we find the term *Erlebnis*, which literally means what has been lived through. The German term conveys the sense of living through a sequence of events that can be a ritual drama, a social drama, or a narrative drama. In addition to meaning living through a situation, experience in the German sense is also a reflection on what has occurred. Whether experience is grasped in the German or English senses of the term, it is always richer than can ever be captured by formal categories, which have a tendency to make experience into something static and synchronic. Experience is something lived, charged with emotion, occurs to an embodied person, and is associated with volition and cognition. Based on accounts from various kinds of religious traditions and what their primary sources suggest, it might be best to grasp experience as a process that occurs within a cultural context immersed within a particular cultural world in which a subject perceives, thinks, feels, and desires, rendering culture, our spider web, an ensemble of various kinds of experiences.

These various types of religious experience can be expressed and preserved by a religious tradition either orally or in writing. In many religious traditions around the world, religious experiences are intertwined with narratives—oral or written—about the history and transmitted traditions of a given culture. The religious experiences appear to be very similar on the surface, but this can be deceiving because the cultural context is always different to some degree.

The effort to discern what these various types of religious experience are exactly and what they mean with any precision is a heroic task for any reader or scholar because the very nature of experience is not evident and the nature of religion is elusive. Religious experiences are located within particular cultures and societies and can be both public and subjective. In either case—public or subjective—experiences are meaningful to the extent of being soaked with meaning. As many narratives agree, religious experiences give a person power that can be exhibited by acute mental and physical powers to do extraordinary things, such as read other minds, levitate, fly, or perform miracles. The acquisition of powers does not negate the fact that religious experiences are attained within a given relational, embodied, social setting and historical context that point beyond an individual experience to something else. The experience itself is self-evident and self-validating for the person having an experience because it is akin to a personal revelation that a person verifies for himself.

Humans experience phenomena at different levels of consciousness. At a lower level of consciousness, we experience things without thinking about them or being only vaguely aware of what we are experiencing, whereas at a higher level of consciousness we are consciously aware about what we are experiencing. Human experience is always embodied, even if a religious experience gives us a sensation that transports us out of our bodies. In addition to being embodied, human experience is also grounded in language, a society, a culture, and historical tradition. This scenario suggests that humans experience and act in complex ways.

When an embodied human being rises to a higher level of consciousness, that person becomes aware that she is conscious of her experience. To be consciously aware of what one is doing, or to be conscious of consciousness, separates humans from other types of animals, even though humans share with many animals a primary consciousness that includes basic attention, perceptions, memory, emotion, action, and awareness. To be aware of conscious awareness involves language and its concomitant complex mental states. Religion is not, however, simply associated with conscious awareness and experience. From a cross-cultural perspective, "religion," as a word or characterization of what people are doing, is rather limited and not totally adequate in some cultural contexts. But it is the term that has been used by Western scholars for a long period of time and is the word most familiar to a Western readership. Thus, until a more accurate term is generally agreed on, it is useful to adhere to what is familiar by retaining the term "religion" for this book.

Mystical Experience

Although "mysticism" is a Western term, there is ample evidence for its existence in a cross-cultural context. It is not to be confused with other profound religious types of experiences, such as trance states, extraordinary visions, or aesthetic sensitivity, even though a mystical experience might also include some of these features. It is connected to an Indo-European language verbal root *muo* (meaning to be mum, mute, or mysterious). The term is associated in Greek culture with mystery cults—Eleusinian, Dionysian, and Orphic—that are called *muein* (literally to close the eyes), suggesting something hidden from perception. After Christian writers applied the term to Jesus, it was adopted later and taken to refer to a deep, profound, direct, personal, spiritual experience, while retaining its earlier association with secrecy and mystery.

In his classic work *The Varieties of Religious Experience*, William James (1842–1910), a Harvard University psychologist, identified four characteristics of mysticism that are still germane today: (1) ineffability; (2) noetic quality; (3) transiency; and (4) passivity. Each of these features needs to be unpacked by defining them. The ineffable quality of mysticism means that the experience cannot be captured in language because it is too profound and mysterious for words to convey its content. Ironically, many mystics acknowledge this difficulty but then proceed to write about their experiences at great length. In addition, the ineffability of the mystic experience implies that it is a direct and personal experience that one cannot impart to another person. Its noetic quality means that the experience involves some new knowledge. The third quality implies that the experience is usually of a short duration, whereas passivity refers to the mystic's conviction that he encounters or grasps a great power over which he does not have control. Subsequent to James, other scholars worked to determine different types of mysticism. At Oxford University, R. C. Zaehner distinguished a threefold typology: (1) panenhenic (nature mysticism); (2) theistic (an intimate relation or union with a personal deity); and (3) monistic (a union with or realization of the single reality of the universe).

In more recent scholarly debates about the subject of mysticism, there evolved two camps: The older one is called the position of viewing mysticism as representing a perennial philosophy, and the other position can be labeled the contextual position. The former position grasps mystical experience as universal and basically the same cross-culturally, although it is common to distinguish the experience itself and its interpretation with the experience being very similar and its interpretation accounting for differences. This popular position has been challenged by those scholars adopting the contextual approach to the subject, which claims that mystical experiences are products of culture, rendering it impossible for the occurrence of a new or original experience. In other words, mystical experiences are completely determined by the culture of the mystic, whereas the weaker version of the contextual position claims that experiences are mediated through cultural filters associated with language, symbols, history, ritual action, and a religious belief system. With this type of emphasis on differences, it is impossible and nonsensical to claim that there is such an event as a pure experience or pure consciousness. From the contextual viewpoint, a mystic is molded by his culture, and any experience is mediated through his culture.

In what is sometimes called the unitive experience, the mystic enters a state of ecstasy, which involves feelings of exaltation, heightened excitement, and bliss. These feelings can become so intense that the mystic loses an awareness of her surroundings and physical body. The experience of ecstasy also gives one the sensation of standing outside of oneself. In this state of ex-stasis, a mystic's consciousness separates from her physical body, creating a sensation of being disembodied that gives one the feeling of being free from the limitations of the ordinary state of embodiment. Attention to mystics from various religious cultures are discussed throughout this book.

The Nature of Religion

When doing cross-cultural studies, it is possible to encounter cultural traditions that do not have a word for religion, even though it is evident to an observer that a particular culture has institutions, structures, and practices that are familiar features of a religion. From a cross-cultural perspective, the scholar is condemned to use imperfect categories, such as religion and experience, to discuss global religious traditions. Nonetheless, religion represents for many people of the globe a way of life that is meaningful and holds the promise of salvation however a particular tradition might define it. By traveling this way of life, a person gains a sense of personal identity, finds a secure location that provides answers to suffering and death within an often hostile world.

A person walks the path of life provided by religion in an embodied condition. The actions required for practicing—praying, fasting, meditating, performing rituals, going on pilgrimage, or being silent—are accomplished by having a body. Humans are able to build temples, churches, statues, or works of art with their bodies. In some religious traditions, the body is a symbol and microcosm of the universal macrocosm. In this way, the human body symbolizes a bridge between nature and culture. Of course, without a body, one could not traverse the path of religion. It is possible for humans to understand their world because they are embodied within a complex set of relationships consisting of bodily, social, linguistic, historical, and intellectual components.

In their embodied condition, humans perform various types of actions that are often related to religious activities of various kinds, such as the following: prayer; meditation; celibacy; ritual; festive; storytelling; singing; bowing; prostration; pilgrimage; preserving scriptures; doing good deeds to help others; begging; asceticism; counseling and comforting the afflicted; healing the sick and infirm. These types of volitional actions are performed purposively for the benefit of oneself or others. Whatever the actions performed—individually and collectively—they are part of an overall quest for coming to grips with a comprehension about the meaning of life. This quest for meaning often takes the actor beyond himself, as evident in certain types of religious experience that enable a person to transcend himself. Within the religious context of ritual, actions are, for instance, often symbolic and allow the meaning of the ritual to become manifested to others. The embodied actions associated with ritual sacrifice, for example, occur in conjunction and interaction with other embodied beings. Even though ritual actions are habitual and routine, they are intentionally enacted by the embodied participants. The symbolic action associated with ritual is profoundly symbolic and allows one access to the mysteries of life. Whether human actions are symbolic or otherwise, they enable religious persons to find meaning and to perform meaning.

Over the past three hundred years of scholarship, religion has proven to be an elusive term to define. A brief review of its use by Western scholars can elucidate its problematic nature. Attempts to isolate primary features of the nature of religion, generally speaking, fall into six types: experiential, substantive, functionalist, family resemblance, postmodern, and cognitive.

An experiential definition represents an attempt to focus on a perceived fundamental religious experience and to construct a theory around it. An early example of this type of approach to religion can be discovered with the work of Friedrich Schleiermacher (1766–1834), a Protestant religious thinker, and his definition of the essence of religion as a feeling of absolute dependence. This occurs when a person encounters something greater than oneself. Another excellent example of this type of definition is Otto's idea of the holy. Using primary sources from the formative Judeo-Christian scriptures and Latin terminology, Rudolf Otto (1869–1937) defines the holy as endowed with power, reason, purpose, love, and good will. The preferred way to grasp the holy is to examine human reactions to it. When the holy is recognized as something other than and transcendent to oneself, it is natural for a person to react to this presence with dread and fascination that causes a human to repel from it with fear but to also feel drawn to its mysterious, overpowering, and wholly otherness. A person with a numinous state of mind recognizes the mystery of the wholly other, developing a feeling of dependence that Otto calls creature feeling or consciousness. For Otto, the essence of religion is to be discovered in a subjective experience of the numinous, which represents a unique, irreducible phenomenon that is an a priori (independent of empirical experience) category. Consequently, religion is something special and separate from every other thing in the world and internal to the experience of a subject. Later scholars reject Otto's definition because it is based on evidence from monotheistic traditions and thus has limited cross-cultural value with cultures that are polytheistic.

The substantive type of definition seeks to identify a basic belief within a religious tradition in order to construct a definition of religion. A good example of this type of definition might be a religion's belief in spiritual beings. Influenced by the phenomenological philosophy of Martin Heidegger, Paul Tillich (1886–1965), a Protestant theologian, defined religion as a person's "ultimate concern." This definition was broadly embraced by scholars of religion for a time during the mid-twentieth century because they recognized its basic neutrality and potential application to religions of foreign cultures.

A functionalist definition of religion attempts to call attention to how religion operates within a particular culture. This type of definition is primarily evident among anthropologists, such as Bronislaw K. Malinowski (1884–1942), who introduced the participant observer method, which required a scholar to live with the people being studied, learn their language, interact with them, describe their culture, and discern how the religion functions within a given society. Distinguishing between magic and religion, Malinowski could still see that they functioned to alleviate anxiety associated with the uncertainty and difficult nature of human life. If religion originated as a response to emotional stress and functioned as a catharsis for people to enable them to cope with the challenges of life, Malinowski equated the function of a religion with its purpose. Magic differed from religion because it was utilitarian and instrumental, was intended to bring about a desired result, such as a cure for a specific illness, and was the precise cause bringing about the desired result, whereas religion possessed no utility and represented an end in itself.

In contrast to the functionalist definition of religion, a family resemblance approach seeks to isolate over-lapping similarities that are similar to each other but not exactly the same in all instances. These similarities can be theoretical (beliefs, myths, and doctrines), practical (rites and moral codes), social (institutions, social behavior, and sacred personages), and experiential (emotions, visions, and trances). The family resemblance approach to the subject of religion was inspired by Ludwig Wittgenstein (1889–1951), a University of Cambridge philosophy professor. Ninian Smart (1927–2001) used this approach for the study of religion, which freed him from having to define the nature of religion. Smart identified six dimensions of religion: doctrine, mythology, ethics, ritual, social institutions, and religious experience. Another scholar influenced by Wittgenstein was John Hicks, who argued that religion could not be defined, although it could be described, because the plurality of religions from a worldwide perspective made it impossible to discover their common essence. The advantage of the family resemblance approach enabled a scholar to account for the similarities and differences between religions. According to Hicks' cross-cultural perspective, religions share a concern for the real, which he thought was a neutral concept that affirmed different types of transcendent belief.

The postmodern position emphasizes the vagueness, uncertainty, and difficulty of arriving at a viable definition of religion because of its unstable and ambiguous nature. If the modern study of religion owes a considerable debt to the influence of Enlightenment philosophy, postmodernism, despite its wide variety, stands opposed to the Enlightenment project because many find it static and not dynamic. Generally speaking, postmodern thinkers stress difference, becoming, contingency, and chance. Postmodernists tend to oppose Western metaphysics and ontology as foundations for things within the world, suggesting that there are no universal truths even though many argue for a multiplicity of truths. For postmodernists, knowledge is incomplete, fragmented, and a victim of historical and cultural forces that no one can harness or control. Humans are at the mercy of discontinuity, rupture, irregularity, plurality, and simulacrum, a hyper-reality that simulates life.

The French philosopher Jacques Derrida speaks about religion as a presence/absence, which he identifies with God. This line of thinking calls attention to the ambiguous nature of religion, which can be understood as an ellipsis (a mark of absence), making religion elusive and difficult to grasp with any degree of precision. Being influenced by the philosophy of Derrida, Mark C. Taylor indicates the elusive nature of religion because it is always eluding our intellectual grasp by virtue of the fact that it is always withdrawing from a student. Nonetheless, the disappearing act of religion allows appearances of itself to emerge even as it continually withdraws. This makes it difficult for the scholar of religion to find it because it is always slipping away, but could appear in strange and unexpected places.

In contrast to the elusive nature of religion for postmodern thinkers, the cognitive approach is grounded in the process of evolution and the findings of cognitive scientists. This line of thinking asserts that religion can be explained by the process of evolution and how it shapes our minds, suggesting that humans have been programed to practice religion because it helps human beings cope with basic survival and other aspects of life. The cognitive approach will be discussed further at a later point when reviewing methodological approaches to the study of religion.

If we retreat to the origin of the modern term religion and acknowledge that it is a term originating in the West, it is possible to find it in the Latin term *religio*, a term referring to the fear of God or other divine beings by humans.

This emotional response to divine stimulation in the ancient Roman mind includes actions associated with rites, although its exact etymology is uncertain. The Roman writer Cicero traces *religio*, for example, to *religare*, meaning to gather together, continuously passing over something, or to read again. Other etymological possibilities are discovered with the term *religare*, which means binding something together. These kind of terminological derivations are indicative of the social nature of *religio*, an etymological result that reflects the practice of religion in ancient Roman culture with its emphasis on the family, society, and state as the context for the practice of religion.

Where does this leave us with a definition of religion? Because there are many definitions and little agreement about the precise nature of religion, does this mean that a student of the subject should jettison all and any definitions of the nature of religion and possibly substitute another term, such as culture or worldview, as some scholars have proposed? We can acknowledge that numerous problems exist with the term religion, but an equally vague or problematic term does not seem to necessarily be the answer, because such terms carry their own baggage and problems. For the purposes of this textbook, I propose retaining the term religion for practical purposes, even if it has limitations in a cross-cultural context. What we can positively affirm is that religion is a complex notion and needs to be understood within a context that reflects its many other associations.

Although this book will retain the term religion, it will not use terminology such as world religions because it owes its origin to scholars working during the historical period of colonialism with its domination and exploitation of Third World countries around the late nineteenth century. This text will also not use the term comparative religion because it also originated around the colonial period and was used by Western scholars to prove the superiority of Christianity over foreign religions, a purpose that also concealed Christian and European universalism that became the standard to measure other religions.

Just because the comparative method was misused during colonialism, this does not mean that we should completely discard it. Comparison is basic to thinking and learning among humans. When we encounter something new—an object or an experience—we invariably compare it to what we already know. Moreover, it is possible to compare similar phenomena in a rigorous way that includes recognizing differences and not simply seeing sameness. By recognizing, identifying, and articulating differences between one religious phenomenon and another, we liberate ourselves from our ethnocentrism and increase our self-awareness, and we free the other by letting the other be who she is, undistorted by us. Comparison can help us progressively to understand the other, although this does not imply that our understanding will be without limits. Our aim must be to understand the other within their cultural context. Finally, religions invite the use of comparison because they have historically compared themselves to other religions and criticized other religions.

Culture and Social Construction of Religion

The spider of the cultural web metaphor that began this chapter is not a single figure but should rather be conceived as a collective social body of creators working as a shared humanity to define themselves, find meaning together, and empower themselves within the context of an often hostile world. Therefore, there are a multitude of creative spiders; and it is their shared life experiences that provide the material to build a web. Within a social milieu, spiders (humans) work to create a viable and vibrant culture by means of their collective intellects, imaginations, religious experiences, and actions that is located within an ever-evolving and dynamic web of meaning. This scenario suggests that humans are not innately religious but learn to be religious by virtue of shared practices and socialization. Within the context of this social process, human instinctual behavior is transformed into more enduring and differentiated forms of communication, organization of social relations, reflection on the meaning of life, and its possible meaning. The social dimension of culture is indicative of a development that points to culture and its other features, such as religion, as a biological necessity.

The social nature of the religious aspect of a given culture is directly related to various types of actions that often intervene in a crisis situation or are embedded in the cultural pattern of life. Social and religious cultural actions are manifested by sacrifices, rites of passage, prayers, pilgrimages, reciting of formulas, chanting sacred utterances, and constructing religious objects such as churches, mosques, and monasteries, as well as icons and paintings. By enabling humans to successfully traverse dangerous situations, these social practices give humans protection, i.e., a means of overcoming periods of crisis, make a person powerful, and promise salvation or liberation. This is not, however, true of all actions, because humans perform most actions in a habitual way. This habitual way of acting can be accomplished consciously, unconsciously, or semiconsciously. But when a crisis arises or something triggers a religious experience, humans tend to snap to conscious awareness. The social aspect of culture and religion puts the individual in relationship to others within her own religious culture and that of foreign others, who have also been busy creating their own religious culture.

Religion and the Problem of Otherness

Imagine a college student of the religions of the globe sitting at his desk typing on his computer, attempting to compose an essay that makes sense and does justice to a foreign religious tradition. Where can you obtain correct information to help you complete your task? You could interview a member of another religious tradition, but you cannot afford the expense of flying to a distant part of the earth. You could find information on the Internet, but this source is not always reliable because anyone can write about Buddhism, for example, without really being immersed in the religion. You could also go to the library to find primary and secondary sources, do the reading necessary, take notes, and return to your computer to compose an intelligent essay. Whether or not you are aware of it, you are writing about a foreign religious tradition as an outsider. This external position puts you at a disadvantage even if you practice empathy (a fellow feeling) toward the other tradition. Your outside position from the religion that you are attempting to understand and write about is one of many fundamental problems associated with the study of foreign religions.

The insider/outsider problem refers to two different perspectives concerning a religion being studied. We can ask the following question: Is the native practitioner or the outside scholar correct in her conceptions of a particular religion? Not all insiders are experts on the religion they practice, and not all scholars truly understand what they study with concepts and methods foreign to the subject. The final written product can manifest a twofold problem: The insiders cannot recognize their religion as depicted by the outsider, and the outsider presents such a biased and distorted version of the religious tradition that it becomes an abstraction. But there is a way to overcome this problem that uses contributions from both sides.

The problem between the insider and outsider can be overcome to some degree by the latter applying his conceptual categories and methods with a light touch and letting the insider tell her story using traditional categories as much as is feasible. This is a narrative approach by which an insider shares her story with outsiders. The story told by the insider is personal, experiential, historical, and communal (social); it is shared in the native language of the insider's culture that is intertwined with the cultural worldview. The narratives of the insider are to be discovered in personal testimony, religious texts of various kinds, historical accounts, biographies, and hagiographical literature.

As the insider is allowed to tell her story, the outsider approaches his subject with empathy and understanding and attempts to share these approaches with readers. The outside scholar uses his critical perspective without superimposing an outsider's viewpoint on the religious tradition being discussed. Thus a narrative approach contributes to overcoming the inherent problem of the insider/outsider when working in a cross-cultural context.

A narrative approach to a variety of religious traditions around the globe also has other advantages because such an approach grounds any discussion in the religious culture being studied. It thus does potentially less harm because it uses a method that is friendlier to a particular culture. Many of the religions covered in this textbook were originally oral cultures in which storytelling and the sharing of stories was a common practice among members, making a narrative approach a continuation of the practice of sharing stories. By using a method employed by the insiders themselves, a narrative approach reduces the chances for the forced imposition of outside categories that might distort the subject. It also needs to be affirmed that any outsider studying and interpreting a religious tradition only offers another perspective that is neither inferior nor superior to that of the insider. The outsider's perspective is just different, and it should be the goal of the outsider (the author of the textbook) to enable an insider to recognize his tradition.

Religion and Intertwined Phenomena

Instead of offering another inadequate definition of religion, this part of the chapter proposes to examine related phenomena that are intertwined with religion that form a web of meaning and what they reveal about aspects of its nature. I concur with previous scholars who have called attention to the social, historical, cultural, experiential, doctrinal, and promise of salvation and/or afterlife manifested by religions. But there are other aspects that need to be emphasized in order to arrive at a more comprehensive grasp of the nature of religion. These interrelated aspects of religion are narrative, power, violence, performance, and play. Even though other features of religion could be chosen, these aspects will serve to illustrate on an experimental basis how elements of religion are intertwined in ways that are not easily recognized. Some of these features of religion have been discussed by previous scholars. Thus, I am not proposing to do anything extraordinary or unique. But I do want to call attention to interconnections between these phenomena and religion with the purpose of helping a reader see the wider connections manifested by the nature of religion.

The single constant characteristic shared by every religion (at least as far as I am aware) is narrative, an oral or written story shared with others within and without a particular religious culture. A narrative usually begins as an oral tradition before being preserved in writing or can simply retain its oral nature and be passed down from one generation to the next as it is maintained in the collective memories of members of a society, representing their collective identity. A narrative occurs within a temporal framework about what occurred at the beginning or some other point in the development of a religion. This temporal aspect of narrative usually takes the form of a chronological sequence, which suggests that it can be historical. The narratives of the major monotheistic religions—Judaism, Christianity, and Islam—tend to be historical in the sense that God breaks into linear historical time and performs acts that affect members of the respective religious cultures. Narratives can also assume the form of myths, legends, epics, ballads, biographies of leading figures, hagiographies, and fictions. What is the overall purpose of these various forms of narrative? Narratives serve several purposes within a religion: pedagogical illustration, spiritual inspiration, behavioral motivation, moral or ethical example, or pure entertainment. Narratives help to preserve the identity of a people and what it means to be a member of a group. Narratives contribute to the cultural continuity of a people and give them direction as they evolve into the future. In summary, narratives tell members of a cultural group who they were, who they are, and who they will be in the future.

Narratives are inherent in the culture and history of a people in a dynamic sense. This implies that narratives are lived by a people and help to define who they are. Humans tell the stories that they live, author these stories, and inten-tionally live these narratives that they pass onward to a new generation. The vast majority of members of a culture, of course, are born into the prevailing narrative of a religion. In this sense, a narrative is pre-given, simply accepted, and adhered to as an established body of facts. It is also possible for a scholar of religion to collect data and construct a narrative about a religion being investigated that not only represents a construction of a religion but also is a construct of the religion through the process of writing about it. Whether it is someone internal or external to a religious tradition creating the narrative, that person assumes to speak and write with a voice of authority.

Even though narratives are preserved in written form or orally within a culture, they are not static entities or museum artifacts; they are, rather, dynamic because they often change over time in response to new challenges or events that are encountered by a culture. Narratives are frequently sub-jected to redaction in the form of deletions and additions to a story line. If one religion encounters a foreign religion, it might borrow appealing aspects of the other religion, which might alter the commonly accepted narrative into something newer.

Many religious narratives reflect a search for power, a ubiquitous feature of religions from a cross-cultural perspective. Not only are polytheistic or mono-theistic gods and goddesses depicted as powerful, even though some divine beings are considered more powerful than others, human actors seek to be near power or to possess it for themselves. The Japanese notion of *kami* (spiritual forces) is connected with both natural and supernatural forces. In Chinese Daoism, the invisible, inaudible, subtle, and mysterious Dao is the ultimate universal, all-powerful principle, while the De (virtue, power) is a force within all things. North American Indians recognize various types of powers: the Algonquian *manitou*, the Iroquois *orenda*, and the Sioux *wakan*. These diverse types of power make it challenging for a scholar to construct a precise defini-tion of power.

For some religious theorists, religion is a quest for power in order to ward off danger and simply to survive. Even though the practice of religion makes it possible for a person or people to gain power to fight off the threat of star-vation, meaninglessness, and death, power is a force that can be used to strengthen oneself or can be shared with others. Power embodies a dynamic drive or impulse that is related to its ability to empower anyone. This points to the inner dynamic of power, although power remains mysterious, elusive, and impossible to accurately measure. Because of its dynamic nature, power influences things and people to move or act in prescribed ways, which can reach a compulsive degree by means of its coercive and prohibitive forces. The compulsive aspect of power can give its owner control over herself, others, nature, or the entire cosmos.

The role of power with respect to religion that is embodied in narratives often proves to be violent in nature. Many cross-cultural narratives relate tales of the battles of divine beings for supremacy, conflicts with demonic forces, and violent adventures of cultural heroes. Violence is dramatically associated with sacrifice, a central religious action in many religions that involves killing an animal or burning some grain that enables people to communicate with divine beings in order to secure their blessings. Besides the ritual sphere, martyrdom is another example of violence in some religious traditions, people becoming models of faith to be imitated by others. The multiple ways that violence appears within a given culture suggest that violence is a relative concept that refers to acts that injure, cause harm or pain, or destroy a thing, animal, or person. Buddhism and Jainism are religions that choose to counter the all-pervading nature of violence by taking a vow of nonviolence that has implications for their diet and lifestyle.

Based on many examples of exerting power and violence, religion is always performed to some degree. Rituals, festivals, pilgrimages, healings, sacraments, magic, divination, or prayer are all examples of performance. Those who perform some type of religious action often play roles before an audience of witnesses. The performance of a ritual, for instance, or the uttering of a word or words makes something happen. In fact, after an animal was sacrificed in ancient Greece and Rome, religious officials checked the entrails of the animal to learn whether or not the offering was accepted by the gods. Among the ancient Hindus, Sanskrit mantras (sacred language formulas) were recited to affect the outcome of a ritual or, equally important, to protect it from errors that might have been committed by unwitting priests, a transgression that could unleash powerful demonic forces that could destroy the participants. The notion of performance mitigates any theoretical bifurcation between thought and action that is characteristic of earlier theories of religion.

Another feature exhibited by religion is play, which is fundamental to human nature and can assume a variety of forms. Play is a voluntary activity, which suggests its freedom in contrast to work and its connection to seriousness, responsibility, and habitual action. For those members of a culture that freely choose to engage in play, they leave the world of work and enter a sphere of make-believe, pretending, and fun. And unlike work, play is disinterested and temporary activity. Play is also an interlude in one's life in the sense that one can break with one's conventional mode of life, such as the observance of a festival. Play enables a person to enter a world apart from ordinary life with its own time limits and spatial boundaries, which is not unlike a football field or a basketball court.

To engage in play is a risky and uncertain endeavor because there is the danger of losing or getting physically and/or mentally injured. Even though play is precarious and dangerous for a participant, it does eliminate doubt because all the players adhere to the same binding rules applicable to everyone. In addition to being dangerous, play is secretive in the sense that not everyone gets to play because not everyone has equal talents necessary for success. It is possible to witness the dangerous and secretive aspects of play in ancient mystery cults of Greece and Rome focused on the god Dionysus/Bacchus. Another aspect of the dangerous nature of play is its ability to deceive, betray, beguile, or delude a participant. Moreover, play is oxymoronic in the sense that it is a dangerous harmlessness. Many cultures have attempted to control the dangerous nature of play by funneling it into competitive games and athletic contests, which can become violent.

Play represents the subjunctive mood ("as if") because it expresses contingent or hypothetical action. In other words, play represents what might be rather than "as-is." This feature of play is expressed within cultures that resort to using masks and strange costumes in ritual contexts in African folk figures like the trickster, among Native American Indian clowns and inner-Asian shamans. Play is also manifested in festivals or the performance of miracles. In addition, play often represents the reversal of hierarchical structures of societies, values, or forms of status, which can symbolize chaos and/or renewal as is often the case with festivals. Within the context of a ritual, secret society, or cult, play is related to language and even the generation of secret modes of communication. Finally, play is dynamic in the sense that it manifests a to-and-fro movement, enabling a player to become powerful or share in a power greater than himself.

Play is closely intertwined with the erotic in many cultures. According to narratives that date to the ninth century CE, the Hindu deity Krishna plays with demons and cowherd maidens in his biography. His play associated with the maidens is expressed in very erotic terms. Beyond its connection with desire and love, eroticism is excessive and potentially subversive because it is characterized by insatiability and consuming desire. The erotic tends to be marginal with respect to the norms of the prevailing society. Eroticism should not be confused with the sex act because it shares more in common with anticipation and fantasy; it cannot be fully satisfied because it represents a disequilibrium that impels a person to call one's own being into question.

Eroticism is transgressive in the sense that it is a desire that is not deterred by a taboo. In fact, the transgression of a taboo fuels its energy by means of eliciting titillation. The erotic can lead to social chaos and violence. The world of the erotic is a madness that cannot be tamed or cured. Within this insane world, the erotic moves toward its final sense, which is death. In some cultures, the erotic moves indubitably toward death and even eagerly anticipates it. Finally, eroticism is a power that can take a person to ecstasy and a state of bliss.

In summary, religion is intertwined with eroticism, power, violence, performance, and play, as well as other features too numerous to discuss at this point. This discussion suggests very strongly that religion is a complex phenomenon that cannot be grasped by some simple reductive definition. Religion is a cultural phenomenon that needs to be grasped as something interrelated with other elements of culture. Scholars have been aware of this complexity to some degree for a long time because they have used various approaches to the study of the subject of religion without exhausting it.

Approaches to the Study of Religion

Because of the complex and elusive nature of religion, it invites a wide variety of methodological approaches in an attempt by scholars of the subject to understand it. These different methodological approaches include some of the following: sociology, anthropology, psychology, phenomenology, history of religions, structuralism, ecology/biology, feminist, poststructural, postmodern, and cognitive. These various methodological approaches to religion reflect the borrowing of methods from a developing discipline, such as sociology, philosophy, or psychology, and applying that method to the subject of religion or a specific aspect of religion. The various methods mentioned were often attempts to apply a scientific method to the study of religion, enabling scholars of religion to be scientific like those in the natural sciences and to have their research and findings respected by the wider academic community. The quest for a science of religion occurred historically in Western universities within the context of a quest for the origins of religion, a search that reflects the presupposition that to know the genesis of something is to understand it. Before briefly surveying the different approaches to the study of religion, we will examine the quest for its origin.

In part, the quest for the origin of religion was shaped by the theory of evolution advocated by Charles Darwin in his book *The Origin of Species*, published in the mid-nineteenth century and revised by Herbert Spencer. Darwin's theory of evolution influenced scholars such as Edward B. Tylor (1832–1917), Sir James George Frazer (1854–1941), Friedrich Max Müller (1823–1900), and Lévy Bruhl (1857–1939). Embedded within the writings of these scholars was a feeling of intellectual superiority over the peoples that they studied. Their writings reflect demeaning and supercilious terminology toward the people they were studying, such as "savage," "primitive," "barbarian," and "archaic mentality." This is hardly an empathic approach to the study of foreign religious cultures. If the goal of the study of religion is understanding the subject, it can be correctly and cogently argued that these scholars took the study of religion astray before it ever had a chance to begin.

Using the evolutionary model to reconstruct the development of civilization, Tylor proceeded to move from the most primitive cultures to the most complex, which implied modern Western societies. Tylor isolated three major stages of human development: hunter-gatherer; a barbaric stage that involved the domestication of plants and animals; and a civilized stage beginning with the art of writing. Tylor conceived of his scholarship as an effort to write a history of the human mind with the ultimate purpose of creating a "science of culture." Tylor begins provocatively by raising the question about whether or not all cultures, even the most primitive, had religious concepts. Tylor wanted to respond to the claim by Andrew Lang (1844–1912) that there were some cultures that had no religion. Tylor used a comparative approach to the study of religion that he grounded in empirical observation and not rational speculation. His method led him to identify animism, a belief that spirits animate living appearances, as the basis for religion in minimally developed tribes. Tylor was intrigued by what he called "survivals," which he defined as processes, customs, and opinions carried forward by force of habit into a new state of society different from the previous state. A basic problem with Tylor's theory is that it suggests something preconceived that he fills with evidence to support it.

From his study at the University of Cambridge, Frazer composed an impressive body of literature devoted to the topic of religion, the most famous of which is *The Golden Bough*, which was originally published as two volumes and grew to twelve volumes. Frazer identified a threefold evolutionary sequence that included: magic, religion, and science. According to Frazer, magic was logically more primitive than religion, which he defined as the propitiation and conciliation of powers believed to be superior to humans. Religion stands in fundamental opposition to magic and science. Magic is necessarily false because it is a mistaken application of the association of ideas. In other words, magic is contrary to logic. Magic mistakenly operates by means of the laws of similarity and contact because it assumes that things that resemble each other are the same. Imitative magic works by injuring or destroying an enemy by harming an image similar to a victim. Contagious magic falsely assumes that things that were once in contact with other things always remain in contact. Frazer concludes that archaic people are neither logical nor scientific. Frazer characterizes the magician as someone who deceives others in her quest for honor, wealth, and power. Frazer's hyperbolic assessment of the archaic mind also embodies an injection of his own political preference for a constitutional monarchy over against the democratic political system common to simpler societies, which means that they are limited by their customs and traditions. It is thus incorrect to portray archaic people as representative of the freest example of humankind, but it is more accurate to grasp them as slaves to the past and spirits of the dead.

In common with Tylor and Frazer, the French theorist Lévy Bruhl compared primitive (his terminology) mentality to modern Western modes of scientific thinking and found, unsurprisingly, that the former's kind of thinking lacked rigor and rationality. He labeled archaic mentally as prelogical reasoning, mystical, and pervaded by a sense of affectional participation. Bruhl argued that prelogical reasoning was indicative of an indifference to logical laws of contradiction, while the mystical meant that primitive thinking was orientated to occult forces, and affectional participation suggested a connectedness with other persons and objects. Instead of experience being regulated by strictly cause-and-effect relationships, the data of experience tend to flow together and associate with each other in complex ways. The law of participation means that some tribes think of themselves as animals or birds, such as the assertion that "I am a red parrot." These people are thus not thinking metaphorically or symbolically because the equation between themselves and a bird implies actual participatory identity.

Max Müller studied languages, comparative philology, and comparative religion. After a teaching career at Oxford, he retired to devote all his energy to editing the famous *Sacred Books of the East* collection that made many of the world's religious scriptures available to a wider audience. Müller published other works that explored issues in comparative religion and attempted to develop a science of religion that would be the last science to be constructed. He saw a necessity for a comparative approach to the study of religion, being inspired by the Latin Church father Basilius, who wrote that the purpose of comparing religions was to learn how they differ and which the better is, a position that few scholars would agree with today. Müller thought that comparative religion could teach humankind value lessons, change our views of other religions, help us to find common ground among adherents of different religions, shed light on the inevitable decay of religions due to contact with the secular world, and reveal the uniqueness of each religion. Influenced by Goethe's comment about studying more than one language, he saw that the absolute necessity of comparative religion was embodied in the following statement: "He who knows one, knows none." Thus, to truly understand one's personal religion entails indubitably studying other religions. Moreover, the exercise of comparison forms the bases of all knowledge. Müller envisioned a science of religion that would assign Christianity its rightful place among the religions of the world, demonstrate the meaning of the fullness of time, and restore unconscious progress toward Christianity. In his broader vision, Müller wanted to reconstruct a *Civitas Dei*, a city of God on earth that will bind together all humankind. In a less ambitious way, Müller conceived of this new science as adhering to the laws of cause and effect and induction as it exposed what he called "Natural Religion," a possession of humankind developing from the combining of moral sensibility with religion.

Social Science Approach to Religion

An early social science attempt to understand the nature of religion was pursued by sociology. In his sociological classic *The Elementary Forms of the Religious Life: A Study of Religious Sociology*, published in 1912, Emile Durkheim (1858–1917), who eventually became a professor at the Sorbonne in Paris, grasped his discipline as a science that was intended to explain the reality of human beings. He agreed with Müller that all religions can be compared because they share common elements, and a religious fact carries the mark of its origins. In a radical statement for its historical time, Durkheim asserted that there are no religions that are false because they are all true in their own ways. Why does he come to this conclusion? Durkheim thought that all religions answered questions about the human condition. But the basic distinction that determines the nature of religion is the distinction between the sacred and the profane. The former is completely separate from the latter, it has a superior dignity, and is wholly other from the profane. The sacred is also taboo. Besides being sacred, religion is communal, leading Durkheim to divinize society and to find the source of the sacred in totemism, an elementary form of religion that identifies a group with an animal species, which reveals Durkheim's embrace of evolution. Durkheim also identified religious phenomena into two basic categories: beliefs that represent states of opinion and consist of representations and rites that are determined by modes of action. In order to define a rite, the researcher must define the belief.

Durkheim's sociological method would be carried forward by theorists such as Max Weber (1864–1920) and many others. Weber published books on the religions of India, China, and Judaism, although he is probably best remembered as the author of *The Protestant Ethic and the Spirit of Capitalism* (1930). Weber moved sociology in a newer direction away from social structure to individually focused studies by adding history to examine roles such as priest, prophet, magicians, shaman, and, most famously, charisma, a gift of leadership and ability to influence others. Weber intended to move away from a positivist, natural science model associated with the work of August Comte, who influenced Durkheim, to something more dynamic, stressing social action over social structure with the purpose of revealing causal connections of social action without neglecting the subjective aspects of a person. Weber developed a historical sociology of religion that led to understanding. Weber also incorporated comparison into his method in order to construct "ideal types," which are configurations of meaning that function as abstractions to assist sociological analysis and enhance understanding. Weber examines the connection between motives and intentions of subjects with their acts and events. This implies that religion is a source for ideas and practices that transcend the phenomenal world with an ability to interact with the social world independently and in unpredictable ways. This dynamic aspect of religion is represented historically by Protestantism (motive) and capitalism (action), suggesting that Protestantism functioned as a source of motivation from which evolved capitalism. On the one hand, this suggests that religion could challenge the inherited order and bring about social change. And on the other hand, religion could play a more conservative role by maintaining the social status quo.

Another discipline of the social sciences is anthropology, which is often linked with sociology. Prior to the career of Polish scholar Bronislaw Malinowski (1884–1942), those scholars who could be labeled anthropologist performed their work sitting in their offices and relying on reports of foreign places by travelers, adventurers, and missionaries, which were tainted by the religious and cultural prejudices of the observers and mistakenly accepted as accurate. Malinowski changed this trend by living with his subjects on a daily basis, observing their practices, learning their narratives, communicating with them in their languages, participating to some degree in their religions, and recording his findings. Malinowski used his approach in places such as New Guinea and the Trobriand Islands. This participant observer approach led to more accurate accounts of the religions of indigenous peoples. By attempting to grasp a society as a functioning whole, Malinowski's name became synonymous with the method of functionalism, an attempt to explain how aspects of a culture function for a people, which made it unnecessary to invoke the theory of evolution into one's analysis. The notion of function was related in Malinowski's method to his understanding of fundamental human needs for survival (e.g., metabolism, reproduction, bodily comforts, movement, growth, and health).

Among the numerous others who followed the lead of Malinowski, there was Victor Turner (1920–1983), who was born in Glasgow, Scotland, and taught at American universities, such as Cornell University, University of Chicago, and the University of Virginia. During his work with African cultures, Turner developed theoretical implications associated with the transitional or liminal stage of a rite of passage by emphasizing the ambiguous status of an initiate. The liminal stage is an in-between period of uncertainty that highlights social transformation and the fluctuating nature of social order. The dynamic nature of society can be seen in the performance of ritual, which Turner equates with social dramas that he identifies with four stages: breach, mounting crisis, corrective action, and reintegration. Another dynamic aspect of a culture is evident with the creation of *communitas* (community), a form of social relationship that lacks structure. Turner identifies three types of *communitas*: spontaneous, normative, and ideological. The spontaneous modality occurs suddenly and does not endure for long. The normative type is influenced by time and the need to organize the first type into a more enduring social system, whereas the ideological type is a utopian model based on spontaneous *communitas*. Turner calls attention to a dialectic that involves a movement from a previous social structure to an anti-structure and returns to the safety of structure, but this dialectical return welcomes back a liminal person who changes and renews society.

Although other anthropologists could be discussed, Clifford Geertz (1926–2006), who did his doctoral work at Harvard and taught at the Institute for Advanced Study at Princeton University for a long time, did fieldwork in both Java and Bali and developed a renowned definition of religion as a cultural system, which helps one grasp religion as a source of meaning and explanation by recognizing that religion is organically interconnected with culture and symbols. Geertz identifies five elements of religion: (1) It is a system of symbols; (2) it establishes moods and emotions; (3) it formulates general concepts; (4) it covers conceptions in factuality; (5) its moods and motivations seem uniquely realistic. If we unpack this definition, it is possible to note that symbols signify something else and point to concepts. There is a system of symbols that forms cultural patterns that constitute sources of information, give meaning, and provide models for conduct. Symbols induce a range of moods that vary in intensity and are transient, whereas motives are directional, persist over time, and are meaningful with reference to goals. A system of symbols creates order. Factuality refers to religious belief that involves a previous acceptance of authority, which is confirmed by ritual. Religion shapes a world that reflects a conception of a self and its interrelationship with the world. According to Geertz, religion provides its adherents a worldview and ethos, a paradigm for behavior, conceptual ideas, and a way of life. Intellectual, emotional, and moral experiences are just some of the meaningful experiences afforded by religion. Geertz's work evokes an image of humans as seekers of meaning, creators of symbols, and conceptualizers. Geertz insisted that an anthropologist adopt the method of thick description, which involved describing the actions of people and attempting to understand what they think they are doing. Geertz acknowledged two steps in the anthropological study of religion: analysis of meaning in symbols and relating this analysis to the social structure and psychological processes of a culture.

Geertz and other theorists are criticized by Talal Asad in his work *Genealogies of Religion: Discipline and Reasons of Power in Christianity and Islam*, published in 1993. Asad stands opposed to a universal definition that is transhistorical. In other words, Asad is against making religion abstract and universal. Asad charges that Geertz confuses and mixes up cognitive questions with those of communication. By insisting on the primacy of meaning, Geertz assumes a theological perspective, according to Asad. In contrast to the sameness that scholars such as Geertz seek to find, Asad stands with the postmodern emphasis on difference.

Trained as an anthropologist, Claude Lévi-Strauss (1908–2009) was inspired by the linguistical theory developed by Ferdinand de Saussure (1857–1913) to create what was called structuralism, a semiological science that adopted meaning as its guiding principle. Lévi-Strauss conceived structuralism as a global approach to the subject of religion and language. By stressing a system of axioms and postulates, he pays less attention to content and meaning. Rather, what is important is structure and the relation between units of meaning. If one takes a mythological narrative, the scholar's task is to decompose it by identifying and charting its most elementary units, which he calls mythemes. Once the scholar breaks down the story into its shortest possible units, these sentences are written on an index card that is numbered according to the unfolding of the narrative. This means that each mytheme unit consists of a bundle of relations that result in revealing a two-dimensional time referent: the synchronic is a given time that represents a horizontal axis that is nonreversible, and the diachronic cuts across time and represents a vertical axis that is reversible and paradigmatic. The vertical columns represent the deep structure of the myth that remains constant over time, even though the myth continuously grows over time with additions and deletions by myth-makers. When the structure of a myth weakens, it dies because it loses its distinctive formal configuration. If one examines the essential nature of a myth, one finds a type of binary thinking that functions to resolve contradictory human problems.

Besides sociology and anthropology, psychology is also characterized as a social science. Needless to say, Sigmund Freud (1856–1939) casts a wide shadow over the subject of religion and its relation to psychology, which he equates with a scientific approach to the subject. According to Freud, religion, ethics, society, and art meet in the Oedipus complex, a theory about the early phases of libidinal development during which a child sexually desires the parent of the opposite sex and feels fear and hostility toward the parent of the same sex as the child. By means of the process of socialization, a child learns to repress these wishes. Freud thinks that the Oedipus complex gives rise to totemism, incest taboos, exogamy, the ritual totem meal, and society itself. The totem animal represents the feared, envied, and loved father, and sacrifice stands for the totem meal. The father represents a model for the construction of a god. Religion originates, however, as a psychological necessity because humans feel helpless against nature's forces. This makes religion an infantile obsessional neurosis. This line of argument leads Freud in his work *Future of an Illusion* to find the psychical origins of religious ideas in illusions that he equates with the oldest, strongest, and most urgent wishes of humankind. Freud does not mean that illusions are false, but they are rather derived from deeply engrained human wishes. In contrast to these human illusions, Freud thinks that science does not give illusions, and thus he places his faith for the future in science. By turning away from religion, humans find mental health. Freud's theory has been criticized for being speculative, fictional, nonhistorical, and nonempirical.

Phenomenology of Religion

During the twentieth century, some scholars began to embrace the phenomenological approach because it promised to offer a scientific way to study religion free of theological biases. The inspiration for this type of approach came from the philosophy of Edmund Husserl. Two essential and influential features of his method are *epoché* and eidetic vision. The former involves restraint or suspension of judgment and the bracketing of beliefs, presuppositions, and prejudices that would influence the resulting understanding. If a researcher brings concepts and constructs from his or her worldview to the understanding of a phenomenon within another culture, this situation leads to distortion of the results. As part of his call to return to the things themselves, Husserl does not argue that the eidetic vision provides the observer with the ability to see the essences that are real, eternal, and superior to particulars. By essence, Husserl means "pure generalities" that manifest themselves to the observer and are pure possibilities that are valid independent of one's experience. A number of Western scholars adopted this method or something similar to it, attempting to study religion in a scientific way.

An example of an adherent to the phenomenological approach to the study of religion is Gerardus van der Leeuw (1890–1950), although he was more directly influenced by the phenomenology of Georg Friedrich Hegel (1770–1831), who held that it is possible to grasp the essence of something by investigating its appearances and manifestations, which are grounded in an underlying essence or unity that Hegel called *Geist* (spirit). In his phenomenology of religion, van der Leeuw refers to three levels of a phenomenon: relative concealment, gradually becoming revealed, and relative transparency that he correlates to three levels of life: experience, understanding, and testimony. He argues that a phenomenon is an object related to a subject and a subject related to an object. A subject does not modify an object and vice versa. The essence of a phenomenon is given by the appearance of an object. A phenomenon appears as a symbol of meaning that offers itself to an observer for interpretation, making phenomenology a science whose aim is understanding and pure objectivity. This methodological approach distinguishes itself from history, psychology, philosophy of religion, and theology.

Van der Leeuw thinks that humans do not accept life as it is because humans turn to religion to improve their condition. This turn to religion reflects humans seeking meaning in their lives, searching for what is superior to them, and striving for power. For van der Leeuw, power is the central concept of religion, belonging to both objective and subjective aspects of religion. Thus, to describe the objectivity of power is to include the subjective response. This suggests that power and the sacred are intimately interwoven. Within a particular culture, power is stored in the deeds, thoughts, and principles of humans. When objects, people, times, places, or actions are charged with power, they become taboo, which functions as a warning to be careful and to maintain a distance from a power. In the method of some scholars, phenomenology overlaps with the discipline of history.

The History of Religions

The history of religions is sometimes called the Chicago School because three of its major representatives have worked at the University of Chicago, namely Mircea Eliade, Jonathan Z. Smith, and Wendy Doniger. During World War II, Eliade was a Romanian diplomat with a membership in the Legion of the Archangel Michael, popularly known as the Iron Guard, a fascist political organization. When the Communists took control of Romania, Eliade could not return to his native land because he would have been persecuted by its new left-wing leaders. He found his liberation in writing scholarly works on religion and numerous works of fiction, which often included religious themes. In the course of his career, Smith frequently criticized Eliade's methodological approach to the subject of religion for being unhistorical and not paying attention to religious differences. Recognizing the complexity of religion, Doniger calls for a tool box type of approach to issues of method. In other words, a researcher uses various kinds of interpretive tools—history, sociology, psychological, literary criticism, philosophy, or feminist theory—appropriate to a particular aspect being investigated.

Eliade defined religion as the sacred, which presented it as distinct and qualitatively different from the profane. This suggests that the sacred is set apart from everything else around it. The sacred is dialectic in the sense that it has the power to transform a natural object into something else. The sacred is equivalent to a power, a reality, saturated with being, and it establishes fixed limits by setting boundaries. The sacred is also ambivalent because it can both attract and repeal, be useful and dangerous, and bring death as well as immortality. He applies his fundamental distinction between the sacred and profane to time and space.

Eliade used what he called morphological classification to organize religious phenomena into proper categories to assist understanding. Morphology is inferred from historical evidence and gives a scholar an opportunity to compare phenomena. Morphology can be used to reintegrate various types of phenomena into its system of associations. What the scholar finds are archetypes that function as models for the actions of humans. It is only human actions based on divine archetypes that give human actions meaning. The scholar must seek and reflect on the structures revealed by the phenomena. What Eliade proposes is an encyclopedic approach to the subject of religion that must go beyond the ordinary historian because the historian of religions must seek the structures of the sacred that are nontemporal. Later in his career, Eliade called for a total hermeneutics that could function as a source for new cultural values because of its ability to change humans and create a new humanism.

Smith stands opposed to Eliade's project because the standpoint of the historian is fabricated within a world in which the historian must stand. Smith views the distinction between the sacred and profane as situational or relational, which shifts according to the map being employed to understand them. According to Smith, religion is both a mapmaking and map-using process characterized by different attitudes toward inevitable differences between maps and territory, which offers basic tools for constructing a world of meaning. The task of the historian is to complicate, not clarify. Religion itself is a quest for power in order to manipulate and negotiate one's space in order to have a meaningful place to dwell.

Smith is also critical of Eliade's use of comparison because Eliade uses it to discover similarity and neglects difference. Since comparison is a subjective experience, according to Smith, it tends to be more impressionistic than a method. Eliade's use of morphology is derived from Romantic natural philosophy that allows for an arrangement of items in a hierarchical series that ignores categories of space and time. When Eliade discovers an archetype, it is a result of a sudden intuitive leap into simplicity. In contrast to Eliade's use of comparison, Smith calls for limited and controlled comparison that is confined to cultural artifacts contiguous in space and time. Comparison has nothing to do with identity but does require a postulation of difference.

Doniger's tool box approach is based in part on her perception of the complexity of religion and allows her an appropriate method for a specific mode of interpretation. She calls her method inductive because it is constructed from the ground up. The scholar must rely on the discovered data, apply history to that data, and then compare the findings. It is comparison that allows us to become aware of differences. A researcher must be aware that evidence has a context that can change the meaning of the data and that a reader also occupies a context. The basic data studied and interpreted exists within a web of meaning that represents a shared humanity and life experience that forms the raw material that one must compare.

Natural Science Approaches

A group of scholars of religion have injected methods associated more with the natural sciences than with humanistic disciplines into their study of religion. These include ecological, biological, and cognitive approaches to the study of religion. There is some overlap of these methodological approaches that differ in degree from one author to another. Ecology of religion is a cross-cultural method that is concerned with the adaptation of a group to a particular environment and what kind of religion is produced by the society. The biological method is more accurately described as a sociobiology that focuses on the coevolution of genes and culture, whereas the findings of cognitive science are applied by scholars to the notion of religion.

An early representative of the ecological approach to religion was Åke Hultkrantz, who imagines a wide scope for his method, which is an attempt to secure new information and not to replace historical or phenomenological approaches to the subject. The ecology of religion is concerned with the environmental integration of religion and the forms of religious expression in different environments. Confining his work to indigenous religions with tribal social systems, Hultkrantz thinks that nature both restricts or impedes and stimulates culture. There is a vital role to be played by comparison in his method in order to discern what one case tells us about another culture in a different environment. For Hultkrantz, religion is tied to cultural structure and the ecological foundations of culture. Hultkrantz refers to three types of religio-ecological integration: primary integration is represented by environmental adaptation of basic cultural features (e.g., means of subsistence, production, or technology); secondary integration stands for the indirect adaptation of religious beliefs and rituals; and morphological integration covers religious features with forms from the physical and biological environment. The procedure of his method includes identifying a cultural type and its social organization, then determining the cultural core and social organization with its type of religion (e.g., monotheism or polytheism). The scholar must be looking for religious change, which the ecology of religion helps her achieve.

If Hultkrantz is an excellent example of the ecology of religion, a strong representative of the biology of religion is Walter Burkert, who is also a scholar of Greek religion. Burkert begins by raising the following type of question: How can we account for the ubiquitous nature of religion and its persistence? In order to help him answer such a question, Burkert incorporates the notion of evolution into his approach in an attempt to search for the origins of religion, which he claims is beyond particular cultures. Burkert defines religion with the unseen and ineffable; it is something that cannot be verified. Religion is manifested through interaction and communication. He finds anxiety, fear, and terror at the origin of religion, which uses biological functions to protect life. While humans resort to and struggle with biological survival, the lessons learned are internalized by humans. Burkert conceives for his reader a form of social Darwinism, a coevolution of genes and culture that gets passed down to others. By becoming embedded into the human genetic code, religion helps humans to survive. Burkert recognizes a paradox here because, on the one hand, survival means adaptability, and religion teaches eternal unchanging truths, on the other hand.

The cognitive scientific approach to religion offers hope, according to some scholars, of uniting the humanities with science. Those scholars adopting a cognitive approach to religion tend to agree that religion exists because of the way that the human mind has been constructed by the process of evolution, representing a biological history of the human species that contributes to the human narrative. The human mind is capable of making distinctions in its environment that get passed to the next generation because they prove useful for survival. Gods and spirits originate in the human tendency toward anthropocentric imagination, which is confirmed by the human tendency to see human faces in clouds or to imagine gods to make our lives meaningful. This suggests that humans socially construct religion and pass it to the next generation.

Scholars using the findings of cognitive scientists argue that there are regions in the human brain that are responsible for religious experience, leading to a mapping of different regions in the brain that are connected to such experience. The other aspect of the brain that cognitive scientists examine is how the human body and brain work to create and release psychoactive chemicals that produce alternations of modes of consciousness. The human genetic structure is also important to cognitive scientists because it helps to construct multiple brain connections that are crucial for religious experience. Another part of the brain/religion puzzle is the chemistry of the brain and its receptors that adhere to chemicals that are produced by the body/brain, creating changes in states of consciousness by enabling nerve cells to communicate with each other.

Pascal Boyer and Harvey Whitehouse are early cognitive theorists, with the latter advocating explicit knowledge in contrast to the implicit knowledge advanced by Boyer. Whitehouse conceives of religion as a culturally specific discourse in which memory plays an important role, forming a general knowledge with social importance. In contrast, episodic memory is more personal, indicating emotional events that have a strong affective component. This type of theorizing about the nature of religion within an evolutionary context recalls attempts to grasp religion in the mid-nineteenth century and represents a continued example of some scholars adhering to the rigors of the scientific method with its unbiased, objective, certain, and falsifiable aspects. Does the cognitive approach to religion mean that the type of religion that a person or society practices is based on their type of mind? This is the type of question that future work will seek to answer. Critics of the cognitive scientific approach to the study of religion argue that this concentration on the human brain tends to neglect the body, language, history, society, and material culture that tend to shape a person. In other words, the cognitive scientific approach is too narrow to grasp the many elements with which religion is connected. And some critics think that developing a true science of religion is delusional.

Feminist Approaches

There is no single feminist approach to religion. There are rather many female voices directed against patriarchy, sexism, misogyny, and general androcentric attitudes. Many feminists view patriarchy as a historical, social, cultural, and political structure of male power. The direct result of this structure of male power is domination, subordination, and marginalization of women. Sexism provides the support for patriarchy, which embodies the ideology of male supremacy. If misogyny is self-explanatory by means of its definition, androcentric attitudes are maintained by relying on the male body as the paradigm for perfection. Feminists also make a distinction between gender and sex. The latter is an inherited biological attitude, whereas gender represents cultural expectations about what it means to have one or the other sexual identity. Feminists tend to agree that gender is socially constructed and needs to be examined in order to understand the role of women in different religious traditions.

Based on the lack of evidence in some instances concerning the roles played and contributions made by women to their religious cultures, feminists have been faced with a job of retrieving and reconstructing this lost heritage about women before being able to reinterpret religious traditions. Sometimes, feminists have been able to find evidence, but they have also encountered absolute silence within some patriarchal traditions, which necessitates their reliance on their own imagination in order to construct a coherent view of women's contributions to a particular religion. Female scholars have also spoken to foreign women about their lives, and this has resulted in new and formerly neglected information about religious traditions. This type of scholarship involves a search for new paradigms for thinking, perceiving, and understanding. Feminists view themselves in part as fighting against bondage to patriarchal attitudes and dominant androcentric perspectives, which represents a politics of knowledge created by men. This situation calls for finding new ways of knowing that will expectantly lead to a liberating paradigm with respect to the study of religion. Feminists provide evidence about the nature of this new mode of thinking by alluding to breaking free of standard rational and objectifying modes of thinking. Some feminists, for instance, want to inject emotion into their approach instead of employing the strictly objective and scientific approaches of males. Rita Gross's emphasis on empathy is an example of this type of an emotional approach. In general, feminists tend to view their work as political and liberating.

Mary Daly is a good example of a radical feminist who directly challenges patriarchal religion and strives to grasp the potential of a women's revolution that includes a transformation of human consciousness. She proposes to castrate the language of the sexist world. By means of her castrating process, masculine symbols and images would lose their credibility. She advocates living on the margins of patriarchal culture to become free of the oppressiveness of the past. In a book like *Gyn/Ecology*, Daly advocates a process of self-discovery renaming for women that she describes as a process of spinning.

In contrast to what they perceive to be a perspective of white feminists, thinkers such as Delores Williams and Katie Cannon advocate a "womanist" (black feminine) position because black women have been neglected and white feminists cannot do justice to the experience of black women, who are equated with survivors and strong figures. Their critique of the racism of white women and men and the sexism of all men is executed within the context of a black woman's experience of racism, sexism, and class prejudice. When making their case, womanist writers exhibit a prophetic, political, and survivalist stance.

Poststructural/Postmodern Approaches

It is possible to distinguish between poststructural and postmodern approaches to the study of religion. Often labeled a poststructuralist thinker, Michel Foucault (1926–1984) adopts some of the linguistic insights of Ferdinand de Saussure (1857–1913) and his theory of signs and signifying along with his reflections on the elements of a language in contrast to the way that it is actually spoken. The previously mentioned Lévi-Strauss applied this theory of language to social groups, whereas Foucault extended de Saussure's theory to history and culture and simultaneously rejected the static aspects of the linguistic model for something more dynamic. In general, poststructuralists reject the subject as a self-contained consciousness, which implies that the individual self lacks presence. Foucault also rejected any assertion that there is a centered or unique place of focus. From this decentered position, Foucault tried to account for the discontinuity of history, its temporal ruptures and factual gaps. Instead of seeking meaning in history, this type of focus led Foucault to stress differences, diversity, and obscuring lines of established communication by calling attention to the many layers of events within discourse, which suggests that history is a series of reinterpretations in narrative form. According to Foucault, the historian can only compose fiction because there are no historical facts. In his earlier works, Foucault used a method called archeology, a purely descriptive method, but adopted genealogy in his later works because it was more diagnostic and enabled him to concentrate on the interrelations of power, knowledge, and the human body. Foucault thought that genealogy, which he borrowed from Friedrich Nietzsche, was a better method for examining the heterogeneous ensemble and gaps of history.

Postmodernism shares some of the same concerns and opinions as poststructuralism, and some writers treat them as separate units of thought, while the latter is sometimes merged with the former. Nonetheless, the term "postmodern" is difficult to define with precision because it represents many voices that do not always agree. The origins of postmodernism have been traced to changes in architectural design; an historical event such as the atom bomb in Hiroshima, Japan, on August 6, 1945; a crisis of narratives that turned knowledge into a commodity that gets produced and sold by, for instance, the computer industry; and loss of the past and accompanying inability to think historically. Whatever its origin, postmodern thinkers point to socio-cultural signs of postmodernism with the loss of traditional household structures, globalization, cultural diversity, urbanization, technology, growth of bureaucracy, simulation of life, liberal democracy, and egalitarianism. If there is a single feature that runs through all these examples, it is the constant flux that they suggest. Another single feature is the attempt to challenge Enlightenment thought by overcoming the representational mode of thinking that occurs when one produces an image for any thought by a person. With representational thinking, the human mind functions as a mirror in a metaphorical way. The diverse assemblage constituting postmodernism implies that it is something plural and not a unified philosophy, although there is a tendency to listen to the German philosopher Martin Heidegger's call to oppose Western metaphysics by thinking about "difference as difference."

From among postmodern thinkers, there is arguably no better example of responding to Heidegger's call than Jacque Derrida (1930–2004), a French philosopher. Derrida is famous for his influential method of deconstruction, a simultaneous process of breaking down and building up a text. By means of deconstruction, a thinker retraces a text to its limits, marks them, leaves a track in the text, and also reveals the track left in the text. The deconstructionist castrates the text because the marks made in the text represent cuts, which is a process of crossing and double-crossing that is exorbitant by nature of exceeding the tracks made in the text. This method, which Derrida refers to as a non-method because it is not reductive like an ordinary scheme, is used to overcome what he calls logocentricism (a metaphysics of presence). Derrida's approach is interested in finding differences as he turns a document against itself. Overall, deconstruction is akin to an inscription that operates to make something evident in order to discern concepts in the text that are cracked by differences and contradictions.

Within the context of Derrida's mode of methodological thinking, religion, a response to the other, is disrupted and subverted. Since religion begins with the presence of an absence, it is both ambiguous and ambivalent, which means that it is impossible to grasp the essence of religion. For Foucault, religion is a mechanism of coercive power. As representatives of poststructural/postmodern thinking, Foucault and Derrida radically alter religion by transforming and destabilizing it. If this discussion of methodological approaches to religion begins with certainty about the nature of the subject, we end with its elusive and absent nature that presents us with a challenge about how to proceed.

In retrospect, these various methodological approaches to the study of religion reflect the multi-dimensional and complex nature of religion. These various methodological approaches imply that religion is not only complex but also manifests a wide diversity that any one or a combination of approaches cannot exhaust because of religion's multiplex nature, which manifests different levels of meaning. These levels of meaning are intertwined with belief systems, practices, cultural ethos, material creations, and goals of a particular culture.

The different ways of methodologically approaching the study of religion suggests a distinction between theory and method. On the one hand, a method is instrumental because it performs a function that is associated with what is logical and conceptual. It helps a scholar of a religion describe in a systematic way what is discovered about a particular religion or religions when comparing one path with another. Method also helps the scholar construct a theory about, for example, a sacrifice or a festival. Based on his findings, experiences, and method, a scholar constructs a theory that unifies what is discovered into a coherent whole that may provide a conditional validity until a better theory is formulated. By concentrating on issues associated with causation, the scholar seeks to explain a particular religious phenomenon, but when the scholar attempts to interpret an encountered phenomenon, he is concerned with the meaning of something. While explanation is related to predictability, the attempt to interpret a phenomenon focuses on possibility. Proceeding from the specific to the general, some theories are inductive, whereas they are deductive when proceeding from general to specific.

In retrospect, the different approaches to understanding religion suggest the complexity of a phenomenon that is cultural, social, narrative, historical, experiential, subjective, and embodied. The nature of religion invites even additional approaches, as evident by the cognitive method. But none of the methodical approaches applied to the subject of religion has been able to exhaust it. Whatever the method used, the study of religion will continue to fascinate scholars and students into the foreseeable future because the narrative of religion is a narrative about humanity.

Problematic Nature of Pluralism and Secularism

At the conclusion of this book, after exposure to religious traditions that have passed into the deep recesses of history, those that are still vibrant today, and those newly developing, it is my expectation that readers would naturally be impressed or at the least aware of the plurality of religions. An awareness of pluralism is the natural result of cross-cultural and comparative efforts to understand the religious ways of other peoples. Pluralism is almost synonymous with religious diversity and is indicative of variety and difference among religions around the globe.

Although it is a cross-cultural given, pluralism is a contributing factor in the rise of secularization, which is in part a subjective feeling that one's inherited religion cannot be a plausible explanation of reality when there are so many competing versions and answers to the problems of life. Even though pluralism tends to be subversive with respect to a particular person's religious convictions, its acceptance tends to enhance the possibilities for tolerance and possible mutual acceptance. From a liberal ideological perspective, pluralism suggests that all religions have a right to their own traditions, belief systems, ritual actions, and spiritual attitudes, a development that upsets those of a much more conservative perspective. Pluralism opens a door to relativism, which undermines claims of superiority, uniqueness, and exclusiveness.

In addition to the threat of pluralism, secularism refers to worldly affairs external to the prevailing religious establishment. Secularism can be traced back to a Latin term, *saeculum* (world, century, age). It implies a process that subverts and possibly replaces religious beliefs and modes of behavior, which creates a cultural vacuum that is filled with worldly ways of thinking, believing, and behaving. The vacuum created by secularism can be filled, for instance, by scientific explanations that can lead to questioning religious values, or the cultural void can also be filled by rationalization that tends to lead to disenchantment with religion. The end result of this process is that the sacred aspects of life are rejected and thus mystery, miracle, and magic are replaced.

Rationalization and its concomitant disenchantment are not the only factors causing secularism. Additional contributing factors of secularism are industrialization, diversity, relativism, pluralism, technology, science, modernization, and egalitarianism. With a focus on lived experience, the philosopher Charles Taylor, in his book *A Secular Age*, identifies three meanings of secularity: (1) public space that is emptied of God or any reference to ultimate reality, even though many people still believe in God; (2) the decline of religious beliefs and practice, with people turning away from God and not attending churches; (3) with a connection to the initial two senses of secularity, its final meaning consists of a situation in which belief in God is understood to be one option among many others. Within this scenario, certainty is loss, and humanism begins to be an attractive alternative.

Religion and Politics

On the morning of September 11, 2001, I turned on the television to learn the final score of the Monday Night Football game and check on the latest news. After turning on the television, I saw a building billowing huge clouds of smoke, a building identified by the news reporter as one of the World Trade towers. As I continued to watch the burning skyscraper, I saw a plane fly into the other tower and set off an explosion. I recall saying to myself "terrorist attack" at seeing the second explosion and reasoning that the same event caused the fire of the first tower. The world would later learn that Muslim extremists had hijacked two American passenger airplanes and deliberately crashed them into the twin towers of the World Trade Center in order to kill as many people working in those structures as possible. When the two towers collapsed because the burning jet fuel burned hot enough to melt the steel structures, the planners of the heinous event were astonished because they did not expect the total collapse of the buildings and shared some laughter over this unexpected happening. Thousands of lives were lost that day in the most heinous terrorist attack in history to that point. The public later discovered that the hijackers took flying lessons on American soil. All things considered, this was a work of evil genius by a pack of religious murderers who justified their actions on religious grounds and denigrated their own religion in the process. Other fundamentalist Muslims hailed the suicidal terrorists as martyrs engaged in a justified holy war against the secular-inclined West. In retrospect, the hijackers and other extremists appropriated and distorted the meaning of holy war in Islam. But what is especially important is that they used their faith to justify their evil. They essentially turned Islam into a political ideology to justify their actions. As illustrated by the 9/11 event, the mixture of religion and politics has often in the course of global history resulted in violence.

The actions of the plane hijackers are just another example of the interrelationship between religion and politics. In addition to Muslim holy wars during its early history and terrorist actions more recently, Europe had its own Christian religious wars, its religious conflicts with Islam to stop its expansion, the Crusades and its attempt to recapture the Holy Lands, the Spanish Inquisition, and World War II. The intertwining of religion and politics is amply illustrated by one man during World War II. That single example is Dietrich Bonhoeffer, a Protestant clergyman, a witness to Nazi depravity, and a twentieth century Christian martyr.

Bonhoeffer was the sixth child of eight siblings born to a psychiatrist and his wife in 1906. Being nurtured in a privileged social environment, the Bonhoeffers were wealthy enough to be insulated from the downward economic spiral experienced by the Weimar Republic. As a young man, Dietrich studied theology with Adolf von Harnack, an acclaimed church historian and liberal thinker, at Friedrich Wilhelms University in the mid-1920s. Then he took a position as an assistant pastor in a Lutheran congregation that exposed him to people from the lower socio-economic level of German society. Dietrich also studied at Union Theological Seminary in New York City; there, he was influenced by the Gospel he heard on Sundays at Harlem's Abyssinian Baptist Church, where he was an assistant pastor. Traveling to the southern states exposed him to racism and conservative politics.

Returning to Berlin in 1931, he witnessed the rise of Nazism. On April 17, 1933, the Reichstag passed a bill that forced the removal of all Jews from civil service jobs. In 1937, his dissident organization for disaffected seminarians near the Baltic Sea was closed down by the Gestapo, the German secret police. After being drafted, Bonhoeffer worked in military intelligence, a position that gave him inside information about internal politics and its anti-Semitism and allowed him to travel unrestricted. Although he was an avowed pacifist, he was implicated in an unsuccessful plot to assassinate Hitler. This act was strongly opposed to his moral values, but he gave a moral justification for the tyrannicide, which he reasoned was a way to save a greater number of lives. Bonhoeffer was arrested and imprisoned before being executed for his part in the unsuccessful plot. During his imprisonment, he smuggled out of prison on pieces of paper his writings, which were collected after his death in a single volume titled *Letters and Papers from Prison*, in which he imagines a religion-less Christianity and other issues for his readers to ponder. Many scholars and others characterize Bonhoeffer as a Christian martyr despite his acquiescence to violence with respect to Hitler and his anti-Semitic policies. Whether Bonhoeffer was right or wrong to resort to violence and violate his vow of pacifism can be debated by reasonable people, but the interrelationship between religion and politics is not debatable.

The term politics comes from the Greek term "*polis*" (city or state) and became "politics" during the use of Middle English in Europe. Normally, politics is a group process whereby people reach agreements and make decisions about how to solve a socio-economic or governmental problem. From the way that it operates, politics is often a struggle for greater influence and power. Starting with the ancient Egyptian rulers, who were considered both human and divine, politics has been interrelated with religion, its narratives, symbols, practices, and striving for power. From one perspective, the ancient Jewish covenant is, of course, a religious agreement between God and His chosen people, but it is also a political document between unequal parties. The Christian Latin Church exercised political power. Constantine (r. 312–327) made Christianity, for example, the official religion of his empire with the purpose of controlling the church and enhancing his own political power. St. Gelasius (r. 392–396), a former pope, advocated the doctrine of two swords, referring to the secular power of the emperor and the spiritual power of the church. The Middle Ages witnessed the church advocating a theocracy (rule of God), a type of government prevalent in Muslim Iran, for instance, at the present.

Buddhism represents a sharp contrast to Christianity and Islam by teaching the renunciation of society and politics. Although the Buddhist monastic community separated itself from the government in kingdoms in India, it was still dependent on the state for support. In turn, the political state gained its legitimacy by its generosity and protection of the monastic community. Indian monarchs often used religious observances and festivals to demonstrate their control and ownership of territory.

In America, its so-called civil religion, which is discussed in a later chapter, weaves together politics and religion into a form of religion that everyone can practice by virtue of being a member of the country. The intellectual developments of black theology, feminist theology, and liberation theology are highly political viewpoints directed at prejudice, discrimination, injustice, and perceived political bondage. If these types of intellectual perspectives represent a progressive stance, conservative religious forces in American have thrown their support to the Republican Party, pushing an agenda that opposes abortion, homosexuality, and gay marriage and supports prayer in public schools and public displays of the Ten Commandments. These conservative groups also insist that America is a Christian nation because it was founded on Christian principles, which makes members of other religions anxious about being able to freely practice their religion as specified in the U.S. Constitution. At times, the rhetoric of conservative groups tends to blur the distinction between the separation of church and state, another religious pillar of the constitution. It is sometimes difficult to differentiate the rhetoric between fundamentalist Muslims and Christians with their intertwining of religion and politics.

Religious Studies: An Academic Discipline

Here you are enrolled in a religious studies course that provides an introduction to and survey of religions around the globe. It is possible that you enrolled in the course because you were curious about the subject matter, because of the reputation of the professor, a friend suggested that you take it, or it meets at a time that fits your schedule. This might be the only course of this kind that you will take at your college or university during your academic career. At the very least, this course will give you something to think about and discuss with your friends. If knowledge is power, you are empowering yourself. Will this course lead directly to or qualify you for a job beyond the confines of your campus? It seems doubtful that such a result will be achieved. This type of religious studies course will, however, broaden your cultural horizons and make you a more interesting companion by giving you something meaningful to discuss on a date. I recall having a conversation some years ago with my heart doctor, who told me that he and fellow medical students would sit around at night and discuss matters of religion, which suggests something about the allure of the subject. But what about the roots of this discipline?

In part, the field of religious studies is an outcome of the European Enlightenment that stressed features such as reason, liberty, equality, tolerance, and common sense. It includes a belief that human nature is basically good despite the sinful nature of humans emphasized by Christian theologians. The Enlightenment also manifests a confidence that humans can improve themselves.

If we examine particular Enlightenment thinkers, we can find implications for thinking. René Descartes (1596–1650) developed methods for critical thinking through his use of methodological doubt in order to secure a foundation on which to erect a philosophy. Descartes argued that he could not doubt his own existence, which he argued could serve as a foundation for his philosophy. What we encounter with Descartes is a thinker searching for first principles and certainty, which later becomes a search for the origins and essence of religion for some.

Descartes' search for certainty was continued by Immanuel Kant (1724–1804), who distinguished between theoretical reason and practical reason with the intention of determining the relationship between reality and knowledge. Kant discovered a unified process of knowledge that consisted of perception (intuition), imagination, and understanding that operated in a cooperative way. It is the human mind that can synthesize sense impressions, unite them, and make them a coherent whole. Perceptions get transformed into experiences by the concepts of our understanding. It is ideas, which are general principles for Kant, which make experience systematic knowledge. Ideas such as soul, God, and world are not given in experience because humans are incapable of understanding metaphysical reality. This point can be grasped by Kant's distinction between the realm of appearance (phenomenal world) that is knowable and reality (noumenal world or thing-in-itself) that is unknowable. But in addition to empirical knowledge, Kant allowed for an a priori form of knowledge, which is unconditioned by experience. Mathematics is the best example of a synthetic a priori type of knowledge. This general philosophical position motivated Kant to distinguish between natural religion, which is shared religious sensibilities, and revealed religion, with its liturgy, theology, ritual, doctrine, and dogma. Kant's position has implications for the study of religion because humans cannot know religion as a thing-in-itself, although they can know and describe phenomenal features of religion.

In response to the Enlightenment discourse about religion, Romantic thinkers gave religion a place in the human heart, making it naturally inherent within humans as a potential that could be developed and refined. A major result of this understanding of religion was that it became something sui generis or unique. As a consequence of its uniqueness, religion could not be reduced to any other phenomena, was conceived as a type of intuition, and was associated with human potential. Romantic thinkers also opposed the overemphasis on rationality by Enlightenment thinkers and stressed the aesthetic and emotional aspects of religion. With the intertwining of the aesthetic and religion, there developed an emphasis on the religious experience of the individual. Romantics tended to relativize religion by asserting that no single religion has a monopoly on the truth and also rendered religion a primarily individual experience. Overall, based on the work of twentieth century scholars, the academic study of religion contains elements of influence from both the Enlightenment and Romantic modes of thinking.

In contrast to its treatment in many theological schools, the discipline of religious studies is an academic subject located within the humanities part of the curriculum in contrast to the social sciences and natural sciences. Being influenced by Enlightenment thought, the academic study of religion is undertaken in a critical, rational, systematic, empathetic, and secular manner. Religious studies is in part a response to Kant's challenge to his readers to know within the context of a free quest for all kinds of knowledge. Intertwined with Kant's call to pursue knowledge, there is a spirit of tolerance exhibited when encountering different subjects and a spirit of optimism that is evident in the conviction that there is nothing beyond the grasp of rational human understanding, with the exception of reality itself. It is these types of attitudes that helped to create the possibility for the academic study of religion.

As part of the legacy of the Enlightenment, the development of higher education exhibits a wide variety of often incompatible visions about its conception. The scientific spirit inspired movements toward greater specialization and compartmentalization in more advanced forms of knowledge. The spirit of science can be uncovered in the German educational system, where a scientific model is advocated for all branches of knowledge. The German term for science (*Wissenschaft*) is broader in meaning than its American counterpart because it suggests an approach to a particular subject that is free of the relativism and positivism evident with the American grasp of science. In contrast to American natural science or empiricism, the highest form of German science is called *Geisteswissenschaften* (sciences of the human spirit), which includes *Naturwissenschaft* (natural science) and is connected with a worldview that represents a synthesis of observations and values. These aspects of the German conception of science are related to an education of cultivation (*Bildung*) that is characteristic of the unique individualism of the scholar.

Moving from the German educational context to the American of the post-World War II era, there is a widespread expansion of institutions of higher education, demands for new technical and professional programs, increased specialization, and influx of secularism. During the 1950s and 1960s, the expansion of higher education also accompanied a growth of the academic study of religion, in sharp distinction to the seminary curriculum emphasizing the study of the primary Western religious scriptures, church history, theology, ethics, and pastoral care courses. Pluralistic course offerings typified religious studies departments as well as the elimination of required courses in religion for graduation and mandatory chapel attendance for graduation requirements. As they evolved in the 1970s and thereafter, college and university religious studies departments moved away from the seminary model of doing religion toward a more inclusive and secular approach. In order to be a genuine religious studies department, it is necessary to include the study of foreign religious traditions, a trend that is resisted by conservative Christian colleges and Catholic universities and colleges that promulgated a strong religious component to their curriculum.

In comparison to the European way of rigorously studying religion, the American constitution helped to shape the study of religion because of its insistence on the separation of church and state. Culminating with the Supreme Court decision in *Abington v. Schempp*, federal courts ruled that it is permissible to teach "about" religion in a state institution because such study is not indoctrination. This ruling also allowed teaching the Bible objectively, critically, and historically as part of a secular education. This type of court ruling accompanied the growth of the study of religion as a serious and legitimate academic subject. Professors of religion stressed the need for multi-interdisciplinary and cross-cultural approaches to the subject. Students benefited by these trends to learn about the pervasive nature of religion in human experience, to learn about foreign cultures, and to gain critical intellectual tools to analyze and understand a rapidly changing world that they will enter after graduation.

The textbook that you are reading is written in the spirit of historical, empathetic multi-interdisciplinary, and cross-cultural approaches to the subject of religion. Throughout the chapters that follow, there is a focus on a narrative approach to the subject with an emphasis on the importance of different types of religious experience, even within particular religious traditions. The use of the term "world religion" has been purposely rejected because of the negative baggage acquired from its inception during the period of colonialism and Western domination and exploitation of Third World countries. Christian bias, convictions about cultural superiority, and European and Christian universalism are also hidden agendas promoted by the term. The term "world religion" implies a religion similar to ours based on a prejudiced assessment by those doing the comparison. Thus, the notion of a "world religion" has exceeded its usefulness as an academic construction and instrument of political domination.

The following chapters will also include a brief discussion about the role of women in a particular religious tradition because women have been neglected in books of this genre. In addition to a consideration of women, each chapter includes a consideration of rituals, material culture, and concerns about the end of time by examining ideas concerning death and the possibility of an afterlife. With a couple of exceptions, this book devotes little time to a discussion about theology. This decision to mostly exclude considerations of theology does not mean that theology does not matter or that it has no place in religious studies. Theology has been downplayed in this book because it is an activity practiced by an elite few, whereas this book intends to include a closer look at the religious lives of ordinary people. Although theology is not stressed in the chapters of this book, the belief system and path to salvation are considered. In various religious traditions, theology is not an appropriate discipline or is considered a foreign subject more germane to theistic systems of religion. Many chapters will consider the worldview of the religion to provide students with the grand vision of a religion.

Suggestions for Further Reading

Arnal, William E. and Russell T. McCutcheon. *The Sacred Is the Profane: The Political Nature of "Religion."* Oxford, New York: Oxford University Press, 2013.

Asad, Talad. *Genealogies of Religion: Discipline and Reason of Power in Christianity and Islam.* Baltimore, MD: Johns Hopkins University Press, 1993.

Braun, Willi and Russell T. McCutcheon. Eds., *Guide to the Study of Religion.* London: Cassell, 2000.

Burkert, Walter. *Creation of the Sacred: Tracks of Biology in Early Religions.* Cambridge: Harvard University Press, 1996.

Daly, Mary. *Gyn/Ecology: The Metaethics of Radical Feminism.* Boston: Beacon Press, 1978; reprint 1990.

Eliade, Mircea. *The Sacred and the Profane.* Trans. Willard R. Trask. New York: Harcourt Brace, 1963.

Fitzgerald, Timothy. *Discourse on Civility and Barbarity: A Critical History of Religion and Related Categories.* New York: Oxford University Press, 2007.

———. *The Ideology of Religious Studies.* New York: Oxford University Press, 2000.

Flood, Gavin. *The Importance of Religion: Meaning and Action in Our Strange World.* Oxford: Wiley-Blackwell, 2012.

Foucault, Michel. *Essential Works of Foucault 1954–1984.* 3 Vols. Ed. Paul Rabinow. New York: The New Press, 1994.

Freud, Sigmund. *The Future of an Illusion*. Trans. James Strachery. New York: Norton, 1975.

Geertz, Clifford. *The Interpretations of Cultures*. New York: Basic Books, 1973.

Gross, Rita. *Feminism and Religion: An Introduction*. Boston: Beacon Press, 1996.

Hick, John. *An Interpretation of Religion: Human Responses to the Transcendent*. New Haven, CT: Yale University Press, 1989.

Hinnells, John. Ed. *The Routledge Companion to the Study of Religion*, Second Edition. London: Routledge, 2010.

Lévi-Strauss, Claude. *Structural Anthropology*. Trans. Claire Jacobson and Brooke Grundfest Schoeft. New York: Basic Books, 1963.

Malinowski, Bronislaw. *Magic, Science and Religion and Other Essays*. Ed. Robert Bedfield. Garden City, NY: Doubleday, 1948.

Masuzawa, Tomoko. *The Invention of World Religions, or, How European Universalism Was Preserved in the Language of Pluralism*. Chicago: University of Chicago Press, 2005.

McCutcheon, Russell T. *Manufacturing Religion: The Discourse on Sui Generis Religion and the Politics of Nostalgia*. New York: Oxford University Press, 1997.

Olson, Carl. *The Allure of Decadent Thinking: Religious Studies and the Challenge of Postmodernism*. New York: Oxford University Press, 2013.

———. *Religious Studies: The Key Concepts*. London and New York: Routledge, 2011.

———. Ed. *Theory and Method in the Study of Religion*. Belmont, CA: Wadsworth/Thomson, 2003.

Orsi, Robert A. Ed. *The Cambridge Companion to Religious Studies*. Cambridge: Cambridge University Press, 2012.

Risebrodt, Martin. *The Promise of Salvation: A Theory of Religion*. Trans. Steven Rendall. Chicago: University of Chicago Press, 2010.

Segal, Robert A. Ed. *The Blackwell Companion to the Study of Religion*. Oxford: Blackwell Publishing, 2006.

Smart, Ninian. *Dimensions of the Sacred: An Anatomy of the World's Beliefs*. Berkeley: University of California Press, 1996.

Smith, Jonathan Z. *Map Is not Territory: Studies in the History of Religions*. Leiden: E. J. Brill, 1978.

Smith, Wilfred Cantwell. *The Meaning and End of Religion: A New Approach to the Religious Traditions of Mankind*. Minneapolis: Fortress Press, 1962; reprint 1991.

Taylor, Mark C. Ed. *Critical Terms for Religious Studies*. Chicago: University of Chicago Press, 1998.

Weber, Max. *The Protestant Ethic and the Spirit of Capitalism*. New York: Scribner, 1930.

2 Ancient Mediterranean Religions

Besides sharing the features of being historically antiquated and dead religious traditions, the ancient Mediterranean religions of Egypt, Greece, and Rome also share other characteristics, such as the following common features: by being polytheistic; not having a single or identifiable origin; orally transmitting their religious traditions; contributing to the maintenance of the social order; being public and communal rather than a private activity; being closely associated with and controlled to a large degree by the state; having their religious cult concentrated in the temple; being born into the state religion by virtue of one's citizenship; participating often in both the state and popular religious cultures; having a popular religion located in both the home and local shrine; and engaging in festival celebrations that create a bond between ordinary citizens and the state religious culture. For readers coming from monotheistic traditions, the polytheism of these religions might raise some questions and problems about reasons for the attraction of many divine beings to a particular religious culture. The Greek author Euripides in his *Hippolytus* (428 BCE) asserts that it is dangerous to focus on only one god. By worshipping the goddess Artemis and refusing the goddess Aphrodite, it is possible, for example, that such a worshipper might be harmed by the offended divine being. In Homer's epic *Iliad*, gods are involved in natural and social occurrences. Not only are Greek gods participants in the war described in the text, but they intervene in human events and punish humans for moral transgressions. Knowing about this type of possibility, it is incumbent on human beings to placate the gods. Moreover, if one deity fails to help a person, that individual can try her luck with another deity. Thus, from the perspective of participants of ancient Mediterranean religions, polytheism had its benefits over monotheism.

Egyptian Pantheon and Creation Narratives

The Egyptian pantheon changed over the very long course of the culture's history. An early version of the pantheon was led by the divine couple Shu and Tefnut, a goddess of moisture, who gave birth to Geb. The pantheon expanded to include Geb and his consort Nut along with their children Osiris, Isis, Seth, and Nephthys. In the Egyptian religious imagination, Geb's recumbent body forms the earth, whereas Nut is a sky goddess whose body extends over that of Geb and Shu ("Emptiness"), associated with the space between earth and heaven. Many Egyptian gods were related to natural phenomena, such as the leaders of the pantheon Amun or Atum and Horus, sun gods. Horus ("Distant One") was imagined with two eyes that were identified with the sun and moon. After the murder of Osiris by his brother Seth, Horus assumed the throne of the divine kingdom, a result that connected him to earthly legitimate kingly succession and authority to govern. In Egyptian art, Horus was depicted as a falcon or as a falcon-headed human wearing a crown or sun disk on his head.

An important goddess figure was Hathor ("House of Horus"), who was connected to joy and erotic love. The term "house" in her name connotes womb. Each morning she gave birth to Re (the sun deity), and swallowed him each evening in the west. There is an ancient narrative about how she and beer saved the world and humanity by accident. Seeking to inflict vengeance on those who plotted to overthrow him, Re commands Hathor, in her aspect as Sekhmet, a frightening, ferocious, and feline figure, to destroy his enemies. After destroying half of the world's population, Re procures an immense quantity of barley beer mixed with a red color and pours it over the earth. When she awakens from her slumber, Hathor mistakes the red-tinted liquid for human blood, drinks it, and thereafter becomes too intoxicated to finish her work, which thereby saves humanity.

Hathor played many roles in Egyptian religious culture, such as protecting women during child birth, and thus she was called "Lady of the Vulva." She appears as a non-domesticated, wild cow that thrives in the marshy areas. When she is depicted as a human figure, she has horns on her head and a sun-disk. She is connected with trees and festive revelry as a result of a state of inebriety. There are narratives of her accepting the dead in the underworld, where she functions as a goddess of fate. As a warrior goddess, she dispenses divine retribution for those who offend the gods. In this type of role she is identified with Sekhmet ("the Powerful One"), a ferocious figure depicted with the head of a lioness. In addition to her fearsome nature, Hathor is also the goddess of more benign actions by serving as a patroness of singers, dancers, and artists.

Another important goddess in ancient Egypt was Isis, whose cult would later be transported to Greece and Rome. She was portrayed as a devoted wife, widow, and mother. Her tears shed in mourning were imagined to be the cause of the flooding of the Nile River. She evolved into the Queen of Heaven. In fact, her name means a throne on which a king sits, which thus closely associates her with the king as his protector. She is also able to heal people and perform magic by, for instance, creating spells used to protect people. Her cunning, clever, and wise nature enables her to learn the secret name of Re. In the narrative, she is depicted collecting drool from the sleeping Re and combines this liquid with earth to create a venomous snake that bites Re after he awakens from his sleep. The pain caused Re to cry for help. Since she is the only deity capable of curing Re of poisonous snakebite, she demands to know his secret name before she cures him, to which Re eventually agrees. By knowing the secret name of Re, she can control and manipulate him, which in turn increases her own power and stresses her role as a trickster figure. Because of the dangerous power of erotic love, Isis domesticates it for the purpose of human procreation. Isis' relationship to her brother Osiris and death will be developed later in this chapter.

Other Egyptian deities included Thoth, divine scribe and moon god, and Knonsu, a god of the city Thebes, who is a good example of a local or regional deity evolving into a national figure. Thoth appears as a baboon or an ibis and was originally associated with the moon, which connected him to time and measurement of years for the purpose of discerning the time of a person's death, which gives him the power to control fate. As the patron of writers, he is associated with books, bestows writing on humans, and gives them the power of speech. Thoth's words are believed to possess magic.

Two significant regional goddesses were Nekhbet and Wadjit. Protecting Upper Egypt, the former was represented as a vulture, whereas the latter goddess is depicted as a cobra and protector of Lower Egypt. The goddess Bastet was represented with a cat's head. This ambivalent goddess can be friendly and cheerful as well as savage and wrathful. The deity Ptah (meaning prosperity, fortune) was the lord of the city of Memphis, capital of the Old Kingdom, who was associated with the fertility of the earth, crafts such as smith or sculptor, and primal creator. The god Min was also connected to fertility, along with serving as the protector of travelers. Wearing a red crown, the goddess Neith was an early goddess of war, signified by a pair of crossed arrows; she was also related to magic, healing, protecting the dead, and the art of weaving. In addition to local and regional deities, there were gods of the underworld portrayed with the head of jackals, including Wepwawet ("Opener of the Way") and Anubis acting as judge and ruler of the dead, who was later succeeded by Osiris during Dynasty 5.

Ancient Egyptians had more than one creation narrative. According to one version, Atum ("the All") created the world when he masturbated and brought order to the undifferentiated mass. Shu and Tefnut were created as the first divine couple. They were respectively related to the breath of life and the moisture of the heavens. In another creation story, it is Ptah, a chief deity during Dynasty 4, who speaks and all things come into existence. Ptah is portrayed as a mummified human figure holding a scepter, representing symbolically life, order, and power.

Greek Pantheon and Creation Narratives

According to Hesiod's Greek work the *Theogony*, Zeus did not create the world, because there was only chaos in the beginning. From this chaos, there arose Gaia ("Earth") and Eros (passion). Gaia gave birth to Uranus (heaven, sky). Then, there came into being a divine generation of the Uranides that included: the six Titans (including Oceanus and Kronos) and the six Titanides (among them were Rhea, Themis, and Mnemogyne), three one-eyed Cyclopes, and three hundred giants. Because he hated his children, Uranus hid them in Gaia's body, who became angry, produced a sickle, and urged her children to punish their father for his despicable attitude toward his children. Among Gaia's children, Kronos was the only child to respond to his mother and act; his action involved the castration of his father while the parent was in a drunken stupor. When Uranus' blood fell on his earthly wife, she gave birth to various creatures. When Uranus' severed sexual organs were thrown into the sea, this resulted in the birth of the goddess Aphrodite.

After rendering his father impotent, Kronos assumed his parent's position and proceeded to marry his sister Rhea, who gave birth to five children: Hestia, Demeter, Hera, Hades, and Poseidon. Fearful of being deposed by any of his children as he had done to his father, Kronos swallowed his children upon their birth. When giving birth to Zeus, Rhea hid him in a cave, substituted a stone wrapped in clothes, and gave the bundle to Kronos to consume. On reaching maturity, Zeus forced Kronos to disgorge his previously swallowed siblings, who gave Zeus a gift of thunder and lightning, which enabled Zeus to command both mortal humans and immortal divine beings. Nonetheless, a long protracted war ensued until victory by Zeus over, finally, Typhon. Then, the major male gods drew lots and divided the world into three cosmic zones: Poseidon presided over the ocean, Hades received the underworld, and Zeus assumed control of the sky. The earth belonged to the three figures in common. Thereafter, Zeus married a series of female figures. With his authority assured, Zeus freed Kronos and made his father king of the Isles of the Blessed, located in the west.

Zeus was not the sole leading figure of the Greek pantheon, although his sexual exploits were often associated with other divine figures. Taking the side of his mother Hera in a dispute with her husband Zeus, Hephaestus, an ugly and infirm son, was thrown by Zeus from Mount Olympus, resulting in him becoming lame in both feet. In later narratives, he binds divine beings with items that he creates, such as knots, nets, and strings that bind others. A famous exploit is his imprisonment of Ares and Aphrodite within an invisible net, prompting other divine beings to laugh at the captured, guilty, and fornicating couple. Hephaestus is the father of the first king and ancestor of the Athenians. Homer depicts him stumbling around on his crippled feet trying to pour wine for the gods, having humorous fun at a handicapped individual's expense.

The Greek pantheon included other important divine male figures. Although given dominion over the ocean by Zeus, Poseidon is associated with horses, and there is a narrative that illustrates this connection. While searching for her daughter, Demeter encountered Poseidon, and he attempted to rape her, but she transformed herself into a mare to escape him. Poseidon succeeded, however, when he became a stallion, and their sexual union created Arion. Poseidon is responsible for the first animal when he shed his semen on a rock from which the animal came. In a different narrative, Poseidon has intercourse with the petrifying Gorgon Medusa. When she was beheaded by Perseus, the horse, Pegasus, and the armed warrior, Chrysaor, sprang from her body. Moreover, Poseidon's dominion over the sea made him a guardian of sailors and fishermen along with being god of the earthquake.

Other sexual exploits of Zeus relate his impregnating the Titaness Leto, who could find no place to give birth because of a fear of invoking Hera's wrath. Finally being accepted on the island of Delos, Leto gives birth to twins, the male Apollo and the female Artemis. Apollo was associated with law, social order, and divine harmony. Apollo is a liminal figure because he is depicted somewhere between adolescence and adulthood, a feature that makes him an ideal candidate as the supervisor of initiatory rites. He was also associated with political institutions, music, and dance. In the epic *Iliad*, Apollo's arrows signify pestilence, but he is also a deity of healing. Sometimes, he is portrayed dancing with his lyre.

Another significant male figure was Hermes, a son of Zeus and the nymph Maia, playing the roles of god, trickster, artisan, and giver of good luck. He became a protector of thieves because he stole cattle from Apollo. Hermes was the protector of flocks, herds, and travelers. Besides his role as messenger of the gods, he invented fire. His association with fertility is the rationale for his being worshipped in the form of a phallus, which recalls his sexual escapades with nymphs in wooded areas, reflecting his connection with the growth of herds of sheep and goats. Hermes does not get lost at night because he knows the way even in the dark and can walk rapidly because of his golden sandals. Since he knows his way around, he guided the dead to the underworld and also became the messenger of the gods.

Some Greek goddesses were also associated with fertility. Artemis, sister of Apollo, was the mistress of wild beasts and functioned as the goddess of child birth, nursing, and teaching. Similar to her brother, she supervised the transition from female adolescence to womanhood. Symbolically associated with light, she was depicted in literature and art with her nymphs hunting. The already-mentioned Hera, wife of Zeus, presided over marriage as its patroness, even though her own marriage was hardly harmonious and blissful because of her husband's philandering adventures. There is a dark side of her nature because she was also the mother of horrific monsters.

Similar to Apollo, the goddess Athena was intimately connected to the Greek city, which she protected from outsiders. According to Greek narratives, she sprang from the head of Zeus already clad in armor. Her origin from her father's head suggests having the attribute of intelligence. In Homer's *Iliad*, she is closely associated with warriors such as Achilles and Odysseus as an advisor. In addition to her martial duties, she was the patroness of the feminine arts of spinning and weaving along with more male-associated crafts like carpentry, being a warrior, and training horses. She is credited with creating the olive tree, horse bridle, and chariot. She also killed a monstrous goat that she skinned and used as her emblem and armor. A narrative also relates her killing and skinning a human giant, Pallas, on the island of Kos, a skin that she proceeded to wear, which serves as a narrative to explain her title as Pallas of Athens.

According to Hesiod's *Theogony*, the goddess Aphrodite originated from the foamy semen of Uranus' sexual organs when thrown into the ocean. She became famous for her connection to sexuality and her own sexual adventures, which got her into trouble. According to one narrative, she was married to Hephaestus, but she simultaneously entered into an illicit affair with Ares. Her husband created a net that caught the lovers betraying him. The two lovers were humiliated when the gods saw them captured in the net and laughed at their predicament. Because of her intimate association with sexuality, Aphrodite was associated with prostitutes and symbolically associated with doves, which were believed to be promiscuous birds, not unlike the goddess.

In contrast to divine beings with a clearly definable gender, the god Dionysus is a more liminal and ambiguous figure. In Aristophanes' *Frogs*, Dionysus is portrayed as an effeminate and cowardly deity who gets involved in grotesque comic situations. There is a reference in another Greek play, the *Bacchae*, of a god with many names. An example of such a name is Bacchus, a god of wine, representing a life force connected to plant, animal, or human life. This force brings madness and potential disaster. There are Greek narratives that associated Dionysus with satyrs, half-human and goat servants of the god, and maenads, wild female followers of the god driven mad enough to kill humans and animals with their bare hands. His liminal nature relates him to male initiation, during which young boys temporarily dress as girls. With his ability to cause ecstasy and madness, Dionysus represents a creative tension between order and disorder. His mystery cult is examined later in this chapter.

As illustrated by their narratives, Greek divine beings often manifested very human traits, such as envy, licentiousness, and amorality. Although they were invisible and immortal, the gods were not particularly loving beings, not eternal, omnipotent, omniscient, or omnipresent. Similar to an earthly ruler, the Greek deities had no guarantee that their power would continue in the future, they could be deceived, and they could fail to succeed. They could become disorderly and petty-minded but still capable of maintaining rules of justice. The Greek pantheon is very anthropomorphic and is populated by figures with defined personalities. Some deities were more prominent than others, according to location, because each Greek city-state had its own pantheon. Within the pantheon of these city-states, there were many local goddesses who got absorbed into the pantheon by becoming consorts of Zeus. The Greek pantheon reflects a twofold division: Olympian gods who reside in the upper sky, on the surface of the earth, under the ocean, and chthonic powers that exist beneath the earth. These underworld powers were, moreover, differentiated into two additional spheres, with one ensuring the earth's fertility and the other representing forces of the underworld and the dead. Another feature of the majority of Greek gods is that they are both benevolent and malevolent, which made them dangerous to humans.

In addition to gods and goddesses, Greek narratives devoted much attention to heroes. The military glory won on the battlefield by heroes gave them a kind of immortality by perpetuating their names and exploits for future generations, as evident by heroes such as Achilles, Heracles, Ajax, Odysseus, and several others. In contrast to the unbridgeable gap between the gods and ordinary mortals, heroes and gods sometimes overlapped with regard to their functions, although a hero's influence was more limited than that of a divine being. An excellent example of a heroic figure that benefited humankind was Prometheus, who was credited with creating humans, stealing fire from heaven for the benefit of humans, and arranging sacrifice to also profit people. According to a Greek narrative, Zeus, an adversary of Prometheus because of his help of humans, punished men with the first woman, Pandora, and her box of evils that is opened to the detriment of humankind. Often depicted guarding oaths and cities, heroes were usually benevolent figures, even though some could be malicious. Their popularity can be partly attributed to the common belief that they were more accessible than the Olympian gods.

Roman Pantheon and Creation

In comparison to Hesiod's genealogy of the Greek gods, the Romans seemed to suggest that the origin of the city of Rome was more significant than any divine pantheon. The origin of Rome relates a narrative about sibling rivalry. The first set of brothers are Numitor, a king, and his brother Amulius, who deposes the king, kills Numitor's sons, and forces their sister, Rhea Sylvia, to become a Vestal virgin. But Rhea is already pregnant, having been impregnated by Mars, god of war, and gives birth to two boys: Romulus and Remus. The twins are left exposed on the bank of the Tiber River. They initially survive when they are suckled by a she-wolf sent by Mars before being rescued and raised by a shepherd and his wife. The sons re-establish their grandfather Numitor on the throne. Then they proceed to establish a city. Romulus chooses the Palatine as the best place to consult the gods, while Remus ascends the Aventine hill, where a flock of six vultures appear to him to serve as an initial augural sign, whereas Romulus sees twelve vultures, which implies to him that he had received the honor of founding the city. Romulus plows a furrow around the Palatine, with the turned up earth representing walls, the furrow standing for a moat, and the plow standing for the gates. After ridiculing Romulus' symbolic creation by jumping over it, Remus is killed by his brother. This origin narrative weaves together cultic elements with its reference to the Vestal virgins, the importance of divination, centrality of protecting the city from all invaders, the symbolic significance of the hills as places near to the gods, and higher locations for communicating with the divine beings. The killing of Remus is a symbolic, cosmogonic sacrifice, whereas Romulus assumes the role of primal sacrificer, founder of Rome, warrior, legislator, and priest.

The most archaic account of the Roman pantheon included Jupiter, Mars, and Quirinus, which was later extended to include Janus and Vesta. Similar to the Greek Zeus, Jupiter was a sovereign figure, associated with thunder, and a guarantor of justice, fertility, and creation, while Mars was the god of war. Quirinus represented the community of the Roman people. Janus is the patron deity of beginnings and is associated with liminal locations such as thresholds and gates. Janus is imagined to be two-faced. Vesta is a goddess figure considered to be close to humans because she is associated with the fire and the hearth in a home. Her sanctuary is round in shape, in contrast to the quadrangular shape of other temples. The round shape of her temple reflects the round earth, which is the source of her power. Although other deities are represented by temple images, Vesta is signified by the fire, which replaced images of her.

The later Romans would add the goddesses Juno and Minerva. Juno's name suggests a vital force with many functions, such as ruling over festivals, fertility, the monthly calendar, and periodic rebirth of the moon. Minerva is considered patroness of arts and artisans. Why did the Romans expand their pantheon? A political or social crisis, an epidemic, or a war might induce Romans to expand their pantheon for practical purposes of seeking assistance to alleviate suffering. During a conflict with another state, a Roman general might, for example, ask a foreign god to join the Roman side in conjunction with a promise to build a temple to the deity in Rome.

Egyptian Belief System

Because the ancient Egyptians developed their culture in relative isolation from other cultures, their religious beliefs did not change very much over the centuries; they enhanced social stability, encouraged a conservative perspective, and helped to create a homogeneous religious ethos. Holding everything together in ancient Egypt was its belief in *ma'at* (order), which represented an identifiable goddess and a central cultural concept. Ma'at is a natural power built into the universe that stands for truth, justice, and order in society; it is normative in all aspects of human life. The origin of the goddess Ma'at is traced back to her being created by Re, the sun god and her father, although she is also known paradoxically as his mother. This connection is explained by the fact that the sun god is bound to his pre-established course in the sky, an orderly path of movement created by *ma'at*. Besides her connection to Re, she is also related to Osiris, lord of the dead, and the judgment of the dead that is conducted in a chamber of the double *ma'at*, essentially life and death.

Ancient Egyptian beliefs reflect the ubiquity of divine power. The concept of god is represented in a hieroglyph depicting a pole holding a flag, which also served as a sign of a holy place. Ancient Egyptians refer to god's beauty, which suggests being ethically and cosmically good. The widespread divine power is also present in humans and animals, which seems to suggest the ease with which to imagine divine beings with human and animal attributes. The appearance of a god can vary and calls attention to various aspects of the god's nature and power. Hathor, for example, is represented with the head of a cow, but when she appears as a female she is depicted with cow's ears; she might also be crowned with a sun disk and a uraeus, a sacred cobra, on her head. This example suggests that anthropomorphic forms and terms are intended to indicate the power of the divine being. This anthropomorphic emphasis means that Egyptians conceived their gods as being akin to humans but with extraordinary abilities. The social life of the gods bears a strong resemblance to human life. The ancient deities lived in an eternity of cyclical time, a location of change and renewal, and a more static, changeless, eternal life. The former is exemplified by Re, the sun deity, and the latter mode of life means to live in the presence of Osiris in the afterlife.

In addition to their relation to *ma'at*, another powerful force is *ba*, an omnipresent power in the world that ultimately resides in heaven. When a god came to the earth, he needed a physical location to reside. The *ba* could reside in a physical form, which is then transformed into a *ka* that enables humans to communicate with a divine being. It is, for example, the *ba* that transforms and enlivens a statue into a *ka*, which is now the physical form of the god while on earth. And like any living entity, the statue needs food and drink offerings for the *ka* from time to time.

Although the gods are not necessarily concerned or engaged with human beings on an everyday basis, this is not true of the king, titular head of a theocratic culture with its religion forming the basis of it. The ancient kings of the First and Second Dynasty (3000–2670 BCE) claimed to be incarnations of Horus, while kings of the Old Kingdom (2686–2125 BCE) declared themselves to be sons of Re, the sun god. This represents a way to enhance the king's authoritative status and power and renders any contenders to the throne enemies of the gods. The primary responsibility of a king is the maintenance of social order and harmony (*ma'at*), without which people cannot thrive. Besides dispensing justice, the king's duties extended to nature with his role overseeing the annual flood of the Nile on which the welfare and survival of the people depends. The divine incarnational status of the king invites ordinary citizens to worship him as a manifestation of divine *ka*, an aspect of the king that was celebrated annually at the temple of Amun-Re at Karnak, while a 30-year reign calls for a festival celebration. These types of religious observances renewed the power of the king. After the death of the king, his *ka* was transferred into his statue, which enabled his royal cult to continue.

The concepts of *ba* and *ka* extended to human nature, where they were embedded in the body of a person, giving each person a firm foundation on which to live. A father is linked to his son by *ka*, a seed that connects different generations, while the *ba*, symbolically portrayed as a bird with a human head, moves easily between earthly and heavenly realms after a person dies. The working of *ka* and *ba* embodied within a human being suggest that Egyptians did not draw sharp distinctions between the physical and spiritual aspect of life, although a belief in an eternal soul is absent in their understanding of human nature. As an embodied being without a soul, a human's body determined to a large degree the quality of one's life, a situation that was especially

Figure 2.1 Temple of Karnak dedicated to the Amun. Waj / Shutterstock.com

true after death and provides a rationale for the embalmment of the body to guarantee its post-existence.

In addition to a person's body, the human heart was considered the organ of life. According to an ancient Egyptian narrative, Anubis unfairly accuses his brother Bata of adultery; Bata responded emotionally to the false accusations by emasculating himself and traveling to the underworld, where he places his heart on a blossom of a cedar tree. His heart carried a message from the aggrieved brother instructing anyone reading it to place his heart in cool water after the tree is cut down. This simple narrative suggests that there can be no life without a heart, the locus of morality and consciousness. When the dead are judged, it is their heart that testifies for or against them. The role of the body and heart in human nature is indicative of the Egyptian belief that there is not a sharp distinction between the material and spiritual aspects of humans. The importance of the human body serves as a rationale for the post-death practice of embalmment to secure a mode of existence after life.

Even though the ancient Egyptians did not have a conception of an eternal soul, they did believe in multiple souls. A person's shadow is analogous to a soul, functioning as a personal protector and spiritual power. There is a soul that is connected to food, a kind of divine vitality or energy. This is the soul that accompanies a deceased person when she travels to the afterworld. If a deceased person loses her soul, she is considered nothing. Another soul is associated with the will to be free, which is depicted as a bird with a human head, holding in its claws a hieroglyphic sign signifying life. An additional soul gets manifested after death. A deceased person gains this soul, which normally resides in heaven, by ritual means. The funeral rites elevate a person and enable her to acquire this spiritual power.

In contrast to historically later Christianity, Egyptians did not believe in original sin, although they did not think that humans were perfect. The important practice of a human was to live a harmonious life in accord with *ma'at* (the cosmic law of order and well-being). The Egyptians' emphasis on destiny and death did not mean that they were fatalistic or pessimistic. They were rather confident that humans could share in the afterlife with the gods, even though they did not develop a cosmic notion of eschatology (last things) and the fate of the world. Death marked a change to another mode of existence and not the complete end to existence, but a type of life that is a mirror image of the present life.

Ancient Egyptians believed that humans and gods could communicate with each other by means of divine oracles, human prayers, and votive offerings. Gods could also communicate their displeasure with humans by sending illness or disastrous events. An example of a deity communicating with a human is the oracle. With the image of the deity on a boat, the god makes itself heavy, causing the bow to dip and the entire boat to shake, movements that indicate the divine will and its message. The success of prayers was enhanced by using an upright stone or pillar engraved with ears to enable gods to more easily hear human prayers. Depending on a human request, the votive offerings could take many forms, such as figurines, plaques, representations of ears, eyes, and phalluses, or amulets. Votive offerings might include mummified animals symbolically associated with a particular deity, such as a cat with Bastet, a baboon with Thoth, or a mongoose with Re. Additional modes of human/divine communication could arrive by dreams, which enable one to gain access to things and people at a far distance. A self-inducing trance state can also transport a person to a distant realm where he can more easily communicate with higher beings. These various types of communication were most often motivated by practical concerns related to illness, social problems, or other difficulties.

Humans were not merely capable of communicating with the gods, but they were also able to sense the presence of divine beings by means of smell, hearing, seeing, or intuition. If a person receives communication that he is under the *bau* (sign of a god's anger), this is reason for concern. Learning about the threat of a god's displeasure with a person is cause for a frightening experience. Anyone under the threat of *bau* is considered to be impure and should be avoided. A person could, however, protect himself against an angry deity by wearing an amulet exhibiting some type of decree. From what has been revealed about divine/human interaction, it is obvious that gods functioned as an integral aspect of ancient Egyptian culture, suggesting no inflexible division between sacred and profane.

During Dynasty 18 (1550–1295 BCE), the leader Akhenaten attempted to transform Egyptian religion from polytheism to monotheism, focusing on the god Atem as an incarnation of the sun and giver of life. After establishing

Atem at his capital at Tell el Amarna, the king discouraged worship of other deities and claimed to be Atem's representative on earth; he was also the only person who knew Atem's will. This attempt had some interesting results because it tried to disrupt the people's direct contact with the deity by inserting the king between the people and god. What saved people was no longer their actions; instead, one's fate depended on one's adoration and obedience to the king. This move to insert the king as a mediator between the people and a monotheistic god did not survive for long in Egyptian religious history. The prominence of polytheism reclaimed its short eclipsed status.

Greek Belief System

According to Hesiod's *Works and Days*, humans are born from the earth into five races: gold, silver, bronze, heroes, and iron. Living like gods, the original humans did not experience pain or have to work; they simply lived a life of pleasure, which came to a conclusion with the fall of Kronos. Because of their failure to sacrifice to the gods, Zeus decided to destroy humans by creating a violent race of bronze. After total decimation of the population, Zeus created a race of heroes, although some died while others went to the Isles of the Blessed. In contrast to this ancient account of Hesiod, there are other Greek versions accounting for the origin of humankind. There are narratives that tell stories about benefactors who assist humankind. A noteworthy figure is Prometheus, famous for stealing fire from heaven to give to humankind in order to cook and keep warm. This transgression against heaven motivates Zeus to punish the thief and presumably humankind for accepting the stolen heavenly property. Zeus' punishment confines Prometheus to a rock, where an eagle eats his liver each day after it regrows from the previous day. The hero Heracles, son of Zeus, would later set Prometheus free.

The Greek poet Homer compares the human situation to windblown leaves scattered on the ground. Homer indicates that the human situation is not only precarious, but it is also ephemeral and a burden. For those that committed virtuous or evil deeds, they were not rewarded or punished. Thus, the ancient Greeks did not believe in original sin or eternal damnation, although narratives provide some exceptions with Ixion, Tantalus, and Sisyphus. The punishment of Sisyphus is diabolically absurd because he is condemned to push a huge rock up a hill only to have it fall back to where it began once it reaches the top of the hill, representing his destiny, whereas Tantalus strives to helplessly reach fruit and water without success. Ixion was a king in ancient Thessaly who was guilty of being impious, a perjurer, and a murderer. He was the first figure to kill a relative, his father-in-law. Zeus agreed to punish him by means of a ruse to welcome the murderer with hospitality, but Ixion coveted Zeus' wife Hera. Zeus sent his guest a cloud image of his wife, with whom Ixion had a sexual relationship that produced a monster, Centaurus, who was half man and half horse.

Each person is given a specific destiny, an allotted time, until one's death. A person's portion is given at birth, a feature of Greek belief called *moira* (destiny, fate), a term that implies a share that one is given that defines one's social status. Death is also a share that is given to everyone. The *moira* is imagined by ancient Greeks as three old women who sit spinning, measuring, and cutting the yarn that weaves together one's life. Since Zeus determines one's fate, *moira* is impossible to alter because any alternative course would be contrary to the universal laws of justice (*dikē*). As a concrete manifestation of a universal order, justice (*dikē*) is a divine law (*themis*). Justice is important and needed because it restrains humans from acting like wild animals. Humans are encouraged to practice *arete* (virtue, excellence), which is associated with not daring to go too far or to exceed accepted social limits. *Arete* functions to lift up a person, which can become dangerous to the holder of virtue because it might infringe on divine prerogatives, which the gods are eager to protect. It is permissible to cultivate one's virtue, but it must be done in a moderate way and not excessively. For those individuals who exceed the limit, they are guilty of *hubris* (pride) and can invoke the wrath of the gods.

In early Greek culture, each person had a *psyche* (equated with breath); its cessation resulted in an external sign of death. This notion later evolved into an immortal soul that left the body at death. A phantom represents an image of a person without consciousness, which is devoid of force in Homer's *Odyssey*. It is phantoms that drink sacrificial blood in order to speak; they are compared to gibbering bats in a cave by the poet.

Another aspect of the Greek belief system is the *omphalos* located at the sacred site of Delphi, a symbolic center of the Greek world connected with the womb. A Greek narrative traces the *omphalos* to Zeus and his freeing two eagles at the opposite ends of the world that eventually meet at the *omphalos*, which is the preeminent oracular site. This is an ancient site at which humans and gods could communicate by the gods sending oracle messages. Priestesses received the revelatory oracles, and drew lots in the form of white and black beans after having asked a question. It was also not unusual for Apollo to inspire a priestess into an ecstatic state, giving her oracular powers of communication. The most well-known Apollonian piece of wisdom is the Delphic message that a person should "know thyself." Another piece of wisdom was "nothing in excess." This oracle was indicative of the advice to act with moderation and self-restraint.

The ancient Greeks, as did the Egyptians and Romans, did not distinguish between the binary opposites of the sacred and profane. The Greeks refer to a sacred month, which consisted of the period before and after a festival. Among the Greeks, space was mapped by their conception of the city-state, starting with the interior of the city and its walls, villages and their agricultural fields, and uncultivated outlying areas signifying forests and mountains, suggesting a special conception radiating outward from order to disorder. The chaotic threat of disorder to the city-state was countered by gods protecting the city gates. The crossroads outside the city was guarded by Hecate, a goddess associated with night-time pathways who can drive humans mad. The Mediterranean cultures tended to identify linear and cyclical concepts of time. The former type of time had beginning and end points, and all creatures were subjected to it. In contrast to the linear notion of time, the cyclical concept of time was inspired by the flow of nature, as evident by the changing seasons and lunar phases.

Roman Belief System

According to Cicero, Romans expressed cultural pride about being the most religious people in the world. Roman religion was antithetical to other religions, conservative, and unconditionally pious. Personal piety was reflected in the importance attached to personal relations and exhibited by meticulous observance of rites. A son, for example, expressed his relationship to his father by obeying and honoring the older man, while disobedience was considered contrary to the natural order. The ancient Romans even took family relations to another level by making them sacred and inviolable. Concurrently, there was a depreciation of the individual because Romans thought that an individual only mattered as a member of the larger group. In the wider cultural picture, as a viable member of society, the individual honored obligations to others and was ultimately devoted and supportive of the state. Personal, social, and state obligations were engrained in Romans because the law earned a religious status and prestige. By executing one's duties, a person was practicing one's religion without doing anything extraordinary other than adhering to the norms of the society and state.

Offering neither ethical rigor nor metaphysical speculation, the Roman religion did condemn willful impiety. The impious person had no right to make offerings at the altar of the gods or appease them in any way. According to Cicero, impiety was viewed as a crime against the gods. For the impious, there was no hope of salvation. The reprobate person could not be saved by either the law or religion. It was not until the final century of the Republic that the hope of personal immortality was accepted, at least for great men, which contributed to the deification of Emperors after they died, enabling their souls to migrate to the celestial realm. The expectations surrounding the death of an ordinary citizen involved joining the community of the Manes (spirits of the deceased), who were also called parents in the afterlife. The dead individual became lost among the ancestors and depended on the piety of her surviving descendants for help, which was expressed by worship at the family tomb at the festival of the dead in mid-February, the Parentalia. In the afterlife, a deceased person encountered the risk of becoming an evil spirit (Lemures). These figures were troublesome, tormented shadows that the living head of a family might have expelled from the family. This pattern of life and death shows two fundamental aspects of Roman religion: The individual never really leaves the family or social structure of the culture whether living or dead, and there is little chance of finding a meaningful religious experience or identity outside of the group.

The individual's loyalty and personal subordination to the state gave the Roman religion a strong political character. This made personal religion difficult and even inconceivable to most people because a single person exists only in so far as that person integrated himself into a larger social and state context. What was considered important by Romans was civic loyalty and a respect for traditions. Thus, a typical Roman did not freely choose his religion but was rather born into the state religion and simply accepted it as the right path of religion.

In addition to their deferential fear of the gods, Romans exemplified a religious pragmatism because Romans expected some type of social or personal benefit to result by means of their offerings to the gods. Deities were closely associated with their office, although the pantheon was not static because foreign gods were adopted over time. In contrast to the Egyptians and Greeks, Romans did not pair their divine beings into couples that acted as a team.

Although most Romans simply followed the tenets of their state religion, there were some individuals who assumed greater responsibility for the welfare of the religion. A perfect example of such people were the six Vestal virgins, who were attached to the pontifical college and chosen by the Pontifex Maximus, leader of the college, at ages from 6 to 10 years old. Once selected, the girls were consecrated for a period of thirty years, during which time they must remain celibate. It was the civic and religious responsibility of the Virgins to keep the city fire burning for the general welfare of the people. It was incumbent on them not to allow the fire to be extinguished. The Vestal virgins were considered powerful because of their celibacy. For those girls that failed to maintain their virginity, the consequences were very severe. Their sexual partners were executed, and the girls were shut up alive in an underground chamber or simply buried alive because their crime was so great. When members reached 30 years of age, they were free to rejoin society.

Mediterranean Family Cult and the Magical

The family cult of Mediterranean religions was centered on the hearth with its fire, a place at which family members could worship their gods and ancestors in an intimate setting. If the gods of the state were remote and uncaring, the gods of the family cult were more intimate, sensitive, helpful, and involved with the family on a daily basis. In Greece, the family cult was, for instance, an economic, social, and religious entity that was led by its father, while the hearth, a symbol of family solidarity, was protected by the goddess Hestia. The importance and centrality of the hearth for the family cult was evident by practices such as walking a new born infant around it soon after birth. The hearth also played a role at weddings to promote fertility and prosperity for a couple. Before cooking a meal, family members would offer a libation of wine to Hestia.

The Greeks recognized two groups of household deities: Lares and Penates. The former were connected to the local geography and offered to protect a family as long as they lived at a specific home. Although lacking names and individual identities, the Penates represented deities of the household that a family can take with them when they move to a new home, whereas the Lares need to be newly acquired when a family moves to a new location. It was the hearth where a family communicated with these figures by making daily offerings in the fire.

The Egyptians and Romans practiced a similar type of family cult. These traditions also communicated with their ancestors. The Romans observed two major festivals to ancestors: Lupercalia in February, characterized by collective purifications, and Lemuria in May, celebrating the return of the dead. These ancestors were fed to appease them and to ensure that they did not take a living person with them. In order to pacify the ancestors, the household leader filled his mouth with beans and spit them out while reciting a formula nine times. This functioned as a message that the ancestors should leave the family.

Egyptians had other means to communicate with the gods. A person could hire a scribe to write a letter to a god to plead one's case. Private prayer, attendance at festivals with the hope of receiving an oracle from a god, and dreams are some of the methods at the disposal of a petitioner. Divination was another popular method used to communicate with the gods for all three Mediterranean religious traditions. And in order to protect oneself, it was possible to wear an amulet. In Egyptian religion, an eye of Horus was worn, for example, to protect oneself.

Not only was the family cult intertwined with the city-state cult by these religions, but these Mediterranean cults used magic to achieve certain ends. In ancient Egypt, magic was represented as a man with upraised arms on his head and personally identified as the god Heka. The individual magician could create evil or protective spells by following a three-part formula: announcing the goal of the spell; making an incantation by assuming the role of a god; giving direction for the performance of the spell. Creating a spell to destroy an enemy, the magician makes a figure of the victim and ritually kills it. This action is then magically transferred to the intended victim after that person has been identified by name. More positive uses of magic involve protecting the less powerful in a family, such as small children and women. Amulets were believed to have a magical quality to protect wearers. Popular amulets were the scarab beetle, which gave life and health, or the *cippus*, a stone image of Horus portrayed as a nude child with side locks, standing on crocodiles. It was common to pour water over the image and then drink the water.

In Greece, magic is similar to medicine in the sense of being a *pharmakon* that has the power to harm or cure. Magic is also believed to be a gift from the gods, although it also acquired negative connotations by portraying a magician as a beggar priest, diviner, and wanderer of the night. The negative nature of magic is enhanced because it represents the art of deception, and its foreign origin in Persia, which gets stressed by the use of foreign language, a reversal of ordinary linguistic usage. The Greek thinkers Heraclitus and Plato contributed to creating a dichotomy between religion and magic, portraying magic as an attempt to persuade the gods, while religion allows gods freedom of choice and invites humans to submit to the will of the gods. There is something coercive about the use of magic because it seeks to constrain the gods by trickery or extortion.

In ancient Rome, the magician performed two basic functions: healing and divination. Over time, divination is transformed from a method of communication to harmful practices intended to damage others. In contrast to Romans, many Egyptian priests served as freelance magicians because of their training in writing and oral communication. The patron deity of these Egyptian priests was Thoth, god of writing and magic. Whatever the Mediterranean culture, when the magician uttered a curse, for example, he enacted a performative utterance that was intended to make something happen by means of the power of the words. In other words, the utterance is automatically effective. Nonetheless, magic and religion were intertwined and not separate aspects of the three ancient Mediterranean religions.

Mediterranean Rites

The most important rite of passage in ancient Egypt was initiation because no formal marriage ceremony existed. The initiation of young boys did not require circumcision for all boys, although it did mark youngsters as socially mature and ready to assume normal social duties. In comparison to initiation, other Egyptian rites were more fully developed and central to the well-being of the culture.

The Greeks had no term equivalent to initiation, although we do hear of young boys being segregated and experiencing harsh treatment, representing the transition stage of a rite of passage. The boys were divided into herds, suggesting that they needed to be domesticated. While in these herds, the boys learned the customs, dances, songs, and arts of war. Among aristocratic youngsters, older men kidnapped them, and retired to the country with the boys, where pederasty, which was accepted as part of the maturation process for the boys, was practiced within the context of an age-based relationship, after which the parties would return to their normal family life.

In ancient Roman culture, a boy became an adult sometime between 14 and 17 years of age. The celebratory rite occurred on March 17, which was the festival dedicated to the god Liber. The youngster exchanged his old clothing, typically consisting of a toga adorned with a purple border and a hollow metal object filled with protective amulets around his neck. This outfit was exchanged for a white toga, which was considered the formal dress of a Roman male. Those fathers and sons from the upper classes of Roman society went to the Forum to offer a sacrifice to Jupiter Optimus Maximus along with an offering of the boy's hair.

The three Mediterranean religions observed sacrifices and annual festivals that were connected to the rhythms of the sun, moon, and the agricultural calendar and production of food. Within the context of Egyptian sacrifice, the chosen sacrificial animal was referred to as the enemy, who was to be punished and simultaneously served as food offered to the gods or an ancestor. While an oxen was still alive, its forelegs were severed and then the animal was sacrificed, which invokes notions of violence, punishment, and slaughter of an enemy.

In ancient Greece, after the animal was purified, the participants received the victim's consent to be sacrificed. After a few hairs were cut from its head, the animal was clubbed, stunned, and allowed to bleed to death. The flowing blood was collected to be sprinkled over the altar. Then the victim was cut open, and its innards were examined by a seer to discern if the gods accepted or rejected the sacrifice. Another method of learning the feelings of the god was to sacrifice either a pig or sheep, place its carcass over the fire, and watch how the tail curled to learn the opinion of the god.

Mediterranean Festivals

The ancient Egyptian seasonal cycle consisted of the inundation of the Nile River that fertilized the farm lands along the river and enabled the growing of grain. This was considered the hot season, a cycle repeated the following year. Not only mindful of this annual agricultural cycle, the Egyptians associated their festival calendar with certain divine beings. Besides the New Year's festival that was intertwined with notions of rebirth and rejuvenation on the eighteenth of the same month, there was also a festival for Thoth. The Opet festival connected the pharaoh with his divine father Amun/Re at the temple of Luxor at Thebes, whereas the pharaoh was annually rejuvenated at the Heb-Sed rite later in the year. During the fourth month, the Choiak or Sokar festival marked the end of the inundation of the Nile and included Osiris, lord of the dead. During the initial day of the fifth month, there took place a festival of rebirth called Neheb-kau. A harvest celebration was represented by the festival of Min, god of fertility, occurring during the ninth month, when the pharaoh cut the first sheaf of grain, stressing his role as a life-sustainer. During the Valley festival, icons of Amun, his consort, Mut, and son Khonsu were transported across the Nile, accompanied by music and dancing. The actions of the divine family were imitated by ordinary citizens as they visited the tombs of ancestors. In addition to their functions ensuring a successful agricultural season and rebirth of the pharaoh, festivals dispensed divine power for the benefit of the people and their social needs.

Festivals in ancient Egypt gave ordinary citizens an opportunity to see and honor the gods, whose worship was normally controlled by temple priests. The public procession of the gods at a festival represented sensory stimulation for ordinary people. At the Feast of the Valley observance, the festival began on the east side of the Nile, where the statue of the deity was transported from one bank of the river to the other by a ceremonial boat, which overall signified a symbolic passage from life to the abode of the dead (the west being symbolically associated with death). During the night of the festival, Amun assumed his ithyphallic form and engaged the goddess Hathor in sexual intercourse that sparked the revival and rebirth of the earth. In addition, the dead and living were able to communicate at the tombs of the deceased ancestors. Participants drank copious amounts of beer and wine, which stimulated revelers to call on Hathor as the goddess of drunkenness.

Unlike the general uniformity of the Egyptian festival calendar, the Greek city-states had different calendars, with the names of festivals coinciding with the names of the months. Adhering to a lunar calendar, the Greeks believed that the waxing of the moon was connected with growth, while the waning moon was related to less auspicious observances. The reinstatement of social and cosmic order was represented by the first festival, called Hekatombaia, during which animal sacrifices were offered to Apollo. A golden age under the leadership of Kronus was recalled by Kronia, during which slaves were freed for a day and even dined with their owners. The birthday of Athens was celebrated with the Panathenaea, which was accompanied with sacrifices and a grand procession from the city to the Acropolis. A several day Athenian festival was marked by the Thesmophoria, allowing married women to leave homes to live in huts within the protective sanctuary of Demeter, from which men are excluded. The festival embodied symbolism of ascent, sexuality, fertility, decay, and new birth. After the women fasted, there was a sacrifice of pigs that recalled the rape of Kore, daughter of Demeter. A final example of a typical Greek festival was the Anthesteria, a spring celebration over three days. The second day of the festival was called the Day of Wine Jugs because it included a drinking contest of red wine. In order to win the contest, a participant must be the first to consume two liters of wine.

The ancient Romans conformed their religious observances around the rising and setting of zodiac signs because these heavenly bodies manifested a divine order, whereas the civil calendar was created by senate decrees. Several festivals were associated with the agricultural cycle and production of food stuffs, which included some of the following: Liberalia (March 17); Saturnalia (December 17); Lupercalia (February 15); and Feralia (February 21). As a reader can tell, most Roman festivals fell on odd numbered days. The Lupercalia traced its origin back to Romulus and Remus and founding of the city of Rome and included a race around the Palatine hill. Many of the Roman festivals concluded with games contested at the Circus. The Saturnalia, festival to the god Saturn, was a popular observance that embodied the spirit of the god of dissolution. This festival included a sacrifice to the god and later added a celebration by senators, a public banquet at which slaves ate before masters, and raucous evening revelries.

The Role of Women

Each of the three Mediterranean cultures covered in this chapter represent patriarchal social systems that assume that women performed actions associated with the home such as cooking, cleaning, nurturing children, spinning, and weaving. Just as the king was the head of the state, the head of the family was the father, who expected his wife to be obsequious and respectful of his place in the family. In contrast to women, adult males had more freedom beyond the home. In these Mediterranean cultures, negative attitudes toward women were embodied in the language and literature of the cultures. We can turn to Greek culture as our sample case to illustrate the role of women.

In Homer's *Odyssey*, Ariadne is depicted betraying her family and father, King Minos, because she falls in love with the hero Theseus, who came to her kingdom to destroy the Minotaur and stop the annual sacrifice to the monster of seven female and male virgins from Athens. The Minotaur was kept in a labyrinth, which was designed by the ingenious Daedalus, who had invented the axe and saw, to protect the monster in its palace. Ariadne gives Theseus a magical ball of string, which had been given to her by the clever Daedalus, to enable the hero to return safely after killing the monster. The victorious Theseus takes Ariadne and her sister with him when he leaves the island of Crete, but abandons the former sister on another island, where she becomes associated with Dionysus. In a similar type of narrative, Medea, daughter of King Acetes and skilled in magic, helps the hero Jason procure the Golden Fleece by killing the dragon guarding it. Jason and Medea flee from the pursuit of the king, but she slows the king down by cutting off pieces of her brother's body after she had cut his throat. Medea and Jason live happily for ten years, but Jason leaves her for the daughter of King Creon. Medea avenges her philandering husband by sending a wedding present to the new bride of a magical robe that becomes a blazing fire and burns the bride to death. Other female figures betray their husbands, such as Eriphyle's betrayal of Amphiaros, a seer, for a golden necklace. While trying to murder her stepchildren in another episode, Themisto accidently destroys her own children.

Some female figures were simply terrifying for a variety of reasons. Moirai (destiny) was considered frightening because one's destiny is uncertain and can lead to anxiety. In narrative accounts, Moirai deceives the monster Typhon, convincing it to take a drug that saps its energy and leads to its death. The Erinyes (furies) are associated with justice, but are also terrifying and merciless. In contrast to Moirai, Graiae (old women) were born old with gray hair. They live under the earth and are associated with oaths. They represent three sisters who share a single eye and a lone tooth. These unattractive female figures guard the road to the Gorgons, marine deities. In the narrative about the hero Perseus, he steals their single eye and makes it impossible for them to see him, giving him access to the nymphs, who give the hero talismans necessary for killing the Gorgon Medusa, a hideous figure who cannot be seen without turning the perceiver into stone. With his three gifts—winged sandals, a sack, and a helmet—Perseus raises above Medusa, uses his polished shield to see her reflection without having to view her directly, severs her head, and puts the trophy into the sack, which enables him to avoid looking at her face. Not everyone is as successful as Perseus navigating by the Graiae, whose terrifying power is used in curses and harmful magic.

Another group of females that evokes negative connotations are the Amazons, a race of warrior women. They are described as women, men-women, barbarians, and flesh eaters, evoking an image of wild carnivores. They were born both the equals and enemies of males and fight on horseback rather than a chariot. In Plutarch's *Life of Theseus*, the Amazons have sex with the barbarian Scythians in public in broad daylight. The society that they create with these men is the exact opposite of Greek society; women made war and served as judges, while men did traditional women's chores, for a complete role reversal of the Greek cultural norms.

Other mythical narratives also depict women with negative associations. Pandora, with her box of evils, is credited with introducing various forms of suffering into the world. In Euripides' *Hippolytus*, a young girl, imagined as an untamed female horse that needs domestication, is given to Heracles by Aphrodite. Then there is the myth of Io and her daughter, Proitos, which compares them to wandering cows. These literary types of images of women reflect social attitudes because women were expected to be yoked by the social institution of marriage and were domesticated and tamed like a horse.

The gender differences of females were recognized from birth in Athenian society because parents hung a woolen fillet on the door of their home for a girl infant, which recalls women's activities associated with spinning and weaving, but placed an olive wreath for a boy, which was also the prize given to a male winner at an Olympic event.

Aristocratic female youngsters were initiated by being secluded and humiliated, learning to dance, participating in physical exercise, and paying attention to their beauty. Besides performing traditional domestic activities, the young girls were required sometimes to go barefoot and trim their hair short and were allowed only a single dress to wear. The exact practices differ with location because in Sparta the period of initiation was longer and more rigorous physically in order for these women to produce strong children. Spartan young girls competed against boys. During the Hera festival, girls ran in races in short dresses and hair, with their right shoulder and breast uncovered. In later Greek culture, initiation rites for young girls faded away and were replaced by the wedding as a substitute for their transition into adulthood.

Because of their monthly menses, women were associated in the popular religious imagination with impurity and pollution in the form of flowing blood. The activity of giving birth was also considered polluting. These attitudes about the causes of impurity even affected attitudes toward the statues of goddesses, which were washed more frequently than those of the gods. These attitudes toward pollution and impurity are also evident in other religions such as Judaism, Hinduism, and Buddhism.

Greek women did have some freedom within the religious sphere of life, even if only for a brief time. The mystery cult of Dionysus allowed women to leave home and join other women to practice their religion. Women could escape their domestic roles and experience brief freedom by entering into a trance state. Taking place in the summer months, the Adonia festival enabled women to gather together to mourn the death of the divine youth Adonis, who was characterized as a result of incest, a coward hiding among the lettuce plants, and a passionate lover. Adonis lost his life while hunting. His cult included ecstatic dancing in the dark and the throwing of green plants into the sea. Popular opinion considered the Thesmophoria festival to be a women's observance. This three-day festival specifically celebrated the procreative role of women so necessary for the preservation of society, although there was no sexuality at the festival. The initial day of the festival was designed to organize it by carrying necessary equipment, food, and piglets to the temple. The female participants built huts in which they lived for the length of the festival. The second day was for fasting, which was characterized by women sitting on the ground without flower garlands. On the third day, fasting ended and women began to behave abnormally by engaging in fake fights, uttering risqué speech, and mocking males. The decaying piglets were placed on the temple altars, expressing the hope for future human and earthly fertility.

Mediterranean Material Culture

The three Mediterranean religious cultures of this chapter left behind some impressive ruins that suggest many magnificent structures during the heights of these cultures. These material cultural legacies include temples, tombs, paintings, statues, and various types of sacred objects. Many of these objects are scattered around the globe and housed in national museums for the benefit of visitors. These objects have become the common property of humankind to enjoy and to learn about the cultures from which these objects originated.

An Egyptian temple was called the "house of god." At the beginning of time, there existed a primordial hill along with the primeval water. These features are recaptured in the temple to the sun-god, where a mound and a pond were located adjacent to the temple. The ancient sun temple at Heliopolis included an ascending path toward the sanctuary, where an obelisk symbolizing the sun stood, with its top signifying resurrection. On an elevated plateau, the temple was built, and, by following its path, a person suddenly encountered the sunlight, whereas later temples gave a visitor a different experience that was more mysterious because of the dimly lighted or dark chambers, but the walls were decorated by scenes from everyday life.

Other sacred objects included statues and sacred boats. Divine statues were often carved in a semi-theriomorphic manner, reflecting the Egyptian belief that divine beings can be portrayed in animal form. The cow's head of the goddess Hathor has already been mentioned, but there were also the falcon's head associated with Horus and Re and the ibis and baboon connected to Thoth, the moon god. Statues constructed in the image of people were an essential aspect of the mortuary cult. In fact, a person could only exist in the afterlife if the statue resembling a person was preserved. Playing an important role in the cults of Osiris and Amun, the sacred boat was used in earthly processions and connected to the beauty of the god; it also played a central role in funeral rites, with its connection to the transportation of the dead to the afterlife. When its statue was absent, the boat could represent the deity and its power of self-renewal.

When people think of ancient Egyptian culture, the image of the pyramids often comes to mind. Modelled on the hill of creation related to the myth of the sun god, these grand structures functioned as the tombs of the pharaohs of the Old Kingdom with the intention of assisting the monarch's wish to participate in the divine afterlife with the gods, operating as a symbol of resurrection.

Another recognizable Egyptian structure has been the Sphinx at Giza, with its lion's body and human head, which is connected to the seat of life. In order to grasp the significance of the lion's body, it is necessary to recall Aker, an earth deity represented as a lion. This animal and earthly symbol represents the victory of life. Egyptian artists created lions back to back along with a sign for the horizon. When depicted in this way, they signify yesterday and tomorrow, respectively connected to Osiris and Re, representing death and resurrected life. Forming a unity, the dual lions suggest the connection between life and death.

Greek temples were built over the *temenos*, a space set aside for gods and heroes that consisted of an altar, possibly a portico for protection against the weather and sun surrounded by a wall or stone columns, an image of the deity to whom the temple is dedicated, divine statues, inscribed monuments, and

Figure 2.2 Sphinx with pyramid of Giza in the background. Cairo, Egypt. Pius Lee / Shutterstock.com

votive gifts. The interior of the *temenos* and its contents were considered the property of the deity, and to steal anything was considered a sacrilege punishable by death. The front of the temple was built in an eastward direction. Within the *temenos*, there existed the *abaton*, a space where humans and gods encountered each other, considered the most sacred part of the temple and restricted to only priests. Representing a gradation of sacred space, the *abaton* was a location reserved for direct contact between the gods and humans, and by extension was a place of divination, divine prophesy, achieving ecstatic states, and healing. A number of temples were located at places struck by lightning believed to have been caused by Zeus, which were believed to represent manifestations of the holy.

Greek temples were distinguished by whether or not they were located inside or outside of the city or town. This basic distinction reflects a tension in Greek culture between cults of gods directly concerned with civic life and exterior cults opposed to the civic order. Thus, interior deities were represented by divine figures such as Athena with her temple on the Acropolis and Zeus' location in the market place, which was associated with political gatherings. Artemis had her sanctuaries outside of the city because of her connection to nature, while Pan represented a herders' god and thus had shrines located external to the city. Poseidon and Dionysus also had temples built to them in the countryside. In addition to this distinction between temples, a distinction was also drawn between altars for gods and heroes. The former's altars were rectangular, whereas the latter group had low, hollow, and circular altars located on the ground. The overall function of these temples and altars was for sacrifice.

Among the Romans, the city controlled the space with the help of augurs, Roman officials, specializing in interpreting omens that they perceive through a process of divination. The augurs would mark an auspicious space with a bronze star and label the location august. In order for a Roman temple to become operational, it had to be completely consecrated. The city of Rome set ritual limits that separated the city from its surroundings, called the Pomerium, which was established by ritual means. It functioned to distinguish the city from other locations and to protect its privileged status in Roman culture. A distinction was also drawn between city-state space and human outlying territory. There was, moreover, a distinction drawn between divine space and human space. Thus, some space was more holy than another. A twofold distinction existed between sacred spaces built by humans and dedicated to a god and other places made sacred by being chosen by god and established by a divine being.

Egyptian Ideas on Death and Afterlife

During the primordial period of Egyptian religious culture, Osiris, son of Geb and Nut, ruled with his wife Isis. Despite a time of peace and prosperity, Seth, a younger brother of Osiris, grew jealous of his successful brother and killed him, dismembered his body, and scattered Osiris' remains over the land. Because of the death of her husband, Isis became distraught and vowed to help her slain husband by tricking Re into disclosing his secret name, finding and reassembling her husband's inert remains, and utilizing the power within the sun god's name to revive Osiris enough to impregnate her. From this act of sexual congress, their son Horus was conceived. This sexual act was painted on the tomb of Sety I at Abydos, depicting the erect phallus of Osiris and revealing Isis as a sparrow hawk on top of the phallus accepting his seed. Isis restores the cosmic order and counters the disorder and violence introduced by Seth by protecting her son. Osiris became ruler of the underworld and judge of the dead. Isis, grieving widow of Osiris, became the focus of a mystery cult that spread to Rome at a later time.

Although usually located in the underworld ruled by Osiris, the abode of the dead was sometimes located in the western desert. When an ancient Egyptian died, she was escorted by Anubis, a jackal-headed deity of embalming and guide for the deceased, to the abode of Osiris. Once in the realm of Osiris, the dead person was ushered into the Hall of Truth, which served as Osiris' courtroom, where divine justice was dispensed. The sisters of Osiris—Isis and Nephthys—mourned for dead people and protected them. Unlike an earthly court proceeding, the deceased recited offenses not committed during life. This odd type of confession was followed by weighing the deceased's heart before the goddess Ma'at, who determined that person's eternal fate. It was believed that evil deeds made the heart heavy and thus testified against a deceased person. The ancient Egyptian imagination conceived this scenario as the human heart being weighed against a feather that stood for Ma'at. Standing near the scales of fate, there was a monster ready to consume the condemned heart. The frightening monster was Ammit ("the Gobbler"), a monster with the head of a crocodile, the forelegs of a lion, and the back legs of a hippo. The trial proceeding was witnessed by and recorded by Thoth, known as the scribe of the gods. Thoth was a moon god, a deity identified with wisdom, and messenger of the gods. If a deceased person passed the trial, Horus then led the deceased to Osiris and two judges for the purpose of rendering a final verdict.

The importance of death in ancient Egyptian culture was emphasized by the literature connected with it. *The Pyramid Texts* date back to the Old Kingdom (2686–2125 BCE). They were discovered on the walls of pyramids. These texts were collected and edited as the *Coffin Texts* during the Middle Kingdom (2055–1650 BCE). These texts were inscribed inside of coffins. Finally, *The Book of Going Forth by Day* dated to the New Kingdom (1550–1069 BCE) and served as a practical, informative guide for the deceased during her afterlife by instructing a dead person how to arrive safely at her destination. This third text was later called *The Egyptian Book of the Dead*. These texts inform readers that Egyptians hated and feared death. They also instruct us that existence after death was not significantly different from life, although there was an expectation that there would be social equality after death. These texts are also indicative of the intimate relationship between writing and religion.

The hieroglyphic script was called "words of god." This style of writing was bestowed on humans by the god Thoth. Writing had the power to create an object or person. Its potency was associated with its divine origin.

After a person died, his body was washed before beginning mummification, a process for those who could economically afford it. The process could take a few months to complete. Many vital organs were removed from the cadaver, with the exception of the heart, because it was believed to be the location of the *ka* that continued to live in a person's heart after death. An organ like the brain was difficult to remove, but the Egyptians used a hook to pull the brain through the nostrils of the corpse. Internal organs were removed, dehydrated, and preserved in jars painted with the heads of protective deities. The body was embalmed before being treated with a powder to dehydrate it. Finally, the body was wrapped in linens, giving the mummy the appearance of a statue.

The funeral ceremony involved a procession to the tomb of the deceased, standing the mummy upright facing the southern direction and exposing it to the light of the sun, symbolizing the life-restoring power of the sun. Then priests opened the mouth of the deceased with the purpose of reestablishing its ability to see, speak, hear, and taste. The slaughter of a calf with its mother present imitated the sound of mourning. The foreleg of the calf was severed and held before the deceased. Dancers wearing tall headdresses performed with the purpose of helping the deceased across the waters to the afterlife. Before the end of the ceremony, funerary objects were placed in the tomb to ensure that the deceased would have items necessary for her next life.

A common tomb had a subterranean burial chamber and a chapel above ground for accepting offerings from the living. The tomb was constructed with a small opening to enable the *ba* access to the body buried underground, whereas the *ka* was believed to stay with the body, and the deceased's shadow resided in its statue. The *ka* was nourished by leaving behind food and drink for it. The interior of the tomb's walls was decorated with paintings and reliefs recalling daily life, creating a familiar world for the *ka* to enjoy. In early Egyptian history, slaves were slain and buried with their masters, but this practice was replaced by simply painting their images inside the tomb, where they were expected to serve their masters. The tomb was protected from thieves by magical means, such as bricks in sets of four that represented the four cardinal directions located at the corners of the burial chamber. Another magical form of protection was curses. Physical offerings were left for the deceased and painted images of food could be left, or voice offerings by means of prayer were an example of a nonphysical offering to the departed.

Greco-Roman Ideas on Death and Afterlife

In Homer's *Odyssey*, the underworld was a dark place that was boring because there was nothing to do. Thus, the afterlife was neither all that unpleasant nor an enjoyable location. The souls of the departed appeared similar to their living form, but retained their negative emotions. The soul could not communicate with the living and could not physically contact the living because it lacks substance. In Homer's *Odyssey*, when a person dies, he is escorted by Hermes to Hades, whose entrance is marked by two rivers: fire and wailing. The deceased is transported across the rivers by Charon and encounters Cerberus, a three-headed dog who guards the gateway to Hades. Some souls suffer awful punishment in Hades because they offended the gods, such as the previously mentioned Sisyphus and Tantalus. The Greeks tied earthly behavior with the destiny of the soul. But there was no real reward for the righteous or no punishment for the unrighteous person. There is a hint of salvation in Homer when Menelaus goes to the Isles of the Blessed. Even though there is no escaping death, Greek thought did not envision a superior mode of life after death. Greek thought did not develop a general eschatology that foretold the fate of the world or humans.

There are references to ghosts in Homer's *Odyssey* who speak to the hero after they receive blood to drink, whose words the poet describes as mindless gibberish. Mistreated souls were the most likely candidates to become ghosts because they might be angry about dying prematurely or some other inauspicious event experienced during life. Because a ghost might inflict vengeance on a guilty person, it was considered prudent to protect oneself. A person could hang a thorny wreath on the door or window of her home. Another method of protecting oneself and placating ghosts was to invite them to the annual Anthesteria festival, where new wine was tasted in early spring, and ghosts were fed on the third day of this observance associated with the deity Dionysus.

In addition to ghosts, Greek literature identifies three sets of figures associated with death: Daimones, Keres, and Erinyes. Daimones were considered spirits of the dead, who are generally benevolent and protect humans from harm. With a hideous appearance and described as drinking blood, Keres were believed to cause old age, death, and inflict misery in general on humans. Hesiod depicts them dragging slain warriors away. The Erinyes guarantee the rights of householders by protecting them. But they also punish those who behave contrary to *moira* (fate, destiny).

Romans believed that it was important for families to integrate the deceased into the world of the ancestors. When someone died, the family was considered polluted and was obligated to prepare the corpse for burial, activities that included washing, perfuming, and clothing it for viewing by neighbors and relatives. Surrounded by incense burners and torches, the deceased was laid out facing the door. Women were hired to mourn the loss by chanting a lament accompanied by musicians playing flutes and horns. Family members rubbed ashes into their hair and wore dark mourning gowns. In order to serve as a sign that a death had occurred, a cypress branch was hung on the door. After a seven-day period, the mourners proceeded to the site of the cremation, a fingertip of the deceased was severed for later interment, a coin was placed into the mouth of the corpse to pay Charon, ferryman over the river to the afterlife, eyes of the departed were opened, cremation executed, and the rite concluded with the family eating together, an act of reunifying the family unit after its loss.

Although cremation was the normal practice for disposal of the corpse, Romans began to favor burial of the departed after 150 BCE. A law passed around 450 BCE by the Roman Senate called the Twelve Tablets was designed to prohibit burial within the city confines. This practice gradually led to the growth of suburban cemeteries and streets lined with tombs outside the city walls.

Mediterranean Mystery Cults

In Greece and Rome, an individual was born into the state religion and did not have to make a conscious choice about what religion to follow. Some individual Greeks and Romans wanted something more from their religion other than the usual habitual type of practice. Some began to feel that the city gods did not respond to their needs, and these gods were, moreover, distant from people. With these types of convictions about their inherited religion, some found themselves open to explore something different and strange and discovered what they were missing in their traditional form of religion in the mystery cults. Some people even joined more than one such cult. Joining a cult enabled a person to find release from social limitations and ordinary concerns and to take a person to a sphere of experience never previously attained in one's life.

Whatever mystery cult a person joined, members found some common features. The first feature that they found in common was the demand for secrecy, a Greek term derived from *myein*, meaning "to close." Within the context of this secret cult, people found a special relationship with divine beings during initiation and a promise of a better life in the present and in the future afterlife. The members were exposed to mythical narratives that related tales of the cult's divinities. These cults also offered a personal ecstatic experience for members that was existentially meaningful. The initial experience for a person might represent a change from initial bewilderment to an experience of wonder as the initiate has an immediate encounter with the sacred. Another prominent aspect of the mystery experience was sexuality, which was manifested in the Dionysus cult with a procession of a huge phallus, a symbol of the deity, during festivals. The initiate gets to see the manifestation of the holy object that gets unveiled for one's experiential benefit. Whether or not to join a mystery cult was an optional, personal decision that a potential member had to make. The city-state religion might have been obligatory, but this was not true of the mystery cult. The initiatory pattern of the cult for the individual stressed a symbolic experience of death to a person's former condition and rebirth into a new condition. Finally, members did not have to reject the state cult because the mystery religions served as supplements rather than alternatives to the prevailing state religion. These various features of the mystery cults do not mean that they were all uniform. These various cults often originated outside of Greece and Rome, in locations such as Egypt, Phoenicia, Iran, and Phrygia, bringing their own narratives with them. The Eleusinian mysteries were, however, an indigenous Greek cult observed at Eleusis in the region of Attica within the territory of Athens.

In the Homeric "Hymn to Demeter," a reader receives a glimpse into the narrative surrounding the Eleusinian cult. As Homer conveys the narrative, Hades, lord of the underworld and with the consent of his brother Zeus, kidnapped Persephone, daughter of the earth goddess Demeter (also called Kore or Maiden), as she picked flowers, with the intention to marry her. This abduction had two witnesses, identified as Hecate, a goddess, and Helios, the sun, who heard her screams. The distraught Demeter searched frantically for her daughter all over the earth, which was her domain. After her futile search, Demeter learns the fate of her daughter from the two witnesses. The grieving Demeter leaves Mount Olympus and wanders the earth disguised as an old woman and joins the royal Eleusinian family as a nursemaid, where she drinks *kykeōn*, a mixture of barley, mint, and water. She agrees to nurse the newborn son of the king, but she decides to make the child immortal by anointing him with ambrosia, drink of immortality, and placing the infant, Demophoon, into a fire each night. Spying on Demeter, the mother of the infant was horrified at what she witnessed. Demeter gives her rationale for her treatment of the child, reveals to the family her real nature as a goddess, demands that a temple be built for her at Eleusis, and promises to reveal secret rites to the people. Then Demeter stops the growth of grain, an action that threatens the people with starvation, and the gods, because this action would also stop the sacrifices. Zeus intervenes and gets Demeter to agree to return to Olympus if Zeus reunited her with her abducted daughter. Hermes is sent to Hades to broker an agreement to release Persephone. Hades agrees to return the daughter, but gives her pomegranate seeds to consume before she leaves him. This act of eating apparently harmless seeds results in obligating Persephone to return to the underworld for a period of time each year. In response to this result, Demeter is placated and teaches the people of Eleusis the mystery rites after restoring the earth's fertility. Demeter promises initiates blessings in their current life and in the afterlife, whereas the uninitiated can expect to encounter complete darkness in the afterlife.

This myth of Demeter and her daughter evokes images of the cycle of agriculture, dangers of a barren earth, the restoration of the earth's fertility, and what a fertile earth means for the welfare of the inhabitants of the earth. These themes are reflected in the mystery cult, which comprised a procession of sacred objects associated with Demeter from Eleusis to Athens by priests and priestesses who were followed by a procession of initiates. The initiates carried a statue of Iacchus and were mocked by masked figures as they crossed a bridge over the Cephisus River. Gates to a grotto dedicated to Pluto, lord of the underworld, were opened for the initiates. Then the participants proceeded to the Telesterion, Hall of Mysteries, for the performance of rituals and revelation of secrets. It is here that initiates received something to drink (*kykeōn*) that sparked hallucinations, disorientation, and/or strange visual experiences. A bath of purification, sacrificing of piglets, eating beans, revealing of a sacred object, and pouring of libations to the dead are actions common to the cult. The participants were shrouded in darkness, forcing officials to operate by torchlight. Initiates were exposed to the goddess Kore (Persephone) as the underworld opened, evoking feelings of initial terror and later joy. The initiates experienced rebirth and received a revelation of the goddess symbolized as an ear of corn, which was displayed before being cut in silence. The cult did not represent attainment of immortality because death continued to be a reality, even though it did not represent an absolute end of life. The symbolism surrounding death suggests a renewal, rebirth, and a new beginning. On the fifth day of the festival, initiates walked from Eleusis to Athens wearing white garments and carrying torches. During this journey, yellow ribbons were tied on their right hand and left leg.

The secret nature of these observances makes it difficult to discern their meaning with any precision, although there are some features that we can comprehend. The sacrifice of the piglets, for example, is related to the pigs of the shepherd Eubuleus that were pulled into the underworld as Hades descended with Persephone. The interrelationship between life and death is obvious. The procession to Eleusis corresponds to Demeter's search for her missing daughter and the blissful joy experienced when she finds her daughter, which symbolizes a transition from darkness to light. When initiates eat beans, this is equivalent to cannibalism because beans were associated symbolically with human flesh, male semen, a female womb, and a child's head for an intertwining of violence and sexuality in the cult.

In comparison to the Eleusinian mysteries, much less is known about Samothracian mysteries, although it did focus on the secret names of gods. At a nocturnal initiation rite, initiates were instructed to wear purple sashes and to confess to a priest the worst deeds that they had ever committed. The purple sashes recalled the hero Odysseus taking off his clothes during a tempest and donning a veil before jumping into the sea that could no longer harm him. At the end of the initiation, new members donned iron rings. The fundamental benefit for the initiate was protection while traveling by sea. Different types of benefits could be achieved with the Bacchic mysteries, focusing on the god Dionysus.

In his *Bacchae*, the Greek writer Euripides tells his readers about female worshippers of the god Dionysus and their fanatical behavior. He relates that the women are driven ecstatically mad by the god to the extent that they tear apart live animals and, finally, the king of the city. The Greek historian Herodotus informs readers about initiates raving uncontrollably at night in the wilderness and released into a mad ecstatic condition. They depicted Dionysus as a deity of dance, wine, and vitality, even though he also embodied lethargy. If Dionysus was a stranger to orderly Greek culture, he also caused initiates to become strangers to themselves through ecstatic experience and transformation into a Bacchos. To the accompaniment of panpipes, cymbals, tambourines, and castanets, which provided the rhythm, the initiates danced in an inebriated state. As a sign that they belonged to Dionysus, initiates were tattooed with an ivy leaf.

These Greek writers were probably aware of the mythical narrative about Dionysus, a son of Zeus and Persephone. While he was a child, Dionysus was lured away by the Titans, gods jealous of Zeus, who killed and consumed most of his body. The goddess Athena was able to salvage his heart, which Zeus fed to Semele to reconceive Dionysus. Even though Dionysus was reborn, Persephone continued to mourn him. Meanwhile, Zeus incinerated the Titans, enabling humanity to arise from their remains. This myth holds together the promise of rebirth after death, the role of violence, atonement to Persephone, and avoidance of suffering after death. In spite of this narrative, Dionysus was considered a stranger to the Greek pantheon and a threat to public order. He was called the "liberator" in Athens because drinking wine removed normal inhibitions and led to uncontrollable behavior, taking initiates to the uncultivated mountainside clothed in animal skins and eating uncooked meat. Participants wore masks to hide their identity to imitate the god depicted in Euripides' *Bacchae*. By leaving the order of the city-state, the initiates got to see the god without his mask, a wondrous revelation of the holy. There was also evidence that this cult also came to the city as all-male participants reveled and wildly processed through the streets. Thus, Dionysus' cult promised something wild and contrary to the public order for participants. Euripides' *Bacchae* paints an idyllic vision as a result of the cult. In this vision, the earth is transformed into a paradise with milk, wine, and honey springing upward from the earth and maenads offering to nurse a fawn by exposing their breasts. But this peaceful portrait is misleading because at the center of this paradise, there are vicious hunters who kill animals and humans and eat their raw flesh.

Another mystery religion was the cult of Meter (Mother). The mythical narrative of this cult tells about the love affair between the goddess Cybele and Attis, a mortal prince and shepherd, who is unfaithful to the goddess. In response to his betrayal of her, the goddess drives him mad, which motivates him to castrate himself and bleed to death. The festival associated with this myth involved cutting a pine tree and wrapping it in narrow bands to resemble a corpse of Attis. Other days are devoted to priests and neophytes dancing and whipping themselves to get blood flowing. Some neophytes cut off their sexual organs and offered them to the goddess. The festival included a procession over a river where the statue of the goddess was bathed. The rite of initiation included being sanctified by the blood of a sacrificed bull.

When this cult arrived in Rome, the Senate confined eunuchs to the sanctuary of the goddess. Roman senators thought that no Roman male had the right to castrate himself or to engage in the frenzied orgies typical of the cult. However, castrated members (*galli*) were allowed to publically dance in the streets of the city once a year wearing female garments, long hair, and amulets. The goddess Cybele received a sacrifice called the *taurobolium*, a rite that involved the severing of the bull's testicles, drenching initiates standing below under planks with the bull's blood, and burying the bull's testicles under the altar. By offending the sensibilities of the Roman establishment over proper civilized behavior and a radical religious cult, it is apparent that the cult of Cybele and Attis challenged the authority of established state religion. Instead of the formalized state religion, citizens now had a choice of joining a cult that encouraged open expression of feelings and emotions, gave one a sense of being reborn, being united with the deity through various forms of self-mutilation, achieving salvation, and being victorious over death.

The mystery cult of Mithras, an Indo-Iranian sun deity, arrived in Rome in the first century CE and lasted until the fourth century, although there is no myth that survived concerning the god or his cult. It is, however, possible to find a myth about the birth of the deity. According to this narrative, Mithras rises from a rock or, in another version, an egg fully formed. He is described holding a torch and a sword. He chases a bull, which is related to the moon, and finally catches and kills it, then proceeds to share it with another sun god. He establishes the seasons of the year and makes crops grow. The act of killing the bull represents the basic image for the cult, which shows Mithras kneeling on the back of the bull, pulling its head back to expose its neck with his left hand, and holding a sword in his right hand to stab the bull. This image assumed a central place in the cult's temples, constructed to imitate caves. In Rome, the cult of Mithras gained popularity with soldiers by stressing brotherhood.

The central ritual act was the *taurobolium* (sacrifice of a bull), and initiates were soaked in its blood by standing under planks over which the animal was sacrificed. The sacrifice included cutting off the bull's genitals. The rite concluded with the cooking and consumption of the animal. The cult identified seven grades that an initiate could attain that corresponded to a planet. The ascending order of grades and corresponding planets were Raven (Mercury), Bridegroom (Venus), Soldier (Mars), Lion (Jupiter), Persian (Moon), Sunrunner (Sun), and Father (Saturn). The cult was exclusively a male movement that appealed to those looking for social advancement by belonging to an elite group and those seeking their place in the cosmos. The grades that can be achieved suggest the ascent of the soul to the highest heaven. Iconic representations of Mithras killing the bull points to the earthly benefit of fertility because the bull's tail is depicted with a sheaf of wheat springing from it, symbolizing also death and rebirth.

According to Apuleius's Latin novel *Metamorphoses*, composed in the latter second century CE, the main character Lucius, a bit of a fool, finds himself transformed into a donkey, a condition that subjects him to various kinds of indignities. He dreams about a goddess who reveals herself to him, eventually identified as the Egyptian Isis. After Isis transforms Lucius back into his human form, he becomes a follower of the goddess and commits himself to her service. Lucius goes through a number of initiations into her cult. His initiation includes fasting, purification baths, avoidance of forbidden foods, receiving secret instruction, and donning linen clothing. Under the cover of darkness,

Lucius goes to her temple, where he has a profound experience before traveling to the underworld, domain of Osiris, where he passes a trial by elements and encounters all the gods. The next morning he is given a clock, a torch, and flowers. After undergoing further initiations, he finally becomes a priest in the Isis mystery cult. The themes of transformation, death, rebirth, and existential experience are all evident in the mysteries of Isis.

From what has been said about the various cults, it is clear that they were open to everyone, represented a voluntary choice, promised unique spiritual experiences, suggested that direct contact with a divine being was dangerous and also desired, transformed members, freed members from the formal established religion of the city-state, and made the divine being more accessible and not as remote and uncaring. The mystery cults suggest that the traditional institutional authority was declining and failing to elicit a positive response to the spiritual needs of people. By joining a mystery cult, a person deliberately placed himself on the margins of the prevailing religious culture and beyond the restrictions imposed by society. The secrecy, danger of the unknown, an opportunity to openly express one's emotions, becoming united with the deity by practicing self-mortifications, and the promise of strange types of experience were all factors that contributed to the feeling of excitement for initiates. The divine beings in the various cults were believed to personally adopt, listen, answer, and be close to initiates, unlike the distant and unresponsive deities of the state religion.

Mediterranean Religious Experience

Egyptians, Greeks, and Romans had similar religious systems with an official state cult into which people became members by virtue of their citizenship. Individuals were also members of the family way of religion. The mystery cults provide an opportunity to participate in an exotic path of religiosity that promised unforgettable experiences. In all three religions, there did not appear to be any apparent conflict between the state and family cults, even though priests had direct contact with the gods and ordinary folks were excluded from and played a passive role in the official cult. Apparently, the cult within the home satisfied people because they could have direct access to the images of divine beings in their midst. People offered praise and gifts to deities within the home, which appeared to give the pious feelings of comfort and reassurance. At other times, people felt fear when possibly offending the gods and were fearful of the event of death. In all three cultures, festivals provided a break from the routine of everyday existence and gave people something to celebrate. For some Greeks and Romans, there was a spiritual thirst for something more exciting and invigorating.

Those Greeks and Romans seeking something more personal and experiential turned to the mystery cults, which provided a way of religion that demanded a personal choice and commitment. When people joined a cult, they were initiates into something secret and mysterious, enhancing their religious enthusiasm and providing then with new sacred narratives and knowledge. Initiates were excited to be reborn into a new condition and promised immortality. Some of the cults evoked experiences of eroticism and aroused one's sexuality. Initiates were encouraged to lose their inhibitions, to go wild, dance, play music, and drink large quantities of wine. Being uncontrolled, members of cults had ecstatic experiences that transported them outside of themselves. These types of experiences were not possible via the state or family cults.

Suggestions for Further Reading

Beard, Mary, John North, and Simon Price. *Religions of Rome Volume 1: A History.* Cambridge: Cambridge University Press, 1998.

———. *Religions of Rome Volume 2: A Sourcebook.* Cambridge: Cambridge University Press, 1998.

Bowden, Hugh. *Mystery Cults of the Ancient World.* Princeton: Princeton University Press, 2010.

Bremmer, Jan N. *Greek Religion.* Cambridge: Cambridge University Press, 2006.

Burkert, Walter. *Ancient Mystery Cults.* Cambridge: Harvard University Press, 1987.

———. *Greek Religion.* Trans. John Raffan. Cambridge: Harvard University Press, 1985.

David, A. Rosalie. *The Ancient Egyptians: Religious Beliefs and Practices.* London: Routledge, 1982; reprint 1989.

Holland, Glenn S. *Gods in the Desert: Religions of the Ancient Near East.* Lanham: Rowman & Littlefield Publishers, Inc., 2009.

Johnson, Sarah Iles. Ed. *Religions of the Ancient World: A Guide.* Cambridge: Harvard University Press, 2004.

Mikalson, Jon D. *Ancient Greek Religion.* Second Edition. Malden, MA: Wiley-Blackwell, 2010.

Morenz, Siegfried. *Egyptian Religion.* Trans Ann E. Keep. Ithaca: Cornell University Press, 1973.

Teeter, Emily. *Religion and Ritual in Ancient Egypt.* Cambridge: Cambridge University Press, 2011.

Turcan, Robert. *The Cults of the Roman Empire.* Trans Antonia Nevill. Oxford: Blackwell Publishers, Inc., 1996.

3 Native American Traditions

According to a Seneca cosmological myth, there lived a great chief and his aged wife in the up-above-world. There was a tree growing in the middle of this world that bore flowers and fruits on which all the people lived. This tree had a blossom that lighted the world above and emitted a wonderful perfume. The roots of the tree were white and stretched to the four directions. In a dream, the chief was given a desire for a beautiful maiden named Mature Flowers, whom he proceeded to marry. But after the wedding ceremony, the chief discovered that his new wife was pregnant, which made him angry about being deceived. Again, in another dream, the chief was commanded to uproot the celestial tree to punish his wife and to relieve his troubled spirit. When the chief uprooted the central tree, it left a huge hole where it had been located. Mature Flowers, new pregnant wife of the chief, sat on the edge of the hole and peered downward. Seeing her sitting by the hole, the enraged chief kicked her into the opening. Before falling into the hole, Mature Flowers grasped some seeds in her hand that had been shaken loose from the celestial tree. While falling downward, she met a bird that emitted fire from its head who gave her a small pot, a corn mortar, a pestle, a marrow bone, and an ear of corn. He told her that she would eat by means of these items because there is nothing to eat below. Knowing about her arrival, the creatures below prepared for her coming: Ducks received her on their wings to break her free-fall, and the great turtle from the underworld made his broad back a resting place. In addition, several animals dived unsuccessfully into the depths to retrieve some earth, until finally a muskrat was successful. Subsequently, the mud retrieved by the muskrat was smeared on the back of the turtle and grew. Mature Flowers dropped many seeds on the earth, and from the root of the celestial tree that she planted there grew a tree with many fruits and flowers, and it also illuminated the world. Finally, Mature Flowers gave birth to a daughter, who was married to the wind, and she gave birth to two sons.

The first son of the daughter was called Good Mind, whereas her evil son was called Warty One. The evil son caused the death of his mother when he emerged from her arm pit. Thereupon, Good Mind buried his mother, and from her burial there sprang stringed potatoes, beans, squash, corn, and tobacco from different parts of her body. As time went on, Good Mind tried to do constructive things, whereas his evil brother attempted to undo his brother's good deeds by creating poisonous plants and thorns on bushes, rattlesnakes, bugs, and worms. Eventually, the two brothers engaged in battle, during which the tree of life was destroyed. As a punishment, Good Mind banished his brother to a great cave. Then, Good Mind created human beings in his own image out of clay and gave them the earth. He also taught them to hunt, fish, and eat the fruits of the land. Moreover, he taught humans to treat each other well and live together as brothers and sisters. After he told them how to make tobacco offerings, he returned to the sky.

This myth about the origin of the world contains a wealth of messages. Before the creation of the earth, there was a paradise from which Mature Flowers is expelled and literally falls. This suggests that creation is given impetus by moral transgression and anger, implying that both of them should be avoided or controlled. The retrieving of mud from the primal depths of the cosmic waters is a common element in Native American cosmological myths, although this is usually preceded by several failed attempts. The myth relates the origin of the earth, humans, and plants necessary for survival. When the animals help Mature Flowers, manifesting her role in the narrative as an earth goddess, this suggests the importance of cooperation between humans and animals and the reliance of humans on animals for survival. The diametrically opposed brothers suggest the struggle between good and evil on earth; their opposition implies that evil is not totally overcome, as suggested by the cave in which the evil brother lives. Before Good Mind leaves the earth, he gives humans a means to communicate with him by means of the tobacco offerings, which establishes a connection between the earth and the heavenly realm. Even though it is possible to find structural similarities between creation myths among Native American societies from different regions of North America, the narratives are often rather different in their details. Myths from the southwest have human beings emerge from under the earth rather than from a being associated with the sky.

This story allows a reader to witness some characteristics of a myth, such as its narrative form about important events in the history of the tribe. Myths deal with meaningful issues of substance for an entire society that explain why things and events appear as they do at the present time. Consequently, myths tell listeners about primordial events that occurred at the beginning of time. By orally sharing these tales, story teller and audience get an opportunity to participate in their culture's internal significance. By telling a myth, the story teller is engaged in a performative act that brings the original actions of the divine beings, cultural heroes, animals, and humans into focus, enabling listeners to relive the ancient happenings and to bear witness to the creative deeds. In fact, the telling of a myth is a social event that reinforces social cohesion.

The myth embodies the sacred history of a society and is connected to ontology (theory of being) because it tells us how something came to be. It is concerned with elements of a culture that are important to human existence such as human relations, food, medicine, sexuality, and death. A good example of explaining why things are as they now appear is illustrated by a narrative from the Shoshoni Indians of Wyoming: In bygone days, long, long ago, the animals were human beings. Wolf and Coyote were the most important. The Wolf—creator figure—and the Coyote were such that Wolf was amenable, while Coyote always tried to do the opposite (of what Wolf did). Wolf pronounced that when a human being died, one could bring her to life again by shooting an arrow under her. But Coyote was of another opinion: "That would not be good; then there would be too many people here, and there is not room for them all. No, let the human die, his flesh rot, and his spirit fly away with the wind, so that all that is left is just a pile of dry bones." The amenable Wolf gave in. But in his heart, he decided to let Coyote's son be the first to die. In this way, Wolf wished that the boy would die, and just because of his wish, it came true. Coyote soon came to Wolf and told him that his son had died. He reminded Wolf about how the latter had said that one could bring a person to life again by shooting an arrow under her. But the Wolf reminded Coyote of how he himself had decided that a person should die for all time. That is why it turned out that way. This myth helps members of a society understand the origin of death.

A myth is also dynamic in the sense that it may change over time in the sense of adding new elements and excising older features within certain limits. If a myth is dynamic in this way and changes, does this mean that myths are false? To a learned twenty-first century student, it might seem that the answer to this question is fairly obvious: It is false. But if you were a member of a Native American society who is living in the myth, which serves as an exemplary model for all significant human activities, the answer is very different.

An example that captures the spirit of the Indian mode of falsity or veracity of a myth comes from two illustrations from Native Americans that live on the plains of North America. In the first instance, Pawnee Indians draw a distinction between "true stories" and "false stories." The true stories are those that deal with the beginnings of the world. Next come those tales that relate to the marvelous adventures of the national hero. Lastly, there are stories dealing with the world of the medicine-men and how they got their superhuman powers. On the other hand, the false stories are those which tell of the far-from-edifying adventures and exploits of the Coyote. Therefore, the true stories are concerned with the holy and supernatural, whereas the false narratives are of profane content. Thus, a myth shares narratives that are sacred and true.

In another illustration from another Plains Indian society that makes a similar point, the Wichita Indians tell a tale about a contest that occurs between a coyote and a man. The contest takes place at night, and the two opponents, sitting beside a fire, tell each other a story in turn. After a period of time, the man is slower and slower at finding a new tale to tell to match the one told by the coyote, whose repertory seems endless. Finally, the human contestant admits himself beaten and is killed by the coyote. Why did the coyote win the contest? He wins because his stories are false, invented, and indefinitely many. The human's stories are true because they tell about things that have really happened. Consequently, there are just so many true stories. Thus, for those living within a particular Indian culture and the narratives of that culture, the myth is a true story about what really took place in the distant past and is simply taken for granted, which liberates a person from having to think about it. The mythical narratives help members of a society understand the past and the present structure of society because they are the foundational accounts that help listeners understand the roots of their culture. By knowing a myth, a human knows the secret origin of things, which gives him power to control, manipulate, or reproduce those secrets embodied within the myth. This magico-religious power can be used to empower himself or to help others.

Worldviews of Native Americans

Myths not only describe sacred irruptions into the world, but they also form a language network that gives a listener a glimpse into aspects of the cultural worldview, although it is seldom the case that a myth manifests a complete worldview. In order to fully grasp a worldview of a society, it is necessary to examine and consider other elements within the mythical network. By examining its many narrative elements, it is possible to discern the worldview of the Tewa Pueblo of the American Southwest.

Before the origin of the world, the Tewa lived beneath a lake, which was similar to the present world but dark. In this place, gods, humans, and animals lived together and death was unknown. The Tewa people had two mothers: Corn Woman (summer mother) and White Corn Woman (winter mother), dividing a year into two parts. While living beneath the earth, a man was sent forth to examine the world above, but he found that the earth was green or unripe. In another quest, the man saw predatory animals that initiated him and accepted him by giving him things necessary for hunting. He returned to the people as a Hunt Chief or Mountain Lion and gave one man an ear of blue corn, which was designed to care for the people during the summer, whereas Hunt Chief gave an ear of white corn to another man, who was to care for the people during winter. These figures constituted the Made People. The narrative identifies a group of social counterparts of the six deities called the Towaé, consisting of six pairs of brothers who have different colors and go in different directions. The initial four pairs picked up some mud and slung it toward each direction, while the all-colored pair found hard ground and saw a rainbow. After the people leave the lake, they become ill. Desperate for a cure, the people opened the Corn Mother only to find the origin of witchcraft and other evils. This necessitated the creation of a medicine man to cure the people. Over time, other cultural figures were created, such as clowns to entertain people, the Scalp Chief to ensure success in warfare, and the women's society to care for the scalps and assist the Scalp Chief. These people became known as the Made People. These three groupings on earth correspond to three more levels of being in the supernatural realm: souls of Dry Food People, supernatural counterparts of the human Towaé, and the Dry Food Who Never Did Become (souls of Made People and all deities present at the origin). Then the people divided into the summer and winter groups, with the former subsisting on agriculture and gathering, whereas the latter group survived by hunting. The people took twelve steps and founded a village, but this place had to be abandoned because of an epidemic that threatened the existence of the people. This original failure was followed by the founding of the six Tewa villages.

The Tewa worldview consists of four sacred mountains, with each associated with a lake or pond. Within the water, there live the souls of the Dry Food People. The supernatural Towaé watch the people from the top of the four mountains, which are considered sacred. Next, there are a group of four flat-topped hills created by the Towaé, who also watch the Pueblo from these hills. Within the circle of the four hills, there are four shrines called souls-dwelling middle places. The final group of four represents the dance plazas within the village. The sacred center of the village is equated with the "Earth Mother Earth Navel Place," a location from which all ritual begins. This worldview incorporates both vertical space (below, middle, and above) and horizontal space, consisting of the center of the village, plazas, shrines, hills, and mountains. The center of the village establishes a fixed point or axis that makes it possible for the three vertical realms and horizontal space to communicate with each other. Thus the Tewa world is located around the cosmic axis, which is the sacred land of the Pueblo in contrast to the undifferentiated nature of profane space. The Tewa origin myth and worldview informs members of the society about the structure of the inhabited world, their place within this world, human social status, and the relationship between humans, animals, and divine figures.

In contrast to the Pueblo, the Plains Indians espouse a worldview that affirms that the world has a round surface. In the four quarters of this world, there reside the four winds. The sky, a location of great powers, represents a great dome over the world. It is the sky and earth that represent the home of sacred life. Parts of the world are joined together by a cosmic pole or world-tree that the Indians identify with the Milky Way, which stretches from the seat of the Supreme Being to the earth. The Milky Way represents the main path of communication between god and humans. This worldview and that of the Pueblos suggest different ways in which peoples orientate themselves and comprehend their world.

Time is also an aspect of the worldview of indigenous peoples. Among the Sioux, there are four kinds of time: (1) daylight; (2) night time; (3) phases of the moon; (4) twelve months that make a year. Time is conceived as cyclical and dynamic; it includes the everyday world and the spiritual realm. The Sioux notion of time corresponds with their nomadic lives based on the cycle of hunting. In other words, cyclical movements of time, migrations of Indians and animals, and the life cycles of animals and birds all move in a cyclical pattern, which gets integrated into the cosmic cyclical movements, creating a harmonious flow of time.

Divine Beings and Spirits

Among Native Americans of the Northern Plains, the Sioux worship the Great Spirit or Great Mystery called Wakantanka. The parts of this name are instructive because *wakan* means sacred and *tanka* means great, large, or big. Wakantanka is not personified, although aspects of it are personified, as when it is called Father or Grandfather. The term *wakantanka* includes a collective meaning in the sense of representing the embodiment of all supernatural beings and powers, which are hierarchically ranked according to groups of four. The superior *wakan* is identified with the sun, sky, earth, or rock, while the associates of the superior *wakan* include the moon, wind, falling star, or Thunder-being. It is useful to know that the superior and associate forms of *wakan* are linked as the sun and moon, sky and wind, earth and falling star, and rock and Thunder-being. These linked entities are called *wakan kin* (the sacred), which are without beginning and are responsible for creating the universe and humans. The third hierarchical category is lower *wakan*, identified by the buffalo, the two-legged (both the bear and humans), the four winds, and whirlwind. Finally, there are those similar to *wakan* such as the shade, life or breath, shade-like, and potency. The third and fourth categories are also called sacred things because they are created by the *wakan kin* and are a part of it.

The Sioux notion of power shares some similarities with the Algonquian notion of *orenda* in the sense that both are impersonal, amoral versions of power. Power is also often imagined as an independent force apart from humans and even supernatural beings, although it is native to some things. A reader will notice as this chapter progresses that power can be gained in many ways. Power can also be used for good or evil, with a shaman representing the former and a witch standing for the latter.

In addition to masculine divine beings, Native Americans recognize goddess figures. Among the Sioux, there is the Buffalo Calf Woman, a giver of social institutions. She plays a major role in the Sioux religion because she gives the sacred pipe to be used in the seven major rites of the nation. She is also considered the mistress of buffaloes and appears as one at times. The buffalo is associated with the earth and its growth. When the buffalo disappear, they are believed to be located within the earth. The Buffalo Calf Woman is also conceived to be an earth goddess, which is symbolized by the red stone bowl of the sacred pipe. The goddess' identification with the earth is symbolically associated with something permanent: the untiring, fruitful womb and foundation of all existence.

Among the Iroquois of the northern woodlands, there are three goddess figures that personify corn, beans, and squash. Each of them is clothed by the plant that they guard and conceived of as very attractive. Once upon a time, a bad heavenly twin sent a devastating blight that destroyed the corn. Indians are reminded of this event in the present time when the wind rustles the corn leaves, creating a moaning sound of grieving. In summary, the corn goddess is the corn itself, is its protector, and serves as the patroness of humans who cultivate it. The cult associated with the corn goddess occurs at the beginning of the planting season when a young virgin scatters grains of corn in the fields. This is done to invoke the assistance of the corn goddess. In this cult, the virgin functions as the priestess of the corn spirit and also represents the corn spirit itself.

An especially interesting goddess figure is Sedna, Eskimo Sea Woman. She lives at the bottom of the sea in a big domed house, which is guarded by seals that bite intruders. In addition to the seals, water creatures swim in and out of the house. The goddess is described as frightening with one eye, a body covered with dirt, tangled hair, a filthy face, and no fingers. She is considered the mistress and creator of sea animals.

Her awful appearance can be grasped by reviewing the Eskimo creation myth. Sedna was a lovely, attractive girl who was wooed by a fulmar (a seabird) with promises of rich food and a bed of soft bearskins. After accepting his offer, she arrived at the country of the fulmars only to discover that she had been deceived because she was given miserable fish to eat and hard walrus hides on which to sleep. When her father visited her one day, she asked him to take her back to her old home. Seeing the plight of his daughter, the father became angry and killed the fulmar, departing with Sedna in his boat. As other fulmars pursued them, they stirred up a heavy storm that frightened the father to such an extent that he threw his daughter overboard. As Sedna held on to the side of the boat, her father cut off her fingers, which swam away as whales, seals, and other marine animals. What the violent myth suggests is that marine animals are a part of Sedna, which possesses serious consequences for hunting because she refuses to release the marine animals to be killed by hunters when they transgress some taboo, such as cooking together the flesh of a sea animal and a land animal, which pollutes the flesh of both animals, thereby causing human eaters of these animals to become impure, a precarious and dangerous status.

In addition to various gods and goddesses, Native Americans believe in a rich array of spirits that are often associated with aspects of the earth or animals. The Ojibwa count among their spiritual beings manitos, who are considered to be powerful beings associated with hunting and the sources of Indian existence. The spirits of the four winds are responsible, for instance, for seasonal changes and weather, whereas the underwater manito is composed of two beings: the underwater lion and horned serpent, who influence the abundance and availability of land and sea animals for hunting. In addition to controlling the game for hunting, the underwater manito causes rapids and stormy waters that can sink canoes. The thunder hawks, controllers of air animals, are spirits that manifest themselves through thunder and lightning and are considered powerful guardian spirits, who often appear to people in visions. The Ojibwa also believe in the owners of animals, who control access to the animals and demand respect and offerings from the Indians. Each species of animal has an owner, and there are also owners of sacred locations associated with springs and waterfalls. Finally, the Ojibwa recognize windigo, a giant cannibal made of ice. He prefers to eat human flesh. In short, he symbolizes winter and starvation for the Indians.

The Northern Saulteaux also recognize a master of animals, whose functions are to preside over the animals in a collective sense or over one animal species. The master sees that no animals are killed unnecessarily and that they are treated with care and respect. After an animal is killed, it must be buried, for example, with appropriate rituals. An excellent example of this behavior is bear ceremonialism among the Saulteaux. Before a hunter kills a bear, he addresses it and apologizes for having to kill it. He might explain to the bear the killing is due to his hunger and his people's need for food. After the bear is killed, the hunter dresses the bear in fine clothing and erects a pole upon which are hung the bear's skull, the skin of its muzzle, and its ears. What is the purpose of such action? It is a means of showing respect for the bear and for the master of the species. The underlying purpose of this action is to assure future game and continued success in hunting by entering into a proper relationship with the animal.

Anthropologists call the intimate association between individuals or social groups with animals or plant species totemism, which includes the belief that members of a totem are descendants of some animal. This motivates a group to assume the name and identities of some mythical animal from which evolve living animals. Thus, members of the bear clan, for example, do not kill bears, although they may eat the flesh and use the hide of the bear if someone from another clan kills the animal. Not only are these animals held in reverence, but they are also called upon in critical situations. At a person's initiation ceremony, each clan member obtains protection from the clan animal.

Native American Indians also conceive of nature spirits, as evident with the Sioux and Cheyenne and their reverence for the Black Hills as the homeland of the spirits. The Shoshoni assume that rock carvings in the mountains are made by spirits. Yellowstone Park is believed to be inhabited by spirits, whereas the Pueblo venerate lakes and other apertures in the earth's surface from which their ancestors emerged. Rocks are also conceived by some Indians as containing spirits. Among the Sioux, all rocks are called Inyan, oldest of divinities and ancestral father of all things and all gods. It is not unusual to find large boulders located in the open plains decorated with paint along with prayers and dog sacrifices directed to them. Moreover, Indians believe that there are spirits in bodies of water, such as seas, lakes, springs, and rivers.

In addition to animal- and earth-related spirits, some societies believe in personal guardian spirits. Among the Pueblo, it is possible to receive a guardian spirit at birth, or it can be acquired by means of visions. Appearing often in animal form, a guardian spirit can protect a person from committing wrong deeds or give a person some kind of gift such as strength or wisdom. If a person transgresses a taboo, the spirit may abandon that person. The spirit might provide one with a fetish like a medicine bundle that contains various items such as animal parts, pipes, rattles, corn cobs, or other things. The bundle serves to protect the owner from physical harm. As time passes, a person acquires the characteristics of his guardian spirit and acknowledges this by painting tattoos on himself to resemble the spirit. In addition, a person might also decorate clothes and weapons with claws, feathers, or fur and adopt the name of the animal, reflecting the intimate bond between the person and the spirit.

Conceptions of Human Nature

The Sioux conceptualization of human nature is an excellent example of how complex and multifaceted it can be imagined. From the Sioux perspective, the universe is composed of a finite amount of energy having two aspects: good and evil. The good aspects of energy are controlled by Wakantanka, whereas the evil aspects are proscribed by *wakan sica* (evil sacred). A human can harness either good or evil energy by propitiating Wakantanka in the former instance or evil energy by appeasing it. If evil energy is subordinate to Wakantanka, a person is subordinate to both. These forms of energy have two aspects: visible and invisible. It is possible to transform visible energy to invisible and vice versa, and both are called *wakan* (sacred). This implies, for instance, that life (a visible aspect) can be transformed into death, suggesting that life and death are both sacred.

Life is manifested in breath (*ni*), and when the breath leaves a person, he dies. In addition to the breath, humans, along with all supernatural beings, objects, and powers—animate and inanimate—have an innate power called *sicun*, which is immortal potency. Acting as a guardian spirit, *sicun* acts to ward off evil, but at death it returns to the supernaturals. Not only does *sicun* account for a person's vacillation between good and evil, but it is also something that one can borrow from another person. In addition, it can be invested in a person through a ceremony, and a person can also accumulate *sicun*, which suggests that a person can increase one's power. The Sioux understanding of *sicun* is paradoxical in the sense that one can give one's accumulated *sicun* to help others, but the more *sicun* that one gives away, the more power one loses.

Another feature of human nature is the *nagi*, a shadow of someone or something; it is the eternal counterpart of every animate and inanimate object. The *nagi* is a spirit that lingers after death when the life breath is lost. With the death of a person, the *nagi* evolves into a *wanagi* (ghost), which is considered dangerous because it grieves for its loved ones left behind and tries to entice its family to join it. In order to appease the *wanagi* (ghost), a relative keeps it for one year, which involves feeding it sacred food. After one year, the ghost departs to the south along the ghost road that is identified with the Milky Way. When the ghost (*wanagi*) reaches its destination, it is met by an old woman, who assesses its actions on earth. Those passing the examination by the old woman pass to a place that reflects their life with *ni* (breath). Those failing the test are pushed over a cliff, and their evil spirits are left to roam the earth, where they endanger the living.

Among the Ojibwa, human nature consists of two souls: a body-soul and free-soul. The former type of soul animates the body from its location in the heart. It can move within or without the body. The body-soul provides intelligence, reason, memory, consciousness, and ability to act and experience emotions. Residing in the brain, the free-soul enjoys a separate existence from the body. It is associated with the senses and can see things from a distance. It not only travels beyond a person during sleep, but it can also warn a person of danger within the context of a battle or a hunt.

Each soul exists apart from the body, and yet each acts in harmony with the body. After death, the body-soul goes to the afterworld, whereas the free-soul becomes a ghost when the body dies. Both souls are eventually united in the afterworld. The soul possesses the ability to metamorphosize into a plant or animal.

The Ojibwa identify other aspects of the human being for importance. The bones are significant, for example, because they hold the body together and thus represent integrity. The name of a person is an extension of a person's identity. Each Ojibwa is given two names: a birth name and a puberty one that is kept secret. A person's shadow is regarded as an integral part of a person.

Role of Women

Female figures play important roles in many Native American Indian cultures. The Buffalo Calf Woman of the Sioux, dressed beautifully in white buckskin, encountered two hunters. One hunter was overcome with lust for her, she called him to her, and they were enveloped by a great cloud. When the cloud lifted, the lascivious man had been reduced to a pile of bones. Thereupon, she instructed the other hunter to assemble the tribe for her appearance to them. When the Buffalo Calf Woman appeared to the excitedly anticipating tribe, she gave them the sacred pipe and instructions on how to use it. Among the Shawnee of the eastern woodland, they believe that they owe their existence and that of the earth to a goddess figure called Our Grandmother. The Iroquois revere three goddesses, identified with corn, beans, and squash, who are sometimes called the Three Sisters, suggesting collectively an intimate connection to the earth and motherhood. The importance of the earth and motherhood carries over into tribal social life.

Although the role of women manifests some differences among Indian societies, there are some common similarities among the various cultures. Among Native American Indian women, there was a tendency for girls to marry young, reaching even to an extent prior to their first menses. During their monthly period, women were considered unclean, and they purified themselves afterwards. Native American women were not chattels and not forced to marry men they found distasteful. Marriage was a secular affair, and divorce was frequent among many tribes, which might simply consist of a process as ingenuous as abandonment of a wife by a husband. The ideal woman was virtuous, an expert at feminine tasks, and physically attractive. Women's work extended beyond the confines of the home. Typically, women of the Plains cultures made clothing, collected and preserved edible roots and berries, erected tipis and dismantled them when the group moved, tanned animal hides, made leather pouches, carried firewood and water, did the cooking, and were custodians of holy objects.

Some Native American tribes manifested a double standard with respect to sexuality. Women were admired and praised for their purity on the one hand, but they were considered social outcasts when they deviated from the ideal on the other hand. Some men abused their wives whether they were virtuous or not, which could lead to a woman divorcing her violent spouse. During the Crow's Sun Dance observance, a married woman of irreproachable fidelity was selected to receive an honorific title as a tree-notcher. Among the Ojibwa, there were female religious leaders, with some becoming healers and artisans because of the visions that they had during life. Some Ojibwa women hunted and became warriors. And under exceptional circumstances, women could become religious leaders.

Not all Native American cultures were patriarchal. The Hopi of the southwest arranged their clans according to a matrilineal model of society. Among the Hopi, women often owned farms and fields. From a symbolical perspective, Hopi women united family, home, and field. Moreover, Hopi women embodied sacredness by means of the concrete and internal phenomena of birth, kinship structures, and property.

Important Cultural Figures

Appearing as the Tricky One among the Winnebago Indians, the spider Inktomi among the Sioux, or the Old Man Napi among the Blackfoot, the trickster is a cultural hero and popular figure because of his many exploits preserved in often violent and risqué narratives. The trickster not only communicates with animals, but he is also responsible for their forms and colors. Serving as a mediator between the supernatural and human realms, he also gives culture to humans, names things, creates language, and plays tricks on humans. A distinguishing characteristic is his enormous penis, which often plays a central role in many narratives.

After teasing a trickster about his colossal penis, a chipmunk is threatened with death by the trickster. In order to save himself, the chipmunk runs into the hollow of a tree. Speaking to his penis, the trickster instructs it to pursue the chipmunk. The trickster probes the hollow tree with his penis, but he cannot reach the end of it. Thus he continues to send more of his penis into the hole to find the end of it, and presumably the chipmunk. Finally, he withdraws his penis, and to his horror he discovers that only a small piece of it is left. Now, being hung like a raisin, he kicks open the log and finds the chipmunk and the remainder of his organ all gnawed up. From the pieces of his dismembered penis, he creates various vegetables and flowers. This narrative ends with the conclusion and lesson of the story: "And this is the reason our penis has its present shape. It is because of these happenings that the penis is short." In this story, it is the trickster that gets tricked.

The Native American trickster can transform himself into any shape, such as the time that he becomes a woman, marries the chief's son, and gives birth to three sons. The trickster may treat his own body as something foreign, a feature exemplified by a story about causing his hands to fight each other or learning from mice how to juggle his eyes. The Indian trickster is often described as carrying his enormous penis in a box that he carries with him as he moves from one absurd adventure to another.

In one such adventure, the trickster demonstrates his insatiable sexual appetite when he spies the chief's daughter across a lake. Desiring to have intercourse with her, he instructed his penis to lodge squarely in her and dispatched it into the water, but it went sliding on the surface, where the women on the other side of the lake could see it. Then he tied a stone to it, but it dropped to the bottom of the lake. Finding the stone with just the right weight, his penis moves beneath the surface of the lake and hits its designated target between the thighs of the chief's daughter. Men and women could not dislodge the trickster's penis, but an old woman recognizes what was happening, and straddles the organ, hitting it a few times with a sharp instrument. When the penis is jerked out by the trickster, the old woman is thrown a great distance. Even though the trickster fails in this narrative, there is a promise that he will return in the future.

There are also narratives that depict the trickster manifesting an ambivalent relation to the animal world. The Old Man, Napi of the Blackfoot Indians, is traveling with his friend, Fox. Because it is a hot day, Old Man's robe causes him discomfort, and he throws it on a large rock. When a rain cloud appears, Old Man sends Fox back to retrieve his robe to avoid getting wet. But the rock refuses to return the robe, which motivates the Old Man to angrily take it back. As they continued their journey, the Old Man and Fox hear a loud noise behind them, turn to see rock rolling after them, and begin to run. In desperation, the Old Man calls the bears and buffalos for assistance, but they are all crushed by the rock, which motivates him to call the night hawks for assistance. Flying over the rock, the hawks break wind over it until the rock is completely destroyed. Arriving at a nest of baby night hawks of the parents that helped him, the Old Man killed them, claiming that the parents spoiled his fun. When the parents discovered the deaths of their baby chicks, they dove on him and defecated on his robe, cutting it to pieces. This narrative combines order and disorder, indicates the ambiguous nature of the trickster, and is indicative of an oxymoronic imagination at play.

The Native American Indian trickster, a wandering vagabond, lives in a world of games that is full of tricks. The trickster reveals that life plays tricks on us, that life is a tricky business, and that survival in the world presupposes being able to be tricky. The trickster takes life as a challenge and makes a game of it. In fact, the necessities of life must be taken and defended by trickery in a cycle in which life preys on life. A tale from the Chinook Indians relates that Coyote conspires with Skunk to feign illness, and when various animals come to sing cures over him, he gasses them. In other narratives, the trickster survives by his own cunning and prowess, as evident by his being a master of camouflage and disguise. In addition to the trickster being able to transform himself into a variety of forms, he is also ignorant and foolish. Sometimes, he not only outwits others, but he also outwits himself.

Another important figure in Native American religion is the shaman or medicine man, who can be defined as a master of ecstasy and curer of the sick with the help of spirits. Receiving his powers directly from the gods and spirits, he acquires his status through personal communication with the supernatural. The medicine man's status is not dependent on his knowledge of ritual but is rather based on his personal charisma (gift of leadership). He treats two types of illness: an intrusion into a patient's body of a spirit or an object and soul loss. In the first type of illness, the object causing the problem is often transmitted by a spirit or an evil person such as a sorcerer or witch. The task of the medicine man is to remove the illness-causing object, which is often accomplished by initially determining the object's position and nature and extracting the object by sucking it out, blowing it away, or massaging it away. In the case of soul loss, the medicine man must find the soul by going into a trance state and sending his own soul to retrieve that of a patient into possibly the land of the dead. When a person loses her soul, she becomes delirious or unconscious. When the medicine man finds and retrieves the soul of a patient, he returns to place it into the body of the sick person and cure her.

There are three means of recruiting a medicine man: spontaneous vocation, by hereditary transmission of the profession, or personal quest. The first means to be called or elected by the spirits. In the second instance, a person assumes the position of his father. The final way may create a less powerful medicine man because he is self-made. Once a man is recruited, he proceeds to be initiated by returning to a condition of being dead and then being reborn. Being educated by souls of dead medicine men and spirits, the medicine man acquires the knowledge to be successful at his profession. The rites performed by a medicine man are not regular but are rather performed by request.

Among the Sioux, the medicine man plays a central role in the spirit lodge ceremony (*yuwipi*), during which he is subjected to being bound and wrapped up. Within the confines of a teepee, the medicine man is tied to the base of a lodge pole, and spirits enter through the smoke hole at the top. When the spirits enter the tent, it begins to shake, which is a sign that the spirits are present. Light visions, confusion of voices, sounds of tappings and steps on the ground, and articles being thrown around are additional phenomena that testify to the presence of spirits. The ritual includes the liberation of the medicine man from his bonds. This is called the rope-binding trick. It includes the medicine man going into a trance state, his soul taking flight, and concludes with the curing of a patient.

In contrast to the healing exercised by a medicine man, the witch is a figure that injures others. Witches share some features and powers, such as the tendency to operate at night under the cover of darkness. The Navaho believe that they wander naked. Witches possess the ability to fly; they can assume animal form such as that of an owl or other type of carrion bird or become a wolf or coyote as the Navaho believe. Because a witch can become invisible, it is only the special eyesight of a medicine man that can identify one. Witches are fond of eating human flesh, a diet that causes them to gather at cemeteries where they wait to consume bodies of deceased people after burial. It is believed that witches consort with demons. It is also believed that a witch is immune to heat because fire is the element of a witch.

There are various ways for a witch to exercise his powers to harm others: touch their victim, use their evil eye, or pronounce a curse. Witches use numerous types of technical aids to accomplish their nefarious goals, such as making a wax image of an intended victim and sticking pins into it, writing a victim's name on a piece of paper and burning it, or using bodily waste (e. g., blood, sweat, urine, vomit, hair, nail parings, excrement, or menstrual blood) when creating a charm, effigy, or potion. In the case of bodily waste, the witch uses any of these elements against a victim by forcing them back onto the intended target, which results in the clogging of the channels of the ebb and flow of the human body and a dissociation of the victim from the world.

A witch symbolizes an anti-social being, who is described as morose, disagreeable, arrogant, ambitious, sly, ugly, dirty, lying, envious, and shifty-eyed. These types of character traits are indicative of the isolated nature of the witch. The witch also symbolizes the anti-human by acting at night, flying or walking on their hands or heads, dancing naked, feasting on corpses, exhibiting insatiable and incestuous lusts despite sexual impotence, murdering relatives, living in the wild with animals, or defecating and vomiting in people's homes. This suggests that a witch lives in a mirror world that is the complete reversal of the social world, and a witch is parasitic in the sense that she blocks or reverses the flow of life.

The Indians' belief in witches performs some important functions in their society. The Navaho society manifests certain dysfunctional aspects of witchcraft beliefs by increasing, for example, fear and violence or opening guiltless individuals to accusations of practicing witchcraft. It is also possible for witchcraft beliefs to embody submerged criticism of a society. From a more positive perspective, witchcraft beliefs can identify those who have violated divine norms. These beliefs contribute to social continuity by pointing to socially disapproved actions, counteracting socially disruptive forces by maintaining a system of checks and balances. Among the Navaho, rich people are expected to be generous, otherwise they may be suspected of witchcraft, which puts social pressure on the rich to live up to social expectations. It is possible that witchcraft beliefs can both express and strengthen group affiliations by accusing outsiders and affirming cultural values and norms by opposing social deviants. These beliefs can provide outlets for aggression, anxiety, and hostility.

This is true among the Navaho because witches become scapegoats toward whom one can direct anger instead of directing it toward relatives, which disrupts family unity. Witchcraft beliefs ensure social obligations such as charity. The Navaho, for instance, care for old people who might otherwise become witches. In a paradoxical way, these beliefs can operate to sever unwanted relationships. Such beliefs can also help to explain unusual situations or fix the cause of an illness, death, or misfortune.

In addition to the trickster, medicine man, and witch, another important figure holding a central role in Indian culture is the clown. This chapter considers the clown separately when it turns to a discussion of the comic element in Native American Indian life.

Material and Artistic Dimensions of Indian Culture

Among the Blackfoot of the American Plains, Thunder is known for bringing rain that makes plants grow and as a stealer of women. In one narrative, Thunder enters the lodge of a man and his wife and strikes them down, rendering the man unconscious, while the wife is abducted. When he regains consciousness the man goes looking for his wife without success after an exhaustive search and concludes that she must have been stolen by Thunder. Being determined to retrieve his wife, the man travels to Thunder's lodge, and all the animals laugh at him because of Thunder's power. But the man meets Raven Chief, who tells the man that his power is superior to that of Thunder and that he will help him free his wife. In order to accomplish this purpose, Raven gives the man some powerful objects that include a raven wing and an arrow. Journeying to the lodge of Thunder, the man confronts him and sees many pairs of eyes that represent the humans that Thunder had abducted in the past. After the man recognizes his wife's eyes, Thunder tries to strike him, but he is repelled by the raven wing. With the arrow given to him by Raven, the man shoots an elk horn arrow through the roof of the lodge, letting sunlight suffuse the lodge. Thereupon, Thunder concedes defeat; the man retrieves his wife's eyes and restores her to wholeness. This encounter ends when Thunder transfers to the man a sacred pipe and gives the man instructions about how to use it to bring rain in the spring.

What the Blackfoot man receives from Raven is a bundle that contains objects that are considered sacred and thus powerful. The contents of sacred bundles vary. Typical contents might include a sacred pipe, a white buffalo headdress, a smaller pipe for smoking during a ritual, skins of certain animals and birds, tobacco wrapped in bird skin, and a rattle wrapped in a prairie dog's skin. Many of these items are painted red. The contents of bundles have two major sources: vision experience of the original owner or vision experiences of successive owners. In order to open a bundle, there is a ritual procedure that is necessary that involves purification of the body and spirit of the owner. This purification process is accomplished by a sweat bath during which the hot stones are placed in a rectangular hole, symbolizing Thunder. The bundle is placed on the top of the sweat lodge with its stem pointing east, signifying the source of life flowing from the sun. A buffalo skull is placed at the western direction of the lodge, recalling the sacred relationship between the people and the buffalo. The Blackfoot give four reasons to open a bundle: the sound of first thunder in the spring, renewing the tobacco in the bundle, transferring the bundle to another person, or responding to a vow made by a person in time of illness or another type of personal crisis. The opening of a bundle is accomplished within a ritual context that includes prayers, songs, dancing, and painting the owner's face red, which identifies him with the meaningful structures that are evoked symbolically in the ritual.

In contrast to the Blackfoot, Crow bundles are mostly associated with warfare. According to Crow lore, a young orphan male fasts in a lonely place. As part of his regimen, he cuts off the first joint of his index finger and prays to the sun for power. Morning Star, Sun's offspring, appears in a vision to the orphan and shows him a powerful arrow and how to use it. Morning Star instructs him to return to his camp and make seven arrows each of a different color, which become the central objects in seven different bundles. Next, Morning Star teaches the young man the ritual and songs appropriate to the bundles. Before taking his leave, Morning Star gives the original sacred arrow to the young man. In summary, bundles are believed to bring their owners both success in battle and good fortune in life.

Besides the power of the sacred bundles, the Crow Indians hold shields in high regard because they promote values associated with the continued existence of the society. The appearance of a shield is given in a dream or waking vision. The shields are considered very powerful, but they are seldom taken into battle because they are too bulky and heavy, although a part of the shield such as a feather or a miniature reproduction of the shield might be taken into battle. A shield signifies various symbolic associations such as a green border on the left side that represents the summer, which is a time for war parties. Dark brown lines on the shield represent bullets or projectiles bouncing off of it. Owl and eagle feathers are tied to the center of it because these birds are considered powerful. The owl had the power of sacred vision because it can see into the future, whereas the eagle is considered the chief of birds because it can fly the highest and can thus see everything on the earth. The whole of the shield represents the buffalo.

For many American Indians living on the Plains, the pipe is sacred because it was given to them by the Buffalo Calf Woman. Among the Sioux, the bowl of the pipe symbolizes the earth, a carved buffalo calf on the pipe represents all creatures, and the wooden stem represents all that grows on the earth. The twelve feathers hanging from the stem of the pipe represents the eagle and all winged creatures, whereas the seven circles represent the seven rites of the Sioux. This description of the sacred pipe signifies the many ways an object can simultaneously symbolize multiple meaningful items. It also helps us to witness that a particular object is sacred because it participates in a source with superior power and force.

Zuni of the southwest and the Iroquois of the northern woodlands live far apart, but they share a common material feature: the mask. Among the Zuni, masks are worn by Kachina dancers made of leather of elk skin or buffalo hide. By wearing the mask, one assumes the personality of the spirit represented, and the mask makes the wearer holy, which means that the wearer must not be touched when wearing the mask. Before the masks are worn, they are invested with spiritual powers by ritual means. These masks are ceremonially fed and carefully preserved. When the owner of a mask dies, it is buried to ensure that supernatural power returns to its origin. In order to wear a mask, the owner must observe certain restrictions: remain sexually continent, avoid contact with white people, avoid quarrels, and have only pure thoughts. The violation of any of these restrictions can cause death to the owner.

In contrast to the leather masks of the Zuni, the Iroquois wear masks carved of wood, which evokes an effect that can be terrifying and humorous. The masks represent spirits of the forest, who are quasi-humans that dart from tree to tree, although they frequently appear to be disembodied heads with long hair. These forest figures promise not to harm humans if they receive tobacco offerings and hold the promise of controlling illness. No two masks are identical, in part, because they appear to the wearers in dreams. All masks share certain features: painted black, red, or black and red, have large, starring eyes made of copper or brass, have long, protuberant, and frequently bent noses, and have mouths that are open and distorted. Moreover, the masks are crowned with long, flowing hair of buffalo mane or horse tails. After a mask is carved and hollowed, it is consecrated by fire and a tobacco offering. After it is consecrated, the mask is considered alive and charged with power for good or evil. Inside of the hallowed mask is a bag of tobacco. Why? There is a common belief that the mask loves tobacco. Since the masks are believed to have power, they must be specially treated with burning tobacco for them, and a mask must not be enclosed in a box. After donning the masks, members of the False Face Society have special powers and can handle hot coals without getting burned with the overall purposes of driving away witches and disease and curing illness.

The connection of the art of carving masks and curing people among the Iroquois is a combination discovered with Navaho sand paintings, even though the paintings are impermanent creations because they are created with colored sand that gets obliterated once a patient sits on it. The aim of sitting on the painting is to transfer the power from the sacred figures on it to the ill person. For an ill person, the curing rite is performed by a priest using pinches of sand from the limbs of the painted deity and applying them to the corresponding part of the patient's body. At the conclusion of the rite, the painting is transferred to the patient, which becomes identified with the sick person, enabling the patient to enter the sphere of the Holy People of the spirit world. This provides the patient harmony and healing.

Ritual Action

The Alaskan Eskimo observe an annual Bladder Festival, at which time inflated, painted bladders of all birds and animals slain during the year are hung on poles. These inflated bladders symbolize the souls of the deceased animals. This periodical ritual is an attempt to repair the relationship between the Eskimo and game owners and to express concern about the availability of animals for the following hunting season. The bladders are returned to their spiritual homes by being placed on a fire or a hole in the ice. This Eskimo rite is an example of a way of communicating with the divine for benefits or to change the human condition afflicted by illness, infertility, enemies, impurity, or anxiety about the future.

It is possible to see these types of outcomes with the Green Corn Rite among the Creek Indians where their houses are cleaned, friendships are repaired, all fires extinguished before a new fire is ignited and medicines prepared on it, purifying oneself, and observing food taboos. The Creek rite represents a New Year celebration, which is a time of peace, forgiveness, purification, spiritual renewal, communion with the spiritual world, and celebration of the forth-coming corn. Indians also observe rituals that are responses to unprecedented events dealing with various types of affliction. Finally, another type of ritual action is performed during critical times of a person's life such as birth, initiation into adulthood, marriage, and death. These are often called rites of passage because a person moves from one station in life to another status.

These various forms of ritual are dynamic and dramatic actions in which participants play different roles, often obscuring for a time underlying social tensions and contradictions and providing a temporary form of symbolic social unification. Ritual is also a vehicle for conveying symbolic truths of the culture and affirms bodily gestures of the participants, giving the body a lesson about where it fits in the world. Besides its unifying and instructive aspects, ritual restricts a participant because certain prescribed acts are required and not others, which implies that a participant does not do what he pleases because there is a pattern to be followed in order for him to reach the aim of the rite.

These comments are evident in the rite of sacrifice. From a cross-cultural perspective of Indian cultures, a typical sacrifice manifests a threefold structure: consecration, invocation-immolation, and communion-purification. Consecration refers to the purification and making sacred of the participants, time, place, and victim. Among some Native Americans, purification is achieved by entering a sweat lodge, where water is sprinkled over hot stones, an action that produces steam and purifies those within the lodge. In addition to purifying the participants, the darkness created when the door of the lodge is closed is symbolically equivalent to a return to the womb, from which they will be reborn, purified, and able to participate in the sacrifice. The second phase of a sacrifice initially involves invoking god and stating the intention of the rite, whereas immolation is the actual killing of the victim. The third phase represents the sharing of the victim's flesh in the case of an animal sacrifice, which confirms the spiritual bond between humans and gods and reinforces the moral and social bonds of the participants. Because participants are considered holy and a danger to nonparticipants, a final purification enables the participants to return to society without harming or being a threat to others.

At one time in its history, the Skidi Pawnee practiced human sacrifice by using a captive girl from an enemy village. The captive was purified with smoke, painted red, and dressed in black. She was lifted onto a scaffold and tied into position. Her captor shot her through the heart using a sacred bow and arrow. Another participant would strike her on the head with a sacred war club. An Indian priest cut open her chest and smeared his face with her blood. As the blood fell, the captor caught the blood on buffalo meat and corn seeds, an action related to ensuring the fertility of the animal and corn for the coming year. Then all male members of the village shot arrows into her lifeless body. The sacrificial victim in this rite also carries away the pollution of the community, and serves as a mediating symbol between the human and spiritual worlds.

In contrast to the Pawnee human sacrifice, there is the Sioux Sun Dance, a form of self-sacrifice. An individual male might decide to participate in this rite for a variety of reasons, such as to fulfill a previously made vow, to obtain supernatural assistance for another person, or to gain the same aid for himself. In order to participant in the rite, a male must possess four major virtues: bravery, generosity, fortitude, and integrity. Because the Sioux society is the custodian of the Sun Dance, it has control over whom it allows to use the rite. If one has the necessary moral virtues, the participant selects a guide to teach the essentials of the rite. With a present, a pipe, and tobacco, the aspirant proceeds to the tipi of the person selected to be his mentor and smokes the pipe with that person. If a teacher refuses to accept the pipe, this is a sign of a negative response to the aspirant and indicates that it is necessary to find another guide. A friend of the dancer is selected to be his attendant. Once a time is selected for the rite, the village invites other Indians from neighboring communities. The candidate is prepared by his mentor with instructions and having his hands painted red in order to handle sacred things during the four days of the rite. The initial three days involve more sacred pipe smoking, announcement of female attendants, women who will chop the sacred tree, a communal feast, decoration of a buffalo head, and invoking the Buffalo god, and a sacred tree is secured after the final blows are administered by two virtuous women. Rawhide effigies of a man and a buffalo are suspended from the crosspiece of the tree. Guns are fired at the two effigies, representing a second symbolic killing, with the cutting down of the tree being the first such killing. This second symbolic act is connected to future hunting success and victory in war.

The aspirant chooses one of four ways to dance: either he gazes at the sun from dawn until dusk; has both his breasts pierced with a knife and inserting wooden skewers under the flesh that are attached to rawhide ropes tied halfway up the sacred pole; has wooden skewers inserted and is suspended between four posts about one foot off the ground; or skewers are inserted and thongs attached to one or more buffalo skulls that he will drag around the dance area. After vowing to dance in one of these ways and being purified, an aspirant dons rabbit skin, which is symbolic of humility, and cries at the center of the sacred site, assuming the sufferings of the people. The dancer successfully completes the sacrifice when his flesh has torn through and is free of the skewers. Bystanders may help by pulling on the ropes. Circumambulating the sun dance lodge four times, the dancer enters the lodge for a final purification and smokes the pipe. The Sioux believe that this sacrifice represents an offering of one's flesh and soul to Wakantanka. This form of human sacrifice is performed for the benefit of all the people. The sun dancers are believed to acquire power, which might be used to cure the sick by a dancer placing his hands on them.

Death and Afterlife

A narrative from the Kiowa Apache relates a tale of the Crow who was angry because he was not given the plumage of the eagle in the early days of the world. He threw a rock in the water saying, "If this comes up, there will be no death; if it sinks, there will be death." Those that heard this story know what happened. Among the Blackfoot, a similar type of myth occurs but with a different cast of characters: Old Man and a woman argued about whether people should die or not. The Old Man proposed a contest: He will throw a buffalo chip into the water; if it floats, then when people die they will become alive again in four days. Although the buffalo chip floated, the woman disagreed and said that one should throw a stone into the water. And if the stone floated, people would live forever; if it sank, people would die forever. Not long after throwing a stone into the river and watching it sink, the woman's child became sick and died. She pleaded with the Old Man to reverse the edict concerning death, to which he replied that he could not undo what had been done.

These two narratives about death form the narrative background for the final rite of passage in a person's life. Whether it is birth, initiation, marriage, or death rites of passage, rites manifest a threefold structure: rites of separation, transition rites, and rites of incorporation. Rites of separation entail being separated from one's former condition, whereas rites of transition are a movement from one position in life to another, such as adolescent to adult, unmarried to married, and alive to dead. Finally, incorporation means being adopted into one's society. The Tewa Pueblo, for example, find the naming mother and her assistant taking the infant outdoors to present the child to the sun and to bestow a name on the infant. Since the next chapter, on African religions, deals with initiation, this chapter will examine some examples of death as a rite of passage.

Among the Tewa Pueblo, the corpse is dressed at death, and its moccasins are reversed because in the afterworld everything is done in reverse. A bit of food is wrapped in cotton and placed in the left armpit of the deceased. Once the body is prepared, there is a wake during which Catholic elements are mixed with native Indian elements. The principal activity at the wake is the singing of funeral dirges in Spanish. The grave is dug the following day. The corpse is taken to the Catholic church for requiem mass and then to the cemetery. After the grave has been dug, a male remains inside it to ensure that witches do not occupy or plant evil objects into the grave. After a priest sprinkles holy water, offers a prayer, and throws a handful of earth with his left hand into the grave, the priest and non-Indians leave. The remainder of the rite involves Tewa elements. A bag containing clothing of the deceased is placed under his head as a pillow. The bag also includes his or her most prized and personal possessions. After the grave is covered, a leader stands at the head of the grave, and tells survivors that the deceased has gone to a happy place. Finally, he admonishes them not to let the death divide the home.

The Tewa believe that the road to the realm of the dead is a rocky and winding way. It is expected that the departed will have to battle beasts of prey along the road. The Tewa believe that the soul of the deceased wanders four days accompanied by its ancestors. Survivors fear that the soul may become lonely and return to take one of them with it. In order to counter this possibility, the Tewa perform a releasing rite that includes going to a shrine to present a feast to the deceased. The leader draws four lines with his left foot at the shrine and again four times on the way back to the house. Participants wash their hands, a symbolic departure from the deceased, and say "May you have life" and reply "Let it be so." The leader then places a hand broom into the fire place to gather ashes to blow it over the people while invoking the protection of spirits.

Among the Shoshoni of Wyoming, the destiny of the dead can involve numerous ends. The dead can travel to a particular location in the other world, remain on earth as ghosts, be reborn again as people, and transmigrate into insects, birds, or even inanimate objects like wood or rocks. In contrast to the Shoshoni, the Hopi buried children in the house, hoping that their souls would be reincarnated in the next child born.

Native Americans generally manifest an attenuated, vague concept of an afterlife. Some Indians conceive the dead traveling along the Milky Way to an ill-defined paradise. For many Indians, there is no state or end to be achieved after one dies because there is no notion of supernatural reward or salvation with a promise of eternal life, and there is not a consensus about the eternal nature of the soul, which could survive for a time only to possibly fade away. An exception to this general pattern is the Pueblos and their notion of a happy afterlife where the dead are joined with *kachinas*, or become clouds that bring rain.

The reasons for ill-defined notions of the afterlife are probably related to the life-affirming attitude of Indians. Rewards are more important in this world. In fact, the Indian way of life is not followed for rewards in eternity. What is important is to make life on earth, about which we can be certain, socially harmonious and happy. This reflects the practical attitude of Native Americans and this-worldly focus. Nonetheless, Indians generally feared the dead because of the dangerous power that the departed were believed to possess.

The Indian's lack of a clearly defined afterlife can also be explained in part by their notion of cyclical time that does not allow for a past or future in their language. A corollary of a cyclical concept of time involves an understanding that death is not the end of life, but rather the beginning of a new mode of existence, which can be on this earth or in a transcendent realm. Individual Indians sometimes hold conflicting ideas simultaneously on the subject. It is possible for a single native to believe that the dead reside in another world, are reincarnated into other persons, or haunt the living as ghosts. Different types of Indians have diverse viewpoints about personal survival after death. Hunting cultures think that there is a happy land after death stocked with an abundance of game, whereas horticulturists tend to believe in a subterranean realm of the dead. Nevertheless, these notions are still vague in particular cultures because it is this life that is really important.

Vision Quest

According to a reported vision of a member of the Crow society, a bird appeared with a white head and came into a man's lodge and sat directly across from him. The bird changed into a man whose face was painted in a certain manner and who wore on his head the skin of the bird that had initially appeared to the man. The bird-man sang a song, and told the man that he would come the next day with his wife to grant the man some power. On the following day, the bird-couple adopted the man and his wife and revealed to them sacred songs and objects. The objects were powerful help when engaged in warfare. Because of beliefs associated with the powerful nature of visions, Native American Indians searched for them in order to empower themselves.

Visions include any of the following: hallucinations; dreams; and unusual auditory or visual stimulus. Indians interpret these phenomena as forms of supernatural communication. Visions have three general results: acquisition of power; advice about what to do in certain situations; and ritual privileges. An individual is motivated to seek a vision at times of disease and death with the purpose of receiving divine help, before war expeditions to become brave, at childbirth in order to discern a name for a child, as an act of thanksgiving, or to realize her unity with all things. Visions can be spontaneous and appear suddenly and unexpectedly. A second type of vision appears after a regimen of fasting and self-mortifications. A particular vision might reveal a wide variety of supernatural beings, such as the terrible Thunder Beings, and concrete representations of animals, which might assume the form of an animal in human form.

The quest for a vision manifests two phases: quest and action. The latter phase is a process by which a person's vision becomes legitimized. The quest for a vision follows a pattern for an individual that begins with a purifying sweat bath and includes actions such as smoking the sacred pipe, holding a nightly vigil, meditation, and visit by a spirit. Other methods include isolation in a secluded place and self-mortification, such as the Blackfoot practice called "feeding the sun," which includes cutting off pieces of flesh and offering it to the sun. Among central Algonquian tribes (e.g., Winnebago, Menomini, and Fox Indians), fasting and not drinking water are performed to become weak and pitiable to the spirits, who, it is hoped, will be overcome with pity and grant one's desires.

The overall pattern of a vision quest is evident among the Sioux, when a person gets the assistance of a holy man. After approaching a holy man with a filled pipe and giving it to him with the stem pointing forward, the seeker points the stem of the pipe toward himself, which indicates that he wants to receive knowledge. Leaving the tipi of the holy man, they face West, with the holy man holding the stem of the pipe toward the sky, announcing that a body is to be offered. Following more smoking and selecting a day to seek a vision, the seeker appears at the lodge of the holy man wearing only his buffalo robe, breech cloth, and moccasins and asks for mercy by placing his right hand on his guide, who asks the seeker the number of days (one to four) that he wishes to lament. The seeker is purified before being taken to a secluded location, where a pole is erected at the center and four more poles at the major directions. After undressing, the seeker walks alone to the top of a mountain, carrying his pipe before him, and laments at each of the poles for an entire day. He prays out loud or silently as he walks the sacred path, forming a cross. At night, he sleeps with his head against the center pole, a representation of Wakantanka, the Great Spirit and source of visions. After receiving a message, the successful seeker returns to the Inipi lodge for a concluding purification. A vision might involve revealing the contents of a medicine bundle.

Visions operate for the seeker in a variety of ways. A seeker could be given or denied rights to a certain social status, prestige, or privilege. Therefore, visions operate to legitimate one's actions and status, to channel behavior in socially approved directions, to raise a person's confidence about assuming higher social positions, to serve as an explanatory device to explain why some have certain powers and status, and to justify decisions about whether or not to organize communal hunts, raids, or dances. A Paiute Indian was a successful hunter, gambler, and lover whose success was attributed to his visions and powers obtained in dreams, whereas another Paiute was a failure who rationalized his lack of success as a result of not having acquired power through dreams.

The Comic Element

According to a Jicarilla Apache myth, the deity Hactcin created all the animals and began to laugh at the sight of so many different kinds of creatures. The animals told the god that they needed a companion. After the animals gathered an assortment of objects and set them before Hactcin, the deity traced an outline of a figure similar to him on the ground. Then, he placed inside the drawn figure on the ground the various objects, which became bones, flesh, skin, hair, and eyes. The figure began to speak, then to shout, and finally to laugh. The dog was glad when he saw the man laugh, jumped on the man, wagging his tail, and ran about happily because of his new companion. The animals thought that man also needed a companion. Hactcin agreed and took some lice given by the animals and put them on the man's head, which caused man to itch and scratch. The scratching made man sleepy. While asleep, man dreamed that a creature like, yet unlike, him was sitting at his side. When he awoke he discovered that his dream had come true. Speaking to the young woman sitting next to him, the man was astonished when she answered him. Then he began to laugh, and the woman laughed, too. And they continued to laugh together.

This story of primordial time is instructive because it is obvious that the Apache give a prominent place to the creation of laughter and a sense of humor. This implies that laughter and humor are critical aspects of human nature. Moreover, laughter and humor are also part of the order of creation. This narrative also suggests something about the nature of humor, which is grounded in seriousness and avoids humor being reduced to cynical contempt or despair. Humor is a boundary notion that lies on the margin between the sacred and profane, the rational and irrational, and cosmos and chaos. The personification of the individual of humor in Indian cultures is the clown.

According to a myth of the Jemez Indians, another Southwestern culture, they emerged at the beginning of time from a hole in the earth. Once on the surface of the earth, they found food scarce and weather inhospitable. Thus, the people began a long, arduous journey to the south, during which many of them died of hunger, while survivors began to despair to the extent of even praying to die. The Moon Mother intervened on behalf of the people and entreated the Sun Father to aid the despairing people. In order to help the people, the Sun Father created the clown by taking a survivor and painting his body with transverse black and white bands, decorating his hair with corn husks, and suspending eagle feathers behind each ear. When the clown began to dance, frolic, and make funny face grimaces, the people forgot their sorrows and became glad. This enabled the formerly despairing group to resume their journey and reach the Rio Grande.

In this narrative of the Jemez Indians, the Sun Father does not rescue the people from cold, hunger, and death. But he does provide a vehicle for coping with these hardships and misfortunes. The original clown enters the life of the people at their darkest hour. And despite the fact that there is little to celebrate, the clown invites laughter and gladness. It is possible to find similar narratives among other Southwestern Indians as with the Laguna and Kere Pueblos, among whom the clown is given a rainbow as a ladder by which to represent the people before the gods. As suggested by the rainbow of the clown, he restores color to life and offers a sign of hope to the people.

The arguably most significant feature of the clown is self-contradiction, meaning that the clown is crude and mean yet gentle and magnanimous, clumsy and inept but also agile, ugly and repulsive but not without elegance and charm. The clown's overall behavior is undignified, unreasonable, and sometimes even idiotic. The Sioux clown (*heyoka*) is identified as someone who had had a vision of a Thunder Being. He can be identified by riding backwards on his horse, wearing his boots on the wrong feet, walking backwards, wearing heavy clothing in the summer and going naked in the winter, and saying yes when he means no. Indian clowns are also often violent.

The Indian clown has contempt for all status by lampooning, for example, a wealthy businessman by wearing a stiff top hat, carrying a useless flexible cane and attaché case. Pueblo clowns burlesque the Kachina dancers by performing out of time and rhythm, whereas Zuni clowns speak Spanish or English before the gods, an activity strictly taboo for ordinary people. A Zuni clown pretends to converse with the gods by means of a fake telephone, even though gods are not supposed to speak. In another witnessed incident, a Zuni clown lampoons a holy man by wearing a bear paw on his left hand, a wolf snout on his nose, and acting crazy. This type of behavior suggests that the clown is an imposter who arrogates human dignity and status. The clown is not merely funny and ridiculous, but he is also frightening and obscene, provoking laughter by a sense of relief. It is reported that among the Hopi of the Southwest, a male clown dressed as a woman went to the plaza of the village with a wash basin and began to wash her legs, spreading them to reveal a huge false vulva. Another Hopi clown dons a large false penis, approaches a female clown, and engages her in vigorous copulation. A clown among the Tewa Pueblo is witnessed snatching off the breach cloth of another clown and dragging him by his penis. Pueblo clowns reach the height of absurdity when two clowns simulate sexual intercourse with a woman with one behind her while the second one copulated with her head. Meanwhile, a third clown masturbated in the center of the plaza.

Besides frightening people and breaking social taboos, the clown is willing to accept being despised by others, being insulted, being tormented, and being punished for his transgressions. Anthropologists have reported seeing Zuni clowns eating various forms of waste, Hopi clowns drinking gallons of aged, foul-smelling urine and telling witnesses how sweet it tastes, and Pueblo clowns eating dirt, excrement, live mice, sticks, and stones. This type of behavior and strange attire points to the clown as a symbol of disorder, which implies that the clown stands outside of order and censure, manifesting contempt for all social order.

In addition to entertaining or frightening people, Indian clowns are connected with medicine and function as healers. They acquire their healing powers by virtue of the violation of a cultural taboo. They also function to grant success in hunting and war, grant good luck in gambling and love, and bestow happiness and prosperity. These positive traits are balanced by their ability to inflict disease and suffering, which render them feared figures within Indian culture.

Nature and Ecology

Many Native American Indians identify themselves with a cosmic totality that they symbolize by the cross, circle, or world-tree. Nature is a part of this unity. It is not entirely true that Indians exist in harmony with nature because they are both a part of nature and apart from it. Indian religions expressed a human alienation from nature because it operates as the Indian's economic source of life. This necessarily means that nature must be exploited for the survival of the Indians, although nature simultaneously represents the Indian's spiritual source of life. Thus Indians manifested an ambivalent attitude toward nature: friendliness because it provides bounty and apprehensiveness because of its potential terrible power. In order to encourage nature to not withhold its bounty, Plains Indians perform, for example, the buffalo dance by dressing like buffalo and becoming the animal in the process. This serves as a way to lure the buffalo to be killed and to thank them for giving themselves to the hunters. Thus, Native Americans manifest a tension between loving nature and exploiting it, although the Indians generally feel dependent on nature and guilty for killing their animal kin.

Indians express a geo-piety that is not a love of nature as a totality but rather a love of particular locations. This means that their veneration of nature is not true in a general sense but rather in a specific way. These particular places are sacred because spirits reveal themselves in these locations. And yet the Indian attitude toward nature is practical because it serves as a means of subsistence, housing, clothing, and transportation. Nature is also something mysterious because it reveals the divine, making it necessary for Indians to care for its well-being.

Native American attitudes toward aspects of nature are revealing, such as the winds among the Cree and Navaho. The Cree imagine the four winds as brothers that surround a hunter and rank them according to their friendliness to humans. Moreover, each wind is associated with a specific kind of weather. The north and west winds are connected to cold, stable weather, whereas the south and east are associated with unstable weather. The winds also affect the dwellings of the Cree. During the hunting season, a lodge, a three-sided teepee, faces east, while the back of the lodge faces north.

Among the Navaho, the wind gives life, thought, and speech; it is behind all good or bad human thoughts and serves as a means of communication between all elements of the living world. When a child is born, it receives wind souls that report to the Dawn Woman about the life of the child. The Navaho believe that the east wind directs one's life, the south wind is our power of movement, the west wind represents one's thinking, and the north winds help one to execute one's plans. In order to provide life and guidance, the Holy Ones send winds to a person throughout one's life. In comparison to these winds, Evil Winds are a source of wrong conduct, which can be countered by the Little Winds that are sent from the four directions and strengthen a person. When a person ignores advice or warnings from the Little Winds, they withdraw their support and guidance.

Millenarianism

In visions and dreams, Wodziwob of the Northern Paiute received messages in 1870 that the Great Spirit would return to the earth with the spirits of the dead, a tremendous cataclysm would occur, and white people would vanish, although their buildings and goods would remain for the use of the Indians. Following the great cataclysm, an earthly paradise would commence during which life would be eternal and food plentiful. An important stipulation specified that only the ancestors of those who believed would return to earth. Wodziwob insisted that the Indians' participation in a ritual dance would hasten the arrival of the ancestors. The dance pattern was an open circle in order for ancestors to enter it and watch the dance. Before the beginning of the dance, participants had to purify themselves by bathing and decorating their bodies with black, red, and white paint. This message represented a revivalistic movement called the Ghost Dance Religion, which envisioned the promise to Indians that their old forms of life would return, white invaders of their land would be expelled, and deceased Indian ancestors would return.

After the 1870 outbreak of the Ghost Dance dissipated, another more spectacular and dramatic movement broke out in 1890 when it came to life, inspired by John Wilson, who was also known as Wovoka, "the Cutter." Wilson was born at Mason Valley in Nevada in 1856. He was adopted by a local farmer named David Wilson. In 1866, he contracted a high fever during which he had a vision instructing him to reinstate the Ghost Dance. Wilson's vision included seeing god and all the previously departed Indians living happy and forever young. The movement began among the Northern Paiute of Walker Lake Reservation in Nevada, promising the return of the dead, a catastrophic end of the world, disappearance of the whites swept up by high winds, and white possessions left behind for the use of Indians. This scenario would be followed by a regeneration of Indian life. In order to bring about this transformation, Indians needed to work assiduously, not to steal, lie, or fight, to love one another, live at peace with the white man, and not to drink whiskey.

Wilson ordered the performance of the Ghost Dance and added an innovation to the dance that resulted in the wearing of Ghost Shirts, which were decorated with feathers, bones, arrows, birds, suns, and stars. The shirt was believed to have supernatural powers and to be impervious to bullets. The dance, a gift from god, needed to be performed for five days at periodic intervals with the overall purpose of hastening the return of the dead. If a performer received visions, they could be painted on the body of the dancer as he danced in a concentric circle with others. The Ghost Dance itself triggered trance states and visions. Overall, the dance symbolized physical healing, spiritual redemption, and the end of the world. It promised no more death, sickness, or old age and a reunion with dead ancestors. Wovoka's peaceful message, however, got lost in the process of diffusion among Indian tribes.

When the Ghost Dance was embraced by the Sioux, it ended in tragedy. Sitting Bull, a great Sioux chief, interpreted the Ghost Dance as a means of returning to power. The United States government was dismayed over his renewed power and decided to arrest him, which resulted in the death of Sitting Bull and others. Two weeks after the death of Sitting Bull on December 28, 1890, three hundred followers of the chief were killed in the

Battle of Wounded Knee Creek, during which many wore Ghost Shirts to make them invincible.

The Ghost Dance movement is a revivalistic type of millenarianism, which is derived from a term from an early Christian movement that expected a millennium, a thousand years in which the world would be at peace and its inhabitants good and happy. Millenarianism needs to be distinguished from eschatology (doctrine of last things), which transfers hope for a better future to a hereafter, whereas millenarianism expects a future and spiritual bliss on earth which will arrive in the foreseeable future. The origins of millenarian movements develop from contact with Western and non-literate societies. When this encounter occurs, disastrous events follow, such as detribalization, conquest of a country or people, destruction of indigenous cultures by whites, collective deportations, or catastrophes. These types of situations cause extreme distress, social and personal crisis, and a sense of precariousness. In response to these negative developments, there arise millenarian movements to meet a need for renewal and catharsis that can take a wide variety of cultic forms.

Another type of millenarian movement is introversionist, a response to an alien and irredeemable world by withdrawing from it. In 1799, the Handsome Lake Religion of the Iroquois was founded by a Seneca prophet named Handsome Lake, which was a syncretistic movement that combined Indian and Christian elements. During the revolutionary war against the British, the Iroquois were also defeated, which resulted in their loss of land, European diseases, alcohol abuse, impact of missionaries, and a tradition of misunderstanding and distrust between the Indians and whites. On June 15, 1797, Handsome Lake had his initial vision while dying of an incurable disease. In a trance, he met four spirits who gave him fruit that healed him. The four spirits urged him to preach a new doctrine of salvation. The fourth spirit was especially significant because he revealed scars on his hands and feet and said that he had been killed by whites. The Christ figure also said that none of his people believed in him, and that he would become the savior of the Indians, who were more worthy of salvation than the whites.

The Handsome Lake Religion adopted some Christian Quaker elements, such as using the Bible as a guide, renunciation of pagan rites, fighting against witchcraft, compassion for the needy, confession and repentance of sins, loyalty and gratitude toward god for gifts received, silent prayer, and introspection. Indian elements included the retention of the Feast of the White Dog, whose flesh served as a form of Eucharist. Indians were encouraged to be true to their traditions. The religion predicted an end time represented by destruction of the earth by means of fire.

Another introversionist movement of Native Americans was founded and promoted by another person named John Wilson, who was also called Big Moon, urging Indians to take peyote, a non-addictive hallucinogenic drug. The peyote could cause nausea, headaches, and vomiting in addition to visions that Indians interpreted as contact with the spiritual world. There were many variations of the ritualistic aspects of the cult centering on a crescent-shaped earthen mound, which was symbolic of the moon. In addition to chewing peyote buttons, which are found around the roots of cactus plants, meetings also involved singing, praying, and playing a drum. The Peyote movement advocated brotherly love, care of family, self-reliance, and rejection of alcohol.

The Indians were taught that the Holy Spirit resides in the peyote that functions like the Christian Eucharist and is identified with Jesus, who was rejected and killed by white people. But Jesus now protects the Indians, who are also victims of the whites. Jesus was believed to be unified with the peyote. The peyote gave Indians visions that reveal all the knowledge needed in life. A Comanche interviewed by an anthropologist said, "The white man talks about Jesus; we talk to Jesus." This is a response that reveals the experiential nature of the Peyote Cult and becomes a vehicle for the expression of a new sense of identity for the Indians. Overall, peyote enabled Indians to maintain their way of life, to sustain the significance of dreams and visions for their culture, and to express a new sense of identity.

It is possible to understand millenarianism as a religion of return because it projects a return to origins in the future that includes the realization of the end time and a renewal of the world, which reflects an attempt to escape a people's current situation. But in order to abolish the present, it is necessary to return to a primordial time. It is a revolutionary program that is intended to renew and reform things, making it anti-cosmic because it is opposed to the established order of suppression. Millenarianism gives people hope for renewal, a kind of rebirth, and a map for transforming the current situation.

Overview of Religious Experiences

In the book *Black Elk Speaks*, a Native American relates the narrative of his life, a story that is about a life that is holy and good. At an early age, he hears voices and then begins to experience visions to which he has a physical reaction, resulting in aching and non-functional legs, arms, hands, and legs that become swollen and a bloated face. Black Elk relates seeing two men, representing powers of the world, in an early vision. A figure identified as Grandfather tells him that in the future Black Elk will have the power to cure people of illness. He also has a vision of himself killing a blue colored man, representing drought, and he has a vision of his people starving. A vision of the bison reveals that they are a gift of the Great Spirit that represents the people's strength, that the people would lose the bison, and that they would need to find another form of strength. From the center of the world, Black Elk sees in a vision the sacred hoop of the people, and in the center of the hoop there grows one flowering tree that shelters all the children. Black Elk admits that it takes him time as he grows older to understand the meaning of his visions.

During his visions, Black Elk is given certain things, such as a view of his life history, after he has a vision of the bay-colored horse. In another vision, he sees twelve black horses and birds, who then turn into other animals, which suggests the interrelatedness of all living creatures. He encounters several Grandfathers who give him a sacred pipe, which can be used as an aid to help one concentrate one's thoughts in the sense of an instrument of meditation. When an Indian smokes the pipe, he comes into contact with spirits, making religious meaning and experience inseparable. During a later vision, Black Elk is given a sacred hoop, a symbol of tribal solidarity, prosperity, and wholeness, along with powers to heal and succeed in warfare. His response to his visions is awe and joy.

The visions of Black Elk are typical of an essential aspect of Native American religious experience that is grounded in a feeling of cosmic harmony in which the world is conceived of as unitary and balanced, populated by supernatural beings, and inhabited by spiritual masters of particular animal species, along with humans, animals, trees, and plants. Within the worldview of many Indian cultures, a world tree symbolizes its unity. An excellent example of this is the Sun Dance post—decorated with an eagle at the top that represents the sky and a buffalo skull on its trunk or at its base—representing the animal and human world, while the offerings of tobacco signify the underworld. This symbolism reflects the three levels of the cosmos.

Within this cosmic harmony, the Indians do not generally draw a sharp distinction between humans and the divine and do not sharply distinguish between humans and animals. As noted previously, the Sioux notion of the Supreme Being stressed not only its power but connection to an abundance of powers and spirits. This harmonious unity also reflects a close relationship between humans and animals as when Indians imitate animals with their dress, dance, actions, and projective mode of thinking. The wearing of feathers, for example, infuses abilities of birds into humans. Besides this primary meaning, the wearing of feathers has secondary significance, such as recalling enemies killed, those scalped, and other deeds. The large war bonnet, a symbol of dignity, probably originated with the Mandan of northern Missouri and spread to other cultures.

In order to live in this cosmic harmony, it is still necessary to empower oneself in order to survive. The quest for power for oneself and others takes the form of visions and dreams. We have noted that the vision quest is done in part to acquire a guardian spirit, a spiritual being closer to the individual than the high god. A successful quest enables a seeker direct contact with the supernatural and an opportunity to share in its power. In Indian culture, visions provide the successful candidate authority among the people. Visions can be induced by various kinds of deprivations, such as extreme forms of fasting, enduring cold temperatures, lack of sleep, or self-inflicted pain. These visions can occur suddenly or gradually. Light visions that testify to the presence of spirits can also be accompanied by automatic speaking and states of possession in the case of shamans, which also serves as proof of ecstatic states of consciousness. It is also possible for trance states to be enhanced by psychotropic plants such as tobacco and peyote.

Before an Indian can have a vision, one must become purified in the sweat lodge, which represents spiritual renewal as the four elements—earth, air, fire, and water—each contribute to one's physical and mental purification. There is no fragmentation of experience into opposing dichotomies, but there is an emphasis on the interrelatedness of things. At the same time, Indians recognize all the differences within the world, but beneath all the apparent differences there is an underlying unity. Indian religiosity reveals to a person her creativity, uniqueness, and identity. The seeker also finds help with her direction in life, having her feelings protected, and understanding her destiny. But the visions are not ends in themselves because one is obligated to live one's life according to a vision, which also has power in a personal sense and also in the sense of gaining a guardian spirit. This chapter has also alluded to the importance of dreams, which are different types of visions that can, for example, play a role in the creation of false faces among the Seneca. And in Navaho sand painting, a rite of re-creation, a patient experiences the complexity and diversity of the cosmos along with its underlying unity. In summary, Native American Indians exhibit a rich variety of religious experiences.

Suggestions for Further Reading

Bastian, Dawn E. and Judy K. Mitchell. *Handbook of Native American Mythology*. New York: Oxford University Press, 2004.

Brown, Joseph Epes. Ed. *The Sacred Pipe: Black Elk's Account of the Seven Rites of the Oglala Sioux*. New York: Penguin Books, 1953; reprint 1979.

———. *The Spiritual Legacy of the American Indian*. New York: Crossroad Publishing Company, 1987.

Gill, Sam D. *Native American Religions: An Introduction*. Belmont, CA: Wadsworth Publishing Company, 1982.

Harrod, Howard L. *Renewing the World: Plains Indian Religion and Morality*. Tucson: University of Arizona Press, 1987.

Hultkrantz, Ake. *Belief and Worship in Native North America*. Ed. Christopher Vecsey. Syracuse: Syracuse University Press, 1981.

———. *Native Religions of North America: The Power of Visions and Fertility*. Prospect Heights, IL: Waveland Press, 1987.

———. *The Religions of the American Indians*. Berkeley: University of California Press, 1981.

Hynes, William J. and William G. Doty. Eds. *Mythical Trickster Figures: Contours, Contexts, and Criticisms*. Tuscaloosa: University of Alabama Press, 1993.

Loftin, John D. *Religion and Hopi Life*. Second Edition. Bloomington: Indiana University Press, 2003.

Ortiz, Alfonso. *The Tewa World: Space, Time, Being, and Becoming in a Pueblo Society*. Chicago: University of Chicago Press, 1969; reprint 1974.

Powers, William K. *Yuwipi: Vision and Experience in Oglala Ritual*. Lincoln: University of Nebraska Press, 1982.

Richard, Gladys A. *Navaho Religion: A Study of Symbolism*. Bollingen Series XVIII. Princeton: Princeton University Press, 1950; reprint 1977.

Sullivan, Lawrence E. Ed. *Native Religions and Cultures of North America: Anthropology of the Sacred*. New York: Continuum, 2000.

Vecsey, Christopher. *Traditional Ojibwa Religion and its Historical Changes*. Philadelphia: The American Philosophical Society, 1983.

4   African Religious Traditions

The sky and earth were originally connected by a rope, which was attached to the tree of creation. The Nuer people (of South Sudan) climbed down the rope from the sky to obtain their food. When people died, they ascended to the sky via the rope. By returning to the sky, the dead were rejuvenated and again returned to earth, a scenario that denuded the power of death and enabled people to enjoy a paradise in the sky. According to the mythical lore of the Nuer, there were two different versions of how people lost the state of paradise. In one version, a mischievous hyena and a sparrow climbed to the sky, where the creator—Kwoth—ordered them guarded in order to prevent trouble, but they eluded their guards and escaped to earth down the rope. Playing a prank on those above, the hyena cut the rope at the bottom, and the remaining segment of rope withdrew to the sky, never to return to earth. In another version of the myth, a girl descended to earth with some companions to get food. She encounters a young man, who originally also came from the sky, with whom she has sexual relations. Because of her amorous feelings toward the young man, she refused to return to the sky and expressed her intentions to stay permanently on earth. The girl's companions ascended to the sky and cut the rope, severing forever the means of attaining immortality.

Either version about how the Nuer lost paradise and immortality explains the separation of the people from god and the current human condition, conveying the origin of suffering, illness, and death. The myth informs readers that there is a polarity between sky and earth and relates that the loss of paradise did not result from disobedience to the creator but rather was a result of accidental and unforeseen circumstances.

The creation myth among the Dogon of Mali is more complex than that of the Nuer, providing symbolic categories to organize the Dogon world and ritual patterns to be followed in order to maintain their existence in the world. These functions of the myth occur in three phases: creation, revolt, and restoration.

Before the creation of the world, Amma, supreme god of the Dogon, existed alone and depended only on himself. He was shaped like an oval egg made of his four collar bones joined together, dividing the egg into four quarters, which contained the four elements: fire, air, earth, and water. The four cardinal directions of space were represented by the joints between the bones. Amma placed 266 cosmic signs, representing his creative thoughts, in the egg. Thereby, he traced within himself the design of the cosmos and its future development. Amma's first attempt to create the world failed and was destroyed by him, whereas the second attempt to create the world was successful. The world was organized according to the image of man. A seventh part of the creation produced a separate segment that rendered the creation incomplete, imperfect, singular, and disorderly. This means that the cosmos includes order and disorder.

The revolt phase of the creation story occurs when the egg is transformed into a double placenta of male and female twins, and Ogo, an impatient male twin, burst forth from his placenta because he feared that Amma would not give him his female counterpart after birth. Amma foresaw Ogo's revolt and removed his twin female to the other placenta. Breaking all the cosmic rules, Ogo intended to secure all the secrets of the universe in order to create another world. In response to Ogo's devious plan, Amma transformed the placenta into the earth in the shape of a human being. Ogo copulated with the earth and defiled it because this was an act of incest, tracing this violation to the placenta that was Ogo's mother. This crass act of incest caused the earth to become sterile, dry, and bereft of its creative potential. The incestuous union resulted in the creation of the first race, consisting of monstrous beings that practiced incest. Ogo's continual transgressions make it impossible to establish agriculture, which make a general purification necessary.

The phase of restoration involved Amma sacrificing another male twin, Nommo, after creating sexual souls for the victim. This version of the sacrifice involved a castration of the victim in which the sacrificer slits the penis and umbilical cord, which separates the victim from both his placenta and penis. After Ogo continued his revolt by returning to the sky and stealing the four sexual souls of his castrated twin and placed them on his own penis, Nommo recovers the souls by using his teeth to circumcise Ogo, which resulted in Ogo's sterility and celibacy. In another version of the myth, Amma slits Nommo's throat, and the victim's blood purifies the earth. After Amma scattered the bodily parts of the victim to the four directions, he was able to regain control over the creative words and signs, re-imposing order, restoring Nommo to life, and making him ruler of the world. From Nommo, Amma also created four spirits that became the ancestors of the Dogon. In a great ark, Nommo and the ancestors return to earth to restore and fructify it, bringing with them all species of animals and plants, elements of human society, and culture. Nommo stepped off the ark to utter creative words that were transmitted to the earth and made available to humankind. Finally, Amma transformed Ogo into an animal called Pale Fox, who wanders the earth searching for his female soul. Pale Fox represents a figure that is always revolting, lives a solitary life, and is incomplete, but he does guide humankind through the mysteries of life by the tracks that he leaves on the earth. In order to purify the earth and revitalize the soil, Amma sacrifices Lebe, an offspring of Nommo, and restores him to life in a snake form, which signifies that Lebe's bones are in the earth and continue to enrich the land.

This complex Dogon cosmogonic narrative suggests that their world oscillates between order and disorder. The phase of creation introduces order in the form of signs, seeds, words, and twins, whereas revolt introduces emotion, irrationality, sterility, and singularity, which are principles of disorder. Finally, restoration mediates the opposition between order and disorder and operates to restore the original order. The myth also relates that the world originated in disobedience by a son of god and not by man, as in the biblical story about the loss of paradise, although humans are descendants of the son of god. The Dogon creation story suggests that the world is imperfect, a version of a fallen realm, and is always in the process of becoming while containing dangerous elements such as darkness, sterility, and death. These negative elements are countered by light, rain, and fertility. The myth also stresses the importance of sacrifice, which is performed periodically to restore the earth, counter disorder, and spread civilization.

The Dogon cosmogony is evident in its social and village structures. Parents are, for example, considered to be Ogo and, ideally, brother and sister. Since this is incestuous, the child's parents are symbolically replaced by the wife's brother and his wife, rendering the child's biological father a stranger toward whom the child can express hostile feelings. Dogon villages are often built in pairs, representing upper and lower villages that conform to heaven and earth or, mythically, Nommo and Pale Fox joined together. The village also represents a pair of Nommo twins with the northern part signifying the head and male meeting place where collective decisions are made. The family houses are the chest, women's huts form the hands, the male sexual organ is the village altar, the female organ is the stone used to crush fruit, and feet are represented by the communal altars at the southern end of the village. A specific home is modeled on Nommo lying on his right side, which is the position of creation, with the kitchen associated with his head, two hearth stones are his eyes, the trunk of his body is the central room, his arms are identified with the storage rooms, and his sexual organ is the entry passage to the work room. The structures of the Dogon society, village, and home, which are based on the cosmogonic myth, suggest how the narrative permeates the entire culture by functioning as a model for organization and rationale for ritual action. The narrative, moreover, gives a reader insight into the Dogon worldview.

Worldview and Concepts of Time and Space

In contrast to the Dogon worldview, the Zulu of Southern Africa conceive of the sky as a blue rock and the earth with a flat surface. The sky stretches from one end of the flat surface to the other, with the vault of the rock resting on the edges of the earth. The earth is supported by four bulls carrying the earth on their horns. Thus, when a bull shakes its head, the earth also shakes, which explains how earthquakes occur. In addition, the sky stands above the sun and moon, which both move along their paths underneath the sky.

The Zulu and other African cultures draw a distinction between mythical time associated with creation and ordinary temporal duration. This occurs when the original cosmic eternity is disrupted by a separation of sky and earth. This separation is sometimes viewed as a fall from the sky to the earth, representing a fall from eternity and pure being to temporality and becoming. The two time states and spatial realms are the inverse of each other: divine/human, sacred/profane, and immortality/mortality. In order to unify them it is necessary, for instance, to join eternity to temporality by repeating creative acts of the gods in ritual action. It is important to note that ritual time is cyclical and not linear. Ritual time is a repetitive and sacred time, a time outside of ordinary time. Since ritual time is also reversible, this implies that people can recover it and repeat it. Thus, ritual time is not orientated toward the future.

In African religious cultures, time tends to be conceived as local and foreshortened, suggesting that it is more microcosmic than macrocosmic. Instead of an indefinite future awaiting an individual, time is episodic and discontinuous. Therefore, time is not linear or unitary. Without a single time scale, there are a variety of times associated with different kinds of natural phenomena and human activities. The multiple forms of time take the appearance of mythical, historical, ritual, agricultural, seasonal, solar, or lunar times. There is almost no future sense of time because its events have not taken place and thus have not been realized. Actual time is represented by the present and past, giving the human perception of time a more backward orientation. This attitude toward time means that it must be experienced to make sense and is thus concrete and specific. The time of day is not calculated by a watch but is reckoned by reference to concrete events, such as milking time for cows, whereas a year consists of two rainy seasons.

Supreme Beings and Spirits

Among the Yoruba of Nigeria, the high deity Olorum remains aloof from the course of history. The Yoruba world is created by his intermediate associates. Olorum is not a god that humans can encounter in a personal relationship. He is imagined to be a secluded, inactive, silent, and impersonal monarch. This remote, distant, and inactive deity tends to disappear from the ritual cult. Olorum is the type of divine being that is replaced by other religious forces, such as ancestor worship, spirits of fertility, or a goddess.

In sharp contrast to Olorum, the Dinka of South Sudan worship a more active and morally omniscient deity named Nhialic. At the beginning of time, he created humans from clay, and he continues to act in the world as the only creator of humans by shaping them in the womb and giving them life. The Dinka believe that he can alleviate major misfortunes for his creatures. Referred to as the father of humans, Nhialic is a more personal deity who cares for humans.

The distant god of the Yoruba is augmented by the goddess figure Oshun. She is described as river-born and associated with cool waters, which helps to explain her vivacious character. She is depicted as beautiful and sweet tempered, with hips like a slow rolling river. Her sensuousness embodies the divine spark in human sexual life and also reveals pleasure. She loves rich gifts of silk, perfume, sweet foods, and jewelry. She is famous as the great coquette who is described as flirting with men and delighting in their seduction. She was the wife of many gods, but none of them could keep her satisfied for any length of time.

In one narrative, she is the wife of Orunmila and is frustrated because he cannot meet her voracious sexual appetites. She decides to wander the bush lands until she arrives at the compound of Ogun Arere, a fierce god of iron and warfare. In order to entice him, she oiled her body with a honey aphrodisiac and danced slowly before him, driving Ogun Arere mad for her. But each time that he lunged for her, she slipped through his oil-covered fingers. Being nearly exhausted, he surrendered to her. She accepted his surrender by giving herself to him. Having become enthralled by her, Ogun begged to see her every day, and she agreed as long as he brought her gifts and sweet cakes.

Oshun's husband becomes suspicious that his wife might be having an affair, which he confirms by consulting an Ifa oracle. Orunmila trains some parakeets to spy on Oshun and to report to him. After Oshun returns from her lover's home, the parakeets sing "Oshun is an adulteress, she sleeps with Ogun Arere." In order to protect her secret affair, Oshun gives the birds some honey aphrodisiac and liquor, which causes the birds to sing to Orunmila, when he returns home, that she is a paragon of virtue and never leaves the house. The husband is still suspicious, and the next day he anoints the bird's beaks with truth-telling oil, which finally reveals the truth.

In another narrative, she is the devoted wife of the god Shango. After living together for a while, the couple parts because of Oshun's love affairs and the god's tempestuous temper. Eventually, Shango loses his military command, wealth, and friends. Thereupon, Oshun returns to him to cook his meals and wash his clothes. Her loyalty and courage inspire Shango to regain his lost glory. During this time of hardship, Oshun's white dress becomes yellowed—and her devotees wear yellow clothes today to honor her. After she accompanies African slaves to Cuba, she becomes known as Puta Santa, the whore saint.

In Yoruba culture, she represents a mother figure in the sense that she gives herself to her lovers much like a mother does to her children, by patronizing and protecting them. Oshun is called the mother of sweetness in part because she possesses the power to bestow children. Thus, barren women seek her aid, while other women pray to her for help with ovarian and uterine problems. She also assists women with difficult pregnancies and childbirth. She is a model for women because she bore many children. Thus, behind the coquette and unfaithful wife, there is a strong mother figure who is closely associated with female devotees.

In addition to gods and goddesses, African religions manifest a belief in spirits. Some spirits are associated with natural objects, such as a rock. Among the Ashanti of Ghana, spirits are believed to animate trees, rivers, and animals and operate as guardians of these things. In the Congo region, there are spirits that are game keepers, who are described as small, dark-skinned, bright-eyed, white-haired, bearded, giving off a bad smell, and living in tree hollows. The Baganda of Uganda believe in spirits that are called "horns" and live in the horns of buffalo and bucks. These horns are used by diviners to call forth spirits.

Among the Nuer, there are spirits of the air above that include the sun after rain, who is the craftsman of god who twists human bodies and deforms them. The son of god is linked with sickness, another spirit is connected to cattle plague, and another is associated with rain, lightning, and rivers. The spirit of war is related to clan spear names and thunder. In addition to these male spirits, there is also a female spirit connected with rivers and streams. Another group of spirits of the above world are those who were once persons struck by lightning. This misfortunate type of person is actually lucky because he has been chosen by god to become a part of god, and although the individual chosen retains his identity before, he is often attached to his own families or lineages.

The Nuer spirits of below include those that have fallen from above. There are four major categories of them: totemic spirits, totemistic spirits, nature sprites, and fetishes. Within the category of totemic spirits, there is a relationship between the spirit and social group. With respect to totemistic spirits, there exists a relationship between spirit and an individual. A person with a crocodile totem is believed, for example, to have some control over crocodiles. A person is expected to have respect for a totem, refrain from harming it, desist from eating it, and to pay it courtesy. Nature sprites are connected to objects to which they are attached. It is believed that their luminosity is evidence of their presence. Finally, fetishes can be pieces of wood. They are considered medicines that talk. They are amoral with respect to action and considered very dangerous. Fetishes can be acquired by purchasing or inheriting them.

Some African cultures have another category of spirits that can be called the living dead, who are deceased members representing five generations. More specifically, the living dead are those living in a state of personal immortality whose process of dying is not complete. These figures are bilingual in the sense that they speak the language of humans and that of spirits and god. They operate to make the spirit world personal by virtue of still being a part of the family and remain members as long as someone has a memory of them. They retain an interest in family affairs, will even inquire about family matters, and function as guardians of family traditions and activities. Since they are considered to be alive, family members leave them food to eat and liquid to drink.

In addition to these divine beings of various kinds, many Africans believe in a mysterious power that is universal. It is possible to view power as working at various levels of life. There is, for example, a power within words that is considered even more powerful when uttered by an authoritative person, such as a parent's curse or blessing, which is even more powerful when recited by a medicine-man, suggesting that power is hierarchically ordered beginning with god and available for humans to tap into. Attempts by humans to tap into power are evident, with numerous people wearing charms and amulets on their person. There is also a power that enables people to walk on fire, send curses, to change into an animal, to kill snakes by spitting on them, to bring inanimate objects to life, or to know secrets. With respect to humans, power is used for curative, protective, and preventive purposes. This African belief in universal power suggests that the universe is something dynamic rather than static.

With their belief in divine beings, there are few if any atheists in African societies. From the state of birth, Africans are convinced that everyone knows that god exists. However, Africans do not hold or promote any creeds. This means that faith is not completely something spiritual; it is rather utilitarian and practical as manifested by expressing beliefs about god through concrete concepts, attitudes, and acts of worship.

Concepts of Human Nature

Before examining specified examples of an understanding of human nature in some African cultures, it is useful to talk in general terms about attitudes toward this issue. Not only are humans superior to everything else in existence, they are also social beings and share a collective identity as a member of a society because the community defines who one is and what one can become, which implies that humans define themselves by means of that which they receive from other members of society. This does not mean that humans do not possess a personal identity with its own needs and aspirations. This situation suggests that individuality and freedom are balanced against the total social context.

In general, traditional Africans believe that humans are attached to the earth. The solidity of the earth is a good guarantee of existence, giving humans something on which to anchor their lives. From the African perspective, the earth is the symmetrical equivalent of the sky. The earth is also considered sacred because it is a nourishing force as well as a place of burial for deceased humans. It is precisely this type of situation that enables us to grasp the significance of the earth as a place where things grow and where deceased humans are consumed by returning to the earth. In this way, the earth unites two opposite poles of existence: life and death.

The African understanding of and necessity for sexuality creates a problem for those who want to practice celibacy. In fact, celibate individuals are treated with contempt and even ostracized by their families and society because celibacy upsets the social and religious order. Likewise, sterile people are despised, and compared to unproductive earth that has no value.

Human spatial symbolism is informative about the way men and women are socially understood. A male is associated with the right side of the body, which is connected with strength and action, whereas a female belongs symbolically to the left, which is related to obscurity and secrecy. From a horizontal perspective, man is in front, and woman is behind. According to a vertical axis, a man is upright, and a woman is horizontal. Based on the realm of activity, a male is linked to the exterior, while a female is connected to the interior. This scenario suggests that the masculine world develops outside of the home, whereas the feminine realm is directed inside of the home. This summary of African bodily symbolism also finds expression in other places around the globe.

The Dogon conception of human nature views a person as a microcosm with the universe being created in the image of a person. As noted earlier, a person contains the basic elements of the universe used to create the world. The four pairs of cosmic grains that are carried on one's collar bones represent the four basic elements and the four directional and eight original ancestors. These cosmic grains also determine one's personality, sexuality, and social rank. It is evident that this condition of a person and that of the world reflect each other. Thus, if one breaks a moral rule, this transgression disturbs the cosmic grains in one's body along with prefiguring a wider social disturbance.

If the individual, social, and worldly realms are disrupted, the disorder can be corrected by ritual means. The Dogon believe that rituals can restore the individual and preserve the general order. In addition, it is believed that rituals help to maintain and revive the world. The types of rituals used to achieve these goals are examined shortly.

Similar to the discussion of Native American Indians in the previous chapter, the Dogon believe that a person has multiple souls, with each soul reflecting a concrete relation between the individual and one's social and worldly environment. When a child is born it has both male and female souls, resulting in an unstable personality until circumcision. It is precisely the rite of circumcision that removes the physical part (prepuce or clitoris) containing the soul directly opposite from the child's apparent sex and makes the child's personality stable. In this way, a person's sexual identity is given by the community. In addition, the child's social and spiritual identities are also given by the community. The child is given an intelligent soul by a clan priest in the form of a secret name, which gives a child a capacity for knowledge and will and conveys to the child the cosmic grains linking that child with the cosmic order. The child is related with the family ancestors because the secret name given by the priest is often that of a patrilineal ancestor, whereas the customary name is given by the patriarch of the joint family, conferring another part of the intelligent soul that gives a child a quantity of life-force. From a child's matrilineal patriarch, it receives a shadow soul, which manifests the maternal side of the child's identity. Moreover, a set of family and regional praise names are given to a child to strengthen its life-force during periods of crisis. If one desires, soul powers can be strengthened by ritual. When a person dies, his sexual soul continues to vitalize the life of the lineage through the life-force transmitted to his descendants. In summary, the Dogon conceive of a person as multi-dimensional and always dynamically developing.

In a similar fashion, the Yoruba think that humans have multiple souls. At birth, the god Olorun gives a person a life-breath soul that contains one's vitality and strength, which is nourished by food and can increase or decrease. A person has a shadow soul that leaves the body during sleep. A person also has *ori* (literally head) and its two complementary aspects, which constitutes the essence of a person's personality or ego and is located in the head, while the other *ori* is located in the heavens, constituting one's alter ego or guardian soul that is called the guardian ancestor, a partial rebirth of a patrilineal ancestor. It is the ancestor *ori* that decides one's destiny prior to being born; it also determines one's character, occupation, success in life, and moment of death.

Based on these multiple souls for the Yoruba, there are some lessons that we can draw. The operation of the souls suggests that life is divinely preordained and sociologically conditioned. Life is also related to personal and spiritual elements that one can control.

The Role of Women

There is a general agreement among Africans that god created males first, which gives males a built-in advantage when viewed from the social hierarchy, making women subservient to their male counterparts. Female inferiority is evident in male discourse when men characterize females as weaker, erratic, frail, and thus unreliable. But these attitudes are tempered by the belief that every woman sustains the entire universe by means of her most inconsequential actions. And possibly because of this type of social attitude, women are taught to respect their feminine natures. The Lele women are, for example, independent and do not hesitate to leave disagreeable and despotic husbands.

Although the domestic sphere is considered their sphere of influence, African women are not entirely confined to their homes. With respect to domestic space among the Epulu culture, the hut is considered a feminine realm to such an extent that only women build and repair huts. Among the Ila, the hut is like a living women, with the hut being symbolically equivalent to a womb. In addition to the home, gardening is done by women because men are responsible for hunting game. Working with the soil links women symbolically with the earth. As a consequence, staple foods are provided by female farming, whereas hunting is a more unreliable source of food.

In general, marriage is a duty for males and females in African societies. Marriage is part of the rhythm of life in which everyone must participate because its overall purpose is procreation, and without the generation of new life, marriage is considered incomplete. As a consequence of procreation, it is believed that the parents are reproduced in their children. Moreover, to have no children means that a male or female is essentially separated from society. With so much at stake, the choosing of a marriage partner is important and is often made by parents negotiating with each other, although a girl or boy can reject a chosen partner. Some parents may decide to use an intermediary to arrange a marriage. Some African cultures allow polygamy because having many wives and children is considered the pinnacle of prestige and social status, which also suggests divine favor. In societies that allow for polygamy, the competition for women can become a major source of friction among men.

When a woman becomes pregnant, which is considered the final seal of a marriage, she receives special care by her family, whereas barren women are considered dead-ends. By virtue of her pregnant condition, a woman is considered ritually impure, which means that she and her husband must refrain from sexual intercourse during a pregnancy. This sexual abstinence may continue after childbirth. A woman is also forbidden certain foods, communicates indirectly with her husband, and must remove from the house any weapons and iron articles.

When a woman gives birth among the Kikuyu, her hair is shaved off, which is symbolic of new life. The placenta and umbilical cord of the infant are buried in the field or near a mother's hut because they are considered symbols of fertility and connect a woman to the fields. The placenta and umbilical cord of the infant also symbolize the separation of the infant from the mother. Among some societies, ritual action may follow a birth.

For those African societies located near a forest area where men can hunt, the spirits of the forest are considered feminine in nature, just like ordinary women. This essential similarity creates an antipathy between them. Thus it is dangerous for women to enter the forest. Sexual symbolism is evident with respect to the village, a realm of women, and the forest, a sphere of men, which tends to view men benevolently. Among the Lele, women must stay out of the forest every third day, and on sacred days women should confine themselves to their village. The restrictions about entering the forest also apply to men on certain occasions. Thus taboos are associated with the forest. These various taboos are intended to keep the village (domestic sphere for women) separate from the forest (natural and male realm) in order to preserve the divine order. This situation also means that a menstruating woman, who is considered impure, prevents her husband from hunting. In fact, among the Matu, a pygmy people, a couple must not engage in sexual relations before a hunt. This implies that there is an incompatible relation between women and forest animals that prevents their relationship. Thus, taboos represent the preservation of distinctions that must be maintained for the survival of all, the avoidance of danger, and the retention of harmony. Cultural taboos play a similar role within village life to maintain social harmony. A man's relationship with his wife, for instance, affects hunting luck. Thus, domestic disputes can harm hunting, good fortune, and social harmony, which puts a village at risk.

Ancestor Cult

In many African cultures, the human drama of life is performed in conjunction with one's ancestors, who are closely intertwined with an individual's life. The intimacy of ancestors and the living is expressed by the attitude that they are heads and parts of the family or community and serve as superintendents of family and communal affairs, even though they are no longer living, from an African perspective. It is not strange that ancestors continue to hold the titles they had while living, such as mother or father. This is even true to a personal extent because ancestors receive worship directed specifically to them. To address an ancestor by name means that the deceased has attributes that are distinctive of a kind of person.

Ancestor worship is socially grounded in domestic, kinship-descent relations and institutions of a culture. It is more precisely a lineage cult in which the oldest living son has the primary responsibility for the rites because he inherited this right and duty when he replaced his father in the social structure. The Tonga, a Bantu society of northern South Africa, believes that ancestor spirits validate the life pattern of the living and bind together potentially divergent kin groups. And the spirits reinforce the principal status changes of the Tonga adult. These features are possible because an ancestor is re-established into the family and lineage by means of ritual. The intimate relationship between the living and the dead is represented in Ashanti culture by a blackened stool within each lineage that serves as a shrine for its ancestors and place to offer food and drink to them.

Nonetheless, the dead present immediate problems for the living because they are considered impure by the fact of their death. The Dogon not only believe that the dead are impure but they understand impurity as death dispersing one's vital force. When they are impure, the dead create disorder, which functions to warn the living. Among the Dogon, millet beer plays a central role, establishing order by the ancestors impregnating the beer, which gives it its intoxicating powers.

Ancestors generally behave in expected and permitted ways irrespective of their earthly characters. A devoted father can, for example, become an ancestor that causes illness and misfortune. Ancestors can be both capricious and ambivalent by being either punitive or benevolent. The ancestors' actions are limited because they can only intervene where they have authority, which is related to their descendants. In the relationship between ancestors and their descendants, the latter owe obedience, economic service, and respect to the former. Among the Lo Dagaa of northern Ghana, a person must return to the ancestor part of any wealth acquired by inheritance, which involves periodic sacrifices of livestock to the ancestor. This practice suggests that the living person is indebted to an ancestor. Thus, if an ancestor is neglected or one practices anti-social behavior, he may punish the living. Among the Lovedu, a Bantu society, a witch is not allowed to kill a person without the consent of an ancestor. When the witch violates this standard, her medicines become ineffective. Despite the close relationship to the living, ancestors also have an independent existence in the form of an afterlife. The Ashanti and Mende of Sierra Leone believe, for instance, that there is a world of spirits where all ancestors live a mode of existence similar to life on earth.

In general, ancestors have authority within a lineage, and the rights and duties sanctioned by them are beyond human challenge. Their presence and authority force survivors to conform to social norms or risk disapproval and punishment. Not only are the living dependent on their ancestors, but ancestors are also dependent on society for worship and the maintenance of their memory. By maintaining the social structure of a society, ancestors symbolize its continuity and the importance of order.

The Ritual Process

The anthropologist Victor Turner, who is known for his field work in Africa and theoretical work on religious phenomena, conceives of ritual as a process, by which he means an enduring system that is not conceptual but is rather dynamic and dramatic. This dramatic social performance exhibits five aspects: (1) the playing of roles by participants; (2) the use of a rhetorical style of speech; (3) an audience; (4) knowledge and acceptance of a set of rules; (5) a climax or end. These social dramas represent either a harmonic or disharmonic process, which implies that these dramas arise in conflict situations, which also reveal a fourfold pattern: breach, crisis, corrective action, and reintegration. This pattern of conflict tends to hide social contradictions within a society, although these factional and schismatic rifts are temporarily symbolically unified. For Turner, ritual forms a symbolic layer on real social processes and an ability to mediate them. Moreover, ritual affirms bodily gestures, becomes a vehicle for conveying meaning to others, and embodies the highest symbolic truths of a society. In addition to affirming bodily actions, ritual helps to explain to the human body its place in the world and enables a rediscovery of true personhood and community as one's self is socially defined in relationship to others. Ritual can also reveal one's uniqueness, unity with others, and worldview. As social unity and personal uniqueness are being affirmed, the individual is also being restricted because only certain actions are required, which are made effective by his adherence to models.

If Dogon sacrifice is a redistribution of life-force for the benefit of everyone, it is modeled on the action of the creator, when Amma sacrificed Lebe to make the earth fertile at the beginning of the world. Besides repeating the acts of the gods and the sacred prototypes established by them, rituals embody a complex variety of symbols. The Ogun festival among the Yoruba includes an offering of kola nuts to the deity, a patron god of hunters. These kola nuts signify friendship and reconciliation, and offering them to Ogun creates an initial bond between the sacrificer and deity. In addition, the offering of snails to Ogun symbolizes softness and smoothness, whereas the sacrifice of a dog symbolically corresponds to Ogun's dualistic nature of destruction and protection because the animal's nature consists of wildness and ferocity in its natural state and friendliness and protection in its domestic condition.

Before they sacrifice an ox, the Nuer rub ashes on the back of the animal, which consecrates it and indicates that its life is dedicated to god. This act also signifies the identification of the sacrificer and the victim, which functions as a substitute for the human. The spear used to kill the oxen symbolically represents the male sacrificer and his virtue and vitality. The purpose of the Nuer sacrifice is to get rid of evil, which is evident when a sacrificer places his hands on the victim, transferring evil to the victim. This ritual action points to the purpose or end of the rite.

The ritual process of a society often includes or presupposes a process of purification, which is necessary before one can engage in a sacrifice. Why is purification necessary? Before engaging in a ritual, an individual is usually in an impure or polluted condition. This is a very dangerous condition for the individual and others because pollution is dirt, according to the anthropologist Mary Douglas, that offends against and threatens social order. Dirt is matter out of place and is unclean, which is the precise opposite of holiness. If a ritual participant performed a rite in a polluted condition, such a person could unleash dangerous forces that could cause considerable harm to many.

Different African religious cultures have a variety of methods for overcoming impurity. Among the Zulu, spitting is a method of purification, which also cleanses one of anger, an ejection of something bad inside oneself. If a Zulu has a disturbing dream, he can spit outside of his hut and not look at the spittle. In another context, elder women spit when discovering that a young girl lost her virginity, and they sometimes spit on the young woman's sexual organ after discovering her condition. A Zulu should spit when she sees improper behavior as a way to demonstrate disapproval, or she should spit when experiencing vile smells. The male emission of semen is another form of purification, but a man does not sleep with his wife for that purpose; he has sexual relations with another woman in order to expel his evil into her. Another method is to take the chyme, a pulpy matter located within a sacrificial animal's digestive area, and to wash one's hands with it, making the hands white just like ancestors'. Chyme is also spattered on the roof of a house and scattered inside the cattle enclosure, which signifies that everything is clean. The purifying power of chyme is related to its coolness, which is associated with the calming of social tension.

The Nyakyusa of Malawi practice an annual purification rite for the cleansing of the entire community that is observed at the beginning of the new year. The rite consists of throwing out the old ashes within the family hearth. The cultural context for this rite is the belief that shades of ancestors come to the family hearth to warm themselves. This close proximity is considered dangerous to the living because they may contract illness brought by the shades to the hearth. It is thus necessary to clear away the old ashes to dispel the dangerous shades. This ritual action is followed by lighting a new fire.

Assuming that the necessary preparations associated with purity have been made and an auspicious date for a sacrifice has been determined by divination, the Yoruba begin their sacrifice to the god Ogun with an all-night vigil at the god's shrine, where large quantities of palm wine and beer are consumed by the participants. The deity is praised by the singing of chants, offering of kola nuts that signify friendship and reconciliation, and presenting of the victim before the shrine. These ritual actions establish a bond between the participants and god. The sacrificial offerings are consecrated by coming into contact with the shrine. The god is invoked by the splitting and casting of kola nuts before the god's shrine to ascertain his divine will. This step is followed by the immolation or actual killing of the victim(s). The Yoruba priest cracks open the snail's shell and pours this onto the god's stone. Then a pigeon's head is wrung off, and its blood is allowed to drip on the stone. Finally, a dog is beheaded and its blood sprinkled on the stone. After being separated from the profane world, these three victims are transferred to the spiritual world as its life-force. The communion and final phase of the sacrifice involves participants sharing the consecrated flesh of the dog, which both renews bonds of unity among participants and reinforces god's relationship to participants.

In contrast to the Yoruba, the Nuer sacrifice only their cattle after rubbing ashes on the backs of the bovines. Nuer males have an intimate personal and emotional relationship with cows, and their importance for the Nuer cannot be overemphasized. Cattle are absolutely essential for food in a sacrificial context, marriage, salvation, sanctification of social undertakings, and overcoming evil, sickness, and sin. Because a cow is given as a sacrificial gift, god gains nothing because the animal already belonged to him. Thus, a sacrifice benefits a human and not god.

Rites of Passage

The conception of ritual as a process is very evident in rites of passage such as birth, initiation, marriage, and death. These events represent changes in a person's existential and social status. These important moments of life that embody change are considered dangerous. It is precisely these rites that protect a person from danger associated with transition states and ensure one's safe passage from one stage of life to another.

The threefold structure of these rites discussed in the previous chapter also applies in the African context.

In the male initiation rites of Kore of the Bambara society of Mali, the period of separation is marked by the boys wearing white gowns. The young boys are led from the village in a single file to the initiation grove in the westward direction, which signifies a symbolic death of the boys akin to the death of the sun each day. These procedures separate the boys from the world of childhood, which is a condition of irresponsibility, ignorance, and asexuality. Being separated from their mothers, the initiates leave behind the profane world and enter a sacred realm in which they will symbolically die and be reborn.

The transition phase of the rite includes five aspects: segregation, initiatory ordeals, initiatory death, instruction, and regeneration. Initiatory ordeals are sometimes painful operations performed on the novices. The Bambara instruct the boys to enter a grove squatting down with their arms extended forward, which commences a process of dissolution and rejuvenations. Elders of the society whip the boys with thorn branches, signifying the pain of leaving their former mode of life, and also flail them with burning torches, which represent the divine illumination of knowledge. The thorns signify the pain of leaving their former life, while the thorn bushes constituting the grove are indicative of the difficulty of penetrating the sphere for everyone except the initiated. In the center of the grove is a tree, symbolizing the creator deity and divine sage. For this ceremony, the grove represents the sky coming to earth. In a stage called the "return of dry excrement," there is a reversal of bodily function and return to the womb for the novices. At this point, the initiates are considered dead, being entombed at the conjuncture where the sky meets the earth. Even though the initiates are symbolically invisible, their mothers bring them food, and elders feed them while the boys remain passive and helpless like a newborn infant. An elder puts iron and wood knives to the initiates' throats, symbolizing death with the former instrument and revival with the wood knife. Sitting at the center of the grove, the novices are covered with a blanket, which represents being enveloped by the sky. After this return to the womb, the initiates are reborn, and teaching begins with elders explaining the significance of 240 objects that represent the totality of things and beings in the universe, which are suspended from a pole. An arrow represents, for example, war, attack, criticism, poison, and hunting, whereas a black piece of cloth symbolizes obscurity, beginning, secrecy, transformation, and primordial knowledge. By means of these objects and many others, the novice learns the meanings and values of his culture.

Among the Dinka, the rite of initiation involves circumcision. The cultural rationale draws attention to the impurity or lack of whiteness for an uncircumcised boy, which renders him permanently polluting because of the dirt beneath his foreskin. This suggests that circumcision reveals the hidden or makes his manhood visible. From the Dinka perspective, the circumcision kills the novice, a result that is compared to a lion devouring the novice. Sexual instruction is part of the knowledge given to the youth by miming copulation with an elder impersonating a female. Each novice is also given a hollowed out cucumber and is instructed to feign intercourse with it.

While an initiate moves through the state of transition, he is a liminal being, which means that he is neither here nor there. This ambiguous, paradoxical condition means that the novice is structurally invisible and thus eludes normal modes of classification. As evident from the shared examples, liminality is akin to death, being in a womb, invisibility, darkness, and bisexuality. It is the rite that makes the progression from the irresponsibility of childhood to responsible adulthood possible and less dangerous. In a sense, the rite of initiation creates an adult member of society.

After dying and being reborn in the transition stage, the novice is incorporated back into society. The Bambara elders lead initiates through a hole in the earth toward the direction of sunlight at the end. Since the hole is a hyena's borrow, an incarnation of wisdom, the novices have symbolically acquired characteristics of the animal. After a final purification, a novice can now safely return to society.

In comparison to the more fully developed nature of male initiation rites, female initiations are less widespread and common than male rites. Where female initiation rites do exist, they tend to have an individual character, whereas male rites are most often collective in nature. What accounts for this difference? Female initiation begins with a young girl's first menstruation. The transition phase of female initiation among the Nandi of Kenya involves older women tying a ligament around a girl's clitoris to stop the flow of blood to it. Then the young girl dances herself into exhaustion. After being taken to the initiation house, instructors insert stinging nettles into the clitoris, which becomes numb and swollen. During the following day, girls are examined for virginity. This is followed by an operator cutting away the clitoris with a curved knife. This type of female initiation is strongly criticized by the American novelist Alice Walker in *The Temple of My Familiar* for its infliction of pain and even death from the procedure. But for the Nandi, the cutting away of the clitoris means that it will not grow long or have branches, children born to an initiate will be normal instead of abnormal, and the cutting unlocks the flow of life. In contrast to the Nandi, the Dogon cut away the clitoris because it represents the male soul, which recalls the culture's emphasis on twins in their creation myth.

Major Cultural Figures

Diviners are essential figures in many African religious traditions because they are often employed to counter witches. According to the Zulu, a person is called to become a diviner by the ghosts of ancestors, which excludes becoming one by choice. The lineage ancestors brood over someone they have chosen to be a diviner and communicate with the chosen person through dreams that are often accompanied by visions. After a person is called to be a diviner, she (most diviners among the Zulu are women) trains with an experienced practitioner and experiences a symbolic death and rebirth. A novice is obligated to catch a wild animal such as a snake that is worn around one's neck. When the snake dies, the novice wears the reptile's vertebrae as a necklace. The novice must abstain from sex and certain kinds of food like eggs, pork, mutton, or bananas. Prior to initiation, a novice sleeps on the earth because it is her mother. In addition to using dreams and visions to foretell the future, a diviner uses bones to discern messages of the spiritual world.

Another important cultural figure in many African cultures is the witch. A person acquires the powers of witchcraft in two basic ways: through the power of another witch or by means of an inherent physical factor. With respect to this second means, the Azande of Ghana believe, for example, that a witch possesses a special organ, which is hereditary, that is located somewhere behind the sternum or attached to the liver. A father passes this condition to his son while a mother transmits it to her daughter. The Azande express pity and tolerance toward those who become witches involuntarily and are not aware of their condition, whereas those who voluntarily choose to become a witch are considered evil and dangerous.

If members of a society are uncertain about the identity of a witch, they can turn to divination, extract confessions, or force a suspected witch into admission by feelings of guilt, torture, fear, or hope of a lighter punishment. The Lo Daga of Ghana force, for example, a suspected witch to drink a mixture of soil and water at an earth shrine. In response to this, a witch's body rebels against the mixture, her belly swells up, and, eventually, the witch dies. The identity of a witch revolves around the fact that witches do not like the cultivated earth and prefer the wild and chaotic bush, a non-human side of the earth. West African societies use iron, an ore linked with the earth, to disclose witches. It is believed that a witch and iron are antipathetic, and a witch will not touch iron because it will burn the witch. Besides disclosing the identity of a witch, ordinary people can take countermeasures against one by burning a piece of thatch from the witch's roof, by burying a bottle of urine that causes a witch to hurry back to the scene of her crime, thus exposing the witch's identity, or by scratching and drawing blood from a witch.

Zulu witches are believed to travel through the air, whereas less able witches ride familiars, usually facing the tail to which they cling. A familiar can be procured by exhuming a corpse and bringing it to life again, by exhuming children, or by capturing a baby baboon that the witch tames. African and Native American Indian cultures share a belief that the witch is an anti-social and anti-human figure. From a more positive perspective, witchcraft beliefs help to explain events. The Azande know that a boy cutting his foot on a stump is a natural occurrence. But a witch is believed to have placed the wood stump in the boy's path. Additional proof that a witch is involved occurs when the wound begins to fester, whereas most cuts heal quickly.

Within the Dogon society, a priest serves as a mediator of Lebe's life-giving force. The typical priest of the Dogon is called a Hogon, wearing a colored tunic and trousers that represent the four cardinal directions and the four elements. The sandals of the priest represent the ark of Nommo, which brought humankind to earth at the beginning of time. The priest's cylindrical shaped headdress is woven in a spiral pattern that corresponds to the path followed by the original cosmic seed. Besides regulating and strengthening the relationship between god and humans by conducting worship services, a priest functions to guard the cultural tradition by keeping its secret knowledge. The priest also functions as an advisor, educator, or philosopher. The priest is often the custodian of the law and its interpreter. In the Nuer culture, a priest might negotiate a settlement in a homicide case by arranging for compensation to the family of the deceased and performing a sacrifice to repair broken social relations. A Nuer priest also conducts the taking of oaths by having a person lick a spear or a metal bracelet as a sign of telling the truth. These types of activities suggest that a priest may formulate social rules and enforce their observance. The priest obtains authority to perform his duties by virtue of his office and submitting to the will of god. As an embodiment of authority, the priest's influence is more than religious; it is also moral, social, cultural, and political.

In contrast to the priest, a prophet tends to receive a personal call to his position, which gives the prophet his authority. Another major difference between a priest and prophet is the personal charisma, an inherent gift of leadership, of the latter, whereas the priest is the possessor of office charisma, which is both connected to his office and is more rational because personal charisma appeals more to the emotions of others. Office-based charisma demands a tempered obedience, while the personal type claims loyalty to the point of personal surrender. In contrast to a priest, a prophet, who is conscious of being a divine instrument, is called to accomplish something, such as proclaiming a doctrine, divine command, or issue a warning about future dire consequences in store for a society. A prophet may receive messages from the divine by means of visions, dreams, or trance states. These forms of awareness arise spontaneously and are received passively rather than being induced by the prophet, who receives no economic reward for his work; he propagates the messages that he receives for their own sake.

In some African cultures, the priest can validate the political power of a king, or he can restrict a king's power. Among the Bemba of South Africa, the priest protects the king through rituals that serve to validate the office of the sovereign, just as refusing to perform rituals can undermine the power of a king. The origin of an African monarch can be due to his being a divine incarnation, a situation in which his power and authority are validated by his divine nature. Not all African kings are divine by nature, although such kings do have the ability to manipulate the gods for the good of his subjects. What happens when the gods withdraw support? A lack of support is manifested by drought, crop failures, wars, and epidemics. What happens when a king becomes old, ill, and sexually impotent? Because the king's body is the dwelling place of the gods, his condition affects his people. The traditional solution to this problem is regicide. In other words, when a king shows signs of declining strength, he is killed to avert possible calamities for the people.

The Shilluk culture of South Sudan uses regicide to protect itself, even though the king is primarily a priestly figure who reigns but does not rule because political decisions are made collectively by chiefs. The Shilluk king functions as a mediator between the people and the forces of vitality, which are controlled by the high god, and acts as a judge in cases of social transgression. But when he becomes ill and loses strength he is killed to save both the people and the office of kingship. Methods of killing a king might include smothering him by blocking his bodily passages, or burying him alive in secrecy along with slaves, wives, or sons of commoners. Because this type of fate awaited candidates for kingship, Nyakyusa candidates for kingship feared being chosen by a council of hereditary priests because the reigns of kings were usually brief. The process of selecting a king includes identifying a fertile person of good character. The Nyakyusa king lives secluded from his subjects, must adhere to numerous taboos such as not walking across a stream because of the danger of triggering a flood, not sitting on a green banana leaf in order to avoid a crop failure, or being restricted to eating only the middle part of a banana in order to avoid widespread hunger. Moreover, the king must not scratch himself in order to avoid bleeding and risk the possibility of regicide by his people.

Playful Elements

A king of the Fon culture offers to give his kingdom to any man who succeeded in having sexual intercourse with his daughter. Men proceed to the deity Fa to receive the power of potency, but instead Legba gives then a red powder that makes them impotent. The men complain to the king, but Legba, a trickster, pleads his innocence before the king. Legba offers to have intercourse with the king's daughter in public, and he deflowers her with ease. Then the king commands that Legba be allowed to sleep with any woman he chooses. This narrative depicts the trickster Legba as an agent of transformation as symbolized by his sexuality; it also manifests his domestication of sex and making it available to the community. When Legba makes sex public, he transforms it into something creative. The narrative helps one to see that Legba is a mediator among the gods, between the gods and humans, and among humans. He is also an agent of disruption and reconciliation.

But he is most importantly tricky. Legba tells, for example, Mawu, a goddess, that thieves are planning to steal yams from her garden. She warns everyone that whoever steals from her garden will be killed. Legba steals her sandals, enters the garden, and takes the yams, leaving sandal prints on the earth. The ensuing investigation does not reveal the culprit until Legba suggests that Mawu is the guilty party, humiliating the goddess when her sandal footprints match those on the earth and causing her to withdraw from the earth for the sky. Before she withdraws completely, she appoints Legba her regent on earth, with the duty to report to her.

While on earth, Legba invents magic and sexuality. After Legba, his sister, and brother receive gifts for singing at a funeral, they sit at a crossroads to divide the gifts. An extra gift is claimed by each of them. Thus, they agree to ask a passing woman to divide the gifts. After the woman decides in favor of the sister, the brother cuts off the woman's head and throws her body into the bush, where Legba proceeds to have sexual intercourse with the cadaver. After two more passing women meet the same fate, Legba becomes a dog, who is also asked to divide the gifts, but the animal buries the gifts in a hole. Thereby, Legba tricks his brother and sister, joins them in violence, creates magic by becoming a dog, and establishes sex in an act of necrophilia.

Ananse is the spider trickster of the Ashanti who is both charlatan and fool, as illustrated by a story about the origin of his baldness. In this story, he steals some beans and hides them in his hat, but they burn his head. Ananse is also wily and stupid, as evident in the tale of detaching his head to bail a stream dry to catch fish. Getting carried away while singing a song, he ends up clapping his detached head to his anus, which suggests his ability to juggle reality.

Moreover, he is a schemer, thief, ingrate, and lecher. But the Ashanti say that he is wonderful because without him life would be boring. It must also be noted that he spreads cultural forces and serves as the archetypical gardener, which is his major activity.

According to Ashanti folklore, the deity Nyame plants a huge garden that becomes overgrown with weeds and nettles. Nyame offers to marry his ninth daughter to whoever can clear the garden without scratching himself when the nettles sting him. Ananse outwits Nyame by only weeding on market days. When people pass by and ask why he has undertaken such a hopeless task, he answers by praising the girl's beauty by slapping and rubbing parts of his own body corresponding to her bodily parts being praised by him. This narrative is indicative of Ananse's socializing the earth through farming and shaping human society.

There are also narratives of Ananse behaving in a radically anti-social way by spreading jealousy. According to an Ashanti tale, Akwasi, a sterile husband who lives apart from his wife, is fearful that someone will take her away from him, prohibiting anyone from seeing or talking to her. Ananse schemes to woo Aso, wife of Akwasi, by taking a huge basket of meat to their home. While the three of them are eating, Ananse distracts them and puts a laxative into Akwasi's food. At the conclusion of the meal, Ananse tells his host that his name is "Rise up and make love to Aso." Then Ananse bars the door of the bedroom located between husband and wife. In the middle of the night, the laxative begins to have its effect. Akwasi answers the call of nature and calls Ananse's false name; Ananse unbars the door to allow the husband to go outside to relieve himself. While Akwasi is relieving himself, Ananse does as he is told. This scene is repeated nine times during the night. The baby of this adulterous union becomes the source of jealously, an anti-social force.

The trickster is a playful and popular figure in many African cultures. For the trickster, life is a tricky game with winners and losers. The playful antics of the trickster enable a student to recognize that humans are more than rational and serious creatures because play includes an irrational quality. Many of the trickster tales are comic and entertaining, which serve as an interlude in the lives of people. The repetitive nature of the trickster story teller creates a temporary and limited order and enchants and captivates hearers of the narratives. The narratives about the trickster are tales that those outside of the indigenous culture can use to enter into the culture of the other and experience an aspect of an African religion that is ordinarily foreign to a researcher.

In addition to trickster narratives, African religion is something that people dance, another aspect of play. Dance is often associated with rites in African cultures by young men and women dancing their initiations. The Samburu culture of northern Kenya have novices dance, for example, in association with their circumcision. Young girls among the Venda of southern Africa dance in a circle, creating a womb. A fetus is symbolized by a bass drum, which is nourished by strenuous dancing symbolizing sexual intercourse. The ashes of a fire signify semen. These overt expressions of sexuality are indicative of human transformation from an inferior condition to a higher status within the society.

Africans dance for a variety of reasons in addition to contexts associated with rites of passage. The Lugbara of Uganda perform a dance, an expression of body language, for the purpose of promoting courtship situations for young people. The Azande beer dance is designed to channel dangerous sexual forces into harmless social patterns. These types of dances express non-verbal sexual messages while also releasing dormant social tension and aggressive feelings that hide beneath the social surface and form a metaphor of sexual relations. As with Native American Indian cultures, African societies perform dances within a violent context such as ensuing war. The Swahili of east Africa perform a dance that is a caricature of a military parade, during which masculinity is displayed and competition between rival groups sometimes results in violence. These examples of different types of dances reflect the ecstatic nature of dance that transports a participant beyond the normal social order. At the same time, dance expresses the energy of the life force that is used to bring people together to celebrate some event or to express collective sorrow. The close relationship between dance and play is evident among the Samburu when they use the term "play" as a metaphor for dancing and singing.

The Role of Healing

A central concern for many African and Native American Indian religions is healing because an illness unsettles a person by interrupting normal social and behavioral routines and undermining assumptions about oneself and the world. Illness can also give rise to questions about the meaning of life and the place of humans in the world. Moreover, many African cultures assume that bodily health is closely associated with spiritual health or even morality. A person's well-being is part of a complex web of social relationships. This implies that physical sickness can be a symptom of disharmony between a person and the world.

If we examine the relationship between healing and culture, it is possible to recognize that illness is culturally defined. The culturally specific nature of sickness enables a healer to treat an illness effectively. A healer's effectiveness is connected to his expertise and past successes, which are often expressed by prestigious titles and credentials. The Lebou of Senegal call their healer "master of knowledge." The role of the healer enables him to assign meaning to an illness, but this outcome assumes that healer and patient share the same worldview.

Sickness presupposes a cause and a method for dealing with it. Causes include object intrusion of a person, spirit intrusion, soul loss, and sorcery. These different types of causes can be countered by confession because an illness can be a direct or indirect infringing of moral codes or violating taboos. There is often an assumption that without confession, healing cannot occur.

Confession, a way to dispel bad thoughts and deeds, is often performed publicly because of a common belief that illness can best be treated in a public way.

Among the Ndembu of Zimbabwe, sickness is sometimes related to anger and aggression of male ancestors, who are motivated to inflict illness on the guilty party because someone violated a law or custom. The Ndembu identify illness with the upper central incisor of a dead hunter. The incisor must be removed by building a shrine. Kin folk and patient are instructed to totally confess their sins, grudges, and grievances. There are a couple of assumptions built into a confession: illness represents something wrong within the society that needs to be reconciled, and illness is caused by harboring misdeeds and evil thoughts. Therefore, secrecy is not healthy.

Another means of healing involves removing it from a patient and identifying it with some object by ritual, symbolic, or psychological methods. The objective is to condense the illness, objectify it, and bind it. Then the sickness can be destroyed or banished. The Yoruba of Nigeria perform, for example, a ritual at a river with the patient donning a white dress, shaving her head, and cutting into her scalp. The healer and patient enter waist deep into the river. Using a dove as a sponge, the healer rubs the patient's body in order to draw out illness and transfer it to the dove, which is then drowned and its body thrown downstream along with the disease. Then, a second dove is killed, and its blood smeared over the patient's head and upper body. It is believed that the second dove transfers vitality and calmness to the patient. After washing and throwing away the blood-stained dress, the patient is rubbed with medicines on shore. Finally, a third dove is killed and its blood splashed over the patient's body before being washed off. Standing on the body of the dove and reciting an incantation, the third dove is thrown downstream while declaring that the dove is carrying away the sickness.

Death and Afterlife

According to Zulu lore, after creating the world, the creator god sent a chameleon to inform humans that they would live forever. But the creator deity changes his mind and sends a lizard to inform humans that they would die. In Zulu culture, the chameleon is renowned for changing its color and thus is associated with deception, a kind of unreliability that reflects back on the god, who is also not fully trustworthy. In other African cultures, the reason for death is related to a mistake or miscommunication of some sort. When death does arrive, African cultures respond to a loss of life by ritual means to help survivors cope and to transfer the deceased to the afterlife, even though the afterlife is not always clearly defined because of the emphasis on the importance of life on earth.

Burial customs among African cultures are another type of rite of passage. It is typical among the Dinka to strip the dead person of decorations and ornaments, shave his head, wash the body, and then anoint it with oil. The corpse is placed into the grave on its side with the head facing west, which is the direction of death. The funeral party crouches around the grave, facing away from it, and pushes the dirt backward into the grave. Straw from the deceased's roof is thrown onto the grave and lit. The smoke blows over the mourners while a ram is held over the fire and killed, and its entrails are sprinkled over the people. Not only does the ram represent the suffering of the mourners, but these final actions are related to purification of the survivors.

In comparison to the Dinka, the Nuer practice actions that are a bit different. The Nuer dig a grave on the left-hand side of the deceased's hut, which is considered the side of evil, and fill in the grave with their backs to it. The earth is leveled, mourners are purified, and a formal ceremony is held from four to six months after burial, which is an attempt to repay the debt owed to death in order to appease it, giving the rite a prophylactic function by protecting the living from the dead. The Nuer can tell if the ghost is content by watching how an ox and cow fall when they are speared as offerings. If the animal falls over cleanly on its right side, this is a favorable sign, while falling on its left side is a negative omen.

The average Nuer finds death dreadful, and people thus rarely discuss it. When a person dies, her flesh, life, and soul separate. The life aspect of a person returns to god, its source of origin. This thus concludes the cycle of life for a person that begins with god and returns to god. The deceased have some type of existence after death, but it is not developed by the culture. Although it is a bit vague, the Nuer believes that the dead exist independently and follow a shadowy mode of existence as a ghost (shade) by means of their soul. This is not some kind of immortality. The only type of immortality recognized by the Nuer is the survival of a social personality by means of a dead person's name. A father, for example, lives forever through his son in a line of family descent. And the memory of the deceased is what keeps that person alive.

After a person dies, the Dogon don masks and dance to frighten away souls and compel them to join their ancestors. It is believed that souls journey northwards to Manga, a Dogon paradise. But the journey is long, hot, and dry and serves as retribution for misdeeds on earth. The journey lasts three years and may require ritual assistance from the living in order for the soul to receive water to slake its thirst and restore its life-force.

A different death scenario is evident among the Lo Dagga of northern Ghana. While the soul is traveling toward the country of the great god, it must cross the River of Death, where the soul needs to pay the ferryman with a fare provided by funeral ceremonies. If the soul has been good, it will cross safely, whereas an evil soul falls through the bottom of the ferry and must then swim across the river. This swim takes three years. Upon arriving in the land of the dead, the soul faces various kinds of ordeals that are determined by the gravity of her misdeeds. If a person has been a witch, she is forced, for example, to eat her own arm and leg before swimming across the river. These ordeals are followed by a final judgment.

Among the Zulu, there is a vague underworld inhabited by shades in which everything is the exact reverse of earthly life. In this underworld, everything is directed downwards. In comparison to life on earth, mountains, trees, fields, and pastures face downward in the underworld. The shades and cattle of the underworld are white in color, which also stresses its distinction from life on earth. In comparison to life on earth, the underworld is an upside-down place.

The Mende of Sierra Leone also believe that a dead person proceeds to a place under the earth where the dead retain their social identity. The departed, however, remain concerned about their survivors on earth. And deceased members communicate with the living by means of dreams, where the dead appear in human forms wearing white garments or are simply painted white. In an African culture like the Yombe of northern Zambia, the dead person is now considered a spirit who can be reintroduced into the house several months after a death by being placed into a valuable object, rendering the deceased a part of the world of its survivors and allowing it to intervene in the lives of the survivors. This type of social practice breaks down the spatial separation of the living and the dead and retains the deceased as an active member of the family unit. Another consequence for the Yombe culture is that the afterlife is essentially of this world and modeled on this world, making it possible for the social order to continue to exist in spite of death. African cultures do not conceive of hell as a place where one goes to be punished for misdeeds committed during life.

The general African attitude toward death is that of a departure and does not represent the complete annihilation of a person. The deceased is commonly said to go home, implying that life is a pilgrimage and that a person's real home is located in the afterlife. The afterlife is conceived as a continuation of life similar to the existence of a living person. This suggests that the deceased person retains his personality, social and political status, sexual distinction, wealth, or poverty. Death is conceived as a process that is completed when the last person who knew the person dies, meaning that the departed is no longer alive in someone's memory. This means that the dying person finally loses his humanness and gains spirit status.

Millenarianism

Ngai, supreme deity of the Kikuyu of Kenya, offered the land to Gikuyu and Mumbi, two original ancestors of the people. The present members of the culture are believed to be descendants of the original ancestors, making them rightful inheritors of the land given by god. Along with this gift of land from the high god, the Kikuyu were also given a prophetic promise that Ngai would assist them during a crisis. From 1952–1956, Kenya was dominated by British colonial rule. This historical period witnessed the ascent of the Mau Mau uprising, a political movement and rebellion framed in traditional Kikuyu cultural values. This movement focused on the importance of the land with the goal of reacquiring their land from the British government. The land symbolically represented the living society and the historical identity of the people living on the land, which supplies their material needs. The land is also associated with the ancestors of the culture, and serves as their mother by nursing the living and the dead. The importance of land is manifested in the tri-colored flag of the Kenya Africa Union, which symbolized the recovery of their land. The black color stands for the people, green stands for the land, and the middle color is red that represents the blood of the people. This suggests that the people are separated from the land by shedding of their blood.

Those joining the movement took an oath of unity, which suggests putting a ritual oath to a political purpose. The oath included major features of male initiation rites in order to enhance, create, and sustain moral solidarity among the rebels. Those of warrior age were administered the warrior or platoon oath. Because the oath involved breaking conventional moral standards, the oath was especially powerful. Besides utilizing the thorax of a slaughtered male goat—believed to be a powerful oath-making instrument—the oath involved performing an act of sodomy with the carcass of the dead goat, making the oath powerful because the moral violation was so vile and repulsive. In summary, the Mau Mau uprising was a nativistic type of millenarian movement because it stressed the value of indigenous cultural elements and attempted to revive or perpetuate selected aspects of the culture.

In 1918, there was a serious flu epidemic in Zaire, formerly the Belgian Congo, during which time Simon Kimbangu, who had been educated at a Baptist mission school, received a message directly from Christ instructing him to convert his fellow citizens. Afterwards, Kimbangu viewed himself as a prophet, but his followers accepted him as a messiah. Initially, he resisted the call and fled to Kinshasa to escape repeated calls. In 1921, the Holy Spirit took him against his will to a sick woman's house, and he healed her in the name of Jesus Christ. Other healings followed, along with restoring a dead child to life. Rumors about his miraculous healing powers spread. He urged people to become Christians, to practice monogamy, and to renounce the local spirit cult. He opposed separation from the mission churches and upheld the payment of government taxes. He also refused to become a leader of a resistance movement against the government. Nonetheless, the government became concerned after people left their jobs, hospitals became vacant, and Catholic missions began to lose some of their converts. Kimbangu's village was now called Jerusalem.

Kimbangu's non-radical religious movement sparked a nationalistic movement that he neither intended nor could control. After his arrest by the government, he escaped, an event interpreted as a miracle. By this time, he was viewed by the people as an African Messiah. He decided to follow Christ's example by returning to his village, now called Jerusalem, in order to surrender to the authorities, but he was betrayed by a local chief and rearrested. His trial concluded with a disciple challenging the judge and asking why Africans could not have their Messiah when white people can have theirs. Kimbangu's death sentence was later commuted to life imprisonment by King Albert of Belgium, even though it was strongly opposed by missionaries and traders. Kimbangu died in 1951.

Having established The Church of Jesus Christ on Earth, Kimbangu was viewed by his adherents as a messianic martyr chosen by God to sacrifice himself for the gospel and his people. Overall, his followers viewed his life as a repetition of Christian salvation history. The religious society sparked by Kimbangu reflects features of a messianic movement with its expectation of a supernatural deliverer who will bring redemption and salvation along with a state of happiness and well-being.

Spirit Possession

African religions are similar in general to Native American Indian cultures in the sense that both tend to stress the need for religious experience that often comes in visions and dreams. These two large blocks of various religious cultures differ with respect to the African emphasis on experiences associated with divine possession and divination.

A narrative among the Dinka is informative about the nature of becoming possessed and responding to this condition with divination. When a young man is born without testicles, it is the cultural custom to place such an infant into the river. But the father of such an infant listened to the pleas of his wife and others and sacrificed a white sheep for the infant to become normal. When the infant's testicles appear, this is interpreted by family members as a divine intervention. When he grows to manhood, he hints about possessing special gifts such as insight and clairvoyance.

When the young man is seized by a free divinity, which is distinguished from clan divinities, he runs around his hut and sings strange songs. He eventually collapses to the ground, where he rolls around and lashes out with his arms and legs. Frenzied movement is interspersed with quieter moments. Those watching could understand what was occurring because they had previous exposure to such unusual behavior. Meanwhile, the young man mumbles unintelligibly. Some months later, he becomes seized again. Others ask him questions to discern who possesses him. Others tell the power possessing him to leave, pat the young man on his back, and lift hands over his head. Another possession drives him into the forest late at night, but he is intercepted just before he enters a river infested with crocodiles. Since he is far from home, the identity of the spirit possessing him increases uncertainty. This type of situation calls for the assistance of a diviner.

The diviner is invited to the home of the afflicted person, and kinfolk sit around the sick person. The diviner is paid for his services. Kinfolk ask the diviner the name of his divinity, and they sing to it. After singing, the diviner begins to shake and feel pain, quiver and tremble, make strange noises, and breathe heavily because the spirit is awakening in his body. Oftentimes, the diviner prescribes a sacrifice be performed to cure an illness.

The Dinka person possessed directly experiences free divinities that make their presence known by causing illness, possessing people, and announcing through the mouths of the afflicted their names and demands. This sometimes occurs during dream states. Some dream states provide knowledge about certain facts that cannot be known in any other way because the divinity communicates with the possessed and through the afflicted to the wider community. Those possessed do not choose their divinities, but are chosen by the spirits. When the divinity Deng, a personification of rain and lightning, is within the body of an afflicted person, for instance, that individual becomes a meeting place where human and spiritual influences encounter each other and live their modes of existence.

Types of Religious Experience

The art of communication between the human and spiritual realms is manifested in the expertise of the diviner, a link between the two realms. In cases of possession, a person loses her personality for a time and assumes the persona of the spirit possessing her. The person possessed may even do bodily harm to herself.

There is evidence that experiences of ecstasy coincide with events such as initiation, rain rites, divination séances, and dancing. Ecstasy involves leaving one's body and society in order to eventually return to them. It is akin to death followed by resurrection. Among the Ashanti, religious experience is more individual than social in nature because a person is called by a spirit or god, which can come during celebrations and religious ceremonies. There are signs associated with a rupture from others that include experiencing convulsions and bodily trembling.

Among the Zulu, dreams are considered important instruments of communication between spirits and humans. These dreams are often accompanied by visions, which can be frightening, unclear, and incomprehensible. Because of the lack of clarity, the services and expertise of a diviner might be needed. A dream can function similar to memory that is lost and restored. By regaining lost memory via dreams, a person expands his identity, frees himself from the present moment, expands his boundaries, and opens new horizons. Dreams can also help a person regain former experiences.

In African cultures, dance can also trigger religious experiences. In northern Kenya, the Samburu, pastoral nomads, as well as the Venda of southern Africa, conceive of dance as a form of play and body language by operating as a metaphor for sexual relations. The Azande beer dance works to channel the forces of sex into socially harmless patterns. In some instances, dance is a means of achieving an ecstatic experience that literally transports dancers outside of normal society.

Suggestions for Further Reading

Berglund, Axel-Ivar. *Zulu Thought-Patterns and Symbolism.* Bloomington: Indiana University Press, 1976.

Douglas, Mary. *Purity and Danger: An Analysis of Concepts of Pollution and Taboo.* New York: Praeger, 1966.

Evans-Pritchard, E. E. *The Nuer.* Oxford: Oxford University Press, 1956.

———. *Witchcraft Oracles and Magic among the Azande.* Oxford: Clarendon Press, 1937; reprint 1972.

Heusch, Luc de. *Sacrifice in Africa: A Structuralist Approach.* Trans. Linda O'Brien and Alice Morton. Bloomington: Indiana University Press, 1985.

Mbiti, John S. *African Religions and Philosophy.* Garden City, NY: Doubleday & Company, Inc., 1969.

Middleton, John. *Lugbara Religion: Ritual and Authority among an East African People.* Washington, DC: Smithsonian Institution Press, 1960; reprint 1987.

Middleton, John and E. H. Winter. Eds. *Witchcraft and Sorcery in East Africa.* London: Routledge & Kegan Paul, 1963.

Peek, Philip M. Ed. *African Divination Systems: Ways of Knowing.* Bloomington: Indiana University Press, 1991.

Pelton, Robert D. *The Trickster in West Africa: A Study of Mythic Irony and Sacred Delight.* Berkeley: University of California Press, 1980.

Ray, Benjamin C. *African Religions: Symbol, Ritual, and Community.* Englewood Cliffs, NJ: Prentice-Hall, Inc., 1976.

Turner, Victor. *The Forest of Symbols: Aspects of Ndembu Ritual.* Ithaca, NY: Cornell University Press, 1967.

———. *The Drums of Affliction: A Study of Religious Processes among the Ndembu of Zambia.* Oxford: Oxford University Press, 1968.

———. *The Ritual Process: Structure and Anti-structure.* Chicago: Aldine, 1969.

———. *Revelation and Divination in Ndembu Ritual.* Ithaca, NY: Cornell University Press, 1975.

Van Gennep, Arnold. *The Rites of Passage.* Trans. Monika B. Vizedom and Gavrielle L. Caffee. Chicago: University of Chicago Press, 1960.

Zuesse, Evan M. *Ritual Cosmos: The Sanctification of Life in African Religions.* Athens: Ohio University Press, 1979.

5   Hinduism

In the distant past, a gigantic serpent enveloped the world causing thirst, hunger, cold, and death. The gods could not help because they were incapacitated and incarcerated by this powerful serpent, Vritra. Unless this serpent was defeated, life was threatened with extinction. The gods brokered a deal with Indra, a warrior deity, to defeat this huge serpent in order to free themselves and release the cosmic waters necessary for life. But Indra was an astute bargainer and extracted a pledge from the gods that he would become their champion after he was victorious. Because they possessed no bargaining leverage, the gods agreed to Indra's central demand. In order to invigorate himself for the cosmic confrontation upon which the fate of the world depended, Indra drank three vats of *soma*, an intoxicating liquid that also had hallucinogenic properties and was used in a priestly sacrificial cult. After a vicious confrontation between Vritra and Indra, the deity is victorious when he splits open the head of the monstrous serpent and the cosmic waters are released.

This bloody and violent creation myth is contained in a body of texts called the Rig Veda, a sacred body of literature written in Sanskrit (literally, "well-formed" or "perfect"), preserved orally for many centuries by families of priests. Scholars have combed this body of sacred hymns for information and hints about early life in India. The narrative of the violent confrontation between Vritra and Indra not only explains the god's rise to pre-eminence in the pantheon, but it also helps to explain the way that room (space) was made by the defeat of the demon, representing the separation between being and non-being, which leads directly to the establishment of the cosmic law that governs everything.

Without the cosmic law (*rita*), there would be chaos and no regular pattern to the cosmos or human life. Even the gods are subject to this cosmic law, unity, and righteousness that supports everything and gives to each entity, from an ant to an elephant, its structure and nature. This law is necessary on the social level to avoid immorality and disorder, and the sacrifice operates because of this inherent law connected to truth and reality. By following this law, humans are established in truth, and achieve a fuller and more harmonious life.

After the successful completion of his violent action, Indra is called the All-Maker. His action is not, however, without an important flaw, because Indra does not annihilate evil for all time. This means that demonic beings continue to exist, especially at night and under the earth. The flawed result of Indra's heroic and victorious action entails that human beings must continue to sacrifice and worship the gods. In short, humans need the gods for protection and continuance of life, while the deities need humans to sacrifice to them in order to sustain their power, creating a mutual giving relationship between two unequal parties that need to cooperate in order to sustain human and divine existence. This kind of mutual generosity is a theme running throughout the history of Indian religious culture.

Ancient Worldview and Divine Pantheon

According to another Vedic hymn, when the sky (masculine principle) rains upon the earth (feminine principle), the latter is fertilized, enabling the earth to support life. Between the sky and earth, there is the neutral atmosphere, which represents the ancient Vedic triple-structured world: sky, atmosphere, and earth, which is constituted by the cosmic law (*rita*). This world represents being, a place where gods and humans live on the earth's surface, possessing light, warmth, moisture, and governed by the cosmic law, whereas non-being is located below the earth in a realm subject to features that are the exact opposite of the earth and inhabited by demonic beings. The great danger to the earth is that the realm of non-being is a constant threat to it and life, which provides a rationale for the continued performance of the sacrificial cult, a way to ensure the continuance of human existence.

The triple structure of the world is also reflected in the pantheon of the divine beings. Besides Indra, different Vedic poets refer to either 303, 33, 3, one divine being, or even 3,003 divine beings. This confusing polytheism is rendered intelligible by its conformity to the triple structure of the cosmos, implying that many divine beings are more active in one realm than in another, although the god Agni, god of fire, is an exception by being active on all levels of the world in the form of fire on earth, lightning in the atmosphere, and the sun in the sky. Within the context of Vedic polytheism, the sky is the sphere of Dyaus, father of heaven; the sun deity Surya; Varuna, who is guardian of the cosmic order; Mitra, who is a constant companion of Varuna; Ashvins, who are described as golden and are harbingers of the dawn; and another solar deity, Vishnu, who is not well-defined at this point in history but is destined to become a major divine being in later Indian culture. The atmosphere is populated by Indra, Vayu or wind, and Rudra, an early manifestation of the later great god Shiva. Agni, god of the sacrificial and home fires, Soma, and various goddess figures, such as Prithivī and Aditi, dominate the earth. There are also other divine beings who play essential roles in the sacrificial cult, such as Vāc (power of speech), Brahman (power inherent in words), and Prajāpati, who is identical to the fire altar and plays a significant role in the ancient ritualistic texts.

The narratives conveying the exploits of these divine figures help outsiders to understand the ancient roots and significance of the idiosyncratic role of the cow within the culture at the present time. The cow's economic value dates to ancient Vedic religion, where it serves as a metaphor for fecundity, maternity, well-being, and beauty. In an ancient Vedic narrative, Indra frees the cows from a cave, symbolic of darkness and ignorance, where they were being held captive and allows them to roam freely, transforming them into symbols of light. Cows also become associated with the primordial cosmic waters and their life-giving powers, become symbolically associated with the earth goddess, and function as a symbol of the unity of life. The cow later becomes a symbol of Mother India. These historical features help to explain the free-roaming cow's significance for many Hindus today.

Ancient Sacrificial Cult

According to an ancient narrative, after Prajāpati's creative actions, his vital breaths leave his body and he disintegrates, needing the assistance of Agni, god of fire, to restore his body by building a fire altar consisting of five layers of bricks. It is upon such an altar that priests make offerings to the divine beings in the form of animals, grains, or *soma*, a drink of immortality. This divine elixir originates in heaven and is guarded by demonic beings, but Indra steals the so-called king of plants for humans and other gods when he is transported by an eagle to its location. The sacrificial drinking of *soma* enables a person to share in the divinity, sacredness, and immortality of the plant, enabling a drinker to also discover mysterious realms and become powerful.

Within the context of the sacrificial cult, various priests function as intermediators between the gods and humans, protecting an individual sacrificer from committing fatal errors by performing the many intricate steps of the sacrifice correctly and reciting sacred *mantras* (formulas) to overcome any mistakes. The fire god Agni also plays an important role by bringing the deities to the sacrifice and taking the sacrificial oblations to the gods. As the sacrifice is executed by the participants, a unity is created among all parties, everyone returns to the source of existence that is identified with the sacrifice itself, everyone participates in the divine power, all are thereby maintained and reinvigorated, and all participants engage in the ongoing process of creation and re-creation of the world. The cosmic significance of the sacrifice is evident by the three fire-altars and the sacrificial stake that symbolically represent three levels of the cosmos. The ritualistic texts stress the importance of repeated sacrifices and necessity for generous gifts to priests for their services.

Sacrificial gifts in the form of food, animals, and land possess a binding force that bonds the giver and recipient. By offering a gift to a priest, the giver disperses herself throughout the world and enters into a procreative union with the elements of the universe. Moreover, since the sacrifice controls everything, to know the sacrifice is to know and control the universe from the perspective of the priests. If the priests depend on the sacrificial cult for their subsistence, what does the patron gain from a life of sponsoring sacrifices and generous giving to priests? The sacrificial patron can gain wealth, power, health, and long life. Wealth is associated with many sons, cattle, and plentiful crops. After death, a patron could look forward to immortality in heaven.

But what mechanism makes the sacrifice effective? A threefold answer is given by the ritualistic texts: The cosmic law (*rita*) governs its operation; *brahman* represents the power inherent in the sound of the *mantra* (sacred formulas or words) repetitively uttered in Sanskrit, a sacred language that is a sonic reproduction of the structure of reality throughout the universe; and the natural power of *tapas* (heat), an entity created by the gods, is the link between the physical (external actions) and mental (interior attitude or faith of participants) aspects of the sacrifice. Therefore, sacrifice represents three things: the truth, a source of knowledge, and reality. Both patron and priest sought to be near this power and to participate in it as much as possible.

Pre-Vedic Period and Vedic Literature

Before the advent of the Vedic literature, there existed the Indus Valley culture (flourished from 2500 BCE to about 1500 BCE) in the northwestern region of India. Two major towns of this culture have been discovered and excavated: Harappa, associated with a river of this name, and Mohenjo Daro (Mound of the Dead), about 350 miles away. For the ancient time period, these were impressive cities, supporting an urban culture of over 40,000 inhabitants.

These locations had a sophisticated drainage system that included internal toilets, garbage chutes, a street sewer system, uniform building bricks, and storehouses for grain. The culture developed a writing script that has not been deciphered to this point in history. The importance of bathing for inhabitants was suggested to scholars by the large pool at Mohenjo Daro.

Archeologists have found terracotta figurines and stones that resemble the male phallus, which might suggest the importance of fertility for these people. Seals depicting humans, domestic and wild animals, and plants have also been unearthed. An especially intriguing seal is a figure seated in a yogic posture wearing a head piece with apparently two horns surrounded by various types of animals. Some scholars have identified this figure as a prototype of the later ascetic deity Shiva, while others view him as a priestly figure. Whatever the correct interpretation of the evidence found by archeologists, the Indus Valley culture began to suddenly decline between 1800 and 1700 BCE for unknown reasons, although some have conjectured about possible floods, drought, epidemic, or military invasion.

Whatever the reasons for its decline, the Indus Valley culture was slowly forgotten and replaced by possibly wandering Indo-Aryan tribes that gradually migrated into the region of northwest India from central Asia through the mountain passes of Afghanistan around 1500 BCE, conquering the indigenous people. This scenario is disputed by other scholars, who argue that Indo-Aryan culture is an outcome of the Indus Valley culture, forming the foundation for the Aryan or Vedic culture that developed later. This contrary position is allegedly supported by evidence of painted gray ware associated with Indo-Aryan culture and indigenous cultures of the area and the lack of archeological evidence related to migrations into India. Other scholars attempt to undermine this scenario by pointing to technology of the migrants. A third position suggesting mutual cultural influence over an extended period represents another possibility.

Whatever the truth about the development of Indian culture in ancient times, there is no disputing the growth of the Sanskrit language that embodied the narratives of ancient India. This language would become the means of communication by the social elite and preserved by a priestly caste. Thus, its narratives tend to present the viewpoint of the more powerful and influential parties of the society.

Even after the development of Sanskrit as the elite cultural language, stories were not written down for hundreds of years, with communicators preferring oral means of transmission. This meant that sacred texts were memorized using a complex method to assist memorization and ensure accuracy. These sacred texts were believed to have been revealed to sages by divine beings. The sages, who were able to touch with their mind and/or heart a deep, mysterious force, were believed to possess an insight or ability to recognize concealed truths. After hearing the messages, the sages preserved the hymns in their memory and passed them on orally to future generations. Due to concerns about inaccurate memory during the passage of time, the revealed hymns were written in order to better preserve them. Because of their divine origin, the Vedic hymns gave unchallenged authenticity and authority compared to other types of literature.

In summary, Indian religious literature is distinguished according to its origin and whether it is revealed (*shruti*) or remembered (*smriti*). Indian classical literature is divided into two major portions:

I. Divinely revealed literature (*shruti*) that does not have a human author. It is rather that which is heard.
   A. Four Vedas
      1. Rig Veda: composed 1200–900 BCE
      2. Yajur Veda: composed 1200–900 BCE
      3. Sama Veda: composed 1200–900 BCE
      4. Atharva Veda: composed 900 BCE
   B. Each Veda contains four sections.
      1. Samhita
      2. Brāhmaṇas: composed 900–700 BCE
      3. Āraṇyakas: composed 700–400 BCE
      4. Upanishads: composed 700–400 BCE
II. Remembered literature (*smriti*) that is not divinely revealed and represents traditional wisdom.
   A. Dharma Sutras: composed 600–200 BCE
   B. Mahābhārata: composed 300 BCE–300 CE
   C. Rāmayāṇa: composed 200 BCE–200 CE
   D. Purāṇas: begin to be composed in 400 CE

Formative Religious/Philosophical Concepts

An inquisitive student goes to his teacher for instruction to inquire about the nature of ultimate reality. The teacher asks him to bring a fig, divide it, and tell him what he sees, to which the student replies, fine seeds. The student is then asked to divide one of the seeds and to tell his teacher what he sees, to which he replies that he sees nothing. The teacher draws the lesson that from this fine essence a huge fig tree arises, and it is from such a subtle essence that the world and the student originate. This is reality that is identical to the student, representing the eternal self of the student identical to ultimate reality.

This narrative dialogue is a typical type of encounter in the Upanishads, a term that suggests sitting near a teacher to receive secret teachings in an intimate and personal relationship in a place apart from society such as the forest. There are some 108 (a sacred number designating wholeness) Upanishads, although thirteen are considered primary and historically the earliest. The Upanishads are called Vedānta (end of the Vedas), implying that they represent the deepest secrets of the Vedas and the culmination and perfection of Vedic thought. These influential texts discuss notions basic to understanding the human situation (e.g., time, rebirth, karma, illusion, ignorance, and liberation), nature of the self, and ultimate reality.

Time, rebirth, and karma are interconnected notions. From the human perspective, time is a mysterious and unpredictable agent of suffering, birth, and death and is responsible for the evolution and involution of the universe. For the Upanishadic teachers, time is cyclic, with an inconceivable beginning and end. This powerful force is imagined to be all-inclusive and endlessly rolls onward in a cyclic pattern. Time is also generally conceived to be destructive, with its six seasons representing its mouths that swallow up creatures. Moreover, time is analogous to a winged horse that carries people away, a noose that binds people, a wheel that ceaselessly revolves, or a power that cooks creatures in a process of ripening them in order to be fit to be swallowed by death.

The cyclic nature of time embodies rebirth or transmigration, which is the cycle of birth and death. According to the earliest Upanishad, the soul is analogous to a caterpillar that passes from one blade of grass to another, suggesting that when the soul, which does not vanish at the death of the body, comes to the end of its life-long journey, it leaves the human body and proceeds to another. And it is the inexorable law of karma (law of cause and effect) that determines what type of body—higher or lower—it inhabits. A good way for a student to conceive of this process is to grasp rebirth as a kind of energy, such as an electrical current or like a bundle of forces fluctuating within an electromagnetic field, with positive and negative charges that are equivalent to good (positive) and bad (negative) charges.

It is karma, conceived as an unshakeable shadow, that determines a person's next mode of being because it is the cause of rebirth. Karma is also more broadly conceived as work, action, rite, performance, or the verb "to make." In the Rig Veda, it is commonly used to designate sacrificial action, although in the Upanishads it refers specifically to the law of cause and effect, which operates in two spheres: physical and moral. In the former sphere it represents a universal law to which everything is subject, whereas in the moral realm it refers to a personal code of conduct. Whatever actions we perform have inevitable moral consequences, implying that humans have the ability to become good or evil depending on their actions. In other words, by performing nothing but good deeds, a person becomes righteous, while evil deeds produce the exact opposite effect. This notion means that any act performed creates a karmic residue that can be meritorious or its opposite. When a person dies his un-activated karmic residues determine what type of body it will have and then passes onto the new body. In this new body, karmic residues determine three fundamental things: the type of body (e.g., human, animal, or insect), the length of life of this new body under normal circumstances, and the affective tone (pleasurable or painful) of experiences a person will have during the life of her new body. There are three types of karmic residues: previous residues whose maturation occurs in a person's present life, residues that will mature in another life, and those that will be produced in the present life and also mature during this life. A helpful way to think about karma is to imagine that it is an arrow in flight that contin-ues until its energy is exhausted unless something, such as premature violent death, obstructs it. The law of karma suggests that an individual can shape her own destiny and make herself.

This entire cycle of time, rebirth, and karma represent the sphere of illusion (*māyā*), according to some Upanisadic sages. From its early meaning associated with a god's or demon's ability to produce illusory effects, to change form, or to appear under deceiving disguises, *māyā* comes to suggest that which is unreal in the Upanishads. When applied to the world, *māyā* implies that the world is unreal because it is temporal and changing, and empirical experiences of humans are only an appearance and nothing of an enduring nature. If reality is singular (Brahman) and the world is dependent upon it, everything else besides reality is relative and dependent, meaning that the world that we per-ceive is unreal (*māyā*). The failure to recognize the true unreal nature of the world is analogous to the proverbial narrative of the three blind men who are placed at different points of an elephant and asked to describe what they feel. Grasping the tail, the first blind man says that it feels like a rope, while the sec-ond man feels the side of the animal and replies that it is like a wall. The final man grasps the elephant's trunk and says that it is similar to a tree. The three blind men of the narrative represent all humankind, who are unable to see things as they are or in their whole. Moreover, humans cannot find reality and certainty within the world, which is characterized by fragmentation, unreality, and uncertainty.

Directly connected to the unreal nature of the world is the notion of igno-rance, which obscures the real nature of the world. The *Katha Upanishad* (2:1–5) compares ignorant humans as living in the midst of ignorance, think-ing of themselves as wise when they are not, wandering about deluded, and led by blind men who are themselves blind. By mistaking the relative things of this world (e.g., wealth and desirable objects) for something real or absolute, humans manifest an entire attitude toward life that is grounded in ignorance, which contributes to our future rebirth status. It is this ignorant attitude that causes our bondage within the world, where humans are captive to what is ultimately unreal. This situation is analogous to wearing glasses with distorted lenses that give humans an incorrect and/or distorted view of the world. When the correct lenses are inserted into the frames of the glasses, humans are able to see the world with genuine insight. If the distorted lenses cause humans to perceive the world dualistically, a prescription for correct lenses helps humans see that reality is one.

The inability to see the underlining unity of everything is also illustrated by the anecdote about the person who sees a snake in the road at twilight and becomes frightened. When the object does not move, the person examines it more closely and discovers that it is a rope and not a snake. Upanishadic sages draw a lesson from this episode: The person encountering the object in the road superimposed the idea of "snake" upon it and was frightened by it, but this notion of a snake was falsely superimposed on it. In order words, there never was a snake, and falsely superimposing the idea of snake over a benign object reflects a person's false knowledge and ignorance. Thus, ignorance must be removed in order to correctly grasp reality, a condition called *moksha* (liberation, release, freedom).

In ordered to be liberated from the cycle of time, rebirth, workings of the law of cause and effect (karma), and ignorance, a person must gain knowledge in order to transcend this cycle of suffering. Are mathematical, scientific, or humanistic types of knowledge necessary for liberation? These types of knowledge are certainly useful but are limited to the empirical world and do not transcend the confines of this realm. Release from the limitations of the world is only possible when a person achieves knowledge of the single reality, Brahman, because by coming to know Brahman, a person becomes Brahman. From the perspective of an analogy, a person's goal is to transform himself from a person who sees many trees or a single tree but is now able to see the entire forest, which means to see the all in Brahman. What is such a person's condition after arriving at this type of knowledge? Such a person possesses no desires because there is nothing more to desire and knows everything because he knows the only unchanging reality. According to the *Maitri Upanishad* (7.6), the released person is not subject to distress, sickness, or death because such an individual attains the all. For the liberated person, the stream of time ceases, which means that rebirth also comes to an end. Karmic energy is burned in the fire of knowledge. Since a liberated person continues to live, what happens to their future karma? This situation is comparable to water that is splashed on the leaf of a lotus flower and simply flows away without clinging to it. In a similar fashion, future karma does not cling to someone who is liberated.

The process of liberation does not occur after a person is dead, but it rather happens while a person is alive. This person is referred to as being liberated while alive. If a person does not achieve liberating knowledge during life, such a person is simply reborn according to her karmic residue. This process of rebirth continues forever until a person attains the necessary knowledge, which also suggests that faith does not play a major role, with the exception of a few texts. The liberated person is desireless, fearless, sorrowless, and painless regardless of the fact that such an individual lives within the world, but the liberated one is not structured by the world, because such a person lives simultaneously in time and eternity. Free of doubt, incapable of evil, and possessor of complete knowledge, the liberated person simply lives out her life. After the death of the body, the liberated person is able to reach a permanent and eternal state beyond the pain and flux of the world. What ultimately makes liberation possible is the nature of the self and ultimate reality from a theoretical perspective.

The Self and Ultimate Reality

According to a revealing narrative in the ancient *Chāndogya Upanishad* (8.7–12), the deity Prajāpati instructs two students who have come to him to learn about the true nature of the self: the demon Virocana and the deity Indra. Prajāpati's initial instruction is that the self is identical to the embodied self in the condition of wakefulness. The demon is satisfied with this answer and happily returns to the demons with his knowledge, which is imperfect, as Indra is insightfully aware of, because the embodied self is subject to fear, old age, and death. Indra returns for further instruction, and Prajāpati leads him by a series of steps that take him through bodily, dream, and deep-sleep forms of consciousness to the final truth that the self is identical to the nature of self-consciousness. This ancient mythical narrative indicates that the self is not limited as are the body and mind, is neither subject nor object, neither knower nor known; rather, it is eternal. From a positive perspective, the self is being, consciousness, and bliss. Since it transcends the states of consciousness associated with wakefulness, dream, and deep-sleep, it is called the fourth, an inexpressible instance of pure consciousness. Beyond the flux of time, the self (*ātman*) is defined as self-luminous, timeless, spaceless, not subject to birth or death, but rather it is eternal, unchanging, and without origin. But the most important feature of the self is that it is non-different than Brahman.

The identity is expressed by an Upanishadic sage saying "That you are" to a student. This short formula embodies the central focus of the relationship between the self and ultimate reality (Brahman). The utterance "That you are" refers to the pure consciousness that underlies a human and the pure consciousness that is the ground of Brahman, suggesting that the pure consciousness of the self is identical to the pure consciousness of reality. If this is the case, it all seems very simple. What is the problem? The fundamental problem for humans that keeps them captive to the cycle of time is ignorance, a lack of liberating knowledge about the unity of self and reality. This situation is analogous to the self being like pure water beneath a dark film over the top of it. Since the pure water is always there, humans need to get rid of the dark film on the surface that hides the pure water. Once the film is removed by liberating knowledge, true awareness dawns, and one is free from all limitations.

Since there is a unity between the self and Brahman, what is affirmed about the self is also true of Brahman and vice versa. In the earlier Vedic hymns, Brahman is identified with the power inherent within words, verses, and hymns. Ancient Indians believed that the uttered word possessed a strange power that contained the essence of the thing denoted. Priests who knew the word were able to control the thing that was identified with the word. As ancient Indian civilization develops, Brahman is frequently extolled as the supreme principle by sages, seeking for the real or the underlying principle of the universe that they could control and thereby become powerful. There existed a basic cultural presupposition that there was nothing beyond the grasp of a knower, suggesting the magical power of knowledge.

If we recall the fine seeds of the fig tree, it is obvious that Brahman cannot be known by sense perception. In another narrative episode, a student is instructed to place some salt in a basin full of water overnight. The next day the student is asked to taste the water from different locations of the basin, and his answer is always the same. The teacher's point is that reality is like the salt because it is all penetrating and all pervading. Due to its mysterious and subtle nature, Brahman can be defined in three basic ways: positive definition, negative definition, or symbolic expression. A positive way to express Brahman is to assert that it is being, consciousness, and bliss. As an unconditional value, bliss means that to know Brahman is to know it as blissful. A negative way to define Brahman is to assert that it is not this and not that. In order words, it is indefinable because it lacks qualities, is impersonal, indescribable, and non-relational. It is indescribable because human conceptual forms cannot exhaust it, its impersonal aspect means that it exceeds both the finite and the infinite, and its non-relational character suggests that it is beyond all relations and yet is the ground that sustains all relations. Finally, it can be represented symbolically as OM, a sacred *mantra* that can be transliterated as AUM, representing waking consciousness (A), dream consciousness (U), and deep-sleep consciousness (M). Beyond the sound of the sacred syllable is the fourth (Brahman) that is partless, beyond empirical relations, the culmination of worldly existence, and non-dual. But finally AUM ends in an ever-remaining silence, or foundation of all sound, which is really the best way to express Brahman.

Path to Liberation

Achieving liberating knowledge sounds simple enough, but its simplicity is deceptive because there is an arduous path to be mastered beforehand. The outline of this path to liberation shapes later religious developments in India. An early account of such a path appears in the *Muṇḍaka Upanishad* (3.1.5) with the following fourfold path: truth, student's life of chastity, austerity (*tapas*), and knowledge. The notion of austerity (*tapas*), a notion that literally means "heat," is especially important and culturally suggestive because it can refer to both a natural heat, such as the heat of a fire or the sun, biological conception associated with embryonic maturation and birth, or sexual desire. Sages compare this natural heat to a hen and the heat that she generates by brooding upon her eggs. But this root meaning of *tapas* as a natural form of heat changes in the Upanishads to refer to the unnatural heat generated by asceticism. When an ascetic practices various forms of *tapas* (austerities), this process is analogous to intellectual brooding similar to that of a hen and a means of purifying oneself by kindling an inner fire of illumination by means, for instance, of practicing intense meditation and other forms of asceticism. The practice of *tapas* is directly related to spiritual rebirth, a process that is compared by sages to a snake that periodically sloughs off its skin. *Tapas* is also connected to achieving immortality, recalling the way a spider emits and draws in its thread and comparatively builds Brahman in the sense of realizing it.

Ascetic practice includes performing Vedic sacrificial rites mentally within oneself. *Tapas* can also take the form of more extreme practice such as lying on a bed of thorns or nails, hanging upside down over a smoldering cow dung fire, sitting under a suspended pot of constantly dripping water, continuously standing on one leg, vowing not to sleep lying down, going without sleep, and many other forms. These extreme forms of austerity are intended to train and control one's body and mind in order to achieve higher states of consciousness.

A by-product of such extreme forms of asceticism is the acquisition of certain powers that both are a result of such practice and render the ascetic a powerful and dangerous figure to ordinary people. These powers include knowing one's previous modes of existence, an ability to read the mind of another person, to become invisible, to make oneself heavy or light, to fly, to see into the future, or possess great strength. The dangerous nature of ascetic powers to others is illustrated in countless narratives. The epic literature tells the story of an ascetic covered by an ant mound discovered by a king and his army. The king spies two round objects prying through the ant mound that represent the eyes of the ascetic and pokes them with a stick, causing the buried ascetic pain and motivating him to curse the king and his army to become constipated and incapable of fighting.

Besides the path already cited, another example of a path to liberation is contained in the *Maitri Upanishad* (6.18) in the form of its six-fold yoga: restraint of breath, withdrawal of the senses, meditation, concentration, contemplation, and absorption. The aim of breath control is to manage the energy released by breathing by progressively decelerating respiratory rhythm in order to penetrate to higher states of consciousness that are normally hampered by common agitated and un-rhythmical breathing. Withdrawal of the senses involves freeing the senses from external objects with the purpose of becoming detached from them. Meditation continues the inward movement into one's inner self and makes it possible to penetrate objects. Fixing one's attention on a single point is the goal of concentration in order to quiet and calm the mind. The practitioner can, for instance, meditate on objects, one's navel, the heart, the tip of one's nose or tongue, a sacred diagram (*maṇḍala*), or a sacred *mantra* (formula), while contemplation refers to a process of reflection. Absorption refers to the unitive experience of realizing that one is the ultimate reality.

These Upanishadic means to liberation are supplemented and expanded by the *Bhagavad Gita*, a part of the larger epic *Mahābhārata* that assumes the form of a dialogue between the warrior Arjuna and his charioteer, Krishna, who is secretly god. During the course of the dialogue between these two figures, Krishna informs the warrior, who is torn between decisions whether to fight his relatives or not for the kingdom that they had usurped by unethical means. Krishna identifies three paths to liberation, and there is an attempt to unify these paths by the writer of the text: paths of knowledge, action (karma), and devotion (*bhakti*). The path of knowledge bears similarities to the path espoused in the Upanishads, while the path of action involves learning to perform deeds free of the binding effect of karma. In short, since it is impossible to live without action, humans can become free of the binding effects of their deeds by dedicating the fruits of all their actions to god. Finally, devotion (*bhakti*) involves surrendering oneself to god, faith in the redeeming power of god, receiving his grace, and salvation defined as a close relationship with god in a paradise. In contrast to some texts of the Upanishads, a follower of the message of the *Bhagavad Gītā* does not become absorbed into god or become god. The final state of salvation represents an intimate relationship between the individual and a personal deity. This represents the difference between a non-dualistic position of many of the Upanishads and the theistic devotional stance of the *Gītā*. In historical hindsight, the devotional position finds much greater appeal to the general public because it is much easier to practice, a person does not have to disrupt his life, and a person can remain within the world, living a normal life full of family, social, and work obligations. In summary, it is this devotional path that is the most prevalent form of religion in India today.

The *Dharma* of the Indian People

During the course of their dialogue, the deity Krishna explains to the warrior Arjuna in the *Bhagavad Gītā* his reason for incarnating himself on earth. Krishna tells the inquiring warrior that he comes to earth from time to time to restore the *dharma*, a term meaning that which maintains, sustains, or supports something that is often translated as law, order, or righteousness. If the term is applied to the universe, it signifies the physical laws that maintain the world, but it is also a term that can mean the order inherent in the nature of things. Thus *dharma* pertains to the physical and moral/ethical world. In the latter realm, it signifies a person's social obligations and duty as a member of a community. Resting on an impressive body of literature, the *dharma* represents the totality of duties for a person or society according to one's caste and state of life. As embodied in this body of literature, *dharma* represents an attempt by sages to organize Indian life.

An influential *dharma* text is the *Laws of Manu*, which opens with a creation myth, relating a narrative about the original primordial darkness, emerging of the Self-existent Lord, dispelling of the darkness, pouring forth his semen, and creating a golden egg, where he is born as the deity Brahmā. After living in the egg for a year, Brahmā split it open and created the world, gods, mind, and body. He also distinguishes right (*dharma*) from wrong (*adharma*), gives creatures pleasure and pain, and bestows a nature on each animal, which allows animals to act as they do. This narrative suggests that the external universe and the interior of creatures are endowed with their particular *dharmas*. If we examine *dharma* metaphorically, we discover spatial metaphors used to express it, such as path, boundary, and departure. Therefore, *dharma* is staying on the right path or within prescribed boundaries along with a direct injunction for everyone to uphold it because it is the right way to live within the boundaries of society.

According to the *dharma* texts, there exist four sources of the law: Veda, tradition, good custom, and conscience. These four sources mean that all *dharma* rests on revelation, a feature that gives it a transcendent character. To affirm that it is founded on tradition suggests that it is based on memory. Good custom refers to the way good people behave in, more specifically, a religious life that is orientated toward the acquisition of spiritual merit, and a conscience shaped by a religious way of life completes the sources.

Being grounded in these four sources, the systematic organization of human life includes defining the four ends of human life, which reflects a realization that humans possess complex personalities that seek to be fulfilled through four channels: personal instincts and natural desires, craving for power and property, anxiety about social security and progress, and the urge for spiritual liberation. The four ends of life that fulfill these four channels are the following: end of acquiring things; end of pleasure and love; *dharma* in the sense of the whole of religious and moral duties; and release (*moksha*). These four ends are not considered contradictory by Indians, even though a superficial survey of them might give a person such an impression. The initial three ends of life are called pursuits of the world, whereas the final end (*moksha*) is an attempt to transcend the world, such as the path pursued by ascetics and yogis.

Recognizing that there are different types of individuals and different physico-psychical stages in a person's life, the four stages of life represent the ethical organization of an individual's life. The four stages of life can be conceived as a planned exertion grounded in the three debts owed by everyone from birth: debt owed to the gods, debt to the seers, and debt to one's ancestors. These fundamental debts are paid by following the four stages of life, identified as student, householder, forest-dweller, and renouncer.

The life of the student begins with initiation between the ages of 8 and 12 and can last for twelve years for the highest caste members. The student's life is characterized by learning, obedience, submission, and celibacy. The life of the householder begins with marriage, when a person's concerns turn to family, vocation, and community. It is the householder stage of life that is the foundation and support for the others. The stage of forest-dweller begins with retirement, when, theoretically, a person's worldly duties are fulfilled, and one takes the time to ponder the meaning of life. Finally, the renouncer represents someone who takes a step beyond the stage of retirement and assumes a meditative and ascetic mode of life. This figure becomes totally detached from the world and assumes the lifestyle of a wandering holy beggar. Such a detached and world-forsaking person is compared to a wild goose, which possesses no fixed abode.

An essential aspect of the Indian *dharma* is the caste system, a complex social system. In a late Vedic hymn (10.90), a primal human being is sacrificed, and castes originate from the various parts of this primordial man's body: from his mouth come the Brahmins, from his arms emerge the warriors, from his thighs originate working people, and from his feet come the servants. Since the body is hierarchically ordered in Indian thought, the members of the highest caste emerge from the upper part of the primal person's body down to the lowest caste, a term that originally connoted color, which may have distinguished the light-skinned Aryans from the darker-skinned indigenous peoples.

The four main castes represent the ethical organization of social life. From a theoretical perspective, castes are not allowed to compete with each other, and members of a particular caste possess a specific nature fitting for their caste affiliation; and it is one's caste that helps a person achieve her nature. The nature fitting members of the Brahmin caste is knowledge associated with rites, sacrifices, and scriptures, functioning as the custodians of the intellectual and spiritual heritage of the culture and administering to the spiritual needs of the people. Priestly caste members have often combined their religious duties with political advice to rulers. Members of the warrior caste are the ruling group who perform the executive functions of state, defend it, and serve as the guardians of social power. The third caste consists of business people and farmers who are responsible for the economic functions of the society by enhancing commerce and providing for the sustenance of the people. The final group is engaged in service and labor types of occupations. This last social group, which includes the largest number of Indians, is called once-born, whereas the initial three castes are called twice-born because they receive birth from their mothers and another birth at their initiation at the beginning of their formal education by their teacher. This means that the once-born are excluded from the initiation ceremony, as are the so-called Untouchables, traditionally the lowest members of Indian society. There are also many subdivisions within the four major castes, resulting from changes of occupation, migration, political, economic, and social factors.

On the village level of Indian culture, the proper name for caste is *jāti* (literally birth), which is geographically and linguistically limited with distinct customs, dress, diet, and behavior. A *jāti* can be conceived as a micro-social grouping, while a caste is a macro-social system superimposed on the village system and arranged hierarchically. The hierarchical ranking of these *jātis*, a self-governing group responsible for its members' behavior and punishment for violations of social norms, determines how members can interact with others and under what circumstances. A person does not normally marry outside one's *jāti* and does not eat with members of higher *jātis*, and members of the upper groups do not accept food from those below them in social rank.

The cultural rationale for such social restrictions is the opposition between pure and impure that forms the principle for social hierarchy. In practical terms, this means that impurity or pollution, a by-product of a systematic ordering and classification, represents a danger to oneself, one's family, and to a lesser extent to other members of one's caste. As members of a caste strive to maintain purity, they have two major options: to perform domestic sacraments, sacrifices, and approved means of purification usually associated with water, while the second means of maintaining purity is to assiduously follow caste regulations, especially those connected to dietary procedures.

Restrictions on the transfer of food between castes depend on the type of food. There are no restrictions on raw food, although cooked food involves numerous restrictions because it is considered imperfect. A staple such as rice is considered imperfect and vulnerable to impurity because it is cooked with water, while perfect food is a product fried, for instance, in butter, a product of the revered cow that sanctifies any food cooked with it or other cow products.

Besides food regulations associated with the caste system, traditional Indian society demands that a person is obligated to marry within one's *jāti* because of concerns for the social identity of children. The observance of marriage regulations means that castes separate themselves from one another and maintain distinctions. There are, however, two categories of inter-caste marriages: when the father is superior in caste status to the mother, which implies being in conformity with the natural order and literally "following the hair," whereas cases in which the father is inferior in status to his wife are considered literally "against the hair" or contrary to caste norms. Although only the first type count as genuine marriages, the status of the children in both cases is considered inferior. There are other types of restrictions, such as having a common ancestor within a certain number of degrees on the sides of both parties. Traditional Indian marriages are arranged by parents, attempting to secure a positive result by marrying their children to good families. Once a possible match is found, families rely on the services of an astrologer to determine if the match is in harmony with the forces of the universe.

The caste system and its inherent inequality has been the object of considerable criticism by Western commentators. During the nineteenth century in India, indigenous reforms called for the end of the system and its injustices. Economic and communicative interaction made necessary by contemporary life in which people of diverse social backgrounds interact on a daily basis make the maintenance of caste regulations difficult to observe and enforce. It is safe to predict that many caste observances will continue to be compromised in the future because of economic and other changes occurring in India.

But from the internal perspective of traditional Indian culture, the caste system has functioned in positive ways despite the external criticism. From the perspective of the upper caste Indians, the caste system has provided a fixed social setting for an individual that comforts a person by giving him some security, because one cannot be removed from one's caste unless one violates its standards. Thus, a person inherits a defined position in society and a constant body of associates to control his behavior and contacts; it also determines to a large degree a person's general occupation. The stability afforded by the caste system means that it possesses the ability to promote cultural patterns, define to a large extent the status of each caste in relation to each other, to integrate Indian society and its often incompatible groups, and to function as a political stabilizer.

Despite its ancient roots, caste is not a static and timeless social system; it has always been a changing social phenomenon, with caste rankings changing and varying according to location. In different regions, caste assumes different forms and meanings, depending on local history and geography.

Origin of Hinduism

The complex sacrificial cult, myths, epic literature, religious/philosophical concepts, cultural *dharma*, and priestly religious and social dominance came to be called Brahmanism and not Hinduism. In fact, early Indians did not refer to themselves as Hindus but rather used terms reflective of community or caste to identify themselves. The term "hindu" can be traced to a Persian word designating the river Sindhu from the time of the invasion by Darius I around the fifth century BCE. The term for this location came to be applied to an entire people but later changed to "Indos" for the river and "Indikoi" for the inhabitants of the region by the invading Greeks in the third century, from which are derived the terms India and Indian, meaning that terms intended to identify Indians originated with foreigners. Moreover, the term "hindu" was used by invading Muslims in the eighth century and was gradually adopted by the indigenous people to distinguish themselves from Muslims. Thus, Indian and Hindu are both of external origin and were not used by indigenous inhabitants for specifically religious reasons. Even though Hinduism was a social construct by foreigners, natives of India began to recognize cultural and political advantages to be gained by having their own identifiable religion similar to Judaism, Christianity, Buddhism, Jainism, or Islam. This development was pushed further by conservative political forces during the nineteenth century advocating the term Hindutva (Hinduness) because its originators envisioned it functioning to unify the various socio-cultural groups that constitute the subcontinent.

An Explosion of Emotion and Sensuousness

Around the sixth century in southern India, numerous devotional poets emerged to compose works that sang the praises of their deities. An interesting female figure was Āṇṭāḷ (literally, "the lady"), who composed poems to honor Vishnu, a theistic deity famous for his many incarnations. According to legend, she was discovered under some leaves sacred to Vishnu by a Brahmin, who received a dream in which Vishnu told him that he preferred flowers offered by Āṇṭāḷ. According to her hagiography, Vishnu arranged for the pair to get married. At the conclusion of a bridal procession to the local temple, the poetess merged into the icon of the god in the temple and disappeared. The poetry of Āṇṭāḷ, who was one among several poet-saints who helped to spread devotion to Vishnu, was preserved along with poetry of other figures and is used in temple rites and festivals today in southern India. A similar development occurred among devotees to Shiva, a deity of interesting contrasts as, for instance, a yogi and householder. These poets and their emotional poems expressed a desire to be possessed by the deity or to possess the divine being. Their emotionalism could be extreme, going to the extent of suggesting that the devotee was mad, an idiot, or possessed. Throughout the poetry of these figures, the many manifestations of god are stressed, along with his unity. The emotionalism of these poets was contagious and swept toward the north, representing a religious devotional revolution that overshadowed Brahmanism, swept away Buddhism as a viable religious option for the greatest number of people, and became the predominant form of Hinduism.

Although devotionalism can be traced back to the Vedas, it represented a new religious energy with new practices and beliefs. The Sanskrit term for

devotion is *bhakti*, which expresses a personal relationship with god characterized by love. Besides its intense emotionalism, it is regional in the sense that
local languages and music are used to sing the praises of god. There is within it
more of a sense of equality in the path of devotion because distinctions based
on caste, age, and sex are obliterated in comparison to Sanskritic Brahmanism,
and it is considered an easy path open for everyone in a benighted, degenerate,
and evil age when it is very difficult to save oneself by traditional means, such
as the sacrificial cult or asceticism.

Devotional Hinduism is very sensual, a feature that is illustrated nicely by
the practice of *darshan* (literally, seeing the sacred). This practice is a common
rationale for a devout Hindu to visit a temple to see the icon of the deity,
which triggers a twofold seeing: The visitor sees the image of the deity and is
seen by the deity. This mutual seeing is a form of communication between the
two parties, enabling a visitor to express feelings, participate in what is seen,
know the other, and touch the other with one's eyes. By seeing the divine
image, a devotee receives the deity's blessing. *Darshan* extends beyond divine
images to include holy places and holy persons, which are often intertwined
with each other in the perceptual imagination of the devotee.

The earlier reference to the revolutionary nature of devotional Hinduism is
evident with the practice of *pūjā* (an invocation, reception, and entertainment
of god as a royal guest) in one's home or in a temple that tends to replace the
Vedic sacrifice, although the practice is grounded in ancient Indian norms of
hospitality that include providing a means to wash, satisfy one's hunger, and
a change of clothing, sharing entertaining stories, and offering a comfortable
place to sleep. In the case of *pūjā*, the image of the deity is the supreme guest
who receives a series of acts of service and respect. A typical *pūjā* service might
include anointing the image with unguents or sandalwood paste, perfumes,
incense, or flowers. The practitioner often waves a lighted lamp before the
image in a clockwise direction with the right hand because it is considered the
auspicious hand, a practice that in some locations of India eclipses the performance of *pūjā*. Before bidding the deity farewell or good night, the image is
circumambulated in a clockwise direction, and poetic verses are recited praising the deity.

Public *pūjās* associated and celebrated with festivals are used by wealthy
donors to assert political power, to display conspicuous wealth, and to express
and raise social status. In prior centuries, land owners have utilized public *pūjā* as
a means of authenticating themselves. The worship at these festivals is inextricably related with competition between wealthy families, local temples, towns,
and villages, with efforts exerted to create a grander and more elaborate celebration that enables one party to triumph over another. The competition focuses on
artistic, social, political, or a combination of these aspects of the *pūjā*.

The sensual nature of devotional Hinduism can include the erotic emotion,
as evident in the life of the female poet Mīrābaī, who was born as a princess
and gained fame by rejecting her husband for her real spouse, the god Krishna.
She refused to worship her new in-laws' deity, neglected her household chores,
and associated with wandering holy people until her exasperated in-laws

decided to poison her, but the poison turned into immortal nectar in her throat because of its previous contact with the feet of her chosen deity. Surviving to compose and sing devotional songs, she wandered like an ascetic. At the end of her life, she is said to have merged with the temple image of Krishna. Many of her poems are about the illicit love affairs between Krishna and the cowherd girls (*gopīs*) of the god's mythology, imagining herself as a *gopī* overwhelmed with love of god. Even more explicitly erotic is the poem of Jayadeva, the *Gītāgovinda* composed in 1170, with the illicit affair between Krishna and his favorite *gopī*, Rādhā, and vivid descriptions of their love-making, which turns the world upside down and makes time stand still.

In addition to the erotic poetry, devotional Hinduism was associated with a new body of literature, the Purāṇas (literally, ancient or old). This vast corpus of literature is characterized by five distinct topics: creation, re-creation, genealogies of gods, sages, and Veda, ages of the world and their regents, and genealogies of kings. There are around twenty major texts, with some extending to multi-volumes in translation. The Purāṇas began to be collected during the Gupta Dynasty from the fourth to the sixth centuries CE, a period of history called a Hindu renaissance, and preserved by Smarta Brahmins, meaning those Brahmins who observed *smriti* (remembered literature).

These rich texts present a new worldview from that of the Vedas, with their four ages called *yugas*, a term that derives from the throw of dice, suggesting that life is analogous to a giant dice game. The ages begin with a period of perfection and proceed to the current degenerate age. This degeneration of ages is symbolically expressed by a mythical cow that begins by standing on four legs until it reaches the final Kali Yuga, when it stands on one precarious leg, a scenario that implies that humans live in a dark age of conflict, quarrel, dissension, and war. The ages diminish with respect to length of time, which mirrors an increasing decline of virtue and an ability to perform good acts. At the end of the four ages, there is a minor dissolution of the world and a return to cosmic non-differentiation that is followed by a major dissolution before the cycle begins anew. In terms of space, the Vedic triple world is preserved but transformed into an egg-shaped cosmos of seven concentric spheres. India is located in the center of this worldview, with Mount Meru, home of the gods, serving as the center of India and central mountain of the cosmos, with its base narrower than its wider summit. In contrast to the world, there is no particular special location or precise number for the hells that are governed by Yama, god of death. It is believed that punishments are temporary because the inflicted pain is succeeded by inevitable rebirth.

Hindu Sectarianism

In the distant past, the demon Bali gained power over the world by practicing asceticism and proceeding to oppress its inhabitants. The demon encountered a dwarf one day who asked the mighty demon for as much land as he could encompass with three steps. The arrogant demon agreed, and the dwarf, an incarnational disguise for Vishnu, covered the earth with his first step, the heavens with his second step, and with no place for the third step the dwarf stepped on the demon's head, driving him into the underworld, where he now reigns. In another myth, an uncontrollable demon gains a boon from the god Brahmā for his success practicing asceticism. The demon requests that he could not be killed during the day or at night, could not be killed by a god, human, or beast, and could not be killed inside or outside of his palace. As the demon establishes a reign of unrighteousness, there is a need for a divine champion, and Vishnu incarnates himself as the man-lion within the pillar of the palace at twilight. Not being man or beast, not being inside or outside geographically to the palace of the demon, and appearing at an in-between time, Vishnu emerges from the pillar as the man-lion and rips the demon's body to shreds as he leaves his palace. These two myths are typical of Vishnu's concern for the plight of human suffering and the need to restore order by means of incarnating himself on earth to fight evil. At the end of the Kali age, he is expected to return riding on a white horse, destroy the invaders of India, and exterminate all heretics, especially Buddhists.

These types of narratives are instructive about the nature of devotional Hinduism because they say something about its spirit and its sectarian nature, with its division into three major sects: Vaishnavism (worship directed to Vishnu or one of his incarnations), Shaivism (worship of Shiva), and Shakta (devotion directed to one of several goddess figures, such as Durgā, Devī, or Kālī). Each of these major divisions has given rise to the development of religious schools of thought focused on one of the deities. Sectarianism stresses devotion to one deity to the exclusion of other divine beings, even though the other deities are acknowledged to exist. The other figures are just not one's personal deity. Thus Hindu sectarianism can be expressed paradoxically as polytheism with threads of monotheism running through it. It is not unusual, for instance, to visit a Hindu temple dedicated to one god but to also find many other deities represented with icons and being worshipped by devotees. The religious goal of devotionalism is to have a personal relationship with god in this life and the next one and not necessarily union with the deity.

The personal nature of devotional Hinduism is especially evident with devotion to Krishna, which helps to illustrate the playful nature of this type of religion. Krishna is the divine player as a child when he aimlessly crawls and steals butter and sweets from women, when as an adolescent he teases the female cow-herders and plays pranks on others, and when he destroys demons in a playful manner. The theme of play in the narrative of Krishna suggests that the gods are complete and desire nothing, although they continue to act. Divine play or sport is a purposeless, spontaneous activity that is not pragmatic but is a blissful and aimless display that dazzles, sometimes terrifies, and ultimately fascinates any observer. If an outsider were to ask: Why did god create the world? A devotional insider would reply that the world is god's playground, which is created in the spirit of divine play. Overflowing with divine bliss and creative power, the world does not demand that we withdraw from it but rather invites humans to participate in a cosmic dance in accord with Krishna's flute, which is an extension of his beauty, an anarchical instrument that breaks down social norms and habitual activity, and represents a call to surrender to him. Another element of divine play is an invitation to dance with Krishna in the so-called circle dance that is conceived as dancing in a circle around the god at the center and also having god dancing to one's right and left sides. Whatever the form of play, there is evidence that god does not act according to the laws of cause and effect, because to act in this way is to work, which is indicative of a shortcoming. Being by nature complete, Krishna plays and invites his devotees to follow his example.

Krishna devotees are given a chance to play during the annual riotous Holi festival during the full moon of March, representing the destruction of the secular order and its renewal. The social order is turned upside down, as is made evident by women beating men with canes and people throwing colored dye on each other, spraying each other with water, and drinking an intoxicant mixed with hashish or marijuana. In sharp contrast to other forms of Hindu religiosity, festivals are an affirmation of life despite suffering, failure, and death, representing a return to a primordial chaos in order to usher in renewal, a relieving of intense emotion, and an expression of joy. All the major deities play pivotal roles in other kinds of festival celebrations throughout the course of an annual religious calendar.

In contrast to Krishna devotion, a different spirit pervades Shaivism, as is evident in narratives of his adulterous character and ascetic nature. Arriving at the retreat of some ascetic sages, Shiva appears naked, smeared with ashes on his body, carrying a begging-bowl, an exposed penis decorated with black and white chalk and red chalked testicles. Driven mad with passion, the wives and daughters of the sages embrace him, forgetting their moral fidelity to their husbands and fathers. Similar to other gods and goddesses, Shiva destroys demons such as Adi, who was difficult to defeat because he won a boon that protected him from being killed if he did not change his shape. Seeking revenge for the death of his father by Shiva, the demon surreptitiously entered the god's palace in the form of a snake and then assumed the form of Shiva's wife. Disguised as the ascetic god's wife, Adi inserted sharp teeth into his vagina, but when Shiva returned to hear his wife tell him that she was driven mad by passion, he recognized a hoax. Fixing a thunderbolt to his penis, Shiva killed the demon when it exploded in the artificially constructed vagina. These types of narratives illustrate the phallic and erotic character of the god.

Various Purāṇa texts describe Shiva as androgynous, a feature that is symbolically expressed in temples by the *liṅga* (phallus) and *yoni* (vagina), representing a paradoxical relationship because the *liṅga* rises out of the *yoni* and does not enter or penetrate it. The *liṅga* and *yoni* represent an iconic form of the deity that is a focus of worship throughout India. The symbolic significance of this iconic representation of Shiva can be traced to a narrative that describes the yogic god absorbed in a trance. A goddess fails to arouse him from his meditation, and he does not notice that she takes the shape of a

Figure 5.1 Krishna playing his flute in the classical three bends posture. Photograph by Carl Olson.

foul-smelling corpse. Then the god takes the form of a *liṅga*, while the goddess takes the form of a *yoni*, and she places the *liṅga* within her as she plunges into the cosmic waters to create. This narrative suggests that the active part of the act of creation is played by the goddess and that both figures are co-creators of the universe.

Besides his *liṅga* iconic form, Shiva is often depicted as the lord of dance, holding a drum in his upper right hand (furnishing the rhythm), a flame in his upper left hand (the final cremation fire), his lower right hand makes the fear not gesture, and his lower left hand points to his raised foot, which represents refuge and salvation. Under his other foot is a demon-dwarf that is being crushed. His face wears an intoxicated smile because his thoughts are absorbed in himself, and the icon is surrounded by a ring of fire that signifies the sacredness of existence and the destruction of ignorance. He wears a male earring in one ear and a female earring in the other, symbolically signifying his androgynous nature. Within his hair are located the sun, moon, a plant symbol, and a symbol of the Ganges River, while a cobra adorns his arm. This dancing god icon signifies the five basic activities of the god: creation, maintenance of the universe, destruction, refuge, and release or salvation, while the dualities inherent in his nature suggest the complementary nature of the opposites and their fundamental unity.

In addition to Vishnavism and Shaivism, worship of the goddess or Shaktism is the third major sectarian division in Hinduism. In the mid-nineteenth century, Ramakrishna, a mad priest of a temple dedicated to the goddess Kālī, received a vision of the goddess on the banks of the Ganges River. He saw the goddess rise from the river as a beautiful woman, give birth to a child, turn into a horrific hag, throw the infant into her gaping mouth, and proceed to eat it. The priest was shocked and terrified by this vision. Nonetheless, this vision represents the two aspects of the goddess: mother and destroyer of life. Ramakrishna's vision of Kālī is typical of her subsisting on the blood, symbolic of life, strength, and vigor, offerings of victims. Religious texts testify to her constant association with death.

In a myth about her origin, she emerges from the forehead of another goddess and proceeds to destroy demons by grinding them with her teeth and howling and laughing as she decapitates the leaders. In another exploit, she assists with the destruction of Raktabīja, a demon with the magical power to instantly replica itself when a drop of its blood touches the earth. This demon is defeated when Kālī stretches out her mouth in order to drink its blood, thereby killing it. In a third narrative, Kālī is the patron goddess of a band of thieves whose leader decides to offer a human victim to the goddess to induce her to give him a son. When the icon of the goddess perceives the saintly nature of the intended victim, she emerges from the image and beheads the leader and his followers, drinks their blood gushing from their severed necks, becomes inebriated from the blood, and, with her attendants, sings and dances while simultaneously playing catch with the severed heads.

This horrific goddess is called the "black one" because of her dark color. Kālī is depicted as naked and immodest, inhabiting the fringes of society, such as the cremation grounds surrounded by jackals, snakes, and ghosts. She holds a sword in one hand, a noose in another, a freshly severed head, and half a human skull that is filled with blood. She is adorned with a garland of human heads around her neck, newly cut hands hang from her waist, and two dead infants form her earrings. These ornaments enhance in a horrific way her physical appearance with sagging breasts, a sunken belly, disheveled hair, large fangs, sunken reddish eyes, and the ever present lolling tongue. Kālī suggests to an outsider something frightening, awesome, and terrible, but to an insider she embodies a primordial being that cannot be circumscribed.

To an insider like the poet Ramprasād (1718–1775), Kālī is a mother figure and saving power. Ramprasād re-interprets her terrible features into something beautiful by juxtaposing the grotesque and the graceful. According to his poetry, Kālī is the mad mistress of a mad world that needs to be saved. Ramprasād refers to the world as a lunatic asylum and heaven as a fair of lunatics presided over by a mad goddess intoxicated with love for all beings.

Besides her popularity among some Bengali poets, Kālī becomes associated with Shiva as his spouse, a role in which she functions as his *shakti*, feminine energy, and active, creative principle of the universe. There are narratives depicting her dancing on Shiva's naked, prostrate body and bringing the god to life as her energy flows into him. There are paintings that depict this scenario with Shiva opening an eye, lifting his head, and his phallus rising as symbolic of the beginning of creation. As Kālī evolves, she also becomes associated with Tantra and its radical religiosity.

In addition to pan-Indic goddesses like Durgā, Kālī, and Shri Lakshmī, consort of Vishnu, goddesses play a very significant role in village life, where they serve as protectors of these small communities up to the present time. Just as no two villages are identical because of ethnic, linguistic, and caste constitution, village goddesses are also different, although they share some common characteristics, such as a concern with agriculture, fertility, wells, animals, marriage, and childbirth. The local goddess figures function as guardians of the villages and their inhabitants, but their influence does not extend beyond the boundaries of the village, a location where it is possible to discover beliefs in ghosts, malevolent spirits, and witchcraft. In some villages, the guardian goddess is Māriamma, goddess of smallpox, cholera, and plague, whose residence might be represented in the village by a stone or tree. The goddess is both the cause of the disease and the disease itself. When a person contracts smallpox, for instance, villagers conceive of the pustules as the teeth of the goddess that she uses to devour her victim. The disease is compared to the goddess becoming hot and making her victim overheated. Pots of water and sugar are strategically placed on the top of the house and under the bed of the victim in order for the goddess to cool herself.

Indian Culture and Women

During the ancient Vedic period of Indian culture, women found themselves locked into a patriarchal society that was life-affirming, family-oriented, and dominated by priestly and warrior classes. The major goals of life were personal desires for progeny, prosperity, and longevity. Women played essential roles in the society, helping males achieve these goals along with offering assistance maintaining social and cosmic order. If the various Vedic sacrifices were connected to maintaining cosmic order, a wife was essential in this role because she and her husband formed a ritual team. In fact, there were sacrifices that were performed only by women that were related to fertility of the earth, a good crop, and husbands for their daughters. However, if a woman was menstruating, she was forbidden to engage in ritual activity because of the cultural conviction that blood is polluting, which places women at a distinct cultural disadvantage. Even though education was restricted for women and mostly confined to domestic duties and responsibilities, there is evidence of some women becoming scholars, poets, and teachers. Despite these exceptions of learned women, most females reached their life's purpose by becoming a mother, a position that has always been highly revered in India.

Traditionally, marriage has been considered the cornerstone of Indian society and religion. In addition, marriage was considered a sacrament and functioned as an initiation for women into adulthood. Another cultural presupposition with respect to marriage was that its purpose was the production of children, especially for males, because the oldest male child was responsible for conducting the funeral rites for his parents. Sons ensured a kind of biological immortality for the father. It was also understood that pleasure associated with sexual relationships can be included as a legitimate goal of marriage, but it is less important than its role as a duty and the propagation of children. Within this scenario, a woman completed her husband because it was only married males who were allowed to perform sacrifices. Husbands and wives were partners in ritual and mutually shared its benefits in the afterlife.

A curious cultural development occurred with the advent of the *dharma* literature because its legalistic minds established the inferior status of women, even though negative attitudes toward women were evident in other bodies of literature. The polluting nature of menstrual blood made women impure for a time each month, which meant that they could not eat with their husbands or cook for them. Women were imagined to be of a lower status than men, which meant that they were subordinated to males throughout their lives. A young girl, for instance, was under the control of her parents. As a wife she was subordinate to her husband, and as a widow she deferred to her sons. Despite the negative cultural image of women and their captivity to the patriarchal social system, they enjoyed high status in Indian culture as mothers, which implies that barren women were considered to be cursed.

The ability to produce children was only part of the cultural model of an ideal wife, a model that presupposed virginity before marriage. The ideal wife was devoted to her husband, protective of him, loyal to him, and sub-missive to him, although the foremost duty of an ideal wife was to obey her husband and to honor him as a god. A wife should get permission to leave the house and interact socially only with family members, holy men, or a physician. A wife was also expected to dress herself in a decent manner. For single-minded devotion to her husband, an ideal wife was rewarded with renown in this life and was reunited with her husband in the next life. The future of an unfaithful wife was portrayed as an especially negative rebirth in her next life.

The epic *Mahābhārata* contains a narrative about Draupadī, who was a polyandrous wife of the five Pāṇḍava brothers; she was cured by a hunter she encountered in the forest who wanted to seduce her. Her faithfulness to her five husbands gave her real power, and because of her power the hunter fell dead. The epic literature relates tales of other powerful women because they have fulfilled the role of the ideal wife. Savitrī rescued her husband, for exam-ple, from the land of the dead, and Gāndhārī was believed to have enough power to burn the entire cosmos.

The power of women can also be traced to their dangerous sexuality. This powerful force was imaginatively associated with a woman's tumultuous sexual drives, being at the mercy of these insatiable sexual appetites, and being una-ble to control themselves. Because of this powerful force, women were threats to the spirituality of men by their ability to divert men from the spiritual path in order to fulfill their own sexual drives. It was commonly believed that only strict control and sexual satisfaction by means of the institution of marriage can channel the dangerous sexual instincts of women. In this sense, the pro-cess of marriage and domestication was created to neutralize women because they constituted a threat to the social and moral fabric of the culture. Within the context of upper caste households, some families practiced seclusion of females, which involved confining them to a particular part of the home that was set apart for only their use and apart from males. From an historical per-spective, the Hindu adoption of this practice might have been influenced by the arrival of Islam between the twelfth and thirteenth centuries, with the intention of protecting women.

Women could enhance their status and influence by taking vows, which enabled them to empower themselves to some degree and gain a bit of per-sonal autonomy. These vows represented a voluntary promise to do something if their wish was fulfilled by a deity. Typical vows involved the well-being of another person—children and/or husband—for health or long life but were never taken with the intention of harming someone. Many vows were accompanied by fasting and sexual abstinence, which give women control over their bodies, promote mental and physical purity, and gain peace of mind and auspiciousness. Vows were often accompanied by ritual art created by women at the thresholds of their homes, consisting of abstract forms with intricate geometric lines and space with the purpose of inviting auspicious-ness into their homes.

If married life represented a happy time for a woman surrounded by her children, widowhood was an unhappy, unlucky, and inauspicious period of life. There was a social stigma associated with widowhood because a woman was considered somehow responsible for her husband's death. Widowhood was marked by dramatic bodily symbolism, such as having her head shaved, no long wearing the red dot mark on her forehead signifying her married status, not wearing jewelry, and being expected to walk barefoot. This bleak and joyless mode of life motivated some women to commit *sati* (immolation on her husband's funeral pyre). A widow ideally declared her intentions to commit the act with her own free will, although, in some locations in India, families of the deceased husband applied social pressure on the widow to prove her status as an ideal wife. Besides proving herself to survivors, a widow purified her husband of bad karma and became a powerful figure in the popular imagination with the ability to curse others and prohibiting certain types of female dressing customs.

Despite the overall traditional status of women, the Hindu religious tradition is marked with numerous holy females exhibiting extraordinary profiles of spirituality. To cite one example, Mahādēviyaka, a holy woman from the devotional Viraśaiva tradition, claimed that the deity Shiva was her true husband. After her jealous husband tried to interfere with her worship of the god, she became a wandering naked ascetic and wrote devotional poetry revealing her amorous feeling for her deity. To cover some of her nakedness, she let her hair grow long, although she referred in her poems to wearing the light of god. Her poems were about love in separation, unitive love, and how her love of god drove her mad.

Dance, Music, and Art

The sensual and narrative features of devotional Hinduism are also evident in various forms of artistic expression as that found in dance, music, art, and temple construction. When humans dance in India, they imitate deities such as Krishna, Shiva, and Kālī. The diverse schools of Indian dance model their performances on religious legends and mythical narratives, enabling them to share these stories with their audience, which is probably a reflection of the origin of dance in temple-centered devotion. Indian dance also expresses a vital energy, a means to celebrate joy about something, to evoke certain emotions, and to bring people together as a community to observe some event. Dancers combine foot work, facial expressions, and elaborate hand gestures to convey a story. The entertainment and religious value of dance is evident, with temple dancers performing before the image of the temple deity similar to courtesans for an earthly monarch. Wandering troupes of richly costumed young boys dance, sing, and act out episodes from the lives of the gods Krishna and Rāma in the spirit of play. Overall, dance is considered a sacred activity and a means of access to the highest spirituality.

Figure 5.2 Icon of Śiva as Nataraja (Lord of Dance). Photograph by Carl Olson.

Dance is accompanied by music because the gods are said to be pleased by them. The goddess Sarasvatī, patroness of learning and the arts, is often depicted playing a stringed instrument. And musicians often worship musical instruments as the body of the goddess and treat them with respect. It is believed that the musician is not an originator of music but is rather its transmitter and preserver because the musician is a conduit through whom the eternal sound, which is identified with the highest reality or Brahman, is struck and becomes accessible to humans. Because of its direct connection to the highest reality, music gives people access to this reality. Within the context of devotional Hinduism, music possesses the ability to evoke the divine presence along with the ability to give ineffable joy, inner calm, and an experience of unity.

In the types of performance mentioned, mythical themes also dominate painting and temple sculpture. This art does not attempt to imitate or accurately depict nature because its primary focus is embellishment, or to depict nature as it should ideally appear. This is executed at first by the artist meditating, for instance, on an image of a deity described in art texts in order to gain a picture of the deity in the artist's mind, which is then copied by the artist in stone. There is thus a revelatory aspect to Indian art that seeks to express divinity, to enable one to transcend human limitations, to create heaven on earth by making the divine immediately perceptible, and to enable a viewer to experience *rasa*, an aesthetic, transpersonal bliss. The various artists and food contain and embody eight types of *rasa* (literally, taste, essence, or flavor): love, humor, sorrow, anger, heroism, fear, disgust, and surprise.

Temples and Pilgrimage

Although there were no temples during the Vedic period of Indian culture, they play a major role in Hindu devotional religion and the material aspect of Indian Hinduism. The Indian artistic spirit is expressed in temple architecture by rejecting the circle because of its naturalness in preference for the square because it represents a refinement of the natural and suggests the perfection of space. With the square for its basic form, the temple is a miniature of a structure from a divine world. The complex pattern of temple squares represents the spatial distribution of the gods of the Hindu pantheon. Temple architecture in the north also reflects microcosmic symbolism related to the layers that constitute a human body with the immortal *ātman* (self) located in the deepest interior of the layers. For temple architecture, this means that the innermost sanctum of the temple that houses the image of the deity is identified with the human self. This innermost sanctuary is called the womb-room because it contains the image or symbol of the deity, and directly above this room is the soaring tower. Other ascending towers suggest that the temple is modeled on a cosmic mountain located at the center of the world that connects the three cosmic regions—heaven, earth, and underworld. The door to the womb-room is carved with an image of the god, gate-keepers at the door-jams, a river-goddess or flowing water are carved into either side of the lintel, which functions to symbolically wash and purify the viewer, who then glimpses the image of the enshrined deity and, ultimately, the essence of herself.

In contrast to the mountain motif of the northern temple, the southern temple's overall conception and structure has a different impact on the devotee. Consisting of seven rectangular walls arranged concentrically, the temple faces south, and each of the gates is covered by a soaring pyramidal structure adorned with images of deities, which often tell stories. As a devotee moves to the interior of the temple and light grows dimmer, he has an experience of descending into his eternal nature.

At the entrance to many temples, Ganesha, elephant-headed son of Shiva, stands guard to protect the interior of the temple. Holding an ax, Ganesha demands that anyone entering the temples must offer her head to get past, which helps to protect the other gods. Ganesha is the paradoxical remover and creator of obstacles, which is the reason for Indian students praying to him for success on exams. This very popular figure is also associated with beginnings, which means that he is worshipped first in private and public ceremonies in order to guarantee success. In addition to these roles, Ganesha is the leader of his father's dwarfish denizens of twilight.

Temples are often located near places of pilgrimage associated with sacred cities and rivers, such as Benares and the Ganges River. Going on pilgrimage is a

Figure 5.3 Khajuraho Temple. Photograph by Carl Olson.

very popular religious activity in India in which anyone can participate, regardless of social and economic status. A sacred place of pilgrimage is a threshold between this world and heaven and can function to launch a person on a journey to heaven. It is believed that rites performed at sacred places of pilgrimage yield bountiful blessings, and a visit can also serve as penance for ethical transgressions. Many Hindus aspire to be cremated in the sacred city of Benares and have their ashes placed in the river because of its direct connection to heaven. A journey to a sacred site is not merely a matter of geography because it also involves an internal crossing within oneself, a pilgrimage of the heart that is associated with truth, charity, patience, self-control, celibacy, and wisdom. In summary, pilgrims become part of the Indian sacred geography, gain good karma or merit, expect rewards, and have a direct experience of the sacred, which can assume the forms of miraculous healing or inward transformation.

Philosophical/Theological Ways to Salvation

While popular practices such as worship of deities, visits to temples, festivals, and pilgrimage were being practiced by ordinary Hindus, an elite group of scholarly men pondered the fundamental problems of life and their solution. Several paths to release from the world were developed that often disagreed with each other. From a conceptual perspective, all Indian schools of thought are paths to salvation, according to members of these schools. Since Hindus have not traditionally distinguished sharply between philosophy and religion, the following discussion follows their lead on this point.

In retrospect, six orthodox schools of thought can be identified, with each representing a distinctive viewpoint: Nyāya, Vaiśeṣika, Mīmāṃsā, Sāṃkhya, Yoga, and Vedānta. These schools are considered orthodox because they accept the ancient Vedas as revealed scripture. The Nyāya and Vaiśeṣika schools are atomistic, pluralistic, realistic, and theistic and are concerned with theory of knowledge and logical analysis. They accepted an atomic theory of matter, a belief in the reality of the world, and a conviction about the plurality of selves and wanted to examine the fundamental categories of reality, and both accepted knowledge as the path to salvation. The Mīmāṃsā school focused on language because Sanskrit embodied the natural rhythms of the universe. The school advocated an identity in difference position that argued that philosophical categories coexist along with differences. The Sāṃkhya school upheld a basic dualism between matter and spirit, and release represented the realization of the misidentification of the self with matter. In short, this involved the self realizing its true nature. Incorporating the metaphysical dualism of Sāṃkhya into its thought, the Yoga school compiled and taught a series of ascetic and meditative exercises that opened the door to liberation. The Vedānta school developed in a few different directions: the non-dualism of Shankara (eighth century), the qualified non-dualism of Rāmānuja (1050–1137), and the unqualified dualism of Mādhva (c. 1238–1317). Non-dualism argues that Brahman is the only single reality, qualified non-dualism contends that the world, self, and Brahman are equally real and distinctive, and unqualified dualism says that there is a basic distinction between god, self, and world. These various schools enable one to recognize the rich diversity of Indian thinking. The messages of Vedānta and Yoga are still relevant in India and the West today. At the same time, these schools of thought embody and promote fundamental concepts identified in the ancient Upanishads, illustrating the continuity and change within Indian thought.

In distinction to those orthodox schools, there stands the path of Tantra, which represents several strands of thought conveyed in a secret tradition that influenced all of the previously discussed sectarian religious movements to some degree. Beginning in several geographical locations around 400 CE, Tantric thought and practice conceived of the human body as a microcosm of a macrocosmic universe, implying that whatever can be discovered in the universe can also be found in the body, such as the sun, moon, water, fire, and planets. The human body consists of a gross body that is accessible to one's senses and a subtle body that is not accessible to one's senses because it exists within the gross body. This perfect and unchanging subtle body is analogous to the universe, a perfect microcosm. By means of breath control, it is possible for a practitioner of tantric meditation techniques to stimulate the centers of the body and finally awaken the lowest center at the base of the spinal column, identified as the *shakti* (feminine energy) or *kuṇḍālinī*, which is usually blocked by a serpent figure. The techniques stimulate the *shakti* to rise up the spinal cord to the top of the head, where it unites with Shiva, transforming a person into an androgynous being and allowing one to regain one's original lost condition. The orthodox, or right-handed school, and the radical, or left-handed, types of Tantra (literally, that which expands knowledge) accept this metaphysical structure.

In order to speed up the process of liberation by stimulating the *kuṇḍālinī*, the left-handed school allows followers to partake of polluting things called the five M's because each item begins with the letter M in Sanskrit: wine, meat, fish, parched grain (probably an intoxicant), and sexual intercourse. The use of these forbidden things and action is intended to demonstrate the underlying sanctity of these things and to call into question preconceived prejudices about what is holy or profane. Within a highly ritualized context for the sexual part of the practice, experts advocate using a low-caste woman without knowledge of the technique, who is symbolically transformed into a goddess for the duration of the rite. The practice takes considerable preparation and control because the male partner must not ejaculate any semen, a counter-productive result. This basic intent is for the male to become aroused and then re-circulate his unspent semen through his body through the breath channels in order to awaken the *kuṇḍālinī* lying dormant and blocking spiritual progress. This type of erotic religiosity is scandalous to ordinary people and an intentional violation of social norms, which is the reason it is considered so powerful and dangerous. It is absolutely essential for a person to secure a *guru* (teacher) to guide him along this dangerous path.

Modern Movements and Figures

Distraught and at the end of his emotional endurance because his beloved goddess would not reveal herself, Ramakrishna, a nineteenth-century holy man, took the sword held by her icon in the temple located in a town outside of Calcutta with the intention of committing suicide, but his life was spared when the goddess manifested herself at the last moment. This holy man might suddenly pass into ecstatic trance states, behave like a child, demonstrate a fear of women and money, assume a feminine attitude at times, and behave like a mad person by demonstrating wide mood swings, acting demented, crying profusely, conversing with and feeding the image of the goddess Kālī in her temple, playing with his own waste, and assuming the role of various gods. His madness functioned as a sign of his holiness. Besides his strange behavior, Ramakrishna practiced life-long religious experiments: Tantra, devotion of the god Rāma, and Vedānta with a master. In addition, he received visions of the prophet Muhammad and Jesus. These religious experiences initiated a catholic attitude toward other religions that enabled him to conclude that all religions are true. From Ramakrishna's perspective, there is a harmony of religions. Although they are not identical, all religions lead to the same goal.

Inspired by his association with Ramakrishna, Swami Vivekananda became the organizer and founder of the Ramakrishna Math and Mission and later the Vedanta Society. At the World Parliament of Religion held in Chicago in 1893 in conjunction with the World's Fair, Vivekananda, a former law student, represented Hinduism, and his speech was positively received by the audience. After this successful event, Vivekananda proceeded to give lectures in America and to establish centers, which represented the first genuine Hindu missionary movement in the West, making Vivekananda a hero on his return to India.

The religious movement initiated by Vivekananda represented one type of response to the colonial domination of the British, which contributed to Indians feeling inferior. The feeling of inferiority was reinforced by Christian missionaries and their criticism of Indian civilization on such matters as child marriage, *sati* (immolation of a widow on her husband's funeral pyre), idolatry, caste system, and other social practices. These missionaries attempted to convert Indians to their version of the truth, but this effort resulted instead in the conversion of Hindus into reformed Hindus by stimulating Indians to rethink their past cultural tradition.

Among the early reformers was Rammohan Roy (1772–1833), who founded the Brāhmo Sabha, a monotheistic movement that developed into the Brāhmo Samāj (Society) when revitalized by Debendranath Tagore. With its focus on a single deity, the society wanted to recapture the ancient *dharma* and the pure theism located in the Upanishads that rejected image worship and advocated human rights. Influenced by Unitarian theology, Roy also rejected the caste system and widow immolation, notions such as rebirth and karma, and practices such as sacrifice and meditation. In 1829, widow immolation was made illegal.

In time, the organization split into conservative and liberal societies, respectively the Adi Brāhmo Samāj and the Bharatvarshiya Brāhmo Samāj led by Keshab Chandra Sen (1838–1884). The latter movement became more concerned with social issues. After a split caused by the marriage of Keshab's daughter to a maharaja and his perceived hypocrisy on the issue of marriage, his movement developed into the Sadharan (General) Brāhmo Samāj and his own Church of New Dispensation in 1897, representing an attempt to synthesize Hinduism, Islam, and Christianity. Keshab became associated with the Bengali holy man Ramakrishna and his religious experiments and spread the fame of the holy man through his newspaper.

Other reform movements stressed other issues, such as the status of women and Untouchables (now called Dalits, "Oppressed"). The Prathana Samāj led by Justice M.G. Ranade (1842–1901) was a good example of this type of society, while the Ārya Samāj was inspired by India's past and led by Swami Dayananda Sarasvati (1824–1883), who wanted to use the ancient Vedas as a guide and rejected post-Vedic developments as superstition. He denied the polytheism of the Vedas and insisted on a single deity behind all the divine names, although he accepted the notions of rebirth and karma and insisted that the caste system was a social institution and not a religious one. These convictions did not stop him from advocating women's liberation, the end of caste abuses, and cessation of conversions by Hindus to Islam and Christianity.

Forming a bond with the Ārya Samāj, the Theosophical Society, founded in New York by Henry Steel Olcott (1823–1907) and Helena Petrovna Blavatsky (1831–1891), made contributions to Indian culture in the nineteenth century by getting involved in the independence movement, in promoting social work, and in aspects of Indian culture. The society promoted Jiddu Krishnamurti (1895–1986) as the appearance of a World Teacher, which was analogous to claiming that he was a messianic figure. Krishnamurti was promoted by an organization called the Order of the Star in the East founded by Charles W. Leadbeater (1854–1934) and Annie Besant (1847–1933). After admitting that he was the expected teacher in 1925, Krishnamurti dissolved the order and renounced all claims to divine status in 1929. He caused a large loss of membership when he resigned from the Theosophical Society the following year.

The Synthesis of Religion and Politics

Confessing in his autobiography to being a shy, awkward, insecure, diminutive, and bookish individual, Mohandas K. Gandhi (1869–1948) overcame his shortcomings and emerged as a major figure in the struggle for independence of India from British colonial domination. His formative years were spent in an area of India heavily influenced by the Jain religion and its emphasis on nonviolence (*ahiṃsā*) to all living entities. He was also influenced by the *Bhagavad Gītā* and its discussion of nonviolence and the path of action. After various experiments with the truth as a young man, a trend that continued throughout his life, he returned to India after his education in England. His career as a lawyer got off to a rocky start, but he eventually secured a position in South Africa in 1893, where he witnessed the legal discrimination directed at Indian immigrants and experienced such injustice first-hand when he was thrown off a train after attempting to sit in a forbidden section. Embracing the cause of indentured laborers in South Africa, Gandhi led protests, gained the trust of victims, enjoyed some modest legal success, and became a hero. While in South Africa, he founded two experiments in communal living called the Phoenix Settlement and the Tolstoy Farm. The objective of these settlements was to produce a new type of human being within a self-supporting community.

During a trip to England in 1913, on his way home to India, he volunteered his service for ambulance duty during World War I. Upon his return to India, he became involved politically in various causes. He was arrested for calling for a work stoppage to protest some controversial legislation, which made him a national figure. More protests and arrests would follow after his call for civil disobedience. His practice of spinning and weaving cloth to help India become more self-sufficient was also part of a program of civil disobedience and nonviolence. During his rise to international fame, Gandhi assumed the guise of a Hindu holy man and became known as Mahatma (Great Soul) and affectionately called Bapu (Father). Gandhi used his ascetic religious persona and charisma to good effect during the "Quit India" movement in the 1940s. His religious persona did not deter a determined Hindu fundamentalist from firing three bullets into his body while he was walking with female companions in the morning; he uttered the name of god, Ram, with his last breath.

Gandhi's thought was grounded in his notion of truth, which he traced to being, and linked it to the moral order of the world, suggesting its indestructible nature. The truth may be singular, but humans live in a world of relative truths. Nonetheless, people must strive to realize truth in everything that they do and say. If humans hold on to the truth in a nonviolent way, they are practicing *satyagraha* (truth-force, soul-force), whose practice implied tolerance, endurance of suffering, and an obligation to accept just laws. Truth-force must be exercised openly and nonviolently, which includes renunciation to harm any living creature. It is also associated with love, charity, truth, and courage, and involves treating others like oneself, being non-attached, willing to suffer, patient, ethically rigorous, self-purified, and ready to die. These basic philosophical concepts form the foundation for social utopian ideals.

Hindu Missionary Movements

Inspired in part by the example of Vivekananda, various examples of guru-centric proselytizing movements became an important feature of Hinduism. A good example is Yogananda (1890–1952), who was cured of cholera as an 8-year-old by looking at a photograph of Lahiri Mahasaya, a holy man, and experiencing a very bright light that enveloped his body and his room. After his cure and education, he made his way to a conference in Boston and stayed in America to teach people *krīya* yoga, a form of science, in his mind, through his Realization Fellowship. In 1946, he published *Autobiography of a Yogi* with tales about his acquiring of powers, telepathic messages from his teacher, and ability to heal.

Another yogic movement was offered by Transcendental Meditation (TM), founded by Maharishi Mahesh Yogi, which became an international movement introduced as a cure and science to remedy the many problems of modern life. The founder stressed an easy technique that anyone could master, involving the control of one's breath to help a person realize Being, a latent power within a person. The practice of transcendental meditation enabled a person to become free from a relative state of experience and transcend ordinary modes of thinking.

There were other guru-centric movements that also enjoyed some success. Living in a cave for sixteen years and taking a vow of silence, Ramana Maharshi (1879–1950) communicated by gestures and his writings. He encouraged others to realize non-dualism and their true identity. A more flamboyant guru was Satya Sai Baba (1926–2011), who was believed to be an incarnation of a previous holy man in the region of Maharashtra. Known for his miracles and healing powers, Sai Baba was famous for producing sacred ash with the wave of his hand and dispensing it to his followers. In 1963, he announced that he was an incarnation of Shiva and Shakti, which is expressed by his name Sai (divine mother) and Baba (divine father). For his followers, his divinity was confirmed by his miracles. Another noteworthy figure is Swami Sivananda Saraswati (1887–1963) and his Divine Life Society, which is grounded in a non-dual philosophy that did not deter him from establishing monasteries, a hospital, and a university. He was convinced of the superior spirituality of Indian culture in comparison to the prevailing materialism of the West. Some guru types of religious leaders quickly appeared before disappearing, such as Guru Maharaj Ji, a young teenage guru and leader of the Divine Light Society, and Bhagwan Shree Rajneesh (1931–1990), who established a religious community in the small town of Antelope, Oregon, which was later renamed Rajneeshpuram, City of Rajneesh. It was not unusual to see the guru surveying his community in a Rolls Royce and disciples bowing as he passed them. This community was ended by internal scandals. Different types of scandals rocked the *siddha* yoga movement found by Swami Muktananda (1908–1982), who taught that a person could be awakened by her internal spiritual energy. This awakening is accomplished by the guru dispensing his grace to a person.

In contrast to Hindu missionary movements that emphasize meditation and yoga, the International Society for Krishna Consciousness (ISKCON) movement is more devotional in nature. In 1965, Swami A. C. Bhaktivedanta Prabhupada (1896–1977) arrived in New York without any money, but he managed to start a movement from a Second Avenue storefront on the lower east side of Manhattan, where he began to recruit followers from the counterculture of the period. Popularly known as the Hare Krishna movement, the founder stressed living in the degenerate kali age, the necessity for the development of Krishna consciousness to be saved, an austere lifestyle, Indian dress, mantra

repetition, and worship of Krishna expressed by devotional singing and dancing. The basic intentions of the practices and communal lifestyle are to fill a
devotee's mind with Krishna, awaken the soul, and return one to God.

In retrospect, Hindu missionaries were not the only export to the West. The abolition
of slavery in the West increased the pressure on nations to find inexpensive
sources of labor for fixed periods of time. In need of work, Indians were induced
to travel abroad to work as indentured laborers and took their religious culture
and social attitudes with them. This global diaspora led to problems of adjustment to new surroundings and customs. Organizations that enabled Indians to
share their culture with those in a similar condition became popular as they
attempted to preserve their identity in a strange place. Communal tensions
caused by caste observation were not unusual as well as internal family problems created over issues of arranged marriages in societies in which this was
not the case. The adoption by the younger generation of Western values also
caused internal problems in families between generations, with the older generation embracing an endangered cultural heritage and younger people turning away from the old ways, a saga that will continue to unfold into the future.

In retrospect, Hinduism is a way of life of rich diversity in language, customs,
ways of being religious, and spiritual experiences. It is even possible to cogently
argue that there is no such thing as Hinduism, which is closer to a convenient
label given to a wide variety of Indian religiosity. Lacking a founding figure like
some religions, Hinduism has no all-binding dogmatic assertions, no single
scripture is absolutely authoritative, no specific religious practice is obligatory,
no specific moral code is binding on everyone, and there is a lack of any single
unifying idea. It is polytheistic, but is more monotheistic to insiders devoted
to a chosen deity. There is no single mode of thinking, because some schools
emphasize empirical ways of knowing, while others stress intuition associated
with the practice of meditation. The advocacy of world renunciation by Hindu
holy persons exists alongside of world affirmation in various devotional movements. Consequently, there is no single valid intellectual or religious position
that is valid for everyone. From an insider's perspective, the wide variety of
thought and practice give one partial glimpses of the truths of the various
traditions, although some schools of thought claim to have definitive answers
about the nature of reality. What is conveniently called Hinduism is also characterized by extreme tolerance with respect to thought and belief, syncretistic,
expansive, receptive, elastic, and resilient.

Religious Experience

There is a richness of religious types of experience in Indian culture that is
truly astounding. The Vedic sacrificial cult must have given participants the
feeling that they were powerful because they could manipulate the sacrifice
that represented a universal secret and the origin of the world, according to
one Vedic creation narrative. It is the knowledge of this intricate sacrificial
system and the ability to manipulate reality that give one a feeling of power

that dispels impressions of insecurity and doubt. Ritual itself can shape and intensify experience because its sequential and repetitive patterns give one assurance that one is in harmony with the cosmos, which was created by a primordial sacrifice. Moreover, Vedic seers received visionary experiences that inspired their composition of hymns.

For the sake of simplicity, later Hinduism can be divided into paths of knowledge and devotion. The path of knowledge assumes the forms of different types of non-dualism (e.g., Advaita Vedānta) and dualism (e.g., Sāṃkhya-Yoga). The type of knowledge required for liberation is not knowing how to do something (e.g., changing the tire of a car), a knowing about something (e.g., the history and culture of a particular country), or knowing why something happens (e.g., motivation for an action or a cause for a disease), but involves an intuitive knowing that gives one wisdom about the nature of reality. Even though these experiences are ineffable, they give the experiencer an out-of-body experience, feelings of being in a state of trance, and/or an experience of unity. There is a tendency in the monistic and dualistic types of experience to lose one's personal identity in the ultimate reality. Nonetheless, the unitive experience in the case of monistic realities is described as blissful, which is a valuable and pleasant experience.

The devotional type of experience often occurs within the religious context of play, emotional excess, and erotic sensuousness. Devotional Hinduism encourages people to engage in the freedom of play, a purposeless, unfettered, unconditioned, and spontaneous activity. Play releases a person's emotions, which are variable. As an adherent plays within the context of Hindu devotionalism, a person might give rise to one or more emotions: (1) repose, calmness, and peace; (2) humility and obedience; (3) friendship; (4) love; (5) erotic love. These various emotions are constituted within the devotional context through interactions between humans and divine beings and humans with other humans. These various emotions are forms of *rasa* (meaning juice, sap, or liquid) that refer to the flavor, taste, or essence of a lived experience. Oftentimes, devotionally associated emotions are triggered by a feeling of the presence of a deity, or it is possible that an adherent feels like he is possessed. It is also not unusual to witness devotees driven to tears of sorrow at separation from their deity or tears of joy when in an intimate relation to their deity. Moreover, devotion to a deity can lead to serving the divine being, or it might involve complete surrender to the deity or being driven mad by the deity.

Suggestions for Further Reading

Babb, Lawrence A. *The Divine Hierarchy: Popular Hinduism in Central India*. New York: Columbia University Press, 1975.

Chapple, Christopher Key and Mary Evelyn Tucker. Eds. *Hinduism and Ecology: The Intersection of Earth, Sky and Water*. Cambridge: Harvard University Press, 2000.

Davis, Richard. *Lives of Indian Images*. Princeton: Princeton University Press, 1997.

Doniger, Wendy. *On Hinduism*. New York: Oxford University Press, 2014.

Eck, Diana L. *Darshan: Seeing the Divine Image in India.* Chambersburg, PA: Anima Books, 1981.

Eliade, Mircea. *Yoga: Immortality and Freedom.* Trans. Willard Trask. Second Edition. Princeton: Princeton University Press, 1969.

Flood, Gavin. *An Introduction to Hinduism.* Cambridge: Cambridge University Press, 1996.

Fuller, C. J. *The Camphor Flame: Popular Hinduism and Society in India.* Princeton: Princeton University Press, 1992.

Harvey, Peter. *An Introduction to Buddhist Ethics: Foundations, Values and Issues.* Cambridge: Cambridge University Press, 1981.

Hawley, John Stratton. *At Play with Krishna: Pilgrimage Dramas from Brindavan.* Princeton: Princeton University Press, 1981.

Kinsley, David. *The Sword and the Flute: Kālī and Kṛṣṇa, Dark Visions of the Terrible and the Sublime in Hindu Mythology.* Berkeley: University of California Press, 1975.

Klostermaier, Klaus K. *A Survey of Hinduism.* Third Edition. Albany: State University of New York Press, 2007.

Kramrisch, Stella. *The Hindu Temple.* 2 Vols. Calcutta: Motilal Banarsidass, 1946.

Lipner, Julius. *Hindus: Their Religious Beliefs and Practices.* London: Routledge, 1994.

Michaels, Axel. *Hinduism: Past and Present.* Princeton: Princeton University Press, 2004.

Olivelle, Patrick. *The Āśrama System: The History and Hermeneutics of a Religious Institution.* New York: Oxford University Press, 1993.

Olson, Carl. *Indian Asceticism: Power, Violence, and Play.* New York: Oxford University Press, 2015.

———. *The Many Colors of Hinduism: A Thematic-Historical Introduction.* New Brunswick, NJ: Rutgers University Press, 2007.

Östör, Ákos. *The Play of the Gods.* Chicago: University of Chicago Press, 1980.

Parry, Jonathan P. *Death in Benares.* Cambridge: Cambridge University Press, 1994.

White, David Gordon. *The Alchemical Body: Siddha Traditions in Medieval India.* Chicago: University of Chicago Press, 1996.

———. *The Kiss of the Yogini: "Tantric Sex" in Its South Asian Context.* Chicago: University of Chicago Press, 2005.

6 Jainism

Descending from heaven, a male child was placed in the womb of a lower-class woman only to be later removed before his birth from her womb to that of an upper-class woman named Trisala, who had had a series of dreams prophesying something unusual. This miraculous birth was initiated by Sakra, chief of kings and gods, who directed a divine leader to cast Trisala and her attendants into a deep sleep in order to execute the successful placement of the embryo into another woman. The rationale for this procedure was that Sakra did not think that great holy men should be born into families of low social class. Because the wealth of the family dramatically increased, the infant was named Vardhamana or "the increasing one." This child later became Mahāvīra (Great Hero) after turning to a life of asceticism, becoming a religious leader and a paradigm for those following him.

For thirty years, Mahāvīra (599–527 BCE) lived a normal life of a householder with a wife and daughter and indulged himself in the pleasures of the world. After his parents died and he had fulfilled his vow to them to not renounce the world as long as they lived, he felt free to ask his brother's permission to become an ascetic. His biography instructs a reader about his rationale for embracing renunciation: The gods requested him to propagate a religion for the world. In order to fulfill this request, Mahāvīra rejected his wealth, pleasure, power, and social position by leaving the world and assuming the ascetic lifestyle. Under the shade of an Aśoka tree at a nearby park, he tore out his hair in five clumps with his bare hands and entered the homeless life of an ascetic. A disputed point in the two major Jain traditions was when he decided to wander naked. According to the Digambara (sky-clad) sect, he abandoned his clothing at the time of his initiation into asceticism, while the Śvetāmbara sect argues that he became naked after thirteen months. Wandering naked like a cow and observing a typical ascetic lifestyle with respect to begging, the length of time one can stay in a village or town, and desiring neither life nor death, he wandered totally indifferent and detached from the world with an unperturbed mind. His wandering lifestyle was not without danger and hardship because he encountered violent people, social and sexual temptations, vicious dogs, cold and hot weather, flies, mosquitoes, thirst, and hunger.

These types of trials motivated his biographers to compare him to an elephant at the head of a battle. From the earliest period of Indian history, elephants have played an important economic, military, and symbolic role in the culture. Appearing on early seals from the Mohenjo-Daro civilization, elephants have been called the "animal with a hand." The Hindu deity Indra rode an elephant, which was also true of human kings, who could direct military operations from an elephant's back. Elephants are associated with creation myths and protect the eight directions against evil demons. From a symbolic perspective, elephants, walking rain clouds, are related to the coming of rain and fertility, which is especially true of white elephants like the one in the story of the Buddha's birth narrative, rendering the elephant a symbol of royalty, power, courage, and fecundity. Within the context of the martial imagery of his biography, Mahāvīra is victorious over his internal and external foes by virtue of the power of his ascetic regimen.

During his wandering, Mahāvīra sometimes invited persecution and suffering in order to consume the accumulation of negative karma on his person. Some of his ordeals were shared with Makkhali Gosāla, another wandering renouncer, who would later separate from Mahāvīra and led the Ājīvikas, a group of ascetics who believed that fate or destiny constituted the essential motive force of the universe, against which humans were helpless. This meant that spiritual bondage would last as long as it was fated, and humans could do nothing to alter their destiny. This materialistic sect affirmed that only matter existed and, thus, denied the existence of eternal souls and the prospect of life after death. Gosāla taught that the accumulation of old karma is fixed and must run its course, and ascetic practices have no influence on this past karma. Asceticism can, however, be used to obstruct the influx of new forms of karma, which means that it is only possible to prevent the influx of new karma. Gosāla's teachings were anathema to Jains and Buddhists, both of whom devoted criticism at this dangerous teaching. Nonetheless, despite their religious differences, Gosāla and Mahāvīra shared some adventures together, such as being thrown into a well for suspicion of being spies and being persecuted by uncouth inhabitants in West Bengal.

As part of his ascetic regimen, Mahāvīra observed a vow of silence, a practice rejected by the Buddha. The observance of silence can be traced back to the ancient Hindu sacrificial cult, where it was practiced by both the sacrificer and priests and was associated with wisdom in the Upanishads. But Mahāvīra's vow of silence was connected to his complete detachment from the world and his message that he was dead to the things of the world.

After following a wandering lifestyle for twelve years, Mahāvīra achieved supreme knowledge and liberation in the thirteenth year after his renunciation of the world while fasting, being exposed to the hot sun, and engaging in deep meditation. This highest state of intuitive knowledge was called *Kevala*, which is described as infinite, supreme, unobstructed, complete, and full. Having achieved this state, Mahāvīra was now referred to as a *Jina* (conqueror) and the last of the *tīrthankaras* (makers of the river crossing). The second term evokes the notion of life being analogous to a great ocean or river that needs to be crossed to attain liberation. Since this is a dangerous and difficult journey, only a heroic effort by a determined and courageous ascetic can achieve it. To overcome this river of pain and suffering, someone must build a bridge for others to follow, which is precisely what Mahāvīra accomplished, earning him the title of Great Hero. In a way similar to the Buddha, Mahāvīra returned to society to share with others what he had achieved and learned by building a bridge over pain and sorrow, and thus enabling others to traverse the bridge and win liberation. The term *Jina* (conqueror) referred to Mahāvīra's spiritual achievement and was adopted by followers, who called themselves Jains. The *Jinas* are not gods, but for ordinary Jains they assume the role of a god in a collective sense.

The Jain tradition does not consider Mahāvīra's achievement of liberation to be unique because he represents the twenty-fourth *tīrthankara* (ford maker) in their religious tradition. Mahāvīra's immediate predecessor was Ṛṣabha, an ascetic followed by Mahāvīra's parents and considered a cultural hero for teaching the arts of cooking, writing, pottery, painting, sculpture, marriage, funeral rites, and other such institutions and practices. This long tradition of twenty-four teachers suggests to Jains that their religion is eternal. The twenty-four *tīrthankaras* (ford makers) are also called *Jina*, an honorific term meaning conqueror, or Arhats ("worthy ones"), suggesting that they are worthy of emulation and veneration. This does not mean that the religion is monolithic, because regional and linguistic variations can be discovered along with differences in practices.

In its early history, Jains won support from the rulers of the Mauryan dynasty (third century BCE), which enabled them to endure and spread from northwestern India to locations in the center of the subcontinent and southern region. In addition to adopting some royal patronage, which was essential for

Jainism's acceptance by the laity and its longevity, Jains incorporated into their religion some royal symbols of the historical period. Jainism also appealed to the merchant class, which was conducive to financial support. Because of disagreements over the role of women, ascetic practices, scriptures, and different interpretations of the life of Mahāvīra, two major sectarian divisions developed, consisting of the Śvetāmbara (white-clad) and Digambara (sky-clad or naked). Based on the example of Mahāvīra's behavior, the former sect insisted on wearing white robes, whereas the latter sect stressed the necessity of nudity for its male ascetics. Both practices were intended to emphasize detachment from the world. The white-colored robes were culturally associated with death because white is the color of death, which evokes the ascetic notion of being dead to the world. In the seventeenth century, the Śvetāmbaras were split by the Sthānakāvāsīs because they rejected the prevailing practice of image worship. Within the Digambara tradition, there was a split caused by the Terāpanthīs in the seventeenth century over the institution of a monastery administrative monk wearing orange robes and having extensive interactions with the laity. This administrator's status as a genuine monk was called into question. During the same time period, the Bīsapanthīs accepted this figure as an authentic monk, along with the Digambaras of southern India.

Besides disagreement over the observance of nudity between the two major sects, they argued over the omniscience of the *Jina*, with the Digambaras claiming that he engaged in no worldly activity and no bodily functions (e.g., eating) and preached by means of a magical divine sound, whereas the Śvetāmbaras view the *Jina* as being involved in normal human activities while simultaneously enjoying omniscient cognition. According to the Digambaras, a woman possesses a body that makes it impossible for her to attain liberation unless she is reborn as a man. The Śvetāmbaras insist that a woman is just as capable as many men and can reach liberation. Another difference between the two major sects concerns the ascetic practice of begging. The Śvetāmbaras are comparatively more liberal because they allow a monk to carry a small pot to beg from door-to-door, to enter a house to eat, and to consume food two or three times a day. The stricter Digambaras do not allow a begging monk to carry a pot or a bowl, accepting offerings in the upturned palms of his hands, allow a monk to eat in a house, and restrict a monk to a single meal each day.

The Jain sects do agree that there is no God who created the world, but there is rather existence without beginning or end. It logically follows that there is no saving deity. The path to salvation is rather achieved solely by human effort. From a sociological perspective, Jains are part of the caste system, although they are not of it. In other words, Jains have traditionally accepted the Indian caste system, even though their literature does not recognize it. In everyday life, Jains organize into castes, marry into them, and observe various caste restrictions and practices. And yet the caste system possesses no religious significance for Jains, who are simply conforming to the social norms of the prevailing Hindu society.

Jain Worldview

From the Jain perspective, the universe is a vast organism, pulsating with life and pervaded by billons of souls, which are pure or capable of omniscient knowledge. In the Jain imagination, the universe is a gigantic human figure, which represents a macrocosmic organism comprising the celestial, earthly, and infernal regions, with the earth located at the level of the waist of the colossal being. Beneath this plane lies the region of hells, which are associated with the pelvic cavity, thighs, legs, and feet, whereas the area of the chest, shoulders, neck, and head represent the celestial region. At the crown of the dome, located at the internal hollow area of the skull, there is the area of supreme isolation (*kaivalya*).

This worldview is complemented by its notion of time, which is represented as a continual series of downward and upward motions of a wheel. There are two divisions of time: an initial golden age of perfection, with six ages or spokes, with the sixth spoke being an uneven age, and a second division that commences with the spokes being in the reverse order. During the initial unfolding of time, there is a gradual process of degeneration until the arrival of the sixth spoke, which is called the Kali Yuga, an evil, corrupt age that is a witness to the gradual diminishment of culture, religion, and human stature. All humans are currently living and suffering in this degenerate age, during which people become smaller, their life span becomes shorter, and truth and knowledge diminish.

During each motion of the wheel, twenty-four teachers appear in succession, which is a process that has occurred from beginningless time and will continue forever. This cyclical concept of time possesses important religious repercussions for Jainism, in the sense, for instance, that the *Jina* is not a founder of a religion but is rather a propagator of a truth and a path to this truth. Therefore, nothing new is taught, and the path to liberation always remains the same, which represents a vigorous argument for the antiquity of the religion.

Jain thinkers have identified three aspects of being in their attempt to depict reality that includes substance (a support for many qualities), quality (experienced as modifications to new and old modes that occur at each moment), and mode (that lasts only a moment and belongs to qualities). In this grasp of being, qualities are always undergoing change and yet reside forever in their substances, which form the ground of support for the qualities and their modes. Therefore, what exists is simultaneously a unity and multiplicity.

In addition, there are three categories of being: a sentient category, a material category, and those that are neither. The sentient refers to a soul that is characterized by consciousness, while the material designates atoms, which possess form, color, taste, and small size. Space, part of the third category, includes three aspects: motion, rest, and time. Space can either be described as having worlds or without worlds. Although both types are continuous and both are infinite, they are distinguished by an ability to provide a location for beings. Jains imagine that a soul and matter are like a fish moving through a water of motion, providing a medium through which movement can occur, whereas rest is comparable to the shade of a tree.

An essential aspect of the Jains' worldview is their understanding of the soul. Unlike indivisible and infinite atoms, souls have dimension and an uncountable number of space-points. Within occupied space, there are an infinite number of souls that exist within the physical limits of its current corporeal shape, which implies that a soul adapts to a particular body it inhabits. Whether a soul is huge or small, its space-points remain the same. This is comparable to a cloth that can be folded into various shapes. Thus the soul is changeable and bound to the world.

The soul possesses three main qualities: consciousness, bliss, and energy. Its most distinctive characteristic is consciousness, which enables the soul to become a knower by energizing perception and knowledge. Energy can generate a vibration of the soul that draws new karmic matter into contact with the soul, serving as a magnet for karma, and can cause modifications of karmic matter by the soul being drawn toward it. In short, energy is a soul's capacity to engage in giving, obtaining, and enjoying worldly objects. Bliss is experienced by a soul through self-knowledge. Although the soul is by nature pure, it can be defiled by other qualities that obscure or block it by means of obscuring karmas. In contrast to consciousness and bliss, energy functions as a meta-quality that is an abstract force.

Within the universe, souls (*jīvas*) or life-monads interact with non-souls (*ajīvas*) in a process called connecting or binding (*bandha*). The former are lighter and tend to rise, whereas the latter are heavy from the weight of karma and tend to sink lower. Thus the non-souls have no life-substance, and their karmic weight pulls down the life-monad that possesses an impetus to rise. These heavy and karmic entities need to be burned away on the path to liberation, enabling the individual soul to rise.

This overview of the soul suggests that humans can have knowledge about reality, but this knowledge is partial and limited. Therefore, a human cannot grasp the entire truth, meaning that no claim of knowledge is unqualifiedly true. The path to discerning the truth is similar to churning curds to get butter by a milkmaid holding a rope in one hand drawing one end taut and slackening the other. The tight end of the rope and the slack end of it means that any descriptions of reality are only partial.

Condition of Bondage

There once was a man who decided to seek a new life in a foreign land to free himself from his abject poverty. While on his journey, he got lost in a forest inhabited by wild animals. The poverty-stricken man became hungry and thirsty, and his situation became life-threatening when he encountered a charging elephant while simultaneously being attacked by a hideous, wicked demoness, who was laughing madly and brandishing a sharp sword right in front of him. Trembling with fear, he searched for a way to escape from his predicament, but the nearby tree was too high and its trunk unscalable. He spied a grass-covered well and leaped into the dark hole to escape and prolong his precarious life. As he leaped into the hole, he grasped a clump of reeds growing from its wall to support himself. Clinging to the reeds, he looked downward, only to see snakes at the bottom of the well. A huge, black, red-eyed python with a gaping mouth was ready to bit him if he fell. The impoverished man was convinced that his life would last only as long as the strength of the reeds lasted. Raising his head, he saw two large mice—one black and another white—gnawing at the roots of the clump of reeds, which constituted his life-line. In the meantime, the enraged elephant knocked over the banyan tree overhanging the well, which dislodged a swarm of bees. While being stung by the bees, a drop of honey fell onto the defenseless man's head and rolled down his face and onto his lips. Having received an instance of sweetness, the poor man forgot all about the dangers associated with his situation and began to crave more honey.

This parable was interpreted by Haribhadra, a seventh-century Jain thinker. According to Haribhadra, the journeying man represents the soul. His wanderings are the four types of existence in which the soul dwells: divine, human, animal, and insect. He interprets the elephant as death; the demoness is old age, and the banyan tree represents salvation. The well is equated to human life itself, whereas the reptiles are human passions that cause confusion, preventing a person from knowing what to do. The reeds are a person's lifetime, during which the soul is embodied in this form. The mice represent the weeks and months that destroy the support of life, while the bees are the many afflictions that torment a person, destroying every moment of joy. The python at the bottom of the well is hell, which seizes a person ensnared by sensual pleasure and inflicts countless pains. Finally, the drops of honey signify the pleasures of life that bind one to terrible suffering. This parable serves as a narrative depiction of the human situation and the difficulty of overcoming the state of bondage in which humans find themselves. It also suggests to a reader that bondage is real and not something that is delusional or simply attributed to ignorance.

In general terms, humans are responsible for their own state of bondage because of what they say, do, and think. The Jains believe that there is no difference between souls of animals, plants, and humans. Each soul is embodied by unspent karmic forces. At the end of each life, the soul departs its body and is reborn into another embodied condition that is determined by one's karma, which operates the process of rebirth. Karma is an inexorable law that implies that each person reaps the negative and positive results of his action. Karma is an impersonal, physical, universal law that operates automatically as the all-encompassing law of cause and effect. It reveals some resemblance to Newton's Third Law of Motion: For every action there is an equal and opposite reaction. But it is also a moral law that affects the soul when a person performs negative or positive actions.

The Jains conceive of karma as a material force that flows in every part of occupied space, a unique understanding of karma in comparison to Hinduism and Buddhism. Karma makes the soul impure by producing vibrations, which are identified as volitional activities that cause the influx of different kinds of material karma. These volitional activities are manifested through the body, speech, or mind, which represent three types of vibrations of the soul. The vibrations alone do not produce bondage but rather draw karmic dust to the soul, and the moisture of the soul enables karmic dust to collect on the soul. This moistening process involves passions, desire, and hatred. The amount of karma sticking to a soul depends on the degree of volition with which an action is performed, and the type of action determines the specific nature assumed by undifferentiated karmic matter. The only time that karma is ineffectual occurs with a dry or passion-free soul that is only true among omniscient, enlightened beings. Besides being compared to acquiring dust, each feature of the soul—physical, mental, and vocal—attracts karma to itself. This can occur intentionally or unintentionally, but when it does, karma degrades the soul.

The following question naturally arises for an inquiring mind: How long will karma cling to the soul? It depends on the degree of the passions that color the original action. When karma gives its result, it then falls away from the soul and returns to its undifferentiated state and into an infinite pool of free karmic matter. It should be noted that there is no actual contact between the soul and karma. If there was such contact, the soul would be material like karma. How does the coloring process operate? Karmic matter gives the soul one of six colors, which depends on the moral character of the act done. The color black is typical of merciless, cruel, raw people who harm others, whereas dark blue signifies someone who is roguish, venal, greedy, sensual, and fickle. The color gray is for reckless, thoughtless, uncontrolled, and irascible actions, while flaming red is for prudent, magnanimous, and devout behavior. Yellow or rose-colored stands for compassionate, considerate, unselfish, nonviolent, and self-controlled actions. The color white represents souls that are dispassionate, absolutely disinterested, and impartial.

Besides this process of coloring the soul, Jains also distinguish two types of karma. A primary type of karma (*ghātiyā*) has a direct negative effect on the soul by determining a soul's rebirth status at death, whereas secondary types of karma (*aghātiyā*) reflect the state and particular conditions of embodiment of a soul. The primary type of karma is related to what soul quality it affects by obscuring perception, knowledge, and energy and defiling bliss. The four secondary types of karma pertain to pleasure and pain of mundane experiences, those determining destinies and body types, those determining longevity, and those affecting environmental circumstances. A person's karma determines one's destiny into one of the major ends: gods, humans, hell beings, and animals and plants, with the lowest form of life, represented by submicroscopic creatures that possess the single sense of touch.

In order to escape the results of karma, it is essential that a person return the soul to its original state, called *kaivalya* (total isolation). In order to achieve this state, the sensual doors of the human body must be blocked to inhibit the influx of karma. The path to accomplishing this takes the form of a strict ascetic regimen. Jain thinkers compare this path to a large water tank that is blocked from any new water supply. With the water tank blocked from any influx of additional water, the contents of the tank will eventually dissipate due to consumption and evaporation because the water (karma) is not being replaced. This type of ascetic practice annihilates the old karma and stops the influx of any additional karma.

Path of Salvation

Because any person questing for salvation begins within the world and an embodied condition, the given world and the bodily needs for food and sex present various kinds of obstacles for attaining the goal of liberation. There are tales that illustrate the problem from the Jain tradition. The following story is a narrative about sexual temptation.

In order to trick a monk from his practice of asceticism, sixty-four *yoginīs*, semi-divine, erotic, female spirits, assume the disguises of religious Jain women. While lecturing to the group of women, the monk is warned by a female follower about the identity of the sixty-four women. The monk confirms this warning when he sees that the eyes of the sixty-four women do not blink, a sign of their semi-divine nature, which motivates him to cast a spell upon them. At the conclusion of the lecture, attendees arise and leave, but the *yoginīs* could not get up and acknowledge that instead of tricking the monk, they instead had been fooled. For an agreement not to harass any other Jain monks in the future, the monk restored them to their normal condition. Instead of creating an erotic atmosphere within which to seduce the monk and keep him from attaining his goal, the *yoginīs* were defeated by a more powerful force directly connected to asceticism of the monk.

The Jain path to salvation is probably best characterized as a way of self-reliance and self-discipline with the goal of awakening a vision or flash of insight. This does not represent a doctrine for the salvation of everyone or an escape from the world that is interpreted in utopian terms as the perfection or redemption of the mundane world. The goal is, however, a release from death and rebirth. The path to the goal is marked by faith that is grounded in the insightful experience into the true nature of the soul, which also enhances chances to learn from ordinary experience such as sense-based knowledge. Thus, this is not a blind faith in a scripture, person, or divine being. Besides awakening a person to the true nature of reality, the insightful vision possesses the benefit of suppressing karmic forces, although it does not completely eliminate them. Another benefit of the vision is to enable a person to cease identifying with her body and its actions. A person realizes that the soul's only pure and proper activity is intuitive knowing, which also gives her an inner peace that promotes pure conduct. A final benefit of the visionary experience is that it reveals the universal community of souls.

If we probe into the nature of the soul, we discover that there is an internal feature of the soul that motivates it to become free, making it an inert catalyst. This aspect of the soul is totally untouched by karma present in the soul, although it waits for the right time to be activated. Once this feature of the soul becomes activated, it redirects the energy of the soul away from delusion and bondage toward insight and freedom. Not all souls possess this feature, however, and thus cannot attain salvation. The Jains do not understand this aspect of the soul as representing a fatalistic teaching because the soul can manipulate karma and achieve a better rebirth in a higher realm. The only thing denied is liberation from the operation of karma and rebirth. And just because a soul possesses the necessary impetus toward liberation, this does not necessarily mean that it will achieve its potential, thus negating any notion of automatic salvation.

In order to stimulate the hidden aspect of the soul and move toward salvation, it is necessary for a Jain to follow a regimen of extreme forms of asceticism, which assumes the forms of external and internal practices. Withdrawing initially from the world, the individual engages in external and internal forms of asceticism. The external type of ascetic practices are fasting, abstinence, collecting alms, abstention from rich foods, mortification of the flesh, and taking care of one's limbs. Internal types of asceticism include expiation of moral and ethical transgressions, politeness, serving one's teacher (guru), study, meditation, and abandoning the body. This entire process is metaphorically expressed as walking on the edge of a sword, or is equated with a fire that purifies because the ascetic roasts himself by means of his asceticism, which is the source of the fire. Taking into consideration the role of clinging karma to the soul, this ascetic process is akin to a bird covered with dust that removes the dirt by shaking itself. This process suggests controlling the influx of new karma and the burning away of past and present forms of karma. This is an arduous process because the soul acts as a magnet for karma to attach itself to the soul.

This life devoted to extreme ascetic practices is best lived within the monastic context. Aspiring Jain ascetics enter a preliminary initiatory period, which is similar to a period of probation, enabling an ascetic to use his/her time to memorize essential texts. A senior monk presides over formal initiation into the order. Among Śvetāmbaras, a novice is given a new name, a pair of robes, an alms bowl, a whisk that is emblematic of nonviolence and a staff, and ascetics entering the Sthānkvārī and Terāpanthī sects are given a mouth-shield to cover that part of the face that might accidently ingest small insects or microscopic life forms. The Digambaras only give the initiate a whisk and water pot for personal hygiene and removable of bodily wastes.

A monk is guided in her life by the three restraints and the five rules of conduct. The three restraints refer to progressive curbing of the activities of the mind, body, and speech. These restraints are manifested by the practice of nonviolence to all living creatures in a monk's everyday life and by observing vows of silence for long periods of time or remaining motionless for equally extended periods of time. The five rules of conduct involve taking care when walking by moving slowly and gazing downward to avoid stepping on insects in an ascetic's path, being careful when speaking by observing a vow of truthfulness, taking care when accepting alms on begging rounds, being careful picking things up and putting them down, carefully performing excretory functions by selecting a place for this action that is free of living things.

These internal and external ascetic practices are grounded in the observance of nonviolence (*ahiṃsā*), an observance that permeates the Jain religion. In Indian culture, violence usually refers to harming others, and it can take three forms: deeds of intentional and premeditated violence; harmful action that occurs either accidentally or may result from an acceptable occupation, much like the difference between a murderer and a medical surgeon, whose basic intentions are rather different; and injury generated by standing in opposition to another person or event. The overall message of Jainism is that care must be taken to minimize all pain.

Jains tend to isolate the essence of nonviolence in the realization that a person is the same as the other, a realization that all living beings are equal because everyone shares a soul. Since all souls are the same, we should not harm others, which holds true for lower forms of creatures. Nonviolence is the primary practice that shapes the lives of all Jains, by being a vow to refrain from causing injury to beings with more than one sense faculty. In summary, nonviolence involves both non-injury to all living creatures and compassion toward them.

The vow of nonviolence applicable to and obligatory for all Jains has some practical implications for them in their everyday life because a Jain should not choose, for example, an occupation that causes intentional destruction of another, which eliminates earning a living by hunting, joining the military, or being a fisherman. The Jain tradition recognizes six respectable modes of livelihood: government work, writing, farming, arts, and various crafts, with the most appropriate being commerce. Besides influencing a choice of occupation, the observance of nonviolence possesses implications for a Jain's everyday diet, which must not consist of animal flesh, which is interconnected to the belief in single-sense creatures that inhabit the universe. Since fermented and sweet substances contain many single-sensed creatures, the consumption of liquor or honey is forbidden. Tissues of certain plants function as hosts for microscopic life, which means a substance such as a fig is also prohibited for food. If food is problematic for Jains, this is also true of water because of the numerous microscopic creatures living within it. How can a person avoid drinking these creatures? Jains assert that boiled water is free of such creatures. Therefore, boiled water is a nonviolent way to safely secure water that adheres to Jain standards. But this does not seem to make any sense because boiling the water destroys the creatures. This conundrum is solved by a division of labor, by forbidding the person boiling the water and killing the creatures to drink the water. Thus the boiler of the water, who acts virtuously, assumes the transgression of the rule of nonviolence for the drinker of the water. The doctrine of nonviolence has important consequences for a monk, who is held to a higher standard of observance than a layperson. The vow of nonviolence means that the monk must become aware of his every action in order to avoid the possibility of committing an infraction. Monks can act appropriately by sweeping the floor to remove any creatures before they sit down; they can move very slowly, never wave their arms about because the air is full of small creatures, or sweep the ground in front of them as they walk when in public.

In addition to the vow of nonviolence, a monk or nun observes four other restraints that are very similar to the Buddhist and the Hindu ascetic paths. The second restraint is to abstain from lying because the act is violent, volitional, and tainted by passions that injure the soul. The third restraint is a vow not to steal that is broadly defined as taking anything not freely given. Not only do acts of theft reflect the presence of greed, they also involve violence. The next restraint is refraining from sexual activities for monastic figures and illicit sexual transgressions for laypeople, which are generally defined as those outside of marriage. It is common to suggest to a layman that he view all women other than his wife as he would his mother or sister and to thus overcome desire for other women. From the Jain monastic perspective, since sex involves passions, it is violent in the sense that it injures the soul, and sexual intercourse kills great numbers of single-sense creatures that live in the body fluids of males and females. Finally, a person must accept the restraint of nonpossession. To be attached to things is to be possessed and deluded by them. For the layperson, this involves setting limits on ownership.

Besides embracing and practicing the restraints, a Jain monastic figure practices meditation with the purpose of attaining insight. The steps to insight include that the bonds of desire are loosened, the soul confronts gross passions and deluding factors, foes of the soul become identified, one becomes aware of forces that control one, a higher state of purity is attained, the duration and intensity of all bound karmas are reduced, and obstructions to insight are prevented from arising. The soul instantaneously experiences a vision of reality, which further reduces karmas that bind a person and cut the influx of future karmas in both quality and intensity. This insightful vision is identical in all souls, although specific results generated are not fixed. The results for a given soul depend upon the type, number, and intensity of karmas that remain.

The awakened soul also provides external signs of its spiritual attainment. If prior to awakening a person grasps the self as identified with external signs of life such as the body and possessions and thinks that it can be an agent of change, awakening enables the soul to turn away from these kinds of concerns. Instead, the soul experiences a mindful reorientation of attention, which focuses on nothing but its own nature, such as the innate and pure qualities of the soul. The awakened person realizes that he is not doing anything in the world except simply knowing it. The awakened one knows objects but does not want to grasp them, residing in a state of seeing the inward self. This awakened state increases his mindfulness and pure awareness to perform morally and ethically pure conduct, moves to a state of constant self-awareness and purity, and develops a strong feeling of identification with all beings, although he is aware of all the diversity among beings. The feeling of mutual identity is grounded in the awareness that all beings possess a soul that can become omniscient, which additionally makes him aware of the worth of all beings and his kinship with them. This realization is related to a feeling of compassion for others, which convinces him that he should help others attain liberation. This transformation of his consciousness is accompanied by a change in his behavior. The bliss associated with awakening leads to ease and tranquility with respect to his outward demeanor. An awakened person is no longer subject to anger or greed and perceives worldly things as transitory and mortal, which is translated into disenchantment with worldly things.

Jain monks and nuns urge others not to foolishly reject the arduous regimen of ascetic practice. The Jain monk Hemacandra compares a foolhardy bird to an ascetic who is willing to practice his difficult discipline despite the visible pleasures of the world for a goal that is invisible. The ascetic is like the bird who steals pieces of meat from the jaws of a sleeping lion. Just as the bird and ascetic are equally fools, the latter is a fool for wisdom and omniscience, whereas the bird is merely a risk-taking fool, opting for a dangerous choice for a momentary form of gratification.

The Jain ascetic life is conceived as a heroic struggle, with the intention of creating an atmosphere for a life devoted to not merely liberation but to the practice of nonviolence and other religious vows and virtues. The Jain tradition imagines the ideal ascetic lifestyle as a wandering mendicancy that is interspersed by brief periods of obligatory residency in a fixed monastic community, such as the annual monsoon season. During these periods of monastic residency, ascetics study texts, perform religious exercise, and preach to the laity. Unable to hold money, not able to grow crops or cook food, and adhering to a strict vegetarian diet, monks must beg for their daily sustenance from the laity. When outside the monastery begging for food, the ascetic follows a pattern of wandering that is called grazing like a cow, which is a metaphorical way to refer to the unintentional way of begging. The Digambara ascetics beg for food only once in the morning and eat only what is placed into their cupped hands by a layperson, which they eat before the donor. Both major sects of Jainism do not eat after dark in order to avoid increasing any chance of accidently injuring other forms of life. Jain ascetics also fast for long periods as a common feature of their overall regimen. In comparison to early Buddhist practice of monastic life, Jains do not attribute special significance to a systematized pattern of meditation. This different emphasis on meditation between Buddhists and Jains is likely due to the Jain belief that the strict practice of asceticism is the most advantageous way to destroy karmic residues.

The radical nature of Jain asceticism is evident by the practice of fasting unto death (*sallekhanā*). This is formalized by renouncing family and friends, rejecting malice toward enemies, and a confession of transgressions. Fasting unto death is the only approved method of ending the life of an ascetic because it does not increase one's passions and is a nonviolent way to end one's life, which Jains do not perceive as a form of suicide. Over the centuries, Jains have carved memorial stones to bear testimony to ascetics who have fasted to death.

An additional nonviolent way to end one's life is to give oneself to vultures, which benefits birds of prey by the ascetic serving as food for them. Jain narratives embody this spirit of self-sacrifice. When a monk witnessed ants dying after eating sacrificial offerings, he sacrificed himself by eating the poisonous alms to save the insects. A general guideline is to perform the act of suicide passively, which is precisely what occurs when a monk waits passively to starve to death. In this scenario, the monk is the sole victim and sacrifice, with the process beginning and ending with himself.

Intended and Unintended Consequences of Ascetic Life

An intended consequence of the ascetic life is taking a vow of celibacy in order to conquer sexual urges that contribute to increased karmic accumulations on the soul and keep it in a state of bondage. According to a sixth century Jain narrative by the monk Jinadāsa, Sthūlabhadra was the son of a minister to the king, and his position in society enabled him to lead a hedonistic lifestyle for twelve years with Kośā, a beautiful courtesan. A malevolent Brahmin manipulated Sthūlabhadra's brother to kill his father, but the innocent brother refused to assume the mantle of his father's leadership. He instead renounced the world. The courtesan remained loyal to her former lover and joined the palace intrigue to destroy the scheming Brahmin.

The narrative now turns to the ascetic life of Sthūlabhadra and three other ascetics, who make different vows before their teacher to practice extreme forms of asceticism during the four-month long rain retreat. The three other ascetics vowed to reside respectively near a cave home to a lion, near a snake's hole, and at the bottom of a well, whereas Sthūlabhadra vowed to live in his former lover's home. His former courtesan attempted to seduce him but was unsuccessful in her erotic efforts. Sthūlabhadra remained resolute in his vow of celibacy, and was acclaimed by his teacher for overcoming the greatest challenge to his celibacy, compared to the other ascetics. This assessment of the teacher was confirmed when the ascetic living near the lion's lair was seduced by the courtesan.

This type of narrative conveys a message about the dangers of sexual activity, the need for celibacy, and the association of sex with violence, forming the context for such a story. Beyond the fact that sexual activity increases passions and further immersion in bondage to the lures of worldly life, sexual conduct is a violent mode of action because the ejaculation of semen leads to the death of numerous life-monads, rendering the ascetic vow of celibacy doubly significant. This type of narrative helps us to see the essential interconnection and reinforcement on each other of two major Jain ascetic vows: nonviolence to all living things and celibacy, which can be viewed as intended consequences of practicing the ascetic path.

In contrast to these intended consequences of following the ascetic path, Jain ascetics encountered an unintended result of their lifestyle by experiencing and acquiring various forms of supernatural powers similar to Hindu ascetics and Buddhist monks and nuns. The fifth-century figure Samantabhadra, a Jain sage and author, gives a list of powers that can be acquired by an ascetic, which includes some of the following powers: ability to become small; extend one's body; make the body light or heavy; adopt any form and any number of bodies at one time; subjugate others; exhibit superiority; and act as one desires without restraints. The acquisition of mental powers is the focus of Umāsvāti, an eighth-century Jain thinker, when he discusses telepathy, clairvoyance, and omniscience and their superiority to extrasensory perception, which is attainable to lower levels of beings that include humans, gods, animals, and beings in hell. Telepathy is the ability to read the minds of others, clairvoyance is the ability to see things outside of the range of normal perception, and omniscience is an all-knowing of substances in multiple modes of the past, present, and future. By existing independent of the senses, these three mental powers are considered innate, although it is only autonomous omniscience that is perfectly innate because clairvoyance and telepathy are related to ignorance. When the obscuring nature of karma is entirely eliminated and an ascetic attains enlightenment, omniscience arises.

A Jain narrative illustrates implications of having superior knowledge with the story of Maheśvaradatta, a wealthy merchant who sacrificed a buffalo to his ancestors and fed the sacrificial meat to his son. An omniscient Jain ascetic told the merchant about the implications of his actions, with consequences for former modes of life. The ascetic tells the merchant that he was feeding his son the flesh of his former father. The merchant's son is also identified as his wife's former lover, and his former wife was now a bitch chewing the bones of the buffalo. From the Jain perspective, this narrative exposes the deluded nature of performing sacrifice and demonstrates the superior mental powers of an advanced ascetic. These types of mental and physical powers are unintentional by-products of the ascetic path, but they should not be construed as representing the goal of the path. As with Buddhist and Hindu ascetic practices, the Jain ascetic's acquisition of powers can function to trap an ascetic within the world and keep the ascetic from attaining her real goal of total liberation.

Laity and Ritual Action

Jain monks and nuns are the elite figures of the Jain religion and function as spiritual paradigms for the laity, who are instructed to follow a weaker version of the ascetic path, although this path does not lead to liberation. Nonetheless, laypeople are an integral part of Jain piety, which is expressed by internal and external manifestations of devotion, often visual, in worship services. Jain textual evidence enumerates eleven stages of spiritual progress for a layperson.

The initial stage concerns right views, which consist of two modes of religious observance: devotional and renunciation. The former involves acceptance of a

Jina (conqueror or fully awakened person) as the ultimate divinity, acceptance of Jain texts as the only valid scriptures, and accepting Jain monks as the only legitimate teachers. The layperson takes refuge with a Jain monk, a practice formalized by an initiatory mantra (sacred formula) that one chants. The arguably most famous utterance is the *Nokār Mantra*. That is the following:

> Praise to the Arhats
> Praise to the Siddhas
> Praise to the Ācāryas
> Praise to the Upādhyāyas
> Praise to all Sādhus in the World.
> This fivefold praise
> Destroys all bad karma
> and of all holies
> it is the foremost holy.

This formula is believed to destroy negative karma. This scenario suggests that Jain devotionalism concentrates on an ascetic ideal—attainment of liberation—and not a divine being.

Laity renunciation is marked by taking various vows, which are understood as basic restraints, a practice that implies that karmic influx can be placed within certain limits. Another aspect of lay renunciation involves avoiding all evil actions, practicing meditation, fasting on particular holy days, observing eating and drinking in a pure way (avoiding certain foods and filtering water), observing sexual continence by day, and working to reach a stage of total continence in the future. It is possible to observe that lay life is conditioned toward an ascetic mode of existence. This becomes more evident as lay renunciation progresses to the stage of abandoning household activity, disposing of one's property and belongings, becoming indifferent to social acceptance or approval by others, and rejecting specially prepared food or lodging. This pattern finally culminates with complete renunciation of all family and social connections. The number of laypeople who can follow this pattern to its successful conclusion is manifested by the relatively small number who actually adopt the life of a monk or nun.

Taking vows is another important aspect of lay life that parallels that of the ascetic. If an ascetic takes the five great vows, a layperson takes the five small vows: (1) choose a livelihood that does not entail violence; (2) do not lie; (3) do not steal; (4) avoid excessive sexual activity; and (5) adopt celibacy during one's mature years. There are also subsidiary vows that include one's behavior with respect to unnecessary movement, excessive gratification, and self-indulgent agonizing. And, like ascetics, laypeople are vegetarian, rejecting meat, fish, and eggs. They are also encouraged to avoid root and bulb vegetables, such as potatoes and onions.

Although vows are important to a layperson, their social and business prestige are derived from their generosity. Many Jain narratives reinforced the importance of generosity. According to one such narrative, a widow lived with her young son in a prosperous neighborhood, earning a meager living cleaning utensils in other people's homes. Her young son was told by other children about *kheer* (a sweet meal made of rice and milk). Bored with the same type of inexpensive meal every day, the young boy asked his mother for some *kheer*, but she replied that she could not afford to buy the ingredients, causing her child to cry. Wanting to please her son, the widow went begging door to door until she had the necessary means to make the *kheer*. While she was fetching water, she left her son with the dish; two monks stopped at the widow's home, and the son saw an opportunity to give them the *kheer*, even though it was a dish that he ardently desired. The monks took the *kheer* and left. The son licked the leftovers, causing his mother to wrongfully surmise that he had eaten the entire amount, because she did not know about the wandering monks. She was angry with her son's apparently gluttonous action and gave him the evil eye, causing him to die during the night. Because of his pure thoughts and generosity, the widow's son was reborn into a better state in a future life as a reward for his charitable deed.

In addition to generosity, the religious practice for most Jains centers on daily rituals and periodic ceremonies. These rites provide social cohesion by bringing families and the wider community together for the purposes of jointly performing ceremonies and enhancing group identity. For laypeople, there are six obligatory duties: practice of equanimity by means of meditation, praise of the twenty-four *tīrthaṅkaras* (ford makers), veneration of teachers, expiation for transgressions, abandonment of the body (e.g., standing motionless for various lengths of time), and renunciation. Among the Digambaras, image worship is conducted by celibate clerics wearing orange robes. A better understanding of lay practice can become more evident if we isolate and highlight some of these practices.

Before an image of an omniscient teacher, a layperson worships any of the twenty-four *tīrthaṅkaras* (liberated, omniscient beings). This primary religious activity of the laity can be performed daily in a Jain temple. It may seem curious to readers to learn that worship directed at these images does not mean that the average Jain expects any help from these holy figures, because these awakened ones are forever beyond human affairs. And to respond to human worship would mean that the *Jina* is attached to humans. Jain worship is more reflective in the sense that the worshipper seeks to stimulate the arousal of *Jina* virtues within herself.

The veneration of Jain images of *Jinas* is exemplified by performing *pūjā* (worship), a practice that does not require a priest. Because the *Jina* is considered far beyond human existence, its unreachable nature makes the presence of a priest unnecessary. Thus, this form of worship can be performed by laypeople individually or in a group. Jain temples that house the images are considered a replica of the holy assembly of the *tīrthaṅkaras* and are a tangible aid to the visualization of such a being. The images are standardized forms that appear in only two postures: standing and sitting in the lotus posture with hands placed palms up, right over left, behind the feet, and covering the genital area of the body. In the standing posture, the image appears erect, rigid, and immobile, with its arms held stiffly down and its knees straight and toes directly forward. For an outsider to the Jain religion, it can be difficult to distinguish one image from another. A Jain knows that distinctions can be made between images by the animals or plants attached to the image. The bull represents, for example, Ṛṣabha (first *Jina* of the present cosmic cycle), Nami (twenty-first *Jina*) by a blue lotus, Pārśva (twenty-third figure) by a serpent, and Mahāvīra by the lion.

A layperson can participate in the ceremony of the five auspicious events, which represents a ritual reenactment of the five primary events in the life of a *tīrthaṅkara* (ford-maker): conception, birth, renunciation, attainment of omniscience, and enlightenment. This ceremony is especially performed when a new image or a set of images are installed in the temple. This ritual is not only intended to sanctify an icon but can also bestow a vision of a *Jina* to the participants. The ritual action involves various acts of adoration, pouring water over the image, and dressing the image, actions that share much in common with a *pūjā* (worship) service.

There are two aspects to a worship service (*pūjā*): external and internal. The latter aspect involves peace of mind and devotion to Jain ideal virtues, which are absolutely necessary before one can begin worship. The external aspects refer to the objects to be worshipped. Although there is a wide variety of practice from one area to another, there are some common features that overlap with other modes of performance.

The lay participant in a worship service enters a temple wearing only three simple pieces of clothing and carrying a plate filled with flowers, fruit, camphor, uncooked rice, and incense. Prior to entering the temple, the lay person purifies her body by taking a bath. Why is purity necessary? It is an expression of reverence, respect, and an acknowledgment that she is about to have contact with something holy. As the worshipper approaches the main shrine, she bows down, utters a litany of names, and circumambulates the image three times with the image always on her right, which is considered the auspicious side. The worshipper then sits on a mat before the image. Using rice grains, the worshipper forms a swastika on a plate or wooden plank. The swastika is a symbol of the four possible rebirth destines. Above the swastika, the worshipper places three dots, which represent the three jewels: true insight, right knowledge, and proper conduct. These three jewels provide a means of liberation from rebirth and bondage, which is also signified by the swastika. At the top of the design, one makes a small crescent with a dot mounted on it, which represents the uppermost portion of the universe with the liberated soul resting within its edge. It is here that the liberated soul dwells eternally in the four infinities of joy, energy, consciousness, and knowledge. The overall result of the three symbols is to suggest liberation from the world and the cycle of rebirth, which is the goal of the worship service.

Once this rice creation is finished, the water ceremony begins by sprinkling holy water over the smaller image in front of the main image, which involves the devotee visualizing herself as Śaka, king of the gods. This role is signified by the application of sandalwood paste on the forehead of the worshipper. Then sandalwood paste and milk are poured over the image, which concludes with the pouring of purified water and flower blossoms over the image. Finally, the image is wiped dry. What this ceremony represents is a reenactment of the ritual bath of the *Jina* atop Mount Meru, a sacred mountain at the center of the universe. The second phase of the *pūjā* (worship) begins at this point by paying homage to the image and offering right substances: water, sandalwood paste, uncooked rice, flowers, sweets, lamp, incense, and fruits. These items respectively signify cleanliness, purity, immortality, passions, contentment, omniscience, fame, and liberation. Sandalwood paste is considered a cooling substance that has the power to subdue passions and destroy karmic influxes. The third aspect of the service involves a garland of victory, during which a worshipper repeats the names of the twenty-four *tīrthaṅkaras*. This is followed by a few moments of silence before the commencement of the chanting of names. The fourth and final phase involves the waving of lamps (*āratī*) before the image in order to remove any harmful karma produced during the service. During the ceremony, members of the Śvetāmbara sect wear a piece of white cloth over their mouths as a show of respect to the *Jina* represented by the icon.

Lay Jains also observe certain holy days during the course of a year, such as the immortal third, a festival that occurs in May/June, which commemorates the first giving of alms to Ṛṣabha, founder of asceticism for this age. Mahāvīra's birthday is celebrated in April/May, and his death is commemorated in October/November. The head anointing ceremony is held every twelfth year, which honors the hero Bāhubali, a son of Ṛṣabha, in the form of a fifty-seven-foot image that is carved from a single rock that stands sixty-eight feet tall. The image stands still doing meditation, and its stillness is enhanced by vines growing on him and the snakes, lizards, and a scorpion living on his body. Digambaras assert that he was the first person to attain liberation in the current time cycle, whereas the Śvetāmbaras deny this and claim that Marubhūti did win liberation after many rebirths as Pārśva. In order to pour the necessary sacred liquids and substances over the image, a huge scaffolding is built behind the icon. By participating in this rite, a person earns great merit.

A Hindu festival called Dīvālī or Dīpavālī (festival of lights) is also celebrated annually by Jains in October-November. According to the Jain tradition, this represents the time of Mahāvīra's liberation. This festival is also important to Jain businessmen, with the start of new account books being marked on a day that signifies the Jain New Year. Jain businessmen and others worship the Hindu goddess Śrī Lakṣmī, a deity associated with wealth and good fortune. It is the hope of businessmen that she will bless them with economic benefits during the forthcoming year.

Another lay practice is pilgrimage to holy places to commemorate events associated with the time when a *tīrthaṅkara* left his body forever, where Arhats liberated non-*tīrthaṅkaras*, or where miraculous events occurred during the lives of great monks. Pārśva and nineteen other *Jinas* died at Summedaśikhara. Ṛṣabha attained liberation at Mount Kailasa in the Himalayas, whereas the twelfth *tīrthāṅkara*, Vāsupūjya, gained liberation at Campāpuri in the Bihar region. These locations are considered sacred because of their connection with Jain ascetic figures. Average Jain householders try to go on pilgrimage at least once during their lives.

In addition to pilgrimage, Jains perform an annual rite of confession that occurs during the rainy season. The Jain confesses his transgressions and pleads for forgiveness by directing confession to a teacher, friends, and family members irrespective of age or gender. As part of the observance, a participant extends his forgiveness to all beings and asks them for forgiveness.

Ritual fasting and gift giving also shape the religious identity of Jains. The Jain who decides to fast does so apart from family in a secluded location. Having taken no food or drink during the day, the fasting person spends the evening hours chanting sacred names or reading scriptures without getting much sleep for a period of nine days. Bathing and even washing one's mouth is prohibited. After this nine-day fast, the Jain returns home to perform a worship (*pūjā*) service at the home shrine. Fasting benefits a practitioner by reducing attachment to one's body and enables one to share the gift of food with others by giving alms to monks. In fact, there are five major gifts that start with fearlessness, a gift to a worthy recipient (e.g., *Jina* idol or a living renouncer), gift of compassion, gift given out of duty, and gift to earn fame. Vows, rituals, icons, *pūjā* (worship), temples, observance of holy days, festivals, pilgrimage, confession, and gift giving that are important features of Jain laity participation in the religion are also to be discovered in Hinduism and Buddhism and reflect a devotional spirit surrounding a layperson's practice of her religion. Thus, the quest for liberation and enlightenment is for the elite religious few because the path is extremely demanding and presupposes renunciation from the world and social associations. Although the lifestyle of an ascetic represents the ideal in Jainism, there is still a place for non-ascetic laypeople to participate in the religion.

The Role of Women

The traditional Jain literature makes it clear that women are sources of temptation and often entice ascetics from reaching the goal of liberation. Hemacandra, a twelfth-century figure, illustrates the problem of women in a narrative about four monks who make different vows pertaining to their means of testing the rigor of their ascetic regimen. The fourth monk vows to test himself over a four-month period by living in the house of Kośā, a lovely prostitute whose walls are erotically painted with murals depicting various types of sexual positions. The monk also vows to eat lavish meals during the same period. Calling attention to the murals on her home walls and flaunting her beauty, the prostitute attempts to seduce the monk, but her continued pattern of enticement did not sexually arouse the monk. Finally, failing to seduce the monk, Kośā falls at the feet of the monk and converts to Jainism, being astonished by his self-control. Within the context of this erotic contest between two mutually opposed figures, the prostitute loses her attempt to seduce the monk and fails at her profession, whereas the monk is victorious. In the end, the prostitute wins, however, because she chooses the path of liberation.

Jain attitudes toward women and their role in society tend to share Hindu and Buddhist perceptions about women. These cultural attitudes shape the conviction that women are limited to a domestic role, with employment outside of the home not approved, with the exception of extremely poor families who are forced out of economic necessity to allow women to work outside of the home. As a consequence of this situation, women are economically dependent on men and have limited influence on the use of family economic resources. But a woman's religiosity can become a family asset in the sense that a woman gains merit for other family members. It is not unusual to find males boasting about their wives' religiosity and claiming they can match their wives by their generosity. Since women are confined primarily to a domestic role, cooking is female work, and this fact of life means that women are involved in violence when cooking or preparing food, an activity that violates the basic injunction of the religion concerning the need for nonviolence. Because of the importance of nonviolence as a defining characteristic of Jainism, women utilize euphemisms such as repairing or amending vegetables instead of cutting or chopping.

Western anthropologists have observed that Jain women play a greater role in the religion than men. A typical woman rises early and performs service before the household shrine, meditates, and takes a set of vows called the fourteen principles that sets limitations on the quantity of food, drink, and household items. Women tend to visit the local temple daily and listen to monks or nuns preach. Women practice asceticism by fasting to develop the spirit of worldly detachment. The length of fasts depends on the auspicious days of the lunar month, festivals, and longer fasts during the year.

Women help to maintain the ascetic lineage by religious practices that are typical for a layperson, which confirms the lineage as a social group. After ceremonies in the temple, women gather to gossip, which gives them news about families within the lineage and information about younger people eligible to marry. Women also play a critical role in the socialization of children and instill them with religious awareness by bringing children to the temple at an early age, teaching them the names of the twenty-four *tīrthāṅkaras*, teaching the avowal of faith, sharing religious stories with them, and imparting a pride in the religion to the younger generation.

A fundamental concern for male Jains is the sexuality of females, which is strictly controlled to guarantee that social relations are not endangered by a lack of discipline and social contact. It is important that economic status is not compromised to the extent of undermining a favorable marriage match, which can have consequences for the unity of the sect and the maintenance of economic resources within the sect in the form of marriage dowries.

As evident in Hinduism and Buddhism, female sexuality is considered dangerous by Jains and must be controlled prior to and after marriage. This is viewed as a means of controlling and consolidating productive resources within the individual family. Moreover, since women give birth to the next generation of inheritors, it is essential to protect the sect against the possibility of pre-marital sex and extra-marital affairs. In the past, many women were protected and confined to the home, restricting a woman's movement and opportunity to encounter males outside of the residence. Female religiosity is also encouraged to ensure a women's sexual purity. Jain heroines who maintain their chastity are celebrated in narratives.

This emphasis on chastity is necessary because sexual promiscuity endangers religious and business boundaries. A wanton woman cannot be married within the community. An impaired reputation of one daughter can affect the marriage chances of other daughters in the household. For social and economic reasons, female chastity must be publicly proven, which can be accomplished by public religious activity with the mother taking the lead and daughters imitating their mothers. Another means of enhancing chastity is to neutralize female sexual desire by engaging in fasting, which is believed to cool sexual desire and transform it into a benign force. It is typical to have a public celebration when a fast ends for a woman and preserve the event in a photo album.

Female ascetics have always been prevalent within the Śvetāmbara sect, a fact that is traced to the nineteenth *tīrthāṅkara*, a woman named Malli. This is denied by the Digambara sect, which identifies the figure as a male named Mallinātha. This disagreement demonstrates a fundamentally different attitude toward women. Among the Śvetāmbara sect, women are more independent and are equally respected like men by the laity and are spiritually equal to male ascetics, although women are considered subordinate to men, as evident by the practice of a head monk performing the initiation ceremony for nuns. But the larger number of nuns means that monks cannot impinge on the authority of nuns.

The Digambara's attitude toward women is more conservative because they hold that women are inherently impure and are born a female as a consequence of past transgressions. According to the Digambara position, women cannot attain liberation because they cannot be reborn into the seventh and lowest hell, which is connected to their inability to perform misdeeds to the same extent as men. Women are unable to renounce all possessions, have inferior debating skills, have an inferior position in society, and run the risk of rape by wandering naked. By means of their bodily structure, they generate and destroy more life-forms than men within their sexual organ, which makes it impossible for them to practice nonviolence. Thus, women are unfit to become monks. In order for a woman to achieve liberation, she must be reborn as a male.

For those women who become nuns, they must endure certain restrictions such as being prohibited from preaching, studying texts on praxis, or performing worship. Reading material of nuns is confined to vernacular devotional literature, and they are forbidden from wandering naked. Even though there are more female mendicants than males, these types of restrictions tend to marginalize women.

Jain Literature

From the perspective of a scholar of religions of India, Jainism and Buddhism represent heterodox movements because they reject the authority of the Vedic scriptures as revealed literature, making them unbelievers and heretics from the viewpoint of orthodox, priestly Hinduism. Jains also did not accept the Hindu gods and goddesses, with some exceptions on the popular level by lay-people. But this does not mean that Jainism is atheistic. It is the case that Jains do not believe in the existence of a creator god and do not think that it is possible for a god to intervene in human affairs, rejecting the possibility that a god could incarnate himself in the world. But since they believe that a liberated soul can become supreme, the Jains are theistic in a limited way. And they venerate holy ascetics who have achieved this liberated status, which is evident in their worship of ascetic icons in temples.

Reading the primary literary sources of Jainism, Hinduism, and Buddhism makes it apparent that there existed a tension between the three major religions. And it is not unusual to find narratives that illustrate the spiritual competition between them. A good example of this tension is evident in the story of a miracle performed by the Jain monk Jindattsūri. Some Hindu priests leave the carcass of a dead cow in front of a Jain temple. In response to this insult, the monk enters the body of the deceased bovine, causing it to rise, walk, and expire again in front of a Śaiva temple, which serves the purpose of polluting the temple and its priests because dead bodies are considered polluting in the Hindu tradition.

For Jains, language does more than relate an interesting story because it also possesses power. According to the commentary of Āchārya Samantabhedra on the *Āpta-Mimāṃsā*, a word possesses its own meaning distinct from other words. Thus each word is distinct and meaningful in its own right, implying that it possesses its own power, as illustrated in the narrative about Mukunda, a Brahmin convert to Jainism who enjoys reciting a text loudly at night, to the consternation of awakened monks. After his teacher convinces him to recite during the day, he annoys laypeople. An irritated layman asks him whether or not he hoped to create a dry stick that would burst into bloom by simply the magic of his words. Receiving assistance from the goddess of learning, he intends to atone and shock others by transforming his dry stick into a blooming flower by the power of his uttered words. It is this type of attitude about the nature of language that informs the Jain literary canon.

Both major branches of Jainism agree that their early scriptures have been lost and are irretrievably a distant memory. The scriptures that did develop after this lost period were finally edited and finalized by Devardnigani in 526 CE. There is thus a long period separating the actual teaching career of

Mahāvīra and the collection of a canon of literature. This canon is considered fluid and thus without fixed boundaries, although the major sects have different versions of its origin. The Digambaras think that the earliest teaching of Mahāvīra consisted of the sound of a *mantra* (sacred formula) that embodied sermons recorded by disciples, whereas the Śvetāmbaras contend that Mahāvīra communicated in a human language. From a wider perspective, Jain literature (*āgama*) is understood as the teachings of omniscient beings, which necessarily means that the texts are thus authoritative and represent an eternal message because of their source in sagacious *Jinas* who have taught the singular Jain message from the beginning of the religion.

The Jain canonical literature includes three groups: *Pūrvas* (14 texts), *Aṅgas* (12 texts), and *Aṅgabāhyas* (34 texts). The first group of texts was lost by the second century CE, but it is believed that later texts embody their contents. This lost literature dates back to the time of Pārśva, according to the Jain tradition. These ancient texts included discussions of the nature of the cosmos, bondage of the soul, astrology, astronomy, and philosophical polemics against rival schools. These texts were transmitted in Ardhamāgadhī, an old Magadhan language. The Jain canon was written prior to the second council held at Mathura around the fourth century CE on palm-leaf. A final redaction of the literature was reached at the third and final council in Valabhi in either 453 or 466 CE.

The twelve *Aṅgas* (limbs) cover subjects such as monastic regulations, doctrine, operation of the law of karma, a reaction to false teachings, and narratives about ascetics and kings. The first text in this collection, *Ācārāṅga Sūtra*, contains an authoritative account of Mahāvīra's life. The fifth text, *Bhagavatī*, includes a tale of the encounter between Mahāvīra and Makkhai Gosāla, leader of the Ājīvikas. This body of literature contains narratives to edify lay followers that are often in the form of tales about the exploits of monks or exemplary laity.

The *Aṅgabāhya* collection of texts, a subsidiary canon, is conceived as a supplement to the *Aṅgas* that owes its origin to monk authors. This impressive body of literature includes the following: twelve *Upāṅgas*; six *Chedasūtras*; four *Mūlasūtras*; ten *Prakīrṇakasūtras*; and two *Cūlikāsūtras*. The first group contains narratives about monks keeping their vows to the extent of fasting to death rather than breaking their vow of not accepting what is not freely given, conversion of a cruel king, the nature of the soul, discussion of the problem of change, ontology, movements of the sun and moon, and narratives about laypeople doing ethical and immoral things. The six *Chedasūtras* focus on monastic life and its rules and regulations. The *Daśavaikālika*, initial work of the *Mūlasūtras*, is a series of lectures about issues pertaining to monastic life composed by Ārya Śayyambhava (c. 429 CE) who wrote it for his son, according to Jain tradition, as instructions about monastic life. An especially prominent work in this collection is the *Uttarādhyayana*, which is asserted to be the final sermon of Mahāvīra. Ten brief texts constitute the *Prakīrṇakasūtras* (miscellaneous texts), which cover topics such as taking refuge, renunciation of food, preparation for death, discussion of food, state of consciousness at death, praise of holy *Jinas*, monastic activities, and other subjects. The *Cūlikāsūtras* (appendix texts) consist of two works: the *Nandīsūtra*, attributed to Devavācaka, and the *Anuyogadvārasūtra*, by Ārya Rakāita. Both works are summaries of previous material appearing in other works. Many of these texts attracted commentaries by monks for the benefit and edification of other monastic figures.

Originating in southern India, the *Anuyogas* (expositions) represent treatises by Digambara monks that have canonical status in that tradition. This body of literature is divided into four categories; the first is the *Prathamānuyoga*, dealing with biographies of holy figures composed by monks such as Jinasena (eighth century), Guṇabhadra (ninth century), and Hemacandra (twelfth century). These types of works were used to spread the religion to laypeople in a popular way by telling stories that illustrate aspects of Jainism. The second category is the *Karaṇānuyoga*, concerned with technical matters dealing with science, cosmology, and astronomy. The third collection is the *Caraṇānuyoga*, devoted to monastic and lay discipline. Finally, the group of texts called the *Dravyānuyoga* concentrate on metaphysical issues pertaining to the soul, being, substance, atoms, and motion. In this category, the work of Umāsvāti stands out; especially notable is his *Tattvārthasūtra*, using the terse aphoristic style of comparable Hindu texts to synthesize the Jain system of thought in 350 verses. The Jain literary tradition also produced works of logic and philosophy as a response to the necessity of debating other competing religious ways.

Later Historical Developments

This chapter has already called attention to the major split of the religion between the Śvetāmbaras and Digambaras over different interpretations of events of Mahāvīra's life, practice, and the role of women. Subsequent historical developments bear witness to additional schisms.

The Śvetāmbaras are the largest group of Jains and are split into three main groups: Mūrtipūjakas, Sthānakavāsis, and the Terāpanthīs. The first group split over disagreements about the use of images for worship. Both the Sthānakavāsis and the Terāpanthīs were inspired by Loṅka Sāh, a fifteenth-century reformer. The former group was opposed to monks dwelling in temples and regarded the worship of images as a violation of nonviolence because of the destruction of small organisms during the pouring on of substances. Being opposed to physical acts that could be harmful to small creatures, they stressed mental worship and adhered to strict ascetic practice. The Terāpanthīs were established in 1760 by Ācārya Bhikṣu, formerly a Sthānakavāsi monk. This group advocated to monks and nuns that they should continue to wear a mouth shield or face mask to prevent inhaling or ingesting small creatures.

Among the southern Digambaras, the Bīsapanthīs (meaning either twenty-fold or universal path) split from the Digambara Terāpanthīs over the issue of authority of monks to administer monasteries. A fundamental problem is that these administrative monks wear clothing because of their frequent contact with laypeople. By violating the injunction of going naked, these figures are not considered genuine monks.

During more recent times, Jainism inspired reformers such as Ācārya Tulsī, who became engaged in the world and promoted Jain values to the wider world, while also stressing the importance of a continual reform of Jain practice. Ācārya Mahāprajñā, another reformer, introduced insight meditation to a wider audience. The Jain teaching of nonviolence had a profound influence on Mahatma Gandhi and his civil disobedience movement to win independence from England, which in turn influenced and inspired Martin Luther King and the civil rights movement in America during the 1960s.

A prominent recent and continuing feature of Jainism is the diaspora of Jains from India to other parts of the world. Early Jain immigrants went to England and East Africa. The first exposure of Americans to Jainism occurred in 1863, when Virchand Raghaviji Gandhi, a Jain speaker at the World's Parliament of Religions in Chicago, spoke as part of the World's Fair that year. But it was not until the 1960s that Jains arrived in America in any significant numbers. It is estimated that there are 25,000 Jains in America, 10,000 in Canada, and 25,000 in England. There are now about 60 Jain centers in North America. Jainism's major umbrella organization is the Jain Association in North America. The purpose of JAINA is to pass its tradition to a younger generation, which gets exposed to a multitude of other religious options. Another feature of this organization is to preserve its past religious heritage by giving lectures and devotional rituals.

Because of the small population of Jains in America, in some areas of the country, they have joined with Hindus to share temples. Examples of shared temples can be found in Pittsburgh and Allentown, Pennsylvania. Contemporary Jains continue to engage themselves in the world by turning their attention to such issues as ecology and social justice. As a consequence of more worldly engagement and the diaspora, there is an acute absence of ascetics, which makes it impossible for ascetics to guide the community.

Religious Experience

It seems wise to place the topic of Jain religious experience into a larger context. It has been noted that the soul is distinct from material nature, which suggests a dualistic viewpoint. However, the Jain position is also pluralistic, because it accepts the existence of a multitude of distinct entities in the universe. We have also called attention to the fact that the Jains do not believe in a creator deity, but they do affirm the eternal nature of the universe, which is expected to continue this way forever and not culminate with some type of final conclusion at the end of time. Jains also define reality as both permanent and subject to change. But their grasp of the nature of reality consists of five categories, according to the Śvetāmbaras, which are identified as the soul and four non-spiritual categories, consisting of motion, rest, atoms, and space, whereas the Digambaras add the sixth category of time.

Within this type of metaphysical context, Jain ascetics strive to become *kevalins*, liberated souls transcending human sense experience. At the moment of liberation, the liberated soul instantly leaves its human body and is simultaneously transported to the roof of the universe, where it exists with other liberated souls but without contact with them. With its achieved state of omniscience, the *kevalin* gains insight into the true conditions of the world, divine beings, demons, and humans. The *kevalin* knows everything about them, even their utmost secrets. Jain texts describe the *kevalin* as living in a state of pure energy, knowledge, and bliss. While the liberated soul exists for eternity in bliss, it now becomes worthy of lay devotion.

Suggestions for Further Reading

Cort, John E. *Jains in the World: Religious Values and Ideology in India.* Oxford: New York: Oxford University Press, 2001.

Dundas, Paul. "Becoming Gautama: Mantra and History in Śvetāmbara Jainism." In *Open Boundaries: Jain Communities and Cultures in Indian History.* Ed. John E. Cort. Albany: State University of New York Press (1998): 31–52.

———. "The Digambara Jain Warrior." In *The Assembly of Listeners: Jains in Society.* Eds. M. Carrithers and C. Humphrey. Cambridge and New York: Cambridge University Press (1991): 169–181.

———. "Food and Freedom: The Jaina Sectarian Debate on the Nature of the Kevalin." *Religion* 15 (1985): 161–198.

———. *The Jains.* London, New York: Routledge, 1992.

———. "The Non-Violence of Violence: Jain Perspectives on Warfare, Asceticism and Worship." In *Religion and Violence in South Asia.* Eds. John R. Hinnells and Richard King. London: Routledge (2007): 41–61.

———. "Sthūlabhadra's Lodgings: Sexual Restraint in Jainism." *Celibacy and Religious Traditions.* Ed. Carl Olson. Oxford: Oxford University Press (2008): 181–199.

Granoff, Phyllis. "The Biographies of Siddhasena: A Study in the Texture of Allusion and the Weaving of a Group-Image Part II." *Journal of Indian Philosophy* 18 (1990): 261–304.

———. *The Forest of Thieves and the Magic Garden: An Anthology of Medieval Jain Stories.* London: Penguin Books, 1998.

———. "Scholars and Wonder Workers: Some Remarks on the Role of the Supernatural in Philosophical Contests in Vedānta Hagiographies." *Journal of the American Oriental Society* 105/3 (1985): 459–467.

———. "Warriors: A Preliminary Study of Some Biographies of Saints and Kings in the Classical Indian Tradition." *Journal of Indian Philosophy* 12 (1984): 291–303.

——— and Koichi Shinohara. *Speaking of Monks: Religious Biography in India and China.* Oakville, New York, London: Mosaic Press, 1992.

Hemacandra. *The Lives of the Jain Elders.* Trans. K.C.C. Fynes. Oxford: Oxford University Press, 1998.

Jain, K.C. *History of Jainism.* 3 vols. New Delhi: D.K. Printworld Ltd., 2010.

Jaini, Padmanabh S. *The Jaina Path of Purification.* Berkeley: University of California Press, 1979.

Laidlaw, James. *Riches and Renunciation: Religion, Economy, and Society.* Oxford: Clarendon Press, 1995.

Long, Jeffrey D. *Jainism: An Introduction.* London: I.B. Tauris, 2009.

von Glasenapp, Helmuth. *Jainism: An Indian Religion of Salvation.* Delhi: Motilal Banarsidass, 1999.

7 Buddhism

According to the *Jātaka* narratives about the previous lives of the historical Buddha, he was born as a rabbit with a remarkable capacity for compassion in one tale. The rabbit encountered a hunter one day, who, due to his inability to catch any animals, was starving to death in the forest. Rather than have the hunter die of starvation, the benevolent rabbit jumped into the hunter's cooking pot, giving up its own life to save that of the hard-luck hunter. In another episode, the Buddha appeared as the leader of a herd of deer who were captured by a king and kept in a pen for the king to shoot for his meal, but the king was unnecessarily wounding many deer. This motivated the leader of the herd to arrange for a deer to step forward and give itself for the king to shoot, alleviating the harm to other deer. This reasonably orderly system worked fine until it was the time for a pregnant doe to serve as the king's meal. She called attention to her pregnant condition and desire to give birth to the fawn that she was carrying as reasons for seeking an exemption to the orderly process. The leader of the herd stepped forward and agreed to take her place as the target for the arrows of the king. Moved by the generosity of the self-sacrificial spirit of the leader of the deer herd, the king released the entire herd. These types of narratives are reminders of the importance of giving for the welfare of others, the radical nature of compassion for the suffering of others, and the importance of reincarnation, and that a person like a Buddha does not just suddenly emerge from any kind of society, but that it rather takes many lifetimes to reach a point at which one is prepared to become a Buddha (a fully enlightened being).

After relating many tales similar to the two just highlighted, the *Jātaka* tales tell the story of the Buddha's final reincarnation as a married man with two children named Prince Vessantara, who is renowned for his generosity. Among the things that he gives away, there is a white elephant, which is culturally considered a very auspicious animal. In response to this action by the prince, his subjects rebel and drive him and his family away. While leading a wandering lifestyle with his family, he encounters a Brahmin, who asks for his children. Not only did Vessantara give away his children, but he also gives away his wife. In some versions of the story, the prince has everything that he gave away in his orgy of generosity restored to him. After the prince dies, he is destined to become the Buddha in his next life.

During the sixth century BCE in northern India, a child was born, according to legend, to a king and his spouse, who was to die shortly after giving birth to the child named Siddhārtha. The child's mother, Mahāmāyā, dreamed about being transported by angels to a mountainous region, where she was purified, clothed, and perfumed before reclining on a divine couch. The couch was circumambulated three times by a white elephant, a symbol of royalty, who struck her on her right side (the auspicious side of the human body) and gave her the sensation of entering her womb. Awakening from her dream, the queen informed her husband King Śuddhodana, who summoned sages to his court to ascertain the significance of the dream, which functioned in part as a predictor of future events. The Brahmin sages tell the king that his forthcoming son would become either a universal monarch or a Buddha, two destinies that depended on what type of life the son decided to follow. Proceeding to the garden of Lumbinī, the queen gave birth while standing and holding the branch of a tree. Some versions of the birth narrative relate that the infant was received by spirits in a golden net and free of any impurity. In a biography composed by Aśvaghoṣa, the infant took seven steps and announced that this will be his final birth because he had arrived to save the world. The seven steps suggested transcendence of the world, time, and space. Seven days after the child was born, his mother died.

The child's body was marked with auspicious signs that were interpreted as signs of future greatness, depending on what path of life he chose to follow in the future. The child grew to maturity amidst grand splendor and unimaginable pleasures. In short, Siddhārtha led a hedonistic lifestyle and lacked nothing. Eventually, he married and fathered a son named Rāhula (literally, "fetter"). This married life continued until he encountered a series of signs that dislodged him from his lifestyle. While riding outside the palace gates on successive days, he witnessed an old man, a sick person, a dead body, and a monk. Disturbed by what he encountered, he wanted to lead a religious life, which his father opposed because the king wanted his son to eventually assume the throne and become the great conqueror predicted of him by sages. But the wishes of his father did not deter Siddhārtha, who proceeded to renounce the world and leave behind his wife, child, and extended family, intending to find answers to his mental and emotional turmoil.

Siddhārtha set forth on a six-year regimen of asceticism that nearly killed him. By living a wandering lifestyle in the forest, Siddhārtha lived a dangerous form of existence in the forest, with meager dietary resources to sustain his body. In the Pali canon, the Buddha confesses that he had become so emaciated that he could reach through his stomach and grab his spinal cord. At the margins of human existence and endurance, Siddhārtha decided to take some food to restore his strength, which was immediately criticized by his ascetic companions. By rejecting extreme forms of asceticism, Siddhārtha developed his own spiritual method, which he called the middle path, that was grounded in meditation, leading to four trance states and eventual liberation from pain and suffering. After being reinvigorated and nourished, the Buddha sat under the *bodhi* (enlightenment) tree vowing not to arise from under it and meditating until he attained liberation. As Siddhārtha progressed spiritually, Māra, a personification of evil and lord of death, arrived at the tree with the intention of disturbing and subverting the sole meditator before he achieved his goal and deprived Māra of a tenant in the realm of the death, showing other humans how to conquer death and rebirth. Māra began by enticing Siddhārtha with heavenly rewards before he sent his hideous army to attack the meditator and natural disasters to destroy him. With the weapons of his army turned into lotus flowers and natural disasters having no effect on Siddhārtha, Māra sent his three daughters—Discontent, Delight, and Desire—but they were of no avail. At the conclusion of their encounter, there occurred an argument over the seat occupied by Siddhārtha when Māra claimed that the seat, which was symbolic of royalty, belonged to him because he has been the most generous. Since an Indian king is by definition generous, the Buddha and Māra were arguing over kingship and who deserved to have dominion over the earth. The Buddha won the debate after he called on the earth to testify to his generosity in his former births, after which Māra retired, defeated.

Siddhārtha continued with his meditation and achieved concentration (*samadhi*), before reaching the four meditations, which involved achieving discursive thought, equanimity, and freedom from anguish or joy. These meditations suppressed desires, evil thoughts, secondary mental activities, and sentiments that have the potential to distract the mind. With his mind concentrated and unified, he attained the four trance states and liberation. Upon achieving the state of nirvana (ultimate freedom) by means of arduous meditation, Siddhārtha became a Buddha (a fully awakened being). This title presupposed that everyone else is asleep to the truth. In order to awaken everyone else, the Buddha spent the next forty-five years of his life wandering, teaching, attracting followers, and establishing monastic communities. Initially, he went to the Deer Park near the sacred city of Benares to deliver his first sermon, known as "The Turning of the Wheel of the Dhamma," where he encountered his former ascetic colleagues and converted them to his path, and they eventually achieved liberation. The Buddha's message was based on his spiritual quest and what he discovered during his search. His message was not to be accepted by faith but was intended to invite others to verify for themselves the validity of his teaching. For this reason, the Buddha requested that everyone should be a "lamp unto yourself" because, ultimately, everyone has to achieve his own salvation.

Long before the advent of Buddhism in ancient India, the country was populated by small kingdoms and countless villages. Kings utilized the talents of Brahmin priests, who served as advisors, and they supported the polytheistic religion of the priests with their complex ritualistic system and sacred body of literature, called collectively the Vedas, which was grasped as a revelation to the seers and committed to memory by members of priestly families. While the Vedas were preserved orally and passed to younger generations of priestly families, ordinary villagers practiced various forms of animism, polytheism, and ancestor worship, although the priests exerted the greatest religious and cultural influence, with the kings exercising the most profound political power. In addition to villagers, priests, and kings, there were various wandering holy individuals who sometimes created cult groups around them.

Social, economic, and political changes slowly evolved around the sixth century BCE. From a social perspective, India developed into more urban centers, although the small villages continued to thrive. Economic changes were hastened by iron tools that allowed for the clearing of more land and the ability to support a larger population. The development of a monetary system, increasing craft specialization, and growth of trade were also part of the economic picture that contributed to a rich merchant class. Political change resulted in the rise of monarchies and empires that replaced local ruling families. These types of changes were reflected in Buddhist texts.

Basic Teachings of the Buddha

Since the Buddha was already liberated when he gave his first sermon in Benares by means of his enlightenment experience, his decision to teach was an act of compassion for those still captive to the cycle of life and death. It is possible to abbreviate his teachings to the term *dhamma* (Sanskrit: *dharma*) as is often done in Buddhist texts. Within the Indian cultural context, *dhamma* can mean the cosmic law that regulates and governs the totality of existence, or it can mean the truth that enables one to break free from the limitations imposed on human existence. From this perspective, *dhamma* is both the source of order within the universe and the means of salvation from the world. The basic intention of the Buddha's *dhamma* (teaching) was to convert listeners to a radical new mode of life in order to lead them to salvation. Buddhists' writings often express this basic intention in a metaphorical way. The Buddha's teachings are called a vehicle, such as a ferryboat, and the river to be crossed symbolizes the river of life. The shore from which one begins one's journey represents a place of suffering and ignorance. The far shore or destination represents liberation and transcendental wisdom. The ferryboat is analogous to the teachings (*dhamma*) of the Buddha, which serves as the means of transporting one to the far shore. But once one's goal is achieved, there is no need for the ferryboat.

If you successfully complete the journey, this does not mean that all your questions will be answered to your satisfaction, because the Buddha left unanswered certain metaphysical questions. During the Buddha's life, a monk challenged the Buddha about such questions and said that he would leave the monastic order if such questions were not answered. The Buddha responded to this monk by telling a parable about a man who was wounded by a poisoned arrow. After his companions acquire a physician to help him, the wounded man demanded to know the caste of the culprit, his name, his clan, whether he was tall or short, his skin color, the type of wood that made the bow, the material used to make the bow-string, the nature of the arrow, and so forth. If one took the time to address all of these questions, the obvious result would be the wounded person's death before all questions could be answered. This parable suggests that there is a high degree of urgency associated with the message of the Buddha because life is short and an aspirant needs to begin practicing his teachings right away.

The initial truth that he discovered and shared with his audience was that all life was suffering, a truth based on his observations of sickness, old age, death, and causality. The initial three observations were connected to the legend of the four signs that he witnessed by the side of the road. The truth about the operation of causality was discovered by the Buddha in a state of insightful trance. Actually, all of these observations are interconnected because they were connected to the law of karma (cause and effect) and the cycle of rebirth (*saṃsara*).

The Buddha's basic insight into the nature of causation means that the cycle of human existence was determined by the law of karma (cause and effect) because the kinds of action that we perform produce either positive or negative karmic consequences that result in some kind of fruit within this present life or a future lifetime in an apparently never-ending cycle. The law of karma was like a natural law built into the universe that operated automatically for actions performed with either one's body, speech, or mind in any of three temporal modes: past, present, and future. If a person was negligent, neglectful, or mistaken when performing an action that harmed another person or creature, the consequences are not as severe as when a person intentionally committed a harmful act. This meant that the Buddha conceived of an intimate connection between a deed or action and human intention. Thus karmic results of actions performed without intention were not as severe as those committed with intention. A slip of the tongue was not, for instance, as karmically consequential as willfully lying or intentionally hiding the truth. The doctrine of karma suggested necessarily that there were no accidental occurrences within the universe. It also implied that everything in the universe was causally conditioned or produced. Therefore, there was nothing in the world, from an apple pie to a zebra, that was not causally produced or conditioned by something else.

Depending on a person's karmic condition during her present and past lives, her future rebirth destiny will be determined by her actions. Even if a person led a virtuous life, this did not mean that her rebirth would result in a favorable condition, because negative karmic consequences from an earlier birth could override the virtuous deeds performed in a person's present life. The important points from the perspective of the Buddha were that this process was unending, led to suffering, and was part of a broader cycle of causation. To be captive to the cycle of rebirth was conceived of as suffering.

The entire process of karma and rebirth was an integral part of a larger process called *conditioned genesis*, a twelve-linked chain of causation discovered by the Buddha. This meant that karma operated within the context of this larger chain of causation and closely interacted with it. The twelve links of causation created a circular chain without beginning and end that functioned as a prison for human beings. The overall theory was important because it explained how suffering arose and how it could be ended. The theory also explained that human existence was determined by innumerable interrelated processes, and it demonstrated how each moment within the process of causation was determined by other conditions. Moreover, the theory of causation demonstrated that everything within the world was impermanent and that all things were interdependent. With its automatic mode of operation and its formation for the context of suffering, causation was a difficult cycle from which to escape. It was analogous to being condemned by a person's action to eternally riding an ever-revolving carousel. When the ride ended, a person changed his vehicle, but he could never leave the carousel that continued to turn because it was fed by the energy of hatred, delusion, ignorance, and greed.

With relentless causation as the foundation of suffering, the Buddha taught that life was unsatisfactory because of such events as the frustration of our desires, sickness, degeneration of our mental and physical faculties, old age, anxiety, fear, and death. Suffering was also connected to change and the temporary nature of things. The passing away of a pleasant event or feeling, for instance, led to sorrow. By clinging to notions like self, I, or ego, a person suffered from conditioned states, which functioned as the support for the initial two levels of suffering. The Buddha taught that it was essential to recognize that the self was nothing more than a combination of ever-changing physical and mental forces without any permanence or enduring substance.

Some readers might protest that the first truth is overly pessimistic and even potentially nihilistic. The Buddha anticipated such objections from his critics. This is illustrated by a narrative about a young woman and her dying baby. After tearfully asking the Buddha for help with her dying child from snakebite, the Buddha felt compassion for her and instructed her to go to each home in the town to ask for a mustard seed from any house that did not experience the death of someone. Holding her dying son to her breast, the woman canvassed the town, asking the appropriate question at each door. Eventually, after her task was completed, she returned to the Buddha without a single mustard seed, because there was no home that had not experienced the death of someone. This discovery concerning the universal nature of suffering motivated her to become a nun and to achieve enlightenment.

The second truth shared by the Buddha was the identity of the cause of suffering that he traced to ignorant craving, thirst, or desire. Humans craved for sense pleasures, existence, and non-existence or no rebirth. Any form of craving was considered counter-productive to a person's spiritual liberation because cravings were examples of attachment and led to rebirth. Even though ignorant craving was the second noble truth, it was not considered the first

Figure 7.1 Icon of the Healing Buddha. Photograph by Carl Olson.

cause of suffering because it was dependent for its origin on something else within the larger context of the entire cycle of causation. However, ignorant craving was centered in the false idea of the self, which entailed eradicating attachment to the self to make any spiritual progress. To think that a person could satisfy her ego represented a fundamental misconception because there was no permanent ego or self to satisfy. From the Buddha's perspective, there was no spiritual substance, soul or eternal self that endured beyond this present mode of existence, which was called the non-self (*anatta*) doctrine. What a person mistakenly assumed to be a self was really a group of five aggregates that consisted of matter, sensations, perceptions, impulses to action, and consciousness that were in a constant state of flux and impermanence, whereas death represented the complete dissolution of these five aggregates, leaving no distinctive physical or mental identity that endured. Therefore, becoming detached from the five aggregates was essential for escaping the world of suffering and pain.

The cycle of suffering ended with the achievement of nirvana as expressed in the third noble truth. In short, nirvana represented the opposite of this world because it was described as uncompounded, unconditioned, causeless, the absence of desire, cessation, the extinction of craving, and the end of rebirth. Being beyond logic and reason, nirvana was unthinkable and incomprehensible. From a more positive perspective, nirvana was absolute freedom in the sense of liberation from evil, craving, hatred, ignorance, duality, relativity, space, and time. If a reader investigates the root meaning of nirvana, it is possible to learn that the term means to be "fully blown out," similar to an extinguished flame of a candle or a match. The attainment of nirvana was analogous to a deathless calm, which was free of decay, aging, and death, that enabled a person to gain an insight into the absolute truth that there was nothing absolute in the world because everything was relative, conditioned, and impermanent within the world. This flash of intuitive insight was an experience that occurred during the life of a person while embodied. With the death of his body, the enlightened person passed away because his life energy was exhausted, but he was not reborn, due to being beyond the cycle of causation.

In order to attain nirvana, a person needed to follow a path that was explained by the fourth noble truth, which the Buddha called the eightfold path. This was described as a middle way between the extremes of asceticism and hedonism. The path consisted of an integration of elements of wisdom, moral/ethical virtue, and meditation. The elements of wisdom were identified as right understanding and thought, which represented understanding of the four noble truths and thought devoid of lust, ill-will, and cruelty. The ethical/moral aspects of the path were represented by right speech, which meant refraining from falsehood and other types of harmful speech; right action, which involved avoiding violence, stealing, lying, sex, and intoxications of any kind; and, finally, right livelihood, which suggested refraining from a mode of occupation that harmed others. The final three steps on the path involved meditation. The sixth step, right effort, involved cleansing the mind of evil thoughts and the prevention of others from arising, whereas the seventh step, right mindfulness, implied becoming astutely aware of one's body and mind. Finally, right concentration involved practicing meditation, which culminated in the four trance states and the intuitive vision associated with the attainment of nirvana.

In retrospect, the Four Noble Truths of the Buddha were apparently modelled on the fourfold pattern of Indian medical science: (1) recognition of a patient's disease by a doctor; (2) making a diagnosis; (3) prescribing a cure; and (4) giving the medicine. Corresponding to this medical pattern, the Buddha's teaching recognizes that life is suffering, the reason for suffering is ignorant craving, the prescribed cure is attaining nirvana, and the eightfold path is the medicine intended to cure suffering. Moreover, a short summary of the Buddha's teachings are condensed into the three marks of existence: suffering, impermanence, and non-self. These three characteristics are typical of all life, without exception. But what about nirvana? The ultimate goal of the teachings is beyond ordinary space and time and is thus without characteristics.

Monastic Community, Precepts, and Refuge

Wandering holy individuals and groups of ascetics have been common in Indian culture, a practice dating prior to the life of the Buddha. These various groups had to contend with the annual monsoon season, which made travel very difficult because of washed out roads and bridges, a situation that necessitated a break for the wanderers. The annual rain retreat became specialized for the early Buddhists after they began to return to and occupy the same habitat as the rainy season began. This practice contributed to the development of monastic fellowships and a curtailing of the wandering lifestyle, which was compared to the single horn of a rhinoceros in the literature and continued to remain the ideal, although the monastery became the practical result because it allowed monks a place of refuge apart from the distractions associated with social life. In fact, the Buddha insisted on the creation of monastic communities. These communities arose from two types of rain retreat settlements: a structure located in the countryside that was built and maintained by monks and another type located in or near a town that was usually supported by a wealthy donor.

The Buddhist monastic community was called a Sangha, a term that referred to the fraternity of monks and the bond of association among them. Theoretically, no religious leader was necessary because the rules guided it. These monasteries were populated by *bhikkhus* (literally, "beggars") because monks supported themselves by begging for food and other necessities of life such as medicines. The monk's begging bowl functioned as a symbol of his lifestyle. Comparable to the life pattern of the narrative of the Buddha, those aspiring to become a monk had to perform an act of world-forsaking. The act of renouncing the world became ritualized over time and consisted of the following: (1) renunciation of caste, kinship, and social rank; (2) acceptance of robes and a begging bowl; and (3) going from home to homelessness. By abandoning the world, a monk exchanged one social system for another. After renouncing the world, a person could be ordained as a novice, an informal affair, which consisted of being at least 15 years old, reciting the three refuges (Buddha, Dhamma, and Sangha), donning the appropriate robes, agreeing to abide by the ten precepts, and having his head shaved. Full ordination involved eight requirements: being a human being; being 20 years old; having permission of parents or wife; being free of debt; being free of disease; being a free person; not being employed by the government; and having a bowl and robes. An eligible person was presented to the assembly of monks. The ordaining monk asked three times if the assembly accepted the candidate. If there was no dissent, the initiate was accepted as a monk, who then chose a spiritual guide with at least ten years of experience within the brotherhood. A monk was allowed to have some personal possessions, which included three robes, a cord worn around the waist, a begging bowl, a razor, a needle, a water-strainer, and a toothpick.

In addition to the begging bowl and robes, the monk's shaven head is one of the most prominent external features of a Buddhist monk. Within the Buddhist context, hair is a bodily by-product analogous to urine, feces, saliva, nails, and skin. These by-products are considered inferior and polluting. The shaven head is analogous to a corpse because the head of a deceased person is shaved before the funeral, an Indian cultural practice before cremation of the body. In a symbolic sense, the ordinary monk is dead to the world while he is also paradoxically alive at the same time. The ordination ceremony transforms an initiate into someone who is both dead and alive, a liminal status that means one cannot die again because one is already dead and cannot be reborn because one is alive. Some Western scholars have interpreted the monk's shaven head as equivalent to celibacy because long hair represents unrestrained sexuality and is associated with semen, which is stored in the hair when a person refrains from sexual relations. According to another scholar, hair is a polluting form of dirt that offends against order and thus represents a form of danger. Thus, shaving the head of a monk sets him apart as a marginal being in relation to society and functions as an act of purification for a monk.

It would be incorrect to think that Buddhist monks were held together simply by a building or need for companionship. The unifying factor was the *pātimokkha*, which etymologically means "bond," representing the basic injunctions of the religion. In the Pali canon, there are some 227 rules, 250 in the Chinese version, and 253 in the Tibetan rendition. In early Buddhism, the *pātimokkha* served as a confession of faith chanted by an assembly of monks that functioned as their bond of brotherhood. The *pātimokkha* was divided into eight divisions involving similar cases. There were, for example, four cases involving defeat or exclusion from the order, which included sexual intercourse, stealing, murder, and falsely claiming to have attained spiritual insight or powers through meditation. Besides these and other violations of the monastic code, the rules encouraged an irenic lifestyle that included manual labor directed toward the monastery and not for personal gain, a prohibition against handling money, simple clothing for bodily protection, sandals made of a single strand, allowing walking sticks for infirm monks, no obligatory solitude, and the forbidding of vows of silence.

The common life of a monk was paradoxical in the sense that he renounced the world and society, but he was still dependent on laypeople to sustain his monastic lifestyle. Buddhist scripture envisioned this relationship as a reciprocity between two groups of givers, with the monks sharing the teachings (*dhamma*) of the Buddha and laypeople supporting the monastery in various ways. But why should the laity support a group of monks who are an economic drain on the community? The simple answer is the following: giving to the monastic community was a meritorious act that resulted in positive karma and improved a layperson's chances to achieve a better state of rebirth in her next life. Moreover, the layperson enhances social stability and order and promotes nonviolence in society.

The Development of Popular Buddhism

From its inception, the Buddhism practiced by a monk was different and in tension with that observed by the layperson. At an early point in its history, the Buddha was so successful at recruiting young men to become monks that texts confirm ordinary people complained that he was making their families sonless (a situation that makes it impossible to conduct traditional funeral and ancestral rites for deceased parents), leaving women widowed (by renouncing the world, kin, and society, a monk becomes dead to the world), and disrupting family lines of succession. In short, the conversion to a monastic mode of life threatens an orderly society. Texts also make it clear that monks held a negative attitude toward members of society by comparing them to dust in the wind. Over a period of time, laypeople adapted to the demands of Buddhism and found ways that they could be engaged with the religion.

Laypeople could listen to religious discourses, observe the five precepts, offer robes, food, and medicine to monks, make pilgrimages to holy sites associated with the history of the religion, worship at *stūpas* (memorial mounts containing a holy relic), and recite the three refuges (Buddha, Dhamma, and Sangha). Many of these actions were considered meritorious and would influence a person's rebirth status. The merit that a person acquires by giving can also be shared with disembodied spirits, although it is impossible to assist those in hell or to alter another's karmic destiny. The merit gained by donors is greater when they give to a more saintly monk. In practical terms, this means that the laity were concerned that the recipients of their generosity be paragons of virtue, which places pressure on monks to excel in their observance.

During his lifetime, the Buddha was a charismatic figure with the ability to convince others of his teachings and was revered for his spirituality. Converts gathered around him, forming a small cult that gradually evolved into a religion, a situation that is comparable to that for Jesus and Mohammad. Monks and laity bestowed honorific titles on the Buddha, such as Bhagavā, which literally means one endowed with great riches, teacher, Tathāgata ("gone there") pointing to his enlightenment, and Mahapurisa (Superman). What sets the Buddha apart from others and makes him an extraordinary male are the identifiable marks on his body: hands and feet like a net, a complexion like bronze, skin so smooth that no dust clings to it, eyelashes like a cow (a beautiful animal), a white hairy mole located between his eyebrows, sexual organs concealed in a sheath, thousands of wheels shaped like spokes that appear on the soles of his feet, and jaws like a lion; he also emits a supernatural radiance from his body, has foreknowledge of human events, and can see into the past and future. This partial list also includes supernatural powers attained as a by-product of his quest for liberation.

These extraordinary powers appear as interesting narratives in Buddhist Pali literature. The Buddha is, for instance, depicted as suddenly disappearing in one tale. In another episode, while others seek a boat to ferry them across a flooded river, the Buddha suddenly vanishes and reappears on the opposite side of the river. A monk is portrayed preaching to a crowd and changing bodily forms from one moment to the next. The Buddha warns monks not to demonstrate these types of powers because they are a mere by-product of the path and are dangerous because they can be used for good or evil purposes. The Buddha is depicted, for example, personally criticizing a monk for levitating to retrieve a bowl from the top of a bamboo pole and then flying around the city three times.

It is not too difficult to imagine monks sharing these types of narratives with laypeople in order to entertain, convert, and teach them. Inspired by the teachings and colorful narratives given to them by monks, laypeople began to direct their devotion toward the Buddha and worship his image, although image worship was probably preceded by symbol worship for several centuries. Somewhere around the first century CE, Buddha images came into existence. Each image signified a different message associated with the teachings of the Buddha expressed by the hand gestures of the statue. Before the image of the Buddha appeared in a layperson's home or in a temple, people could direct their devotion to a monk who was slowly being deified by monks and laypeople, which was at odds with the portrait of a human being achieving his own salvation. It is historically ironic that others are now asking him to save them.

Besides devotion directed to images, laypeople also embraced *stūpa* veneration, a practice that apparently dates to the period after the cremation of the Buddha's remains and their distribution to several parties. A *stūpa* is an artificially constructed memorial mount that contains the relics (ashes, bone, hair, tooth, or robe) of the Buddha or a saintly figure. It was believed that the relic makes the deceased symbolically present. The literature traces the origins of the *stūpa* to the Buddha, who is depicted giving his permission, in a text that narrates his final nirvana and death. When a *stūpa* is ritually empowered, it becomes the body of the holy person in the sense that the base of the *stūpa* represents the Buddha's legs, the dome is his torso, the central axis is his spinal column, and the top is equated with his head. In the case of the Buddha, his spiritual charisma is contained in the *stūpa* and animates it. When laypeople go on pilgrimage or visit a local *stūpa*, they are performing a meritorious deed by circumambulating it with the right (auspicious) side of one's body toward the object. In addition to the merit acquired by visiting and worshipping a *stūpa* or an image, a layperson receives *darsan*, a physical-spiritual seeing and being seen. The devoted layperson sees, for example, the image of the Buddha, and it in turn sees her because the image is alive. This process of seeing enables a person to participate in the holy charisma of the Buddha and to communicate with him. This type of evidence shows that laypeople play an important role in the success of Buddhism to shape the lives of its adherents inside and outside of the monastery. In fact, it is the devotional spirit of Buddha expressed in the lives of ordinary people that eventually enables Buddhism to become a global religion and more than an enclave for elite monks.

Early Buddhist Canon

Formative Buddhist scriptures were not considered a form of divine revelation by early Buddhists because the historical Buddha was a mortal human being and not a god, sharing his teachings about the nature of human existence and its solution. The Buddha, a charismatic figure, taught and shared his message orally in the language of local dialects and Old Māgadhī, which was the primary language of his teachings and eventually made its way to Sri Lanka. The preserving of the Buddha's oral teachings in a written form began around the middle of the first century BCE because there was a decline of reciters, war, and famine. The Sri Lankan monastic community preserved the teachings on wood products and palm leaves bound together by leather strips, forming books written in Pali. Prior to being preserved in writing, a series of councils were held after the death of the Buddha to establish the authenticity of his message. These councils resulted in the organization of Buddhist literature into, initially, two baskets: *Vinaya-pitaka* (basket of monastic discipline) and *Sutta-pitaka* (basket of discourses). In the second century BCE, a third basket was added called the *Abhidhamma-pitaka* (basket of additional teachings).

The *Vinaya-pitaka* contained the rules and precepts that guided monastic life. The term "*vinaya*" literally means "to lead away from." By adhering to the rules, a monk was led away from evil, the trap of sensual pleasures, and egoism. In fact, the rules are an assault on the ego in order to prepare a monk for liberation from the cycle of causation. In the *Vinaya-pitaka*, there are narratives often associated with the origin of a rule triggered by an action. When the Buddha was alive, monks would seek his opinion, which made the regulation valid. After his death, rules were considered valid if they could be traced back to the Buddha, or monks would use his previous rulings as their guide to decide on new cases. The *Sutta-pitaka* contained the Buddha's discourses, and the term *sutta* was metaphorically connected to weaving and connotes a thread or thong of leather or string used to hold together the pages of the text. Many discourses contained introductions with the location at which it was spoken and a list of those in the audience, and then proceed with the sermon of the Buddha. This structure suggests that monks were concerned about accurately transmitting the Buddha's teachings and establishing an orthodox tradition. The *Sutta-pitaka* was arranged according to length, giving us long and middle-length sayings in addition to those arranged by contents and numerical groupings, as well as a collection of minor works.

The third collection of texts included in the early Pali canon was the *Abhidhamma-pitaka*, which consisted of the prefix "*abh*," meaning "above," implying what is beyond or superior to the *dhamma* (doctrine/teaching) that it was analyzing. In comparison to the *suttas*, the term suggested greater authority. The *Abhidhamma* literature represented a scholastic analysis of material from the *Sutta-pitaka*, suggesting that it referred to an analysis of the teachings or an understanding of them. This literature tended to be technical because it probably originated from a list of doctrinal topics that were used to collect and preserve concepts and teachings of the Buddha. The literature indicates a wide variety of scholastic viewpoints. After the creation of the three baskets of literature, learned monks wrote commentaries on the texts. An excellent example of this trend in the fifth century CE was the work of Buddhaghosa, a monk who also authored *The Path of Purification*, a very influential text that both summarized the Buddha's teachings and explained them.

Missionary Buddhism

The Buddha sought to convert others to his message by the power of his charisma and teachings in order to convince others to renounce the world and lead a monastic life in order to devote full time to meditation and achieving salvation. But there is no evidence that he envisioned his path spreading beyond northern India. Buddhism did, however, spread beyond India to areas of South and Southeast Asia. The impetus for the wider missionary character of Buddhism can be historically attributed to King Aśoka, a figure who converted to Buddhism late in his life after defeating an enemy in a bloody conflict that disturbed his conscience. Aśoka was famous for erecting pillars in north India that spread the message of Buddhism. In addition to holding a third or a fourth council (according to some recent scholarly opinion), Aśoka transformed the Buddha's teachings into a missionary movement, an event that began with sending his son Mahinda to Sri Lanka, where he converted the king of the island, who subsequently converted the entire island to Buddhism. From this island conclave, Buddhist monks spread the religion to Myanmar (formerly Burma), Thailand, Vietnam, Cambodia, and Laos. The early history of Buddhism in these countries was diverse and eclectic, with a mixture of Buddhism, Hinduism, Tantra, and indigenous animistic traditions. Eventually, Buddhism also arrived in China, Korea, and Japan, which are developments that will be considered in future chapters on religions of China and Japan.

The Role of Women in the Buddhist Tradition

The depiction of women and their proper role in society within Buddhism was similar to that inherited from the Hindu tradition. Thus, we need not repeat what was discussed in another chapter. The Buddhist tradition does, however, provide us with some interesting cases that show women asserting their identity. Within its cultural time and place, Buddhism was more revolutionary and egalitarian in comparison to ancient Hinduism.

An essential way that Buddhism was different from Hinduism in its treatment of women to some degree was evident in the narrative of Mahāprajātī, maternal aunt of the Buddha. She approached the Buddha and inquired about establishing an order for nuns but was refused by the enlightened one. Not disappointed at her initial failure, she decided to use Ānanda, a faithful attendant and confidant of the master, to intervene for her to press the Buddha for authority to establish an order. Arguing for the aunt, Ānanda got the Buddha to admit that women were capable of attaining enlightenment. With this hard-won admission to his credit, Ānanda got the Buddha to approve an order for nuns, although the Buddha foretold that Buddhism would only last five hundred years in India instead of the one thousand that it would have lasted without the inclusion of women. This simple narrative about the origin of an order for nuns exemplifies ancient cultural attitudes toward women while also indicating some improvement in the lives of women by giving them a choice about their future careers, showing that the teachings of the Buddha were for everyone and indicating that women were the spiritual equals of men.

Buddhism also represented social changes for women by advocating more respect and authority in their homes: not being forced into marriage, enjoying more equality in their marriage, and being allowed to manage, give away, and inherit property. Buddhist women could retire from life to meditate and study Buddhist scriptures. They could thereby become preachers and teachers. When a woman became a widow, she did not have to be reclusive, suffered no moral degradation, and did not endure disastrous social status as a widow. Nonetheless, women were still negatively depicted in many Buddhist texts dating to the appearance of written literature, which were products of monks influenced by prevailing male attitudes toward the opposite sex.

Monkish narratives related tales of sexually voracious females who seduced or raped unsuspecting monks while they are asleep or too ill to resist. Women are portrayed as dangerous to males and unable to control their tumultuous sexual drives, which need constant satisfaction. In the *Jātakas*, women are depicted negatively. In one story, an old, blind hag was flattered by a young student. In order to escape with her new lover, the hag attempted to kill her son, who had tended her faithfully over the years. In another narrative, a woman is rescued from a flood by an ascetic; she seduces and marries him. But later she deserts him for a robber chief and tries to murder the ascetic to be free of him. If these two examples indicate that women are untrustworthy, unfaithful, and unethical, men are portrayed in contrast as noble, loyal, generous, and holy. This type of depiction of women in such stark negative features not only reflects ancient cultural attitudes toward women but is also evidence of the monkish attitude toward women as a dangerous threat to a monk's monastic purity, which stands in sharp contrast to the innate unclean nature of women because of their menstrual cycle. The narrative evidence makes it clear that the fault for transgressions resides with women and not innocent monks.

These types of attitudes shaped the monastic code, in which women were made institutionally subordinate to their male counterparts. A nun must treat every monk as her senior and superior, even if he just entered the order. Nuns owed monks homage and respect and were forbidden to revile or admonish any monk, but these attitudes need not be reciprocated by monks. A nun could not teach monks, but nuns were required to receive a lecture from a monk every half-month. When a woman was a nun candidate, she was asked if she was a woman. This might seem to be an unnecessary question about something that would appear to be rather obvious, but the purpose of the question was intended to ensure against the admission of eunuchs. A nun's entry into the order meant that she followed the same life of poverty typical of a male. There were some minor differences, such as the necessity of wearing a bodice, an inner garment that covered her body from the collar bone to above her navel for the purpose of hiding her breasts. This particular clothing requirement is traced directly to a directive of the Buddha after it was reported to him that a nun's breasts were exposed when a strong wind blew up her robe, and laypeople laughed in response to the sight. Similar to monks, nuns shaved their heads, turning them to unisexual or asexual beings just like monks, to an external observer.

Buddhist narratives also testify to extraordinary women in the tradition. There were some eminent teachers, some nuns attained enlightenment, and other wealthy women supported the monastic community with their generosity, according to stone engravings made on Buddhist monuments that date from the third to second century CE. In an early tale, Somā, daughter of a chaplain of a king, was tempted by Māra, lord of death, who reminded her of her limited intellectual and spiritual capacity and why it was important for her to submit to his temptations, but she still emerged victorious over this symbol of evil, a narrative that parallels the victory of the Buddha over Māra. The spirituality of nuns is evident in the *Therīgātha* (Psalms of the Sisters), representing compositions about enlightenment from more than seventy nuns.

In the countries of Sri Lanka, Thailand, and Myanmar, which are associated with the Theravāda Buddhist tradition, the order of nuns has ceased to exist today. The religious vacuum has been filled to some degree by laywomen who have chosen to lead a monastic style of life without getting ordained, while still deciding to observe the basic ethical precepts. In Sri Lanka, the women do not want to become nuns because they want to remain free of male domination. It is a bit ironical that these laywomen practice celibacy, which gives them social and religious autonomy. In these South Asian countries, lay nuns assume a marginal status in their societies because they are not fully ordained and not full members of common social life.

The Spread of Mahāyāna Buddhism

The Buddha lived and taught during the beginning of the Mauryan period (546–324 BCE), which was a time of empire expansion and of social, economic, and political change. After the Buddha's death, a council was called to preserve his teachings, with the purpose of establishing an authoritative canon. Later councils were called to address disputes over monastic regulations and doctrinal issues. Within a hundred years after the death of the Buddha, the movement that he established began to split, initially over various issues of monastic discipline and later over issues of doctrine. At one point, some eighteen different schools existed, which was evidence of the diversity within Buddhism, a trend that continued throughout its history with many different and often competing schools and movements. This type of historical evolution of the religion was indicative of its many branches spreading from the trunk of a single tree, a metaphor for the historical Buddha. Thus Buddhism was not a centralized or monolithic religion; rather, it was a religion of widespread diversity.

It is not possible to assert with absolute certainty that any of the early schools represented precursors of Mahāyāna Buddhism. It appears to be more likely that the Mahāyāna school arose between 150 BCE and 100 CE as a loose community of individuals and groups adhering to particular texts. With its roots in India, Mahāyāna spread north to Tibet and east to China, Korea, and Japan. Within the overall umbrella term of Mahāyāna, there were many different schools that often represented very different views about the nature of Buddhism. A new type of wisdom literature emphasized the notion of emptiness, the philosophical insights of Mādhyamika, and the thought of Yogācāra.

The wisdom (*prajñā*) literature represented texts (*sūtras*) by different unknown authors of various lengths, with some texts titled according to their length. Among the shorter works, there were such texts as the *Heart Sūtra* and the *Diamond Sūtra* that were composed between 300 and 500 CE. The format of these texts represented a continuous dialogue between the Buddha and other figures like disciples, gods, spirits, or humans. These texts were believed to represent the word of the Buddha, an association that gave these texts their authority.

According to the *Heart Sūtra*, the ultimate facts of reality are, for instance, called *dharmas*, of which there are two types: conditioned (generally the world of causation) and unconditioned. There are only two unconditioned types of *dharmas*: nirvana and space. The text proceeds to teach that there are two ways of viewing *dharmas* (elements of reality) that are essential for a person's salvation. The first way is an act of differentiation that involves breaking apart the apparent unified ego or self and its experiences and being able to recognize that wisdom views the aggregates that constitute the self as something constructed by the mind, whereas ignorance imagines a unified self. The second step involves an act of depersonalization that eliminates all references to ego, me, or mine. Finally, there is an act of evaluation in which one realizes that the Buddha's teaching about the self is superior to an unenlightened and ordinary understanding of the self.

But when a person really views the *dharmas* (elements of reality) he sees them in their own-being (*svabhava*), a term that can refer to the essence of a thing. A good example would be to say that fire is a thing of which heat is its essence (own-being). The term is also used to refer to an essential feature of a thing in the sense that own-being embodies its own mark. An example would be to assert that consciousness is being aware. A third usage of the term is to claim that it is the opposite of other-being, which means that the former is dependent only on itself, whereas other-being is contingent and tied to conditions. It is possible to illustrate this point by noting that heat is an essential feature of fire, although it also depends on fuel, oxygen, and other elements. To truly have own-being (*svabhava*), a thing must possess full control over itself that is independent of conditions. But what is the point of this torturous type of philosophical exercise?

The author of the text wants to make clear that *dharmas* (elements of reality) are empty of any own being, which means that they are not ultimate facts in their own right. They are merely imagined, because each *dharma* is dependent on something other than itself for its existence. In and by itself, it is nothing. Therefore, elements of reality (*dharmas*) do not exist as separate entities, have no relationship to other entities, are isolated, and are not made or produced, because they have never left original emptiness. The most that a person can assert about *dharmas* is that they have a nominal existence as mere words. In fact, from the perspective of an enlightened being, *dharmas* (elements of reality) are empty. Therefore, the notion of emptiness conveys the idea that what appears to be something is really nothing. These appearances are analogous to a dream state.

The *Heart Sūtra* develops a three-stage dialectic that begins with the five aggregates that mistakenly give a person the false sense of a self, and each is identified with emptiness. The text makes it clear that emptiness is a transcendent reality when it states the following: "Form is emptiness, emptiness is not different from form, neither is form different from emptiness, indeed, emptiness is form." Even though emptiness is beyond all that is, it is also immanent, which suggests that it is also identical with its exact opposite—for instance, the five aggregates that constitute the self.

The basic insights of the wisdom texts were made more systematic by the Mādhyamika school, inspired by a brilliant philosophical monk named Nāgārjuna (c. 150–250 CE). Inspired by more idealistic Mahāyāna texts like the *Gaṇḍavyūha Sūtra* (Flower Ornament Text) and the *Laṅkāvatāra Sūtra*, the Yogācāra school, which was founded in the fourth century by the monk Asaṅga and his brother Vasubandhu, attempted to correct some of the perceived shortcomings of the Mādhyamika school, which did not address issues such as the process used by the monk to create objective fictions, error, how memory occurs, the identity of experiences that are free from discrimination, and the origin of suffering.

In a fashion similar to the Buddha, Nāgārjuna envisions a middle way between affirmation (is) and negation (is not), occupying a transcendental position that is beyond concepts and speech. This middle way clings to neither existence nor non-existence, implying a position of total detachment in which no philosophical view is ultimate. The ruthlessness of Nāgārjuna's dialectical method is intended to put an end to all theorizing, knowing, and philosophizing. From his perspective, this is the practice of the perfection of wisdom (*prajñāpāramitā*), which is equivalent in Mahāyāna Buddhism to the attainment of nirvana.

A crucial feature of understanding the thought of Nāgārjuna is coming to grips with his distinction between conventional truth and ultimate truth. The first kind of truth deals with knowledge that is valid for practical purposes. It is useful to know, for instance, that rice and bread can satisfy a person's hunger and that a stone is uneatable and will not cure one's hunger. But this everyday type of knowing has its limits because, when a person pushes it, there is a tendency for it to become self-contradictory or illusory. Why is this true? It is due to ignorance (*avidyā*), which tends to obscure the real nature of things or constructs a false appearance. This does not imply, however, that ignorance possesses any reality, because it is in fact characterized as unreal (*māyā*), much like a mirage in the desert or a pregnant virgin. In contrast, ultimate truth is a non-dual type of knowledge that represents an intuition devoid of content. Beyond ordinary knowledge or rationality, it represents a dissolution of the conceptual aspect of the mind. The freedom suggested by this type of truth does not necessarily imply a complete rejection of conventional truth, because a person still finds it pragmatically useful to know how to cook, what to eat, how to use a hammer, how to communicate, and many other valuable forms of practical knowing that get us through the day successfully and may even improve our lives.

With the dawning of the realization that all distinctions are empty, a person's mode of awareness is transformed. Such an awakened person sees things as they really are in fact, which means to see things as empty (*śūnyatā*), which suggests an intuitive vision of everything as swollen or lacking in self-existence (*svabhāva*), a feature that is non-contingent and without relation to anything else. Wetness is, for instance, never encountered apart from water or moisture. Therefore, wetness is created and is not self-existent. The lack of self-existence (*svabhāva*) represents the true nature of all things. This does not suggest that emptiness is a superior viewpoint, something in itself, or represents ultimate reality, because Nāgārjuna defines emptiness as empty. This means that emptiness is insubstantial and imperceptible. This suggests that emptiness checks the inclination to transform phenomena into something substantial by means of conceptualizing them and making them something that they are not. The wisdom that a person gains from the intuitive insight into emptiness releases a person from attachment to things, to dissolve any absolute notions about something, and to realize that one attains nothing. However, the intuitive insight does destroy illusion created by attributing self-existence to things, and it affords a person freedom, detachment, cessation of problems, and purification from things like hatred, fear, greed, and anxiety.

In contrast to the Mādhyamika school, the Yogācāra school more clearly defined the problematic nature of the human condition by specifying craving (*taṇhā*) as the root cause of misery, although craving needs a subject (craver) and an object (something craved) for it to be effective. The other basic problem is ignorance (*avidyā*), which exists because humans regard the objectifications of their minds as a world solely independent of their minds. In order to overcome this problem, humans need to realize that their minds are the source of all objectifications. If you can imagine an animal with the body of a zebra, the legs of an elephant, the tail of a peacock, and the head of a lion, it would be possible to create an object of such a strange creature. The objectification of such a weird creature could be traced directly to our minds, suggesting that this false creature is nothing more than a phantom created by the mind. Just as humans can create strange creatures by using their mental powers like imagination, they can also make strange creatures or objects disappear without a trace. The Yogācāra philosophers claim that this type of mental operation occurs all the time with the objects of the external world and the world itself. Thus the only thing that truly exists is the mind-only or consciousness-only.

It is neither possible to become aware of this from the standpoint of a mentally constructed level of reality nor from a relative level of reality, because the former fabricates objects and the latter is dependent on a duality of a perceiver and a thing perceived. It is essential for one to reach perfect knowledge and to see things as they really are in fact in the fulfilled state of reality that is beyond all discrimination and duality. The fulfilled state means to see everything as mind- or consciousness-only, which implies that the fundamental dichotomy between subject and object is extinguished as a person's consciousness sees only consciousness. With the identity of the seer (mind or consciousness) with itself by the extinction of an external object, there arises an identity of the consciousness and object. Yogācāra thinkers call the negation of the seer no-mind and the negation of the object nothing-grasped. This represents the end of thinking that objectifies or conceptualizes. A person's thinking is now characterized or equated with wisdom. Thus, if a person can still conceive of a subject and an object, such a person is not liberated and does not possess wisdom. But the truly wise person who sees consciousness-only does not allow craving to arise because such a person is liberated from objects as well as a self that craves objects. Consciousness-only is pure in the sense that there are no objects and the person is not even conscious of consciousness. Moreover, pure consciousness is equated with sheer emptiness.

If there is consciousness-only or just mind, how can a person account for the variety of ideas and impressions that exist in her mind? Why can different people agree that a particular object represents a chair and another object a glass?

The Yogācāra thinkers account for such questions by pointing to the store-house consciousness (*ālaya-vijñāna*), which is a kind of repository for ideas and impressions associated with the activity of the mind that is traced to a beginningless past. Since the beginning of time, every human who has ever lived has made deposits in this store-house consciousness in the form of universal and private seeds. The former type of seeds accounts for things that we recognize and share in common, while the latter signifies differences. In addition, there are pure and impure seeds, which along with the other types of seeds are deposited on the store-house consciousness in a process called perfuming, which affects other types of consciousness. In its perfected state, gained by the practice of yoga and meditation, the store-house consciousness represents pure consciousness, which is equated with the state of nirvana.

The central paradigm of the ideal person in Mahāyāna Buddhism is the *bodhisattva* (literally, enlightened being) who counters the ideal of the *arhant* (fully enlightened being) or *pratyekabuddha* (literally, solitary Buddha) in the Pali text tradition, which were thought to be self-centered and selfish ideals because they were only concerned with their own salvation, whereas the bodhisattva vows to save all beings. Actually, the term bodhisattva is a bit misleading because she is a figure that progresses to the brink of enlightenment but does not fully enter nirvana because such a person possesses compassion for everyone and stays within the world to teach and lead others to liberation. Thus, it is best to conceive of the bodhisattva as a person destined to become a Buddha (a fully enlightened being).

It is likely that the ideal of the bodhisattva was historically influenced by Hindu devotional movements with their emphasis on love of deity, service to others, and fervent devotion, which were elements that could also be discovered in the Buddhism of lay supporters from a formative period in Buddhist history. In comparison to the earlier history of Buddhist holy persons, the Mahāyāna school advocated the ideal of the bodhisattva to counter the person of the *arhant*, a fully enlightened being who teaches, and the ideal of the *pratyekabuddha*, a person enlightened by himself who does not teach. Since the *arhant* and *pratyekabuddha* seek liberation for themselves, the Mahāyāna school depicts them as selfish and egotistical ideals, because neither of them is really concerned with the spiritual condition of others. By advocating the ideal of the bodhisattva, the Mahāyāna school wanted to counteract the solitude and the cloistered, passive, placid, and inert type of monastic life characteristic of the other types. In short, the bodhisattva is a person who works for his personal salvation as well as that of others. The bodhisattva also strives to help others find welfare and happiness within the world. Therefore, the fundamental focus of the bodhisattva is within the world instead of escape from the world.

If life is suffering and humans are captive within the world, is not the this-worldly focus of the bodhisattva misplaced? This question is best answered by the theoretical context in which the bodhisattva operates. As the Mādhyamika school makes clear, if everything is emptiness, this is also true of the world of rebirth and nirvana. Since the world of rebirth is equivalent to nirvana due to their shared emptiness, they are non-dual and without distinction. Moreover, because there is only one, non-dual reality, everything is a part of the one reality. Hence, all human beings and other creatures are tied together, interrelated, and interdependent parts of a single reality. Since this is the theoretical situation in which the bodhisattva finds herself, this forms the rationale for helping others and for being orientated toward the world rather than being motivated to flee from it.

From within the context of emptiness (although strictly speaking there is no such context) and the limitations of language to express it adequately, the bodhisattva demonstrates his commitment, determination, and resolve to assist others by making four fundamental vows by which he lives. The initial vow is to save all beings. Secondly, the bodhisattva vows to destroy evil passions and, thirdly, to learn the truth and teach it to others. Finally, the bodhisattva promises to lead all beings toward enlightenment. In addition to these four vows, the bodhisattva is expected to develop and practice a series of perfections (*pāramitās*), culminating with the perfection of wisdom that is equivalent to achieving nirvana.

Transmission of Buddhism to Tibet

There is little known about the pre-Buddhist history of Tibet, often called Kangchen (land of snows). According to a Tibetan narrative, primordial waters gave birth to an awful ogress, a creature of irrepressible emotion and sexual impulses, and a meditating monkey, an incarnation of the merciful bodhisattva Avalokiteśvara. Believing that she was alone on the earth, the ogress wept profusely for a mate, alerting the monkey to her presence. The contemplative monkey left his cave because he felt sorry for the ogress, and they had a sexual relationship that resulted with the birth of six offspring without tails, sparse hair on their bodies, and the ability to walk upright.

From the perspective of a historical narrative, the introduction of Buddhism from India north to Tibet can be grasped in two disseminations of the religion. The initial dissemination occurred in the seventh century CE during the reign of Songtsen Gampo (c. 618–650), who was portrayed as an incarnation of the bodhisattva Avalokiteśvara for the purpose of spreading Buddhism. The king appeared to have been influenced by his two wives: Bhṛkutī, a princess from Nepal who brought an image of Akṣobhya (literally, "Imperturbable One") Buddha to Tibet, and Wen-ch'eng, a daughter of the Chinese emperor who brought a statue of the Buddha with her. Songtsen Gampo built the first Buddhist temple in his capital of Lhasa, developed a legal code based on Buddhist ethical principles, and sent scholars to India to study.

Buddhism was also promoted by another king, named Trisong Detsen (c. 740–798), who was believed to be an incarnation of the bodhisattva Mañjuśrī (literally, "Gentle Holy One"). The king invited learned Buddhist scholars from India, such as Śāntarakṣita (c. 705–798), but they were forced to leave Tibet when the local angry spirits caused natural disasters. In order to subjugate the local spirits, a great tantric master named Padmasambhava was invited to Tibet, and his efforts were successful, but he was also forced to leave the country when he became a victim of anti-foreign sentiment. In 775, the Samyé Monastery was consecrated, giving Buddhism a tenuous foothold in Tibet. During Trisong Detsen's reign, the controversy over gradual versus sudden enlightenment was allegedly settled by a debate, with the king judging the contest in favor of the gradual approach and also decreeing that the Mādhyamika school would be the preferable way followed in Tibet.

The first dissemination of Buddhism in Tibet ended in persecution by King Lang Darma (r. 838–842), who closed monasteries, required monks and nuns to return to lay life, and severed contacts with Buddhism in India. The persecution drove Buddhism underground, and eventually the king was assassinated by Belgyi Dorje, a Buddhist monk, which led to political chaos, collapse of the dynasty, regional fragmentation, and the demise of Tibetan power in central Asia.

The second dissemination of Buddhism into Tibet had more enduring consequences. By the end of the tenth century, political stability enabled kings to revitalize Buddhism. Not only did kings send students to study in India, but they also invited famous Buddhist masters to Tibet, such as Atīśa (982–1054) in 1042, whose disciple Dromten (1008–1064) founded the Kadam school, and Marpa (1012–1096), who was another student of Nāropa (1016–1100), a great tantric master and teacher at Nālandā University located in northern India. Marpa inspired his disciple Milarepa (1040–1123), who in turn influenced Gampopa (1079–1153), a founder of the Kagyupa school.

Buddhist monasteries were looted and monks killed after Tibet reneged on paying tribute to the Mongols, but this negative development gave way to something positive for Buddhists when the Godan Khan agreed to allow a Tibetan representative at his court around 1274, was converted, became a protector of the religion, and made the leader of the Sakyapa school, Gūnga Gyelsten (also known as Sakya Pandita, 1181–1251), the regent of Tibet. This began the practice of monastic leaders assuming responsibility for the social and political welfare of the Tibetans.

By the late fourteenth century, Tibetan Buddhism had fallen into decay, but it was to experience a major reform initiated by Tsong Khapa (1357–1419) and his reformist movement, which emerged as the Gelugpa (Order of Virtue) school. This reform started a spiritual revival, as evident by the construction of the Ganden Monastery in 1409, and it was symbolized by the ceremonial yellow hats and robes of the monks in contrast to the red-colored attire of the unreformed monks. Further construction followed before Sonam Gyatso, leader of the school, was given the title Dalai Lama by the Altan Khan, which initiated the reincarnation doctrine associated with the Dalai Lama. During the life of the fifth Dalai Lama, Tibet became unified for the first time, with the support of the Mongols. This period also witnessed the building of the Potala Palace, as residence of the Dalai Lama, in Lhasa, capital of Tibet.

The position of Dalai (Great Ocean) Lama (teacher), a term of Mongolian derivation, evolved in Tibet from the notion of the bodhisattva and his vow to save all beings. Because the bodhisattva dies without fulfilling his vow to save everyone, it is necessary for him to return to earth, adopting an incarnated form until his vow is completed. The Dalai Lama was believed to be the incarnation of the bodhisattva Avalokiteśvara (literally, "The Lord Who Looks Down"), who sees the suffering of humanity and responds with compassion, within the Gelugpa sect, Order of Virtue. The term was initially applied to Sonam Gyatso (1391–1474) by Altan Khan, a Mongol ruler of Kokonor. The title was applied to two predecessors before being applied to all subsequent incarnations, including the fourteenth Dalai Lama (b. 1935) living in exile in northern India. When a Dalai Lama dies, it is the duty of the sect to identify the child in whom he is currently incarnated by looking for signs, consulting the oracle at Nechung monastery, and consulting a lake south of the capital of Lhasa associated with the patron goddess of the Dalai Lama to look for a vision in the lake. Once a child is identified, he is tested to verify the procedure by exposing him to articles associated with the previous Dalai Lama. When a successful search is concluded, the boy is enthroned and begins his education, but does not assume a leadership role until he is mature and becomes the leader of a priestly state. Until he becomes mature, regents run the country. The concept of the Dalai Lama gives Tibetan Buddhism a way to pass religious authority and charisma to later generations.

After a period of international isolation, Tibet became a British protectorate before it lost its independence in March of 1959 when the Communist Chinese invaded the country. This event caused the fourteenth Dalai Lama to flee into exile in India. The Dalai Lama became a spokesperson for a free Tibet and a major international figure espousing peace and nonviolence. His efforts for international peace won him the Nobel Peace Prize in 1989. From his residence in Dharmasala, India, the Dalai Lama seeks to find a solution to Chinese domination of Tibet.

The Way of Tibetan Buddhism

Buddhism in Tibet did not reach its mature form until the end of the fifteenth century CE, absorbing as it developed ritual elements, magical attitudes, and local spirits. The Tibetan way is labeled Mantrayāna (sacred formula vehicle) or later Vajrayāna (diamond vehicle). Tibetans translate *vajra* as *dorje*, meaning "lord of stones," which is used in ritual to signify the active male principle (*dorje*), and a bell represents the female perfection of wisdom or emptiness. This male/female symbolism reflects the influence of Tantra on Tibetan Buddhism, representing a philosophy of the non-duality within the context of the appearance of dualities. Besides Tantra, the Tibetan Buddhist tradition is also composed of Mādhyamika and Yogācāra thinking. A fourth major tradition forming Tibetan Buddhism is the Bön-po religion, a form of inner-Asian shamanism that existed in Tibet before the advent of Buddhism that was allied with nature worship because the people believed that spirits inhabited mountains, rocks, meadows, and water. Shamans used various types of divination devices to determine their influence on human events and exorcised and placated demons and spirits. Because Mādhyamika and Yogācāra have been previously discussed, we will concentrate on Tantra influence on Tibetan Buddhism at this point.

According to Tantric thought, the human body is the abode of all truth, representing a microcosm of the macrocosmic universe. Within the material human body, there is a subtle, innate body representing a psycho-physical complex that consists of fine breath power, which serves as a vehicle for mental energy. This innate body consists of four centers, a nerve system, and mind. The goal of Tantric practice is to circulate and unite energy in the central nerve and to get this energy to flow upward and unite with the innate mind, which represents a union of emptiness (śūnyatā) and compassion (karuṇā). Emptiness is equivalent to wisdom (prajñā), and compassion (karuṇā) represents skillful means (upaya). The former is passive, conceived as female, symbolized by the lotus flower, identified with the left nerve, and underlies all the diversity of the phenomenal world, whereas the latter is active, conceived as male, symbolized by the thunderbolt (vajra), identified with the nerve on the right side of the body, and accounts for differences in the world. Finally, wisdom and skillful means form a unity of emptiness and existence. This non-dual unity is equated with supreme bliss.

It is common for Tantric texts to stress their secretive nature. It is also common to assume that Tantric practice is for advanced monks who have exhausted or advanced beyond previous forms of meditative practice and reciting of mantras, such as the famous Mani mantra: *Om Mani Padme Hum*. *Mani* means jewel and is equated with the *vajra* (diamond), *Padma* means lotus, and *Hum* cannot be translated, while *Om* stands for the totality of sound and the totality of existence. The Tantric method presupposes that the meditative process focusing on body, speech, and mind can be hastened by a more radical procedure involving illicit sexual relations.

The use of desire to achieve liberation stands in opposition to the need in the Buddha's teaching to control ignorant cravings. But Tantric adepts think that the energy of a female partner can be used to untie the knots within you that block channels of energy. This sexual method is metaphorically expressed as a union of the lotus and *vajra* (diamond scepter). Some Tantric authors refer to this method as the "worship of women." The method involves a male recognizing his female partner as a divine goddess. This recognition involves a woman entering a *maṇḍala* (sacred diagram) and sitting in front of the male figure, who worships her with flowers, incense, offerings, and lamps; he prostrates before her, circumambulates her in a clockwise fashion, and engages in sexual intercourse with her. This is followed by acts of service directed to the female, such as rubbing her feet, cooking for her, feeding her, and prostrating before her, which are expressions of the male's subordination to his partner.

Regarding any substance or fluid that might issue from his partner as holy, the male must be willing to touch and ingest her waste. Some writers refer to these types of practice as worshipping the female organ, which is compared to lotus petals. The male must continue the worship until the female signals that she is satisfied.

This type of erotic play is intended to stimulate the flow of the woman's sexual fluid, which means honey, nectar, or wine. The female's sexual fluid is the nectar that ultimately confers the omniscience of Buddhahood. During sexual intercourse, each participant absorbs the other's fluid, which is metaphorically expressed as the mingling of the red and white essences. At the final stage, partners relinquish attachment to pleasure and meditate on emptiness. The Tibetan Buddhist adoption of tantric methods and concepts adds to the diversity and richness of the religion.

Ritual, Festival, and Cultic Activity

Throughout South Asia, villagers offer worship and celebrate important moments of the Buddhist narrative. Major observances include the Buddha's birth, enlightenment, first discourse at Benares, and nirvana. The Visakha Puja (Buddha's Day) combines the Buddha's birth, enlightenment, and death because they each took place on the full moon of the month of Visakha. In Thailand and Myanmar, evening activities predominate, with people gathering with lighted candles and glowing incense to circumambulate the monastery three times. The beginning of the monastic community is celebrated because it represents the completion of the three refuges (Buddha, Dhamma, and Sangha). These types of rites take place within a cultural context of animism, a belief in multiple spirits that are called *phii*, malevolent spirits, in Thailand and *nats* in Myanmar, providing an interesting blending of Buddhism and local folk traditions.

Villagers in Thailand organize and sponsor a rite called Somdet, honoring a monk by means of investing him with titles, which is considered a mark of communal appreciation for the monk's piety and services. There are eight grades of titles that can be bestowed on a monk, with Somdet being the lowest and also the name of the ceremony. The selected monk receives a gift of silver inscribed with the names of the honoring village and monk. The length of the silver depends on the degree of the title. At the beginning of the ceremony, the monk to be honored is carried on the shoulders of villagers, a procession led by the chief priest, carrying a stick akin to a sacred wand. Before the monk is led to an altar, male villagers lie flat on the ground for the monk to walk over them on the way to the altar, which is believed to benefit the males because it allows them to acquire merit and drives away illness. The monk to be honored kneels on a stone slab before the altar. On the altar is a long hollow piece of wood carved in the form of a Naga, a water serpent. While other monks chant blessings, three candles are lit and placed on the Naga's head, and water is poured into the serpent's groove, which falls on the monk's head.

Then the monk is taken to the preaching hall, a presentation is made, and the monk substitutes his wet robes for dry garments. The major lay sponsor reads the inscription on the piece of silver. The ceremony ends with blessings being given by the honored monk to the assembly.

The symbolism of the ceremony is a hybrid mixture of Buddhism and folk culture. The handling of valuable objects (silver in this case) is a violation of monastic regulations. Paradoxically, the honored monk is purified with water and simultaneously fertilized because the water poured on the monk symbolically seeps through the serpent's poison bag, which is akin to milk, a fertility symbol. Moreover, the water pouring aspect of the ceremony enables ordinary people to pay respect to their superiors, symbolizes transfer of merit, and purifies the honored monk. This rite is informative with respect to the monk's role in the village, which represents a respected and venerated status.

Another type of rite performed in Thailand is called Sukhwan, which means calling the *khwan*, a person's life soul that primarily lives in the body but can leave it. This rite refers to binding the life soul to the body in order to make a person whole at crucial times during one's life, such as rites of passage, when one is in transition to a new social status, or other points of transition during one's life. The rite consists of tying a piece of thread to a person's wrist. This type of village rite reveals a belief in one or more souls despite the traditional teachings of the Buddha about the non-existence of a permanent soul or self.

In some instances in Thailand, a festival called Loi Krathong, which marks the end of the monastic rain retreats, is an expression of gratitude to Phra Upagutta (Pali, Upagupta), a monk who protected Aśoka's 84,000 *stūpas* from Māra's attempt to destroy them. In addition to preaching about the *Vessantara Jātaka*, small boats of banana stalks are set adrift to float on rivers or ponds illuminated by candles, with incense and coins placed on the boats. Children swim to the boats to retrieve coins. Besides its connection to Upagupta, Thai Buddhists also believe that the offerings are associated with a narrative about the Buddha when he left footprints on a sandy shore that a serpent (*naga*) king wanted to worship after the Buddha's death.

Within the context of Tibetan culture, ritual incorporates magical elements. The Chöd rite is a perfect example of this trend, which is performed to invoke the protective power of a deity against the possibility of being poisoned or getting leprosy. The person being protected dances in the form of a goddess to destroy erroneous beliefs. After identifying his passions and desires with his body, the person offers his body to *ḍākinis* (female spirits) and visualizes his body as a fat, luscious-looking corpse. After mentally withdrawing from this vision, the subject watches the goddess Vajrayogini sever his head and convert his skull into a container, into which she tosses chunks of his bones and slices of his flesh. By reciting mantras during this event, the subject transmutes the entire offering into pure nectar and begs the supernatural beings to devour it raw. This rite embodies compassion to all hungry beings and a realization of the emptiness of the body.

In Thailand and other South Asian countries, it is typical for young boys to be ordained Buddhist monks for a predetermined amount of time, which can amount to a few weeks or months, without any intention of becoming a professional monk. Young boys between the ages of 12 and 18 become monks briefly because they want to earn merit for a dead relative. At the end of their tenure as monks, the young boys return to society—without any negative stigma attached to their return to society—to resume a normal pattern of life. In fact, the boy's return is ritualized by the boy giving flowers and candles to thank those who officiated at his ordination, although this is performed at a predetermined auspicious date and time. After the brief ceremony, the ex-monk remains in the monastery for one or more nights to clean the residence, with the purpose of removing any sins that he might have committed as a monk.

A vigorous cult of amulets exists in Thailand, representing miniature busts of the Buddha or famous monks believed to possess sacred or supernatural power. The amulets are attached to necklaces and chains and worn around the neck by men and women. They can be purified with holy water, propitiated with offerings, and worshipped by a person pressing her palms together in reverence. It is common for wearers to put the amulet on in the morning and recite a sacred formula to it. Then, using both hands, the wearer transfers its power to her head. If an amulet loses its power, a wearer can ask a famous monk or holy person to touch it and thereby restore its potency. A wearer is motivated to don an amulet because it offers personal protection and prosperity and reminds one of the virtues of the Buddha and the saints.

South and Southeast Asian peoples have weaved together the Buddhist religion and the village agricultural calendar into annual festivals. The Songkrān Festival, a New Year celebration of Thailand, is characterized by giving food to monks, cleaning homes, washing one's hair, and exploding fire crackers. The local statue of the Buddha is bathed by villagers, which is believed to wash away their demerits and show respect. An enormous sand *stūpa* is built that symbolizes new beginnings. Deceased ancestors are invited, commemorated, and given merit. Young people bathe and wash away the sins of their elders, seek their forgiveness, and receive their blessings. When the sand *stūpa* is completed, it is topped by three flags symbolizing the three jewels of the Buddha, Dhamma, and Sangha. A white cord is attached to the sand mound and the Buddha image in the temple, which charges the *stūpa* with power, signifying personal regeneration and reordering of the world. Young people engage in water sports to cast away the old and engender the new. Activities on the fourth day are informal, with people paying respects to the Buddha's image and freeing caged birds and fish to earn good merit.

The villagers of Thailand also celebrate the Bunangfai (Rocket Festival) to solicit rain. Sections of bamboo are packed with black powder and reinforced with rope to create either of two types of rockets: respect or wishing rockets. If a rocket flies straight and high, the omens are considered auspicious, but when a rocket fails, its firer is hit with mud. The launching of a second rocket gives way to ritual license and rowdiness. Monks do not participate with those who are ecstatically possessed by spirits.

Taking place in February-March, there is the observance of the Bun Phraawes festival in Thailand for merit making and harvest celebration. Humans and spirits are invited to listen to the story of the Buddha's life. The name of the festival is derived from the story of Vessantara, the final incarnation before Siddhārtha becomes the Buddha. By listening to the narrative, villagers receive merit and fulfilment of their wishes. Uppakrut, a serpent (*naga*) lord, is invited to attend because he helped defeat Māra and protect King Aśoka's *stūpas*. People demonstrate their gratitude by holding this festival in order to get the serpent to protect the village and bring rain.

In Myanmar, the Taungbyon Festival is a national celebration that is observed at the end of August, recalling the lives of two brother spirits. This festival is very riotous, with its invitation to overeat, gamble, and indulge in sexual play. Drunkenness is common among men, along with sexual banter, teasing, and fondling of female backsides. After offerings are made to spirits, many people dance to entertain the spirits and to soothe them. By wearing spirit costumes, dancers symbolically represent the spirits. The festival includes the bathing of images at the river, where some people observe this action from boats. Young men engage in sexual banter and shout obscenities at girls in other boats. The festival concludes with the destruction of a spirit tree, and people carry fragments away to bring good luck. These kinds of festivals mix together elements from the folk culture and Buddhism. Some of the folk elements were present before the arrival of Buddhism and often are contrary to the spirit of Buddhism. Festivals periodically turn a society upside down, renew the society, refresh the people, and represent a positive attitude toward life that is far removed from the spirit of the first noble truth, which characterizes all life as suffering.

The same type of development is found in Sri Lanka with the syncretism of Buddhist and Hindu elements. A striking example is the Kataragama cult that Sinhala Buddhists have adopted and transformed, with monks taking control of the sacred area. The annual festival recalls the dramatic narrative of the procession of Skanda to a Valli Ammā shrine for fifteen nights. This reenactment celebrates the sexual union of Skanda, a son of the Hindu deity Śiva, with his mistress. The festival commemorates the washing of the deity's clothes polluted by sexual intercourse. Participants play in the water of the river by splashing each other, which is considered a celebration of the god's passion and sensuality. This type of glorification of sense pleasures represents non-Buddhist features.

Buddhism and Death

As Buddhism developed in various cultures, it became closely associated with death rites that have a twofold purpose: representing a rite of passage for the deceased and attempting to secure a good status for the dead in the next world.

The second purpose of the rite is accomplished by merit-making and its transfer. Buddhist monks play the roles of mediators between death and rebirth and absorb and neutralize the dangers associated with death and its polluting nature. In Thailand, villagers make a distinction between normal and abnormal death because the form of death is vital for the fate of the soul. An abnormal death occurs unnaturally, suddenly without warning, or caused by childbirth, accidents, homicide, or disease. These types of death cause the soul of the deceased to seek vengeance on the living.

Mortuary rites involve preparation of the corpse by bathing it, using thread to tie hands and feet together, laying it on a mat facing west, inserting a coin into its mouth, and sealing the mouth with beeswax, which enables the dead to buy her way to heaven and purchase necessities there; a pair of flowers and candles are placed in the deceased's hands, and other bodily openings are closed with wax. A white cloth, symbolizing death, is used to lower the corpse into the ground. A red cloth is used to cover the coffin and is taken home after the ceremony; its color represents normal life and its continuation. A procession to the grave is led by monks who hold a long cord attached to the coffin, while puffed rice is thrown on the ground. The dispersal of rice is intended to motivate spirits to welcome the dead person in the next world, to prevent spirits from entering the coffin and making it heavy, and to lure the spirits to the cemetery and away from the village. The coffin circumambulates the funeral pyre three times in a counter-clockwise direction because death subverts normal procedures. While on the pyre, water is poured over the corpse, and monks pour coconut juice on the face of the deceased. After the funeral pyre is ignited, mourners go to the monastery before returning home because it immunizes survivors from the dangers of death. Monks visit the home of the deceased for three nights to chant for protection and blessings for the living. On the third day after the cremation, the second phase of the rite occurs, with a palace being created for the deceased to live in during its afterlife; gifts are given to monks to create merit for the deceased, bones are collected, and ashes are raked to find the coin placed into the mouth of the deceased, which is used to counter spirits. Bones are placed into a pot, a hole is poked in the white cloth in order to release the soul, and the pot is buried. The rite concludes with food offerings to monks.

In comparison with Buddhist-dominated cultures of South and Southeast Asia, Tibetan Buddhists' treatment of death is especially elaborate. Tibetan monks talk about external and internal signs of death. External signs appear on the human body, which include pain, confused speech or mind, disturbed dreams, and change of flesh color that are omens of inevitable death. A sure sign of death is evident if one simultaneously urinates, defecates, and sneezes. When fingernails and toenails become bloodless, a person will die in nine months. A person will die in three months if the hair on one's neck grows upwards. Teachers insist that external signs are basically emotional, whereas internal signs can be discovered through an interpretation of breathing or through the interpretation of dreams. If one dreams that one is riding a tiger, fox, or corpse, this is a sure sign of impending death. There are also secret signs, distant signs such as different forms of one's shadow, near signs such as gums growing grimy and black, and various types of miscellaneous signs such as snapping one's fingers and getting no sound.

Tibetan monks composed a manual of death that is intended to be read aloud in the presence of the dying or deceased person. This text is the *Bardo Thödol*, that is well known in the West as *The Tibetan Book of the Dead* in English translation. The purpose of reading this text aloud was to give instructions to the deceased about how to navigate through the three intermediate phases (*bar-do*) of dying, death, and rebirth, with the goal of attaining liberation. Tibetans believe that there is a forty-nine-day period after death that is very dangerous for both the deceased and survivors. The term "*bardo*" literally means "between two" because there are three intermediate stages: The briefest period happens at the moment of death; the second stage is the *bardo* of reality; and a third stage appears when reality is not recognized. During the first stage, a profound state of consciousness enables one to recognize a clear light as reality, which immediately liberates one from rebirth. The second stage begins when one cannot recognize the clear light as reality. The disintegration of personality at death reveals various wrathful and peaceful deities in sequence over many days. During the third stage, the stage of mundane existence dawns and reveals that one must begin rebirth in one of the six realms (e.g., gods, demigods, humans, animals, hungry spirits, or hell).

The Tibetan Book of the Dead originated with Padmasambhava, although it was not revealed until the fourteenth century, when it was discovered by Karma Lingpa. The text belonged to a category of Tibetan literature called *terma* (literally hidden treasure) because it represented hidden texts due to religious persecution that began in the ninth century CE. These hidden texts were intended to be rediscovered later by *Tertöns* (treasure discoverers) with the help of female spirits. These hidden texts were believed to have been hidden during the initial diffusion of Buddhism into Tibet by the Indian monk Padamasambhava and discovered at a later date. Until discovered by a *Tertön*, these texts were protected by spells from discovery by undesirable people. Overall, the *terma* phenomenon represented the possibility of periodic renewal within Tibetan Buddhism.

Tibetans have invented methods of avoiding or cheating death. A good way to avoid death is to create a thread-cross by crossing two sticks and connecting them to colored thread to form a diamond shaped cobweb, which forms a demon trap. Similar to flies getting caught in a web, spirits are captured in the thread-cross. Once the demons are trapped, the thread-cross is abandoned in a remote, lonely place. Fearful of impending death, a person can cheat death by having a dough figure resembling him, using color associated with particular demons and mixed with elements such as a person's excrement, clothing, mucus, saliva, tears, hair, and nails. After being empowered by six mantras (sacred formulas), the figure is cast into a river with the intention of getting the demons to chase or accept the substitute. If this method is successful, a subject averts death for three years.

A typical Tibetan funeral is restricted to family and others indicated by a favorable horoscope. An astrologer discerns an auspicious date for the funeral. The deceased's body is bound with ropes into a crouching posture with the head placed between the knees and hands placed under the legs. If rigor mortis occurs, the bones must be broken to get the desired bodily posture. The procession to the site of the funeral is led by monks chanting mantras, blowing horns, beating drums, or ringing bells and followed by relatives, friends, and finally the square coffin, which is led by the chief priest holding a long scarf tied to the coffin.

Tibetans observe five means of corpse disposal. Embalming is reserved for grand *lamas* (teachers), while cremation is restricted to high priests. The corpse is consumed by animals after it is stripped of clothing, placed face down on a slab of stone and tied to a stake, or the corpse is butchered, with the flesh given to vultures and other animals to eat. To view this procedure as a barbaric way to dispose of a corpse is to take it out of its cultural context within a country in which the ground is frozen much of the year. Thus, the disposal of the deceased by animal consumption is best interpreted as an adaption to a people's environment. Any remaining bones are buried. A fourth method involves grinding a deceased's bones into a fine powder after the flesh is consumed by animals or birds. Finally, for the very poor, cadavers are thrown into a river or a place of waste.

Material Culture of Buddhism

Monasteries and temples of diverse styles are typical of Buddhism in South and Southeast Asia. In Thailand, a monastery is called a *wat*, an area for the worship of the Buddha by monks and laypeople. The structure of the Thai *wat* consists of an inner part called the Buddhavāsa, an area used by monks and laypeople for worship, and an outer part called the Sanghavāsa, an area used only by monks. These internal and external parts of the monastery form two concentric circles around the central Buddha relic.

A typical Thai *stupa* (memorial mound) consists of three parts: base, central dome, and top, which symbolizes the three jewels of the Buddha, Dhamma, and Sangha. From the perspective of Buddhist cosmology, it represents the three realms of the world: sensuous, form, and formless. The *stūpa* symbolically represents the center of the world, which unifies the three realms that provide its vertical orientation. The horizontal orientation consists of the four Buddha altars located at the four major directions and four guardian *yaksas* (spirits of the earth and wealth) at the four minor directions. The entire structure represents a miniature cosmos.

Arguably, the most famous *stūpa* is the structure at Sanchi in Madhya Pradesh, which was built during the Shunga period of Indian history (first

Figure 7.2 Gate to the Great Stupa at Sanchi. Photograph by Carl Olson.

century BCE to first century CE). In addition to holding relics of the Buddha, the complex tells the narrative of the Buddha, including his life as Chaddanta, an elephant, that is contained in a *Jātaka* tale of one of his former births. At the eastern gate of the complex, a carved crossbar relates the story of his departure from his home and family, whereas the crossbar of the north gate depicts his defeat of Māra's army. In these types of examples, the narrative of the Buddha is literally carved into stone for illiterate people to be able to read his story, making the major events of his biography accessible to everyone.

In addition to monasteries, temples, and memorial mounds, images of the Buddha and bodhisattvas are prevalent in Buddhist countries. Before an image of the Buddha can be worshipped, it needs to be consecrated. This process includes two major elements: instructing the image and charging it with power. Resting on a raised platform, the head of the image is covered with a white cloth, a symbol of his act of world renunciation, and its eyes covered with beeswax. Then the image is instructed in the Buddha's personal history by monks by means of chanting and sermons, which also empowers the image. This process of empowerment of the image is enhanced by nine monks who sit in a semicircle around the image, meditating. Sitting before the monks are their bowls, which are connected to the image by sacred cords, functioning as conduits of power from the monks to the statue. Female renunciants prepare honey-sweetened rice balls that commemorate the food that sustained the Buddha for forty-nine days. At dawn, monks remove the white cloth and beeswax, which symbolize the Buddha's enlightenment, and three mirrors are turned around to face outward instead of toward the image. The three mirrors recall the three super forms of knowledge experienced by the Buddha, which includes knowledge of former lives and states of rebirth of everyone. At the conclusion of the consecration of the image, it is ready to accept offerings. Offerings are not given directly to the image, because gifts are intended to be offered to the memory of the Buddha.

Within the context of Tibetan culture, besides images of the Buddha, there are many metal and stone images of holy persons. Tantric practice is celebrated by the so-called *yab-yum* (literally, father and mother) image of two divine beings fornicating. Beyond the physical act of sexual congress, this image symbolizes the female passive principle of wisdom (*prajñā*) and the active male principle of skillful means (*upaya*). Tibetan artistic expression is also evident with *thangkas*, which are scrolls depicting holy figures, deities, and episodes from Buddhist narratives. These colorful paintings are executed in a variety of styles and are used to adorn homes and temples. An often-related form of Tibetan artistic expression is the *maṇḍala* (sacred diagram), although it is used for meditation purposes. Often representing the symbolic world of a deity that is flanked by four entrances at the cardinal directions, *maṇḍalas* can be of any size and hung on a wall or created on the ground with colored powder. Sitting near the sacred diagram, a yogi visualizes entering its outer ring of fire, which destroys the yogi's impurities. By entering the second ring of diamonds, the yogi achieves the indestructible quality of enlightenment. The third circle consisted of eight cemeteries that destroy eight distracting modes of consciousness. Finally, the fourth circle consists of a ring of lotus flowers and a land of purity. Standing at the center of the cosmos, the yogi encounters the central deity, who represents emptiness and with whom the yogi identifies.

Tibetan Buddhists are also famous for creating and using prayer wheels of various sizes. Prayers are written in Tibetan script and placed into a cylinder within the wheel. When the wheel is turned, this action is equivalent of a person reciting a prayer. This type of practice harkens back to the early Buddhist injunction "to turn the wheel of the dharma." Another device used for reciting prayers is the prayer flag, an inscribing of a prayer on a piece of cloth attached to a stick that is placed in the ground. When the wind makes the flag wave, this is equivalent to reciting a prayer. Tibetans also use rosaries to count personal prayers made of 108 beads, a sacred number dating back to ancient Hinduism. Tibetans also use protective charms that consist of a written mantra (sacred formula), which is used in mental practices of visualization likened to a whirling in the heart of a deity of the Tibetan pantheon. Another devotional type of object used in Tibet is the *chortens* (*stūpas*) constructed to hold images of holy persons or the deceased in charm boxes that are sealed within the larger *chortens*. Besides these smaller objects, Tibetans have also constructed impressive monasteries and structures like the Potala Palace, residence of the Dalai Lama in Lhasa.

An artistic treasure and wonder of the Buddhist tradition is Angkor Wat in Myanmar, which was originally a temple complex dedicated to the Hindu deity Vishnu. After Khmer kings embraced Buddhism, it was transformed into a Buddhist temple in 1431. When the capital was moved to Phnom Penh the site was abandoned until it was re-discovered by western scholars in 1860, which commenced a restoration project and a reclaiming of the site from the jungle vegetation. The complex was constructed over a thirty-year period, combining elements of Hindu and Khmer art. This pyramid structure covered 200 acres surrounded by a moat. The temple incorporated serpent-shaped balustrades with an ascending complex of terraces and small buildings surmounted by five towers, representing the peaks of Mount Meru of Buddhist cosmology, the symbolic center of the world.

Another impressive wonder of artistic construction is evident in Borobudur, located on the island of Java, dating to the eighth and ninth centuries. The entire site was constructed on the model of a sacred diagram (*mandala*). The walls of its five terraces are carved with images recalling Buddhist narrative lore. The site includes three circular platforms holding seventy-two small *stūpas* around a massive central *stūpa*. Directional bodhisattvas grace the lower terraces, but are outnumbered by the bodhisattava Vairocana on the fifth terrace. The complex is structured to enable a pilgrim to progress by ascending it, a symbolic journey from the realm of rebirth to that of nirvana.

Angkor Wat and Borobudur are indicative of religious structures that manifest a close relationship between the religion and kingship. These structures are microcosmic models of the larger Buddhist universe. Within their *mandala* design, religion and the socio-political order are unified and governed by a righteous king, which evolves into a cult of the divine king. These impressive structures also suggest a synthesis of cosmology and kingship, creating a location where the Buddha is present. And the presence of the Buddha creates a sacred land and links the king with the Buddha. It is the king who actualizes the Buddha's presence, and the Buddha's presence in the form of his relics legitimates the monarch.

Buddhism Arrives in the West

The beginning of the Buddhist mission to the West was preceded by colonialism and Western domination of traditional Buddhist countries. Western nations imposed their political and military power, subjugating less powerful countries for economic exploitation. The Western maritime powers introduced their worldviews, economic systems, educational ideas, technologies, and religions into these countries. These Western national impositions brought with them various types of Christian missionaries, who proceeded to criticize the foreign customs of the people that they encountered and attempted to convert them to the Christian truth. In this process, local people were made to feel inferior, ignorant, and backward. Some of the subjugated people did convert to Christianity, but the vast majority took refuge in their own religion. Reactions also included reforming their native traditions as a response to criticism by Westerners. Some of these reform movements reacted with their own mission to the West, where members had been prepared to be open-minded, tolerant, and curious about these strange ideas and customs by their own intellectual Enlightenment period.

If the purpose of the eighteenth century Enlightenment in the West was an attempt to free human beings intellectually, it played an unwitting role of introducing Buddhism to the West by providing a rationale for Buddhist scholarship and thereby opening minds to the acceptance of Buddhism. Scholarship inspired by the Enlightenment was grounded on the scientific method and the rational analysis of empirical data, which stood in contrast to other forms of knowledge that were culturally relative instead of being genuine knowledge. The Enlightenment assimilated empiricism, cultural relativism, pluralism, eclecticism, and social reform. These elements were inspired and guided by the values of liberty, equality, and human rights, which were believed to have scientific validity.

The German Enlightenment figure Arthur Schopenhauer (1788–1860) became the first Westerner to declare publicly his affinity for Buddhism, and he inspired Richard Wagner to compose an opera on the life of the Buddha. In order to promote Buddhist scholarship in Germany, Karl Seidenstücker, a Pali scholar, founded the first Buddhist society. The most outstanding early German Buddhologist was Hermann Oldenberg. who labored editing and translating Pali texts and publishing *Buddha, sein Leben, seine Lehre, seine Gemeinde* (1881). In 1888, a German convert to Buddhism, Subhadra Bikkshu

(Friedrich Zimmermann), published the initial edition of *Buddhistischen Katechismus*, a German version of a catechism originally created by Henry Steel Olcott (1832–1907), co-founder and first president of the Theosophical Society. George Grimm (1868–1945), influential author of *The Doctrine of the Buddha, the Religion of Reason* (1915), was widely read, and he called his interpretation "Old Buddhism," suggesting the original teachings of the Buddha, in which he taught a doctrine of the self beyond concepts. Another important German contribution to spreading knowledge about Buddhism was made by Hermann Hesse when he published *Siddhartha* (1922), which was devoted to relating the life of the Buddha. In contrast to these intellectuals, Paul Dahlke (1865–1928) was a German organizer known for building the "Buddhist House" in Berlin and Frohnau, a temple and meditation center in 1924.

Germans became better acquainted with Zen after World War II through the influence of Eugen Herrigel's book *Zen in the Art of Archery* (1948). Zen meditation centers were established during the 1970s, while Jōdo Shin also established a presence along with the *vipassanā* meditation center opened in 1961 in the vicinity of Hamburg. Anagārika Govinda (1898–1985), a German convert and follower of the Tibetan ecumenical Ris-med movement, founded a lay order in the 1970s called the Arya Maitreya Mandala. In addition, Edward Conze (1904–1979) made valuable scholarly contributions to understanding the Perfection of Wisdom literature.

The Enlightenment also inspired Buddhist scholarship in France, with the philologist Eugène Burnouf publishing *Introduction à histoire du bouddhisme indien* (1854), which argued that Eastern religions were part of a single tradition originating in India. There also developed a Franco-Belgian school of Buddhology represented by Louis de la Vallée Poussin, who translated the *Abhidharmakośa* and other works, and Etienne Lamotte (1903–1983), who was a Catholic priest and prelate of the pope's household. Lamotte made valuable contributions to Buddhist scholarship with his five volume translation of the *Great Treatise on the Perfection of Wisdom* by Nāgārjuna, other Mahāyāna texts, and his study *Histoire du bouddhisme*. Less a scholar than a religious adventurer, Alexandra David-Néel became famous for her trip to Lhasa, capital of Tibet, in 1924. She wrote over 30 books about her travels and Buddhist thought. She also became the confidante of the crown prince of Sikkhim, Maharaj Kumar Sidkeon Tulku, after accepting an invitation to visit the royal monastery, and she also encountered and questioned the thirteenth Dalai Lama twice.

In 1929, the first Buddhist society in France, Les ams du bouddhisme, was founded by T'ai-hsu, a Chinese reformer, and Constant Lounsbery. By 1984, three Vietnamese temples were opened by Indochinese refugees. During the same time period, forty-six Tibetan centers and five Zen centers were established, along with two Theravāda monasteries. The French interest in Buddhism has raised questions in the national press about the country losing its historical Catholic identity and turning to a new religion. The French Buddhist Union (during the 1990s) estimated that there were 600,000 to

650,000 Buddhists in France, with French converts consisting of 150,000; these figures do not include Buddhist sympathizers.

During the nineteenth and twentieth centuries, when Buddhism spread to the West, there were three major movements with many subdivisions: ethnic, missionary, and immigrant. The ethnic type of Buddhism was concerned with its own group and excluded Westerners. The ethnic Buddhists came to the West for economic reasons. Chinese immigrants who arrived in California in response to the Gold Rush were a good example of such a group. Missionary Buddhists sought to convert Westerners to their religion. Zen, Tibetan, and Vipassana Buddhism were excellent examples of the missionary impetus, with its emphasis on meditation practices. Finally, immigrant communities from Vietnam and South Korea constituted the final group.

It could be argued that there was even a fourth type of movement that enhanced the spread of Buddhism to the West made by Western scholars. In 1881, T. W. Rhys Davids, a former member of the Ceylon Civil Service, founded the Pali Text Society for the purpose of translating original Buddhist texts into English and promoting Buddhist scholarship, and he established the Buddhist Society in London in 1907, along with a branch in Ireland. This latter society published a journal, *Buddhism*, in England in 1926, which was replaced by *The Middle Way* in 1945. Davids and his wife Caroline collaborated to introduce Buddhism to the West through their writings and lectures. In addition to the work of the Davids, the Royal Asiatic Society was established in 1823 to promote scholarship on Asian cultures in general by publishing a journal, sponsoring public lectures, and holding conferences. The scholarly dispersion of information about Buddhism and other religions was also given impetus by Friedrich Max Müller, a German born Indologist who taught at Oxford University, by his editing of the series Sacred Books of the East (1879–1894); he edited another series of texts in Sacred Books of the Buddhist beginning in 1895 and translated the popular *Dhammapada* from Pali.

Of all the types of Buddhism introduced to America, Zen was arguably the best known and popular during the twentieth century. Zen Buddhism was represented at the World's Parliament of Religions during the Exposition in Chicago in 1893 by a Rinzai Zen abbot named Shaku Sōen (1858–1919), whose impression was muted by the limitations of his command of the English language in contrast to the positive impression made by Vivekānanda (1863–1902), representing Hinduism. Nonetheless, Sōen made friends with Paul Carus (1852–1919), a scholar of Eastern religions and publisher of Open Court Press, and introduced him to a disciple named Daisetz T. Suzuki (1870–1966), who did more than any other single figure to introduce Zen to a Western audience by reinterpreting it and adapting it to his audience. Suzuki gave courses at Columbia University in New York City, and he lectured widely in America and European cities. Zen was introduced into Germany by Rudolf Otto of the University of Marburg, who was famous for his classic work *The Idea of the Holy*. In 1928, Zen halls appeared in San Francisco, and the following year in Los Angeles. The first Zen Institute was founded in New York in 1931. From these locations, Zen centers spread to other American cities and rural areas, a development that was also true for Tibetan Buddhism, with its Naropa Institute founded by Chögham Trungpa in Boulder, Colorado, combining meditation practices with Western subjects.

During the 1960s, Buddhism was embraced by the so-called Beat Generation by such figures as Jack Kerouac, Allen Ginsberg, and Gary Snyder. Kerouac composed a fictionalized account of their religious adventures in *Dharma Bums* (1958). After lamenting the destruction of his generation by means of drugs and madness in his poem *Howl*, Ginsberg traveled to the site of the Buddha's enlightenment in India, visited the Dalai Lama, and eventually met Chögyam Trungpa in 1970. After becoming a disciple of Trungpa, Ginsberg taught at the Naropa Institute. Snyder also found employment teaching Buddhism after spending seven years in a Zen monastery in Japan, being inspired by the writings of D. T. Suzuki. This period witnessed the spread of Buddhist thought by the cultural popularizer Alan Watts, who also stared in videos made by the Hartley Foundation. Watts, born in England and immigrating to America during World War II, was an Episcopal priest and chaplain at Northwestern University for five years before turning to lecturing and writing about Buddhism and Taoism.

The 1960s was a time when religious studies departments began to grow at colleges and universities around the country. Many of these departments offered courses in various Eastern religious traditions. The introductory world religions courses attracted many students and helped to support courses specifically in a more narrowly focused subject such as Buddhism. Graduate programs grew to meet the demand for qualified college instructors.

The growth of public interest in Buddhism was not merely reflected by college course offerings, because those professionals teaching the subject organized groups devoted to the scholarly study of the subject, such as the International Association of Buddhist Studies founded in 1976 and the Buddhist section of the American Academy of Religion, where scholars could gather to share their research at conferences. The promotion of Buddhist scholarship has been enhanced by the creation of publishing houses devoted to the subject, such as Shambhala Publications, Snow Lion, and Dharma Publishing International. The entire Chinese Buddhist canon is being translated into English by the Numata Center for Buddhist Translation and Research located in Berkeley, California, which is a project that will make a major contribution to the dissemination of Buddhist literature to a wider audience. In summary, Buddhism is being studied in institutions of higher education, being practiced by many people, having its literature translated and published, being often in the news, and appearing on Internet websites. In the early twenty-first century, Buddhism has become ubiquitous in America and other Western nations, moving beyond the original *bodhi* tree in India to become a major global religion. During its journey westward, it has changed, adapted to new cultures, and offered spiritual help to many people looking for answers to the problems of life.

Religious Experience

In the narrative about the Buddha's attainment of nirvana, there is a reference to his four trance states prior to attaining enlightenment, which is made possible by an intense concentration of the mind. The trance states are also preceded by freedom from the five hindrances (coveting the world, hatred and desire to injure, stupidity and slothfulness, excitement and misdeeds, and doubt), resulting in feelings of joy and peace before the beginning of the trance states. Each trance state is higher than the previous condition, with the discarding of desires and unwholesome thoughts in the first state and replacement of joy and happiness. The second state represents the suppression of intellectual activities and the development of tranquility and one-pointedness of mind. Joy disappears at the third state of trance, but feelings of happiness and equanimity remain. In the final trace stage, happiness and unhappiness, joy and sorrow are abandoned, leaving just equanimity and awareness in a condition of complete detachment from the world. Wisdom dawns, giving one insight into the nature of things and verifying the validity of the Four Noble Truths.

With the fourth trance state and advent of wisdom, there is nirvana for the seeker. Nirvana represents the cessation not only of suffering and rebirth, but it is also the end of the Buddhist narrative because it is impossible, theoretically and existentially, for it to be the subject matter of any narrative. Nirvana brings the story of a person's life to an end. Nirvana does not occupy a location in the drama and flux of history because it exists beyond spatiotemporal locations. This suggests that nirvana, which is indescribable and beyond reason, is not equivalent to becoming or nonexistence; it cannot be produced or caused by any person or process. If nirvana represents the cessation of narrative, it is also the termination of consciousness. And yet Buddhists assert that nirvana exists and can be known. However, it is not possible that a person can define it, designate its nature, or characterize it by means of discursive thinking. Try this experiment for yourself: Assume that you are a turtle, and think how you might begin to describe the experience of dry land to a tuna? Well?

Nirvana, which literally means to be fully blown out like the flame of a candle or to have the flame's fuel exhausted, is something permanent and eternal; it stands metaphorically outside of change and time. Does this mean that a seeker's consciousness comes to an end? The orthodox Buddhist response is that a person's consciousness is transformed at the precise moment of enlightenment, although consciousness ends when an enlightened person's body ceases to exist at the end of one's physical mode of existence. It must be remembered that nirvana is only reached during life, and, at the end of life, one proceeds to final nirvana. Moreover, the attainment of nirvana by cultivating insight meditation reveals the unreality that grounds our conventional view of life in the world; for instance, there is no self or soul, everything is constantly changing, and it is impossible to locate any essence within the world.

In the Mahāyāna school of Mādhyamika, nirvana is defined as empty (*śūnyatā*) because it has no self-nature, no essence, or inherent existence. Although it lacks independent existence, it does represent the perfection of wisdom and highest achievement for a bodhisattva by means of an intuitive insight that is liberating. The Yogācāra School did not think that the Mādhyamika position could account for something such as memory and error, assuming a consciousness-only philosophical perspective, whereas the Mādhyamika School represents a non-position because emptiness is defined itself as emptiness.

Whether one takes a Theravada, Mādhyamika, or Yogācāra position and path to enlightenment, nirvana, however one treats it, makes it impossible to affirm the existence of deities. Thus, beyond this world, the notion of nirvana makes it theoretically impossible for a person to accept the existence of one or many gods and/or goddesses. Even though the monastic traditions of both major branches of Buddhism deny either theism or polytheism, the Buddhism practiced on the popular or folk level is polytheistic, with veneration leading the way over local deities and spirits from the indigenous traditions. This type of impetus contributed to the rise of Pure Land schools, which will be discussed more fully in future chapters, where ordinary people were promised the possibility of attaining a kind of paradise from where they could work to achieve nirvana within the midst of splendor. But the attainment of the Pure Land is gained by faith and grace of the bodhisattva and not by any intuitive insight into reality.

If the formative, elite tradition of the Buddhist monk is world negating, the way of Pure Land (which will be covered more fully within the context of the religions of China and Japan in following chapters), folk, or devotional forms of Buddhism are more world affirming. This is evident by practices that express the joy and love of life with the worship of the Buddha, cult of relics, participation in festivals, and taking security in the three refuges. This scenario suggests the wider array of Buddhist religious experiences that is not simply confined to the realization of nirvana.

Suggestions for Further Reading

Anderson, Carol S. *Pain and Its Ending: The Four Noble Truths in the Theravāda Buddhist Canon*. Richmond: Curzon, 1999.

Bartholumeuz, Tessa. *Women Under the Bo Tree: Buddhist Nuns in Sri Lanka*. Cambridge: Cambridge University Press, 1994.

Collins, Steven. *Nirvana and Other Buddhist Felicities: Utopias of the Pali Imaginaire*. Cambridge: University of Cambridge Press, 1998.

Gombrich, Richard F. *How Buddhism Began: The Conditioned Genesis of the Early Teachings*. London: Athlone, 1966.

———. *Precept and Practice: Traditional Buddhism in the Rural Highlands of Ceylon*. Oxford: Clarendon Press, 1971.

Harvey, Peter. *An Introduction to Buddhist Ethics: Foundations, Values, and Issues*. Cambridge: Cambridge University Press, 2000.

Kalupahana, David J. *Causality: The Central Philosophy of Buddhism.* Honolulu: University of Hawaii Press, 1975.

———. *A History of Buddhist Philosophy: Continuities and Discontinuities.* Honolulu: University of Hawaii Press, 1992.

Olson, Carl. *The Different Paths of Buddhism: A Narrative-Historical Introduction.* New Brunswick, NJ: Rutgers University Press, 2005.

Powers, John. *Introduction to Tibetan Buddhism.* Ithaca, NY: Snow Lion Publications, 1995.

Swearer, Donald K. *The Buddhist World of Southeast Asia.* Second Edition. Albany: SUNY Press, 2010.

Tambiah, S. J. *World Conqueror and World Renouncer: A Study of Buddhism and Polity in Thailand against a Historical Background.* Cambridge: Cambridge University Press, 1976.

8   Sikhism

The Sikh religion is rooted in the Sant movement in northern India, begun in the thirteenth century by various holy men and women who wandered the area singing poems about the wonders of their gods. Because it does not have a precise meaning or term with which to translate it, the term "sant" is ambiguous, although the English word "saint" is often used to translate it. The term "sant" is rooted in the Sanskrit verb "to be," which connotes what is real or true, terms that evoke the inner meaning of "sant." Some Sant poets worshipped God with attributes (*saguṇa*), while others were devoted to God without attributes (*nirguṇa*). The latter poets were very critical of anyone who approached God through iconic representation or mythical narratives. Many of the poets came from humble social backgrounds, although Mirabai, a female

Sant, was born a princess of a Rajput family. According to legend, she wanted to be the wife of the deity Krishna. After an arranged marriage to a Rajput prince, she caused problems for her in-laws because she neglected public social decorum, refused to worship the family goddess, and associated with holy men. Her uncompromising loyalty to Krishna and rebellious demeanor motivated her mother-in-law to attempt to murder her, but the poison was turned into nectar by Krishna, and in another episode a poisonous snake was transformed into a stone by her deity. Escaping from her husband's family, she traveled to holy places associated with Krishna and wandered, singing her poetic creations. Her life culminated with her merging into a temple icon of Krishna and never being seen again.

Another Sant devotee of Krishna was Sūrdās (b. 1478), a blind poet who had clairvoyant powers, as became evident when he divined the location of two valuable coins hidden by mice. He led an itinerant lifestyle composing emotional poems about Krishna's amorous adventures, while other poems expressed the distress of the cow-herding females with the disappearance of Krishna, their anguished search for him, and their emotional responses to being separated from their deity.

In contrast to Hindu Sants who worshipped God with attributes, other Sants preferred focusing on a deity without attributes. This group includes Ravidas (c. 1500), Kabir (1398–1448), Nāmdev (1270–1350), Eknāth (1548–1600), and Tukarām (1598–1649). Ravidas was, for example, an Untouchable leather worker, which is considered polluting work because it brings a person into contact with the impure hides of dead animals, from the holy city of Benares. Some themes in his poems reflect his social origins, such as a critical attitude toward those who treat others like trash. From his perspective, it is only the absence of love in one's life that makes one an Untouchable. In fact, everyone is an Untouchable in relation to God because of His very nature. Numerous legends were created that are indicative of his superiority over Brahmins despite his lowly origins. In such an episode, the king of Benares brought Brahmins and Ravidas into the presence of a royal icon in order to settle a dispute and announced that he would value the claim of whoever could show that God inclined in his direction. In response to the Brahmins' chanting of sacred Vedic verses, which had no effect, Ravidas began to sing and asked God to reveal Himself as the one whose nature is to rescue the fallen. The image jumped directly into the poet's lap. In another popular episode, Ravidas' right to preach was challenged by Brahmins. The two sides agreed to allow the river goddess, Ganges, to decide the case by throwing something into the river to discern whom she supported. The Brahmins tossed in a piece of wood, but it sank like a stone, whereas Ravidas threw a stone into the river, and it floated. In addition to these kinds of narratives, themes of his devotional poems expressed humility, the need for confession, and the irrelevancy of caste for one's salvation.

Similar to Ravidas, Kabir spent most of his life in Benares belonging to a lowly weaver caste, with parents who apparently converted to Islam, as reflected in the chosen Muslim name of their son. Kabir's poems express disdain for Hinduism and Islam. In his poems, he refers to a Satguru (primal teacher) who is identified with the voice of God within the human soul. This God cannot be named or described because the deity is devoid of attributes, qualities, and form. Therefore, God can never be an object, rendering Kabir critical of iconic representations of God and sacrifice. Emphasizing inward experience in his poems, Kabir suggests that God may reveal Himself to a devotee by means of his grace, assuming that a person is prepared to receive it. This requires preparation, which Kabir identifies with the path of love, although one can anticipate long periods of anguish associated with separation from God. In spite of a person's love of God, revelation comes at divine initiative and suddenly, which Kabir depicts as the arrow of the divine word discharged by God that slays the devotee. When a person is dead, she finds genuine life in a mystical union with God, an ineffable experience of dissolution in the divine.

Many pious legends and miracles surround the life of Kabir. In one legend, he responds to a test from God to weave cloth until the supply is exhausted and then goes into hiding because he cannot provide food for his family, which is supplied to them by God. Another narrative finds Kabir being constantly in demand from adoring admirers, and he associates with a prostitute in order to separate himself from the admiring public, only to offend people. He cures a priest at a distant temple by pouring water on his own feet. His spiritual power is also demonstrated by legends of him resurrecting two deceased individuals. End-of-life narratives depict him attaining immortality and disappearing from his funeral, leaving the bountiful flowers in place covering his now missing body.

The poems of some of these Sants appear in the *Ādi Granth* or *Guru Granth Sāhib*, which is the primary sacred book of the Sikhs. In general, the Sants stressed love and synthesized dissenting elements of prior Hindu/Islam religion, such as devotional aspects of Hinduism, hatha yoga of the Nath Yogis movement, and an influence from Sufism, a form of Muslim mysticism.

The Nath Yoga influence on the Sant movement is evident in its conviction about the irrelevance of caste for salvation, the folly of advocating a sacred language and body of scripture, and the uselessness of temple worship and practice of pilgrimage, although the Sikh movement would ignore some of these restrictions. The focus on interior devotion was of central importance. At the same time, Sants were critical of the Nath Yogi movement for its overt asceticism and practice that does not lead to liberation from the cycle of karma and rebirth.

Overall, Sants who worshipped God without attributes denied the Hindu incarnations of God. The Sants rejected religious ceremonies, caste distinctions, sacred languages, and scriptures, which did not endear them to Hindus. Like Muslims, the Sants were monotheist in their formative tradition and attached no value to celibacy or asceticism, although they did place importance on the need for a teacher (guru). They were convinced that everyone could be saved by devotion to God, expressed by the constant repetition of God's name, which assists a person to remember God and to become absorbed in the divine name. And because the Sant community included women, low-caste figures, and embraced people from the lowest level of the social hierarchy, the movement represented a potential threat to the sociological structure of Indian society.

From a historical perspective, the Sant tradition elevated the status and power of the guru to previously unmatched levels. The guru became a mediator and conduit to God. The guru represents the promise to devotees that it is possible to directly communicate with God. Any assumed monopoly of religious knowledge or right of access to God by elite office holders ceases with the guru assuming the role of a mediator. The notion of the guru is used by Sikhs in four senses: God as guru, teacher as guru, scripture as guru, and community as guru. Moreover, the Sants also created a religious environment that influenced the development of what came to be known as Sikhism. Into this religious environment of northern India, there was born a child named Nanak, initial guru of the Sikh movement.

Sikh Founder Nanak

Nanak (1469–1539) was born a Hindu into a merchant caste (Khatri) in the town of Rai Bhoidi Taluandi, 40 miles southeast of Lahore, Pakistan. His father, Kalu Bedi, was a revenue superintendent for the Muslim owner of a village, and his family lived in a Muslim community. During his early life, Nanak encountered Muslim intellectuals and holy men. At age 19, he married Sulakni and had two sons, playing a role as a spiritual preceptor to others in the community and singing praises of God with local groups. As an adult, he lived with his sister, Nanaki, and her husband in Sultanpur and worked at a local grocery store.

When he was 30 years old, he had an enlightenment experience that transformed his life. According to accounts of this occurrence, he failed to return home after his normal morning ablutions at a local river. Village members found his clothes on the riverbank and assumed that he had drowned. They proceeded to drag the river to retrieve his body but without success. After being missing for three days, Nanak re-appeared but remained silent about what had happened to him. When he did speak the next day, he uttered an enigmatic statement: "There is neither Hindu nor Muslim, so whose path shall I follow? I shall follow God's path. God is neither Hindu nor Muslim, and the path which I follow is God's." Nanak explained that he had been taken to the court of God and escorted into God's presence, where there was a cup filled with nectar, and he was commanded to drink it. God informed Nanak that He had bestowed the gift of His name upon Nanak, and was told that his mission in life was to reveal the name of God to the world.

Many aspects of Nanak's life are only known from the perspective of hagiographical narratives that are not trustworthy historical documents, but these

tales do inform readers about the way that the Sikh tradition chooses to understand his life. A consistent biographical feature of his life is his travels with
Mardana, a Muslim companion from his youth, who earned a living recording
family genealogies. As they journeyed together, Nanak would sing devotional
songs, and his Muslim companion would accompany him by playing his *rabah*,
a stringed instrument. During one journey to Mecca, Nanak fell asleep with
his feet toward the holy Ka'ba. Seeing this violation of religious etiquette,
a Muslim official charged Nanak with irreverence toward this sacred object.
In response, Nanak instructed the official to turn his feet toward the proper
direction, but every movement of his feet resulted with the Ka'ba turning with
his feet.

According to Sikh lore, Nanak traveled widely for two decades, visiting various holy shrines and pilgrimage sites associated with Hindu and Muslim figures. After his many journeys, he assumed the status of a householder in the
1520s and gradually became the leader of a religious community at a location
that became known as Kartarpur in the Punjab region. This community would
eventually emerge as an independent religion. His earliest followers were relatives and some members of the Khatri caste, although his movement would later
include members of the Jat caste, made up of lower-caste members of mostly
farmers, and some Muslims. Followers would assemble at the house of the guru
(teacher, leader) to sing the praises of God, a devotional practice called *nam
simran* that consists of repeating God's names. This shared practice gave followers a sense of being part of a close-knit community of common believers.

But what is it that constitutes the identity of a Sikh? The term "Sikh" literally means pupil. But a genuine Sikh is someone who abides by the teachings
of the gurus and keeps their teaching constantly in mind. The full identity of a
Sikh would emerge out of its history of struggle, violent confrontation with the
Muslim Mughal Empire of north India and hill tribes, and the features specified by Guru Gobind Singh, tenth and final guru in the lineage.

When Nanak taught others, he did so seated on a *gaddi*, a specially reserved
teaching seat. If someone wants to know Sikhism's teachings, such a person
should concentrate on the guru's utterances, which were orally preserved in
the memory of others, were later collected and written down, and are regarded
as scripture. Before he died, Nanak chose his successor—Lehna—on the basis
of the man's humility and obedience. After praising his chosen successor,
Nanak initiated him as guru to the community by placing five coins and a
coconut before the successor and bowing at his feet. This gesture was intended
to signify that the coconut represented the created universe and its hairs stood
for vegetation, whereas the five coins signified the five universal elements: air,
earth, fire, water, and ether. The coins also symbolized the skill of humans.
Nanak gave Lehna a book of his own hymns, which indicated the new guru
being entrusted with the divine message, and a woolen string symbolizing the
spirit of renunciation. Then, Nanak renamed his chosen successor Angad,
which is a pun on the word for limb (*ang*). The term means a "part of me" and
suggests that the new guru possesses the prior guru's spirit and being.

Various legendary narratives demonstrate Nanak's superiority over Nath Yogis. According to one narrative, when Nanak sits under a withered banyan tree where Nath Yogis typically gather it suddenly springs to life because of his presence. According to another legend, when Nanak flies through the air, he travels three times as fast as his Nath counterparts, which implies that Nanak does not desire these powers for their own sake. In a tale about Nanak and a great Muslim saint, the king's skull refuses to explode during his cremation to release his soul. Astrologers are summoned for their expertise, and they determine that the king was guilty of lying and predict that the skull will break once a true holy person enters the kingdom. A Muslim saint bows to Nanak, because the saint thought that Nanak should walk into the kingdom first. When Nanak enters the kingdom, the king's skull instantaneously breaks open, releasing his soul. These types of narratives are intended to distinguish Nanak from members of other religious paths and even to distinguish him from the succession of gurus to follow him.

Sikh Tradition of Gurus

The chosen successor to Nanak was Guru Angad (b. 1504, guru 1539–1552), as previously discussed. Angad had been a devotee of the Hindu goddess Durgā, and then converted to the Sikh path during his twenties. Known for his humility, Angad was also renowned for his meditation, austerities, and abstinence. His name means "limb," suggesting that he was a part of Nanak and expresses his close relation to the founder. A narrative relates how Nanak tested the loyalty and obedience of a group of followers by taking them to the wilderness and producing silver and gold coins. Many present seized all the coins they could hold and thus disqualified themselves. With only two Sikhs remaining, Nanak proceeded to a funeral pyre and commanded them to eat the corpse under the shroud. After one Sikh fled, Angad lifted the shroud and discovered Nanak, resulting with him passing the test of successor. Besides imparting an ascetic spirit to Sikhism, Guru Angad is historically significant as a consolidator of the movement by keeping the community united for thirteen years. He is also accredited with collecting all the hymns of Nanak for the first time. Angad's succession to leadership of the community came at the expense of his two sons, which motivated Guru Angad to move to Khadur. In retrospect, Nanak chose the best person that he could find as the second guru, but others would select relatives to succeed them in the history of the movement.

Because of the irreligious nature of his two sons, Angad appointed as his successor a convert named Amar Das, who had originally encountered the devout daughter of Nanak while singing a hymn authored by Nanak and asked to meet her father. After succeeding Angad, Guru Amar Das followed the pattern of married leaders, which tends to affirm the householder life instead of the ascetic lifestyle, and assumed residence in Govindwal, making it a new center for the movement. He also constructed a water tank with eighty-four steps leading down to the water at Goindwal with the intention of creating a place of pilgrimage for Sikhs. The eighty-four steps correspond to the eighty-four rebirths in the Hindu cycle of existence. Amar Das also divided the Sikh community into twenty-two units under the direction of provincial leaders. This type of organizational move was necessitated by more members being born into it and the guru becoming more remote from followers because of the expansion of the movement. Guru Amar Das established a system of preachers and supervisors over local communities. He also appointed some women to preaching duties, who were called *peerahs*, a Punjabi word for "chair." And he emphasized the free, communal meal as a way to express unity and equality within the community. By participating in this meal, a member would thus find himself seated near members of lower castes. In addition to compiling hymns, he introduced festival days to be regularly observed by the community. On the political front, he persuaded the Mughal government to repeal a tax it imposed on pilgrims going to the city of Hardwar. The Mughal Empire was under the enlightened leadership of Akbar at this time, who took an interest in the Sikh movement because he had hopes of uniting Hindus and Muslims within his empire.

Before he died, Guru Amar Das nominated his son-in-law, Jetha, to be his successor. The new successor took the name of Ram Das, slave of God. This guru (b. 1534, guru 1574–1581) was historically significant for founding the city of Amritsar (literally pool of *amrit* or nectar), which was destined to be regarded as the holy city of the Sikhs. Ram Das' son later built the Darbar Sahib, a place of worship and pilgrimage, which stood on the site that is now occupied by the Golden Temple. Ram Das introduced some social reforms, such as prohibiting the practice of *sati* (immolation of a wife on her husband's funeral pyre), prohibiting the veiling of women, and allowing widows to remarry. Ram Das also composed a wedding hymn that now constitutes a major part of a typical Sikh marriage ceremony. By introducing these changes related to women, Ram Das helped the Sikhs define their own distinct identity in comparison to Islam and Hinduism.

In order to organize a growing movement, Guru Ram Das appointed *masands* (means "thrones" or "raised platforms"), who acted for the guru by supervising particular communal groups of devotees. The *masands* functioned as spiritual guides and collected donations. Later *masands* would enrich themselves and corrupt the system and would later be disbanded by Guru Gobind Singh, the final guru. The guru also instituted rites of passage for birth, marriage, and death.

During his life, Ram Das groomed his son, Arjan, to become his successor, which made him the first guru to have been born a Sikh. Guru Arjan (b. 1563, guru 1581–1606) reigned during an expansion of Sikhism characterized by missionary activity and the conversion of many small landowners. Arjan instituted a tax on the community to raise revenue for construction of large reservoirs to counter an annual threat of drought. He also built the Harmandir at Amritsar, a building with a doorway on each side, intended to signify openness to all four castes. Because the building was constructed on a lower level than the surrounding area, it was necessary for a worshipper to step down and to recognize that God is attained by bending low in submission and humility. Moreover, Guru Arjan built three towns to complement Amritsar: Taran ("raft over the world ocean"), Kartapar (city of the Creator), and Shri Hargobindpur, located on the Beas River.

In addition to his successful building projects, Guru Arjan produced an authoritative collection of hymns that included compositions of the initial three gurus, those of his father, and his own works. Under the instruction of Guru Arjan, Bhai Gurdas completed the collection of hymns in August of 1604, a volume known as the *Ādi Granth* and considered the primary Sikh holy text. The compiling of an authoritative text countered the problem of other counterfeit texts in circulation. This text embodied the spirit and worldview of the Sikhs and made them equal to other religious traditions with sacred texts. Guru Arjan was prolific hymn composer whose compositions have been collected in a text known as the *Sukhymanī Sāhib*. Moreover, under Guru Arjan, Sikhism was developing toward a theocracy.

Before he could conclude his leadership of the Sikh movement, Guru Arjan was killed by a new Muslim ruler. The Mughal Emperor Akbar, renowned for his liberal attitude and tolerance of other religions, died in 1605, ushering in a complete reversal of attitudes toward other religions. The new Mughal leader was Jahangir (r. 1605–1627), who was resentful toward Arjan for his success converting Muslims to Sikhism. Arjan also provoked the displeasure of the new emperor when he supported the monarch's son for the throne. His death was interpreted by Sikhs as martyrdom, an event that contributed to the defining of Sikh identity.

Guru Arjan was followed by his son Hargobind (b. 1595, guru 1606–1644), who acted on his father's concern for an army to protect the community, marking a time when all subsequent gurus would be selected from the male line, whereas the initial three leaders had appointed loyal disciples to succeed them. Hargobind is credited with originating the practice of male Sikhs carrying two swords, representing power within the political realm (*mīri*) and spiritual realm (*pīri*). These swords carried meanings originating with a Sufi term for "religious teacher" or "pious person" and the other meaning "commander of the faithful" from the title Amir from the Arab tradition. Current Sikhs refer to them as sword and cooking pot to mean the protection of the oppressed and feeding the hungry. Hargobind also devised a pennant for his troops that became the flag of Sikhism. The importance of temporal and spiritual powers was expressed with the construction of a fort and court across from the central shrine called the Harimandir Sahib, a building known to Sikhs as the Akal Takht (Immortal Throne). During his reign, members of the Jat caste became a majority of the community, passing the Khatri caste in total members. Because he lost all of his sons, with the exception of the youngest with a withdrawn nature, Hargobind chose Har Rai, youngest child of his eldest son, to succeed him.

Chosen at age 14 to be a successor to his grandfather, Har Rai (b. 1630, guru 1644–1661) was known for keeping alive animals that he captured in his gardens, grew herbs, and was interested in medicine. His gentle disposition was celebrated in narratives. According to one such story, while walking in a field, he accidentally brushed a flower with his clothing and broke its stem. Full of remorse for the flower, he tucked in his clothing on future trips in the fields. He made a calculated mistake of supporting Shah Jehan—originator of the Taj Mahal, built in memory of his beloved wife—in a Mughal power struggle, who lost to his son Aurangzeb (r. 1658–1707). Aurangzeb proceeded to imprison his father and ordered the closing of Hindu schools and demolition of temples within his kingdom. Renowned for his ruthless nature, Aurangzeb forced citizens to convert to Islam, re-imposed a pilgrim tax, and imposed a tax on non-Muslims that provoked a civil war.

Guru Har Rai was succeeded by his 5-year-old son, Har Krishan (b. 1656, guru 1661–1664), who died of small pox, although he was able to name his great uncle, Guru Tegh Bahadur (b. 1621, guru 1664–1675), a personal name that means "brave sword." Tegh Bahadur was known for his bravery against Mughal forces, whom he defeated in battle, and his care for the hungry, as evident by his popular nickname, "brave cooking pot." A nephew attempted to assassinate him and was later pardoned. After Tegh Bahadur was summoned to the Mughal court for protesting the emperor's policy of forced conversions to Islam, Aurangzeb had him imprisoned. Tegh Bahadur watched as four of his companions were executed in his presence when they refused to convert to Islam. He was given a similar choice and accepted death by his refusal to convert on November 11, 1675. Sikhs viewed his death as martyrdom, and saw him as a man willing to accept death for his faith and religious liberty.

Guru Gobind Singh and Creation of the Khalsa

The martyr for Sikhism, Tegh Bahadur, was succeeded by Gobind Singh (b. 1666, guru 1675–1708), an educated man, skilled horseman, and soldier who was chivalrous and generous. At an assembly of the faithful, he announced a plan to replace their weakness with strength and unity. The plan was based on loyalty to the guru. At the gathering, he asked men to come forward to give their heads to him, a request that he made with a drawn sword. After some hesitation, one brave man came forward and was led to the guru's tent. After the guru reappeared alone with a blood-stained sword, four more men proceeded to the tent. These men would later be known as the beloved five or cherished five. After Gobind Singh emerged from his tent with the five men, they were given a concoction of water and sugar prepared in an iron bowl and stirred with a two-edged sword, which served as their initiation, which was followed by many others. The guru also proclaimed a code of discipline that included the following injunctions: a rejection of tobacco; rejection of eating meat of animals slaughtered in Muslim rituals; and to avoid sexual relations with Muslim women. These rules created a new brotherhood called the Khalsa (Pure Ones) that was intended to prevent them from following rival leaders.

The initiates were instructed to wear or carry on their person five symbols: uncut hair, a comb, a steel wrist guard, a sword, and short breeches. These were called the Five K's because the items all begin with the letter "k." The uncut hair harkens back to practices by some Hindu ascetics, although the meaning of the practice is different for Sikhs, who are instructed to regularly wash their hair and comb it twice a day. Hair is culturally significant in India because it is associated with male vigor and potency and is considered a divine gift and, thus, a symbol of holiness and strength within the context of Sikhism. In fact, God is imagined to have long hair. The long hair is adorned by a turban, which gives Sikh males a distinctive appearance and sets them apart from others. The turban is intended to function as a symbol of a religiously committed male, sig-nifies social cohesion, and represents social identity. Along with the hair, the comb symbolizes orderly spirituality modeled on the divine order established by God and an orderly society, just as the comb constrains the hair and makes it orderly. From the Sikh perspective, there is a very close relationship between a comb and hair that enables a person time for self-reflection when combing the hair.

The pair of short breeches, intimate apparel, must not extend below the knees; it signifies modesty, moral restraint, and continence. The term for breeches (*kacha*) is etymologically related to "underarm" (*kacch*), which sug-gests something not normally visible. Within the context of Sikh history, there is probably a connection with the breeches and a military need to mount and dismount one's horse rapidly when fighting. The breeches are also associated with virtues reflecting modesty and sexual restraint.

Within Buddhist and Hindu culture, a bracelet is connected with royalty. When Sikhs wear the bracelet on the right wrist, the steel wrist band signifies constraint, represents vows and beliefs taken in the name of God, stands for service to others of the community, and reminds Sikhs of their unity with God and the Khalsa. Beyond its practical purpose of protecting the sword, the steel bracelet represents divine unity. Even though it might remind males of their dominance in the culture, the bracelet both controls the power of the sword and protects it. The bracelet and sword do not represent antithetical aspects of the Khalsa because the former shares in the identity and function of the latter. The sword symbolizes dignity and self-respect along with a readiness to fight, but only in self-defense or for protecting weak and oppressed people. A Sikh is instructed to use his sword only as a last resort when all other means of defense have failed.

The introduction of the Five K's represents a Sikh remaking of the human body by breaking down the prevailing Indian cultural conception of the body as hierarchically ordered, with the head representing the higher aspect and the feet being associated with the lowest part of the body. The Khalsa ideal views the upper and lower parts of the human body as parallel to each other, which represents a radical break with the prior cultural tradition and freedom from its mode of thinking about the body and dress code. The Sikh view of the body as something parallel is connected with martial virtues such as bravery, courage, chivalry, and self-control. The Sikh transformation of the conceptualization of the body is part of an attempt to also develop a new sense of the self, which is a process of remaking what it means to be a Sikh subject, as distinct from Muslims, Hindus, or Buddhists.

In addition to the Five K's and turban, all initiated males adopted the name Singh (lion), a rapacious animal traditionally associated with royalty and strength. Women were admitted to the Khalsa brotherhood and adopted the name Kaur (princess). Women embraced ideals of sexual and caste equality. For the Sikhs, these new names signify that everyone within the community is part of a royal family that rejects the former caste system and its hereditary occupations based on a person's birth. A person's place in society is now defined by membership in a spiritual community.

According to Sikh tradition, Guru Gobind Singh was stabbed by a Pathan male who was associated with the Vazir Khan in the small town of Nander on the Godavari River. The knife wound was stitched, but a few days later the stitches broke, and Singh died. Before he died, Guru Gobind Singh installed a copy of the *Granth Sāhib* as his successor and guru of the religion by placing five coins and a coconut before a copy of the sacred text and announcing that his life marks the end of the line of gurus.

Because he established the Khalsa, a case could be made to support the claim that Guru Gobind Singh was the most influential guru since Nanak. He is the singular figure who completed defining the nature of a genuine Sikh, which endures to the present time. His creation of the Khalsa was likely motivated by the corruption of several *masands*, administrative deputies acting for the guru, an event announced around 1699. By terminating the authority of the administrators, Guru Gobind Singh made followers directly connected to him—and not to subordinates—through a sacred text, which now became the center of devotional focus. The Sikh tradition of ten gurus did not begin with Nanak because it is grounded in God as the primal Guru, although Nanak was the first human guru. This scenario suggests that there has been a tradition of commonality that can be traced to the spiritual inspiration grounded in God and transmitted through the ten gurus by God. The narratives of the ten gurus reflect a rejection of any claim that Sikhism is either a sect of Hinduism or Islam or a synthesis of Hinduism and Islam. Finally, the Sikh narratives indicate that transmitted divine inspiration ends with Guru Gobind Singh and becomes embodied in the holy text, the *Guru Granth Sāhib*.

Sikh Literature

The holy scripture of the Sikhs is called the *Ādi Granth* (meaning original text), consisting of devotional hymns composed by Nanak, five other gurus, and other selected Sant poets such as Kabir, Namdev, and Ravidas, for a grand total of 1,430 pages. Sikhs also call the text the *Guru Granth Sāhib* or the *Sri Guru Granth Sāhib*, consisting of the honorific terms *śri* and *sāhib*. Early in the Sikh tradition, these hymns circulated freely in different collections until

Guru Arjan compiled them in 1604 into a volume called the *Kartarpur*. The contents of the text are identified as utterance (*bani*), utterance of the guru (*gurubani*), and divine word (*shabad*). The religious hymns comprising the primal, sacred text is composed of *shabads*, hymns of varying length, and *shaloks*, couplets. It is written in the Gurmukhi script and purposely not in Sanskrit, which is the classical language of India, with the intention of making the verses accessible to everyone. In summary, the *Ādi Granth* represents the manifest body and actual presence of the guru because the guru's words and spirit are considered incarnated into the text.

The text is organized chronologically, beginning with Nanak and other Sikh gurus and ending with the Sant poets. The hymns of Nanak are labeled Mahala 1, hymns of Guru Angad are called Mahala 2, and so on. The exact meaning of "Mahala" is obscure, although in Islam the term means principality or abode, conveying a location where the Divine resides. The term is also associated with the body, implying that gurus have different bodies, although they share the same spirit as Nanak. There are 31 divisions in the *Ādi Granth*, reflecting musical measures called *rags*, which means to color with emotion. When a hymn is recited, it is intended to evoke a specific type of mood or create a certain type of atmosphere. The contents and structure of the text encourage humans to sing it rather than simply read it, which suggests that the text is intended to be performed.

Within the Indian cultural context, sound is believed to have power to purify one's mind and lead one toward a spiritual path. The Sikhs contend that *rags* exist eternally and are not created. Because of their basic nature, they can be discovered by inspired poets and musicians. The musical harmony that is inspired represents a copy of the Divine harmony of the universe and enables a person to attune herself with this primal harmony. From Guru Nanak's perspective, music can be used to inspire devotion, to give expression to the inexpressible nature of God, and to show humans how to relate to the Divine harmony pervading the universe.

At the beginning of the text, one encounters the Mul Mantra, a basic creedal statement: "One Reality is," which is considered the most sacred utterance because it expresses God's unity and omnipotence. This primal mantra, a derivative of the mantra OM in Hinduism, represents the number 1 and the letter "O," which is called 1-Oankar by Sikhs. Also prior to the hymns is the "Japji Sahib," a devotional hymn of Divine praise following the Mul Mantra. Devout Sikhs recited these two utterances daily upon awakening in the morning, whereas the "Sodar Rahiras" is a prayer that is recited before one retires for the night.

These various internal features of the *Ādi Granth* indicate that it is more than an ordinary book. It is a special book because it embodies the words of God, an abode of the ten gurus, and the Divine in material form. Based on Guru Gobind Singh's decision to end the succession of gurus with his reign, the text becomes the eternal and living guru for the community. The significance of the text is evident in the early morning in temples, when Sikhs treat it with great respect by having it located on a seat of embroidered cushions, awaken it, and later retire it for the evening, similar to Hindu practice for icons.

Another body of Sikh literature is the so-called *Janam-sākhis* (birth stories). These tales represent hagiographical literature of dubious historical value. There are two collections: the Bala collection, a group of narratives about Nanak and his musical companion Bhai Bala, and the Purātan group, which represents another version that was discovered in 1872. The second group presents various miracles in a more subdued way. Although these narratives lack indisputable historical value, they do give one a glimpse into the impact of Nanak's teaching, the communal nature of these teachings, the nature of worship, and aspects of communal life. The *gur-bilas* is another collection of hagiographical narratives recounting the heroic exploits of the sixth and tenth gurus, whereas the *janam-sākhīs* ("life testimonies") are narratives about the life of Nanak.

The final text of importance for the history of Sikhism is the *Dasam Granth*, a text attributed to Guru Gobind Singh that was accepted as equal to the *Ādi Granth* before being eclipsed by the older text. The *Dasam Granth* consists of 1,428 pages representing four types of compositions: (1) autobiographical works of Guru Gobind Singh; (2) four devotional works; (3) two miscellaneous works; and (4) mythical narratives, as well as popular anecdotes. The term *dasam* means tenth, which reflects Guru Gobind Singh's place in the lineage of the gurus. This body of writings also contains a letter written by Guru Gobind Singh titled the "Zafarnana" that is addressed to the Mughal Emperor Aurangzeb. The letter informs the emperor that the guru is fighting the hill chiefs of the Punjab and not attacking the emperor. He also criticizes the emperor for not providing safe passage to his family. Before the two men could meet, the emperor died and was succeeded by Bahdur Shah, who met with the guru the following year.

There are some exceptions, but the bulk of the *Dasam Granth* was finished around the later 1690s. It was composed in verse using a variety of meters and is written mostly in Brajbhasha, which became a prestigious literary language of an old Hindi form of language in Gurumukhi script. The text consists of several parts, beginning with a prayer intended to be spoken called the "Jap Sahib," meaning to pray or recite. The various parts of the text represent a curious collection, which has given rise to disputes about what parts were composed by Guru Gobind Singh and why they are included in a single text.

The *Bachitra Natak* (Wondorous Drama) is a part of the text that comprises sixteen chapters and deals with genealogy, birth, and life. It gives the impression of being autobiographical because it is written in the first person. A king predicting that he would be reborn as Nanak during the final age of the Kali Yuga is part of the content, along with a discussion of the Sikh gurus within the context of the four *yugas* theory of time typical of Puranic Indian culture. The four *yugas* reflect the decline of the dharma (traditional teaching and order of society), a scenario that is evident with the failures of Hinduism and Islam to address and rectify the problem of cultural and religious decay. This dire situation calls for a new effective way to live. The pattern of Sikh gurus and their teaching about the unity of God is a viable response to the situation created by the four cosmic *yugas* of decline, although these gurus should not be considered incarnations. They do, however, perform a similar function associated with restoring righteousness and defeating the forces of evil.

In contrast to this part of the text, the *Debī Charītra* and *Chandi Charitra* devote considerable attention to Hindu goddesses and their exploits. This extensive attention to goddesses does not fit into Sikh theology and gives rise to various questions about authorship and intention. These texts are a bit polemical because the demons that fight the goddesses have Muslim characteristics, which seems to be a clever way to critique a group of antagonists. This critical portrait of Muslims just might be the overall purpose of these two parts of the text. This line of argument is supported by the portrayal of goddesses defeating demons inspiring Sikh warriors to defeat Muslims, and attention is directed to the goddess Durgā's vehicle the lion (*singha*), which is, of course, the name given to initiates joining the Khalsa. These parts of the *Dasam Granth* are not, however, intended to promote goddess worship by Sikhs. They do reflect this period of Sikh history and the dominance of Muslim political hegemony over northern India during this time period.

In addition to these sections of the twenty-eight sections comprising the *Dasam Granth*, there are other sections that deal with legends and narratives from classical Indian epic literature. There are also narratives about human character and dangers associated with unbridled lust. In many of these narratives, women are depicted in negative cultural stereotypical patterns, although some women are portrayed heroically. Overall, the *Dasam Granth* depicts Sikhs as heroic fighters for justice and protectors of Indian culture.

Nanak and His Message

It is commonly believed that Sikhism is a blend of Hindu and Muslim beliefs, and there is some truth to this opinion. The Hindu influence is evident by Nanak's reworking of some elements of the Sant tradition, although he reinterpreted that religious tradition along the lines of his own personality and experience. Nanak was also influenced by Sufism, a mystical movement within Islam, and Islamic religious beliefs concerning the unity of God, a revelation in the created world, the paradox about the transcendence and immanence of God, light symbolism associated with God, and the doctrine of grace. Nonetheless, true belief exceeded either Hinduism or Islam because they were both fundamentally wrong. Thus, it is incorrect to interpret Sikhism as solely a synthesis of Hindu and Muslim religions.

Arguably, the most essential feature of Nanak's teaching is God's unity. Along with an emphasis on God's transcendence, these positions necessarily reject any hint of duality or pantheism. A consequence of God's oneness is that His essence is beyond all human categories, but He can be truly known only in experience. Nanak's conception of God depicts a deity of grace to whom one responds with love. Nanak also stresses that the many things within the world are all expressions of divine unity, a notion that is connected to the concept of revelation throughout the created universe. In comparison to Nanak's deity, the Hindu gods are nothing more than creations of the genuine God, and are described as deprived of all functions and subject to illusion and death. In place of the Hindu deities, Nanak's God is creator, sustainer, and destroyer.

With respect to the Sant distinction between *saguna* (conditioned and manifested) and *nirguna* (absolute and unmanifested) aspects of God, Nanak argues that the latter is the primal, absolute, unconditioned, and devoid-of-attributes God to whom he prays. In this *nirguna* or absolute aspect, God is unknowable because He is completely beyond the range of human comprehension. But God does not wholly exceed human perception because He endows Himself with attributes that bring Him within the compass of human understanding. By means of His own will, God becomes *saguna* in order for humans to know Him. And it is by knowing Him that humans can enter into a unitive relationship with Him. Since God is immanent in all creation, He is not completely unknowable and is specifically immanent in one specific part of creation: the human heart.

According to the Sikh understanding of the beginning of the world, there was originally undivided darkness for countless eons. There was neither earth nor heaven. There was only the infinite order of God, implying that apart from God, there was nothing. God created the world when it pleased Him without any visible support. In fact, God created Himself. This self-existence of God affirms His absolute nature beyond which human understanding cannot go. God does not merely create the universe, but He also watches over the world and cares for it, which are activities that reflect His sustaining activity. He can also destroy what He has created and sustained. According to Nanak, God is the sovereign of the universe, which means that He wields absolute authority and possesses unqualified power. Nanak also defines God as omnipotent and eternal, features that sharply contrast the nature of God with the unstable and impermanent nature of the universe.

God is without beginning and beyond time because He is always firm and wholly constant, which implies that God is not subject to death and rebirth. Nanak insists that God is formless, suggesting that He is uncreated, unborn, and never incarnated. These features of God mean that He is not an incarnation and can never become present in an idol, as believed in Hinduism. According to Nanak's conception of the *nirguna* way of understanding God, it is important to stress that He is ineffable, which means that an authentic human response to God is a combination of awe, fear, and wonder before the One who is beyond human comprehension. Moreover, God is ultimately responsible for the unitive experience that represents the climax of the salvation process, although humans must participate for there to be union and release from the world.

God, an infinite singular deity, dwells within each individual, rendering the transcendent one intimately associated with humans. A major implication of this position is that everyone is equal. But this theological position does not mean that God is contained within any form, because such a claim would contain and confine God. Nonetheless, God is everywhere and unrestricted. This theology does not imply that Nanak promotes a pantheism. He insists that God cannot be reduced to any type of form because God is always transcendent, although God makes the world pulsate with energy and potentiality.

Nanak conceives of God as a communicative guru who connects with humans by means of his word, a soundless noise that is equated with the mystical sound that is heard at the climax of hatha yoga. Synonymous with the word is the name of God, although a distinction is sometimes drawn between the name and the word of God because the word is a medium of communication while the name is the object of communication. All that God represents is captured by His name, which is equal to the Truth.

Guru and Divine Order

The series of ten historical Sikh gurus (teachers) are genuine figures, but the paradigm for them is the divine guru, God. In Sikh thought, the divine guru is identical to the Word (*Śabad*). Functioning as a guide and exemplar, God's personality inhabits each religious leader in the succession of the ten gurus. But with the death of the final guru—Gobind Singh—this divine personality merges into scripture and community.

The Sikh notion of the divine order (*hukam*) is intended to explain how it is possible to apprehend the truth. All forms are created by the *hukam*, a principle that determines the giving of different forms and accounts for distinctions. Even though the *hukam* represents a regular and consistent pattern that governs human existence and the movement of the universe, it is beyond description, implying that humans cannot totally comprehend it. By understanding this divine principle that governs the existence and movement of the universe, a person is led to the destruction of self-centeredness because one has grasped the primal, constant principle that functions in a predictable pattern and is thus absolutely dependable. The *hukam* is connected with the revelation of the nature of God and thus identical to the Word (*Śabad*). When a person recognizes the divine order, that person perceives the truth. For an individual, this means that everything that happens is predetermined and occurs because God wills it. Therefore, by God's command both good and evil happen.

God's determining of everything is tempered by the divine gift of His grace, which enables a person to hear the voice of the divine Guru. Although this gift of grace is a prerequisite and is necessary for salvation, it does not guarantee salvation, but it does give an initial and prerequisite illumination. Disciples are urged to live their lives in accordance with what it imparts. Sikh literature also adds further implications and meanings for the gift of grace that include making a disciple aware of being accepted by the divine Guru and receiving His blessing. The divine gift of grace liberates a person to act according to love and transforms a person into someone who discovers the meaning of existence.

The Human Situation

Nanak was very concerned with the human condition because of human attachment to the world, problems associated with human nature, human entanglement in the working of karma, being caught in *māyā* (illusion), and death. Humans are not merely attached to the external world but also demonstrate that they are trapped by interior pride, self-centeredness, sin, death, and rebirth. In order to attain release from this external and internal maze that can only lead to further rounds of rebirth, it is essential for a person to transcend one's condition in order to gain salvation.

Nanak often uses the term *man*, a term derived from *manas* (mind) in Sanskrit, to refer to the human subject in a very broad sense, which includes human intellect, memory, ego consciousness, heart, and soul. With this inner sense of mind, a human makes decisions of an ethical/moral nature. A human also uses the mind to meditate, to apprehend the truth, and to love God, although the mind can also serve as the origin of negative human qualities such as lust and anger. The mind is also the location of the moral law inscribed on one's heart that enables one to know right from wrong. The mind of an unreformed person is unrestrained and impure. And yet within the realm of creation, humans are unique because they possess the ability to discriminate and to voluntarily enter into a relationship of love with God.

Besides the problems already mentioned, Nanak focuses on the dilemma of what he calls self-centeredness or self-reliance (*haumai*), which works to dominate the mind of an unreformed person and causes suffering. This forms a pattern of behavior that determines the life of a person and taints everything that she does, even righteous actions. The trap of self-centeredness involves imprisoning a person in illusion, doubt, and rebirth. By grasping with one's intellect the nature of self-centeredness, this awareness begins to give one a glimpse into the door of salvation. Nanak calls a person *manmukh* because that person is self-absorbed, listens to the voice of her own mind, and neglects to hear the truth-speaking voice of the guru. The *manmukh* is a person who chooses falsehood and remains in bondage within the cycle of death instead of opting for truth, freedom, and life. In sharp contrast to the *manmukh*, Nanak promotes the *gurmukh*, a person who obeys the instructions of the guru and is God-minded.

Even though there is something good imprinted on the mind of a human at birth, the mind is dangerously influenced by five evil impulses: lust, anger, covetousness, attachment to worldly things, and pride. Operating in a complex tandem, these five impulses give rise to falsehood and violent actions, resulting in negative karma and endless rebirth. If these five negative impulses characterize an unreformed person, ignorance is another feature that shapes a person and his fate. When a mind is dominated and entrapped by these aspects, it is also subject to illusion (*māyā*). Nanak does not mean this in the sense of a cosmic illusion that implies that the world is unreal, or that humans accept this unreal world as something genuine. What Nanak means by illusion is that the world is real, but humans accept the world as something permanent when in fact it is impermanent. What the world offers to humans, who are blinded by ignorance, forgetful of their true nature, and going astray, is false and deceptive because it keeps humans separated from God and subject to continued rebirth. If a person accepts the world as something valuable, such a deluded person also accepts duality, which necessarily stands in opposition to unity. From an existential perspective, it involves accepting death and rejecting life. The unreformed person suffers from a disease that, if left untreated, results in death, a phenomenon that can be reduced to separation from God.

Path of Salvation

The attainment of salvation consists of two necessary events: God's grace and an individual's own effort to eradicate all the negative things that make gaining salvation impossible. Nanak emphasizes an inward devotional approach to the path that rejects common features of Indian religiosity, such as caste, social status, idolatry, bathing at pilgrimage locations, ascetic practices that promote abandoning the world, and leading an itinerant lifestyle. Rather than fleeing from the world, Nanak stresses striving within the world to achieve one's goal but not to be captive and affected by the world. The Sikh's journey to salvation is imagined to be an inward pilgrimage that is characterized by love. The type of love that Nanak conceives to be useful is related to certain corollaries: fear of God, surrender to God, and singing God's praises. Fear of God is combined with recognition of His infinity and absolute authority, whereas surrender means an unconditional submission in faith. The singing of God's praises involves repeating the name of God (*nām simaran*) in one's heart, which purifies the mind/heart, keeps God's name on the reciter's mind, and enhances remembering God's name. It is not sufficient to repeat the name of God in a mechanical matter, because it is essential to understand the implications of the word and to meditate on it. By meditating on the name of God, this word reveals the absolute, eternal nature of God and invites submission to Him. This type of meditation must be executed in love and ideally performed in one's thought, word, and deed.

The meditative repeating of God's name is the interior path advocated by Nanak that concentrates on the omnipresence of the divine name and also includes singing devotional songs. These types of religious practices bring the devotee into harmony with the divine rhythm and instruct a person that one does not have to renounce the world or to practice any other ritual observance. The repetitive name of this devotional exercise leads to an experience of an immense awe (*visamād*) that is intimately related to an ecstatic condition. A person's mind becomes overthrown, becomes redirected, and dies as it is purged of evil passions and egoism (*haumai*). Now free of karma and illusion (*māyā*), the mind conforms to the divine order that vibrates across the universe. Along with a sensation of joy and peace, a person ascends to higher levels of comprehension and experience.

Sikh thinkers have identified five stages of ascent toward a devotee's goal, with each stage representing a deeper experience and attainment of a higher level of being: piety, knowledge, effort, fulfillment, and truth. The first stage is a realization of the interrelationship of everything in the universe. The second stage undermines self-centeredness and gains a sense of being at one with all that has been created by God. The third stage represents the soul becoming more attuned to God and passing beyond what can be described. The fourth stage of fulfillment represents a realization of God that brings a person peace and equanimity. The individual moves beyond error, doubt, death, and rebirth and is filled with spiritual power, enabling her to feel God in her heart. The final rung is equated with truth and entering into union with God. The devotee enters into accord with the divine order (*hukam*), which is the ultimate end and purpose of human existence.

The union with God suggests three results for a person: a unitive experience of the human mind with the being of God, a cessation of rebirth, and awareness that the union with God escapes one's attempt to describe it because it is so profound. Sometimes, this union is expressed as a uniting of the individual light in the light of God, which suggests that the soul is dissolved and absorbed in God.

Rites of Passage

The Sikhs practice four major rites of passage: birth, marriage, initiation, and death. After the birth of a child, many families recite a prayer of thanksgiving and give the newborn a taste of nectar stirred with a sword. A name for a child is chosen randomly by opening the *Guru Granth Sāhib* to any page and taking the first letter that appears on the left-hand page to select an infant's name. Infant males have the name Singh (lion) added to their arbitrarily selected names, whereas female names are followed by a second name Kaur (princess), following a practice instituted by the tenth guru.

Many marriages are arranged by the parents, which follows the cultural custom in India. It is typical for the prospective couple to separately have their hands, arms, and face smeared with a paste consisting of turmeric, flour, and oil. This action is accompanied with traditional Punjabi wedding songs. A day before the wedding is the time for the bangle ceremony, which involves a maternal uncle giving the bride gifts that include ivory-colored bangles to wear on her arms, while the groom is given gifts of clothing. At the beginning of the wedding ceremony, the couple sits before the sacred text, during which prayers and blessings are offered along with a sermon on the role of marriage. At the conclusion of a statement by the couple and a prayer, the bride's father unites the couple by taking the hem of the groom's shoulder scarf and giving it to his daughter. Holding the scarf, the bride follows the groom as he circumambulates the sacred text four times in a clockwise direction, with their right sides toward the text. This act prefigures a wife's subordinate status to her husband throughout their married life. At various points of the ceremony, sacred verses are sung and read. This ceremony represents a spiritual union of a single soul in two bodies, from the Sikh perspective.

The initiation rite represents induction into the Khalsa for men and women. Initiates purify themselves by bathing and washing their hair, removing all jewelry, and wearing the Five Ks. The formal part of the ceremony occurs before the *Guru Granth Sāhib*, as with the marriage rite. As part of the rite, a mixture of sugar and water is poured into an iron bowl and stirred with a two-edged sword; using a cup dipped into the bowl, an initiate will drink four times. This drink is considered a sacred nectar that recalls the nectar offered to Guru Nanak when he received his vision of and call from God. This sacred drink is intimately related to a fully initiated Sikh male, who is called "nectar bearing." Male initiates accept the external and internal insignia associated with initiation into the Khalsa.

The importance of the initiation rite and associated practices are evident when drawing distinctions among Sikhs. Those initiated into the Khalsa as "nectar bearing" represent a minority. Those Sikh males called "hair bearing" represent those who do not cut their hair but have not undergone full initiation, a category that epitomizes the vast majority of Sikhs. The Sikh male who shaves and cuts his hair embodies a third distinction, whereas an initiate who cuts off his hair is considered in a fallen state, as is evident by his being called *akhalsa* (non-khalsa) and thus not an orthodox member of the religion.

The final rite of passage is a cremation, which usually occurs on the day of the death. This is a male affair, because women are forbidden from entering the cremation grounds. In a ceremony led by the oldest surviving son, participants continuously read from the sacred text for two days. At the conclusion of the cremation, mourners return to the home of the deceased for a communal meal. Many of the details of the marriage, initiation, and funeral rites reflect the influence of Indian culture on the Sikh community.

The Traditional Role of Women

Another feature of life that has influenced attitudes among Sikhs is the prevailing ethos of Hindu and Islamic patriarchal culture and their conceptions of the proper role of women in society. Hindu, Islamic, and Sikh cultures view the proper place of women as being in the home and being subordinate to their husbands. This subordinate, inferior, and obedient status is embodied in the Sikh wedding ceremony when the bride follows her husband around the sacred text and is instructed to accept her husband as her lord and master. Like upper caste Hindus and Muslims, some Sikh women practiced *purdah* (seclusion at home) and *sati* (immolation on their husbands' funeral pyres) during the nineteenth century. In all three cultures, women must not misbehave, because non-approved actions bring dishonor and shame to a family, which is then obligated to punish the offending female. The unequal status of women is deeply engrained in the culture because it follows social rules of hypergamy, which considers the bride and her family socially inferior. Any children are considered property of the father. Women are also set apart and excluded from the interior of a temple when having their menstrual period because flowing blood is considered polluting, a source of pollution that is also attributed to women by Muslims, Hindus, and Buddhists in India.

The deeply embedded nature of negative attitudes toward women is evident in narratives of the *Dasam Granth* constructed by Guru Gobind Singh. The "Charitro-pakhiam" is a part of the text about the nature of human character, especially about the evils of lust. In these narratives, we find tales of untrustworthy women with insatiable passionate attitudes. In order to meet with their lovers, female subjects manipulate others to help them by giving them wine, cannabis, and opium. When lustful women are caught engaged in a tryst, they commit lies and fabricate fantastic stories. To avoid being caught in some instances, women murder husbands, parents, and others; they don disguises themselves or disguise their lovers as, for example, an ascetic. Another tale relates the story of a woman who, after stealing money from her father at the prompting of her young lover, left her parents to run off with her lover, leaving a letter telling them that she had gone on a pilgrimage. She returned to her parents many years later after exhausting the money she had stolen. Her father was duped into thinking that she had acted righteously and piously when she gave him some money that she claimed to have earned performing religious acts.

But not all the narratives concerned with character depict women negatively, because there are also tales about women who are skillful and cunning fighters. According to one such story, a woman assumes the place of her husband after locking him in a cellar to protect him from harm. After valiantly fighting and defeating his enemies, she frees her husband, returns his turban and horse, and tells him farewell, because she has witnessed his inabilities and proven her own military prowess. Another narrative about self-sacrifice also depicts its heroine positively. While conducting a siege of a fort, the leader is killed by a woman, who also loses her husband and son. Enemy fighters subdue her and inform her that she would now become their slave, to which she agrees. She insists, however, on cremating the remains of her husband and son. During the cremation ceremony, she pulls an enemy solider into the blazing fire with her. This tale is a good example of a woman fighting to the very last moment of her life, a narrative that suggests something heroically positive about women.

Other aspects of Sikhism improve the status and treatment of women, because they are not required to wear a veil, they are allowed to read the sacred text, they can be initiated into the Khalsa, and motherhood is highly regarded. Discrimination against women is not supported by Sikh theological reflections because God is considered both male and female or without any gender.

Some Sikh feminist writers have returned to study the *Guru Granth Sāhib* to find aspects that reflect more positively toward the image of women in the early history of the religion because there are features of the text more conducive to a different portrayal of women by calling attention to more positive depictions of them. Some feminist Sikhs reinterpret, for instance, the Five Ks, a male-dominant aspect of the religion. The long hair expresses, for instance, a female mode of spirituality, beauty, and a social norm. Something similar can be affirmed about the comb. The breeches are an item that is necessary for both genders and undermine sexual distinctions that attempt to justify sexual inequality. The bracelet is feminine because it evokes images of female ornaments used to adorn the female body. Finally, the sword is reinterpreted as feminine because it is associated with divine wisdom and is not primarily an androcentric symbol.

Worship and Festivals

The Sikh location for public worship is the *gurdwara*, a term that literally means "by means of the guru's grace" or "the door of the guru." This term can be applied to any building that houses the sacred text, *Guru Granth Sāhib*, although the preeminent *gurdwara* is the Golden Temple at Amritsar. The temple does not contain any images or icons. It is usually open all day, with people visiting in an informal manner for as long as they wish to stay. The temple is not operated by an ordained priesthood because Sikhism is a lay organization, although there are *granthis* present who are readers and custodians of the sacred text, the fundamental object of devotion.

Before entering the temple, all entrants must cover their heads and remove their shoes, although socks are permissible if they are only used to visit the

Figure 8.1 The Golden Temple. Amritsar, Punjab, India. Curioso / Shutterstock.com

temple. People must wash their feet if they are dirty. The location of a temple can be recognized by the triangular saffron flag attached to a pole. The flag is symbolic of *khanda*, a member of the Five K's, emblematic of a double-edged sword. When entering the temple, a visitor must bow before the enthroned sacred text to the degree that his forehead touches the floor. There are no distinctions made according to a person's caste or social status or whether a person is a member of another religion or an atheist.

Worship in a temple begins with the ritual opening of the sacred text called "making the light manifest," followed by the singing (*kirtan*) of hymns. In addition to a possible sermon, members recite verses from the hymn named *Anand Sāhib*, originally composed by Guru Amar Das:

> The Khalsa shall rule, no enemy shall remain.
> All who endure suffering and privation shall be brought to the safety of
>   the Guru's protection.

Following the recitation of this hymn, members utter the *Ardās*, a Khalsa prayer of petition, which is followed with salutations. Finally, *hukam* is performed by randomly opening the sacred text and reading the hymn that appears at the top of the left-hand page. A formal service concludes with a reading from the concluding pages of the sacred text and ends with a communal meal at the *langar*, a room where people sit in rows that do not distinguish socially among people. This represents a joyous conclusion to the worship service. During the evening, the ceremony of *sukhasan* ("resting comfortably") is performed, which represents the closing of the sacred text for the day.

The central role of the sacred text is evident throughout worship. The text is available to worshippers for seeing (*darshan*), also a prominent feature of Hindu devotion in a temple, which not only includes viewing the physical text but also includes acts such as listening, reading, singing, and simply being in its presence. The other major essential feature of the worship service is *kirtan*, singing sacred verses accompanied by musicians playing drums (*tabla*) and harmonium, a key board instrument, and led by three singers.

Sikh devotional worship also includes going on pilgrimage to sacred places associated with the history of the religion and observing important anniversaries. Generally, there are five such places of special importance, which are called seats (*takhīs*). The primary place for pilgrimage is the Akal Takht that faces the Golden Temple in Amritsar. The other four locations are connected to incidents in the life of the tenth figure, Guru Gobind Singh. The Patna Sahib is the location in Bihar where he was born. In Anandpur, there is Keshgarch, where he instituted the Khalsa. The location where he died is Hazur Sahib in Nander, and his place of rest is Damdama, located near Bhatinda. In addition, there are other sacred places of pilgrimage associated with the lives of earlier gurus. The anniversaries that are observed are connected to important events in the history of the religion, such as the birthdays of Guru Nanak and Guru Gobind Singh. The martyrdom of Guru Arjan is also commemorated by the faithful.

There are also a number of festivals that mark the year for Sikhs. The start of the annual agricultural cycle and the New Year are celebrated at the Baisakhi festival, which is marked by rejoicing and visiting temples. This festival marks Guru Gobind Singh's inauguration of the Khalsa in 1699. Common features of this festival include washing the triangular flag and the saffron-colored cloths wrapped around the flag pole. The sacred text is also paraded through the streets and accompanied by singing of devotional hymns.

A festival originating with Hindus and shared by Sikhs is the Divali, Festival of Lights, at which lights are lit at night. It is also observed by merchants, who close their account books for the year, similar to Hindus, and householders clean their homes and give away sweets. Divali is especially meaningful for Sikhs because it commemorates the release of Guru Hargobind from his imprisonment by the Mughal Emperor Jahangir. During the evening, the Golden Temple is illuminated to mark the festival. An important festival for Hindus is Holi. On the day after this significant Hindu festival, Sikhs observe Hola Mahalla, a festival that is traced to Guru Gobind Singh and is observed by military exercises. Among other festivals are the following: Lohri, which marks the end of the short winter; Basant Panchmi, a spring festival; and Rakhari or Raksha Bandhan, which is marked by a girl tying a ribbon on her brother's wrist and him promising to defend her honor throughout his life.

Popular Sikhism of the Village

Sikhs living in villages in the Punjab share many features with Muslims and Hindus living under similar circumstances in India. Sikh villagers seek pragmatic results to their everyday problems and thus attempt to manipulate reality to their advantage, which is also a feature of Hindu and Muslim village life. Within this village world, goddess devotion plays a central role, along with practices and beliefs associated with the veneration of saints, spirit possession, belief in evil spirits, and making use of astrology and divination. These sets of beliefs and practices have long been at odds with orthodox Sikhism.

Sikh village folk worship Hindu goddesses such as Sitala, goddess of smallpox. She is represented by a clay image of a naked female riding a donkey, or she is believed to inhabit a local tree. Although she is normally cool, when she turns angry, she becomes overheated and attacks innocent victims. When her victim develops pustules on her skin, this condition is treated by a curing process consisting of a cooling process of the goddess and victim by means of water and cooling foods.

Villagers often venerate Sikh, Hindu, and Muslim saints by making pilgrimages to their shrines. Sakhi Sarvar is a typical saint worshipped by Sikhs. According to his biography, he was abused at home and traveled to Baghdad, where he received the gift of prophecy from three saints. When he returned to

India, he got married and educated himself. He became famous for his mira-cles, which attracted a large following. In one miracle, he created a well by striking the ground with his staff, and its water is believed to cure leprosy. In other miraculous acts, he killed a lion with a slipper and resurrected a dead horse. People believed that he could cure blindness, impotence, fever, and boils. However, envious kin became jealous of his fame and decided to kill him. When he died in 1174, his burial place became a shrine that attracted the faithful. Pilgrims make offerings at his shrine, while musicians play and dance there. Besides saints, villagers venerate special trees, streams, or rivers.

Villagers routinely believe in spirit possession and that evil forces can invade one's body, which may trigger disease. The afflicted person relies on a diviner or holy person for cures. There are also evil spirits that operate at night. These male spirits are described as casting no shadows and do not touch the ground with their feet when moving. Female spirits are associated with former women who have died while pregnant or within 40 days of childbirth. Normally, these female spirits have a hideous appearance, with feet facing backwards, although they can become beautiful to entice men.

Various superstitions exist about cures for snake bite, asthma, rheumatism, fever, or earache, consisting of a special soup. In order to control their hus-bands or others, women resort to charms carried on their person. By means of astrology and divination, it is possible to discern favorable days for doing things and know what the future might have in store.

Art and Material Culture

Overall, Sikh art is aniconic and focuses on religious themes such as the Divine Name, the heroic nature of the Sikh path as exemplified by its adherents, the need to fight for justice, and the role played by martyrdom in shaping the tra-dition. The *Guru Granth* has served as an artistic center of artistic focus and expression grounded in Sikh devotion. There are numerous versions of the *Guru Granth* that are illustrated with figures and illuminated with artwork. The historically earlier versions of the text are adorned with signs and emblems. Other versions of the sacred text are illuminated or are adorned with floral designs, while others are illustrated manuscripts with figural embellishments.

In spite of the aniconic nature of Sikh art, portraits of human subjects based on episodes of the Jamasakhis literature find their way into manuscripts. There are also examples of the portraits of Sikh gurus that are painted in the courtly style of the Mughal court artists. With respect to these types of paintings, Sikh gurus resemble Mughal royalty, when they are depicted with parasols and attendants reminiscent of the Muslim court.

Functioning as the principle shrine for Sikhs and considered the most sacred place within the Sikh religious world, the Golden Temple plays a symbolic role as the center of the Sikh world. It achieved its current name after Maharaja Ranjit Singh arranged for gold leaf to be placed on its upper two stories. Its golden dome is reflected within the pool of water in which it is constructed, making for a lovely sight at any time of the day. The temple is also called the Harimandir Sahib or Darbar Sahib; it represents the spiritual presence of the guru. It is built on a lower level, forcing devout visitors to descend steps to enter and worship, which is symbolic of the importance of approaching God with humility. The central shrine is open on all four sides, which suggests that the temple is open to everyone regardless of a devotee's socio-economic status.

Located immediately adjacent to the Golden Temple is the Akāl Takhat, which represents the temporal authority of the religion. The term *takhat* refers to a throne where temporal or political activity occurs. This building enables leaders to gather to discuss issues of socio-political import for the wider community. Thus, these two buildings represent the dual roles of the guru: spiritual and temporal.

Reform Movements and the Sikh Diaspora

It would be a serious mistake to conceptualize Sikhism as a monolithic path of religion, because its history suggests a dynamic and changing historical way with a broad variety of opinion about its teaching and path. Some early sects espoused an ascetic lifestyle. The Udasis, for instance, trace their lineage back to Siri Chand, a son of Guru Nanak, who advocated a path of renunciation and celibacy and did not acknowledge the Rahit (basic injunctions defining an orthodox Sikh). Ascetic discipline and celibacy were also stressed by the Nirmala sect, whose teaching was heavily influenced by Vedantic monistic thought. Sect members also donned saffron robes and worked as itinerant preachers.

There are two Niramkari groups: Asali Nirankaris (true N's) and Nakali Niramkaris. The former group traces its origin to Baba Dayal (1783–1855) and was centered in Rawalpindi until the partition of India in 1947. The sect stresses mental worship, using a silent method of *nām simaran* and supporting the teachings of Guru Nanak.

The ecstatic cries uttered during ritual performances help to define the Namdhari (called *kūk* or "shriek"), whose most renowned guru was Ram Singh (1816–1885), a preacher of a renewed Khalsa. The British did not trust Ram Singh and exiled him to Burma, where he died. The members of this sect are strict vegetarians, vigorously advocate cow protection, and wear white home-spun clothing with a white woolen scarf around their necks that is used as a rosary, and males secure their turbans horizontally across their foreheads. They treat the *Ādi Granth* and the *Dasan Granth* as equally important. Sect members also conceive of Ram Singh as a reincarnation of Guru Gobind Singh.

Some Sikh sectarian movements are rather conservative, whereas some groups are selective about what they observe. An example of the latter is the Sahaj-dhari Sikhs, because their males cut their hair and fail to acknowledge the Rahit (Five K's) that defines an orthodox Sikh. In contrast to the Sahaj-dhari, the Nihangs (meaning literally "free from care" or "free from worldly concerns") call themselves the only true members of the Khalsa. Even though their origin is obscure, they represent a division of four armies with their separate commanders. Most of the members are unmarried, which frees them from family ties and responsibilities. Male members wear high turbans crowned with a piece of cloth known as a standard or flag, a remnant of their military organization. Another conservative sect is the Nanaksar Sikhs, who accept the sacred text as literally true. An additional conservative group is the Damdami Taksah, who uphold a strict Khalsa position and a conservative school of theology. During the 1970s and 1980s, they were led by Jarnail Singh Brindranvale.

The Singh Saba Movement, a reform organization, strictly observed the Rahit code, which conservatively defined the basic beliefs and conduct of the Khalsa as established by Guru Gobind Singh. In the 1840s, British forces won two conflicts against Punjabi armies, giving the British an opportunity to annex the Punjab in 1849. During the following years, there was a steady decline of Sikhism, as the British simultaneously predicted its eventual demise. The decline of Sikhism was evident by the following of Hindu caste conventions, neglect of its belief system and personal appearance, and adoption of Hindu modes of worship, with the installation of idols in the Golden Temple. After four young Sikhs announced their baptism at a mission school, a number of Sikhs met to create a society that would protect and revive the religion in 1873. This group was matched by another, more aggressive organization in 1879 located in Lahore. The more aggressive Lahore group attracted intellectual figures to its ranks, whereas the older Amristar group was more conservative. Even while they pursued their own programs of action, the two groups united to form the Chief Khalsa Diwan in 1902. The group located in Lahore became the Tat Khalsa (True Khalsa), which was more exclusively orientated toward Khalsa identity, whereas the center in Amritsar became known as the Amritsar Singh Sabha, a movement that was more influenced by Christianity and British criticism of general religious practices in the country. Indian religious practices were portrayed, for instance, as irrational, superstitious, and contrary to genuine Sikhism. The movement denied that Sikhism was a branch of Hinduism or Islam.

After many years of loyalty to the British, the political relationship between the Sikhs and British began to tear apart. The break in their relationship came in April of 1919 after several days of unrest over British policies, culminating with the Jallianwala Bagh Massacre. According to accounts of the horrific event, Brigadier General Reginald Dyer placed Amritsar under martial law, but the annual Baisakki festival drew many people into the public realm. People were trapped by British soldiers within an enclosed area. Dyer ordered his men to fire into the trapped crowd, and 379 were killed, while many others were wounded. This action sparked passage of the Gurdwara Act in 1925, which replaced those in charge.

During the mid-eighteenth century, the Sikh diaspora began with members going abroad to serve as soldiers or police officers in places such as China, Malaysia, the Middle East, Africa, and Europe. By the late nineteenth century,

Sikhs went abroad to work as indentured laborers in Uganda and Kenya. These travelers tended to live in larger cities, in contrast to their former rural lifestyle. After World War II and rapid industrial growth, the demand for labor motivated many Sikhs to seek economic benefits afford by this situation. In addition to economic factors, political events such as partition and the political turmoil caused by the Indian government's attack on the Golden Temple and assassination of Prime Minister Indira Gandhi by her Sikh bodyguards motivated some Sikhs to leave India. The dispersal of Sikhs around the world was aided by more liberal immigration policies by host countries.

Life in foreign countries did not always go smoothly for Sikhs looking for a better life. Many Sikhs were forced to leave Kenya in 1968 and Uganda in 1972 when they were expelled as a result of policies favoring Africans. Numerous Sikhs went to Britain as political refugees, only to encounter caste discrimination by Sikh compatriots of the predominant Jat caste. Sikhs that migrated to Canada encountered disagreements over the leadership of the local temples, leading to strong disputes between contending pro- and anti-Khalistan groups.

The first Sikh temple constructed in the United States was located in Stockton, California, in 1915. During the early years of migration to America, Sikhs experienced overt racism, labor discrimination, social exclusion, and riots. When labor leaders attempted to expel Asians from working in lumber mills, riots erupted in Bellingham, Washington, in 1907. The city of Los Angeles prohibited Asians from purchasing homes in 1910, and, later, the 1913 Alien Land Law excluded non-American citizens from owning or leasing land. And a 1923 decision of the Supreme Court—*U.S. v. Bhagat Singh Thind*—put a halt to immigration from Asia, although more recent history has witnessed a more open policy toward immigration from Asia.

In 1971, Harbhajan Singhkhalsa Yogiji (also known as Yog-Bhajan) established the Sikh Dharma of the Western Hemisphere (3HO Sikhs) in America. Its educational branch was termed 3HO (Healthy Happy Holy Organization). Members are distinguished by wearing white apparel. In addition, women wear turbans along with men. Its ordained ministry leads members to practice a simple and rigorous life of yoga and meditation.

Religious Experience

From a simplistic perspective, Sikh religious experience is a devotional path that eventually culminates in a direct experience of God and liberation from the cycle of death and rebirth. Sikh leaders reject the techniques of yoga and asceticism because they are ultimately futile practices. In place of these types of techniques, Sikhs advocate using God's name, serving the guru, and maintaining association with the servants of God. More precisely, these techniques include repeating the divine name, singing hymns, and meditating on the divine name at a more advanced level of practice, seeking to become harmonious with the divine name. These Sikh techniques are indicative of a personal relationship with God and other members of the community. The Sikh path involves adjusting one's life to the harmony embodied in God's name.

In his *Japji*, Nanak specifies five stages of attainment of liberation, during which God's grace is present at each point. The initial stage is *dharm khand*, a state into which everyone is born, a condition during which one practices duty and piety. The second stage (*gyan khand*) is a stage of awareness or knowledge that involves a deeper grasp of reality, which makes one aware of the mysterious nature of the mystery of God and the vast nature of the universe. Third, the realm of effort (*saran khand*) represents one's mind and intellect becoming more adjusted to God, which is the final stage during which human effort and insight are effective. This is followed by the fourth stage of grace (*karan khand*), by which one attains peace and realizes the true nature of life, that the essence of God is also equivalent to the genuine nature of a person's own self. Now the mind is controlled and its limitations are contained, resulting in a "God-minded" person, who is the only truly free person. Finally, the realm of truth (*sach khand*) is the realm of ultimate experience, which cannot be described by language because it stands for the formless and everlasting essence of the *Nirgun* (formless) nature of God, enabling one to perceive the world from the viewpoint of the God, the Eternal Being.

Nanak also calls the fifth level of attainment *sahaj*, a point at which the human soul reaches equipoise and tranquility. The human soul is now beyond the cycle of rebirth. This state is described as a blissful, peaceful, and joyous experience. Nanak associates this experience with wonder and rapture as the human soul peacefully blends harmoniously with the Eternal One. This experience occurs when one is alive, making a person someone liberated while alive and beyond the cycle of rebirth.

Suggestions for Further Reading

Cole, W. Owen and Piara Singh Sambhi. *The Sikhs: Their Religious Beliefs and Practices.* London: Routledge, 1978.

Jakobsh, Doris R. *Sikhism: Dimensions of Asian Spirituality.* Honolulu: University of Hawai'i Press, 2012.

McLeod, W. H. *The Sikhs: History, Religion, and Society.* New York: Columbia University Press, 1989.

———. *Sikhism.* London: Penguin Books, 1997.

Obereoi, Harjot. *The Construction of Religious Boundaries: Culture, Identity and Diversity in the Sikh Tradition.* Delhi: Oxford University Press, 1994.

Rhinehart, Robin. *Debating the Dasam Granth.* Oxford and New York: Oxford University Press, 2011.

Singh, Nikky-Guninder Kaur. *Feminine Principle in the Sikh Vision of the Transcendent.* Cambridge: Cambridge University Press, 1993.

———. *Sikhism: An Introduction.* London: I. B. Tauris, 2011.

9   Chinese Traditions

According to ancient Chinese cosmology, creation of the world does not originate from nothing but is rather created from some already existing matter. The ancient Chinese worldview imagines the world in the following way: Earth is square; the sky is round, held aloft by four or eight giant pillars fastened by cords to the sky's canopy, or the cosmos is supported by four immense mountains. This world is the only one of its kind. Moreover, there is neither a creator god nor a divine will that guides creation. This general viewpoint is enhanced by the myth of Pangu, a firstborn and dying god.

Not being precisely a god or fully human, Pangu is a giant who shares the cosmic powers of heaven and earth. Since he is the first to die, the creation of the world is a direct result of the metamorphosis of his dying body. According to one version of this narrative, as the firstborn approaches death, his body is transformed into aspects of nature, such as wind, clouds, thunder, sun, moon, stars, water, plants, trees, and rivers. The mites on his body are touched by the wind and become black-haired people. According to another myth, the goddess Nügua constructs humans from yellow earth and mud, which polarizes humankind into rich aristocrats made from yellow earth and poor commoners made from mud.

Ancient Chinese cosmology situates China at the center of the world, with its capital located in the middle of the kingdom and the royal palace situated at the center of the capital, which is the precise place of the center of the world. It is here that heaven and earth can communicate with each other. In the capital, there is located the *ming tang* (ritual palace), which is built on a square base signifying the earth, functioning as a center of the world and calendar. The structure is covered by a round roof, which symbolizes heaven. As the year progresses, the emperor, son of heaven, moves from one part of the palace to another, placing himself at the quarter of the palace demanded by the calendar. By following this movement, the emperor successively inaugurates the seasons and the months. At the end of the third month of summer, the emperor assumes a position at the center of the *ming tang* (ritual palace), incarnating himself at the center of the world and the connection between heaven and earth. This cosmology includes two concepts of time built into it: a cyclic notion of time with no beginning point and the linear time of human history.

The cosmos operates according to the theory of *yin-yang* and their alterations. The female principle *yin* is described as negative, receptive, and passive; it is low and thus akin symbolically to the earth. *Yin* represents cold and cloudy weather. The masculine opposite principle is *yang*, which is described as active, positive, and aggressive; it is said to be high and is akin to heaven. It suggests sunny and warm weather. These two alternating principles are complementary and represent a cyclical totality constituted by their conjunction. While one principle is dominant, the other one is recessive. At the summer and winter solstices, *yin* and *yang* begin to give way to one another. These times of the year are especially dangerous to humans, and call for special precautions with respect to how a person conducts herself. This alternating cycle enables us to recognize a close correspondence of human affairs with the processes of the world, giving the rhythm of the universe cosmic and social aspects.

The cyclic pattern of *yin-yang* is intertwined with the five agents' theory, which holds that the basic constituents of the universe are wood, fire, earth, metal, and water. Rather than concrete substances, these five agents are conceived as abstract powers. These agents are constantly replacing each other in an endless succession by overcoming each other. Wood (meaning plant life) grows, for instance, out of—and thus overcomes—soil, metal cuts wood, fire melts metal, water extinguishes fire, and soil dams up water. When this final phase is reached, the cycle recommences. Overall, each agent succeeds another in exercising a dominant influence over both human and natural events. Each of the agents occupies a space and controls certain forces of nature. Wood is located, for example, in the eastern quarter and controls the forces of spring and production, whereas fire occupies the southern quarter and controls the forces of summer and heat. In the western quarter is located metal, which controls the forces of autumn and destruction, while water occupies the northern quarter and controls the forces of winter and cold. The earth is located at the center and includes all the elements, which form a network of relationships that ties together human and nonhuman parts of the cosmos into a single fabric. Since a disruption of one element can produce inevitable effects elsewhere in the cosmos, it is thus possible for human conduct to exert a powerful influence for harmony or disharmony. Therefore, human action can have serious consequences, because humans are microcosms of the macrocosmic cosmos. There are two basic ways to maintain and ensure harmony: performing good moral behavior and correct performance of ritual. Overall, this worldview is holistic and all-embracing.

The ancient Chinese tend to look backward when seeking a golden age, which is typical of Eastern forms of religion, whereas Western religions tend to be orientated to the future and a better age to come, with notions such as a coming messiah and final judgment before the end of the world. For the ancient Chinese, there are three demigod rulers of a golden age of antiquity: Yao, Shun, and Yü, who are perfect rulers. This golden age did not represent a material paradise but rather denoted perfect government, in which each of these figures abdicated leadership to the next best person instead of some family member, serving as a paradigm for the enlightened reign of an ideal sage-ruler.

The basic cosmogonic myth is often associated with a sequence of myths relating the origin of items needed for survival and organization of human life. The Fire Driller discovers fire and the art of cooking. Fu Xi and Nügua, male and female deities depicted as two human figures linked by their serpentine lower bodies holding, respectively, a carpenter's square and compass, serve as exemplars of marriage. Depicted carrying a red whip, Shen Nong, a farmer deity, is credited with teaching humans agriculture and pharmacopoeia, whereas Chi Yu invented metallurgy and weapons, making him a god of war. Musical instruments were invented by Ti Ku, and Cang Cong taught humans the way to raise silkworms.

In addition to items and knowledge needed for social welfare, ancient Chinese mythical narratives contain stories about savior and destructive figures. Zhu Long, who is part human and serpent, alleviates darkness in the northern region with the divine light from his eyes and is called the Torch Dragon. Nügua repairs the cosmos after it returns to chaos when its four supporting pillars collapse by creating five-colored stones to repair the sky, using the severed feet of a giant sea turtle to support the four pillars, and destroying a black dragon. Cosmic destruction is averted in another myth by Yi, the archer, when he saves the earth from the sun, while Kun, a descendent of a deity, saves the world from a flood, instructs people how to renew the soil, and establishes the mythical Xia dynasty.

Countering creative actions, there are destructive actions such as the murder of the sky god, Bao Jiang. The primal archer Yi plays the role of a villain by killing the Lord of the River and abducting his wife; he is assassinated by his clansmen, who cook his body and attempt to force his son to eat him. By refusing to eat their father, the sons were also killed. The Yellow Emperor is the foremost warrior deity and defeats a series of enemies. He defeats, for example, his brother, Flame Emperor, in a struggle for total supremacy after originally agreeing for each of them to rule half of the world and turns his brother's hide into a war drum in order to introduce terror into governing.

In addition to various male divine figures, ancient China embraced female deities such as Nügua, who is famous for her 70 transformations, which reflect her creative powers of change and renewal of the cosmos, but she loses her independent status when she later becomes the consort of Fu Xi. In contrast to Nügua, the Weaver Maid is a star connected to another star called Draught Ox, and they are linked together as unhappy lovers. The Xing Queens are two daughters of Yao and become wives of Shun. After their husband dies, the sisters drown in a river and become its spirits. When she was born, the Woman Chou was scorched to death by ten suns. She is associated with the crab, a symbol of regeneration. Woman Chou dresses in green clothes, is a virgin, and lives on top of a mountain. A final example is the Queen Mother of the West, a goddess of the wilds who lives among wild beasts. The Queen Mother is described with unkempt hair, a panther's tail, and tiger's fangs, and is surrounded by a retinue of feline beasts and birds. She is an avenging goddess and can bring plagues. In contrast to these attributes, she can also confer immortality on humans, which is symbolized iconographically by the basket of peaches of immortality in her right hand.

These mythical narratives not only explain the origins of the world and important cultural features, but they are also indicative of a rich polytheism that becomes enhanced when Daoism gets established. The Chinese religious tradition is a complex blend of three indigenous elements—Confucianism, Daoism, and folk religion—along with Buddhism, an imported religion from India. These various religious paths are not mutually exclusive, although there were times in Chinese history when they were in tension with each other, which sometimes led to persecution of mostly Buddhism, in part because of its foreign origin and strange ideas that were considered contrary to the Chinese social values. As these traditions co-existed and intermingled, it became possible for an average member of Chinese society to simultaneously observe aspects of each way consciously or unconsciously. To the average person, this type of practice did not seem contradictory. Each of these traditions will be treated separately for the purpose of understanding them, but it must be remembered how they are intimately intertwined.

Confucianism and Way of the Sage

Born around 551–2 and dying in 479 BCE in present Shantong providence, Confucius spent his life developing his philosophy and attempting to find a ruler who would accept his philosophy and use it to rule his kingdom. Because he was unsuccessful in finding such a leader, Confucius concluded that his life-long work was an abject failure. What Confucius could not foresee was the way his thought shaped an entire civilization. He also could not conceivably see that he would become the center of a religious cult, even though he was not a religious teacher. He did see himself, however, as a conservative figure who tried to preserve and transmit an old tradition that was basically ethical.

His ethical thought was shaped by a belief in, worship of, and sacrifice to a supreme deity, who was connected to a reverence for ancestor spirits. Confucius' ethical thought was grounded in his conviction that society needed to be organized on the model of the family, and practical economic needs emphasized the importance of mutual friendliness and assistance. Finally, the harmony and peace of society were best promoted by a careful regulation of all human relationships. Confucius viewed these elements as part of an old tradition that he sought to preserve and transmit. In this way, he was a conservative person who looked to the past for guidance in his attempt to create a harmonious society led by a sage, who was the perfect man and true gentleman. Thus, he was no revolutionary figure and no religious teacher, even though he appears to have been a deeply religious person. He was, however, skeptical about the existence of spirits and ghosts that were so widely accepted by ordinary humans, refused to discuss questions about survival after death, and was reluctant to discuss the nature of heaven. In short, his focus was on this world and interpersonal relationships.

Confucius believed that all humans (with the exception of women) are equally endowed at birth, although they become different by practice. Because humans are naturally equal, they are malleable, and any differences between humans do not affect their ability to perform beneficially as members of society. Humans are free of innate defects such as original sin. This means that given the right kind of education, humans can grow morally and ethically. The later Confucian thinker Mencius says that a person is like a tree. If a person receives the right nourishment, this person will grow to his utmost potential. All humans are born with a mind that can function in two ways: It can evaluate the requirements of a situation and can command proper action. The human mind not only discriminates between right and wrong, but it also approves or disapproves. When a person's actions are in accord with the commands of one's mind, a person is able to enter into communion with heaven.

For Confucius, a human is a social being and is shaped to a large extent by society. In contrast to Buddhism and Daoism, Confucius thinks that it is wrong to become a hermit or a monastic recluse, because one is rejecting one's natural social nature, while it is also wrong to simply follow the crowd. A person's social identity is supported by the five most important personal and social relationships: (1) relation between father and son; (2) relation between elder brother and younger brother; (3) relation between husband and wife; (4) relation between elder and younger person; and (5) relation between ruler and subject. It needs to be noted that the latter person in each pair is inferior in status to the former. The five relationships are governed by appropriate dispositions, which include filial piety by a son, respect by a younger brother, obedience by a wife, deference by a younger person, and loyalty of a subject to a ruler. These basic dispositions are reciprocated by superiors by showing, respectively, kindness, nobility, respect, humanness, and benevolence.

Confucius expounds five major ethical concepts: *li* (ritual, ceremony, and courtesy), *ren* (humanity), *zhong* (conscientiousness and loyalty), *shu* (altruism and reciprocity), *yi* (righteousness), and *xiao de* (filial piety and brotherly love). The virtue of *li* consists of two Chinese characters: an influence coming from heaven and a sacrificial vessel, indicating its original meaning of sacrifice. The term includes all customary and socially accepted rites by which a person should conduct her interactions with others, such as burying one's parents according to its precepts. Confucius conceives of *li* as singular because it is in harmony with the *Dao* and acts as a restraint on a person's proclivity to act contrary to it. It is essential that human actions follow the already established pattern of *li*, with the inter-social goal of having one's gestures coordinating harmoniously with those of others, which must be done effortlessly and spontaneously. From Confucius' perspective, a smooth-functioning social life is analogous to a classical Chinese dance performance, during which all the movements are well coordinated. A person's actions are not innate but rather depend on prior learning, just as one might learn to dance. The outward display of *li* is not sufficient without internal feelings of sincerity and reverence. When a person is shaped by *li*, that person becomes truly human. Because ceremony is public, shared, and transparent, it enables a person to be open and receptive toward others.

The Confucian virtues reach their summation with *ren*, in the sense of perfect goodness, human heartedness, or humanity. The Chinese character is composed of two characters: "man" plus "two," which literally means man to man-ness and consists of loving others according to the golden mean: do not do to others what you do not want them to do to you. This socio-ethical injunction also means to put oneself into the position of others, whereas its opposite is an unsettled, un-tranquil, and disturbed condition. *Ren* and *li* are two aspects of the same thing, in the sense of directing our attention to social patterns of conduct and relationship, although *ren* cannot be realized until a person learns *li*.

By practicing *ren*, a person is also practicing conscientiousness (*zhong*) and altruism (*shu*). Conscientiousness means to serve others with all one's heart, while altruism entails putting oneself in the place of others. Doing what is fitting and right is righteousness (*yi*); it is the "oughtness" of a situation, in the sense that one acts in a certain way because it is the right thing to do.

Rather than a fixed law, righteousness accords with socially accepted standards of human conduct, which is a way that will produce the greatest well-being and happiness for a majority of people. These virtues are connected to filial piety, which involves conducting oneself in such a way that one's parents have no cause for anxiety except for one's health. This virtue entails respecting and revering one's parents and obeying them as long as their demands accord with what is right.

These virtues accord with the *dao* (way) of heaven. This way is not a matter of choosing; it is more a matter of knowing the way and following it. The way is the path that humans ought to travel because it is ordained by heaven. The goal of the way is not to arrive at some place but rather to follow the way without effort and correctly, a path characterized by love, righteousness, propriety, reciprocity, loyalty, and wisdom. The path leads to harmony. This suggests that the goal of the way is reaching a condition of following the way by simply treading the path.

What Confucius means by the way is fairly clear, but his conception of heaven is a bit vague because he refused to speculate about it. Confucius did not view heaven as an anthropomorphic being, because it is more akin to a universal moral force. Intimately associated with the way (*dao*) is the decree or will (*ming*) of heaven, which is the way ordained by heaven. The will of heaven is a purposeful force that serves as the guiding principle of life, which humans seek to understand in order to conform their lives to it. By trying to do what is right without thinking about success or failure, we never fail, because we are doing our duty in a righteous way, which makes us happy and free from anxiety. Confucius does not mean to say that *ming* is deterministic or fatalistic, because humans can either accept or reject it.

By following Confucius' teaching, a person can become a perfect gentleman (*zhong zi*) or noble-minded person, which is a more practical and attainable character, unlike the holy sages of ancient times, who managed to achieve a divine status. The more realistic genuine gentleman carries the three marks: goodness, courage, and wisdom. This is a possibility for all men that is not dependent on one's birth but does depend on conduct and character. It is individuals with the best ethical character that should assume positions of leadership.

Because the world is not a paradise or perfect place, a process of degeneration occurs from the top down to the bottom of the social structure. Therefore, Confucius recognizes a need for a method that he calls the rectification of names. According to Confucius, every name possesses its own definition, which designates the nature of a thing, representing its essence or concept. Thus a ruler, minister, father, and son must act in life in accordance with the definitions of their names. By them performing their duties, there will be no disorder in the world. According to Confucius, this process must begin from the top, because this is the location where the discrepancy between actualities and names originates.

Later Developments

Born a few years after the death of Confucius and sharing the humble origins of the sage, Mozi (c. 470–391 BCE) became convinced that Confucius' teaching could not resolve the root social problems. Mozi rejected the Confucian method of the rectification of names, which Confucius thought established an ideal world of universals because it was established without regard for practical consequences. Since institutions, artifacts, and principles of a society originate in practical needs as a response to specific problems, a realm of universals does not solve any problems. Music, for example, is a waste of time because it interferes with producing food and clothing, while war is also deplored because it disrupts society, decimates the population, and is unprofitable. Mozi argues that the remedy for war and other social evils is universal love.

Because humans cannot practice universal love with their original natures, they need to be dyed by universal love without degrees. Having nothing to do with the emotions, love is purely a thing of the mind, representing a principle of all-embracingness that treats everyone alike, which goes beyond the thought of Confucius. How can a person be convinced that this is the best path? Mozi responds with his doctrine of enlightened self-interest, which means that people must be made aware that universal love is useful and is a way to practice *ren* (human heartedness). Moreover, the usefulness of universal love is all around us because it enriches the country, increases population, establishes good order, prevents war, and obtains the blessings of the spirits.

Mozi claims that universal love is the way of heaven, which loves all humans impartially. In sharp contrast to Confucius, Mozi's notion of heaven is personal, righteous, and loving. Heaven also possesses a will, punishes evil, and rewards goodness. In contrast to Confucius, Mozi also opposed the concept of an impersonal fate. Since rewards and punishments are sent by heaven and the spirits, they are determined by the conduct of humans and not fate.

In retrospect, Mozi founded the only school in ancient China named for an individual and is the only person to have established a religion. He also founded a strictly disciplined organization capable of military action. Mohism developed in two directions: a religious organization and a scientific and logical system of thought known as Neo-Mohism. By the third century BCE, all Mohist schools disappeared, because of their dogmatic philosophical stance, condemnation of all pleasure and emotions, and authoritarian system of government, with its fixed rules to be followed.

A different Confucian spirit was offered by the sage Mencius (372–289 BCE), who was born in northeastern China, studied with Confucian thinkers, and tried to put his philosophy into practice with an administrative position. His philosophy is a reaction against Mozi, whom Mencius viewed as insidious and pernicious. Mencius compared himself to an ancient sage-king who controlled a flood and brought peace to the world. Not lacking for self-confidence, Mencius thought that he was the only one with the ability to perpetuate the Confucian tradition.

Mencius argues that human nature is good, although not perfect, and needs to be developed. Humans are naturally good because they possess the essential virtues. There are no external forces that hinder the development of these innate virtues. He compares a person to a tree that receives the right amount of nourishment to grow to its utmost potential, a process that makes a person fully human. What makes this possible is the mind of a person, which overlaps with the heart and its emotions, desires, ideas, intentions, and tendencies. Mencius speaks about four innate minds in a person that correspond to the major Confucian virtues: commiseration, reverence and respect, shame and dislike, and the approving and disapproving aspect of the mind.

Mencius makes a unique contribution to Confucian thought with respect to an understanding of heaven, which is the universal lord of the world, creator, and regulator of laws that govern humans. He argues that the will of heaven can be known through the will of the people. Heaven is personal, responsible for the order of the world, intelligent, a vague spiritual force, ethical, a source of human nature, and a way. By knowing one's nature, one comes to know heaven. And since all men are by nature good, all men are potential sages. In ancient China, women were not conceived to be able to attain the status of a sage.

Role of Women in Classical Chinese Culture

According to a narrative about a contest for supremacy between a matriarchal and patriarchal society, the people made a man known as the Lord of the Granary their leader. During his wanderings, he encountered the Salt Goddess, who asks him to live with her, but he refused her offer. During the night, she came to sleep with him. At dawn she turned into a flying insect, and along with a swarm of other insects, turned the day into night. This confused the Lord of the Granary, who could not see where he was located for several nights. He asked for a green silk cord and presented it to the Salt Goddess as a belt, with an offer to live together. After the Salt Goddess accepted and wore it as a belt, the Lord of the Granary stood on a sunlit rock and shot arrows at her belt, killing her. Then the sky cleared as far as he could see. In this narrative, the male figure tricks the female into thinking that they could be equal but then destroys her to maintain his supremacy. This narrative reflects the social structure of classical Chinese society, with women assuming an inferior condition in comparison to men.

The inferior status of women in classical Chinese culture is grounded in the cosmic order, where the feminine *yin* is identified with the earth and with all things lowly and inferior. The feminine *yin* force is further characterized as yielding, receptive, and devoted. Although *yin* is inferior to the masculine *yang* force, the *yin* force is still indispensable to the proper working of the universe. Therefore, from a cosmic perspective, women are the complementary opposites of men.

The Chinese character for a wife shows a woman with a broom, reflecting her domestic role in life. The typical woman is educated at home, where she learns good manners and domestic skills like sewing and weaving. At 15 years of age, a girl received a hairpin that marked a coming-of-age ceremony. By 20 years of age, she is expected to be married, a condition in which she is expected to serve her husband, whose duty is to manage his wife. The correct relationship between a husband and wife is based on harmony. Besides stressing formality and reserve in marriage, Confucianism also emphasizes that a wife should be devoted to her husband and be responsible for her spouse's moral character.

The ideal woman is chaste in the sense of integrity and honor, and there are numerous stories that illustrate a virtuous wife. According to one such story, a widow does not leave a burning room because a chaste woman does not leave the house at night unless accompanied by a matron or governess, perishing in the fire rather than violating social decorum. In another story, a woman disobeys her mother's request to return home because she would rather stay to nurse her husband's case of leprosy. A third tale relates the predicament of a married woman whose father is captured by an evil person who threatens to kill the father if she does not allow the evil man to kill her husband. In order to avoid having her father or husband die, she pretends to cooperate by informing the evil person of the location where her husband will be sleeping. Taking the place of her husband in bed, she is killed instead of her husband. Thus, this chaste woman remains faithful to both her husband and father.

Traditional Chinese women have their inferior status because they are also associated with pollution, in the sense that they emit unclean substances or liquids from their bodies, and because of their further connection with birth and death. Primary unclean bodily fluids include menstrual blood and postpartum discharge, whereas secondary unclean substances include urine, feces, pus, and mucus. Female bodily fluids are associated with dangerous power. This is especially true with blood that emerges during childbirth, which is connected to the notion of Thai Sin, the placenta god and child's soul for four months after birth.

In addition to her role as a giver of life, a woman has more contact with the realm of the dead than men. Since women are periodically unclean due to their menstrual period, they are allowed contact with unclean spirits of the dead and their world. Some women worship malevolent spirits to avoid harm and not for gaining supernatural assistance. This scenario gives us a glimpse into a hierarchy of spiritual beings, with clean, high gods worshipped by men and lower spirits and ghosts worshipped by women.

Traditional Chinese women are not without power. Their most significant power is the ability to produce children. This is especially true with male children, who ensure that offerings to ancestors will continue after the death of their father. It is also known that even newly married women attempt to manipulate their husbands and even act to subvert and disrupt them. Even after menopause, a woman's power can threaten male dominance in the village setting by her talking about the males, which may cause a male to lose face. Older women can also exercise influence through their sons by controlling them through their persuasive power.

A curious custom in Chinese culture that began between the Tang and Song dynasties and was accepted among the upper classes by the twelfth century is the practice of foot-binding. Starting when a girl is around 7 years old, bandages are tied tighter around the child's feet until they become broken and deformed, creating very tiny feet that are called "lotus hooks" because of their association with beauty. There are two reasons for this practice: Tiny feet are equated with beauty, and they arouse male desire. This custom resulted in painful walking, a restricting of a woman's movements, and confining of women to the home.

Family and Communal Religions of China

The most basic level of religion in traditional Chinese culture is the family cult, which is expressed in ancestor worship and the kitchen stove. The next level is the communal cult, then the state cult, and personal religion, which is secondary to the family cult, involving Daoism or Buddhism or a combination of them for specific purposes. An individual most likely participates in all four levels of religion during his life. The closest term that the ancient Chinese had for religion is *zhong-jiao*, which is very revealing about their way of religion. The character for *zhong* depicts a house or a shrine in which an altar is constructed to offer sacrifice. From depicting a sacrificial shrine, *zhong* evolves into ancestral worship. The character *jiao* depicts a teacher holding a staff while giving instructions to his pupils, an image that stresses three things: authority of the teacher, obedience of the student, and the necessity of discipline. The term *zhong-jiao* literally means "the ancestral teachings," even though the term was used separately in ancient China.

Virtually every home in ancient China possessed an ancestral altar that held wooden spirit tablets, each one representing a deceased ancestor. The presence of these tablets indicates that the dead continue to occupy a place within the family activities. This ancestor cult embodies two parts: mortuary rites immediately following death and those rites that maintain the long-term relationship between the living and the dead. The mortuary rites are performed for the benefit and salvation of the soul, which includes reporting the death to the proper governing authorities in the underworld, such as the earth god, city god, and others. This reporting facilitated admittance of the soul into the spirit world. Since the deceased have passed into another form of existence, some personal effects are placed in the coffin, taking the form of paper horses, boats, and houses along with clothing and money. A typical funeral service involves scattering of paper money at the head of the funeral process to ward off evil spirits. Daoist and Buddhist priests might be hired to chant scriptures during the funeral, with the intention of assisting the spirit to travel to the happy land of the Western Heaven and help the soul to pass through the ten courts of judgment in the underworld. These rites are intended to stabilize the relationship between the dead and the living, to protect the living, and to demonstrate that survivors depend on the spirits for protection and blessing.

In addition to the ancestral cult, the kitchen god and his wife are important figures present at the center of family life, represented by their picture. The kitchen god is represented as a white-bearded old man dressed in a mandarin costume seated on an armchair, with his wife standing at his side feeding the six domestic animals: horse, cow, pig, sheep, dog, and chicken. As the head of the family deities, he governs the house. He is offered a meal three times a year: his birthday, the third day of the eight month, and the twenty-fourth day of the twelfth month. It is believed that he reports to the Jade Emperor, who governs the earth and heaven, once a year about everything that has occurred in the house during the year. The kitchen god and his wife keep a register in which they record all the family's actions. Depending on the report, the Jade Emperor increases or diminishes the family's share of happiness for the following year.

In contrast to family religion, communal religion is consciously organized, whereas family religion is the result of biology. What gives communal religion its cohesiveness is common interests, a body of social rules, shared values, and practices. Chinese peasants worship agricultural gods associated with the forces of nature, such as wind and thunder, rain and flood (represented by various dragons), deities of insect control, and deities for protecting domestic animals and trees. At local temples, people prayed for good crops and protection from epidemics. Patron deities are common among craft and trade groups. The goddess Tianhou, a patroness of sailing, was born, for instance, in the tenth century CE. She could perform miracles as a young girl, and, unlike most Chinese women, she refused to marry. Sailors encountering danger at sea claim to have seen her apparition, which leads their ship to safety. Various trades maintain a meeting place with a sacred altar, an image of their patron divine being, and scrolls containing the names of deceased members.

Communities gather for fairs and festivals. Fairs are intended to enhance rural trade and to entertain people with peep shows, puppet shows, magic shows, acrobatic and boxing performances, storytelling, and fortune telling. Because sexual segregation is relaxed during fairs, men and women are able to mingle together and talk. Chinese festivals reflect important dates of the agricultural cycle. A very important celebration is the New Year festival, because this time marks the moment when *yin* and *yang* make contact at the winter solstice, when *yang* is reborn. This festival includes the hanging of cocks and hens on gates and doors to appease the power of *yin* and to harmonize both forces. Other festivals involve thanksgiving, exorcism of demons, lunar observance, spring, purgation and lustration, and numerous others. Chinese festivals are affirmative, a joyful time during which excessive eating, drinking, dancing, and singing take place and harmony is also maintained.

Chinese Divination

From ancient times, divination was practiced at all levels of Chinese religion and permeated the religious culture. Divination was used to gain foreknowledge about what was to happen to a person, family, society, or the state. When one had this foreknowledge, it was possible to decide what should be done to counteract undesirable future occurrences, or to be in accord with supernatural forces gave one chances to produce positive results. Divination also played an important role as a way for a person to keep in touch with deceased ancestors in order to learn their needs in the afterlife and to help them. The ancient Chinese used animal shoulder blades or tortoise shells as divining devices by beating or heating them and interpreting the meaning of the cracks, or they used stalks of different lengths.

Later methods of divination included astrology, to discern the order of the twenty-eight star constellations and to access the movement of the five planets along with the sun and moon. Consulting almanacs was another method to guide and give advice for daily life. The almanacs helped one to arrange actions according to the four seasons and adjusting to the equinox and solstice. Another method was associated with the five elements theory, with the objective of making certain that they do not become confused and to discover what changes will arise with respect to the five planets. The interpretation of a person's dreams was also a way to divine the future.

Presupposing that the cosmos was a functioning organism and not a static entity, the *Yijing* (Book of Changes), a text that was a Confucian classic and part of its canon, was a diviner's manual that evolved from eight trigrams, a combination of broken and unbroken lines placed atop another line. The eight trigrams corresponded to natural phenomena: heaven, earth, wind, lakes, mountains, fire, water, and thunder. The broken lines of the trigram represent *yin* (feminine principle), while the unbroken lines stand for *yang* (male principle). Each line is a symbol, and the diagrams are symbols as wholes. The diagrams change from symbols to being invested with power. This development suggested that they changed from representing change to bringing about change. The original eight trigrams developed into sixty-four hexagrams. This was done by placing one trigram over another. The theory behind the trigrams portrayed the universe as being in a constant state of change and transformation, whereas the term *yi* in the book's title signified "easy." But underlying this continuous flux, there was the Dao, which did not change.

The philosophical theory behind the *Yijing* demonstrates the interrelationship of the three major religions of China and their contributions to divination. Because Confucians held that there is a correspondence between heaven, earth, and humans, there are signs all around us that can be discovered that reveal what will happen. Confucians also believed that humans can directly influence cosmic changes with their foreknowledge of human destiny. In addition to the Daoist grasp of change and transformation, the Buddhist theory of causality also made a contribution to the development of divination.

Besides the *Yijing* text, another mode of divination is *fengshui* (literally meaning winds and waters), a Chinese form of geomancy that is designed to determine an auspicious site for constructing a home or burying a deceased person. Supporting this practice of divination was the conviction that the topographical features of the earth manifest the principles of *yin* and *yang*. The literal meaning of *fengshui* as "wind and water" is indicative of the two most common examples of vital energy (*qi*). This life energy or power is present in all things and beings. If one's vital energy is strong, one's life is also vigorous, whereas a weak vital energy means that life is weak, ill or old. Its total loss means death. The basic presupposition concerning vital energy is that it is necessary to nourish and cultivate it for a good and healthy life. The movements of the vital energy affect land, mountains, and rivers, suggesting that their different shapes and forms result from vital energy and the *yin* and *yang* genders of it. By divining the nature of the land, it was possible for a person to synchronize one's actions with nature and thereby to achieve or maintain harmony with nature.

The Chinese State Cult

Besides a person's personal religion, family, and communal religion, every citizen is considered a member of the state cult by virtue of a person's birth into the state. Many of the rites are performed by the emperor, who is considered the Son of Heaven, assisted by his nobles and government officers. These state rites are performed for the benefit of the people and the well-being of the empire, even though they did not participate in these rites. Those people outside of the official state observances are mere observers. The emperor operates as the intermediary between Heaven and the people. These rites ensured the continued harmonious relationship between Heaven, earth, and humans.

The state cult observes three categories of sacrifices. The great sacrifices performed only by the emperor are made to Heaven, earth, imperial ancestors, and spirits of land and grain. The medium type of sacrifice is made to the sun and moon, rulers of former dynasties, the patron of agriculture, the patroness of silkworms, and numerous spirits of earth and sky. Finally, the lesser or smaller sacrifices consist of some thirty different rites, such as those to minor gods.

Occurring on the day of the winter solstice, the sacrifice to Heaven is performed at the round-shaped southern altar, which features *yang* (odd) numbers in its construction. On this shortest day of the year, *yang* forces are believed to begin increasing in strength, and *yin* forces begin to decline. The rite occurs in nine stages, a supremely *yang* number. The sacrifice to the earth takes place on the summer solstice and is performed on a square altar to the north. The square nature of the altar is indicative of its limitations when compared to the boundless expanse of Heaven, whose round nature symbolizes harmony and perfection.

These grand sacrifices and others adhere to ritual rules (*li*), which are creations of ancient sage kings and are consonant with the social and moral worlds.

The rules express the utmost reverence toward human or divine beings, evoke deep moral feelings of mutual respect, and represent the best way to harmonize society and the cosmos. The ultimate instrument of harmony is music, an embodiment of perfect beauty and goodness. Reflecting the inner qualities of a human, music incorporates dance-like, ritual movements as it expresses joy. If ritual defines the external structure of the individual, music provides inner harmony, operating as a microcosm of the harmony that exists between Heaven and earth. The imperial rites are culturally significant because they justify the political power of the emperor, establish administrative authority over the state, maintain peace and harmony, and uphold civic values, inspire faith in the government, and enhance public morals during times of crisis.

The state religion is governed by a board of rites that controls erection of temples, monasteries, and convents; it also controls heretical sects and the size of the clergy. Its main function is to prevent religious groups from threatening the socio-political order. State control extended, for instance, to deities, to the point of coercing rain deities, which are most often conceived of as dragons. If prayer, dance, or appealing to the deity's sympathy does not work to produce rain, authorities take more extreme measures by directly threatening the rain deity. A supplicant might throw himself onto a burning pyre and tell the deity that it must produce rain or suffer the sin of causing the supplicant's death. Gods that do not produce positive results for the people might have a magistrate revoke the deity's titles, demote the god, close its temple, or banish it to a distant place. People might expose the deity's image directly to the blazing sun to give the deity a taste of what the people are enduring, hopefully gaining its sympathy. Other coercive methods included whipping magic stones. The rationale for this type of action is related to *yin-yang* theory, in which *yang* produces heat and dryness. The *yang* must be forced to reduce its energy and allow the *yin*, which produces cold and wetness, to function. If this type of coercion does not succeed, it is possible to whip the image of the deity or take a more desperate action by destroying the image of the deity. When these types of methods succeed, they manifest the power of the emperor and his officials.

In summary, Chinese ethnic religion, which can be called Confucian in a broad sense for lack of a better identifying term, is orientated to this world and tends to be pragmatic in the sense of doing what is necessary for positive this-worldly results. As noted with various previous examples, Chinese Confucian religiosity is nonexclusive in the sense that individuals and social groups embrace various types of religious practices and ways of religion, which are intertwined with Confucian, Daoist, Buddhist, and folk ways, without attempting to reconcile their differences. Neither are people overly concerned about apparent contradictions related to incongruencies and paradoxes in their beliefs and practices. The way that average people practice their religion is simply the way that their ancestors have always practice their religion. And since religious practices have withstood the test of time, it is collectively concluded that there is no need to change for the sake of being up-to-date or innovative.

The Chinese religious tradition calls our attention to the relatively permeable boundaries between life and death. Its this-worldly perspective is often characterized by an emphasis on issues of well-being and health in the present life and the next life. The focus on issues related to health and general happiness reflects a concern for the enduring fate of a person. Traditional Chinese religiosity did not stress attaining eternal salvation or what occurs at the end of time, even though these concerns were evident in Daoism and Buddhism. These future events were just not central to the concerns of ordinary people, because they were focused on finding solutions for present problems.

Daoist Tradition

According to the Daoist classic the *Zhuangzi*, which bears the title of its author, who lived between 370 and 286 BCE, myths can be used to convey meaning that cannot be directly expressed. The narrative of the Big Fish and the Big Bird from this text is an excellent example of the use of myth to communicate meaning. This narrative relates the tale of a huge fish living in the northern darkness that changes into an enormous bird, which flies off with its wings resembling clouds. The measureless bird sets off for the southern darkness, which represents the lake of Heaven. In this narrative, the fish symbolizes a creature that can be captured and lives in darkness—ignorance. The fish is analogous to the reader of the myth, but it has the capacity to transform itself. When it becomes a bird, this signifies its freedom and transcendence. The overall message is that it is possible for everyone to be transformed by knowledge. What is important to know for a Daoist? The answer is simple: the way of the Dao.

The nature of the Dao can be discerned by reading the classic *Daodejing*, a text that dates to around the fourth or third century BCE. The authorship of this text is attributed to Laozi, a legendary figure, although internal analysis of the text points to several authors of different parts of it. The text is divided into two sections, consisting of chapters 1–37, known as the *Daojing* (Classic of Dao), and chapters 38–81, known as the *Dejing* (Classic of De). Traditionally, there have been two major versions of the text: the He Shang Gong and the Wang Bi, with both dating to around the middle of the third century CE. The work became a Chinese classic during the Han Dynasty (206 BCE–220 CE).

The second major classical text is the *Zhuangzi*, an anthology of philosophical thoughts, aphorisms, and allegories composed by several writers, having often different philosophical opinions. This text is dated by scholars to around the late fourth century BCE, but its compilation dates to about the second century BCE. Three sections of this text have been identified: inner chapters (1–7), outer chapters (8–22), and miscellaneous chapters (23–33). Scholars have attributed the inner chapters to Zhuangzi, the Daoist sage. From an original text of 52 chapters, the text was edited and reduced to the 33 current chapters by the Jin dynasty scholar Guo Xiang (d. 312 CE). An important feature of this text is the rejection of rational analysis in favor of a direct intuition of the world as a whole. This type of intuition of an undifferentiated whole implies that the whole cannot be captured by distinctions made by language. Zhuangzi also espouses a radical relativism that counterbalances all values.

The Chinese character for the term Dao has three elements: a road, a human head, and a human foot. Thus, it can be translated as path, road, or way, but it later comes to mean method, principle, truth, or reality. When it is used as a verb, it means to direct, to guide, or to establish communication. The *Daodejing* informs its reader that the Dao comes into existence by itself, exists before heaven and earth, and represents the mother and ancestor of all. It is not only the source of all life; it is also the storehouse of all things. It is described as mysterious because it is invisible, inaudible, and subtle; it is also all-pervading, all-embracing, and present everywhere and in all things. The Dao is nameless because it is not concrete and has no divisions, distinctions, or characteristics.

The function of the Dao is its being, whereas its essence is its non-being, respectively equivalent to the named and the nameless. Being and non-being are also phases in the movement of the Dao. The cycle of the Dao gives birth at first to non-being, which in turn gives birth to being before returning to non-being. On the human level of existence, people are born, mature, and grow old before returning to non-being. Thus, by perishing, being produces non-being. In summary, being is a co-principle of non-being when it is fully developed. Moreover, these co-principles give birth to each other. Non-being is not only prior to being, but it is also more powerful and makes being function. This situation is analogous to a wheel with its hub, which is empty and allows the spokes to unite and form a wheel.

The Dao is, moreover, natural, and brings all things into existence and governs them. It operates in a regular pattern, which makes it immanent within the world and not aloof from it. Because of the mysteriousness of the Dao and the difficulty of saying anything intelligible about it, the text reverts to symbols, such as saying that it is empty or like a piece of un-carved wood. To affirm that it is empty suggests that it is without characteristics and particularity. By comparing it to an uncarved block of wood, this refers to what is simple, plain, and without color or markings.

The notion of *de* is composed of three elements: the verb "to go" or "act," heart/mind, and an eye, which means to look. In addition to referring to a correct or honest state of mind, *de* is Dao endowed in individual things. In other words, *de* is what makes things different from one another, whereas Dao is common to all things. Representing the function of Dao, *de* is a force within things; it is a potency within things, an inner power that expands outward. They are related in the sense that the *de* follows Dao, representing the perfection and harmony of original nature. In summary, Dao and *de* denote unity within multiplicity. This point is illustrated by a centipede, according to the *Zhuangzi*, because from a relative viewpoint the insect has many legs, but from a higher point of view, there is unity within the multiplicity.

A life of *de* (virtue) is characterized by deep love, frugality, and not daring to be ahead of the world. These are practices that lead to courage, generosity, and leadership. A life of *de* means to be tranquil, content, humble, accepting disgrace, being low and submissive, and weak. Overcoming strength or hardness in the long run, weakness is an outward expression of real strength and is compared to water, which is soft and weak but can wear away hard objects like rocks. This life of simplicity and harmony is unspoiled, like an uncarved block of wood, and leads to being one with the Dao, or to becoming enlightened.

The path of a Daoist to his goal involves getting beyond the egotistical, selfish and evil level of human nature to a deeper level, which is characterized by an underlying harmony that is his original nature. In order to become aware of this deeper level of a person's nature, an aspirant is instructed to practice nonaction (*wuwei*), which does not mean a state of inertia or a refraining from action. By its very nature, action is more *yang* than *yin*, which implies that there is always a danger to over react. In order for action to be harmonious, it must be counteracted by its opposite, non-action (the *yin* feature of action). More specifically, this means to never be violent or aggressive, suggesting that a person's actions have the qualities of nature and water.

With respect to non-action, there are three fundamental presuppositions of the Daoist position: All action gives rise to reaction, violent and artificial activity causes chaos, and natural human activity brings harmony. This involves not doing anything that is not natural or spontaneous and avoiding artificial action, which is defined as acting to disrupt harmony, while actions based on selfishness and greed cause chaos. A person can harmonize things by following the Dao. What, then, is the spontaneous and natural way to act? Daoists must not strain, have no ambitions, have no desires, support things in their natural state, be free from their own actions, and act without intention. Non-action enables us to achieve non-differentiated knowledge, a path that demands unlearning and getting rid of the burden of prior, useless knowledge. Instead, one must return to one's original nature, which leads one to endurance, longevity, and eternal consciousness by controlling one's breath and senses.

With regard to the path, the second chapter of the *Zhuangzi* refers to forming the way by walking it. As one walks, one brings into being the way, suggesting that the way is not a static path but is rather an evolving process. The way to cultivate the Dao is a "wandering freely beyond." This phrase does not mean that one wanders about aimlessly but rather moves outward and away from what is familiar to oneself in order to see how the other perceives things. This does not mean that I lose my previous perspective. This free and easy wandering is not simply a shifting of one's position or changing one horizon for another; it is more akin to an expansion of one's perspective.

It is possible to attain a condition of enlightenment in a gradual or sudden way. The former way is achieved through a method of quietude. This is a movement of reversal that is equated with the way of the Dao, which is a returning to one's roots or non-being. When one embraces quietude and turns within oneself, it is possible to find tranquility, which is akin to a traveler who leaves no track or trace. Sudden enlightenment is achieved through intuitive knowledge, a seeing that enables one to recognize the unity of the unnamable and the nameable, or to see within nothing the ten thousand things. Whether it is achieved suddenly or gradually, enlightenment enables the sage to identify with the Dao and assume its attributes. This condition involves achieving a state of namelessness, selflessness, and speechlessness in which one's being and thinking are the same and to see the multiplicity in their unity. This is a state of complete harmony.

From a metaphorical perspective, the Daoist sage dies to his profane face, which is nothing more than an artificial mask given by history and culture drilled into a plain surface, in order to return to his original condition of no-face. The condition of no-face means to return to one's face before birth, which is a metaphor for returning to the Dao and becoming identified with that beginning, a vast emptiness.

The importance of non-face is illustrated by the myth of the emperor of the south and the north who meet periodically in the center in the territory of the faceless Hundun, who treated the emperors generously. Trying to reciprocate Hundun's generosity, the emperors drilled seven openings in his head to make him appear like others. After they bored a hole each day, Hundun finally died on the seventh day. What does this narrative mean? The emperors of the south and north are equivalent to dual principles, whereas Hundun is the third thing needed for creation because he harmonizes the polarities into a perfect form. The meeting of the southern and northern emperors occurs during the age of paradise, a period before the creative rupture or death of Hundun and the age of complete harmony that establishes the profane world, a secondary creation that is exemplified by a world of face and civilization. The fall from paradise is represented by the decision of the southern and northern emperors to civilize Hundun and give him exterior openings that reflect the human condition, but he is already virtuous. By boring the faceless creature, the emperors make Hundun human. In contrast, Daoism is concerned with a reversal of this process and a return to a state of facelessness. This process of reversal involves returning to the Dao, the primordial source and root of life without form.

Popular Daoist Pantheon

The popular or folk Confucian/Daoist polytheistic pantheon was hierarchically ordered, with heaven or Dao at the top of the structure. The popular pantheon was inclusive of many deities, representing many levels and features of life. In contrast to Confucian divine beings, Daoist deities did not depend on bloody animal sacrifices. The Daoist divine figures responded instead to the petitions made by ordained priests. From the Daoist perspective, the gods and goddesses were emanations of the Dao, which suggests that they were not only less important than the Dao, but they were believed to eventually die and get reabsorbed into the Dao. Because of the nature of the Dao, the boundary lines between nature, divinity, and humanity are not sharply differentiated. Since these boundaries are permeable, it is possible for a person to deify herself and be venerated as a Daoist immortal.

With the Dao accepted as the ultimate principle, there was no singular divine being ruling over the divine pantheon, although by the Tang dynasty (618–906) the Three Purities were depicted as ruling figures and portrayed as men sitting on an elevated platform. Each of these iconic figures holds something: The host holds a circular object representing unity; the first guest holds a scepter that represents cosmic power and a wish fulfilment; and the second guest holds a fan that depicts paradise and immortality. Located beneath the Three Purities was the Jade Emperor, supreme ruler of the cosmos, who was assisted by the Three Officials in charge of heaven, earth, and water and the Five Emperors, or rulers of the five directions.

In addition to governing the world, the Jade Emperor personally manages heavenly and earthly affairs. He is depicted seated on a throne and dressed in a long robe embroidered with dragons, symbols of rain and fertility. Members of the Jade Emperor's family play significant roles, such as his son Second Lord of Quality, who employs the Celestial Dog to drive away evil spirits. Goddess Horse-Head, a secondary wife of the Jade Emperor, looks after silkworms. Young girls call upon Seventh Young Lady, a daughter of the Jade Emperor, to learn beforehand the identity of their husbands. The court of the Jade Emperor includes, for example, Wang, the Transcendental Official, who serves as the gate-keeper of the palace, turns away intruders, goes on missions, and executes guilty people. He also guards Daoist temples and is depicted dressed in armor and holding a gnarled staff. The court also includes ministers, generals, and other guards. The Grand Emperor of the Eastern Peak administrates authority over the earth and humans by setting the time for birth and death of humans and being in charge of destiny, fortune, honors, and affluence. His scribes keep registers of all births and deaths. Around the first century CE, this figure became the god of the dead.

The pantheon contains two popular figures. The first such figure is the Queen Mother of the West, who is responsible for the orchard where the peaches of immortality grow. There are times when she holds a banquet that admits only invited guests at which she gives away the peaches, transforming the eater of the peaches into an immortal. The second popular figure is Laojun (Lord Lao), who is identified as the defied sage Laozi.

The Chinese pantheon also includes gods of administrative districts, such as gods of walls and ditches that operate as protectors of towns and cities. Some of these figures have humble origins, as illustrated by the Little Fan-bearer. In a fit of anger, a king put a boy to death for accidently hitting the king with the fan while performing his duties. The ghost of the boy appeared to the king and frightened him. In order to placate the spirit, the king named the ghost the god of the district. The gods of walls and ditches have subordinates that they direct, such as the gods of localities responsible for city streets and villages.

More intimately associated with the people are the family gods, such as the aforementioned kitchen god, who is depicted with his wife standing at his side as he sits in an armchair in mandarin dress. The wife is also feeding the six domestic animals: horse, cow, pig, sheep, dog, and chicken, whereas her husband's duty is to govern the house. Before his house shrine, there is an empty cup and a pair of chopsticks. The kitchen god is offered meals three times every year: on his birthday, the third day of the eight month, and the twenty-fourth of the twelfth month. Having kept a registry of the family's activities, once a year he reports to the Jade Emperor what has transpired within the house, a report that determines the share of happiness for the family during the following year. Other intimate divine figures are the Gate Gods, Lord and Lady of the Bed, who protect married couples, and the Goddess of the Latrine-Ditch. As the second wife of a district official, she was the victim of the first wife, who killed her in a fit of jealousy by throwing her into a latrine, and the Jade Emperor made her the divinity of this place. The pantheon also includes gods of professions, trades, and guilds.

It is hardly surprising that agricultural deities are part of the pantheon. The Great King Pa-cha, for instance, destroys locusts and other harmful insects. Dame Horse-Head is the patroness of silkworms. According to Chinese lore, she was a young woman when her father was abducted by pirates. Her mother vowed to give her in marriage to anyone who could retrieve her husband. The family horse overheard this vow and left to retrieve the husband, but the father refused to allow the vow to be concluded. The husband killed the angry horse, skinned it, and hung its hide to dry at the door of the home. When the young girl passed near the hide, the horse came alive, wrapped itself around her, and abducted her. Ten days later, the horse hide was discovered hanging on the branch of a mulberry tree, and the young girl had become a silkworm. Then the Jade Emperor took her to heaven and made her a concubine.

Other divine beings are associated with illness and healing. There are also deities that specialize in protecting women and children, such as the Princess of Multi-colored Clouds and Guanyin, a Buddhist goddess who brings children into the world and heals them when they get sick. In contrast to these benign healing figures, there are deities associated with the various hells, with Yama serving as their king. In Hindu mythology, Yama is the first person to die and thus made the Lord of Death, a feature that confirms the inclusive nature of the Chinese pantheon.

The Daoist pantheon includes various ranks of immortals, which include ghosts, humans, terrestrials, and spirits. Specific immortals have been emphasized by different movements at certain times of Daoist history. There are many popular narratives about one group called the Eight Immortals, an invisible group that does not receive formal worship and does not fit into any system. They are fundamentally unapproachable and do not eat human food, and no type of sacrifice can make them manifest themselves. They are described as wandering about drunk, a condition that causes chaotic confusion. The arguably most famous of the Eight Immortals is Lü Dongbin, described as a carefree social dropout with a preference for a wandering lifestyle in the mountains instead of an official government career. Another especially popular figure of folk Daoism is Zhongli Quan, depicted holding a sword and accompanied by his familiar, the spirit of a willow tree. Zhang Guolao is a third immortal of the eight, who is portrayed as a very old man accompanied by his magic mule, which the immortal could fold up like a piece of paper to easily carry the animal when not riding it. The only female of the group is He Xian Gu, who is depicted holding a basket of magic mushrooms, peaches, or a lotus flower. Born the daughter of a druggist, she is seduced in the mountains and makes love for three full days, but her lover never ejaculates even once. She learns the secrets related to pressure points on the body from other immortals and applies the correct amount of pressure during their next sexual encounter at just the right moment, releasing her lover's seminal fluid, which is pure *yang*, that serves as a powerful drug of immortality for her.

Daoist Cults of Immortality

Later developments in Daoism revolved around a quest for immortality while living on earth. This quest assumed three forms: use of expeditions to find the Isles of the Blessed (Penglai), alchemy, and hygiene. The Isles of the Blessed are a magical location situated in the East. Another paradise is located to the West called Mount Kunlun, which is governed by the Queen Mother of the West, who guards the Turquoise Pond and orchard where the peaches of immortality are grown. When these peaches ripen, approximately every thousand years, a large feast is observed and the fruit is eaten, and consumers of the peaches become immortal. These paradises embody a concern by Daoists for power to manipulate cosmic processes, healing, good health, and self-divinization with the quest for immortality. These results are also evident with the external and internal forms of the quest for immortality.

Alchemy is called the outer elixir (*waidan*) and involves restoring the body to health and longevity by balancing the principles of *yin* and *yang* within the body. This quest for bodily harmony utilizes elements such as cinnabar and gold to restore the body to its original state, when *yin* and *yang* were indistinguishable from each other. The alchemist attempts to convert cinnabar into gold, a perfect and incorruptible metal that is equated with *yang* (the masculine principle). It is believed that gold can preserve bodies from corruption, which is the rationale for eating and drinking from gold bowls and burying a person in clothes adorned with gold. The overall objective is to prolong life indefinitely by ridding the body of harmful vapors that are the cause of aging, illness, and death.

The hygiene school is called the inner elixir (*neidan*) because it operated from within the body to achieve a material immortal body. This goal could be achieved by replacing a mortal body with an immortal one during the course of a person's life, which is accomplished by developing and giving birth to a new internal body that will survive the death of the worldly body. This quest for an immortal body is set within a microcosmic (human body) and macrocosmic (exterior world) conceptualization. The human head is equated with the vault of heaven, feet represent the square earth, right and left eyes are respectively the sun and moon, veins are rivers, the bladder is an ocean, and bodily hair is equated with the stars and planets. The human body has three centers, located in the head, chest, and abdomen, and within each center is a field of cinnabar, the essential ingredient for the drug of immortality. Within the fields of cinnabar, there dwell 36,000 gods, with one deity presiding over a field of cinnabar. These gods are necessary to preserve life and thus need to be made happy by a person in whose body they dwell. Since the gods detest the smell of wine and meat, it is essential that a person avoid using them.

Besides the many gods located in the human body, there are three worms located in each cinnabar field that cause old age, sickness, and infirmity, which obstruct the quest for immortality. The three worms are identified as Old Blue, who dwells in the head and causes blindness, deafness, baldness, rotten teeth and bad breath, White Maiden, who dwells in the chest and causes heart problems, asthma, and melancholy, and Bloody Corpse, who is located in the lowest field and causes intestinal problems, dry bones and skin, and rheumatism. These three worms live on five kinds of cereals: rice, millet, wheat, oats, and beans, suggesting that a person should refrain from eating these cereals. Theoretically, a person lives only on breath and saliva. For a male practitioner, this means that his purified breath is united with his semen in the lowest cinnabar field, which produces a mysterious embryo that develops into a new body within the old one. When a person dies, this new, immortal body is released, using either a spiritual technique or a sexual technique.

The spiritual technique involves entering into a positive relationship with the gods within the body by leading a pure life and doing good deeds. This path uses meditation and a vision of a chosen deity to achieve ecstasy and to see the Dao in one's spirit. The realization of the Dao produces wisdom and changes the body and spirit. At this point, the body is penetrated by the Dao and unites body and spirit. Since the body is completely like the spirit, there is no longer any life or death because a person realizes one is not different from the Dao.

The sexual technique focuses on uniting the *yin* and *yang* in order to nourish the vital principle. This method presupposes that normal sexual relationships lead to a shorter life span. Because a person's essence resides in the lower part of the abdomen, it is necessary to increase life-giving fluid by stimulus without losing it. During sexual intercourse, the male must not ejaculate but must rather return his essence to the brain and rejuvenate it. What is occurring within a practitioner's body is that the *yang* force is being nourished by the *yin* force of the female partner. Positive benefits of this practice can be increased by using a succession of sexual partners as long as the male does not ejaculate, which is a result that is counter-productive. According to Daoist legend, the Yellow Emperor had intercourse with 1,200 concubines during an evening without injuring his health. The choice of female partners is important, because a woman who knows the procedure may benefit herself instead of her male counterpart. It is believed that younger women bring the utmost benefits for a male; some experts recommend pretty girls, while others advocate a woman with a harmonious voice, small bones, and sexual areas and armpits that are not too hairy. Some experts say to avoid women with, for example, thick skin, very thin bodies, masculine voices, hairy legs, cold sexual parts, those who eat too much, and those with bad-smelling armpits. The sexual technique stresses the female aspect of life, accepts equality between male and female, and is convinced that health and longevity need the cooperation between males and females. The sexual method also presupposes a metaphysics of sexual alchemy, with males and females, respectively, representing heaven and earth and repeating the original sexual act performed at the beginning of creation.

The Arrival of Buddhism

Buddhism began to arrive in China with immigrants around the first century BCE by way of two routes: a northern path along the commercially important Silk Road and south via a sea journey from India to China. Because Buddhism was not indigenous to China and was associated with foreigners, these features aroused criticism from already established Confucian and Daoist figures because it failed in the following ways: It was a foreign barbarian creed and not a cultural product of China; it was detrimental to the authority of the government, social stability, and prosperity of the state; its monastic life was useless, unproductive, and a violation of acceptable social behavior; and it represented an attack on filial piety. The Buddhists made counter arguments by claiming, for example, that filial piety is in the Buddhist canon and developed an apocryphal literature with narratives about Buddhist monks practicing this Confucian virtue. A monk named Shanzi, for instance, encountered a blind, childless couple, and chose to be born their son in order to serve them. The son was accidentally killed by the king. The blind parents were overcome by grief when they uttered an act of truth over the corpse of their son: If he was a paragon of filial piety, let him be restored to life. The Buddha heard this act of truth and restored the son to life. This type of narrative enabled Buddhists to claim that their notion of filial piety was superior to the Confucian ideal, because the Buddhist notion was aimed at universal salvation and included all previous ancestors. Gradually, Buddhism found a niche for itself in Chinese culture, although there were periods when it suffered persecution.

Because China was already a highly developed culture, Buddhism did not exert an overpowering influence as it did in countries such as Myanmar, Thailand, and Sri Lanka. In fact, Chinese culture influenced aspects of Buddhism. The bodhisattva Avalokiteśvara was, for example, a figure who cared for the suffering of humans and responded to cries for help from humans. Known for his boundless light, he also escorts the dead to the Pure Land, where they will be reborn. Around the tenth century CE, he is transformed into a female figure, Guanyin, who was a giver of children. By the fourth century CE, there was an active Maitreya cult with the objective of enabling devotees to be reborn in the Tushita Heaven and to see their deity. At around the thirteenth century CE, Maitreya, a Buddhist figure to come in the future to usher in the final age, appeared as a fat, laughing monk, who was called the pot-bellied Maitreya or the laughing Buddha. This figure was based on legends of the life of a tenth century monk who was popular with the local people for being a barometer for the weather. He also carried a hemp cloth bag on a stick over his shoulder and wandered begging for food. His rotund belly signified prosperity, and he was often associated with children, reflecting the Chinese ideal for a large family. Another bodhisattva figure of importance was Mañjuśri, whose name meant "gentle or sweet glory." He was imagined to be a youthful figure, a crown prince of *dharma* (teaching). He appeared to humans in dreams, and hearing his name reduces a person's time in the cycle of rebirth. By worshipping him, a person was born into the Buddhist family, received his protection, and reached enlightenment by meditating on his icon.

Along with Confucian and Daoist sages, Buddhist monks became engaged in the political fortunes of the country in spite of monks insisting that they were a separate, self-governing entity within the country, but Buddhism and other religions were subordinated to the state bureaucracy. The close relationship between Buddhism and the state apparatus was evident when chapels were erected in the palace, and monks recited sacred texts for the protection of the state. In addition to Buddhism's political role, Buddhist monasteries made important economic contributions to the state by way of land holdings, leasing land to farmers for cultivation, and wealthy families enjoyed tax-free status by constructing a Buddhist temple on their private burial grounds by means of the practice of merit cloister. Some monasteries became involved with industrial enterprises through water-powered mills, used to produce flour for consumption and sale; presses were used to produce oil for cooking and fuel; monks lent articles to borrowers and charged interest on them; and monasteries functioned as hotels for traveling state officials or candidates taking the civil service exams.

Buddhist monasteries were also centers of education. Public lectures often used narratives to convey some message. According to one narrative, a young man set off to make his fortune after his father died. The son left a portion of his inherited property to his mother, another to be distributed to the poor, and a final part to be given to Buddhist monks. After her son left, the greedy, evil mother disregarded his wishes. The mother abused and chased away monks when they came for alms and set dogs on needy people to keep them away from her. After amassing a fortune, the son returned home and discovered that his mother had not executed his instructions. The mother swore that she was telling the truth when her son questioned her and claimed she would descend into the deepest hell within seven days if she was lying. The son believed his mother. After seven days, she died and was reborn in hell, where she suffered interminable forms of torture. The son observed for three years the mourning period for his mother. Thereafter, he became a monk and attained enlightenment. His enlightened status enabled him to see his father in one of the heavens, but he could not find his mother. The Buddha helped him locate his mother and explained why she was in hell. Receiving power from the Buddha to be able to visit his mother in hell, the son encountered her, and she confessed her sins. With the Buddha's help, the son was able to get his mother reborn as a female dog that ate impure stuff all day. Further help of the Buddha and pious actions of the son resulted in the mother being reborn into one of the Buddhist heavens. This tale functions to highlight and praise the filial piety of the son.

Buddhist Schools in China

Several schools of Buddhism developed in China after the fall of the Han dynasty in 220 CE. These schools included some of the following: Huayan, Tiantai, Pure Land, and Chan. The Pure Land School attracted the greatest number of adherents among the laity because it offered the easiest way to practice Buddhism without becoming a monk or nun, calling for faith instead of meditation in order to be reborn in this paradise. Pure Land Buddhism was based on either a longer or shorter version of a primary text, the *Pure Land Sūtra* (Sukhāvativyuha). The longer version of this text stresses that to achieve rebirth in the Pure Land, it is necessary to perform meritorious deeds, have faith, and exercise devotion to Amitābha, bodhisattva of the west, known to save many people, whereas the shorter version of the text requires only faith and prayer for admittance into the Pure Land. Reaching the Pure Land is not an end in itself, because it was from this location that a person could meditate undisturbed and attain nirvana, even though the place was described in a materialistic manner manifesting beauty, precious jewels, and sensual pleasures. It was taught that rebirth in the Pure Land guaranteed a stage of non-retrogression and eventual enlightenment.

Tanluan (476–542 CE) was the first master of the Chinese Pure Land lineage and was probably the originator of the practice of reciting and meditating on the name of Amitābha, a practice that frees a person from sin because the name has an inherent, creative power that can purify one's mind. Tanluan distinguished between self-power and other-power. The self-power person has a dualistic view of reality and thinks that one can achieve liberation by rigorous practice, an attitude that manifests arrogance and pride. The other-power person operates from a non-dualistic perspective and relies solely on Amitābha. This type of distinction suggests that rebirth in the Pure Land is due to the power of Amitābha for a person who sincerely desires to be reborn there.

Another leading figure in the Pure Land movement was Daochuo (562–645), who illustrates the path in a narrative called "Two Rivers and the White Path." The narrative relates that everyone is traveling toward the west, while to the south of the road is a river of fire. To the north there is a river of water. Between the two deep and wide rivers, there is a white path that is only four or five inches wide. At every point of the white path, fire and water threaten to inundate everyone, rendering rest on the path impossible. Robbers and wild animals are also a constant threat to the traveler, making it impossible to turn back. Being convinced that one is confronted with only death, the pilgrim decides to go forward to the west. From the eastern shore, one hears words of encouragement urging one forward. A voice from the direction of the western shore promises to protect the person, although thieves call the person back and plant doubts in one's mind. Paying no heed to the thieves, the pilgrim goes ahead, reaches the western shore, and escapes evil. This narrative informs a listener that one is threatened on all sides, what lies ahead is unknown, and it is necessary to make a decision. The narrative thus suggests a process of conversion. Because of the decline of Buddhism, being remote from the time of the Buddha, and personal weakness, humans discover that this is the only way at this historical moment to achieve salvation. The easier doctrine and practice that is advocated by Pure Land Buddhism make it very popular among the largest number of adherents, and it promises them a reward for sincere practice, rebirth in a blissful paradise.

In contrast to the popularity of Pure Land Buddhism among the wider public, the Huayan and Tiantai schools appealed to a more elite, monkish audience. The founder of the Huayan School (Garland School) was Fazang (643–712), and he used the image of a golden lion to make an important philosophical point about the nature of reality. The gold of the statue of the lion was pure, perfect, and brilliant, even though it was devoid of form. It assumed whatever form was assigned to it. Being the primary cause of the lion, gold made the creation of the lion possible. The secondary or contributing cause was the figure, representing the realm of things, which symbolized the dynamic phenomenon represented by the creation of the artist. The major point that Fazang was attempting to make was that principle and phenomenon were interconnected, which implies that everything in the world arose through a combination of these two sets of causes. Fazang also intended to inform readers that each thing within the world embraces other things, resulting with the mutual identity of all phenomena. This position meant that all dynamic phenomena were manifestations of static principles. Ultimately, what made this possible was that everything was empty.

Another way to discuss emptiness was developed by the Tiantai sect, which also wanted to call attention to how everything is interconnected and unified. This school was established by Zhiyi (538–597 CE), who named it after a mountain called, in translation, "Heavenly Terrace." The school based its teachings on the *Lotus Sūtra*, which it claimed was the apex of Buddhist teachings. The school was eclectic by attempting to include all periods and schools of Buddhism within a single, all-comprehensive system. The school offered a re-interpretation of Buddhist history and texts, with the Tiantai school representing the fifth and final period, which united all ways into one vehicle and emphasized the absolute identity of opposites. Humans cannot see this unity because of their condition of ignorance, which can be countered by practicing concentrated insight, representing a process of emptying the mind of delusions, passions, and other obstacles to lucid understanding. It was insight that enabled a person to see the genuine nature of reality, in which all things are empty. This is illustrated by the doctrine of the 3,000 realms, which suggests that all things in the universe form a unity, and the 3,000 realms can be known in one instant of consciousness, implying that the world is immanent in one moment of thought.

Chan Buddhism

The Chan school traces its lineage to the legendary figure of Bodhidharma, a south Indian member of the Brahmin caste, who allegedly arrived in Canton in 470. According to legends, he devoted nine years gazing at a wall meditating, until his legs fell off. At one point during his meditation practice, he cut off his eyelids so that his concentration would not falter. Bodhidharma's discipline attracted the attention of Huike (487–592 CE), who asked the master to adopt him as a disciple, but Bodhidharma continued to practice and ignored the aspiring disciple. Huike stood outside of Bodhidharma's cave in the falling snow without success. Finally, he desperately cut off his arm and presented it to the master, who finally accepted Huike as a disciple and later, successor, after Bodhidharma's death. Other legends have Bodhidharma crossing a river on a reed and meeting with the emperor. There is no way to discern what is factual or fictional concerning his life. These narratives do point to the importance of meditation in this school, as does the name Chan, a derivation from the Sanskrit term *dhyana* (meditation).

The Platform Sūtra of the Sixth Patriarch is a seminal text of Chan Buddhism, a narrative that gives us a glimpse into the life of an important figure in Chan's history, even though it is probably a fictionalized account of his life. According to the narrative, Huineng lived as a young man with his widowed mother in poverty. On a particular day, he overheard someone reciting the *Diamond Sūtra*, an event that awakened his mind and motivated him to seek a master to guide him toward enlightenment. He journeyed to the monastery of the Fifth Patriarch and asked for permission to join, but Hongren asked him how this young man, essentially a barbarian, could expect to attain Buddhahood. Huineng replied to this insult by saying that there are no differences in the Buddha-nature, although our bodies are different. After gaining admittance to study with the master, the days passed until the Fifth Patriarch, seeking a worthy successor, asked his monks to return to their rooms to look into themselves, and to write a verse of poetry that would reflect their state of enlightenment and let him see it. If an awakened monk was found, he would become the Sixth Patriarch. The head monk wrote a verse on a wall at midnight that depicted the mind as something passive and inert like a standing mirror that must be continuously wiped clean. The dust particles on the mirror-mind were obscurities and passions aroused by desires, images, and thoughts. The Fifth Patriarch read the verses and concluded that they had some merit, but the author was judged to have not reached enlightenment; the patriarch encouraged the head monk to think about his composition and to write another one in a few days.

Huineng, an illiterate person, heard a monastic acolyte reciting the verse on the wall and concluded that the writer was not awakened. Huineng dictated a verse for the acolyte to write on the southern wall. When the Fifth Patriarch read these verses, he knew that he had discovered his successor and secretly invited Huineng to his quarters, where he gave the monk a lesson on the *Diamond Sūtra* that triggered a full enlightenment experience. The Fifth Patriarch gave Huineng the *dharma* (teaching) and robe, signs of the transmission of his authority to his chosen successor. Huineng's verses indicated that he was iconoclastic because there was no place for dust to cling and argued that self-nature was already pure or self-transparent. In other words, the mind was already enlightened, although it was deluded and prevented us from seeing its true nature.

A central teaching of the Sixth Patriarch is that meditation and wisdom form a unity, which he compares to a lamp (meditation) and its light (wisdom). This unity enables a person to see her original nature, which the Sixth Patriarch refers to as "no-thought," which eventually becomes "no-mind" in Japan. What is no-mind? It means that the mind adheres to no object; it is also directed to no object and thus motionless but also perpetually active because its brightness reflects continuously. No-mind consists of no conscious mental activity, which makes it like the absolute and universal Buddha-nature, the non-thinking mode of thought, which is equivalent to the no thought prior to thinking. This awakening occurs suddenly and immediately.

In contrast to Chan Buddhism, the Tiantai and Huayan schools favor an interfusion of appearance and reality in their philosophy. In response to these schools of Buddhism, Chan argues that these principles are never fully grasped by the human intellect but must instead be personally and directly experienced. From the Chan perspective, the approaches of the Tiantai and Huayan schools represent an intellectual search for the truth that divides a human being into something transcendental and concrete. This is dangerous for two reasons: by seeking the transcendental, one abandons the concrete, and by remaining in the concrete, one is unable to transcend it. In order to avoid either danger, Chan states that nothing is transcendental apart from the concrete. During ordinary daily activities, the Chan monk is engaged in the concrete and simultaneously transcends both the concrete and transcendental, rendering them unified and recognized as the same in one's life. Even though the Chan monk lives in time and space, he is not limited by either of them. Before one is enlightened, one sees a mountain as a mountain and a river as a river. During the process of attaining enlightenment, mountains are no longer mountains, and rivers are no longer rivers. When a monk achieves enlightenment, mountains are once more mountains, and rivers are once again rivers. Therefore, Chan emphasizes concentration on the concrete experience rather than on an abstract principle. This is stressed by insisting on the direct transmission of the teachings from the master to a student.

A disciple's inner state is expressed by the notion of potentiality in action. This notion is illustrated by a narrative related to a process of selecting an abbot for a monastery. Because he is not selected to be the abbot, a senior monk angrily protested to the master Bozhang when he learned the identity of the monk to be appointed abbot. The master challenged him to answer a question to prove his worthiness to succeed the master. Bozhang points to a pitcher and asks the upset monk to identify it by not naming it a pitcher. After an inadequate response, the master asks Lingyou for an answer; Lingyou proceeds to kick over the pitcher, proving his talent as a worthy successor to the master. The answer of the upset monk is too intellectual and gets entangled in words. Thereby, he reveals no depth of inner cultivation, because he wants to argue over whether or not the pitcher should be called this or that. By knocking over the pitcher, Lingyou reveals his inner enlightenment and freedom from intellectual or rational entanglements.

A Chan narrative captures the spirit of its teaching style in the Chinese context. According to this narrative, two monks were arguing over the possession of a cat within the monastery. The Master Nanquan seized the cat, saying that if either monk said the right word he would spare the cat. Since neither monk could respond, he ruthlessly cut the cat in half. When Zhaozhou returned in the evening, the master told him about the incident. Zhaozhou did not say anything. Instead, he removed his sandals from his feet, placed them on his head, and walked out of the room. The master replied: "If you had been here, you would have saved the cat." If this episode is analyzed, it is possible to see that the master was attempting to sever the monks' attachment to the cat and their state of bondage to the world. Although the master violated a basic Buddhist precept to practice nonviolence, he was justified because he had a higher purpose to achieve and accepted the negative karma of his action. Zhaozhou's apparent arbitrary placement of his sandals on his head is intended to express that in the realm of reality, worldly values are subverted, and his spontaneous response reflects the spirit of Chan.

Encounter dialogues are also part of the overall Chan method of teaching. Consider the following two brief dialogues: When a monk asked Dongshan, "What is the Buddha?" Dongshan said, "Three pounds of hemp." In another dialogue a monk asked Yunmen, "What is the Buddha?" Yunmen said, "A dry piece of excrement." What kind of sense can be made of these encounters and the different responses to the same question? The words used to trigger his enlightenment are not intellectual and logical assertions, which Chan masters refer to as "dead words." The Chan masters advocate "living words" that are irrelevant and illogical answers. An insightful response by a student to a question of a master is intended to reflect simply what is on a student's mind at that moment. This type of effortless answer is not contrived or thought out, being without artificiality or intention.

In order to bring a student to the moment of enlightenment, Chan masters devised some unusual methods of teaching. Among these unique methods is the *kung-an* (*kōan* in Japanese), which represented enigmatic sayings and dialogues of old masters that do not make rational sense. These encounter dialogues are given to students in order for them to meditate on them and discover an answer to them. A famous *kung-an* used many times is: Why did

Bodhidharma come to China from the west? Student answers are varied and make no sense because the response of the student does not coincide with the question. There is no adequate answer to the sound of one hand clapping, or how to get a goose out of a long stem vase without breaking it or killing the goose, or what one should do if a snake swallows a frog. Other unusual teaching methods include shouts to a question, or raising a finger as a response to a question. The master Linji is famous for his infliction of beatings and violence on students. Other methods included abrupt negations, using opposites, such as saying "finger" to a question about the moon, or one-word answers, such as replying to a question about the nature of Dao with "go."

In Chan Buddhism, all monks are required to perform manual work. Chan monks clean the monastery and cook. They work in the fields growing rice, cutting bamboo, and growing tea plants. Manual labor makes Chan monks less dependent on donors and helps to counter a charge that they were social parasites. In fact, manual labor becomes an integral part of spiritual discipline and extended the meaning of meditation. Labor also counteracts lethargy and depression caused by sitting in meditation for extended periods of time.

Chan Buddhism tends to be iconoclastic, suggesting that all idols must be smashed. Idols can be one's ego, a scripture, doctrine, a deity, a miracle, or even the Buddha. This chapter previously referred to master Yunmen identifying the Buddha with human waste. The master Linji urged monks to kill the Buddha and any patriarch in order to be absolutely free from any attachment. Many of the dialogical encounters of Chan figures are humorous and reveal colorful masters. Chan masters have compared their path to that of a bird that leaves no track or trace, and where you meet no one.

Buddhist Folk Religion

Besides developing Chan and other schools, Buddhism imbedded itself into the folk culture with the development of new movements and practices. An excellent example in the twelfth century of such a movement was the White Lotus Society, which began as an independent association of clergy and laity who were devoted to attaining rebirth in the Pure Land. There were many branches of this movement, but its major characteristics were the following: It was radically syncretistic, combining various forms of being and practice; it had a congregational structure; it held a concept of a lay priesthood; it incorporated elements of folk shamanism, with both male and female figures who had the ability to exorcise evil spirits; it used Daoist and magical techniques; it had a dualistic eschatology (doctrine of last things) during which good and evil were in conflict; it incorporated Amitābhist elements, such as repetition of mantras, hope for rebirth in paradise, and emphasis on divine compassion; it adopted the Eternal Mother, who gave birth to yin and yang and the original pair of humans; it was syncretistic at the social level because sect leaders were evangelists holding imperial titles and it lacked sexual distinctions, embraced equality of women and men, and allowed women to hold leadership roles;

and it was populist in the sense that everyone could be saved. Membership in the movement involved simply paying a fee and approval by the leader or by a deity itself through divination. The new member's name was written on a piece of paper and burned in order to be entered on the heavenly rolls. Salvation was, however, conceived as a return home to the Eternal Mother, who weeps for her human children because they live and suffer in a sea of bitterness.

The eschatology of the White Lotus Society represented an interesting blending of Buddhist elements within its doctrine of the three world stages: the past controlled by the Lamplighter Buddha seated on a green lotus, the present dominated by Sakyamuni seated on a red lotus, and the future that is to be introduced by the coming of Maitreya seated on a white lotus. The sect believed that they were at the end of the second period. The arrival of Maitreya involved the enthroning of a pious ruler who would preach the Buddhist doctrine and recreate time. It will also be a time when heaven and earth are in harmony and there is no aging, no birth or death, and no distinctions based on gender. This period would be called the Great Way of Long Life, when everyone will live for 81,000 years.

Folk Buddhism was also involved with festivals, such as the Lantern Festival, which recalls a time when altars were erected for Buddhist, Daoist, and local gods and set on fire. Only the Buddhist scriptures did not burn, which motivated the emperor to order lights to be lit that day to commemorate the light of the Buddha. Other festivals included All Soul's Day, which recalled a son's search for his mother in hell and occurred during the month when ghosts of the dead returned to earth, the Buddha's Birthday on the eighth day of the fourth month, and Vegetarian Feasts that lasted seven days.

Besides these examples of festivals, folk Buddhism included practices such as releasing rites, when aquatic creatures and birds destined to be cooked were set free to gain merit. This activity was promoted by narratives to promote the practice. A man bought some centipedes, for example, to release, but only one of them was alive. While sitting with a friend one night, he saw a centipede on the wall, tried to drive it away, and failed. After inquiring about its identity, he preached the Buddhist teachings to it. After he finished, the centipede slowly crept out the window. There was also an active cult of relics associated with the veneration of parts of the Buddha and holy persons of the religion.

Folk Buddhism advocated healing cults that were indebted to Daoist and Buddhist meditation techniques and integrated with Confucian theory. This type of cult conceived of illness as a disequilibrium. Thus, healing was a restoration of order and harmony.

Another feature of folk Buddhism was the creation and distribution of morality books that contained ethical aphorisms or lists of specific moral acts that should be performed. A person could consult the book to discern what good deeds one should do and what bad actions one should avoid, representing a mixture of Confucian and Buddhist values and presupposing the law of karma. By keeping a daily tally of his deeds, it was possible for a person to determine the nature of his account, because each good or bad deed was assigned a maximum number of one hundred or a minimum of one, a process that worked automatically.

Chinese Material Culture

It is an irony of Chinese Buddhist history that the religion, from its conception, rejected the material world and its objects, music, and sensual pleasures, because they represent fetters that bind one to the world and delude one's mind. Early monastic regulations discussed the use of material items at great length. Within the Buddhist milieu, certain objects became sacred and were believed to possess power, which tended to make the religion tangible and proximate. Some of these material objects included relics, *stupas*, icons, clothing, hair, rosaries, temples, monasteries, scepters, books, chairs, and tea. Similar types of material spiritual objects can be discovered in Confucianism and Daoism.

For the most part, ancient Chinese did not believe that the bones of an extraordinary person were special, although there was a minority opinion that believed that the spirit of a person was preserved in a person's bones, which necessitated crushing the bones of an enemy's ghost and scattering them to avoid being haunted by that person. But various Buddhists introduced the importance of relics into China. According to a legend, the Indian king Aśoka is portrayed collecting, distributing, and enshrining relics within *stupas* (burial mounds) during the Zhou dynasty (ca. 1000–256 BCE), but the relics were neglected and forgotten until Chinese followers discovered the remains. As Buddhism evolved in China, the alleged relics of the Buddha were supplemented by eminent Chinese monks. These relics were believed to emit power and light and have the power to produce miracles, implying that Buddhist practice transforms the body. Related to the cult of relics, a Chinese innovation was the introduction of mummification of the bodies of eminent monks. Average people were attracted to relics because it gave an adherent an opportunity to stand in the presence and be near a holy person and to vicariously participate in power of such a person.

During the early years of the first century, the worship of icons gained importance just prior to the cultural impact of Buddhism. Icons of the Buddha enabled people to enter into the presence of the Buddha, offer gifts, and ask him for assistance. Icons were used in rituals, and monks and nuns could confess transgressions of the monastic code before them. By contemplating an image, this meditative practice functioned as a tool for visualization of the Buddha, because it was a repository of power. These icons were not lifeless material but manifested a power and higher reality. After a ritual process of consecration and the painting in of the eyes, the icon became animated. A mirror was used to dot the eyes because there was a restriction about looking directly into the eyes of the image.

Among the Chinese populace, there was hostility and skepticism toward icons. According to the *Biographies of Eminent Monks*, dated around the sixth century, an image of the Buddha was unearthed from the palace grounds. A man moved it to a privy and then urinated on it, calling his desecration of the image "bathing the Buddha." Soon after this incident, his body broke into boils, and his penis caused him considerable pain. His suffering caused him to repent and recognize the truth of Buddhism, resulting in his cure. This embrace of icons was not shared by the Chan tradition, because of its opposition to venerating them. The iconoclastic spirit of Chan is exemplified by Danxia Tianran (739–824), who burned a Buddhist image to keep warm on a winter night, using the image as a metaphor for destroying ignorance and attachment.

In traditional Chinese culture, clothing often visibly defined a person's role in life. The geographical region of Chinese Buddhist monks could be recognized by the color of their robes. The rules specifying the composition of the three Buddhist robes were rather complex and differed according to the school. The three robes signified a rejection of the three poisons—greed, anger, and ignorance—and symbolized Buddhas of the three times—past, present, and future. The robes also symbolized the monastic lifestyle of the wearer and transmission of the teachings. According to Buddhist legend, a fetal robe was given to a disciple of the monk Ananda. This narrative related that an infant was born wearing a monk's purple robe, which looked like a thin layer of skin. When he matured, the purple robe covered his body, and he wore it when he became a monk, suggesting that he was destined to become a monk. Eventually, the purple robe became a mark of moral distinction and virtuous service.

Daoist priests used vestments on ritual occasions, such as the preceptor robe, made with wide, open sleeves that hung down to the area between the lower calf and ankle. Ritual garments were a red color with black borders, while others were multi-colored and ornate. The vestment collar has three sections, a masculine (*yang*) number that corresponds to other things classified in threes. The vestments manifested multiple layers of meaning with, for example, eight trigrams associated with the eight directions, or the Luotian heaven, a location below the three heavens where the Jade Emperor resides, depicted on the back of a garment.

In classical China, long hair represented the cultural fashion among men and was associated with a person's health, according to medical texts, whereas hair loss was an indication of old age. Before the advent of Buddhism in China, criminals were the only group with shaven heads. The shaven heads of Buddhist monks and nuns were indicative of renunciation. In contrast to Buddhists, Daoists grew their hair long, pulled it into a top knot, and secured it with a hair pin made of wood.

Buddhist monks devised a string of beads for counting prayers and chanting that eventually spread to the laity in order to steady the mind, assist with concentration, and lead to nirvana or a place in paradise. The Buddhist rosary was made of 108 beads, representing different afflictions that one was attempting to overcome, and was ideally strung together by a virgin. The rosary was made of nine substances and contained a large bead at the center, which notifies a user of having gone through the ring once. The central bead represents Amitābha, while the string holding the beads together represents the empathic bodhisattva Avalokiteśvara.

Buddhist and Daoist priests used a scepter, a curved stick made of metal or jade and often embedded with precious gems. It was used to keep time to music, used as a pointer or lecture baton, and used when debating or lecturing. From an emblem of authority, it later became a symbol of marriage, with couples exchanging them.

In ancient China, teachings and narratives were transmitted orally and eventually preserved in writings transcribed on bamboo and silk, which were replaced by paper in the first century CE. This Chinese invention would become the standard material for making books. In Daoism, texts were controlled by different families, whereas Buddhist texts were protected, preserved, and copied within the context of monasteries. It was not until the Tang dynasty (618–906) that wood-block printing would emerge and replace the scroll as the standard format for books. The Buddhists, Daoists, and Confucians venerated certain books because they had power to save people from calamity and ward off demons. The act of making a book was akin to performing a religious act of service and an act of merit creation. A Buddhist text like the *Lotus Sūtra* explicitly states that the text has the power to save people when they hear or read it.

The three major and overlapping religious traditions created monasteries and temples. Daoists preferred mountainous locations for their buildings because mountains were locations where *yin* (earth) and *yang* (heaven) came closer together and manifested the Dao. Mountain retreats enhanced opportunities for sages to seclude themselves from the distractions of the world and were associated with the symbolism of ascent, although not to the extent of neglecting or forgetting the earth and its representation of the feminine principle.

Death and Afterlife

From the perspective of the *Zhuangzi* text, death is nothing more than a change from one mode of existence to another. If we view life as a way to find happiness, there is no reason why we should not find happiness in a new mode of existence. Thus, death is a natural result of life. By feeling sorrow or bitterness toward death, we increase human misery and violate the principle of nature. After the death of his wife, Zhuangzi is found singing and beating time on a bowl. A friend questioned him about his apparent odd behavior. Zhuangzi replied that he grieved for his wife, but then he realized that there was a time before she was born, a time before she had a body, and a time before she had a spirit. Amidst everything, a mystery occurred, and she had a spirit, then a body, then another change resulted in her birth, and finally she died. This is similar to the changes of the four seasons. Thus, there is nothing to lament, because change happens, but it is still possible to attain a state of neither life nor death. This type of attitude toward death influenced Chinese culture, along with contributions from Confucianism and Buddhism. The subject of death is an excellent place to witness the synthesis of the folk tradition with the three major religions.

In traditional Chinese culture, old people prepare early for death by retiring to their native home, resigning themselves to a more passive role in society, caring for grandchildren, and giving more attention to religion, and might have an active interest in preparing their coffin or tomb. When an elderly person is dying, he is moved to the main hall of the home, where he symbolically joins his ancestors, represented by tablets on the family altar.

In classical Chinese thinking, each person has two souls: a *hun* soul and a *po* soul. The former type of soul leaves the body and wanders freely, and death is considered a moment when the *hun* soul leaves the body on a permanent basis. The *hun* soul might reside in an ancestral spirit tablet, and it eventually makes its way to heaven, whereas the *po* soul goes to the earth at death and resides in the grave. The *po* soul can become a *guei*, a ghost or demon, if it is mistreated, angered, or disturbed by survivors. Thus, caution needs to be exercised by survivors not to offend the *po* soul. When a person dies, survivors perform the ceremony of *zhaohun*, a summoning of the *hun* soul to return to the body. This act gives the soul an opportunity to return before a person is declared dead. After the death of a person, the *hun* soul is invited to inhabit an ancestral tablet and to assume its place with prior ancestors.

When a *yin* soul becomes a demon, it evokes fear and caution in the living, who feel a need to protect themselves. Several modes of defense can be employed to protect oneself and those dear to one, including wearing charms and amulets or placing them in the home. Parents give children derogatory names to protect them, a practice intended to fool the demons into thinking that the children have little value. A person can hire a professional Daoist demon fighter, who uses incantations and sword-waving to drive demons from a home. A professional can also exorcise demons after they possess a person, an action that is interpreted as a triumph of the masculine (*yang*) force over the feminine (*yin*) force.

The funeral rites represent a rite of passage and serve a twofold purpose: to guarantee safe passage of the deceased's soul to the spirit world and to prevent the contagious misfortune of death from spreading to survivors. The belief in the contagious nature of death is evident in the custom of "double-death day" rituals. If someone dies on a double-death day according to the almanac, a special rite is performed to prevent another death in the family. This rite involves sacrificing a cock to counteract the omen of a second death. An alternative ritual method is to place a red cloth or paper above the neighbors' doorway to ensure their safety.

The actual funeral rite involves washing the body of the deceased and sending white cards to announce the death to relatives and friends. Being considered the opposite of the life-giving color red, white, a symbol of death, is used to express sorrow. A temporary ancestral tablet is set up, measuring a foot long and made of paper that identifies the deceased. When guests, arrive they pay their respects and give presents of incense, spirit money, and real money to defray funeral expenses. The corpse is dressed with longevity clothes, and jade or other jewels are placed into its mouth. The family may have to wait weeks or months for an auspicious day, according to divination results, to perform the actual funeral rites. When a person dies, it is essential that a diviner determine, by means of geomancy (*fengshui*), the correct position of the grave in order not to disrupt the harmony of the earth.

The actual funeral includes a grand procession: A sedan chair located in front of the coffin is carried for the soul of the deceased, lanterns illumine the way to the grave, and a container of rice symbolizes the fate of the deceased and the family. The procession also includes musicians, priests, and people carrying banners, while the mourners walk behind the coffin trail. The coffin is lowered into the grave, accompanied by doleful tones of mortuary music, somber chanting of priests, and wailing of mourners. The eldest son sacrifices to a local earth god, kneels in front of the grave, and holds an ancestral tablet. A dignitary is invited to dot the ancestral tablet, an act that signifies that the tablet is now the actual residence of the soul of the deceased.

Within a year of the funeral, a permanent ancestral tablet is made to replace the paper tablet. This foot-long, thin tablet includes the name, any titles, and death day of the deceased. This permanent tablet joins the other ancestors of the family. Ancestors are considered to be powerful and protective of the family, but they are also vulnerable because they are dependent on sacrifices offered by survivors, creating a relationship that is interdependent, with ancestors functioning as mediators between Heaven and humans.

During ancient times, souls were destined to go to the Yellow Springs, a kind of netherworld that was not well defined, although it did suggest the earth because of the color yellow. This early notion of an afterlife was succeeded by a more elaborate underworld under Daoist influence. Another notion of the afterlife was represented by the isles of the blessed (*penglai*), which were believed to be located at a faraway distance. Buddhist influence included sacred mountains in the west, a direction that became associated with paradisiacal realms. Visions of heaven and hell originating in Buddhist, Daoist, and folk traditions became paradigms of the real world, with its hierarchically constructed institutions and social order. On the one hand, this made heaven similar to a government bureaucracy, whereas hell was akin to a worldly judicial and prison system. In addition to judges, the jailers of hell were ghoulish and fierce demons who tortured convicted inmates, although this situation did not represent eternal punishment or permanent damnation. Relatives of the deceased could reduce a sentence with money bribes of the jailers just like similar figures in the world, which was indicative that release could be possible for an ancestor.

The Buddhist tradition made important contributions to the way that heaven and hell were conceived by the Chinese. The Buddhist notion of rebirth influenced the notion of hell, because people would be destined to assume another life at some point. Furthermore, the Buddhist notion of karma introduced a dimension of justice and punishment into the conceptions of heaven and hell. The Buddhists' notion of the transfer of merit enhanced the ability of the living to influence the suffering of a deceased relative. Moreover, the Buddhist conception of Maitreya, a messianic figure, introduced the notion that such a figure would come at the end of time, an idea foreign to Chinese culture prior to the advent of Buddhism.

Types of Religious Experience

Embedded into ancient Chinese religious culture, there is the emotional response of awe and dread associated with ordinary people encountering ghosts and other supernatural beings. Many narratives recall such encounters with the supernatural. It is not unusual to find tales of ghosts making noise in Chinese literature by weeping as a way to protest wrongs suffered during life or death, which is usually a way to communicate with the living, seeking some type of redress. There are also narratives that are informative about the afterlife and how Buddhism, for instance, can help a ghost. In one such tale, a suddenly deceased male meets the wife of his uncle in the underworld and is given a tour of the place by a white-robed monk. From the flames, he could hear someone call his name, only to discover that the ghost was a former student, admitting that he was in hell because he transgressed Buddhist monastic regulations regarding drinking wine and eating meat, and asking the visitor to help him. The former student even gives precise instructions to the visitor, which include copying the *Diamond Sūtra* and placing it in a public location where everyone can see it, which will enable the former student to be reborn a beast and work toward becoming a human being again in a future life.

In addition to the fear triggered by encounters with ghosts and other supernatural beings by ordinary mortals, harmony is a predominate theme in Chinese religions, from the social harmony of the Confucians, to becoming harmonious with the Dao of Daoism, and to the harmony espoused by many Buddhist schools. The development and practice of Confucian virtues leads to harmony similar to a ritual dance, during which everyone knows and executes one's part in synchronization with others. By embodying and practicing these virtues, a person is in accord with the way of heaven. For Daoism, harmony is a returning to the beginning of life when one was unspoiled and identifying with the Dao that is without beginning or end, a state of facelessness akin to an uncarved block of wood.

The Daoist sage forgets her previous accumulation of knowledge. This is metaphorically a cleansing process of the mind of all impurities, which allows the Dao free access. In addition to other practices, forgetting enables one to unburden oneself and to become identical with the Dao. The perfected person is completely at ease in the Dao and floats along with it, going wherever it takes her. This fasting of the mind leads to an experience of quietude, an undisturbed and non-agitated condition, during which one is in harmony with one's inborn nature. There is also an experience of emptiness that represents a translucent compatibility with whatever comes. The sage also experiences trance states that lead to an enlightened state, which can be gradual or sudden. The gradual type of enlightenment is achieved through a method of quietude, a movement of reversal that is identical to the way of the Dao, whereas sudden enlightenment comes through intuitive knowledge, a private awareness of one's innermost being that unlocks the secrets of non-being, which enables one to see that the unnamable and the namable are identified, or to be able to see within nothing the ten thousand things.

The sage has now reversed ordinary life and achieved an experience of complete identification with the Dao, which is akin to what is called a tranquilization in chaos. This experiential condition is like being a rotating wheel, a symbol of that without beginning or end. Consequently, its birth is its beginning and end, while its death is its end and beginning. An insight dawns that life and death are human terms but are meaningless from the standpoint of eternity. Moreover, the rotating wheel symbolizes the natural equality of things and the natural principle of change.

Several Buddhist schools of thought seek differently expressed unitive experiences. The Huayan position represents a philosophy of identity in difference. Fire and ice are, for example, identical because both are empty, while they are also products of conditions (e.g., heat and cold) and have no self-existence or self-nature. This means that things are simultaneously empty and existent, and nothing enjoys an independent existence because everything depends on something else for its coming to be. The experience of enlightenment arises when one realizes that all phenomena are empty. This experience is analogous to awakening from a dream and realizing for the first time that the objects of that dream have always been unreal. With the awakening experience, delusion is stripped of its apparent reality. The enlightened person experiences a mind that is as calm as a tranquil sea; erroneous thoughts cease, one is free from hindrances and bondage, and one does not dwell within the cycle of life and death, and the liberated person can see the interdependence of everything. The Tiantai school uses the *Lotus Sūtra* as its foundational text, but it espouses a similar experiential awakening as the Huayan school and need not detain us any further.

In contrast to these two representatives of Chinese Buddhism, the Pure Land school stresses the experiential phenomena of conversion, visualization, and faith. Conversion can be accompanied by associated phenomena, such as feelings of joy, hope, being speechless, rapture, ecstasy, and communion with Amitābha. Visualization practice refers to contemplating the Buddha, the Pure Land, Amitābha, and his attendant bodhisattvas, which helps one to realize a spiritual tranquility. In Chinese Pure Land Buddhism, faith is an adjunct to meditation. A person must believe that her chosen Buddha makes a vow to save everyone and believe that he is both willing and able to save her. A firm faith has three features: sincerity, a strong conviction about one's own wretchedness, and the intention to transfer one's own merit to the Pure Land

and vow to be reborn there. When a person of faith dies, she is escorted to the Pure Land by Amitābha.

The enlightenment experience associated with the Chan tradition can be illustrated by a dialogue between a student and a master. Once, when master Mazu and his attendant Baizhang were walking together, they heard the sound of some wild ducks fly by. The Master inquired about the source of the identity of the sound. Baizhang replied, "Wild ducks." Then the Master asked, "Where have they gone?" The attendant said, "They've flown away." The Master then grabbed Baizhang's nose and twisted it. The attendant cried out in pain. The Master asked, "When have they ever flown away?" At the utterance of this remark, Baizhang attained enlightenment. The dialogical encounter suggests that when a person sees the ducks flying in space and time, such a person puts himself into space-time relations, which implies that one is not in the absolute present and is not free. When the Master twisted the student's nose, this act was intended to redirect the student's attention away from the ducks, and awaken the attendant to the absolute present. Since there is only the absolute present, there is no space or time. The monk is no longer subject to causation but rather experiences the oneness of all things and discovers his true nature. This experience is at once a seeing and a not-seeing because subject and object are nondual. The profound nature of this experience means that it cannot be captured by or expressed in language. It is best to remain silent.

Suggestions for Further Reading

Adler, Joseph. *Chinese Religious Tradition*. Upper Saddle River, NJ: Prentice Hall, 2002.

Bokenkamp, Stephen. *Early Daoist Scriptures*. Berkeley: University of California Press, 1997.

Bruun, Ole. *An Introduction to Fengshui*. Cambridge: Cambridge University Press, 2008.

Ch'en, Kenneth. *Buddhism in China: A Historical Survey*. Princeton: Princeton University Press, 1964.

Ching, Julia. *Chinese Religions*. Maryknoll, NY: Orbis Books, 1993.

Coutinho, Steve. *An Introduction to Daoist Philosophies*. New York: Columbia University Press, 2014.

Eskildsen, Stephen. *Asceticism in Early Taoist Religion*. Albany: State University of New York Press, 1998.

Faure, Bernard. *The Rhetoric of Immediacy: A Cultural Critique of Chan/Zen Buddhism*. Princeton: Princeton University Press, 1991.

Feuchtwang, Stephen. *The Imperial Metaphor: Popular Religion in China*. London: Routledge, 1992.

Jordan, David. *Gods, Ghosts and Ancestors: Folk Religion in a Taiwanese Village*. Berkeley: University of California Press, 1972.

Kieschnick, John. *The Impact of Buddhism on Chinese Material Culture*. Princeton: Princeton University Press, 2003.

Kohn, Livia. *Laughing at the Dao: Debates among Buddhists and Daoists in Medieval China*. Princeton: Princeton University Press, 1995.

——. *Introducing Daoism*. London: Routledge, 2009.

Komjathy, Louis. *The Daoist Tradition: An Introduction*. London: Bloomsbury, 2013.

LaFargue, Michael. *Tao and Method: A Reasoned Approach to the Tao Te Ching*. Albany: State University of New York Press, 1994.

Maspero, Henri. *Taoism and Chinese Religion*. Trans. Frank Kierman. Amherst: University of Massachusetts Press, 1981.

Overmeyer, Daniel. Ed. *Religion in China Today*. Cambridge: Cambridge University Press, 2003.

Robinet, Isabelle. *Taoism: Growth of a Religion*. Trans. Phyllis Brooks. Stanford: Stanford University Press, 1997.

Saso, Michael. *Taoism and the Rite of Cosmic Renewal*. Pullman: Washington State University Press, 1972.

Thompson, Laurence G. *Chinese Religion: An Introduction*. Fourth Edition. Belmont, CA: Wadsworth Publishing Company, 1989.

Wright, Arthur. *Buddhism in Chinese History*. Stanford: Stanford University Press, 1959.

Yao, Xinzhong and Yanxia Zhao. *Chinese Religion: A Contextual Approach*. London and New York: Continuum, 2010.

10 Japanese Traditions

Before the existence of anything, there was a primordial chaos that contained a life principle, suggesting that heaven and earth were originally united. Eventually, heaven became purer and lighter and rose upward, whereas the earth became grosser and heavier and moved downward, resulting in the separation between heaven and earth. Between heaven and earth, a sprout of vegetation springs up that becomes a god called Heavenly Central Lord, who is the leader of a triad that also consists of two subordinate figures, named High Producing and Divine Producing. Eventually, this triad vanishes and is followed by similar triads for several more generations until the emergence of a primordial couple named Izanagi (male principle) and Izanami (female principle). This original parental couple, both husband and wife and brother and sister, descend from heaven to the earth, creating the islands of Japan by dipping their jeweled spear into the ocean, bringing mud to the surface attached to the spear, and shaking off the mud adhering to the spear, thereby creating the islands of Japan. From their union, they also create many other gods, nature, and ancestral spirits, who are all called *kami*.

While touring the land, Izanami speaks first, which represents a ritual transgression because of her female nature and the injunction that a male must speak before a woman within a ritual context, resulting in their punishment. Their ritual error is punished with the birth of a leech as their first child, which they set adrift, and they start again to produce life. This time the male figure, Izanagi, speaks first, and a more auspicious result is achieved, although Izanami tragically dies during the birth of the fire spirit. A distraught Izanagi travels to the underworld to find her, only to become polluted when he discovers merely putrid decay and maggots covering her body. Izanagi turns around, leaves the underground, and purifies himself by diving into the sea, an action that produces another generation of deities. When he washes his left eye, he produces the sun goddess, Amaterasu; washing his right eye, he creates the moon god, Tsukiyomi; and from his nostrils arises Susano-o, god of the hot summer wind. Because of his fiery nature, Susano-o threatens crops, and he generally acts contrary to his sister, Amaterasu, by subverting irrigation of rice fields. Susano-o nauseates his sister by leaving his excrement, a form of pollution, on her throne. This gross and impure act of defecation offends and angers Amaterasu, who retires to a cave and bars its entrance, plunging the world into darkness. This situation motivated the *kami* (spirits) to collaborate on devising a plan to extricate her from the cave. The *kami* erect a *sakaki* tree outside of her cave and hang a mirror high on the tree, placing jewels on the middle branches and decorating the lower branches with white and blue ribbons. The Terrible Woman of Heaven is recruited to perform a lewd dance, which causes loud noises outside of the cave, motivating Amaterasu to inquire about the source and reason for the loud noises. After she emerges from her seclusion, she is unable to return to the cave because clan ancestors erect a rope that prevents her return to the hiding place. Finally, her brother is fined and banished to the underworld for his act of pollution.

Before finishing the narrative, there are some themes that are important for Japanese religiosity and need to be highlighted. The narrative reflects polytheism, the importance of purity and pollution, the social subordination of females to males, as evident by ritual rules concerning who should speak first, and the importance of the sun for life on earth. The mirror and jewels become part of the regalia of the emperor, and paper on the tree anticipates practices at a Shinto shrine. Finally, the narrative suggests the divine origin of the Japanese islands and a reverence for nature and reflects the close relationship between the people and *kami*.

As the narrative continues, Ninigi, grandson of the Sun goddess, becomes the ruler of public and divine affairs. Descending from a mountain, Ninigi carries the three sacred treasures: mirror, sword, and jewel. These three items would become associated with the imperial regalia and serve as symbols of Japan. The great grandson of Ninigi was Jimmu, first emperor of Japan and a member of the Yamoto clan, alleged to have lived around 660 BCE. This means that Amaterasu is the ancestor of the emperor and Japanese people.

This overall narrative suggests that Shinto, the way of the *kami*, represents the ancient and indigenous religious tradition of Japan, land of the *kami*. The narrative also suggests that Shinto possesses no founder, no single creator god, and no formal organization. Shinto also lacks any consensus collection of sacred texts or an official set of doctrines.

From a wider historical perspective, the Japanese religious tradition represents an interweaving of several religious traditions: Shinto (an indigenous tradition), folk religion, Buddhism, Daoism, Confucianism, Neo-Confucianism, and Christianity. With the exception of Shinto and folk religion, the other religions were imported from Korea, China, and the West. The interweaving of these various traditions created a dynamic situation at different periods of Japanese religious history because Shinto and Buddhism vied for and achieved predominance at different historical periods. Whatever the historical period, there was a close interconnection between the nation, its identity, and religion because religion pervaded everyday life. The Japanese also envisioned a close relationship between humans, divine beings in the form of *kami*, and nature. The observance of purification regulations permeated everyday religious life, along with the religious nature of the family.

The Japanese ideal embodied a harmony between humans, gods, and nature. The close relationship between the three entities extends to such an extent that humans can become gods or Buddhas. Moreover, unlike the major monotheistic traditions—Judaism, Christianity, and Islam—there is no hierarchy of gods, nature, and humans. The center of religious devotion was the home, where a small shrine (called the god-shelf) was used by a family for daily prayers. Water, salt, or fire were used to purify a person before performing rites. From its basis within the family, Japanese religiosity stressed local observances of festivals, which reinforced village or town unity. But there were also individual expressions of religious devotion to figures, such as Jizo and Kannon, who were Buddhist bodhisattvas, represented by their images in villages and along roadside shrines. If you were a fishermen or tradesmen, you could direct your devotion to specific types of *kami* related to your profession. An individual could visit a local shrine or temple when ill or under duress for help. The family-centric and local nature of Japanese religiosity also included a close relationship to the nation. From ancient times, the sun goddess, Amaterasu, watched over the Japanese islands.

Types of *Kami*

The term "*kami*" is a word of uncertain origin that generally connotes that which is superior, extraordinary, and mysterious. *Kami* are not omniscient or omnipotent. Although *kami* are superior to humans with respect to knowledge and power, they represent spiritual forces devoid of specific shape and thus can only manifest themselves if called to assume some shape. The vehicles that are necessary for a *kami* to reveal itself are called *yorishiro*, which can assume the forms of natural objects such as trees, stone, flags, pillars, mirrors, or swords. *Kami* can also reveal themselves through human beings such as shamans, who are called *miko* and were predominantly women in the early tradition. A more permanent dwelling place for a *kami* is the spirit body (*shintai*), which becomes an object of worship within the innermost sanctuary in the form of a mirror, sacred wand, jewels, sword, or wooden image. *Kami* generally function to maintain harmony, a positive manifestation of their power, but they can also cause negative destructive events in the form of malevolent spirits (*goryō*).

Not only are *kami* ubiquitous in the world, but they also manifest a wide variety of types, such as the following: natural forces (e.g., trees, stones, water, or storms); divine beings; food; abstract procreative powers; humans (e.g., the emperor); and clans (*uji-gami*) and villages, which function to protect kinship groups. Clan *kami* are also spirits of place such as a village or neighborhood, whereas other *kami* are more widespread. The cult of Inari (the rice spirit), for example, is centered in a *kami* of food, while the fox is a messenger of the *kami* of food that usually guards the Inari shrine.

Some *kami* represent imported Buddhist and Daoist deities, while others are demonic and vengeful spirits. Among the most evil demons (*ori*) are invisible figures, whereas other freakish figures are described with three eyes, horns on their heads, huge torsos, and a variety of colors. In addition to these evil spirits, there are ghosts, and the fox spirit, which is especially feared because it can possess people, make them ill, or kill them. Another strange figure is the grotesque birdman (*tengu*), who is benevolent. Many *kami* are ancestral spirits, a type of *kami* that originates with the soul of a person, which is transformed into a *kami* after death. Among examples of Buddhist figures that have become *kami* are various bodhisattvas (enlightened beings), such as Amida, ruler of the Pure Land; Kannon, who is a protector of children, departed souls, and women during childbirth; and Jizo, who is also concerned with children and protector of those who suffer pain. Besides Buddhist figures who become *kami*, Hachiman is a Shinto *kami* who gets integrated into Buddhism. Prior to his association to Buddhism, Hachiman is a popular indigenous deity who represents a warrior god and becomes the patron *kami* of the Minamoto clan, leading them to victory over the Taira clan, which brought the Heian period of Japanese history to an end in the twelfth century. At some point, Hachiman becomes a Buddhist bodhisattva figure and is believed to be an incarnation of Amida. It is to Hachiman shrines that families take boys to be purified for the first time. It is these types of figures that suggest a dynamic syncretistic religious situation at work.

Finally, there are heavenly *kami* such as Amaterasu, sun goddesses, and earthly *kami* such as Okuninushi, a guardian deity of Japan and its emperor, who protects the symbolic items of imperial sovereignty—a sacred mirror, magical sword, and fertility jewel. The so-called "Heavenly Person" (Tenjin) is a human deified after he served as a brilliant administrator and scholar, who had been falsely accused of misconduct while in office. Even though Shinto is polytheistic, the benevolent and malevolent types of *kami* are believed to

Figure 10.1 Steps to the temple of the Shinto Kami Hachiman. Photograph by Carl
     Olson.

harmoniously cooperate with each other. In addition to these various types of
kami, Japanese religious history manifests various types of Shinto.

Types of Shinto

There are five major forms of Shinto that have existed during the course of
Japanese religious history: syncretistic Shinto; state Shinto associated with the
imperial house; shrine Shinto; sect Shinto; and folk Shinto, which will be
discussed later. The first type of Shinto reflects events of the medieval period,
when Shinto was eclipsed by Buddhism but appropriated many aspects of
Buddhism into its structure, resulting in the increase of the popular appeal
of Buddhism to ordinary people. In addition to incorporating Buddhist features, medieval Shinto also adopted elements of Confucianism, Daoism, and
Neo-Confucianism. Shinto leaders borrowed Confucian ethical concepts, but
they also adopted the Daoist cosmology, religious calendar, divine beings, festivals, and use of protective charms. They also incorporated into Shinto Neo-
Confucian philosophical notions along with Buddhist philosophy, cosmology,
rituals, objects of worship, and sacred language formulas. During the Tokugawa
period (1600–1867), Japanese leaders adopted Neo-Confucianism because
they were convinced that it could serve the state by controlling the people,
enhancing social stability, and creating an orderly state. Neo-Confucianism
was adopted as the necessary knowledge needed for the state educational system and also became part of the state Shinto cult, which stimulated a restoration of national Shinto.

State Shinto was focused on the emperor, who performed rites for the imperial ancestors, and included elements from shrine Shinto. State Shinto is actually an artificial conception owing its origin to a political creation during the Meiji (1868–1945) era. In the prior period of the Tokugawa regime, leaders maintained a rigid social system that was based on social rank and class according to strict Confucian principles. The Tokugawa leadership isolated Japan from foreign maritime powers from the West. Wanting Japan to become a modern state, the leaders of the Meiji Restoration stressed contact with the outside world and restored the position of the emperor to pre-eminence by emphasizing his essential importance along with the mystique of his divine ancestry. The overall objective of this policy was to unite the nation around the symbol of the emperor. This process included the replacing of Buddhism by Shinto as the official state religion in 1871 and integrating the ancient religion into the power structure of the state by giving its priests and institutions financial support and a privileged status. The decision to demote Buddhism in favor of Shinto was related to the fact that the former religion had been a branch of the feudal Tokugawa government. Buddhism was also perceived to be financially corrupt and to spiritually manifest a state of decay. In addition, Shinto represented the old imperial religion, stressed social cooperation, and encouraged an absence of individualism among people. State Shinto thus made subordination to the emperor and state a virtue.

State Shinto did not have complete autonomy when it got restored as the official state religion, because religious policies were determined by the state political authority. Among its other characteristics, state Shinto was a religion of ethnocentric nationalism that finally culminated in Japan's entry into World War II. Even though traditional Shinto had been tolerant of many kinds of beliefs and practices, state Shinto did not share such openness and tolerance, because it could not deviate from its new pre-established norm. After Japan's defeat in 1945 by Western allied forces, the emperor was forced to deny his divinity, and the concepts that the Japanese people were superior to other races and destined to rule the world were also rejected. The Japanese were directed to turn to a love of humankind instead of their family and country.

In contrast to the imperial aura of state Shinto, shrine Shinto revolved around *kami* and their shrines, even though there were no fixed shrines in ancient times, because *kami* were believed to live in remote places. When it was time to perform a rite or celebrate a festival, a temporary enclosure was built by participants in the shape of a square, arranged with a sprig from a sacred tree located at its center. The entire enclosure was separated by a boundary of straw rope. In contrast to this temporary shrine, a more permanent enclosure was marked by a rock border. Humans needed to invoke *kami* to visit such places, although at a later date, humans believed that the *kami* resided in more permanent structures. The builders of shrines needed to adhere to approved principles, which included the naturalness and simplicity of the location, the necessity of using plain lumber and avoiding superfluous decoration, and taking into consideration the site's harmony with nature. With a location secured, *kami* could be represented in an image, although a mirror was used more often than an image. The *kami* associated with a given location were ranked according to whether they were enshrined or not enshrined. There were also distinctions between the enshrined *kami*.

Shrine Shinto included three kinds of rites. The first category was external rites of preliminary purification, such as avoidance of all foods, with the exception of those prepared over a ritually pure fire. This first category included taboos related to death and flowing blood, which means that a menstruating woman or people with a recent death in their family were expected to refrain from shrine worship. Internal purification and exorcism represented the second category of rites. In order to cleanse a person of pollution, the Shinto priest would wave a purification wand over the worshippers. The third category included rites of dedication that began with the offering of sprigs from a sacred *sakaki* tree. This kind of rite was originally associated with the offering of the first fruits of the harvest but became an honoring of a *kami* as a guest. The dedication offering included food and drink accompanied by musical and dance performances.

Between the nineteenth and twentieth centuries, Sect Shinto evolved into thirteen distinct religious groups. The *kami* of the various sects were identical to figures of traditional Shinto, although they were founded by different charismatic personalities with a shamanistic inclination. The sects, which were independent entities, tended to share a concern with life in the world and were heavily dependent on agrarian communities for support. These various sects represented a wide variety of practices, such as mountain worship, faith healing, purification, Confucian focus, and revival groups. In retrospect, state, shrine, sect, and folk Shinto are interrelated and often not easily identifiable as distinct entities.

Not only did these types of Shinto overlap with each other, Shinto also incorporated various elements of Buddhism. It was not unusual for Shinto shrines to be located in Buddhist temples and vice versa. Buddhist texts were chanted at Shinto shrines. Shinto gods were worshipped alongside Buddhas and bodhisattvas, and Buddhists claimed that *kami* were manifestations of universal Buddhist powers and that Shinto manifested Buddhist truths. As Shinto and Buddhism became more intertwined, it became difficult to distinguish them. This integrative religious scenario united the new (Buddhism) and the old (Shinto) together into a system called *jingu-ji* (shrine and temple).

Shinto Belief System

The Shinto belief system imagines a three-dimensional structure of the universe. Male and female *kami* reside on the highest realm, the Plain of the High Sky. Humans and other animate beings live in the Manifest World, located in the middle of the universe, while the Nether World or lowest realm is the location for unclean and evil spirits. These three realms constitute the Shinto worldview and play a role in the Shinto religious imagination when dealing with the *kami*. The Shinto worldview also expresses a sensitivity to nature, a necessity for purification, and simplicity. Within the Shinto worldview, there exists a benign harmony that is present in nature and human relationships with *kami*, nature, and other humans. Moreover, there is an invisible vital force (*ki*) that permeates the spiritual and physical realms with its life-giving power. The Shinto worldview manifests a concern for the interconnectedness of each aspect that constitutes the whole and not just a single part, an emphasis that helps to explain the lack of individualism within society.

If we examine the Shinto conception of human nature, we discover that all human beings have the same nature, which is characterized as fundamentally good. The differences in the core human nature are attributed to the extent to which a person pursues moral/ethical principles. This attitude implies that there is no innate evil, such as original sin, in a person. A human represents a social being who is always in the process of becoming or growing toward that person's final maturity, an understanding of human nature that necessarily means that human nature is not something static. But what about a person's origin? Shinto believes that humans did not fall from a primordial state of blissful existence. A human rather receives her life from the *kami* and is thus a child of the *kami*.

This *kami* parental relationship with a person has important implications, because it suggests very lucidly that the world of humans and that of *kami* overlap each other, and that human beings have the flesh of *kami* in their bodies. This means that there is no estrangement between a person and the *kami*, although the human sense of well-being and happiness is exactly the same for the *kami*. In addition to being related to the *kami*, a person is intimately related to the cosmos as an integral part of it. Within this context, the cosmos is a community of living beings all sharing the *kami* nature. These points help one to understand that a human is a part of the cosmos and the rhythm of nature, which is intellectually and emotionally grasped as an essential harmony between a person and nature. Since this unity and harmony characterizes their relationship, it is incumbent upon a person to cooperate with nature and not to attempt to coerce or conquer it, because the cosmos and its contents are all divine gifts. This line of thinking about the cosmos, nature, and humans means that there is no dualism between the material and spiritual in the Shinto worldview and conception of human nature.

The ancient Japanese distinguished between four kinds of soul, including the following: rough or violent soul; quiet, tranquil, or mature soul; luck soul; and mysterious spirit. The first and second souls are often combined in the popular imagination. The soul represents the identity of a person and participates in the divine cosmic activity of things. In popular Shinto religion, the life of a soul follows a commonly shared narrative. The body of an infant receives its soul four months before its birth. On the seventh day after birth, the newborn infant is officially presented to the family and given a name. On the thirty-second day after the birth of a boy or the thirty-third day for a girl, the infant is taken to a Shinto shrine, introduced to the *kami* associated

Figure 10.2 Japanese cemetery in Tokyo. Photograph by Carl Olson.

with the shrine, and thereafter becomes a member of that shrine. After the death of the body, a human may assume various forms, even becoming a monster or ghost. The souls of those who have experienced a sudden and violent death are considered especially restless and angry and thus dangerous to survivors. These troubled souls need to be appeased by the living with offerings of food and acts of purification. It is believed that a soul lingers in the house after death for forty-nine days, but it departs after this period to a place of peace and comfort. And after thirty-three years, the soul becomes a *kami*, which represents the soul's final stage of happiness and its ability to protect the well-being of the surviving family members.

The Shinto conception of death is that it is a continuation of life, implying that a person continues to exist after death. Within the cultural context of this belief, there is also no end of the world and no final judgment day. Any notion that the soul must be delivered from sin or that one needs a savior is foreign to Shinto. The Western notion of reaching a final goal or paradise is also not part of the Shinto religious ethos. The only goal recognized by Shinto is the welfare and flourishing of its people in a wider social sense. These remarks should not mislead one to assume that Shinto is without an ethical core, because the exact opposite is true.

The fundamental presupposition of Shinto ethics is that life is a continual blessing. Humans and *kami* share a common attitude toward life that is called *makoto*, which is defined as honesty, sincerity, conscientiousness, or truthfulness. Its practice makes a person true to his total situation. *Makoto* also means that one is in harmony with the *kami* and thus following the way of the *kami*

(*kami-no michi*). This is a way that a person should travel during his life, which is analogous to a cosmic path and way of nature. *Makoto* also involves discovering the truth by searching one's heart. The ideal for a person is to have a pure heart and mind (*makoto no kokoru*). The center of feeling and thinking for a person is the heart and mind (*kokoru*), a response to other people and things devoid of blind emotion; it represents a union of the subjective and objective, a cognition with affect and vice versa. From an ethical perspective, Shinto does not espouse a fixed and universal set of laws concerning right and wrong. Rather, each person must discover his own way of the *kami*, even though what one ought to do is not an individualistic decision; it must be a decision reached within a communal context because there is no such thing as an absolute ethic given by a divine authority. The traditional Shinto ethic tends to be situational and relative to a particular time and place. How, then, does Shinto deal with the problem of evil?

In Shinto, a human being is not tainted by original sin, nor can someone violate God's will. The term *tsumi* is probably the closest thing to sin in Shinto, but it is actually more accurately translated as "offense" or "defilement." Various types of transgressions are caused by external factors, such as ritual or physical impurity, moral faults, or calamities. An ethical/moral offense is an act that is unworthy of someone living her life according to the way of the *kami*. This implies that evil is a lack of natural harmony. How can harmony be restored and defilement cleansed? Evil can be removed by ritual purification, which leads to being mended, set right, or rectified. A person is simply responsible to live a sincere life and have respect for the *kami*.

The way of the *kami* is an ethical path that also involves the importance of maintaining face when interacting with others in a public manner. The Shinto conception of ethics is not grounded on guilt but rather on shame. To perform an act that causes shame involves the loss of face, which not only affects the individual actor but also reflects negatively on his parents and ancestors and brings disgrace to his biological lineage. When a person is shamed, he can atone for his mistake by bowing deeply, ritually giving a gift, or committing suicide, in extreme cases.

Purity, Pollution, Ritual, and Festival

When Izanigi went to the underworld to search for his wife/sister, who died during childbirth, before the historical period, he contacted death, which polluted him. After this misfortune, he purified himself by bathing in the sea. This foundational narrative forms the basis for the Shinto emphasis on the necessity for purification, which is especially evident prior to coming into contact with the *kami* or after contact with a source of pollution. The method of purifying oneself is simply to pour water from a clean source, for instance, over one's hands and to also rinse one's mouth, which purifies a person internally and externally. This renders one's body fit to approach the *kami*. Other means of purifying oneself include fire and salt; the latter is white and associated in the Japanese imagination with sea and renewed life. The importance and role of purification runs throughout Japanese culture and encompasses ordinary customs, such as removing one's shoes before entering a house, taking a daily bath, not mixing white rice with other foods, and using virgin chopsticks. Since the interior of a home is considered sacred space, it is mandatory for residents to keep it clean and free of pollution. A resident wants to maintain a harmonious balance between the interior and exterior of a home.

Before a person can approach a shrine with the intent to worship the *kami*, purification is absolutely essential for both personal and communal forms of worship. By the practice of faithful actions in daily life, a person transmits and follows the will of the *kami*. The communal aspect of worship manifests being in awe and thankful for what one has received from the *kami*, which can be accomplished by reciting prayers or singing about the joy of life. For what I presupposed was a typical act of worship, I watched people at a Shinto temple dedicated to Hachiman, warrior *kami*, approach the sanctuary to make a small monetary offering, ring a bell attached to a long rope, or clap their hands twice, which was done to get the attention of the *kami*. A typical visitor bows next, with hands pressed together. It is safe to assume that the person silently asks for a favor before clapping her hands again to signal the end of the prayer. This devotional act embodies the spirit of simplicity characteristic of Shinto.

Within the context of communal worship, an officiating priest summons the *kami* to descend to the shrine (*yorishiro*) by means of invocations. When it arrives, it is offered food and drink, often in the form of *sake* (rice wine). Often using a *miko* (female medium), the *kami* are induced to provide answers to questions about the welfare of the community. At other times, the *kami* of the village is transported in a palanquin around the village, which is a public presentation of its presence. Petitionary prayers are recited by community members in order to implore the *kami* to favorably arrange the future of the village, if necessary, for a beneficial outcome. For some events, purified girls, who are called *miko* girls (shrine virgins), perform a dance known as *Kagura*, a celebration of the renewal of the life cycle. Some *miko* function as female mediums and are contacted for problems related to illness, war, natural disasters, or assistance with marriage decisions. The *kami* communicate with the community through the female mediums, a pattern that reassures the members of the community. An important part of the ritual occurs when the priest dips a branch from a sacred evergreen tree and waves it over the people, an action representing the *kami's* blessings.

The Japanese term *matsuri* means festival ritual, although some scholars think that it includes the meaning of "to wait" for the *kami*, while others think that it means "to join" or "to be united." According to the *Records of Engi*, there are three types of ritual festivals: greater, middle, and lesser. Within the greater festival category, there is the harvest festival; a middle-level festival is praying for a good harvest, monthly festivals, and those for a new rice crop. Lesser festivals include propitiating the wind *kami* for help achieving a rich harvest, decorating *sake* casks with flowers, a festival to appease the fire *kami*, a festival for road *kami*, and a festival connected to particular *kami* shrines. The New Year Festival is, for example, a three-day event that is marked by house cleaning, with the intention of beginning the New Year unpolluted. Other features of the festival include dispensing gifts to superiors, making a special soup and pounded rice cakes, and visiting a shrine or temple with the purpose of making offerings and praying for prosperity and good health for the coming year. Several festivals culminate with a public procession of a portable *kami* shrine around the neighborhood, with the intention of allowing everyone along the parade route to visually see the *kami* and to sanctify the local area.

In classical Shinto, the emperor and *sake* (rice wine) play significant roles in rites. Shinto temples house large vats of aging wine for use in ritual. Rice wine is offered to dead ancestors and *kami*. At the beginning of a new business or political activity, new barrels of *sake* are opened for good fortune. *Sake* also plays a role in some purification rites. When *sake* is consumed by a group of people, it functions to socially unite them. The traditional role of the emperor, who is believed to be a direct descendent of the Sun Goddess, Amaterasu, in Shinto, manifests his dual role as political leader and priestly figure. Strict taboos surrounded his office and person, as did imperial symbols, such as the sacred jewels, mirror, and divine sword. The emperor was attuned to the will of the *kami* by means of direct communication, dreams, states of ecstasy, or divination. The emperor was expected to obey the directives of the *kami* because its words contained power and potency.

Literary and Material Culture

Shinto has never had a sacred, revealed body of literature in its history, but it is not devoid of other types of literature. The *Kojiki* (*Record of Ancient Matters*) was composed around 712 CE. The *Nihonshoki* (*Chronicles of Japan*, which is also known as the *Nibongi*) was composed in 720 CE and reflects life during the Nara Period (710–794 CE), but it is written in classical Chinese, with poetic parts in archaic Japanese; it presents the genealogies of several clans, with each genealogy traced back to a particular *kami* from which the clan directly descended. The *Nihonshoki* and *Kojiki* favored different rival clans, with the former promoting the claims to divine descent of the Izumo clan against the latter's favoring of the Yamato clan. Both clans claimed direct descent from the goddess Amaterasu, a divine ancestor used to support claims about the emperor's divinity. Therefore, the purpose of tracing their lineage to the goddess was to fortify the dynastic claims to legitimacy of each clan by tracing its lineage to a particular *kami*. In addition to these works, the *Manyoshu* (*Collection of 10,000 Leaves*) dates to around 760 CE, representing a vast anthology of poetry focusing on different topics. Provincial chronicles are represented by the *Fudoki*, commissioned in 713 CE, which conveys legends of local *kami*. The fifty volumes of the *Engishiki* embody the Shinto law code and date to around the late tenth century CE; this work includes ritual prayers (*norito*) and liturgies used in public services. These prayers or incantations confirm an already existing relationship between humans and *kami* that serves to appease them and gain their favor and blessings.

Village, household, roadside, and temple shrines are typical locations for *kami* shrines. These shrines can be simple or slightly more elaborate. The Grand Shrine at Ise near the Isuzu River is a major complex that is a frequent destination for pilgrims. This is the most ancient, sacred, and revered site in Japan, which houses the *Naiku* (Inner Shrine), dedicated to the goddess Amaterasu. Another important structure is the *Geku* (Outer Shrine), dedicated to Toyouke, goddess of the harvest.

The larger Shinto shrines (*jinga*) are readily recognizable by their sacred gateway (*torii*), which consists of a pair of posts that are topped with two crossbars. The *torii* is intended to mark the boundary between the impure, external, and secular realm from the internal sacred space of the shrine and presence of *kami*. The sacred gate is also a place that one leaves and to which one returns after contact with an awe-inspiring power. The gate gives one an experience of intimacy with a sacred world, other people, and empowerment of oneself. Another type of marker of a sacred location is the sacred straw rope (*shimenawa*) made of rice straw that is tied to a tree, calling attention to the location as a *kami* site, even though the *kami* is not believed to reside in the tree. What makes it possible for a *kami* to inhabit a tree is that it is already something material and spiritual. In folk Shintoism, the relationship between the spiritual and material can be external, internal or a combination of both of them. The interdependence of *kami* and the world suggests that the world is full of *kami* and power, and that they would be incomplete without each other.

Figure 10.3 Shrine at Komyo-ji Temple in Kamakura. Photograph by Carl Olson.

Figure 10.4 Shinto priests performing a wedding ceremony in Kamakura. Photograph by Carl Olson.

The larger shrine consists of a sanctuary containing the image of the *kami* dedicated at the site. There are also an oratory, storehouses, restrooms, and outer buildings for the purpose of reciting prayers and making offerings to the *kami* by visitors. Finally, there is a stone trough containing pure water for purification. The Shinto shrine complex in the city of Kamakura contains a raised pavilion with a roof that is open for public viewing and is used for weddings. The material used to constitute a Shinto shrine is believed to be infused with a spiritual power (*tama*) that does not compromise or change the material or the spiritual aspects of the complex. In Shinto, materiality and spirituality exist interdependently with each other.

Buddhism in Japan

Buddhism was not indigenous to Japan; it arrived in Japan via Korea in 552 CE after a delegation from Korea's kingdom of Paekche arrived with an image of the Buddha and several scriptures as gifts for the imperial court during the reign of Emperor Kinmei, although there may have been prior unofficial contacts between the two cultures. Whatever the historical case, a continuous wave of Chinese Buddhist influence followed these initial contacts. Initially, Buddhism was practiced by Korean immigrants, but it was gradually accepted by upper class families, by the imperial court, and finally the state. Buddhist scriptures were, for example, recited for members of the royal court for cures from various types of illness and dangers associated with childbirth.

A historically important figure encouraging the Japanese acceptance and establishment of Buddhism was Prince Shotoku (573–621), second son of the emperor, who made the city of Nara a center for the foreign religion. It was during the Nara period (710–784) that Buddhism became a national religion because of the support of the devout Emperor Shomu (r. 724–749), who ordered the temple—Todaiji—built to contain a large statue of the Buddha. In 741, he ordered that two Buddhist temples be constructed in every province to accommodate monks and nuns, whose duty was to recite sacred scriptures that would enhance social and economic welfare for the people. The Nara era emperors thought that Buddhism would improve Japanese life and form a solid moral foundation for the country.

During the historical period covering the seventh to the eighth centuries, six Buddhist schools of thought entered Japan: Jojitsu (625), Sanron (625), Hosso (654), Kusha (658), Kegon (736), and Ritsu (738). These schools tended to be scholastic and promoted one or more Buddhist scriptures that were considered the secret teachings of the Buddha, creating an extension of the six sects during the Chinese Tang Dynasty. The Sanron school, for example, taught the abstract philosophy of Nāgārjuna with his interpretation of the middle way, Mādhyamika, between the extremes of being and non-being, which culminated in no permanent philosophical position because emptiness was a non-dualistic stance. The old Yogācāra school of "consciousness-only" was represented by the Hosso school. The Ritsu school stressed monastic discipline, even though it did not adhere to all Indian rules for discipline.

As the Nara period evolved, Buddhism became increasingly decadent and corrupt. Some priests and temples became very wealthy, with some priests getting involved in the political machinations of the period. The royal patronage of Buddhism sparked the construction of imposing temples and monasteries. Buddhist wisdom became associated with the healing Buddha. According to the *Sūtra of the Golden Light*, the Japanese religion was united with the government by means of the Buddhist Law (*dharma*), which also functioned to protect the country. From the city of Nara, the capital of the country moved to Kyoto in 794, which began the Heian era (794–1185).

During the late Heian period, Buddhist monks personally reached out and interacted with ordinary people and thereby endeared themselves to the populace. Kūya (903–972) was such a monk from Mount Hiei; he was famous for dancing through the city streets with a tinkling bell hanging from his neck. This pioneer of Pure Land Buddhism would publically utter the name of Amida and encouraged others to sing and dance with him. Because of his public antics, he became known as "the saint of the streets." Ippen (1239–1289) employed similar methods, believing that the grace of Amida was present everywhere. The faith-based movement was aided by Ryōnin (1072–1132) and his promoting of *nembutsu* (repetitive chanting of Amida's name). Agreeing with the spirit of Kūya, Ryōnin, and Ippen, Genshin (942–1017) painted scenes of the torments of hell along with the glories of the Pure Land and espoused having trust in the saving power of Amida.

During the Nara period (710–794), there lived a multi-talented monk named Kūkai (774–835), a scholar, poet, sculptor, painter, calligrapher, and inventor born into an aristocratic family who got involved in political machinations of the time and was disgraced, a situation that was probably a factor shaping Kūkai's decision to become a Buddhist monk. Before he became a monk, he studied at a Confucian institution. At 17 years of age, he wrote a book on three religious traditions: Confucianism, Daoism, and Buddhism. In this book, he depicts the superiority of Buddhism. In 804, seeking a unifying vision for Buddhism, he took a hazardous ship voyage to China with royal financial support. At the Chinese capital of Chang-an, he found a master, Hui-kuo (764–805), who was so impressed by the young Japanese man that he adopted him as a disciple. Kūkai was honored when his master died, because he was chosen to write the funeral inscription. After two years in China, which Kūkai spent securing esoteric scriptures, training, and being initiated, he returned to Japan and eventually established the Shingon sect in 816. Shingon means true (*shin*) word (*gon*), representing a Japanese rendering of the Sanskrit term "mantra." After receiving numerous honors in Japan, Kūkai asked the emperor in 816 for permission to build a monastery on Mount Kōyo, which eventually became a center for his own sect. In 822, Kūkai became abbot of the Tōdaji, a prominent Buddhist temple, and became known posthumously as Kōbō Daishi (Propagator of the Law).

Kūkai devised what he called the Ten Stages, which was intended to mark the major stages of life and religious teachings. The initial two stages were identified as Confucian and Daoist, but the Shingon esoteric teachings represented the culmination of Buddhist thought. He equated the Vairocana Buddha, who was more than a vision of the historical Buddha, with the totality of everything that is without beginning or end. He asserted that Shingon was superior to other religions and forms of Buddhism because it represented the esoteric or private teachings of the Buddha, whereas other schools are the public (exoteric) teachings. Therefore, Shingon represented the secret, mysterious, and inner experience of the Buddha. Even though the teachings were secret, they can be attained by everyone. From Kūkai's perspective, Shingon denied that the world was consciousness because mind and matter are inseparable. This school of Buddhism synthesized Buddhist concepts with Chinese *yin-yang* theory and later incorporated aspects of Shintoism.

Kūkai became an expert in two *mandalas* (sacred diagrams): the Womb Mandala and the Diamond Mandala. The diamond *mandala* represents the essence and unchangeable nature of reality like the hard and stable nature of a diamond, whereas the womb *mandala* is considered soft, changing, and active, which is the exact opposite of the diamond. The womb points to the multiplicity of phenomena, while the diamond represents the unity of phenomena. When they are separate, they stand for the dual aspect of reality; but when they are considered together, they represent the essential unity of everything. This unity is symbolized by Vairocana (in Japanese, Dainichi). By meditating on these *mandalas*, one transforms the powers of the divinities within the *mandala* to oneself.

For a Shingon monk practicing the esoteric way, the magical use of *mandalas* (sacred diagrams), *mudras* (hand gestures), and *mantras* (sacred formulas) played an essential role in the attainment of one's goal. Kūkai referred to the three mysteries associated with the body, speech, and mind, which are directly associated with hand gestures, sacred utterances, and methods of perceiving truth by means of wisdom. These methods were rooted in the Tantric tradition in India with its emphasis on symbols and esoteric formulas that were secretive. The hand gestures function as the seal of the *mantra* being simultaneously recited. In other words, the hand gestures guarantee the efficacy of the sacred utterances. The hand gestures suggest the three mysteries: thought, word, and act, which are grounded in Vairocana and represent different ways to approach the one reality. Thus, thought, word, and act are different expressions for an essential unity, which is analogous to ocean water, which is always salty regardless of where one takes a taste of the water.

Kūkai taught that the key to esoteric knowledge was contained in the *Mahāvairocana Sūtra*. In Shingon temples, fearsome statues of figures with menacing postures, glaring eyes, sharp teeth, and weapons appear on the altars. A typical such figure is Fudō, who is described as colored blue with a ferocious facial expression, surrounded by flames, and carrying a sword and a rope to fight evil. These terrifying figures are explained as representing the malevolent side of actually benevolent deities, which manifest a higher unity beyond the dualistic world. The sect performs esoteric rites for healing the sick and protecting women giving birth.

In addition to Kūkai's religious convictions and expertise with esoteric methods, he also believed that artistic expression was a path that revealed the true significance of the esoteric scriptures. The esoteric, mysterious, and aesthetic aspects of Shingon are best expressed through art. These arts included painting, sculpture, music, literature, gestures, actions, and other aspects of civilization. His emphasis on aesthetics was intended to express and create what was beautiful, and what was beautiful was part of the nature of the Buddha.

In addition to Kūkai, another monk unsatisfied with Buddhism of the Nara period was Saichō (762–822), who also traveled to China to seek genuine Buddhism, with the intention of establishing this true religion in Japan. Saichō found this truth in China and founded the Tendai school upon his return to Japan. He was honored posthumously as Dengyō Daishi (Great Teacher) by his country.

Saichō was Kūkai's student until their cordial relationship fell apart when the former wanted to make Shingon a mere appendage of Tendai. From the perspective of this school, truth is embodied in the *Lotus Sūtra*, which makes its path superior to all others, and its discovery is aided by meditation. Since everyone possesses the non-dual Buddha-nature, it is potentially possible for everyone to achieve enlightenment. Because everything is Buddha-nature, it is possible to achieve a more sympathetic and insightful understanding of nature.

Saichō embodied his teaching within a framework formed by the five periods of the teaching and eight doctrines. By means of Kūkai's teaching, Saichō organized Buddhist teachings into five historical periods that culminated with the final truth, which he identified with the *Lotus Sūtra*. The eight doctrines were a typology of different religious approaches to salvation in the history of Buddhism that again culminated with the perfect text of the *Lotus Sūtra*.

As the Shingon and Tendai schools gained favor with the Japanese nobility, they were, however, compromised by wealth and power. By the twelfth century, wars among competing armies led by shoguns became common, and political power shifted from the royal court at Kyoto to ruling feudal groups, who established their first government at Kamakura, which became the name of this period of Japanese history, beginning in 1185 and ending in 1333. During this troubled period of history, Buddhist temples became economic centers,

Figure 10.5 Daibutsu Buddha in Kamakura. Photograph by Carl Olson.

with their own armies of monks. With the decline of the court and nobility, financial support for Buddhist schools waned and led to a weakening of Shingon and Tendai schools. The political and social turmoil of the period gave impetus to the theory of the "decline of the law" and a fear about the imminent end of the world. This dire scenario created an opening for new schools of Buddhism that could respond effectively to the situation and address the needs of large numbers of people.

Pure Land Buddhism

During the Kamakura era (1185–1333), there was a perception that Buddhism was corrupt and had declined, a period of war and suffering had arrived, and the end of time was imminent. In addition to this bleak situation, humans were perceived to be weak and degenerate to the extent of not being able to achieve salvation by means of their own efforts. Into this dire historical context and religious vacuum, there evolved Pure Land Buddhism as a response to the miserable situation under the leadership of men such as Honen (1133–1212), founder of the Jōdo Pure Land sect, Shinran (1173–1263), a disciple of Honen and founder of the Jodo Shinshu (True Pure Land) sect, and the controversial Nichiren (1222–1282).

Honen, a renowned scholar within the Tendai school, recognized that abstract and complex philosophical texts did not speak to or could not help ordinary people suffering from forces beyond their control. At 42 years of age, Honen thought that he found a way to help common people when he turned to Pure Land teachings as a response to difficult times. He rejected the notion generally accepted in Buddhism that difficult forms of practice lead to salvation, because ordinary people were not capable of arduous forms of meditative and ascetic practice. His basic problem was to devise a way of coping with the decline of the law, a notion that referred to the decline of Buddhist teachings and the impossibility of attaining nirvana in the current degenerate historical period. The decline of the Buddha's teaching had evolved from an initial ideal age, when practice and liberation were possible, to a second period that witnessed people practicing the religion knowing that enlightenment was impossible, and to the final degenerate age, when no one practices the religion, which awaits the final disappearance of Buddhism. This teaching about the decline of the law should not be confused with a notion like original sin, because it is not an aspect of human nature for Honen but rather something external to humans.

Honen developed his grasp of the dire situation by further distinguishing two paths of religion: a Holy Path (*shōdō*) and the Pure Land Path (*jōdo*). The first distinction was called *jiriki*, implying reliance on an individual's strength, whereas the other path was called *tariki*, which suggested reliance and the strength of another. Taking into consideration the appalling nature of the times, Honen reasoned that a path on which a person relies on herself is impossible, and thus a path on which one can trust the strength of another figure was a wiser choice in a degenerate age. Therefore, Honen instructed people to throw themselves at the mercy of Amida, bodhisattva of the Pure Land, and rely on his grace to be saved. But how does a person trigger this grace?

Honen discovered an answer to this question about the origin of grace by using the mythical narrative about Hōzō, a tale about the bodhisattva Amida in a prior lifetime. In this narrative, Hōzō vowed to postpone his liberation until everyone could be saved. In order to make salvation possible, he invented the *nembutsu* (a practice of chanting the name of the bodhisattva). This was the best practice for this degenerate age because it was easy, took little effort, did not rely on the chanter's strength for ultimate success, and was something that everyone can do. This method and its benefits implied that everyone can be saved by the grace of Amida. A person was instructed to repeatedly chant "namu Amida" or "namu Amida Butsu," meaning "I put my faith in Amida Buddha." The repetitive nature of chanting fostered the growth of belief, focused the mind on a single thing, and enabled the chanter's mind to become absorbed in Amida. According to Honen, chanting can be compared to the reflection of the moon in water, which enabled the image to either rise freely upward or to shine down on the water.

Shinran, a disciple of Honen, shared exile with his master because of his teachings, rejected Tendai Buddhism like his master, and converted to a devotional path. His marriage and lack of remorse about breaking basic Buddhist precepts resulted in him being called, pejoratively, "Bald Head." Shinran accepted many of the teachings of Honen, but he radicalized some of them by emphasizing certain features. If the world was, for example, in a state of decay, it was impossible for a person to perform a single good deed, because all deeds are self-centered and involved in passion. Because it was absolutely impossible for a person to perform one good deed to bring about his salvation, any attempt to win salvation for himself was indicative of having an ulterior motive, such as a desire to be saved. A person's only hope was to throw himself on the mercy of Amida by chanting his name a single time with utmost sincerity, while additional chanting was merely an expression of gratitude. In fact, an evil person, imagined by Shinran, might have a better chance of gaining salvation than a virtuous person, because a wicked person might be more acceptable to Amida and more inclined to give himself completely to Amida, while a good person might think that she has a better chance of salvation because of her good deeds. This provocative line of thinking was intended to call attention to the importance of faith, which Shinran linked to chanting.

Besides its intimate relation to chanting, Shinran identified three elements of faith: a sincere mind, trustfulness, and a desire to be reborn in the Pure Land. He drew a further distinction between two types of causes: a passive cause that was the light of Amida, which he connected with wisdom, and an active cause of faith, which he identified with the name of Amida. Although the passive cause also referred to a religious experience of being illumined, faith was finally a gift from Amida, which Shinran came to believe was very rare as he grew older. Shinran also argued that faith involved a believer achieving a recognition of his inherent Buddha-nature, a state of egolessness, from Shinran's perspective. Despite their differences, the messages of Honen and Shinran found a welcome reception among lower-class families living in the countryside, creating greater numbers of Buddhist adherents who were not the socially and politically connected elites following the older, predominant, major sects.

The Buddhist devotional movement was given a different emphasis by Nichiren, a controversial, uncompromising, and prophetic figure during his life. Believing that he was reforming the Tendai school, Nichiren revived a focus on the *Lotus Sūtra*, an embodiment of the truth, and recommended chanting the *daimoku*, or title of the text. He gave this practice the status of the only genuine practice and a doctrinal foundation that made it the only way to salvation. With a sacred text and a practice of chanting its title as his foundation, Nichiren criticized Pure Land Buddhism, politicians, and major temples. He argued that the *Lotus Sūtra* should be adopted as the foundation for a state religion, and those who did not adhere to the text were heretics. He was finally arrested in 1271 and sentenced to exile on the island of Sado, located in the Sea of Japan. A hagiographical narrative relates that he was nearly beheaded for his outspokenness, only to be saved by an object streaking across the sky that terrified his executioners. He also suffered through a second exile, which he interpreted in the light of bodhisattva Never Despising, a figure suffering in the *Lotus Sūtra* who became the historical Buddha in another lifetime. Like this figure, Nichiren viewed himself as propagating the truthful message of the Buddha in this final age. Using other bodhisattva figures from the text, Nichiren identified his efforts to these religious figures and traced their teachings to an original, primordial Buddha, who even preceded the historical Buddha. After he was pardoned in 1274, Nichiren was asked when the Mongols would invade Japan. His prediction that they would invade within a year proved to be accurate. Japan was saved from an invasion when the Mongol ships encountered very bad weather.

Zen Buddhism and Meditation

Because Japanese monks who traveled to China to study were members of the Tendai sect, it was not unexpected that those who were exposed to Zen teaching in China would return to Japan with a Zen Buddhism that was more akin to a hybrid religion. A good example of this trend was Dainichi Nōnin (n.d.) and his creation of the Daruma school by synthesizing Zen with the teachings of Mahāyāna texts, reflecting more esoteric practices. Another good example of this phenomenon was Myōan Eisai, who was educated as a Tendai monk and later given credit for founding Zen in Japan after a second trip to China in 1187. Having authority to establish the Rinzai tradition in Japan, Eisai encountered resistance from the hierarchy of the Tendai school, but he was able to make progress because he was protected and supported by the shogun Minamoto Yoritomo, enabling him to establish a monastery in Hakata in 1195, although his version of Zen was practiced along with esoteric ritual of other sects. Eisai was never able to create a genuine and independent Rinzai school.

In contrast to Eisai's incongruous brand of Zen, Enni Ben'en (1201–1280) developed a type of Zen that was more undiluted and more independent than the hybrid Zen of his predecessor. A contemporary of Enni was Shinchi Kakushin (1207–1298), who became famous for bringing the *Mumonkan* collection of *kōans* from China back to Japan. This collection and the *Hekiganroku* helped monks and nuns fix their concentration on one thing, which amounts to language meditation on enigmatic sayings of old masters or dialogues between them and their disciples. The ultimate objective of this method was to help meditators recognize the futility of all intellectual attempts to realize their goal and to trigger an enlightenment experience.

During the thirteenth century, Dōgen Kigen (1200–1253), another pilgrim to China in search of the truth, returned to Japan to reside at Eisai's temple, Kennin-ji, only to become dissatisfied with the hybrid version of Zen that he found there. Dōgen had attained enlightenment under the guidance of a master from the Caodong school. He intended to offer a purified Zen free of Tendai and Shingon Buddhist esoteric/magical features. After settling at the Eihei-ji temple, Dōgen established the Sōtō school. Just before he died, Dōgen wrote his multi-volume classic, the *Shōbōgenzō* (*The Treasury of the True Dharma Eye*) in which he expounded on his non-dualistic philosophy written from the perspective of an enlightened master. From his non-dualistic position, he asserted that the Buddha-nature was equivalent to all existence, including plants, animals, and the inanimate world.

Dōgen directed his non-dualistic way of thinking to the method of seated meditation, which for him was superior to language meditation provided by *kōans* of the Rinzai sect of Zen. He asserted that seated meditation (*zazen*) was the primordial form of Buddhist spiritual life. He gave his interpretation of this practice an odd twist when he claimed that meditation is not a technique by which one comes to realization and thus not the cause of *satori* (enlightenment) because seated meditation was already realization, even when one first begins to sit. Seated meditation is the non-thinking mode of consciousness, a thinking of the unthinkable. The non-thinking mode of consciousness stands opposed to a way of thinking that weights ideas or a not-thinking mode that negates thinking. Non-thinking is a more fundamental mode of consciousness that is not intentional, meaning that it is free of affirming or denying and simply accepts the presence of ideas and things by just letting them be their pure presence as they are without adding anything to them. Non-thinking is equivalent to emptiness, rendering it objectless, goalless, formless, and purposeless.

What Dōgen means is probably best illustrated by a narrative case from the *Mumonkan* collection of *kōans*: It is like a man up a tree who hangs from a branch by his mouth; his hands cannot grasp a bough, his feet cannot touch the tree. Another man walks under the tree and asks him the meaning of Bodhidharma's coming from the West. If he does not answer, he does not meet the questioner's need. If he answers, he will lose his life. At such a time, how should he answer? Dōgen takes this case and analyzes it by stating that the man hanging from the tree is not simply suspended in space but is rather suspended in emptiness just as the questioner, tree, and question itself are hanging in emptiness. In a sense, the answer given by the man suspended from the tree is not really different from the question. Nonetheless, the non-thinking mode of consciousness, a realization seeing that is non-dual, allows one to gain insight into a complex situation and to find a pragmatic solution.

In another case from the *Mumonkan*, the Zen master Sekiso asks the following question: From the top of a pole one hundred feet high, how do you step forward? The answer is that one must step forward from the top of the pole and manifest one's whole body in the ten directions. Dōgen uses this anecdote to illustrate that non-thinking involves a leap, a step beyond the top of a hundred foot pole. For Dōgen, this means to cast away both body and mind, which is thinking the unthinkable. This does not mean that the body is a hindrance to enlightenment; it is rather a vehicle through which enlightenment is realized. When Dōgen refers to the casting away of body and mind, he means that the ego completely disappears from consciousness. Therefore, the leap from the top of the hundred foot high pole is not a negative action; it means not to cling to any preconceived or personal views. By casting away body and mind, a person suspends all relative thinking and worldly opinions. This path leads to an experiential verification of the already existing enlightenment within oneself and a cultivation (practice) that authenticates what is present. When a meditator casts off body and mind, her original face will be manifest. In other words, the enlightenment is the shining forth of Buddha-nature.

As Buddhism developed in Japan, it did not attempt to replace or subvert Shinto and the folk tradition. In fact, their shrines and divine beings were evident in each other's temples, Buddhist temples were located near Shinto shrines and temple complexes, and *kami* and bodhisattvas of the Buddhist tradition were sometimes synthesized into individual religious figures. This type of close co-existence and unity is evident with Sōtō monasteries adopting their own local *kami* to protect them. Zen monks ordained these *kami* and chanted scriptures to them, although the *kami* lacked the Buddhist precepts necessary for enlightenment. This endearing type of relationship gave birth to narratives concerning monks and spirits. The monk Rogaku lived, for example, in poverty for many years before a stranger approached him one night requesting to be ordained. The stranger confessed to having been reborn into a realm of reptiles and asked the monk to have compassion for him. After the monk administered the basic precepts, the reptile spirit instantly attained liberation. Wishing to thank the monk, the former reptile lead him into a valley and told him to build a temple there. As he looked downward, Rogaku saw the body of a large white snake. When the villagers heard of the departure of the snake spirit, they eagerly came to help the monk build his temple. This is a single example of many similar stories.

Zen and Japanese Culture

Zen has had an enormous influence on Japanese culture once it got established as part of the cultural fabric. This cultural influence is evident in a variety of artistic ways, which include ink brush painting, calligraphy, poetry, the tea ceremony, Nō theater, and the martial arts of swordsmanship and archery. These various artistic ways are to be performed by the artist, which parallels the religious path and involves a progression of a mastery of rules and techniques to the awakening experience. Therefore, art can be used as a way to attain enlightenment. When an artist reaches a point of no-mind, he possesses free artistic creativity in both his life and art. Zen-influenced art is formless, spontaneous, trackless, and immediate emptiness. It is ideally without intention and flows immediately and formlessly from a mind in touch with emptiness. This type of art does not point to something else; it points rather to itself in the here and now and immediately enables an artist to express reality. In summary, the artistic way is a path for creating an enlightenment experience in the midst of phenomenal existence.

From an aesthetic perspective, this art prefers irregularity over uniformity, simplicity over complexity, perishability over permanence, and suggestion over certainty. Its basic aesthetic categories favor sadness mixed with melancholy for the transient nature of things, what is old, faded, or lonely, the simple and unpretentious beauty of great depth, and the profound, remote, and mysterious. These aesthetic aspects of Zen that influenced artistic expression are evident in the various artistic ways.

Zen gardens are considered a landscape painting executed in natural materials such as stones, water, sand, trees, and plants arranged in an angular and asymmetrical style. Actual rock gardens are called a dry landscape, which is intended for meditation, forming a visual *kōan* for the seated meditator. In contrast, ink landscape paintings seek to penetrate beyond the senses and rational mind to nature's essence. The artist's technique must flow thoughtlessly and without effort, using very absorbent rice paper and black ink because they are more expressive, giving a viewer an illusion of color, and tricking a viewer into supplying her own colors.

The Nō theater productions stress what the actor does not do, which suggests an interval between two or more spatial or temporal things. A room is, for example, a space between the walls, a gap, or opening. The slow motion movement of the main actor attempts to create space on the stage, a liminal place where nothing is done but is where the most interest is located. This observation also applies to ink landscape paintings in which the unpainted part is what commands the greatest interest. The Nō actor attempts to rise to a selfless level of art to a state of no-mind, which is a state of consciousness in which the dichotomy between actor and audience is overcome. There is a Zen influence on the architecture of the theater because the stage is a platform of polished wood that is undecorated and covered by a roof resembling that of a temple. With its disregard for space and time and use of obscure language and abstract gesturing, Nō performances represent a non-representational kind of theater. In a typical play, plot is deliberately suppressed, and an emotional experience or state of mind (e.g., hatred, love, longing, fear, grief, or happiness) is presented by being described. The theme of the play rarely grows or gets resolved during the performance. By utilizing masks, dances, poetry, and slow-motion movements, a play is subtle, reserved, and suggestive. The stillness that is created represents a perfect balance of opposing forces.

The art of poetry is another artistic path, which is insightfully expressed by Bashō (1644–1694), a student of a Rinzai master, who had an enlightenment experience when he was 40 years old. He was an itinerant composer and wrote poems about a muddy melon, a flower, a frog jumping into a pond, or a sunrise. Bashō's *haiku* poetry expressed that the eternal existed within the mundane. A typical *haiku* poem consisted of just seventeen syllables in Japanese and often contained a reference to the time of the year, referring to an eternal element and an ephemeral element represented by something like a flower, chirps of insects, songs of birds, or scents of blossoms. Bashō rarely expresses his own sensations and feelings, but he presents and gives a reader the name of things. This is a selfless poetry that suggests the interpenetration of all things, freedom, humor, and simplicity. A good example of his poetry is the following: "Now, as soon as eyes / Of the hawk, too, darken / Quail chirp." This poem suggests that nighttime is coming, and the quail begins to chirp because the hawk can no longer see its prey. The poem expresses Bashō's sensitivity to the interplay of life in nature, where a quail prudently hides during the day because it does not want to be a meal for the hawk, and just as the hawk must prey on a defenseless bird, the quail preys on equally vulnerable insects. The poem also suggests a universe that changes, as exemplified by light and then darkness; it is at the edge of the transition from day to night that we find experience.

Included in the artistic ways to liberation are the martial arts of swordsmanship and archery. The aspirant learns and masters the techniques of the discipline that merge a person with the sword into a harmonious unity that can react instantaneously and instinctively, rather than thinking about his actions. The mastery of the art of archery is different from swordsmanship in the sense that the archer strives to become detached from the weapon because the archer must concentrate completely on the target, implying that the archer must forget technique, bow, and arrow and draw and not strive for accuracy. This is achieved by intuitively applying correct form or, more precisely, non-form. When the string of the bow is pulled and then released, the arrow flies toward its target without any deliberation by the archer. It is clear that these various artistic ways are integrated with the religious path to form a harmonious unity.

Japanese Folk Religion

It is not usual to find Buddhism encountering the folk religious tradition in narrative form. According to a hagiographical tale, the Zen Buddhist master

Ikkyū was on a ferry on his way to the city of Sakai when he was questioned by a *yamabushi* (a member of a magico-religious fraternity of mountain ascetics and a leading character in the folk religion of Japan) about the Zen monk's ability to perform miracles. Acknowledging that Zen Buddhism could attest to having performed many miracles, Ikkyū asked the ascetic what kind of miracle he had in mind. Invoking deities, the ascetic made Fudō, a fierce protector of Buddhism, appear on the boat surrounded by a halo of dancing flames, to the utter astonishment of the other passengers. With a ferocious face, the ascetic ordered everyone to offer Fudō a prayer, a command that made the passengers uneasy except for a completely unruffled Ikkyū. The fearsome mountain ascetic challenged Ikkyū to deal with his miracle, to which the monk retorted that he would produce a miracle from his own body to issue forth and extinguish the flames of Fudō. Thereupon, Ikkyū lifted his robes and began to urinate all over the flames, counteracting the ascetic's magic until the image of Fudō had melted away. At the conclusion to this astonishing display of magic and counter-magic, the other passengers bowed to the Buddhist master and acknowledged his victory over the mountain ascetic.

Although this humorous encounter depicts a victory for the Buddhist monk, the *yamabushi* represented in the narrative was a member of the Shugendo movement, a syncretistic phenomenon combining folk, Shinto, and Buddhist elements located in the mountains, where these ascetics could practice their lifestyle without being disturbed. The intention of ascetic practice was to gain superhuman powers prior to descending from their mountain retreats and ministering to the local populace. In addition to ascetic practice, the Shugendo movement was connected to pilgrimages to sacred places and mountains, where religious festivals would be observed.

In addition to mountain ascetics, Japanese folk religion also reveres another religious specialist playing the role of the shaman, who is often a woman. It is the shaman's duty to minister in a personal way with those in need of help. In order to be a successful shaman, it is necessary to train with a previous shaman, along with an ability to enter into a trance state and communicate with the dead. The role of shaman is sometimes filled by blind women. The shaman operates by making an offering to her guardian spirit, reciting a liturgy, entering into a trance condition, making contact with a spirit, and allowing the voice of the spirit to communicate through her mouth to her client, who typically wants to learn what would please the departed spirit.

Similar to folk religion in other religious traditions, it represents an amalgam of old superstitions, magico-religious rites, and customs of common people and contains elements borrowed from Shinto, Buddhism, Confucianism, and Daoism. Folk religion is devoid of doctrines or organization. Its adherents neither seek to win converts nor to propagate faith. It is transmitted by long-established customs among people united by community and kinship ties. Folk religion provides a framework for the development of the major paths of Shinto and Buddhism, which have accommodated their ways to and gained acceptance from those practicing the folk religion. Folk practice includes, for example, practices such as divination, spirit possession, and shamanistic healing. The worship of household and village deities represents an outcome from the interaction between indigenous folk and Shinto elements. Simultaneously, the practice of Buddhist chanting is, for example, also embraced by folk religion.

Japanese folk religion enables ordinary people an opportunity to be intimately related with and protected by *kami* by means of simple practices. Amulets are useful for protection and specific purposes, such as success, good health, business success, or childbirth. It is common for the shrine, identity of the *kami*, and desired benefit to be written on a small piece of white paper tied to a string. It is also possible for a person to write a request on a small wooden plaque, which is then hung from a special rack at the shrine. An alternative to this practice is to hang a plaque on a tree branch or a string attached to two poles. These types of practices suggest a personal relationship to a *kami* and a social solidarity that is recognized by relationships that bind people to *kami* and others within a community. In Japanese culture, this suggests that a person is intrinsically communal even when acting as an individual.

If one looks at ancient evidence of folk religion, there is proof of the existence of phallic worship. In some locations, a large wooden phallus is carried in procession from the male shrine to a female shrine and repeated in the opposite direction as people rejoice. A rural shrine might have, instead, two large ropes of opposite genders. These types of practice signify features that appeal to an agrarian culture with concerns about fertility. There are also superstitions concerning possession by fox or dog spirits. Another form of superstition relates to one's year of birth, because during the year of the elder horse, for example, a woman born in that year will be more powerful than her husband, causing him to die young.

Folk rites are primarily concerned with ancestral festivals and agricultural rites. The Flower Festival in April finds people climbing to the top of a nearby hill or mountain, where they eat and drink together and gather wildflowers before they return home. It was originally believed that the mountain *kami* followed the flowers back to the homes of the participants. This celebration reflects human harmony with nature. In addition to rites of passage typical of many cultures, folk religion observes rites of exorcism and purification. An example of a ritual of purification is the Doll Festival, held in March, which features girls and a tiered display of customized dolls, symbolizing nobles and ladies of the ancient imperial court. The families of the girls celebrate their daughters' growth and maturity by drinking a toast of *sake*.

Japanese folk religion embodies two systems of belief: the guardian shrine system (*uji-gami*) and the human-god system (*hito-gami*). The former system is based on the family or clan and is characterized by particularism and exclusion of other families. The primary function is to integrate all family members—living or dead. It operates to maintain and integrate the political and economic autonomy of the family. The system works by establishing a contractual relationship between the *uji-gami* and its clan. The power of the *uji-gami* is directly evident by the political, economic, social, and cultural circumstances of the family members to which it is limited. In comparison, the *hito-gami* system is grounded on a close relationship with a particular *kami* and a religious specialist such as a shaman. Both of these figures demonstrate strong individuality, creating a kind of super family because they play the dual roles of disintegration and reintegration. This system has an overt character in contrast to the other system, which implies that it is inclusive rather than exclusive. This means that followers are not restricted to a fixed social family. Instead of biological generation or geography, the *hito-gami* system is based on a relationship between a *kami* and a particular person. In the final analysis, the folk religious tradition is intertwined with the major religious traditions of Japan, which are also interrelated with each other, and it becomes difficult to draw clear differentiations between the various complementary religions.

Japanese folk religion, Buddhism, and Shintoism, with which folk tradition is intertwined, exhibit many local and regional differences, resulting in a remarkable diversity. But this widespread diversity of religious practice also suggests a homogeneity. Large national shrines exist and are destinations for those going on pilgrimage, but the vast majority of shrines are local or regional. Instead of regretting this regionalism, folk religion celebrates it. The local and regional nature of folk religion is centered in the family, village, and occupation of the populace in an informal way in contrast to the formal organization of national religions such as Shinto and Buddhism. Folk religion is related to the yearly calendar, which demonstrates a concern with important agricultural dates and memorial rites for those departed. During the New Year observance, homes are consecrated by cleansing them, a pine branch is hung on the gate of a home or a tree is erected in the yard, and cooked rice is placed at the entrance of a home. These kinds of practices and observances give folk religion a dynamic quality and provide people with direct access to spiritual resources to prevent or respond to problems associated with daily life.

Women and Japanese Culture

The *Nihon ryōiki*, a ninth-century collection of didactic stories, contains many tales in which women appear in diverse roles. According to one narrative, a village woman lived as a concubine, a social position inferior to that of a wife, but she was a pious person, had a pure heart, attained enlightenment, and kept a clean house. Being poor, she had little money to feed her seven children and was forced by her economic situation to weave vines to clothe them. Her exceptional religious status achieved under very difficult circumstances was noticed by gods and spirits, and they transported her to heaven for her dedication to the religious life and motherhood despite her lowly status.

In contrast to this virtuous woman, other narratives recount stories about women who are evil because of their lascivious lifestyle or neglect of social virtues necessary for a harmonious society. The latter problem is illustrated by a narrative of a daughter who does not practice filial piety for her parents. The daughter dies without seeing her parents again, a punishment for her neglect of an important family duty. Another tale relates a woman being punished for her prior licentious life and not caring for her children. As a punishment, she is reborn in hell with a very painful breast illness. A Buddhist master helps her by finding her neglected son, who atones for his mother's sin by reciting scriptures and making images, and she is pardoned. In such stories, the law of karma is used to support cultural values and encourages practicing meritorious Buddhist customs.

Despite the prevailing and dominant patriarchal cultural in which Japanese women lived, they were not always depicted as evil, because males were also often portrayed as unethical or unreasonable. The *Nihon ryōiki* contains a tale about a pious woman who goes to a local temple to perform a rite of repentance before a statue of the Eleven-Headed Kannon. Unable to find his wife on returning home, her husband proceeds to the temple, where he falsely accuses a priest of seducing his wife. The husband takes his wife home and sexually violates her. But the husband is punished when an ant bites his penis, killing him, which again demonstrates the working of the law of karma for the husband's unethical behavior toward his wife and the priest. In another episode, a blind widow with a daughter attributes the loss of her eyesight to evil deeds in a prior life. She prays to the Healing Buddha to restore her eyes so that she could properly care for her daughter. Two days later, her daughter sees a sap like that from a peach tree oozing from the image. After the mother eats the sweet sap, her sight is restored. These types of tales suggest that Buddhism did not simply reject women, even though some of its literature is misogynist.

In addition to the Buddhist discourse about female inferiority, there is a social discourse that indicates that women were a commodity used to perpetuate the family lineage, making a woman's body valuable because of its procreative potential. Another type of discourse represents a pervasive misogyny associated with notions of fear, evil, and impurity. This prevalent negative attitude toward women is grounded in the Buddhist tradition that holds that women experience five obstructions (e.g., coveting the world, hatred and desire to injure, stupidity and slothfulness, excitement and misdeeds, and doubt) and cannot achieve salvation in a female body, implying that a woman had to be reborn a man in order to achieve liberation. This masculine attitude and the injunction that women had to be instructed by men did not constrain women, who were not simply passive actors of patriarchal Buddhist teachings, because there is evidence that they resisted the prevailing teachings. If monks were teaching about the inferior status of women, why would females freely chose to become nuns?

Some females looked for alternative lifestyles to the traditional role of motherhood. Those choosing to become nuns gave themselves a measure of autonomy and freedom from traditional social obligations and domestic roles. Prior to becoming nuns, some women had shamanistic abilities, which some monks interpreted as a different type of skillful means employed to save people. Female religious roles were inextricably connected to a common social belief in the spiritual power of women, a power associated with a woman's reproductive ability.

Instead of becoming nuns, other vocational choices open to women were assuming the role of a shaman, medium (*miko*), courtesan, or singing nun. Some *miko* led an itinerant lifestyle, combining religious roles with entertaining and/or prostitution. Traveling female puppeteers also combined entertainment with sexual activity. In addition, there were women who danced to their own poetry and dressed in male attire. It is likely that these wandering females spread legends about sexually active feminine figures such as Izumi Shikibu, sufferer of a venereal disease. While she was married, she had an affair with a prince and his younger brother. She also had a second husband, a provincial governor, during a period in which she had an incestuous relationship with Dōmyō, a Buddhist priest, who was a child of her affair with a courtier. She later learned that the priest was her son.

These kinds of women choosing an alternative lifestyle and traditional mothers were considered powerful and dangerous. The power of women was traditionally traced to their procreative capabilities, but the danger associated with them originated with menstruation, which made women impure for part of each month. There is, however, evidence that women viewed menstrual blood differently than males, because they thought it was purifying and sacred for its apotropaic power. Because of menstruation and its ability to pollute an area, women were forbidden to enter into, reside in, or perform religious acts within the confines of a temple, shrine, or ritual site or to recite sacred mantras. This danger can extend to the next life, as illustrated by a tale of a monk who visits hell and encounters a hungry ghost who tries to devour him, but the monk is saved by Jizō, a popular Buddhist bodhisattva, who reveals to the monk that the ghost is his former mother.

During the medieval period in Japan, there were two types of convents: a building for girls cloistered from childhood from good families and convents for widowed nuns who chose to become nuns later in life because it was difficult for widows to remarry. But even widow nuns were socially pressured to exhibit fidelity and chastity and to pray for the souls of their deceased husbands, suggesting a continuation of their subservient social status to males. In fact, some women opted to become nuns because it was an easier way to get a divorce. It is, however, possible to discover Japanese rhetoric of equality within Tantra and Zen. Tantra espouses a more positive view of the feminine because it assists one to attain liberation, whereas Zen denies any gender difference because everything is empty. Therefore, a woman can achieve enlightenment and need not be reborn a man.

In more recent times, a woman suffering from guilt related to the loss of an infant by abortion (traditionally considered murder because of the conviction that life begins at conception), a stillborn fetus, or miscarriage can partake in memorial rituals called *mizuko kuyō* (nourishing a water child). This memorial service includes offerings of light, food, flowers, incense, and prayers to Jizō. A bereaved couple buys a sculpted stone statue about two feet high that resembles a Buddhist monk, or more accurately a child-monk. These statues are left within the temple and given a posthumous name, which is inscribed on a mortuary tablet to be taken home or left at the temple.

Christianity and the Japanese State

Christianity was introduced into Japan by Roman Catholic missionaries in 1549 led by Saint Francis Xavier, a famous Portuguese member of the Jesuit order. Christianity evoked confusion and incomprehension among the populace and was labeled a foreign religion. Therefore, the Catholic missionaries did not succeed in converting many Japanese to their religion. Along with their religion, the Portuguese also brought European goods for trade. In 1587, the powerful leader Hideyoshi ordered the expulsion of the missionaries and their foreign religion because he wanted to consolidate power within a central authority that he could control and did not need any competition for Japanese loyalties. In response to this type of edict, Christian converts went underground and survived as a small, secret cult. Later Japanese rulers continued the persecution of Christians to the extent of producing martyrs. In 1639, Portuguese ships were prohibited from visiting Japan as the country entered a period of isolation from foreign influence.

During the Tokugawa period (1600–1867), every Japanese family was ordered to belong to a Buddhist temple, which was a further attempt to eradicate Christianity and control the population. Contrary to what one might think, this action was not inspired by Buddhism but was rather promoted by Neo-Confucianism, which was considered an excellent philosophy by which to run a government because it stressed stability and order. In fact, the state educational system strongly reflected this philosophy originating in China. Even though this system might seem to favor Buddhism, it ironically stimulated a restoration of Shinto.

The movement away from feudal Japan was represented by the Meiji Restoration (1868–1912), marking the abolition of shogun rule and the elevation of the emperor as head of the central government, along with a constitution, elected officials, and national armed forces. The capital was moved from Tokugawa to Tokyo. The prior state support of Buddhism was now replaced by patronage to Shinto and the encouragement of a vigorous nationalistic spirit focused on the cult of the emperor's divinity. Buddhism got eclipsed by Shinto because it was perceived to be too closely identified with the prior Tokugawa regime. The Meiji state ordered the separation of Buddhism and Shinto, as evident by the removal of Buddhist statues from Shinto shrines, an action that also called for the purification of Shinto shrines. Orders were also made for all citizens to register at a local Shinto shrine, which came to articulate a new and ominous nationalistic militarism that would culminate with a disastrous defeat and its accompanying public disillusionment after World War II.

During the post WWII period, the majority of Japanese people lost their attraction for Shinto, which they blamed for the war's destruction of the nation. Meanwhile, Shinto and Buddhist temples lost their landholdings, which undermined an important source of income. With the instigation of freedom of religion in a new constitution and disavowal of the emperor's divinity, the door was opened for the development of new religions, which were not associated with the war or its aftermath, were not stuck in the past, and offered hope for a better future. This scenario created competition for new adherents.

Advent of New Religions

In 1838, Miki Nakayama (1798–1887) had a very ill son and called a popular exorcist to hopefully provide a cure. It was common for this exorcist to use a female medium, who went into a trance to identify the malevolent spirit that needed to be exorcised. But for this healing ritual, the medium was not available, and Miki took her place as the medium. After going into a trance state, Miki received a divine revelation, resulting in a *kami's* permanent possession of her; the name of the *kami* was Terri Ō-no Mikoto (Religion of Heavenly Truth). The term *terri* meant "heavenly wisdom." Using Miki as its medium, the *kami* demanded that she become its instrument in order to spread its message for as long as she lived. This scenario essentially transformed Miki into a living, embodied *kami* and a founder of a new religion, which motivated her to create her own rites and scriptures. Even though this new cult was located in the countryside, its message was quickly spread, and people with illnesses and personal problems gravitated toward her for relief. This new religion became known as Tenrikyo, a way of religion with its roots deeply in the folk Shinto religious tradition.

Other new religions originated in the cities of Japan, and some of them found inspiration and authority in the *Lotus Sūtra*. An excellent example of such a movement was Soka Gakkai (Value Creation Society), founded by Makiguichi Tsunesaburol (1871–1944), a former teacher who envisioned a triad of beauty, benefit, and goodness within his new theory of value. Although values are subjective, relative, and can be created, the truth must be sought regardless of the fact that it is objective and absolute. He identified absolute truth with the *Lotus Sūtra*, the teachings of the Buddhist prophet Nichiren, and ardent faith, which forms the foundation for the creation of values necessary for a happy life. In addition to emphasizing the creation of values and reforming of society, the movement practiced morning and evening chanting, which enabled members to experience the Buddha's presence. The founder died in prison, but the movement's other leader, Toda, was released from prison in 1945 and increased its membership by instituting an appeal to Japanese youth to convert others, using an aggressive method called "breaking and subduing." In the mid-1960s, the religion became involved in national politics with its Clean Government Party and has spread to 114 countries worldwide.

Another movement that was inspired by the *Lotus Sūtra* was a lay organization founded by Kotani Kumi and his sister-in-law, Kubo Kakutarō, called the Reiyūkai Kyōdan, which practiced faith-healing and ancestor worship. A lay bodhisattva in the text served as a model for imitation. Those revering and reciting the text were promised mundane happiness. Splitting from the Reiyūkai Kyōdan, another lay organization was the Risshō Kōsekai (Society for Success in Establishing the Right), which was established by Niwano Nikkyō and Myōkō Naganuma. They regarded the *Lotus Sūtra* as the final and most perfect message of the Buddha. These founders stressed the importance of inter-religious dialogue, international peace, and nuclear disarmament. This faith-oriented movement also emphasized the bodhisattva ideal of leading a moral life, cultivating wisdom, postponing Nirvana, and leading a life of service to others. These ideals are based in the meditative practice of continually chanting the name of the *Lotus Sūtra*.

A new Japanese religion that became infamous was Aum Shinrikyō (Supreme Truth Movement) because its leader, Asahara Shoko, taught about the imminent end of the world and the role of violence. Releasing sarin gas in the Tokyo subway system, the members of the movement were able to injure and kill many passengers in 1995. This heinous act, along with other murders and kidnappings, was a prelude to the coming end of time that was predicted to arrive in 1997. In the aftermath of the subway attack, the cult leader and some members were arrested, convicted, and sentenced to death. The movement insisted on extreme forms of asceticism for new recruits, worship of the goddess Amaterasu, and stressed loyalty to the imperial family, participation in rituals, flower meditation, and the traditional tea ceremony. At least four other groups have broken away from this radical movement, although they do not teach the sudden end of the world.

Religious Experience

For an adherent of Shinto, religious experience springs from a feeling of awe inspired when encountering the mystery and wonder of the natural world and the *kami* that animate it. Not only is the individual struck by the mystery, but one is also motivated to respond to the experience with an exclamatory reaction, an "ah" moment. In order to grasp how *kami* and oneself are part of a common identity, one must be truthful, genuine, and sincere (*makoto*). Otherwise, without being who she truly is, it is impossible to understand how a person can reflect *kami*, and how a person can recognize that she and the *kami* are part of each other.

External objects stimulate a person's response after being processed by his senses within his heart and mind (*kokoro*). This experience is not simply a mental or feeling event but also includes somatic and physical aspects. Heart and mind can be conceptualized as a response that happens within the intersection between the world and a person. The responsive aspect of the heart and mind calls attention to the inter-dependence between the world and individual. This suggests that the heart/mind is not a blind emotion; it is rather an affective cognition, being both objective and subjective, which, in turn, implies that physical existence is united with spiritual existence. By having this type of experience, one realizes that there is a spiritual power that is infused with the material aspect of the world that preserves the integrity of both the spiritual and material. Moreover, this type of religious experience is a celebration and embrace of life rather than a fleeing or renouncing of life beyond the confines of the walls of a monastery. The ideal Shinto religious experience is neither a faith in some deity nor a creed to which an adherent must hold, whereas Pure Land Buddhism is more about faith and the grace of a savior figure, as discussed in the previous chapter.

The Zen Buddhist tradition recognizes the *satori* (enlightenment) experience as the goal of a person's quest. The Rinzai school tends to stress the suddenness of enlightenment. Hakuin is an excellent seventeenth century representative of the Rinzai school who provides readers with an account of his experience as a 24-year-old monk. While on his path to enlightenment, Hakuin recounts that he could not sleep and forgot to eat, and a great doubt manifested itself to him. He imagined being stuck on a giant sheet of ice and unable to move. He thought that he was crazy, with only the *kōan* remaining as he floated through the air, a condition lasting for several days. Finally, he heard the sound of the temple bell, which caused the ice to break. He was without self or bell, a pure experience of non-thinking that rendered him just the experience of hearing the sound of the bell within a pure presence.

In this state of pure presence, Hakuin could hear the sound of a single hand clapping, a famous *kōan* that he invented, because he was in a place where reason was exhausted, words were inadequate and thus terminated, any conceptualizations were blocked, the realm of illusion was shattered, and the cycle of birth and death was overturned. When the sound of a single hand clapping enters one's ear, what is it like? In an uncharacteristic personal statement for a Zen master, Hakuin states, "All is vast perfection, all is vast emptiness." The monk has cast off his body and mind and is free from them. This enables one to see into one's own nature.

Hakuin's membership in the Rinzai sect of Zen placed a greater emphasis on the use of *kōans* as expedient devices to assist a person to concentrate on a single thing, whereas Dōgen's Sōtō sect placed a greater focus on seated meditation, which involves casting off body and mind, forgetting the self at the moment of the enlightenment experience, and a release and transcendence of normal consciousness. By casting off body and mind, a meditator is not involved in a negative activity, but is rather ridding himself of preconceptions, personal views, and all relative modes of thinking. For Dōgen, enlightenment also involves the disappearance of the ego from consciousness, while the experience is simultaneously a conscious, luminous experience that includes an awareness of being. Once a meditator has achieved enlightenment, he has authenticated his Buddha-nature. Seated meditation is not, however, the cause of enlightenment, because practice (seated meditation) and realization (*satori*) are identical. This non-dualistic enlightenment realization is always present and everywhere, during which the Buddha-nature shines forth, revealing one's original face. Dōgen insists that enlightenment must be continually confirmed in practice because awakening does not happen just once; it must be ever-continuing and ever-renewed.

Aesthetic experience also plays an important role within the overlapping folk, Shinto, and Buddhist traditions in the Japanese tradition. When a person perceives, for example, an object in nature, it is possible for the perceiver to have an emotional response to it. This can be understood by the aesthetic category of *aware*, an emotional response of sadness because one realizes, for instance, that beauty must die. Thus, as a sight or sound fades, the artist becomes cognizant of its passing away. Another aesthetic experience that is intertwined with *aware* is *yūgen*, which suggests something profound, remote, and mysterious. The sense of *yūgen* cannot be captured with one's intellect because it refers to what is unknowable, invisible, sublime, and subconscious. By gaining a glimpse of something mysterious and strange, it is possible for the perceiver to catch a glimpse of something eternal within the world of flux.

Suggestions for Further Reading

Anesaki, Masaharu. *History of Japanese Religion, with Special Reference to the Social and Moral Life of the Nation*. Rutland, VT: Charles E. Tuttle, 1963.

———. *Nichiren, the Buddhist Prophet*. Cambridge: Harvard University Press, 1916.

Bellah, Robert N. *Tokugawa Religion: The Values of Pre-Industrial Japan*. Glencoe, IL: The Free Press, 1957.

Bloom, Alfred. *The Life of Shinran Shonin: The Journey of Self-Acceptance*. Leiden: E. J. Brill, 1968.

Bodiford, William M. *Sōtō Zen in Medieval Japan*. Honolulu: University of Hawaii Press, 1993.

Bowring, Richard. *The Religious Traditions of Japan, 500–1600*. Cambridge: Cambridge University Press, 2005.

Breen, John and Mark Teeuwen. *A New History of Shinto*. Oxford: Wiley-Blackwell, 2010.

Dumoulin, Heinrich. *A History of Zen Buddhism*. Trans. Paul Peachey, New York: Pantheon, 1963.

———. *Zen Buddhism: A History*. Vol. 2. New York: Macmillan, 1990.

Earhart, H. Byron. *Japanese Religion: Unity and Diversity*. Third Edition. Blemont, CA: Wadsworth Publishing, 1982.

Eliot, Charles. *Japanese Buddhism*. New York: Barnes and Noble, 1959.

Kasulis, Thomas P. *Shinto: The Way Home*. Honolulu: University of Hawaii Press, 2004.

———. *Zen Action/Zen Person*. Honolulu: University of Hawaii Press, 1981.

Kitagawa, Joseph. "The Buddhist Transformation in Japan." *History of Religions* 4, 2 (Winter 1965): 319–336.

———. *On Understanding Japanese Religion*. Princeton: Princeton University Press, 1987.

———. *Religion in Japanese History*. New York: Columbia University Press, 1966.

Sansom, George Bailey. *A History of Japan*. 3 vols. Stanford Studies in the Civilizations of Eastern Asia. Stanford: Stanford University Press, 1958–1963.

———. *Japan: A Short Cultural History*. New York: Appleton-Century-Crofts, 1962.

Saunders, Ernest Dale. *Buddhism in Japan: With an Outline of Its Origins in India*. Philadelphia: University of Pennsylvania Press, 1964.

Swanson, Paul L. and Clark Chilson. Eds. *Nanzan Guide to Japanese Religions*. Honolulu: University of Hawaii Press, 2006.

11 Zoroastrianism

Emigrating from Eastern Europe during the third millennium BCE, Indo-European tribes reached Central Asia, from where they continued south, reaching the Iranian plateau around the second millennium. Some tribes conquered northern India and settled there, while other tribes continued into Iran, where the Medes settled in the northwest, Persians settled in the southwest, and Scythians continued to lead a nomadic lifestyle. At some point, the Indo-European tribes split from those that would become the Indo-Iranian tribes. The original unity of both groups is suggested by some similar linguistic terminology and their penchant for calling themselves Aryans (noble, pure, and lighter skin colored). The indigenous natives were deemed barbarians because they were unable to speak correctly and were darker skin colored and were considered demonic because they worshipped false gods. The original inhabitants of the conquered lands were gradually assimilated into the alien cultures by means of adopting a new religion. The first description of Iranian religion was given by Herodotus, a great Greek historian of the fifth century BCE, when he observed that Persians did not erect statues of their deities, did not build temples, performed sacrifices associated with fire in the open, and exposed dead bodies in order to dispose of them rather than burying or cremating them.

During the second millennium BCE, Indo-Iranians adhered to an ethnic religion, a tradition reformed by Zarathustra, a priest, prophet, and reformer stressing the worship of a divine being called Ahura Mazdā. Strictly speaking, Zarathustra lived and operated within a pre-existent religious tradition and thus did not establish a new religion, although he did introduce some new ideas. Depending on what text is examined, scholars have arrived at several approximate dates for the prophet: One is 630 BCE, because he lived 300 years before the Greek general Alexander the Great overthrew the Iranian throne in 330 BCE. The *Bundahishen*, a ninth century text, gives 588 as his date of birth, whereas another text, the *Denkard*, sets his date of birth at 618 or 628 BCE. Another scholar appoints a time period of 1700–1500 BCE for his life and claims that he lived prior to the Indo-Iranians conquering the area, around 1200 BCE. During the Sasanian period (226–641 CE) of Iranian history, the name Zarathustra was changed to Zoroaster after contact with Greek culture around the fifth century BCE, which helps to explain the name of the religion at the present time. In addition, this same historical period witnessed the name of Ahura Mazdā being changed to Ohrmazd and his arch rival Angra Mainyu becoming Ahriman.

The earliest references pertaining to Zarathustra outside of Iran were made by the Greek writer Xanthos of Lydia (mid-fifth century BCE), who was later quoted by Diogenes Laertius in his work *Lives of the Philosophers*. In a discussion about wondrous happenings associated with religious prophets, Zarathustra is mentioned in the Greek work *Philippika* as well as in other works, such as Pliny the Elder's *Natural History*, Porphyry's *Life of Pythagoras*, Clement of Alexandra's *Stromata*, and Apuleius' *Florida*. These types of works referred to Zarathustra as a teacher of philosophy, astrology, alchemy, and magic.

These early portraits of Zarathustra were eclipsed by a European eighteenth-century view that depicted him as an Eastern alternative to the perceived rigidity of the Western tradition. It was later in the century when Mozart's protagonist Sarastro appears as a philosopher, with features shared with Zarathustra in the "Magic Flute" of the European musical composer. European Freemasons used Zoroastrian symbolism to promote their movement. While in Paris, Benjamin Franklin (1706–1790) introduced the French philosopher Voltaire (1694–1778) to Zarathustra and the Masonic Lodge in the city. Franklin also wrote favorably about Zarathustra on January 13, 1772, to the president of Yale University and recommended that the university purchase the writings of the prophet, which had been translated by the French scholar Anquétil Duperon. Zarathustra was also mentioned by German and English Romantic poets in their works. And Friedrich Nietzsche (1844–1900) portrayed the prophet as an example of the German thinker's superman. In his work *Ecce Homo*, Nietzsche depicts Zarathustra as a prophetic figure who represented the first person to struggle against evil and transform morality into a metaphysical force.

The Traditional Narrative of Zarathustra

In any event, Zarathustra's birth was depicted to have occurred at both the midpoint of world history and at the center of the world. According to the *Denkard*, a historically later Pahlavi text, Zarathustra ("he who can manage camels") was created by Ahura Mazdā and sent to his earthly mother by way of the sun, moon, stars, and home fire. Zarathustra's pregnant mother was attacked by demons in the form of plagues, and demons deluded the minds of villagers, who accused the pregnant woman of sorcery. Prior to her becoming pregnant, the desperate demons attempted to frighten the parents into not having sexual relations. Nonetheless, this demonic activity was unsuccessful, and Zarathustra's pre-existent soul was miraculously transmitted to his parents, whose home was surrounded in light. He was born into the Spitāma clan ("of the brilliant attack"), breeders of horses, while his father was named Pouruśaspa ("of the spotted horse") and his mother, Dughdōvā ("milkmaid"). After his mother received his sacred, igneous, luminous, and spermatic fluid (*xvarenah*), she was enveloped by light, and her home appeared to consist of light. This birth event was not a virgin birth, even though it was certainly an extraordinary event and was told to indicate the special nature of the prophet. Actually, Zarathustra was the middle child of his parents who had two older and two younger sons. When he was born, the first thing that Zarathustra did was laugh because he foresaw the forthcoming of fortune and well-being. Zarathustra's post-birth trials matched his pre-birth challenges, because an evil priest attempted to kill him, but his hands turned backward and withered. Zarathustra also had to repel an attacking wolf and dispel demons from the earth. Around the age of 20, Zarathustra left his parents to lead a wandering lifestyle. At one point of his life, Zarathustra asked God for immortality; God endowed him with wisdom, which he used to see visions of life with and without children and concluded that it is joyful to have children. He became convinced that having children was superior to immortality. In addition, God instructed Zarathustra to marry if he wanted to be admitted into paradise.

At 30 years of age, Zarathustra received a revelation from Ahura Mazdā at the time of the spring festival, on his way to fetch water for the *haoma* ceremony by walking into the middle of the stream. Returning to the bank of the stream in a state of ritual purity, he received a vision of a bright shining Being, who revealed himself as Vohu Manah (Good Intention), a figure who leads the reformer to Ahura Mazdā and five other radiant figures. It was from this heptad that he received his revelation, which also served as a call to serve God, to which Zarathustra adhered. After this revelatory gift, Zarathustra, a poor married priest, did not convince many potential converts about his message. In fact, his lone convert was his cousin, which did not deter him from attacking traditional priests in the name of his deity. The threatening reaction of these old priests motivated Zarathustra to flee the area, but he took refuge with Vishtaspa, a chief of the Fryāna tribe, who was converted to Zarathustra's message and offered the prophet friendship and protection. Neighboring monarchs insisted that Vishtaspa return to the old religious tradition. This disagreement ended when Vishtaspa was victorious on the battlefield and established Zarathustra's teachings over everyone. Zarathustra's attack on the traditional Iranian religion criticized its practice of bloody sacrifices, orgiastic rites, and the immoderate use of *haoma* (literally, "that which is pressed"), a hallucinogenic liquid that apparently stimulated visions.

After the conversion of Vishtaspa, there is little known about the life of Zarathustra. We do know that he married three times, a common custom among Iranian priests. He sired three sons and three daughters with his initial two wives, whereas the third wife was childless. Zarathustra's youngest daughter married Janaspa, who was primary counselor to the king and renowned for his wisdom. Not much else is known about his life until he dies.

The Zoroastrian tradition preserved two traditional narratives pertaining to the death of Zarathustra: He was killed by a rival priest during the performance of his normal duties, or he met his end with others during an attack on a fire sanctuary. In reflective hindsight, accounts of Zarathustra's life are not historical versions of the life of a prophet. These biographical narratives represent a cross between hagiography and local legends of a unique figure. The accounts of his biography do, however, accurately reflect the Zoroastrian conception of the dualistic, cosmic conflict between the forces of good and evil, with the prophet representing a bulwark against the onslaught of evil and the preservation and promotion of the good. The cosmic battle between the dual forces for supremacy on earth is also suggested by the symbolic use of light versus darkness and the role of purity and impurity in Zarathustra's biographical narrative.

Zoroastrian Literature

As is true in many ancient cultures, Zoroastrian literature was preserved orally for hundreds of years before being committed to writing around the sixth/ seventh century CE. A textual timeline divides the literature into the following: Old Avestan (dating from mid- to late-second millennium BCE); Young Avestan (dating early to mid-first millennium BCE); Old Persian (dating to late sixth/fourth centuries BCE); Middle Persian (dating between 300 and 1000 CE); and New Persian (dating 1000 CE to the present). The distinction between the *Old Avesta* and *Young Avesta* relates to the different dialects in which they are written. The Avestas are considered to be sacred texts, but only a quarter of them have survived; they consist mostly of ritual hymns. The Old Avesta texts contain seventeen hymns known as the *Gathas* in six collections, which are attributed to Zarathustra, although he probably had a direct voice in five of the six collections. The *Gathas* are part of a longer text called the *Yasna* (Sacrifice) of seventy-two chapters, which are recited daily. In the *Gathas*, Zarathustra gives some personal information about himself. In these hymns, he shares his joy and anguish, even though these hymns suggest being used in a ritual context. The contents of the *Gathas* embody Zarathustra's gift of the revelation and his response to it. The Old Avesta also contains some prayers and the *Yasna Haptanhaita*, or "the worship of seven chapters."

In contrast to the Old Avesta texts, the Young Avesta texts represent works written by generations of anonymous priestly composers. It includes the *Yashts* (hymns) to deities that are presented as quotations of Zarathustra. Many of the hymns are associated with specific periods of the liturgical calendar and are recited at appropriate times during the year. The later *Yashts* are dated to the Achaemenian period (550–330 BCE). The hymns of the *Yashts* reflect a personal relationship to God and stress the importance of righteousness and significance of the coming last age and its consequences. The Young Avesta literature also includes the *Videvdad* (Law against the Demons), or the *Vendidad* in its Pahlavi linguistic form, a text concerned with ritual impurity, means of avoiding impurity, and ways to rid oneself of impurity. This collection of prose texts about purity and impurity is really about countering the forces of evil associated with impurity. The *Visperad* (for all the Lords) consists of borrowed passages from the *Videvdad* and *Yasna*. A collection of commonly uttered prayers are contained in the *Khordeh Avesta* (Shorter Avesta), whereas the *Sirozah* supplies a list of various deities related to the days of the monthly calendar. The *Hadokht Nask* (sayings) provide vivid descriptions of the soul's fate after death. The final two works are the *Herbadestan* and *Nerangestan*, which focus on priestly concerns and organization.

Zoroastrian Middle Persian texts (also called Pahlavi literature) includes: the *Bundahishn* (Creation), which focuses on creation and its four 3,000-year eras and contains diverse material related to the heavenly court, apocalyptic visions, and pre-Zoroastrian mythical material; *Zand*, which is a commentary on earlier Avestan texts; *Menog-i Khrad*, a book on heavenly wisdom; the *Shayast Ne-Shayast*, a text about ethical/moral injunctions and purity regulations; and the *Arda Viraz Namag*, which relates tales about Viraf's journey to the world of the righteous and evil people in the afterlife. These texts and the earlier Avesta texts were dubbed the "*Zand Avesta*" by nineteenth-century European scholars because they mistakenly conflated "*Avesta*" (basic text) with the term commentary (*Zand*). Another notable text in Middle Persian is the *Denkard*, a work containing historical episodes of the religion. After a long oral transmission and preservation of the texts, the complete twenty-one books of the Avesta were composed in Iran during the Sasanian dynasty (c. 224–651 CE), but large portions of the collection were destroyed during political conflicts. These various texts combine elements of the religion of Ahura Mazdā and the polytheism of the ancient Indo-Iranian religion.

Creation of Good and Evil

According to an early version of the Zoroastrian creation narrative, the gods made the world from formless matter in a series of seven stages. The initial stage of creation was represented by a sky of stone that functioned like the shell of a turtle. The bottom of the shell was filled with water. The third stage witnessed earth resting on the primal waters. During the fourth and fifth stages, an original plant appeared at the center of the earth, and a bull was created. In the sixth stage, humans appeared. Finally, the sun was created, representing the fire above the earth. In fact, fire was a hidden element in the other stages, acting as creation's life-force. With these stages completed, the gods performed a sacrifice by scattering the essence of the plant over the earth, which gave birth to additional plants on the surface of the earth. Then, at the margins of the earth, mountains appeared, and the earth was divided into seven regions by the rains. Living in the central region of the earth, humans were separated from the other six regions by seas and forests. The entire created world was governed by order (*asha*), which established truth and justice among humans.

According to the historically later Pahlavi texts, creation took a duration of 12,000 years. During the initial 3,000 years, the world of thought was created. Over the next 3,000 years, the world of the living was created without opposition. The third creative duration of 3,000 years represented a mixture with the world of the living associated with the good being assaulted by the forces of evil. The final 3,000 years represented a return to the time of origins that was free of evil. But where did good and evil originate? Early in the creative process, good and evil originated from two spirits, which the narrative depicted as sleeping twins. The good spirit (Spenta Mainyu) was the life-giving twin, whereas the evil spirit (*Angra*, which literally means dark or black) gave off a smelly stench.

This creative scenario is viewed in the Zoroastrian tradition as an opposition between order (good) and chaos (evil). The created universe owes its order to Ahura Mazdā's use of the principle of *asha*, a product of the omnipotent deity that he produced from his thought, which is both a principle and a divinity associated with the seven Bounteous Immortals. Everyone can witness its visible form during the day because it lights the sky. The opposing principle represents the cosmic lie (*angra*), which is a cosmic form of deception that deceives humans and gods about the true nature of the cosmos. Chaos continually attempts to subvert Ahura Mazdā's creation. This universal conflict between good/order and evil/chaos represents a battle that has been raging since the very beginning of the created cosmos. And it is a struggle that each member of the Zoroastrian community must fight until the end of time. It is precisely this cosmic dualism that shapes the conceptual world of Zoroastrianism and affects the way that a member acts within the world.

Worldview of Cosmic Oppositions

The Zoroastrian worldview manifests a couple of fundamental cosmic oppositions. There are two dimensions of time: infinite and finite. And there are two dimensions of space: invisible and visible. Space and time are inextricably connected within a space/time continuum that is considered sacred. Infinite time is an eternal duration without beginning or end. What makes infinite time a pure duration is its endurance forever and its complete lack of change.

Infinite time is the source of finite time, which manifests a transient duration. Invisible space is ontologically prior to the visible. Although invisible space cannot be captured by the eyes, it is, however, accessible to the mind's eye. The invisible space and infinite time are *mēnōg* (spiritual), whereas *gētīg* (material) represents visible space and finite time. The *gētīg* represents, then, the material universe of ever-changing particulars. The material aspect of the universe is dependent for its existence, meaning, and order on the invisible or spiritual *mēnōg*. The material is always superior to the spiritual because the spiritual endows the material, creating two states that form a single totality. All finite time and visible space are considered the good creation of god. Therefore, Zoroaster depicts a cosmic dichotomy between the forces of good and the powers of evil, a theme that runs throughout his teaching.

Divine Pantheon

Dating to the reign of Darius I (522–486 BCE), an inscription was left with the name of Ahura Mazdā engraved on it. Another inscription refers to King Artaxerxes II (405–359 BCE) worshiping the gods Ahura Mazdā, Mithra, and the goddess Anāhita. It is also possible to find bas-reliefs that depict Ahura Mazdā, who is generally conceived anthropomorphically as a winged disk that is often crowned with the bust of a bearded figure surrounded by imaginary animals, such as winged lions, bull-men, or scorpion-men. There is also evidence that ancient Iranians worshipped three ethical deities: Ahura Mazdā (Lord of Wisdom), Mithra, and Varuna. The last two mentioned deities are also prominent during the Vedic era in India. They function as protectors of the covenant and oath and bind people to *asha* (order). Mithra had a close connection to warriors, who would invoke him before battle. Mithra is described as never sleeping and possessing a large number of eyes and ears, reflecting his power to know everything. Living on top of Mount Harā at the center of the earth, Mithra frees the earth each dawn of evil by going forth each morning to clear a path for the sun, a symbol of truth and the good.

Because Ahura Mazdā created the other gods, when a person performs an act of worship, it is ultimately directed to the originator of all the gods. Thus Ahura Mazdā can rightly be called the God of gods. Among these other divine beings, there is Airyaman, a god of healing and harmony; Sraosha (literally, "readiness to listen"), a warrior god depicted with a mace who was the first to offer sacrifice and to recite the *Gathas*; the goddess Ashi, who is a constant companion to Airyaman and sends rewards to humans; Rashnu ("the straightener") who serves as a judge in the afterlife and favors everything straight, including human behavior and crafts; Ardwī Sūrā Anāhitā, a goddess identified with the heavenly river; Tishtriya, representing the star Sirius (the dog star), who fights drought and is personified as both the demon Apaosha and the Witch of Bad Seasons; and Werthraghna, a warrior deity, a companion of Mithra, who could appear in any of his ten shapes, such as wind, bull, white horse, rutting camel, or boar. The deity of wind is Wāyu, a god of the between space through whom the souls of the deceased must travel after the demise of their bodies. The sacrificial drink of *haoma*, which is called *soma* in India, is a deity who keeps death away, because it is the liquid of immortality.

Because of its importance to Zoroastrians, Fire (Ātar) is a deity that deserves special attention. With its multiple functions and meanings, Fire is a complex notion in the religion. On one level of meaning, Fire represents *asha* (order, righteousness, truth), which is an attribute of Ahura Mazdā as well as something that he created. There is thus a close connection between Fire and *asha*. Ahura Mazdā is also identified with fire, which is associated with both his essence in the form of light and the principle of righteousness. When Ahura Mazdā appears as fire, as for instance the sun, this is considered an epiphany of wisdom.

When Fire is within its container, it represents the greater fire, the sun, that rises and sets each day according to the operation of *asha* (order), which also regulates the time and seasons of the world. Because of its regal status, Fire deserves the utmost respect from believers. This attitude of respect is reflected by the necessity for a person to never turn her back to it, and it must be protected from pollution and corruption. This is accomplished by purifying oneself before having contact with fire, and a priest must cover his face with a cloth to prevent his breath from polluting the fire. In short, Fire must be kept free of all actual and potential pollution. There are additional rules to be observed with respect to Fire that include not allowing a Fire to die once it has been created. Thus, to deliberately extinguish a Fire is to commit a serious transgression. When a Fire is consecrated, Ahura Mazdā becomes present, representing his divine light, and *asha* (truth) is also rendered present.

Within the ritual context, Fire makes *asha* accessible to the faithful by eating the sacrificial offerings. This scenario suggests that Fire receives the sacrificial offerings and distributes them to the other deities. In the roles of accepter and distributor, Fire maintains harmonious relations between the gods and humans. It also serves as a symbol on the earth of Ahura Mazdā (Wise Lord). Finally, because of its power, it functions to combat evil, personified as Angra Mainyu. These types of characteristics suggest that ritual has an ethical purpose.

Another category of divine beings is the Amesha Spentas (Holy Immortals). The term *spenta* means that which possesses power. They are directly or indirectly considered emanations of Ahura Mazdā and are collectively known as *yazatas* (beings worthy of worship). Most of these benign divinities were worshipped before the arrival of the prophet and are considered interdependent but distinguished by functions. In the Avesta literature, they are arranged in a hierarchical order. They begin with Spenta Mainyu (Holy Spirit), Arta or Asha (Justice, Good Order), Vohu Mainyu (Good Thought, Right Inspiration), Kshatra (Empire), Ameretāt (Immortality, Eternal Life), Armaiti (Devotion, Right-Mindedness), and Haurvatat (Wholeness, Integrity). These figures should not be confused with personal deities because they are more akin to deified values or cosmic forces that function to assist Ahura Mazdā. The initial four are essential for a successful and thriving kingdom.

It is possible to unpack the seven aspects of the Amesha Spentas and their relation to Ahura Mazdā. Spenta Mainyu (Holy Spirit) does not have any independent existence apart from Ahura Mazdā and serves as an augmenting spirit to Ahura Mazdā during the process of creation. It also nurtures divine self-realization, which is directly connected to the creative process. The Holy Spirit enables Ahura Mazdā to disperse himself throughout his creation. Asha (Order) represents the universal law that is directly associated with truth and righteousness and is represented by fire on earth. Vohu Mainyu (Good Thought) is activated by Ahura Mazdā during creation and enables one to recognize the holy nature of God. In the sacrificial cult, it is symbolized by the sacrificed victim. Kshatra (Good Empire) points to the need for prudent authority on earth and avoidance of indiscriminate violence, whereas Armaiti (Devotion, Right-Mindedness) represents faithfulness and religious dedication. Even though she transcends limits imposed by the sacred area, this feminine spirit is symbolized by the sacred ground of the ritual area. Haurvatat (Wholeness, Integrity) and Ameretāt (Health/Immortal Life) are often depicted as a pair, with the latter concerned with vegetation in a ritual context and the former associated with water. The seven Immortals are associated with the seven creations in Pahlavi literature. These seven should abide in a human in order to give a person power over evil. These qualities of Ahura Mazdā are the furthest removed from him, but they become especially important after death. As emanations and aspects of Ahura Mazdā, the Amesha Spentas (Holy Immortals) represent at least three things about God: Ahura Mazdā is transcendent, but the Holy Spirit also makes him immanent, protects humans through the holy seven creations, and represents the good creation, which is countered by evil and demonic beings.

Standing opposed and undermining the good represented by the Amesha Spentas (Holy Immortals) there is Angra Mainyu, a destructive spirit and counter force to the good and twin brother, the Wise Lord. Angra Mainyu is a rival of the Wise Lord, which makes him of equal rank. In order to grasp the world's nature, it is essential to reconsider the creation of the cosmos. In the beginning, Ahura Mazdā brought everything into existence in a disembodied or immaterial condition (*mēnōg*). Then he bestowed material (*gētīg*) existence on what he created in the first step, which was considered advantageous because it provided form along with solidity and sentience and served as the battlefield where the conflict between good and evil occurs in the future. But this second development set the stage for the assault by evil, Angra Mainyu, who marred and polluted the different forms of creation. Examples of such destructiveness are that fire was sullied with smoke and some places on earth became deserts. The divine good countered this subversive activity by using evil for the benefit of the earth by, for example, scattering the essence of plants to create more and different plants. In a sense, Ahura Mazdā initially created a static world, whereas Angra Mainyu's introduction of death and decay into the world gives it a dynamic dimension. After the original creation and attack by evil, a counterproductive power in the world, there is now a mixture of good and evil that characterizes history, although evil continues its assault on the world, having been lured out of infinite time into finite time, where it can now enter into battle with the good. Within this mixture that characterizes the narrative of history, humans must not only worship Ahura Mazdā and the Spentas but must also introduce them into their hearts. In summary, the good and evil spirits are antagonistic but are also complementary forces, although Ahura Mazdā is the sole sovereign deity of the universe.

From a Zoroastrian theological position, it is not possible to imagine God, representing the good, without its contrary, evil, just as it is impossible to imagine beauty without ugliness or heat without cold. In later Zoroastrian thought, Angra Mainyu becomes known as Ahriman, and Ahura Mazdā is called Ohrmazd. Moreover, the Zoroastrian tradition tends to revere deities as personified abstractions, a dominant feature of Indo-Iranian religion. Nonetheless, there is also a link between the abstractions and concrete phenomena. In summary, Zoroastrianism can be conceived as a devotional monotheism, although not a pure or radical one, because it includes an interweaving of a dualism between good (pure) and evil (impure) with a polytheism, a situation that can give one the impression that it is contradictory.

The Righteous Person

In the Zoroastrian vision of human nature, humans are composed of body, spirit, and soul. The human body is a divine creation, and its full development is supervised by Sarvatā, a member of the Amesha Spentas who also ensures the integrity of the body. If the human body is divinely created and thus considered good, when the body becomes infirm or suffers from some disease, it is compromised and put at risk. What explains such a situation? The Zoroastrian answer is that sickness of the body is a punishment inflicted on the body by a malevolent agent of the forces of evil, the Lie or cosmic confusion (*drug*). Moreover, death or decomposition of the body reflects impurity and violation of the integrity of the body. Death is viewed as a victory of evil, and decomposition of a corpse is attributed to a demon called Druj-i-Nasush.

The second aspect of a human is the spirit (*manah*), which is a force of life, representing a quasi-divine power that distinguishes a person from animals. The spirit enables a person to acknowledge himself as a member of a just community. The individual and community are capable of doing good acts or committing evil deeds. Since individuals have free will and spirit, they are responsible for their actions.

The third element constituting a human being is the pre-soul (*fravashi*) that both pre-exists and post-exists the person. The Avesta literature also refers to a breath soul (*urwan*) and vision soul (*daēnā*). The soul is created immortal by God. In addition, the soul guards a person and attempts to stir a person to perform moral and ethical actions that determines her later destiny in either paradise or hell. The human soul also witnesses a person's actions and assists

Ahura Mazdā to guard the universe against evil. When humans choose evil, they are acting contrary to the wishes of God.

In order to assist humans to make the right choice, God provides them with the means to guide them. The first such divine gift is a mind that can be used to motivate a person to select the right choice with respect to his deeds. The faculty of desire enables a person to discern right from wrong. Referring to a need for fire, Zarathustra intends to affirm that such a need reflects the truth of his message. Thirdly, God gives an individual conscience that enables him to understand the revelation. Conscience enables a person to accept or reject the revelation and to continue to work with God to usher into existence the renovation or perfection of the universe. Ahura Mazdā also gives humans insight, a noetic faculty that helps one to follow the truth. By noetic quality, Zarathustra suggests a sense of intuition, a supplement to an individual's intellectual ability. An intellectual type of knowledge supports intuition. Finally, Ahura Mazdā bestows wisdom on an individual when he is established on the ethical right path, assuming that one applies insight and intuition to ethical issues. These gifts from Ahura Mazdā are intended to help humans overcome evil and restore the world to its primordial perfect condition in concert with the actions of God.

Zoroastrian Worship

Prayer is the most common form of worship for a typical Zoroastrian, whose duty is to pray five times a day, during the times of sunrise, noon, sunset, midnight, and dawn. Ideally, prayer should be performed in the presence of fire, which symbolically represents Ahura Mazdā and righteousness while one stands before a fire. Before one prays, she must perform ritual ablutions to purify herself. Since one can pray before any clean or unpolluted fire, there is no religious obligation to visit and pray at fire temples, which are equally accessible to men and women. By praying to Ahura Mazdā, a worshipper joins God in his cosmic combat against evil. Zoroastrian prayers are similar to *mantras* (sacred formulas) in Hinduism and Buddhism because they assume the form of chant formulas.

At fire temples, it is the daily duty of priests to keep the fire burning in the temple. Priests wear only white, a symbol of purity, and cover their faces with a white mask when near the fire in order to protect the fire from pollution that might be inadvertently defiled by a priest's breath or saliva. Only Zoroastrian males can become priests, an occupation that is usually hereditary. The priest functions as an intermediary between God and the people and represents the people before Ahura Mazdā. When a fire is made unclean or a new fire is created by a priest, he performs a ritual to purify the fire by reciting prayers, holding a ladle of wood chips over the fire, a symbol of divine presence, but not making contact with the fire. Zoroastrian priests do not typically preside over a congregational form of worship conducted at specific times during a day.

Just as there are three grades of priests, there are three grades of sanctity for fire, with the middle grade called "fire of fires" and the highest grade named "victorious (*varahram*) fire," which involves combining fires from sixteen separate sources. There is also a third type of temporary fire (*jashans*) for the purpose of praise or thanksgiving. The central place of fire in Zoroastrianism is related to a belief that fire possesses power over evil and that it is a way to combat Angra Mainyu, the personification of evil.

There are three major types of worship services in Zoroastrianism. The *Yasna* ceremony is a typical form of worship, usually directed to a specific deity. It is performed when the sun is rising in the early morning. This is the fire that symbolizes righteousness and order (*asha*) and includes the dissemination of light and warmth over God's creation. This represents the daily struggle for combating against and dispelling of the darkness associated with the forces of evil by injecting truth and righteousness into the world each morning. The *Yasna* rite gathers together the basic elements of the cosmos: fire, water, plants, animals, humans, and holy utterances.

As Zoroastrianism developed, it excluded animal sacrifice, but it retained the old Indo-Iranian sacrifice of *haoma* (Indic *soma*) by purifying, pounding, extracting the sap, straining, and mixing the sap with milk and water. *Haoma* was a sacred liquid that was characterized as igneous, luminous, vivifying, and spermatic, suggesting that it had life-giving powers. According to an ancient contested epithet, *haoma* means "the one who keeps death away," which reinforces its association with life. This drink of immortality was imbibed by the priests, enabling them to enter a state (*magga*) that transported them beyond the human condition. In other words, the priests drank the liquid and were transported into a state of ecstasy by the hallucinogenic properties of the liquid. Meanwhile, the consecrated food and drink gave off a pleasant aroma that was believed by the faithful to satisfy Ahura Mazdā and other divine beings. While under the influence of the drug, priests had visions and enjoyed ecstatic experiences that gave them illumination. In later Zoroastrian history, *haoma* would be replaced by a combination of plant juices, water, and milk.

The two other typical forms of *Yasna* (worship) are the *Visperad* (worship of all the masters) and *Vendidad*. The former ceremony is dedicated to Ahura Mazdā as the master of everything for the celebration of the seven holy days of obligation. Its major difference with the *Yasna* is the addition of twenty-three short pieces of liturgy. The *Vendidad* is performed during a night-long service that is read aloud. As a book of the *Avesta*, it means the "code against demons," which includes regulations for maintaining ritual purity along with other material pertaining to ritual. Scholars refer to these three forms of worship as inner ceremonies in contrast to an outer ceremony such as the *Afrinagan* that praises Ahura Mazdā for his beneficence toward the world and its inhabitants and functions to connect the spiritual world and material world.

Zoroastrian worship is performed to achieve four general purposes. The first is to purify the world. Second, worship is intended to strengthen the relationship between the spiritual and material realms by creating a circumstance that evolves into a unity. Third, worship is performed to praise and glorify God. With the fourth purpose, it is possible to recognize that Zoroastrian worship embodies and reflects an eschatological spirit, because it is performed to weaken and ultimately defeat evil forces threatening the order or righteousness (*asha*) of the world. And the individual worshipper and priest play an active role in this eschatological drama occurring in the universe. This suggests that the individual Zoroastrian, who becomes a teammate of God, has an important role to play in a cosmic conflict between forces of good and evil. When the forces of good are victorious, the salvation of the world and its inhabitants will be ushered into reality.

Rites of Passage

Zoroastrians have traditionally observed three major types of rites of passage: initiation, marriage, and death. A distinction is drawn between males and females with respect to initiation because the former are formally initiated between the ages of 12 and 15, whereas females are initiated by their husbands during the wedding ceremony, because real life for a female commences when she is accepted by her father-in-law's home fire. The male initiation ceremony is called the *navjote* (new birth) or *sedra-pushun* (putting on the sacred shirt), a rite that fits into a larger cosmic narrative that reflects the cosmology and eschatology of the religion. To be born suggests that biological birth merely confers upon a child a bare form of physical existence. But a man is a being who has a spiritual essence that points to God. While living on earth, a man lives in exile from his true home in heaven with God. In order to enter a path that will lead him to his true home, it is essential that he spark his spiritual essence to get it to develop and become an un-extinguishable light.

The actual initiation ceremony involves stripping the childhood clothing from the youngster and then bestowing upon him a sacred garment and cord. Before receiving these items, he is given a sip of a consecrated liquid consisting of bull's urine to internally purify him. The white color of the garment (*sedra*) signifies purity and innocence. This shirt is loose fitting and contains a small pocket at the location of the neck for the symbolic storage of good deeds. The cord (*kūsti*) of wool consists of seventy-two threads, which is modeled on the same number of chapters of the *Yasna* text. The sacred cord is wrapped three times around the youngster's waist in order to remind the boy of his devotion and the threefold ethical requirements to cultivate and perform good thoughts, good words, and good deeds. These reminders are reinforced when an initiate prays before the fire because he unties the cord when he prays and reties it when he concludes his prayers. In addition to the sacred shirt and cord, the initiate learns his real, secret name and is presented to the fire, which both recognizes him and adopts him.

A marriage ceremony is performed before the family hearth with a fire burning in order for the fire to function as a witness to the rite or at the courtyard adjoining a fire temple. During the ceremony, the fire will receive offerings and operate to guarantee the union of the couple. The marriage ceremony begins with the bride, family, and friends traveling to the home of the groom to offer gifts to his family. Thereafter, the groom's party goes to the bride's home for the actual ceremony. The groom is welcomed at the home of his bride's father with gifts of coconuts and eggs and his forehead is marked with a red vertical mark that signifies the sun, whereas the bride receives a forehead mark that symbolizes the moon. This suggests that the rite unites the conjunction of opposites and prefigures the joy and grief that the couple will encounter during their marriage. With the singing of songs and fire burning, the groom joins his bride on chairs facing eastward. A curtain initially separates them, signifying two separate people, while the removal of the curtain represents their union. After the bridal couple sprinkle each other with rice that suggests a symbol of fertility, the pair join hands, and a knot is tied around their hands by a priest.

The rite of passage for a deceased person is intended to isolate the corpse, because it is impure, and to assist the soul. Zoroastrians do not traditionally bury, submerge in water, or cremate a dead body because they fear polluting the earth, air, or water or even contaminating fire. Cadavers are rather abandoned on rocks, cliffs, or remote areas to be devoured by carnivores, especially vultures, during the earliest tradition but were later placed on circular enclosures known as "towers of silence" (*dakhma*), which are round structures that are open to the elements. The interior of an open tower consists of three concentric chambers: an outer circle for males, a middle circle for females, and a central circle for children to be laid in. In traditional Zoroastrianism, a lower sub-caste handled the dead and their disposal.

The ceremony includes washing the deceased with unconsecrated bull's urine and wrapping the body in a cotton shroud that is conveyed by an iron bier, which is accompanied by praying priests and followed by mourners to the tower for final disposal. After vultures clean away the flesh and organs, the bones are bleached by wind and sun. A general funeral guideline is to dispose of the corpse within twenty-four hours after death. It is believed that the soul lingers on earth for three days, and thus priests recite prayers and perform ceremonies to assist the soul to make its transitions to another realm. These death ceremonies are continued monthly for a year before becoming an annual observance for thirty years.

Role of Women

During the early history of Zoroastrianism, members of the religion began to anthropomorphize abstract concepts and attribute genders to them. This process influenced how people were perceived within the culture. A rather stark example was the attribution of masculinity to *asha* (righteousness) and making *druj* (evil) into a female. Biological genders were also given to Ahura Mazdā (male) and the evil Angra Mainyu (female). Other demonic creatures were regarded as female, such as Drukhsh Nasuch, a ghoul associated with corpses and the ability to pollute humans after they die. Some female figures were associated with Ahura Mazdā, such as the Amesha Spentas (holy immortal spirits). These original female spirits functioned as a counterforce to hunger and thirst and operated to heal and restore afflicted humans to health. Their early feminine gender affiliation was gradually changed to a neutral status during the medieval period. Another example is Āzi (lust), a demonic spirit related to Angra Mainyu with an early masculine gender, who became a mistress of the demonic Angra Mainyu during the medieval period. Āzi's name was changed to Jahikā (Jēh), and this transformed figure became the primordial whore, being given credit for introducing lust to humanity. This cultural process of feminization of negative features within the religion was carried over to the conceptualization of the afterlife. After the death of a malevolent person, his evil soul encounters a naked Jahikā, whereas a righteous person meets a beautiful girl who escorts the deceased to paradise. These various examples work to reinforce the masculine conviction that women are more closely associated with evil.

Taking into consideration the importance of ritual for the religion and the emphasis on purity, these types of negative female attitudes may have originated within the female biological phenomenon of menstruation. According to Zoroastrian lore, when the demoness Jahikā revived Angra Mainyu in hell after his defeat by Ahura Mazdā by kissing him on his face, she began to menstruate, which suggested that flowing blood was something demonic. From its origin in a grateful kiss from one evil being to another, Jahikā transferred menstruation to future generations of women, becoming a monthly sign of affliction and unfortunate fate for females. Because monthly menses pollutes women for a period of time, women are cursed by their biology and barred from performing rituals in order not to pollute the ritual actions, the sacred space, and other participants, a scenario that could prove catastrophic for everyone. Needless to say, women were also excluded from the ranks of the clergy because of their connection in the popular imagination with flowing blood and evil.

Despite these negative attitudes toward women, they were still considered an important part of the community. By the age of 15, boys and girls received initiation, which made them adults for religious and legal purposes. This age also marked a time when girls were considered old enough to marry. Similar to other cultures, such as India, early marriage tended to increase the chances that a girl was a virgin, a cultural expectation by the groom's party at the time of marriage. Zoroastrians placed a high cultural value on marriage because the offspring became members of the community and increased its numbers. Thus, induced abortions were prohibited, and sexual intercourse with a pregnant woman was also forbidden because of a possibility of harming the developing fetus. Similar to other patriarchal religious cultures, women were expected to embrace the role of motherhood for the good of the religion.

Importance of Purity and Pollution

The distinction between purity and pollution is based on a basic cosmic and ethical dualism between righteousness and evil that is often called the "lie" (*drug*). In the beginning, Ahura Mazdā created a world that was characterized as good, whereas evil was the work of Angra Mainyu, a personification of evil, who uses imperfect and impure substances, such as sin, dust, dirt, stench, excrement, disease, decay, and death, to pollute the perfect and pure creation of Ahura Mazdā. Thus, the ultimate source of pollution is negative forces that arise from evil. This scenario suggests that pollution is not a relative force or dialectical process, because it is rather absolute in the Zoroastrian worldview, although it can be countered by the good created by Ahura Mazdā, who is the antithesis of the evil spirit.

Pollution takes various forms, with bodily refuse being the most obvious, including such items as excrement, flowing blood, menstrual blood, semen, dead skin, saliva, urine, nails, and hair. These types of bodily waste must not touch water or fire, which are sacred phenomena. When nails, hair, or skin are part of one's body, they are considered pure. For example, when nails are cut, they must be properly disposed of. Otherwise, a group of giant demons can use them to create weapons of war.

Dead matter such as animal carrion or a human cadaver is very polluting. When someone dies, that person's body is immediately attacked by the Corpse Demoness. Zoroastrians also believe that the cadaver of a righteous person is even more susceptible to impurity than that of an evil person because the latter type of person is already corrupted by evil forces. A less obvious example of an impure bodily product is exhaled breath. When a person exhales his breath this act is analogous to excrement that can pollute a fire or the earth. As a precaution against the potential pollution by breath, a Zoroastrian priest dons a mouth and nose mask before he approaches a sacred fire.

These various kinds of pollution involve practicing certain types of behavior to individually counter the threat of pollution. Since saliva is unclean, Zoroastrians refrain, for example, from spitting. Orthodox believers neither drink from a glass or bottle that has touched the lips of another person, nor do they eat from a common dish. Maintaining silence is common among Zoroastrians when eating food or drinking liquids. The act of male urination is performed while squatting and not standing as a sanitary precaution. The sexual relations between couples are restricted because of spent semen or menstrual blood. As a general rule, semen ejected for the purpose of procreation is considered pure because it is released for the purpose of reproduction. When a woman is pregnant or nursing an infant, sexual intercourse is forbidden, because the child might be harmed. Couples are also forbidden to have sexual relations during a woman's menstrual period or three days after it ceases. During her menstrual period, a woman is forbidden to prepare food. Another consequence of these types of beliefs about purity, which is symbolically imagined to represent wholeness, is physical injury or defect marking a person. These types of bodily deformities or disfigurements are considered marks of the evil Angra Mainyu inflicted on an unfortunate victim. This observation helps to explain the requirement that priests are required to be physically perfect.

There are fundamentally two means that humans can use to counter pollution: taboos/prohibitions and ritual purification. The former involves, for example, adhering to dietary rules. The general dietary restrictions are built on consuming only the flesh and products of pure beings or plants, while those products that originate from unclean sources are prohibited. In addition to the clean and unclean sources of foods, there are those products that have been neutralized by Ahura Mazdā, such as honey. Pollution can also be countered by the gaze of a dog, which is considered a clean and righteous creature that possesses the power to drive away demons. Moreover, if a person gives a dog food in the name of a deceased person, the departed will be nourished in the other realm.

The ritual of purification involves three steps: recital of *Avesta* verses by both the priest and person being cleansed; an internal purification of body and soul by drinking consecrated bull's urine with a pinch of fire ash added to the liquid; and external cleansing of the entire body by using unconsecrated bull's urine that is followed by a washing of the entire person with water. Bull's urine is considered—whether consecrated or unconsecrated—a purifying fluid because it is a product of a sacred animal, whereas water can be traced back to the good created by Ahura Mazdā. People can also purify themselves by confessing their sins. From a wider perspective, purity guidelines and rituals are intended to help an individual Zoroastrian support the Wise God battle evil in the cause of righteousness. Thus, rites of purification do not merely cleanse a person, but they also reintegrate a person into the community and grant her the hope of salvation. In sum, purification of body and soul are prerequisites for admittance into heaven.

Fire and water play important roles in the dichotomy between purity and pollution and in Zoroastrian eschatology. Fire and water, which are respectively the male and female elements of the world, are extremely vulnerable to pollution and must be protected by humans. Ahura Mazdā used fire when he created humans and animals, which thus makes it a sacred element. And the final renewal of the universe at the end of time involves using the medium of fire, an object of worship, to accomplish this, whereas water will help to cleanse humans for the final battle and victory over evil.

What makes human beings obligated to engage in this struggle against evil is the covenant between Ahura Mazdā and humans. Evidence for this covenant is found in the *Bundahsin* (Book of Primal Creation), a Pahlavi language text dating from the ninth century CE. According to the narrative of the text, humans agree to assist the increase of righteousness and combat evil forces by their earthly actions. The victorious side will witness the separation of good and evil, the defeat and expulsion of the forces of evil, and the final restoration of the original, good, perfect universe, which will be fit for human inhabitation, resulting in a heaven on earth. This indicates that human beings must not assume a passive role in this cosmic confrontation for the welfare and future of the universe but must rather fight on the side of the Wise Lord and his forces of righteousness. When divine and human victory is achieved, cosmic order will reign supreme because everything will be purified, while the disorder exemplified by impurity will be overcome.

Eschatology

From a discussion about a future cosmic battle, it is an easy transition to a consideration of what happens at the end of time. After the death of the body, the soul goes on an arduous journey on a path that leads to a precipice spanned by what is called the Chinvat Bridge, which is guarded by two dogs. This represents a bridge of separation, because righteous and wicked persons are differentiated on this bridge, which widens for a righteous person but narrows like the edge of a knife for an evildoer and causes such a person to lose his balance and fall into hell, a dark pit of torment. While crossing the bridge of separation, the ethical person encounters a beautiful maiden named Daēnā, a reflection of her good deeds and source of comfort in the next life, whereas the evil soul encounters an ugly, vile, stinking hag dressed in rags. The soul of the wicked is destined to fall into a dark, icy place, while the ethical soul safely crosses the bridge to the House of Songs, a place inhabited by the righteous. The realm of the dead is governed by Yima, who was the first human to die and had the responsibility to build a dwelling place for the dead.

Zoroastrian eschatology includes the resurrection of the body when the soul and body of an individual are reunited, but this occurrence does not happen immediately after death; it happens at the end of time within a paradise described as celestial and luminous, where God sits on a golden throne while devotees sing his praises and enjoy sensuous things. Some souls that are not judged good or evil await in a neutral type of place, a kind of limbo. The end of time is also marked by cataclysmic destruction of everything by fire or flood. This cataclysmic event is prior to God's reestablishment of the original golden age, signifying a renewal of the cosmos. The souls of the dead must endure a decisive trial when they are judged by a tribunal presided over by Mithra and other divine beings. According to some sources, Ahura Mazdā alone decides the fate of the soul by weighing its deeds. According to a later revelation, the world is fully restored to its original perfect condition, free of evil by gods and humans. The moment of perfection is called the *Frashegird* (meaning Healing and Renovation), marking the end of history and utter cessation of evil. The *Frashegird* is a realm of endless joy and happiness, which represents a return to the original material condition, when the human soul is reunited with the body and restored to an unblemished condition within a genuine kingdom of god.

Another element of Zoroastrian eschatology is the Saoshyant (literally "one who is strong"), a world savior. According to a Zoroastrian narrative, this savior is the product of a miraculous conception, although he is not a divine figure, because he is born of human parents. The son will be the product of the seed of the prophet that will be preserved miraculously in a lake, where it is protected by the pre-existent spirit (*fravasis*) of the righteous. In the future, a virgin will bathe in the lake and become impregnated by the seed hidden within the lake, giving birth to a righteous son. This narrative about the savior's birth is consistent with the concept that humans will participate in the grand cosmic battle, and it follows Zoroaster's assertion that someone more important and greater will come after the prophet. This figure is a person who arrives at the end of time and utters a warning about the coming end of the world, which is expected at any moment in this degenerate world. The *Yasna* literature informs us that Zarathustra refers to himself as a benefactor who will come later to bring benefits to humans. In short, Zarathustra is calling attention to himself as an eschatological figure. There is little doubt that Zarathustra expected the end of time during his life, which gives his teaching a sense of urgency.

With respect to his overall teachings, Zarathustra wove together the spiritual and material. He recognized a moral component in the physical. From his perspective, the material and spiritual were moving toward the goal of the re-creation of the world, which would represent a state of happiness and harmony. He exhibited a nostalgia for a past primordial time that existed before the damage inflicted by the evil Angra Mainyu and his malignant forces. He was convinced that human beings could retrieve that perfect state of life previously experienced during a primordial time prior to the progressive degeneration of creation over time. Thus, Zarathustra was both forwarding looking toward an end time and also was nostalgic for an original pristine time that was harmonious and perfect in every way.

Heretical Challenges

Arising in Babylon around the fifth century BCE, there developed a doctrinal controversy called Zurvanism, which was named after time (*zurvan*). At the center of the controversy was a question about how to understand Ahura Mazdā's relationship with Angra Mainyu, which was sparked by a reference in the *Gathas* to the two spirits as twins. The Zurvanites reasoned that they probably had a parent, which they contended was Zurvan (Time), a prior, remote deity and parent of the two twins. From the Zoroastrian perspective, this suggested that good and evil originated from the same source. Moreover, there is less distinction between good and evil. As a consequence of this position, Ahura Mazdā gets demoted to a lesser status, and human free choice is compromised by a more deterministic position in which time exercises its control over human life, making it impossible for a person to shape her own destiny by correct ethical choices. Therefore, Zurvanites embrace time as the origin of the twin spirits. By compromising much of the Zoroastrian position, they were revealed to be more preoccupied with events such as the fate of a person and society, which were under the control of the inexorable decisions of time.

During the early Sasanian period (226–641 CE), Manichaeism, a religious movement named after a prophet renowned as Mani (216–276 CE), arose to challenge Zoroastrianism, even though it used the names of Zoroastrian *yazatas* (divine beings worthy of worship) for the deities of his own divine pantheon. Mani was an Iranian noble who believed in God and the Devil, the existence of heaven and hell, a final judgment after death, the possibility of eternal life, and the final defeat of evil. His religion prospered in Iran after the ruler Shapur patronized the religion, but accession of another ruler resulted with Mani's arrest and execution.

Because the world was almost totally evil, Mani was rather pessimistic about the world. Because of his assessment of the world, Mani advocated renouncing the world and leading an ascetic life, which committed one to a celibate lifestyle. By taking such a path of religious life, a person would refrain from contributing to any further misery in the world. Mani also stressed a path of knowledge that was grounded in a fundamental dualism between God and matter. Mani's teachings were wrapped within an apocalyptic vision of a cosmic battle between the forces of light and darkness. In sharp contrast to Manichaeism, Zoroastrianism is opposed to asceticism and emphasizes the importance of the family. For these and other reasons, Zoroastrian priests called the Mani movement a heresy.

Zoroastrian Diaspora

After the invasion of Iran by Muslims in the seventh century and subsequent pressure to convert to Islam or be taxed and persecuted, life for ordinary Zoroastrians became very difficult in Iran, a disadvantage not encountered by Jews and Christians because they had sacred scriptures, while Zoroastrians were not recognized to be people of the book by Muslims. Being subjugated and persecuted, Zoroastrians sought a way out of their dilemma. Some Zoroastrians converted to Islam, while others emigrated to western India, where they found a home and became known as Parsis (Persians), an identity that continues to the present time in India.

Within the Indian cultural context, Parsi lore recounts a smooth transition, adaptation, and integration into the local culture, a mixture of Hinduism and Islam, with some exceptions. Parsis accomplished this by calling attention to their beliefs that coincided with Hinduism and adapted some of their cultural customs to accommodate indigenous Hindu sensibilities. During the sixteenth century, the Mughal Emperor Akbar, a Muslim ruler with a liberal and tolerant attitude toward other religions, was impressed by the Parsis' faith and rewarded a member of the Parsi community with a gift of 200 acres of land after learning about the religion. In 1158, Akbar incorporated two Zoroastrian elements into his syncretic cult: the Zoroastrian calendar names for the months and their veneration of fire and the sun. The ability to adapt to the culture of India was carried forward into the nineteenth century, when Avestan texts were translated into Gujarati, a regional language of western India.

The British acquired Bombay from the Portuguese in 1662 in order to create a trading port in southern India. The new authorities encouraged Parsis to move to the area by enticing them with gifts of land. Between 1672 and 1674, a tower of silence was built to accommodate deceased Parsis. As they became more urbanized, Parsis became increasingly wealthy, which resulted in their rise to social and political prominence during the British period. Parsis continued to adjust their religious practices to Indian culture, with two major results: They ceased to sacrifice cows or consume beef to placate Hindus and gave up pork products to appease Muslim sensibilities. These types of adjustment continued into the twentieth century, when Zoroastrians also discontinued sacrificing sheep, goats, or chickens. They even founded the Parsi Vegetarian and Temperance Society in Bombay, a further example of their accommodation to Indian culture. Parsis also encountered internal challenges to their religion with their emphasis on endogamy, which tended to preclude proselytism as a way to increase their numbers, a social feature of the religion that became a serious problem in the twentieth century, when their death rates exceeded their birth rates.

During the nineteenth century, the Zoroastrian community in India was challenged by Christianity, introduced by the colonial powers. Non-empathetic Christian missionaries accused Zoroastrians of belonging to a polytheistic, nature-worshipping religion and being followers of a dualistic religion. Zoroastrians were also assaulted for rejecting revealed texts, having no sacred texts of their own, and having the credibility of their prophet called into question. Around the early 1860s, Martin Haug, a German philologist teaching at Pune University, not only translated the *Gathas* of the prophet but shocked Parsis by informing them that these hymns represented the only historical words of Zoroaster that can be trusted. Reformist Parsis rejoiced at this development, because Haug's thesis could function to justify rejecting the old teachings and habitual behavior that conflicted with nineteenth century enlightenment ethos.

Besides the nineteenth century changes induced by urbanization and Christian missionary criticism, Parsis also encountered the introduction of Western education and science, which both collided with Zoroastrian beliefs. Again, internal tensions within the religion were caused by the increased wealth of some families, which sharply contrasted with the modest economic means of priestly incomes. By faithful adherence to their religious tradition, Zoroastrian priests gave the appearance of being backward, ignorant, and poor. Some reformist Zoroastrians responded to this situation by recognizing a need for modern education and scientific knowledge. The need for reform was answered by Naoroji Feerdoonji, who founded the Young Bombay Party and the Zoroastrian Reform Society around the 1850s with the intention to confront orthodoxy and religious prejudices that hinder progress. In 1854, Mulla Firoze Madressa established the Kadmi (ancestors) movement to encourage education and pursuit of scientific knowledge. The Parsis also responded to Christians by imitating them and creating schools, hospitals, and orphanages operated by Parsis.

In 1885, Henry S. Olcott and Madame Blavatsky, co-founders of the Theosophical Society in New York, arrived in Bombay and spread the influence of their esoteric movement. Olcott expressed high regard for Zoroastrianism and its simple ethical message, urging Parsis to retain and embrace their rituals, although his embrace of Hindu and Buddhist teachings tended to subvert Zoroastrianism. The influence of Olcott and Blavatsky sparked an imitation of their organization by Parsis in the form of the Ilm-I Khshrooom (Knowledge of Spiritual Satisfaction), an early twentieth-century Zoroastrian Theosophy movement. The occult movement taught that fire was divine wisdom, a means of communicating with God, and a source of blessings. These types of attitudes were combined with theosophical convictions about the usefulness of vegetarianism, the operation of reincarnation, and the grasping of different planes of existence. Some have argued that embracing theosophy undermined Zoroastrianism.

The twentieth century witnessed the drive for Indian independence from Britain, which increased urbanization for Parsis and created hostility toward Parsis because they gave the impression to Hindus of thriving economically during British rule, while others suffered social and economic deprivation. During the 1930s, Hindus boycotted Parsi farms in Gujarat, forcing Parsi farmers to sell their land. This situation caused an exodus from the countryside to urban Bombay. A similar type of scenario was occurring in Tehran, where Muslims were critical of Zoroastrianism for centuries for their polytheism and fire worship. Because the practice did not fit into modern modes of life, Zoroastrians were forced to cease performing their traditional way of disposing of the dead. Again, Zoroastrians were forced to adjust their religion to criticisms from outside of the community.

India's campaign for independence in 1947 had negative consequences for Parsis because some of them discovered themselves living in Pakistan, a newly created Muslim state. This gave renewed impetus to their diaspora by motivating them to emigrate from Pakistan to England, Canada, and the United States, although the vast majority of them remained in the East.

From the 1960s, the Zoroastrian population has declined because of emigration, intermarriage, and a low birth rate. India holds the single largest concentration of them, at around 70,000, whereas the United Kingdom has a population of about 7,000, North America 20,000, and other countries 6,000. These types of numbers are the result of often hidden historical, political, and economic changes. Due to adjustments to new situations and challenges during recent centuries, Zoroastrians have had to make religious accommodations. As they made reforms, aspects of the traditional religion were compromised, subverted, or rejected.

Whatever the future holds for Zoroastrianism, its past influence on Judaism, Christianity, and Islam is evident in these monotheistic religious traditions. The Zoroastrian influence can be traced to such beliefs as history coming to an end, the notion of individual and general judgment by a divine being for each soul and community, the notions of heaven and hell, a future resurrection of the body, and the reuniting of the soul and body to enjoy life everlasting in a state of paradise. The strong emphasis on the necessity of leading an ethical life in Zoroastrianism also finds echoes in the monotheistic religions, although their differences with Zoroastrianism are rather dramatic.

Religious Experience

Zarathustra called his followers to make a choice between good or evil. Faithful members of the community were urged to fight against evil and get engaged in a cosmic struggle. Nothing short of the fate of humanity and the world was at stake. Therefore, humans have been created to help Ahura Mazdā struggle and fight against the forces of evil. Humans can contribute to this battle by performing good deeds, uttering good words, and cultivating good thoughts.

By following this religious path, a person can attain wisdom, the highest religious value. In this context, wisdom is not an abstract kind of knowledge but is rather a creative way of thinking that both discovers and creates the structures of the world. This wisdom is both initiatory and eschatological. After death, the soul experiences crossing a bridge, ascent to heaven, judgment, and meeting one's own true self. Moreover, the soul reaches the primordial lights, or paradise.

The performance of ritual sacrifice also contributes to the overall goal of defeating evil. The eschatological aspect of sacrifice performs a theological mediation that results in the purification and spiritualization of the world. During the ritual process, the sacrificer acquires the condition of *maga*, an ecstatic experience that results in illumination. While enjoying illumination, the sacrificer participates in the separation of one's spiritual essence (*mēnōg*) from one's physical nature (*gētīg*). This is often conceptualized as a recovery of purity and innocence prior to the mixing of the two essences. In general, the sacrificer contributes to the restoration of the primordial condition and thus participates in the transfiguration of the world and the work of redemption.

Suggestions for Further Reading

Boyce, Mary. *A History of Zoroastrianism.* Vol. 1. Ed. Handbuch der Orientalisik. Leiden: E. J. Brill, 1975.

———. *Zoroastrians: Their Religious Beliefs and Practices.* London: Routledge & Kegan Paul, 1979.

Choksy, Jamsheed K. *Purity and Pollution in Zoroastrianism: Triumph over Evil.* Austin: University of Texas Press, 1989.

Clark, Peter. *Zoroastrianism: An Introduction to an Ancient Faith.* Brighton: Sussex Academic Press, 1998.

Hinnells, J. R. *Zoroastrianism and Parsi Studies.* Aldershot: Ashgate, 2000.

———. *The Zoroastrian Diaspora.* Oxford: Oxford University Press, 2005.

Rose, Jenny. *Zoroastrianism: An Introduction.* London: I. B. Tauris, 2011.

Skjaervø, Prods Oktor. Trans. and Ed. *The Spirit of Zoroastrianism.* New Haven: Yale University Press, 2011.

Stausberg, M. Ed. *Zoroastrian Rituals in Context.* Leiden: E. J. Brill, 2004.

12 Judaism

The ancient patriarchs of Judaism are identified as Abraham, Isaac, and Jacob. During the ancient period, Abraham migrated from Mesopotamia to the land of Canaan in the area of Palestine. According to biblical accounts, Abraham worshipped a monotheistic deity, who tested the patriarch's faith by requiring him to sacrifice his son Isaac, a favorite child born to Abraham and his barren wife in their old age. Abraham was torn between his God's demands and love of his cherished son. Just before Abraham applied his knife to sacrifice his son, God intervened to save the child's life and was satisfied with the proof of the old man's faith. According to Jewish tradition, God enters into a covenant, an event that helps to define the nature of Judaism, with Abraham by offering protection in exchange for the obligatory circumcision of all males as a sign of entering into the covenant. By giving a piece of himself, a male not only enters into the agreement with God, but one also becomes symbolically clean, because the foreskin is a sign of dirt. In order words, circumcision is a visible sign of a male's membership into an exclusive covenant.

With the demise of Abraham, Isaac and Jacob assumed patriarchal leadership roles. Jacob had twelve sons, who eventually came to represent the twelve tribes of Israel. During a famine, Jacob's family migrated to Egypt, where they enjoyed royal favor prior to being enslaved by a new king. In the meantime, a male infant was placed in a basket and abandoned in the bulrushes, recovered, raised, and trained in Egyptian circles (Exodus 2:1–10). The Exodus narrative continues with Moses stopping an Egyptian from beating a Hebrew slave. Fleeing Egypt, Moses journeys to the land of Midian, where he meets and marries the daughter of Jethro, a priest. But the crucial event of Moses's life occurs when he encounters a burning bush that is not consumed by the fire and hears God's voice calling Moses to save the Hebrews from their bondage. In response to his overpowering experience, Moses summons the courage to ask God his name so that Moses can tell the people who precisely sent him and why they should take his message seriously. Why did Moses ask for God to identify Himself? Within the Jewish culture of the period, it is important to know the name of someone, because the character and identity of a person is embodied within and expressed by his name. In response to Moses's question, God responds: "I am who I am" (Ex. 3:14). This means, in Hebrew, that Moses should tell the people that YHWH (the Lord) sent him. Yahweh informs Moses that he is the God of Abraham, Isaac, and Jacob. God also informs Moses that "I will be with you" (Ex. 3:12).

Thus, instructed by God and affected by the plight of the Hebrews, Moses entreats the Egyptian king to give his people their freedom. Scholars have identified this king with Ramses of the Nineteenth Dynasty around 1290 BCE. When the king refuses Moses's request, the narrative explains this as God acting to harden the Pharaoh's heart. Throughout the encounter and contest between the Pharaoh and Moses, it is always God who is in control, by influencing the Pharaoh's disposition, by being behind the miracle of the rod of Moses becoming a serpent when cast to the ground, and by sending plagues to the Egyptians that represent water turning to blood and sending frogs, gnats, flies, cattle plague, boils, hail, locusts, darkness, and the death of their firstborn (Ex. 11:1–8). These undesirable events are described as signs and wonders, which are visible evidence of the presence and purpose of God. Under the leadership of Moses, the Hebrews leave Egypt in haste, although it is actually God who guides the journey as a pillar of cloud during the day and a pillar of light at night to enable people to see the correct path; it is a cloud and fire that serve as symbols of God, who leads the people on a circuitous journey toward the Red Sea. God sends a strong eastern wind to drive back the sea and makes the sea dry land, but clogs the chariot wheels of the pursuing Egyptians, who are drowned.

The freed Hebrews leave slavery behind them, but they must bear another burden, evident by their forty years of wandering in the wilderness of Sinai. With scarce water and little food, their life was precarious, which led to constant complaints, discontent, strife among themselves, disenchantment, and rebellion against Moses. They wanted to know if God was with them or not (Exodus 17:7). The people struggled against hostile desert tribes. At the same time, the Hebrews wandering in the wilderness were not without divine guidance, because flocks of quails would appear and, miraculously, *manna*, a sweet, sticky substance produced by insects, would appear during the early morning and also provide a source of food.

As the Hebrews despair, Moses ascends Mount Sinai, where God offers the prophet a covenant that unites this revelation with the deliverance from Egyptian slavery. In Exodus 19:4–6, God instructs Moses in the following way: "'You have seen what I did to the Egyptians, and how I bore you on eagles' wings and brought you to myself. Now therefore, if you obey my voice and keep my covenant, you shall be my treasured possession out' of all the peoples. Indeed, the whole earth is mine, but you shall be for me a priestly kingdom and a holy nation.'" These words of God are indicative of Israel's election by God to a special status in contrast to other religions in the region. Related to this special calling and its requirement to be holy, the Israelites are called to decide whether to accept or reject the covenant. Moreover, the biblical passage quoted from Exodus inexorably links together the deliverance from Egypt and the revelation on Mount Sinai. These combined happenings are called the Exodus event, in short. These events occur in history, suggesting that Yahweh is primarily a God of history. Unlike the nature deities of other tribes of the region, the Israelite God is not a personification of nature. Yahweh acts and reveals himself on the theatrical stage of history.

Under Joshua's leadership, the Israelites attacked and were victorious over the Canaanites, claiming their land as theirs. In time, the Israelites established a monarchy led by Saul, David, and Solomon. After the death of Solomon, they split into two kingdoms: Israel in the north and Judah in the south. The northern kingdom fell to the Assyrians (722 BCE), while the southern kingdom became a vassalage of Assyria before being overpowered by the Babylonians (587 BCE) and taken into captivity. With the rise of the Persian Empire, the Israelis were free to return to their homeland where they rebuilt Jerusalem, which occurred around 450–400 BCE under the leadership of Nehemiah and Ezra. After two centuries of Persian rule, the Israelites came under the control of Greece because of the conquest of Alexander the Great (332 BCE). The Hebrews endured the imposition of Hellenistic culture. Finally, the Jews revolted under the leadership of the Maccabees (164 BCE). After this period of independence, the Jews were conquered by the Romans, who undermined the center of Jewish religion at the time when they destroyed the temple in Jerusalem.

Judaic Sacred Literature

For many centuries, the narratives of the Jewish patriarchs and Exodus event were passed orally from one generation to another. Thus the ancient Jews did not have a single sacred scripture but rather had a collection of 24 separate books that were eventually called the Bible (Greek *biblia*, "books"). This collection of distinctive books was not called the Old Testament, a designation that can be traced to later Christian writers, which represents a prejudicial and theological position, suggesting an old, worn out, and inadequate message that is now superseded by the Christian message, which now fulfills the old prophecies. In other words, the Christian scriptures represent the culmination and promise of the prior Jewish texts, and these former texts are therefore old and outdated. In general terms, the separate books of the ancient Jews represented an evolving and edifying narrative about God's interaction with his chosen people and his actions to assist them in history.

This dramatic narrative related the major themes of Israel's faith, which included the promise of the ancient patriarchs to be faithful to their God, the divine deliverance of Israel from Egypt, divine guidance while wandering in the wilderness, receiving of the law at Mount Sinai by Moses, and the inheritance of the promised land. This entire scenario of events is often shortened to the Exodus event, which is actually a series of events that depicts God's redemptive efforts for his chosen people and simply a matter of political liberation from servitude. The Exodus event, during which time God acted in history and made it meaningful, functions as the sign of his revelation and divine presence. If one places the significance of God's actions in history within the context of the other religious cultures in the region and their cyclical concept of time, this Jewish linear conception of historical time—past, present, and future—represents a unity of time, because the present moment has meaning because of what happened in the past and the present is moving toward a meaningful conclusion sometime in the future. In comparison to other religious cultures, with their cyclical concepts of time tied to the agricultural temporal pattern, the Jewish notion of time is a major worldwide cultural change that would directly influence Christianity and Islam, which also sets Jewish thinking apart from Eastern religions such as Hinduism and Buddhism. In summary, the Jewish narrative of God's active intervention in history shapes the Jewish understanding about what God has done (past), what God is doing (present), and what God will do (future), which unifies the three moments of time into a meaningful configuration.

After the oral transmission and preservation of their Scriptures, the Jews decided to preserve their books into a single collection. The ancient Jews referred to their collection of books as Tanakh, an acronym for its three major divisions. The term Tanakh is derived from the first letters of all three divisions: Torah (Law), Nevi'im (prophets), and Kituvim (hagiography). The initial, most important, and authoritative division is the Torah (Law), also meaning "instruction," "teaching," which includes the so-called Five Books of Moses or the Pentateuch: Genesis, Exodus, Leviticus, Numbers, and Deuteronomy. Scholars also refer to the Pentateuch as the Hexateuch, which is derived from the Greek term meaning "five scrolls" (five books plus Joshua). From the Jewish perspective, the Torah represented God's gift to the people of Israel. The gift was, however, conditional upon the people's acceptance of the divine commandments and their obedience to them as the chosen people.

God's narrative gift to his chosen people was given to them in Hebrew, a divine language. Nonetheless, that the Jews lost the language before the Bible was finalized is evident in the Book of Daniel, which was composed in Aramaic, a language spoken by Jesus and his disciples. By the post-Exilic period of Jewish history, Aramaic became the preferred language used to translate the Jewish Scriptures, and second century BCE marked a time when many Jews read a Greek Septuagint or an Aramaic version. An oral tradition preceded the Jewish Scriptures, which assumed the form of the scroll (Isaiah 34:4) or a roll made of papyrus, leather, or parchment (Jeremiah 36:14; Ezekiel 2:9). Hebrew writing used Canaanite characters, which were eventually replaced with an Aramaic form of script known as the "square script." On the one hand, the process of writing was accomplished by using metal implements for the hard surfaces of stone and metal. On the other hand, a stylus was used for writing on clay or wax, a brush for various materials with paint or ink, and a reed pen with ink.

The prophetic literature is divided into the earlier prophets of Joshua, Judges, Samuel, and Kings, while the later prophets are Isaiah, Jeremiah, Ezekiel, and the twelve minor prophets. Finally, the mixed collection is called Ketubim (writings), which includes works such as Psalms, the Song of Solomon, and the moral stories of Job, Ruth, and Esther. The writings also include the wisdom of Proverbs and Ecclesiastes, and the historical Ezra-Nehemiah and Chronicles, with both sets of works representing two texts in a single collection. The final collecting, fixing, preservation, and canonization of the Pentateuch occurred during the Babylonian exile (Ezra 7: 14, 15), which was a period centuries removed from the events recounted in the books.

Modern biblical scholars view the Pentateuch as a composite work representing several major traditions that have been woven together. Scholars have identified four main literary strands that are signified by the letters J, E, D, and P. The J literary contribution represents the earliest source, originating from the period of the early monarchy (950 BCE), whereas the E sources can be dated to the time of the Northern Kingdom (about 750 BCE). The best example of the D literary strand is the book of Deuteronomy, which dates from the period of the Southern Kingdom (about 650 BCE or even later). The P source refers to priestly influence and dates from the time of the fall of the nation in 587 BCE.

The J source represents the Yahwist position found in Genesis and Numbers. The J writer is dated to the tenth century BCE during the united monarchy, with its center in Jerusalem. The Yahwist source stresses the anthropomorphism of God. When reworking the Jewish tradition, the Yahwist combined

Mosaic narratives with stories concerning creation history in Genesis and synthesized traditions from the patriarchal era. The E source represents the Elohist source, which is found in Genesis and Numbers and dated in the ninth century BCE at the northern court of the divided kingdom. The E writer stresses God's transcendence. Being prominent in Leviticus and Numbers, the P source is priestly in origin and dates to the sixth century BCE. The P source is attributed to Jerusalem priests during the period of the Babylonian exile, and portrays God as even more transcendent than the Elohist. Finally, the D or Deuteronomic source dates to the seventh century BCE and shaped its message in Deuteronomy and 2 Kings. The D source focuses on Jewish deliverance from Egypt and the Sinai covenant.

After the Babylonian exile, Jews were allowed to return to their homeland around 444 BCE. Ezra is credited with editing the Pentateuch, reorganizing people's lives around the Torah (Law), witnessing the building of the second temple, and contributing to the reestablishment of the priestly cult centered in the temple. Alexander the Great won Jerusalem and favor with its Jewish inhabitants, but his early demise caused Judah to fall to the Ptolemies of Egypt. The powerful influence of Greek culture and its adoption by many Jews caused the eclipse of Hebrew. This embrace of Hellenism by the Jews promoted the translation of the Torah into the Greek language. According to tradition, seventy scholars worked on the translation, which is known as the *Septuagint* (a Latin term for seventy).

The entire Pentateuch assumed its present shape around 400 BCE. The Pentateuch's written stage was preceded by at least three centuries of oral transmission, and it came to be recognized as the written Law (Torah). The only standard for the Jewish religion was the Torah, which represents the written and oral divine revelation. In the Torah, God reveals his nature, his purpose, and what he intends humans to do. Hebrew Scriptures identified the Torah with wisdom (Proverbs 8: 12). In contrast to the Pentateuch, the Prophets and Hagiographa literature became canonized after the destruction of the Second Temple in 70 CE by the Romans. The Prophetic books and Hagiographa are considered tradition by rabbinic scholars and help to explain the Pentateuch. In fact, the Prophets represent a continuous tradition that began with Moses.

Along with the written Law, Jews recognized an oral law that was developed by the Pharisaic teachers and their successors, who came to be known as "rabbis." The oral law took the form of scriptural exegesis. Rabbinic law was summarized in the *Mishnah* (Review), while the *gemara* (completion) consisted of reports of broad discussions about the Mishnaic text, which was the basic text of the oral Torah. Dating to around the third century CE and containing legal teachings of the Tannaim (teachers), or earliest rabbinic authorities and transmitters of the unwritten law, the *Mishnah* is a collection of originally oral laws divided into six orders according to subject matter, devoid of direct reference to the Pentateuch (written Torah). In general, the *Mishnah* codified the oral tradition in a more permanent form in writing and elaborated the law. It should not be conceived as a systematic body of law intended for practical use but rather should be understood as an instrument for the study of the law.

In addition, rabbinic Judaism gave birth to the Talmud, which contains analysis and elaboration of rabbinic lore (*aggadah*) that is prominent in the collection known as *Midrash*, which originated in the academies of Palestine and Babylonia. Within the Talmud, legal (*halakhah*, which means "the way or procedure") aspects dominate the text. These are laws that are prescriptive for human conduct in the sense of a right legal procedure for living life. The Talmud is a collection of six orders of the *Mishnah* that are subdivided into sixty-three tractates. The six major divisions are called the following: seeds (agriculture); festivals; women; damages; holy things (ritual); and purifications. There are two Talmuds: Palestinian and Babylonian. The latter encyclopedia collection became more authoritative over time. Each Talmud consists of the Mishnah of Rabbi Judah and one or more bodies of commentary.

The term *Midrash* means interpretation or commentary. Although rabbis presupposed that biblical scripture could not be altered, they still wanted to understand its significance by attempting to resolve contradictions within particular narratives or between one passage compared to another. Rabbis conceived of the Bible as consisting of three parts: Law (Torah), Prophets, and the sacred writings. They used the acronym Tanakh to represent the corpus of Hebrew Scriptures. The oldest datable rabbinic document is traced to Rabbi Judah the Prince shortly before 220 CE. The first generation of rabbis were called Tannaim (Aramaic for "repeaters" or "teachers"). Two major schools of interpretation were led by Hillel and his contemporary Shammai, whereas alternative Tannaitic traditions were called *Tosefta* (Aramaic for "addition"), suggesting footnotes that serve as commentaries on individual problems in the texts. With the same structure as the *Mishnah*, the *Tosefta* often provides the biblical bases of a rule or a reason for it, which the *Mishnah* rarely gives. Therefore, it exceeds providing supplementary notes and often serves to amplify the *Mishnah*. An example of a public letter was called *Teshuvah* (literally, "return," meaning a response), which was a corpus of rulings made when specific communities wrote to the rabbis for opinions on legal matters.

In retrospect, the rabbinical schools did not adhere to a theory of prophetic inspiration but rather thought that every syllable of the revealed Scriptures represented truth and authority traceable to the word of God. Rabbinic scholars did not advance the concept of a progressive revelation because the revelation to Moses was complete and final, even though it was possible to discover contradictions in the Scriptures. In the final analysis, there were no substantial differences.

Jewish Belief System

During its ancient history, the Jewish faithful were known as Israelites or Hebrews. It is not until the book of 2 Maccabees, during the Greek domination from the later second century CE to around the start of the third century, that the term "Judaism" appears in written form, giving it a rabbinical origin. It can be historically related to the completion and acceptance of the *Mishnah*, which was redacted by the Patriarch Judah. Within 2 Maccabees, Judaism is a term used to distinguish Jews from other people.

Despite the late use of the term, the centerpiece of Judaism is the covenant, which includes both a demand and a promise: "You shall be my people and I will be your God." By accepting the agreement, the lives of the people have a goal and history, and they have meaning within a context of trust and security. In addition, faith of the people is grounded in history, a location within which people practice the religion. To be admitted to this covenant requires a willingness to subordinate oneself to the will of God; it has nothing to do with natural kinship. Despite the patriarchal period, which is considered by Jewish thinkers to be a prologue to the Exodus event, the Exodus is an act of God in historical time and space that is a sign of God's revelation and presence and marks the genuine beginning of Judaism. During the eighth century, Amos (3:1–2) depicts the people of Israel as a family united together by God's act of deliverance from Egypt.

The covenant has social implications for the Israelite tribes because it gives the twelve tribes a sense of solidarity with each other and to the will of God, which forms the bases of their social unity. With respect to history, the covenant reflects its most decisive motifs: election, covenant agreement, and divine lawgiving. In contrast to the polytheistic religions of the time and their emphasis on the spirits of nature, election makes Judaism exactly opposed to them. The historical covenant is also a personal relationship between Yahweh and his chosen people, which stands in sharp contrast to the non-personal relationship between polytheistic followers and their gods. From a Jewish theological perspective, the covenant represents a gift of God's grace that God enters into freely and can dissolve at any moment.

There are two types of covenants: parity and suzerainty. If the parity covenant is reciprocal, the suzerainty type is more unilateral because it is made, for example, between a monarch and his vassal. The vassal is obligated to obey the conditions of the covenant. By adhering to its conditions, the inferior party finds protection and security. Thus, the suzerainty type of covenant is an agreement reached between unequal parties. And this relationship between unequal parties typifies the Sinai Covenant because God's sovereignty is not confined by the agreement, being completely free to either initiate or terminate the covenant.

As the covenant God of his chosen people, Yahweh is defined as a personal and immanent deity. By revealing his name to Moses, God wants to reveal the truth, to be defined, to be distinctive, and to be individual. The Israelite deity is thus not some nameless condition of being and not an abstract figure with whom no one can enter into a personal relationship. The revealed name of Yahweh suggests that this God opens himself and gives the faithful access to him. A consideration of the importance of a name in Middle Eastern cultures of the historical period is instructive, because a name is directly connected to a person's mode of existence. Therefore, knowing the name of someone means to enter into a relation with a person's being.

Besides being personal and immanent, Yahweh is spiritual, transcendent, and powerful. The power of Yahweh points to the awe-inspiring terribleness of God, which leaves an individual awestruck. This overpowering experience of Yahweh is neither an incomprehensible rage nor an irrational force; it is experienced as a self with a personal will. Moreover, God's power is exercised on behalf of Israel, and it is possible to find evidence of God's power in creation, the order of the universe, and the course of history. Since nothing can obstruct God's purpose, his omnipotence is connected with the end and purpose of history.

Within the context of the other polytheistic religions of the Middle East of the historical period, Yahweh declares his oneness, which sets him apart and is unique in comparison to other divine figures. The very first commandment of the Decalogue in Exodus (20:3) makes this perfectly clear and incumbent on believers to accept as part of the covenant. The *Shema* of Deuteronomy (6:4) further confirms this aspect of Yahweh: "Hear, O Israel, the Lord is our God, the Lord is One." In addition, Yahweh is described as the God of all the kingdoms of the earth. Thus, in comparison to Yahweh, other gods are nothing (I Kings 8:60; Jer. 2:11). God's singular nature necessarily implies that he is not androgynous and does not need to be complemented by a female consort. In comparison to Yahweh, the prophet Isaiah (2:8; 10:10) proclaims, the polytheistic deities are nothing.

A feature that Yahweh does share with other religions of the region is his wrathfulness, although a new factor is introduced by Judaism, with sin identified as the cause of God's displeasure, which triggers his wrath. Jewish good fortune is grasped as divine favor, while misfortune reflects God's wrath. In the book of the prophet Amos (3:6), every misfortune is identified as a product of the power of God's wrath. The prophet Hosea (11:9) makes it clear that God's wrath is not reflective of despotic caprice or blind rage. Yahweh's wrath is limited to the sphere of retributive justice, which suggests that punishment and forgiveness are not mutually exclusive, because paying a penalty constitutes a remission of sin. This pattern of thinking implies that divine wrath is transient when compared to God's loving-kindness and righteousness.

The loving-kindness (*ḥesed*) of God is directly connected to the covenant relationship, where it is sustained by both parties, making it an alternative in different situations (Genesis 24:12). Loving-kindness, a spontaneous expression of love, points to God as the father and shepherd of his chosen people. In conjunction with loving-kindness, God's righteousness is related to keeping the law in accord with the specific issues of the covenant. God is not only the guardian of justice but also protects the righteous against injustice within the covenant (Jer. 11:20). Jewish prophets through the centuries have warned the Israelites that the covenant was in jeopardy.

The love of God is developed by the prophet Hosea (11:4; 6:6) by making love the ultimate basis of the covenant relationship. Using the imagery of marriage, Hosea intends to say that the relationship based on law is now displaced by a living fellowship characterized by love. Moreover, Hosea sees the eventual triumph of love over everything. Direct evidence of God's love can be discovered by looking into a mirror because all humans have been created in his image. And the utmost gift of God's love is his revelation.

Connected to God's love is his mercy, which counters his wrathful aspect. God's mercy is all-embracing, as evident in Psalms (145:9). Along with mercy, there is God's justice. His mercy and justice form a unity in his nature. God's mercy and justice are characteristics of a personal God and extend beyond mere divine attributes, pointing to his redemptive actions. This loving, merciful, and just deity is a national god, but he is not a leader of a pantheon like Assyrian, Egyptian, Greek, or Roman deities. Yahweh is a jealous God who does not allow his chosen people to share their worship with other divine beings. All human worship must be directed to Yahweh because he is the only real and universal deity.

If love invites or implies an intimate relationship between the two unequal parties of the covenant, the holiness of God separates him uniquely apart from human beings. An early piece of evidence of God's holiness appears in I Samuel (6:20), when Samuel refers to the God of the ark. The emphasis on the holiness of God means that he is unapproachable because he is completely other and perfect when compared to created beings. That Yahweh is holy suggests the perfection of his being and sharpens the contrast of his nature to that of the created cosmos. The holiness of God has important consequences for humans, captured by a passage in Leviticus (19: 2): "You shall be holy, for I the Lord your God am holy." The command for Jews to be holy separates them and their God from other peoples and their deities.

In relationship to Yahweh, there stand human beings, as in the narrative of paradise, where life is akin to a primal innocence, as suggested by the nakedness of the inhabitants. This beautiful and harmonious place is ruptured when Eve induces Adam to pluck off and eat an apple from the tree of knowledge, thereby violating a law of God, who drives the couple from paradise as punishment for the violation. This narrative about original sin means different things to Jewish and Christian thinkers. For Christians, original sin scars the primordial ancestors of humankind for all time, rendering humans fallen beings in need of redemption, whereas original sin is a marginal notion in rabbinic thought, although there is a recognition among rabbis that it disrupts an inner divine unity within a person. The ancient rabbis called attention to the fact that humans have a free will and moral responsibility. But humans have two inclinations: one makes a person capable of doing good deeds, whereas the other pulls a person in the direction of evil. Under the guidance of the law, the rabbis are optimistic that humans can perform good actions and avoid the strong pull of the evil inclination within their nature. Due to the influence of Hellenistic culture, rabbinic thinkers adopted the Platonic doctrine of the pre-existence of souls.

When a Jew transgresses the law she can restore herself to good standing by repenting her sins. The Hebrew term for repentance is *teshuvad*, which literally means "turning" or "returning." Three stages of repentance are recognized: admitting wrong behavior, being genuinely sorry for wrongful action, and promising not to repeat the sin. By seeking forgiveness for transgressions of the law, the act of repenting is intended to transform a human life.

Judaism considers sin to be impure because it stains the individual, similar to getting dirty, rendering one unable to uphold the covenant. The human body is a temple that needs maintenance and protection against impurity. The distinction—purity and impurity—dates back to the ancient Israelite religion where this plays an important part in the flood story. Genesis (8:20) informs a reader that God orders Noah to take clean and unclean animals and tells him that only clean animals can be sacrificed. In Leviticus (19) there is a holiness code that broadly covers aspects related to cult and morality. Leviticus distinguishes between clean and edible animals and their opposites. All edible animals must conform to a specified classification, which divides all animals into groups that have divided hooves and chew their cud. The pig and its products are not allowed because the pig has the divided hooves but does not chew its cud. In the case of fish, they must have fins and scales, which eliminates eels and shellfish from the Jewish diet. According to Leviticus (12), female bodily emission of blood from either giving birth or menstruation makes a woman unclean for different periods of time and calls for purification. When a woman is unclean, she must neither touch anything holy nor enter a sanctuary. Leviticus (15) instructs a reader that when a man emits semen, he becomes impure and must regain his former condition. The male's discharge also pollutes the bed, for instance, on which he laid. Moreover, anyone coming into contact with the bed will be polluted. Thus both the male and the bed must be made clean by washing.

Besides bodily emissions, the Hebrew Scriptures indicate that there are other sources of pollution, which include such things as a corpse or someone with leprosy. These examples, of course, have nothing to do with morality. Purification is achieved by washing, whereas high degrees of pollution can be purified by sacrifice. By committing a sin, an unclean person can be restored to purity by atoning for one's transgressions and seeking the forgiveness of God. According to Ezekiel (36:25–26), water can purify the sinner, but God gives the sinner a new heart, replacing the former heart of stone with one of flesh and placing the divine spirit into a sinner.

Rabbinic Judaism

Before the Roman destruction of the temple in Jerusalem in 70 CE, Judaism was represented by four major sects. On the margins of Judaism, the Samaritans were distinguished by what they accepted as valid scripture. Unlike other Jewish sects, the Samaritans rejected prophetic literature as part of the Hebrew

Bible. They accepted instead only the first five books of Moses. They also continued the practice of animal sacrifice, which was rendered difficult after the destruction of the Jerusalem temple.

Representing a separate group from the main body of Judaism, the Essenes were an ascetic, cloistered group led by a high priest called the Teacher of Righteousness. In order to practice their interpretation of the necessity for purity, they retired to the desert in order not to compromise their way of life. This ascetic adhering group produced the Dead Sea Scrolls, which were eventually discovered in jars located in caves near the Dead Sea at Qumran from 1947–1956. Sect members read the old narrative of Judaism preserved in the Torah as the model for the future. When reading the sacred Scriptures, the Essenes did so through the lens of apocalyptic expectations about the fast-approaching end of time. They envisioned an apocalyptic climax of history when angels would join them to fight a final battle between the children of darkness and light at the end of time. The Essenes' eager embrace and expectation for the apocalyptic conclusion to history was also evident in the spirit of the Jesus movement, to be discussed in the next chapter.

Another Jewish sect was the Sadducees, a group that represented the upper socio-economic structure of Judaism. According to 1 Kings (1: 39), Solomon, king of Israel, appointed Zadok to be high priest, an influential position passed on to his descendants. As a party of the priestly establishment, their power and influence was dependent on and centered in the temple, but with the destruction of the temple, their power waned in Jewish society. They also represented a powerful conservative force in Judaism, as evident by their practice of literal interpretation of the law without any possibility of deviation by means of new interpretations. A later minority of Sadducees became hedonistic and assimilated themselves to Roman culture.

The Pharisees represented the fourth major sect of the pre-rabbinic period. In contrast to the Sadducees, the Pharisees wanted to render the law more humane in order for people to live according to its dictates. Instead of the upper-class appeal of the Sadducees, the Pharisees appealed to the people in the middle class and interpreted scripture more broadly, although they were punctilious concerning guidelines for purity and tithing. Additional differences between the Sadducees and Pharisees were marked by disagreement over literal interpretation of the law. They also disagreed over the nature of scripture, which the Sadducees conceived as the sole authority, whereas the Pharisees promoted scripture and tradition. And they differed over the resurrection of the dead or retribution after death, a belief that the Pharisees accepted as an article of their faith, while the Sadducees argued that there is no evidence for such a belief in scripture. From within the Pharisee sect, brotherhoods developed that were not strict in their interpretation of the law. After the destruction of the temple, the Sadducees and Pharisees evolved into the rabbinic movement that revolved around the synagogue.

In contrast to the earlier sectarian battles and their dogmatism, rabbinic Judaism defined itself in opposition to the former sectarian groups, reinvigorated

Judaism, and preserved its identity. The term "rabbi" means "leader" or "great one," but later evolves to mean "teacher." The rabbi's vocation was to study, interpret, and write commentaries on the law. Any male Jew could become a rabbi; rabbis were educated in what eventually would be called a *yeshiva* (sitting, session). When a male student graduated, he would be ordained a rabbi. Although the rabbi studied the law alone or in dialogue with others, public worship took place at the synagogue.

Judaism has not been a religion that seeks to evangelize its message and convert others to its faith, which can be attributed to its early ethnic nature and the Jewish existence as a minority community throughout its history, bound together by a covenant with God, often in foreign nations. Rabbinic Judaism did, however, set three conditions that had to be met by anyone converting to the religion. The rite of circumcision was necessary for male converts. This was followed by ritual immersion or baptism in the faith and an acceptance of the commandments of the religion.

Rabbinic Worship and Rites of Passage

When God created the world, he created something distinct each day. Humans were created on the sixth day, an event representing the culmination of God's creativity, while on the seventh day, God rested. The sixth day represented the arrival of Adam (Hebrew for "man") and Eve (Hebrew for "living"). The primordial couple is portrayed as innocent, naked, without shame, surrounded by abundance, and, thus, needing nothing. But they lose their place in paradise because they disobey God's commandment not to eat from the tree of knowledge of good and evil. The ancestor of all subsequent women, Eve, falls prey to the inducement of the serpent to eat the forbidden fruit and become wise and immortal—in short, to become like God. Eve persuades naïve Adam to eat the fruit, which violates God's commandment, leaving the divine being no choice but to expel the couple from paradise. After their expulsion, the primeval couple becomes aware of something new—shame and guilt.

This myth, celebrated by Western artistic expressions of creativity, can be interpreted from a few different perspectives. This narrative of Adam and Eve can be understood as a prologue to God's covenant with Abraham and Moses. It suggests that there are severe consequences for the human party who does not abide by the conditions of the covenant. Western feminists have called attention to the negative portrayal of Eve as the conduit of evil and argued that this picture of Eve contributes to a prejudicial stereotype of women as nefarious temptresses. From a third perspective, God's creation of the world has theological consequences because Yahweh's creation is performed within history. Being a creative work executed within time, Yahweh's actions cease to be myth, becoming instead historical actions, from the rabbinical perspective.

As descendants of Adam and Eve and members of the Exodus covenant, the faithful Jew owes gratitude to God for his life and for being chosen for inclusion into the covenant. Jews repay God by prayer, a form of communication between Jews and Yahweh that evokes a network of symbols and narratives that are packed with meaning. The repetitive and rhythmic nature of prayer is evident in Jewish practice because an observant Jew prays before going to sleep at night and when awakening in the morning. In addition to these times of prayer, a Jew should pray another three times a day in a fixed pattern. But whenever a person prays, she must have the right spiritual intention. Otherwise, prayer becomes a mechanical exercise that is insincere. Besides having the right intention before reciting a prayer, there are also other restrictions that must be observed. The content of a prayer must not be idolatrous, which would include, for example, prayers to angels or intermediary beings. It is, however, permissible to petition God for a special favor, just as long as it does not adversely affect others.

Before engaging in prayer, a faithful Jew dons a prayer shawl (*tallith*), which is shaped like a large rectangular piece of cloth with fringes located at the corners, as stipulated by law (Numbers 15:37–42). Males are required to cover their heads when praying by using the prayer shawl, before the Middle Ages. Since the Middle Ages and into the modern era, a skullcap has been used to cover the head, which has been called *kippah* (cap) or *yarmulke* in Yiddish. In addition to the skullcap, Jewish faithful also don a *terfillin* in prayer, which are a pair of black cube boxes about two inches high. These black boxes are connected to leather thongs that are secured to one's forehead and one's upper arm facing one's heart, wrapping the thongs around the arm and fingers. Besides pointing to the heart and suggesting sincere intention, the black box on the forehead operates to remind a practitioner to concentrate his mind on the reciting of a prayer. Inside the boxes, there are scriptural passages that explain their purpose and use. The securing of the black boxes echoes the biblical command to bind the Torah (law) on the hand and between the eyes. The book of Deuteronomy (6:5–9) records Yahweh commanding Jews to love him with their hearts and souls, and then saying with respect to prayer to bind them to one's hand and forehead as bodily signs. Additionally, a person should write these messages on the doorposts of their homes. These rolled up scrolls (*mezuzoth*) contain the *Shema*, a fundamental Jewish prayer that the dweller touches as he enters the home.

In the narrative about creation, Yahweh rested on the seventh day, and Jews honor God by keeping the Sabbath, as required by Exodus (31:16–17), as a day of rest; anyone daring to work on this day should be put to death. The requirement to keep the Sabbath, a sign made between Yahweh and his chosen people, is a part of a perpetual covenant to be followed by the faithful. Preparations for the Sabbath include cleaning of the home and individual, preparing the meal, and lighting of candles. In addition to the observances at home, many Jews attend the synagogue toward the end of the Sabbath to celebrate Havdalah, a boundary-marking observance that includes the use of wine, a braided candle, and a spice box reminiscent of the sweetness of the day. A song wishes everyone fortune for the coming week. Invariably, the service includes a reference to Elijah, a former prophet and current messianic figure. A particular synagogue may use the services of a cantor, a professional singer and leader of prayers, who has the ability to change the chanting style called for by either the Torah or Prophets. In addition to the roles of the rabbi and cantor, the laity play a major role in a typical service at the synagogue.

With respect to rites of passage, we find four major observances: birth, initiation, marriage, and death. The birth of a male involves the rite of circumcision and removal of the foreskin on the eighth day of life as a sign that one is now a member of the covenant agreement between the patriarch Abraham and Yahweh. The male initiation rite occurs during the teenage years and is called Bar Mitzvah ("son of the commandments") for males; the rite for females is called Bat Mitzvah ("daughter of the commandments"). The male rite is characterized by reading, in Hebrew, a scroll of one of the Pentateuch Scriptures. The youngster is now considered an adult member of the community, with ritual and moral responsibilities, and can count toward constituting the quorum of ten essential for a prayer group.

Having become an adult, a Jew is encouraged to marry. Unlike some ascetic strains in Hinduism, Buddhism, and Jainism, which insist on the observance of celibacy to free a person to practice her path to liberation by eliminating the attachments and obligations associated with marriage, Judaism advocates marriage as a wise choice for members. Marriage is encouraged as practically a religious duty, an injunction that should be grasped within the context of the covenant, because a child born to a Jewish mother is automatically a member of the covenant. Rabbinic scholars also advocate marriage because it—socially and personally—fulfills a person. And there is no negative stigma attached to sexual pleasure. In fact, rabbinical scholars insist that marriage is necessary for both procreation and pleasure.

Death is the final rite of passage recognized by Judaism. According to some versions, a person is visited by the angel of death, who carries out God's order concerning death in an impartial way for both the righteous and the wicked. In ancient Judaism, if a person died peacefully, it was said that he was gathering with his ancestors. In some areas, family members were buried together in underground caves, with their bodies placed on bench-tombs until the bodies had decomposed, at which time the bones of the deceased were collected and placed into a repository and interred beneath the benches. In modern Judaism, burial practices have changed, with a deceased person being buried in a plain coffin. Because no embalming is allowed, burial is done as quickly as possible, although funerals and weddings are not permitted on the Sabbath. After the death of a family member, an announcement is made about the time period for the family to receive guests, which extends over seven days after the deceased has been buried. Family members don somber clothing, and mirrors in the home are covered. If a father has died, the eldest son honors his father's memory by reciting the Kaddish, a prayer praising God and associated with death, every day for a year. The proper observance of death comes with some ancient restrictions that prohibit offering tithed food to the dead, based on Deuteronomy (26:14). The same text (18:11) forbids consulting ghosts and spirits or seeking oracles from the departed, because these practices are examples of superstitions. The text (14:1) also forbids extreme forms of mourning, such as self-laceration, which was common among other religions of the region.

Traditionally, Jews have been opposed to cremation or embalming, as practiced by other religious cultures. Jewish thinkers explain the avoidance of these types of practices is because they prevent the natural decomposition of the body. In addition, cremation was not adopted by Jews as a method of the disposal of a corpse, because they objected to something being consigned to flames that was considered to be created in the image of God. In the case of embalming, this practice was considered unnatural and thus rejected.

Jewish Eschatology

The Hebrew Scriptures offered neither a concept of immortality nor a clear image of life after death. The general ancient consensus was that God shaped the human body from earth and animated it with the breath of life, according to Genesis (2:7–8). When a person dies, he becomes a dead breath, according to Numbers (6:6), and the body returns to dust. Along with these ideas about the afterlife, there was also the notion that when someone died, he descended to Sheol, a dark place of death, where everyone is equal because of the acknowledged universality of death. In the book of Isaiah (14:15), Sheol is called the pit, and the place is partly described as a place of worms (14: 9–11). Within this dark pit, the deceased are estranged from God. According to the book of Job (10:26), it was a location of deep shadows and darkness. Job also referred to its confusion because there is no order, only chaos (10:22). Job also stressed that there was no return from it (14:17) because the deceased will descend, not arise again, and not return home (7:9–10). What mattered to ancient Jews was continuing to exist in one's descendants, because there was no promised paradise or bodily resurrection for the righteous.

Later literature accepted the idea that, after death, one became a shade, with a type of material existence and the hope of resurrection. The earlier notion of resurrection was used as a metaphor for the restoration of Israel after the Babylonian exile. Within the prophet Ezekiel's vision of a valley of dry bones (37), which represented the entire house of Israel, the bones reassembled, grew flesh and skin, came alive, and stood erect through the power of God. The passages describing Ezekiel's vision do not include a concept of the resurrection of individuals but rather a social or collective resurrection of a people. In a similar fashion, the book of Isaiah (26:19) refers to the dead living and their bodies rising. Isaiah (25:6–10) says that God will make a great feast on Mount Zion and will swallow death forever. This type of this-worldly vision is expanded when Isaiah (65:20) perceives a new heaven and earth where people will live to be a hundred, although they will continue to be mortal.

The book of Psalms (16:9–10) supports a belief in a beatific afterlife and refers to God ransoming a person's soul from the power of Sheol. And yet the universality of death is recognized by the same body of Psalms (49:12, 20), a common fate for everyone, with exceptions granted to Enoch and Elijah. In contrast to the visions of Psalms, I Enoch (22) sees the souls of the dead waiting for judgment in a mountain cave in which the souls of the righteous are separated from the wicked. Likewise, the Wisdom of Solomon subscribes to the Greek notion of an immortal soul (1:23), while it is the body that weights down the soul (9:15).

In the apocalypse of Daniel (12:2), a text composed after the outbreak of the Maccabean wars, which represented a revolt against Greek hegemony, "apocalyptic" comes from a Greek term that means "to uncover or reveal." The book of Daniel is a sealed book (12:4) because it uses a spiritual code language embodied within bizarre visions, mysterious symbolism, and supernatural occurrences, although its primary theme is God's revelation concerning the end time. The apocalypse of Daniel (12:2) refers to resurrection. The text recounts a vision of four successive empires—Babylonian, Median, Persian, and Greek—with each succeeding empire becoming more evil and brutal. The rapid increase in evil becomes associated with speculation with regard to the end of time. Daniel reports in chapter 7 seeing four beasts arising from a watery chaos, with the final one being the most horrific, with ten horns. These beasts represent the four successive empires: Babylonia is represented as a lion with eagles; Median is a bear with three ribs in its mouth; Persia is depicted as a leopard with four wings and four heads; and the Greeks are portrayed as a beast with ten horns. A third vision gives Daniel a glimpse of the coming kingdom of God. The book of Daniel will be examined further, in the next chapter, on Christianity.

The so-called little apocalypse of Isaiah (24–27) portrays the Last Judgment, when Yahweh will judge all nations. The apocalyptic vision begins with a cosmic catastrophe, with the earth being turned upside down, the sun and moon being eclipsed, a reign of universal chaos, and the righteous of past generations being raised from the dead. The book of Isaiah (9:1–7) makes it clear that the Messiah, who is not mentioned in Daniel, would come from the lineage of David and would come to restore David's kingdom (11:1–9). When this occurs, the wolf and lamb and the lion and calf will live in peaceful harmony, while the bear will graze with the cow and the lion and ox will eat straw.

In rabbinic Judaism, these various visions were fashioned into a coherent teaching about eschatology. For the rabbinical thinkers, there is a bodily resurrection, along with the soul being reunited with its body. The rabbinic pattern of eschatology includes a messianic period of national restoration, a new aeon of God's kingdom, and a celestial hereafter in which the soul eternally enjoys the vision of God. During the Middle Ages, there evolved the belief that in the period shortly before the appearance of the Messiah, the prophet Elijah will return. Elijah's task is to prepare the people for an imminent crisis, identified with the appearance of the Messiah. According to ancient Jewish Scriptures (2 Kings 2:1–18), Elijah was transported in a fiery chariot to heaven after choosing Elisha to be his successor. In Jewish narrative literature (*aggadah*), Elijah is recognized as the forerunner of the Messiah and becomes a hero of Jewish folklore, where he is portrayed as a hero of the poor. On the eve of Passover, he is believed to assist the poor for the seder meal. His expectant presence at the meal is symbolized by a cup placed at the center of the table and leaving the door open for him to walk into the room to announce the arrival of the Messiah. When the Messiah arrived, Elijah would anoint and reveal him to everyone. Among several different possibilities, the rabbinical tradition expected that Elijah would restore to Israel three things that had been concealed with the ark before the destruction of the temple: a jar of *manna*, water for purification, and the flask of anointing oil.

During the Hellenistic period, Jews expected the arrival of a kingly, warrior figure who would lead Israel to victory over their oppressors. There was an expectation that this figure would be a son of King David. The apocalyptic visions of the book of Daniel did not specify the need for a Messiah, a term that has its origins in the Hebrew term *mashiah* (anointed one). The term harkens back to the practice of pouring oil over the heads of kings, prophets, and priests, which was a Jewish custom and not a Greek practice. When the Hebrew term was translated into Greek, it became *christos*. Overall, Jews expected a political figure and not the suffering and dying person of early Christianity.

Festival Observances

The traditional festival calendar of Judaism represents a synthesis of an agricultural calendar with historical events. The ancient Jews observed a lunar calendar, with each month beginning a new moon. If placed in a sequence, many of the festivals would provide one with a historical summary of defining events of ancient Judaism. Such a list of festivals and their historical connections would provide a student of Judaism an insight about how its members comprehend themselves and their notion of salvation history.

The New Year (Rosh Hashanah) was a festival introduced after the Babylonian exile. The Day of Atonement (Yom Kippur) began after the Babylonian exile as a penitential observance. These festivals are marked with the blowing of the *shofar*, a ram's horn. The symbolism of the horn conveys the image of a wakeup call for the people to arise from their moral/ethical slumber and also invites Jews to recall their positive deeds of the past year.

In ancient times, Sukkoth marked the conclusion of the autumn harvest period. Sukkoth can be translated as booths or tabernacles; it refers to the old practice of camping in one's fields to protect them from harmful creatures. This agricultural festival evolved into an observance at which Jews built small shelters outside of their permanent homes. They sleep in these shelters during the eight days of the festival, recalling an even more ancient agricultural observance.

Hanukkah (dedication) is a festival that celebrates the historical event related to the rededication and purification of the temple in Jerusalem in 164 BCE by Judas Maccabee. Unlike other holidays, it does not have any biblical source, but it is based on the narrative about the Maccabees in the Apocrypha literature. This festival falls in December around the period of Christmas. Rabbis enhanced the festival in a more spiritual way by altering it into a joyful experience of divine deliverance by means of a miracle.

Another significant festival associated with an historical event is Passover, which recalls the liberation of the Jews from Egyptian bondage into the children of God. It is also a spring festival, representing renewal and rebirth that is observed by spring cleaning of the home. The liturgy of this festival is called *Haggadah* (narrative), which interprets the Exodus events. The unleavened bread (*matzah*) that is baked for this observance recalls the moment when the ancient Jews departed from Egypt on short notice under the leadership of Moses, making it impossible for the bread to rise in such a brief time. The unleavened bread is known in rabbinical circles as the bread of liberty.

Originally celebrating the barley harvest in late spring, which was observed by consuming only dairy products, the festival of Shavuoth (Pentecost) also celebrates the gift of the Torah to Moses on Mount Sinai. In contrast to this spring festival, there was another in late summer called the Ninth of Ab, a day of fasting from sunset to sunrise, which is historically associated with the destruction of the first and second temples. Besides observing fasting, a Jew is to refrain from wearing luxurious jewelry or clothing, which includes a ban on wearing leather.

The theme of deliverance is also celebrated by Purim, a minor festival, known as the Feast of Lots because it recalls the casting of lots in order to determine the best way to massacre Jews. Since it is based on the book of Esther, this book is read aloud. The narrative recalls the liberation of the Jews from Persian domination. Esther's wicked enemy was Haman, who gets hung while she wins a reprieve for her people. As the book of Esther is being recited, children make noise whenever Haman's name is mentioned by the reader. The festival is marked by the exchange of gifts in the morning, while merrymaking traditionally occurs in the afternoon, with excessive drinking accompanying the celebration.

Material Culture

The book of Exodus (33:7–11) refers to the tent of meeting, which was a tent pitched outside of an encampment by Moses. It was a place at which Moses could communicate with God and would be joined by others wanting to speak with God. Exodus describes Moses walking out of the camp toward the tent on the outskirts of the camp and people standing in front of their own tents. When Moses entered the tent of meeting, people would witness a pillar of cloud descend and stand at the entrance of the tent while Moses spoke with God. The tent represented the manifestation of a transcendent God on earth.

The book of Exodus (25:10–22) also refers to another sacred object identified as the Ark of the Covenant, which scholars seem to think was originally a portable throne on which God sat invisibly. The ark represents the presence of God among his chosen people. This material object stands in sharp contrast to the images of deities among the polytheistic cultures of neighboring peoples. As the Ten Commandments make absolutely clear, there are to be no images of Yahweh made by any human. The text specifies its dimensions, wooden material, the use of gold to adorn it, the poles used to carry it, and its mercy seat, to be used to carry the covenant agreement. Overall, the ark signified the nearness of a transcendent God. More specifically, the mercy seat represented a footstool of God's throne and was conceived as a place at which God encountered the priestly representative of the people. According to Deuteronomy (10:3), Moses made the original ark, and it was brought to Jerusalem by King David, according to 2 Samuel (6:2–4).

As important as the tent of the meeting and the Ark of the Covenant were to ancient Judaism, the temple of Solomon was arguably central to the cultic practices of the religion. This temple was built according to Phoenician architectural patterns, with a courtyard in front of the structure that held an altar. Two huge pillars flanked the eastern door. The temple consisted of three parts: vestibule, sanctuary, and inner shrine. Ordinary people worshipped in the court outside in the vicinity of the sacrificial altar. The main sanctuary contained sacred furniture, such as the seven branched golden candle-sticks, a table for show bread, and a small altar. This room was large, with a height of 45 feet, and covered with a flat roof supported by huge cedar beams. With latticed windows located on either side, the room was dimly illuminated, evoking a sense of something mysterious. Carvings of palm trees, flowers, and cherubim adorned the walls. Beyond the small altar, stairs led to a raised room located behind a small double door, which covered the holiest spot in the temple, which was lined with cedar wood but had no windows, making it absolutely dark, which heightened the sense of mystery and holiness. Within this dark room, there were two large cherubim standing about 15 feet high. Beneath their wings, the Ark of the Covenant stood, representing Yahweh's throne.

With the rise of Rabbinic Judaism after the destruction of the temple in 70 CE by the Romans, the temple was replaced by the synagogue, which comes from a Greek term meaning "assembly" or "gathering." This place for public worship was built as either a longhouse, a long rectangular room, or as a basilica, a building modeled on the Roman municipal type of architecture. The building was constructed for the congregation to face Jerusalem while praying. During a typical service, the Torah was placed before a niche, which was carved or painted into the wall, before the worshippers. As Judaism evolved, the Torah niche developed into a more elaborate piece of furniture called the Holy Ark, which contained the law scrolls. Later in the tradition, the ark became a lamp. During religious services, the Torah was read from a rostrum, which might be located in the center of the congregation. Within a Jewish home, the eastern direction toward Jerusalem was designated by a plaque (*Mizrah*, meaning East in Hebrew). During the vicissitudes of the course of history, the synagogue was an essential institution for the preservation of Judaism, forming a location at which people can enter into a bond of social union on a regular basis. Thus, the synagogue was more than a building and formed a gathering place for the faithful.

Making its appearance as an important symbol of Judaism, there was the six-pointed star, which arose during the Middle Ages. This star recalled the shield of King David of biblical times and now adorns the national flag of Israel. A final example of Jewish material culture is the *menorah*, a seven-branched candlestick. Exodus (25:40) recounts that its pattern was given by God to Moses on Mount Sinai and was intended to provide light for the interior of the temple. The *menorah* used for Hanukkah in households constitutes a nine-branched object whose central light is called the *shamash*, the serving light, because it is used to light the other candles. According to a rabbinical narrative, the Maccabees entered the temple in Jerusalem and found the *menorah* unusable, which motivated them to use their spears to create a temporary *menorah*. This action transformed weapons of war into implements of peace. With the *menorah* and Star of David, we have two good examples of members of a religious culture creating meaningful objects that are based on divine models.

Women and Judaism

According to the narrative of Genesis, Eve was born from the rib of Adam, succumbed to the wily cunning of the serpent, and seduced Adam to eat the fruit of the Tree of Knowledge. This narrative suggests that women are inferior to men, have weak wills, are easily manipulated, and cannot be trusted. This narrative is the product of a patrilineal culture and patrilocal households. Among ancient Israelites, the lives of women were circumscribed to the home and market, where they could cook, work the loom, clean, or buy food, whereas the lives of men were more public. The lives of women were restricted in other ways. According to Exodus (21:7), a father could sell his daughter into slavery. Some laws in Exodus (25:11–12) protect men, as when a woman grabs a man's testicles during an argument; for this violation of the male anatomy, a woman is punished by having her hand cut off.

The ancient Israelites were concerned about a woman's sexuality because they were worried about the stability of the family. They were convinced that female sexuality could be controlled by early marriage soon after a girl reached puberty. Because of the dangerous nature of female sexuality, a girl had to be under the control of her father and passed to the control of her husband when married, becoming her husband's property. Therefore, adultery amounted to a violation of property rights of the husband. The book of Deuteronomy (22: 13–21) demonstrates, however, a concern about protecting women from false charges.

A high value was placed on virginity. Any virgin seduced and losing her virginity was considered to have lowered her economic value for her father, and he was to be compensated by the offender (Exodus 22:16). Because male descent lines must be kept pure and unconfused, the general rule in ancient Judaism was virginity before marriage and lifelong monogamy. This guideline was a bit uneven because a male could have more than one wife, while a woman must be monogamous, although the husband had to provide equally for the first wife and subsequent wives (Exodus 21:10).

The inferior status of women was mitigated to some degree by legal rights. Besides being distinguished from slaves, a woman could not be divorced without a substantial reason, although a woman was forbidden from initiating a divorce, according to Deuteronomy (24:1–4). In the case of rape, Deuteronomy (22:25) specifies that the penalty is death, while the rape of a virgin (2:28) requires recompense to the father for lowering the value of his property.

In general, a woman's value is measured by her ability to produce offspring. With motherhood as the epitome of her purpose in life, a woman who is barren is considered cursed, and barrenness was accepted as a grounds for divorce. Later in her life, a barren woman had no one to care for her welfare. According to textual evidence, women followed other occupations other than motherhood. The book of Jeremiah (9:17) calls attention to professional mourners, Ezra (2:65) refers to women serving as temple singers, Ruth (4:161) mentions nurses, and Genesis (35:17) mentions midwives. These socially acceptable forms of employment stand counter to working as a prostitute, devoid of social status. Deuteronomy (22:18) associates women with sorcery, which the text calls an abomination. Due to her ritual impurity associated with her monthly menstrual cycle, a woman was excluded from the priesthood, even though she had to adhere to the same moral and dietary regulations as her male counterpart. This type of restriction is followed by rabbinic Judaism, when the *Mishnah* excludes women from centers of holiness.

Overall, the Jewish attitude toward women could be ambivalent. Genesis (2:24) refers to the marital bond as becoming "one flesh." Kabbalistic mysticism stressed the female aspect of divinity with its notion of the *Shekhinah*, although this is mitigated by describing its feminine aspect as passive and susceptible to demonic influence. Ecclesiastes (25:24) says that a woman is the origin of sin, and the reason that we must die. Finally, woman are considered dangerous, as illustrated by the narrative of Samson being duped by Delilah (Judges 16: 4–21). These negative and positive attitudes toward women are very similar to other religious cultures of the same time period.

Jewish Mysticism

In the book of Ezekiel (1:1–28), the central figure is a priest administering to fellow Jews in exile around 571 BCE who becomes an important prophet, warning Israelites of their sins. The first chapter of this book opens with Ezekiel's account of his vision, when the heavens open to reveal visions of God. Ezekiel recalls a strong wind, a bright cloud, and flashes of fire. In the middle of this, he spies strange creatures of human form, each with four faces, four wings, straight legs, feet like those of a calf, and human hands under their wings. Their four faces included that of a human, a lion, an ox, and an eagle. In the middle of these weird creatures he sees a fire, with flashes of lightning issuing forth. There is also a wheel near each of the four creatures, which formed a chariot with the ability to move in any of the four directions. As the creatures moved, the wheels moved simultaneously with them; if they ascended, so did the wheels. Ezekiel also witnessed a dome over the creatures from which issued a voice. Above the dome, he could see a throne with a human form sitting on it in shining splendor. In this ecstatic vision, Ezekiel sees the chariot-throne with God sitting on it; God proceeds to give the prophet his commission to warn the Israelites about their sinful ways and the dire consequences that awaited them if they did not change their behavior.

Ezekiel's ecstatic vision served as inspiration to Jewish mystics, whose beliefs came to be called Merkabah (chariot) mysticism. These early mystics strived to duplicate the vision of Ezekiel by making an ecstatic (outside one's body) journey to the divine throne room, where the mystic could see God in all his glory. It is significant to acknowledge that a mystic did not experience a unitive experience with God, because the mystic's awareness of God's otherness is never blurred, and she never loses her identity.

These kinds of ecstatic experiences are described in a body of literature called the *Hekhaloth* books, which were edited in the fifth and sixth centuries. The journey of the mystic described in these texts recalls proceeding through heavenly halls, a journey that is restricted by numerous gate-keepers. The soul can only progress by knowing the secret names, introducing the importance of esoteric knowledge into the mystic path of ascent to the divine throne. The role of an esoteric knowledge inspired detailed descriptions of God's body that recall the fifth chapter of the Song of Solomon. The mystical texts even provide descriptions of the enormous dimensions of God's organs, and the secret name of each organ is also given in the text, which is intended to help the mystic get past heavenly guardians. Merkabah mysticism did not, however, concern itself with cosmogonic speculation typical of the later Kabbalism.

Reaching its apex at the end of the thirteenth and early fourteenth centuries, another form of mysticism developed in southern France and Spain, called Kabbalism, which literally means "tradition," implying that it represented the true interpretation of the Hebrew Scriptures. According to the *Book of Bahir*, Kabbalah also means "acceptance" in the sense of being accepted by God. From a historical perspective, Kabbalism developed in three phases: (1) the work of Abraham Abulafia (1240–c.1291), what is called prophetic Kabbalism because he compared his mission to the prophet Isaiah, pretensions that alienated him from more orthodox Kabbalists; (2) the *Zohar*, representing a speculative movement; and (3) the movement of Isaac Luria (1534–1572), which stimulated messianic speculation.

Abulafia's primary aim was to untie the knots that he believed bound the soul, separating it from a cosmic stream of life that flows through the entire creation. This implied that the soul needed to escape the limits imposed by its sensory perceptions and emotions in order to concentrate on the spiritual.

His proposed method for achieving this condition was to meditate on the Hebrew alphabet, because it had the power to produce a new state of consciousness. A prerequisite for meditation is a form of Judaized yoga that culminates in prophetic ecstasy, during which time a mystic encounters his own self. During the ecstatic experience, the seeker becomes God's anointed one, and during a brief period of his ecstatic experience, a person becomes his own Messiah.

Contemporaneous with Abulafia's work, there was the *Zohar*, a text whose title is derived from the book of Daniel (12:3): "Those who are wise shall shine like the brightness (*zohar*) of the sky . . . like the stars forever and ever." The authorship of the text is disputed, with some scholars tracing it to Rabbi Simeon bar Yohai, a renowned third-century figure, or to Moses ben Shemtov of Leon (1250–1305) living in Granada, Spain. Nonetheless, the *Zohar* represents the foundational text of Kabbalah.

A central feature of the *Zohar* is the concept of the *Sefiroth*, which originated in the *Sefer Yetsirah* (*Book of Creation*), which dates to the period between the third and sixth centuries and depicts the *Sefiroth* as living numbers that are conceived as divine emanations. But in the *Zohar*, the *Sefiroth* loses its numerical significance and becomes grades or degrees of creative power of a divine manifestation. They are identified as the creative names that God gave to himself, making them attributes and agencies of God. The *Sefiroth* represents the hidden world of divine language that forms the bases of the phenomenal world, representing the hidden aspect of the Godhead and the means of his self-revelation to humans. Moreover, the *Sefiroth* can be conceived as emanations of divine light whereby a transcendent God becomes immanent in the world and is active in the souls of human beings.

If the *Sefiroth* represents the emanations of God, the *En-Sof* (the infinity) is the inner most being of God; it stands for God's hiddenness, because he is devoid of qualities and beyond human knowing, although it is also possible to know God. Kabbalists use a piece of coal to point to what they mean because a piece of coal can exist without a flame. The latent power of the coal manifests itself only in union with the flame and thus in its light. In a similar fashion, God's attributes are emanations of light in which the hidden nature of *En-Sof* manifests itself. There are ten fundamental attributes of God, which are at the same time ten stages through which the divine life pulsates back and forth. The *Sefiroth* are considered a single great name of God, but they are divided into three triads, while the tenth *Sefiroth* represents the harmony of the totality. This tenth principle that unites the others is called *Malkuth* or the Kingdom of God. The tenth and unifying *Sefiroth* is also called the *Shekhinah* (presence).

In Talmudic literature, the *Shekhinah* literally means the in-dwelling of God in the world. What in the Hebrew Bible is called God's face in rabbinical usage becomes not only an aspect of God but also receives a feminine character, as evident in descriptions of the queen, daughter, or bride of God, while the *Sefiroth* is referred to as the offspring of the union between God and the

Shekhinah. Moreover, it is the archetype of the community of Israel and the mother of each individual Israelite.

According to the Kabbalistic narrative account, before humans fell from grace, there was a complete unity between God and the *Shekhinah*. After the fall symbolized by the expulsion of Adam and Eve from paradise, this fundamental unity was ruptured, replacing harmony with discord. Thus, sin has had a destructive result and influence because it has caused the exile of the *Shekhinah*. This notion of the exile was rooted in the Talmud, where it meant that God's presence was always with Israel during its periods of exile. However, the Kabbalists interpreted the exile of the *Shekhinah* as meaning that a part of God was exiled from the divine nature and represented a separation of the masculine and feminine principles in God, which was metaphorically referred to as the separation of the Tree of Life from the Tree of Knowledge.

Since the world and levels of beings were interrelated for the Kabbalists, the *Shekhinah* was also conceived as the dwelling place of the soul, which is said to pre-exist in the divine realm and whose task after descent to earth was to reunite itself with God. From the Kabbalistic perspective, the union of God and the soul was a reunion of the feminine and masculine principles. Thus, the exile of the *Shekhinah* was symbolic of a person's guilt and sinfulness, which a person must seek to end by uniting with God.

By conceiving of Jewish life as cosmically disrupted, Isaac Luria (1534–72), a prominent Kabbalist, was able to make sense of the tragedy of Jewish life. According to Luria, God contracted himself in order to make room for the world that he created. Luria perceived this as a dangerous process, because God had to also remove his perfection, which caused a fracture in the divine sparks that get intermixed with the gross and evil material of creation. It is the duty of the mystic to help God return the divine sparks to their rightful place. The mystic can accomplish his task by means of meditative practice, pious actions, and ritual acts.

Jewish Heresies

Around the beginning of the seventeenth century, Jews were invited to migrate to Poland to live and work by its impoverished nobility, who sought to utilize Jewish acumen for business affairs. Jewish business men managed large estates, collected taxes, stimulated trade, and developed industry, which led to greater wealth for Polish nobles. In addition to their economic usefulness, Jews served a political purpose by acting as a buffer between the Poles and Prussians and townspeople and village peasantry, while being protected by the crown. Besides becoming economically prosperous, the Jews enjoyed considerable autonomy because they had their own courts and synods fully recognized by the government. Nonetheless, external dangers existed, such as the Catholic clergy, who organized mob violence against the Jewish community. But as the Jews became more prosperous and recognized as a vital economic factor, the violence ceased. Over time, the Polish nobility and Jews became wealthier, which made the social situation of the Jews in Poland more precarious. Because Polish peasants were economically drowning to death under oppressive taxes and forced labor imposed upon them, the peasants vented most of their anger on the Jews. Led by Bogdan Chemelmicki and his Cossacks, a revolt was launched against the Polish lords and Jews in 1648. Horrific massacres were inflicted on Jewish citizens. During the decade of 1648 to 1658, it is estimated that seven hundred Jewish communities were completely destroyed.

This type of violent historical disaster created an emotional and insecure environment, which contributed to various Kabbalists' notions pertaining to the birth of messianic expectations, implying that many Jews believed that their sufferings at this time heralded the coming of the Messiah. The *Zohar* had predicted that in the year 1648 the Messiah would appear, which set the stage for the expected appearance of such a figure. It was not mere coincidence that at this time Sabbatai Zevi (1626–76), a follower of Lurianic Kabbalah, announced that he was the Messiah in 1666, which sparked adherents to embrace him. The Turkish sultan perceived the movement as a danger to his position and imprisoned Zevi. While incarcerated, Zevi, a false messiah, was given a choice of conversion or death. When he decided to convert, his disillusioned followers rejected him and his movement, returning again to the misery of despair.

Before the memory of Sabbatai Zevi had begun to fade, a new heresy arose with the appearance of Jacob Frank, an unlearned and unscrupulous adventurer. Frank proclaimed himself the incarnation of Sabbatai Zevi. He was heralded as the Messiah risen from the grave by the people. Frank wanted to establish a new religion that would be based on the *Zohar* and not on the Hebrew Bible or Talmud. This betrayal of the Jewish tradition shocked the whole of the religion.

Besides these two heresies, Enlightenment thought threatened the future of Judaism by introducing a wave of religious nihilism. Some became convinced that the Hebrew Bible and Talmud did not contain the seeds of salvation because the hope of the future rested in secular wisdom. Diatribes were directed at the synagogue and the sacred Hebrew language, leading to despair and creation of a spiritual wasteland. The religious vacuum created would be filled by the rise of the Hasidic movement.

Hasidic Mystical Movement

Hagiographical literature relates many tales about the founder of the Hasidic movement known as the Baal Shem Tov (Master of the Holy Name). It is alleged that he could speak to animals and heavenly beings in their own languages. He is credited with restoring the life of a bride who died on her wedding day. In another episode, he laughs three times about what was occurring in a village some distance from his location. His disciples are puzzled by his odd behavior because there was nothing humorous occurring where they surrounded their leader. Gathering some of his mystified disciples called Ḥasdim (pious ones), he took them by wagon to the home of a pious, humble, poor Jew to show his followers what the villager did that was so humorous. In addition to these types of mystical powers possessed by the Baal Shem, he embodied a simple joy and celebration of life. This unpretentious joy for life is illustrated when he takes the scroll of the Torah in his hands and begins to dance with it, surrounded by his followers.

In one of the few writings that he left for future generations, composed as a letter and dated New Year's Day in September 1746, the Baal Shem Tov writes about an ascent of his soul and the wonderful visions that he experienced during his ascent. In the Garden of Eden, he saw, for instance, many souls, who were in a state of rapture. The repented souls invited him to ascend with them, and he agreed to accompany them. He proceeds step by step and enters the palace of the Messiah. There he sees the Messiah studying the Torah with rabbis and saints, within the midst of great rejoicing.

The so-called Baal Shen Tov was born Israel ben Eliezer (c. 1700–60) into a religious wasteland characteristic of Europe of the historical period. His life was grounded in the divine and introduced a robust optimism into Judaism by injecting a burst of religious enthusiasm into it. He lived with and for his followers, and they conceptualized him as a personification of the Torah. During his life, he did not separate the sacred and the profane, because he believed that every profane act can be made sacred. The Hasidic movement centered on the Hasidic leader (zaddik, literally the "righteous one"), who represented the center of the community. The Hasidic leader was not like the biblical Noah, who walked with God and was mainly concerned with his own salvation. The Hasidic mentor was more similar to Abraham, a selfless leader who walked before God, suggesting that he ministered to the needs of the people. According to the Hasidic movement, the Torah finds its completion in the zaddik, who loves and studies it, becoming a living Torah.

The righteous leader mediates between heaven and earth, enabling heaven to reach the people. By clinging to the zaddik, the people join themselves to him, and thus are raised with him to God with the hope of being delivered to heaven. The zaddik also acts to restore the harmony of creation, which is accomplished by spiritualizing the people, implying that the zaddik and the people are incomplete without each other. But the most essential characteristic of the zaddik is humility, which is actualized by the negation of the self and his love of the people.

Hasidism teaches that people occupy different rungs during life and that there is no area of life in which God cannot be served. This means that there is no division between the sacred and the profane. In fact, the profane ordinary acts of eating, drinking, and speaking can become holy acts. What is important is that the zaddik must have the correct intention (kavanah), which also means to be completely concentrated on God. It is the gift of concentration that turns a profane act into a holy one. The highest level of concentration is a gift of God that leads to complete abandonment of the self and to a high degree of ecstasy, which unlocks the meaning of life. It is at this moment that one experiences uninterrupted thought and communion with God and transcends personal ecstasy.

Modern Jewish Movements

Modern Judaism in America falls into three major movements: Conservative, Reform, and Orthodox. Founded in Germany in 1819 by Leopold Zunz (1794–1886), Conservative Judaism was influenced by Enlightenment philosophy, which motivated it to think that change is justified by historical precedent, assuming a middle position between Reform and Orthodox forms of Judaism. By seeking historical justification before introducing an innovation, this movement did not reject traditional forms of Judaism. The Jewish Theological Seminary was founded in Pittsburgh in 1885, although the Orthodox did not recognize its ordination of rabbis. The Orthodox rabbis also do not recognize rulings made by Conservative Jews concerning issues such as female ordination, divorce, and conversion. Reform Jewish leaders defined the movement in the "Pittsburgh Platform" as a "declaration of independence." Among its innovations were elimination of a head covering when praying, only the ethical elements of the Torah were considered binding, God's commandments were ethically important, the importance of Israel was eclipsed, and anticipation of the arrival of the Messiah at a future time was replaced with its fulfillment in America.

Believing that traditional rituals and observances were the best to follow, Orthodox Judaism was not comfortable with innovation. Orthodox Jews conducted worship in Hebrew, observed Sabbath obligations, insisted on kosher meals, and observed proper gender roles. Orthodoxy is less a turning back to an earlier age than it is an attempt to balance religious tradition with modernity.

Influenced by Moses Mendelsohn (1729–86) and his Enlightenment philosophy, with its emphasis on rationality, Reform Judaism encouraged the faithful to absorb German culture because it would not affect the essence of the religion. The leaders of Reform Judaism attempted to make it more relevant to the historical period. Many of its reforms were in liturgy, introduction of choral singing, and recitation of prayers in the vernacular. Despite these liturgical innovations, Reform Judaism remained theologically conservative, even though it emphasized diversity and tolerance, the obligatory nature of religious practice, and responsibilities to the state of Israel.

In contrast to these Jewish groups, Zionism was a movement that was both political and religious, arising in mid-nineteenth century Europe amidst the rise of nationalism, anti-Semitism, and a longing for social freedom. Theodore Herzl (1860–1904), a Viennese Jew, is credited with founding Zionism, named for God's dwelling place on a ridge in Jerusalem. Herzl, a news reporter, covered the trial of Alfred Dreyfus (d. 1935), a French army captain charged with selling state secrets to Germany. Herzl noticed the overt anti-Semitic prejudices that influenced the trial and came to the conclusion that only by establishing a new Jewish nation could Jews become secure.

The modern movement of Zionism thus represents a return to the ancient land of Israel that is combined with nationalism reminiscent of Europe of the time. Before Zionism became a reality, the sentiment surrounding it was expressed in the words of the Passover *seder* meal with the refrain of "next year in Jerusalem." This type of wish is testimony to the existence of a spiritual nostalgia to return to the holy land, a journey that would include a revival of the Hebrew language that would re-unite Jews into a single culture. The Zionist ideal combined a secular conception of Jewish self-emancipation along with the religious messianic hope for a redemptive restoration.

Besides the influence of Herzl, Moses Hess (1812–75), a socialist thinker and theorist, published *Rome and Jerusalem* in 1862 in which he called for a Jewish state founded on socialist principles. Eventually, this type of thinking developed the idea of the *kibbutzim*, collective agricultural settlements that still exist today. They enable farming areas to be economically self-sufficient. The Zionist movement was nurtured by the Holocaust and a desire to be secure from a similar type of event in the future. During World War II and after it, many Jews spread around the globe, leaving European anti-Semitism behind them. Many Jews migrated to Palestine and had to fight an army consisting of troops from seven Arab states. Victory gave the Jews an opportunity to create the state of Israel, the only viable democracy in the region.

The Holocaust

In his award-winning novel *Night*, Elie Wiesel (b. 1928) describes in moving detail how the German Gestapo took over his town, rounded up all the Jewish people, and shipped them by rail to concentration camps. In short, powerful sentences, Wiesel recalls the horrific ordeal and how he and his father struggled to survive. Wiesel recounts the hanging of two Jewish adults and a young boy by the Nazis at Auschwitz. Before being hanged, the two adults cried out "Long live liberty," but the child remained silent. Coming from a location behind him, a youthful Wiesel could hear someone ask where God was, and then heard another voice say, "He is hanging on the gallows." At a later point in the novel, Wiesel sees himself in a mirror and can hardly recognize himself because he looks like a corpse. The prisoner's depth of despair is shown in another of his novels, which depicts Jewish males putting God on trial and finding the deity guilty for allowing this horrific genocide.

During the 1920s, there was no grand plan to exterminate Jews, based on Hitler's book *Mein Kampf* in Germany. After Hitler gained power in 1933, the persecution of Jews began with a boycott of Jewish-owned businesses. In 1935, other forms of discrimination followed, stripping Jews of citizenship, looting their stores, forbidding them from entering businesses and government services, imposing social isolation, and making it easy to identify Jews by requiring them to wear a star on their outer clothing. German leaders taught that Jews were racially inferior, while Germans represented a superior race—the Aryan myth—that must maintain its purity and not be contaminated by the impure Jews. During the Olympic Games of 1936, the German government reduced its overt action against the Jews to present a benign demeanor to the outside world, but the persecution continued after the games.

Many Jews fled Germany for other countries, but the conference of 1938 at Evian, France, made it clear that other nations did not want to absorb the Jewish refugees. There were some Jews who were confident that a nation like Germany, which had produced great philosophers, theologians, poets, novelists, musical composers, and artists, could never engage in mass murder. After the Nazi invasion of Austria in 1938, the assault of Czechoslovakia, and invasion of Poland in 1939, the Nazi authorities devised the final solution, which involved the creation of a sophisticated bureaucracy designed solely to exterminate human vermin regardless of their age or gender. The so-called "final solution" involved collection of people by the civil authorities, transportation by train, placement into gas chambers, and cremation sites where one's body would be reduced to ashes. The names of many of these extermination camps—Auschwitz, Treblinka, and Buchenwald, for example—live in infamy in the collective memories of Jews today. Some Jews avoided being gassed to death by being strong enough to work, some women were forced into prostitution for the pleasure of German soldiers, other Jews were forced to endure dangerous and painful medical experiments, some Jews were gunned down and buried in mass graves, and deceased Jews had their gold fillings extracted before being buried or cremated. There were some Christians who worked secretly to subvert the Nazi killing machine and to save as many Jews as they could, and some were killed by the Nazis for their heroic and empathetic efforts. Critics argue that Western governments knew more about the scenario of mass murder and should have attempted to do more, such as bombing the railroad tracks taking victims to concentration camps. In the final analysis, the Holocaust was efficient enough to approximately exterminate a third of the Jews in the world. Many of the Jews who survived the concentration camps experienced feelings of guilt about why they survived and so many others perished. A close friend of mine had a mother who survived a concentration camp, and it was not unusual for her to awake during sleep, triggered by a nightmare related to her experience. Obviously, her horrific experience still haunted her.

In light of the consequences of the Holocaust, this tragic event convinced Jews that in order to be secure, they needed their own sovereign state where they could practice their religion, preserve their language, and follow their own customs. With the support of the WWII Allied Forces, the United Nations voted to partition Palestine, creating a Jewish state within the midst of several Arab states.

Experiential Aspects of Judaism

Even though the ancient Israelite religion and worldview are shaped by the covenant with God, which represents a close bond between God and his chosen people, the fundamental religious experience manifests a dialogical relationship between the chosen people and their God. During the course of this ancient dialogue, both parties ask questions and respond with answers within the context of this intimate dialogue. Israelites experience God as a personal figure who cares about them. This interrelationship between humans and their single God also involves being in dialogue with each other, which is often manifested as mutual obligation. The interaction between God and humans manifests itself as an actual experience of God or an emissary. In Genesis (15), the message of God comes to Abraham in both visual and auditory forms.

In another powerful incident in Exodus, Moses sees the burning bush that is not consumed by the flames and hears God's voice. Moses responds with fear, awe, and wonder, being overpowered mentally and emotionally by the experience. An earlier part of Genesis relates the trancelike experience akin to sleep that is experienced by Adam before Eve is formed from his rib. The religious experiences of Abraham, Moses, and Adam are neither simply supernatural events, nor are they solely natural events. These types of events and the experiences that they trigger are considered the work of God. The ancient Jews did not distinguish sharply between natural and supernatural events.

Exodus (24) relates a narrative about Moses and other elders beholding God in a vision of the heavenly realm. The book of Isaiah (6) also manifests a visionary experience that enables the prophet to see God and his throne, where the seraphim cloak God's face and feet, which means that he does not directly see God. Ezekiel also describes a vision of the divine realm that includes seeing angelic figures, burning coals of fire, lightning flashes issuing from the fire, and the divine chariot.

Besides visionary experiences, textual evidence allows a reader to witness religious experiences that are connected to acts of annunciation from God. In Genesis (18:1–15), Sarah gains knowledge of God's plan for her to give birth to a son in her old age and responds with laughter, but comes to learn that nothing is impossible for God. Again, in Genesis (16:7–14) Hagar, an Egyptian slave of Sarah, is driven away because the former treated Sarah with contempt because she was barren, while Hagar became pregnant. An angel appears to Hagar and tells her to return to Sarah as her slave, but promises Hagar to increase her progeny in the future. According to Genesis (25:22–23), after Isaac's prayers to God for divine assistance to enable the barren Rebekah to conceive, she receives a message directly from God that she will give birth to two sons, Esau and Jacob. In this narrative in Genesis (28:10–17), Jacob steals Esau's birthright, which rightfully belongs to the firstborn. Jacob escapes the vengeance of Esau, lies down to rest on the earth, and falls asleep, to dream about a ladder that extends from earth to heaven. In his dream state, Jacob sees angels ascending and descending the ladder. He hears God repeat the terms of the covenant. Upon awakening, Jacob is fearful and awestruck after seeing the gate of heaven and hearing God's reiteration of the covenant. While escaping the wrath of his brother and the stress of the situation, Jacob directly and personally experiences the holy, the wholly other. In these various examples, it is possible to witness ways in which Judaism renders religion a personal relation between an individual and God. This is a relationship that does not simply occur in isolation but includes a social context of a fellowship of a religious community.

The auditory messages and visions continue with the different forms of Jewish mysticism. An aspect of these types of religious experience that is emphasized is the ecstatic nature of the experience, which enables an individual to transcend one's body. In contrast to Kabbalistic mysticism, Hasidism embraces the ecstatic experience and adds joy, celebration, playfulness, and fellowship to the mystical experience. In both cases, the dialogical relationship between the mystic and God is not lost but is rather enhanced in such a way as to unite others in a fellowship that celebrates one's relationship to God and to others.

Suggestions for Further Reading

Boyarin, Daniel. *Dying for God: Martyrdom and the Making of Christianity and Judaism.* Stanford: Stanford University Press, 1999.

Buber, Martin. *The Legend of the Baal-Shem.* Trans. Maurice Friedman. New York: Schocken Books, 1969.

———. *Tales of the Hasidim: The Early Masters.* Trans. Olga Marx. New York: Schocken Books, 1947.

———. *Tales of the Hasidim: Later Masters.* Trans. Olga Marx. New York: Schocken Books, 1948.

Dresner, Samuel H. *The Zaddik.* London: Abelard-Schuman, n.d.

Jacobs, Louis. *Jewish Mystical Testimonies.* New York: Schocken Books, 1977.

Magness, Jodi. *Stone and Dung, Oil and Spit: Jewish Daily Life in the Time of Jesus.* Grand Rapids, MI: William B. Eerdmans Publishing Company, 2011.

Moore, George Foot. *Judaism in the First Centuries of the Christian Era.* 3 vols. Cambridge: Harvard University Press, 1927.

Neusner, Jacob. *The Way of Torah: An Introduction to Judaism.* Third Edition. North Scituate, MA: Duxbury Press, 1978.

Niditch, Susan. *Ancient Israelite Religion.* New York: Oxford University Press, 1997.

Peters, F. E. *The Monotheists: Jews, Christians, and Muslims in Conflict and Competition.* 2 vols. Princeton: Princeton University Press, 2003.

Scholem, Gershom. *Major Trends in Jewish Mysticism.* New York: Schocken Books, 1956.

Segal, A. F. *Rebecca's Children: Judaism and Christianity in the Roman World.* Cambridge: Harvard University Press, 1986.

Trepp, Leo. *Judaism: Development and Life.* Third Edition. Belmont, CA: Wadsworth Publishing Company, 1982.

Wolfson, Elliot R. *Through a Speculum that Shines: Vision and Imagination in Medieval Jewish Mysticism.* Princeton: Princeton University Press, 1994.

13 Christianity

Every Christmas season in the West and other parts of the world, the birth narrative of Jesus of Nazareth is retold and celebrated in church liturgy and with choral performances. It is a simple and imaginative narrative that has captured the hearts and minds of Christians for centuries. The Gospels of Mathew and Luke give the fullest account of the circumstances of the infant savior's early life. These texts share a story of love, hardship, miraculous happenings, and joy.

The authors of the Gospels of Matthew and Luke thought that it was necessary to provide Jesus with a genealogy that traced him back to David and Abraham, two pillars of ancient Judaism, which is appropriate because Jesus was a

Figure 13.1 Ely Cathedral in Ely, England. Photograph by Carl Olson.

Jew and prophecies predicted that the Messiah would come from the lineage of David. Before the Gospel of Matthew discusses the birth of Jesus, it relates that his mother was impregnated by the Holy Spirit while having been betrothed to Joseph, who is depicted as a righteous man unwilling to embarrass his wife but planning to quietly divorce her. During a dream, an angel appeared to Joseph to inform him of the origin of Mary's pregnancy, the name of the child, and his destiny. During the reign of Herod, Jesus was born in Bethlehem, an event that was revealed to three wise men. After meeting with Herod and promising to inform him about the location of this special child, the three wise men proceeded to follow a star that identified the house sheltering the infant, where they worshipped him and offered him valuable items but did not report back to Herod after being warned in a dream, returning to their home by an alternated route.

After the departure of the wise men, Joseph is warned in a dream to flee with his wife and infant to Egypt because Herod intended to kill all infants, being fearful of having one of them grow to maturity and destroy him. Joseph and his family remained in Egypt until the death of Herod and avoided the slaughter of innocent male children under 2 years of age. Again, Joseph received another message from an angel after Herod's death to return to the land of Israel, while another message told Joseph to settle in the town of Nazareth.

In comparison to the Gospel of Mathew, the Lucan narrative begins with the birth of John the Baptist, prior to which his father Zechariah was informed of the coming son by an angel inside the temple where he worked as a priest and told him that he would be struck dumb until his wife gave birth, despite their advanced ages. The Gospel of Luke introduces the story of the annunciation to the Virgin Mary, who has a difficult time believing that she could become pregnant without a husband, but the angel informed her that anything is possible with God. The writer of Luke includes a story about Mary's journey to the home of Elizabeth and how the infant leaped in the latter's womb when the two women met. Luke relates the birth of John the Baptist before turning to the birth of Jesus. Luke informs his reader that a Roman census was the reason for Joseph and his pregnant wife to journey to the town of Bethlehem, where the child was born in a manger because no other accommodations were available due to the census. An angel announced this special event to shepherds, who proceeded to worship the infant in the manger. Similar to a typical Jewish male infant, Jesus was circumcised and given his personal name. Afterwards, the family returned home to Nazareth. When Jesus turned twelve, Luke recounts, there was an episode in the temple where Jesus was found by his parents asking teachers questions and demonstrating understanding, to the astonishment of others. Luke then turns to the ministry of John the Baptist and his preaching about the urgent need for repentance, because the end time is coming at any moment. The narrative of Jesus in the Gospels has a large gap because we know nothing about his life after reaching his twelfth year of life until his ministry begins.

The Gospels continue with the beginnings of Jesus' ministry, the beginnings of the Jesus movement, his baptism by John, and the execution of John, who is portrayed as a precursor of Jesus. The Gospels relate the teachings of Jesus, his miracles, the gathering of disciples, the Last Supper, his betrayal by Judas, and his conviction, imprisonment, passion, and death on the cross. The latter part of the narrative of Jesus is a tale of denial, deception, betrayal, and violence inflicted on an innocent man by being nailed to a cross that he is forced to carry to the location of his death. But this sorrowful tale ends with the empty tomb where his body had been placed after his death. According to Mathew, Mary Magdalene and another Mary go to the tomb, an earthquake occurs, and an angel descends, rolls back the stone blocking the tomb, and sits on it, frightening the guards, then announces to the women that Jesus has risen from the dead, invites them to see the interior of the empty tomb, tells them to inform Jesus' disciples, and announces that Jesus will appear to them at Galilee. The key event for Christians is the resurrection, which represents the victory over death. It is safe to say that without the resurrection or Easter event, there would be no Christianity, and the Jesus movement would have been a short-lived religious cult that probably would have had a minimal historical impact.

Scriptures of the Formative Christian Tradition

The early Christian community did not possess its own sacred book. The early Jesus movement had a charismatic figure who taught with authority, and having him in their midst was sufficient for ardent followers. In fact, a claim to have a sacred book would probably have struck them as strange. After the death of Jesus, the situation for the early community changes, and the oral traditions surrounding the life and teachings of Jesus begin to be edited by writers and arranged into coherent narratives to give them some sense of permanency. It is not too farfetched to affirm that the early community did not think that it needed a sacred text. The members of the early Jesus movement did make use of Hebrew texts, although it tended to read them as prophecies of the Christ figure. From the perspective of his followers, Jesus did not bring a scripture. His actions, charismatic persona, and message represent his revelation, or "Good News" (gospel) to the faithful. The dawning of Christian scripture evolved unevenly because it lacked a self-conscious effort and a consistent deliberation about what constituted a scripture.

This chapter began with an overview of the life of Jesus in the synoptic Gospels (Mark, Matthew, and Luke). But the letters of the Apostle Paul were the earliest extant Christian literature, which date from around the mid-first century, although there was an oral tradition that consisted of the life and teachings of Jesus that was circulated within the early community and shared with others for the purpose of converting them to this infant religious movement. In contrast to this oral tradition, which is comparable to the early Jewish, Muslim, Buddhist, and Jain movements, Paul's writings in the form of letters to various congregations were preserved and gathered into a collection after his death. These letters were called "letters to the seven churches" because seven was a symbol of holiness in the ancient world and, in its context, implied the entire church. Although the letters are addressed to particular congregations and their problems, Paul's message is intended for a wider audience, an evolving community, and considers its struggle to survive in the hostile socio-cultural environment of the Greco-Roman world. To argue for the authenticity of his message, Paul claimed that his authority came directly from Jesus, the resurrected Lord and Savior.

Paul's letters were intended to be read aloud to an audience, which was also true of the Hebrew Bible and other documents that later came to constitute the New Testament. Within the context of the ancient Greco-Roman world, all reading was performed aloud, as Paul instructed his letters should be read (1 Thess. 5:27). The sense of a text was thus to be gained by listening to its being proclaimed. When Paul's letters were read aloud, for instance to a church community, the letters evoked the apostle's presence.

In contrast to Paul's letters, the Gospels are more akin to narratives and interpretations of the life and teachings of Jesus. The term "gospel" is derived from the Greek word *evangelion*, which means "good news"—in the New Testament, this becomes the good news of salvation, rather than its prior meaning, associated with the welfare of the emperor. The authority of these texts was grounded in the words and deeds of Jesus, which were preserved by memory and transmitted orally. The Gospels were composed by anonymous authors who named their works after disciples of Jesus to give them unchallenged authority. These Gospels consisted of Mark (composed c. 65–70 CE), Matthew and Luke (c. 80–90 CE), and John (c. 90–100 CE). Representing efforts to collect and codify various traditions about Jesus and sayings attributed to him, each Gospel writer sought to interpret the meaning of Christianity for his specific constituencies. The anonymous authors derived their authority from the various communal traditions rooted in the teachings and deeds of Jesus. During their formative period, the Gospels were considered valuable historical testimonies; it was not until later that they were considered scripture. The traditions about Jesus were preserved by memory and circulated orally.

If the four Gospels are compared with each other, striking differences emerge between John and the synoptic (meaning that they present a common view) Gospels. Few of the events in Jesus' life recorded, for instance, in the synoptic Gospels are discovered in John. Besides missing events, the location and chronology of Jesus' ministry are different in John, along with style and language. The close literary relationship of the synoptic texts reflects another problem associated with their similarities. There is general agreement among scholars that Mark is the earliest Gospel and that Matthew and Luke used it as a foundation for their Gospels. In addition, the writer of Mark was not precisely an author but rather a redactor, connecting units of an oral tradition that he inherited from others in the Jesus movement. Scholars tend to agree that much of Mark is discovered in Matthew and Luke; the arrangement and sequence of material support a theory of dependence on Mark, and numerous parallel passages indicate that Matthew and Luke tried to improve on Mark's literary style and language. Material missing in Mark is also found in Matthew and Luke. What accounts for the absent material in Mark? Scholars have rejected the possibility that they borrowed from each other and have concluded that it would be more reasonable to assume they used an independent source. German scholars dubbed this source *Quelle*, which was abbreviated to "Q." This means that Matthew and Luke used two sources: Mark and Q. Textual scholars think that Q was probably a written document because of the verbal agreements between the two Gospels. Scholars also tend to think that Q (dated around 50 CE) existed prior to Mark. In addition to Mark and Q, Matthew and Luke both had access to oral or written traditions independent of Mark: these are called M and L sources.

Scholars arrived at this general consensus about the Gospels by using three types of criticism: source, form, and redaction. Source criticism examines the origins of the texts, whereas form criticism is a discipline that goes behind the written sources to examine the period of the oral tradition. Redaction criticism is an analysis of the editorial work in relation to sources. It is concerned with determining what and why certain editorial decisions were made.

In addition to the four Gospels and letters of Paul, what came to be called the New Testament also included the Acts of the Apostles, letters of Peter, James, and Jude, and the Book of Revelation, which was attributed to John, author of the Gospel of the same title. As the Christian church developed, numerous prescriptive lists of authentic texts existed in many Christian assemblies. These various lists were called canons (Greek *kanones*, meaning measures or standards), so called because they were connected with criteria associated with authenticity. The formation of the fourfold Gospels occurred, for instance, by the late second century and was generally accepted by the faithful in the third century CE. The Gospels gained spiritual status as a group rather than as individual texts, a development suggesting their authority was grounded in their collective nature.

If the early period of the primitive Christian church emphasized the oral nature of Jesus' message, why were the Gospels committed to writing? New Testament scholars have offered several plausible reasons for a turn to writing the Gospels. These reasons include the death of the apostles, or dying of those closest to Jesus during his life, and becoming fearful about losing the tradition of Jesus. In addition, the formative church wanted to know how to deal with persecution by learning from Jesus. The primitive church also struggled to define and understand itself apart from Judaism. And the early church wondered how it could appeal to the Gentiles without losing its original Jewish identity. Finally, the problem associated with the delay of the *parousia* (second coming of Jesus) and the end of the world served as motivating factors to commit the Jesus message to writing.

What Paul and writers of the Gospels proclaimed was the *kerygma* (a Greek term meaning to announce or proclaim), representing the content of the early Christian message. An assumption has been made that there was a unity of the Christian message in its scriptures among the earliest generation of Christians. This claim to kerygmatic unity is probably unwarranted, because if message summaries are compared, the evidence points to a variety of opinions concerning the *kerygma*. So-called kerygmatic statements presuppose that God has acted decisively in Jesus for the salvation of humanity, which has ushered into history a new age. Moreover, the kerygmatic messages include references to Jesus' humiliation, his death, and the exaltation associated with his resurrection.

Although Christianity was an apocalyptic (from a Greek term meaning "to reveal") sect within Palestinian Judaism and Jesus was a Palestinian Jew, the world of the New Testament was dominated by Greek language and culture; the language itself had been transformed from classical Attic Greek into *koinē* (common) or Hellenistic Greek, which became the language of the New Testament. Using material such as papyrus, parchment, or wooden tablets, Christians preferred the codex (book-like), previously used for letter-writing and record-keeping, over the scroll employed in Judaism or for Greek literature. Scholars have offered several reasons for the adoption of the codex, such as economy, compactness, convenience, ease of reference, or usage of an already familiar medium and practical means of communication. A four-Gospel codex was used to preserve the best-known and widely accepted texts for everyday usage as handbooks for the Christian community.

As New Testament texts gained canonical status, the issue of a sacred language never really developed, because Christian scripture spread quickly and into a variety of vernaculars. This situation changed when Jerome translated the Bible into Latin during the fourth century. The Latin version of the scriptures became the sacred language of the Roman Catholic Church until Martin Luther, a former Catholic priest turned Protestant reformer, translated the Bible into German, with the purpose of making the text more accessible to ordinary people, in the sixteenth century.

Basic Teachings of Jesus

Before reviewing what Jesus affirmed, it might be wise to discern what he did not claim to be or represent. Firstly, Jesus did not claim to be a Christian for the simple reason that none existed during his lifetime; he was rather a Jew. He did not establish a religious order, sect, or church, although he was the primary focus of a cult. Being a charismatic figure with a gift for communicating with others and persuading them to believe in his message and to act on it, Jesus shaped the hearts and minds of many listeners to his teachings. During his teaching career, Jesus warned about the end of time but did not attempt to predict a precise date for such an event. He also does not invite others to look for signs of the end (Mark 8:11f). Except for in the Fourth Gospel, Jesus does not invite others to believe in him. Moreover, he does not proclaim or identify himself as the Messiah. Instead, he points to the one who is coming in the near future. Finally, he was not a political or social reformer, although some people viewed him in these terms. Jesus' focus was directed less to this world and more toward a future mode of existence beyond this troubled sphere. This observation does not mean that Jesus was uncaring about personal suffering in this world. The many miracles attributed to him and his message of love are indicative of a religious leader who cares for the plight of others.

The Gospels depict a religious teacher criticizing others for certain types of behavior, practices, and beliefs. Jesus was opposed to public displays of piety because he thought that it was a vehicle of pride. He denounced those who were obsessed with insignificant matters of the Jewish legal code and also denounced legalism typical of such individuals. Jesus also criticized fragmenting of the Jewish law. He was opposed to the belief that by doing good deeds, one had a claim on God. He denounces those who seek to separate themselves from others by practicing a kind of puritanism and manifesting a holier-than-thou attitude. Finally, Jesus denounces avoidance of sinners, which is a form of behavior that is related to puritanical attitudes of those who would prefer to be separated from sinners.

In response to aspects of Jewish thought and practice, Jesus offers some radical new elements that include reaching out to sinners. Jesus adopted a new form of religious authority. Prior to the life of Jesus, Jewish prophets spoke with an authority derived from God, with claims such as "Thus said the Lord," whereas Jesus said "I say" (Matt. 5:18). When Jesus uttered these words, they caused a scandal for his Jewish listeners and critics because only God can speak with authority, from their perspective. Another new element introduced by Jesus is the *kairos*—the present time that affirms that the Kingdom of God is at hand (Mark 1:15). Within the context of ancient Judaism, these radical features of Jesus' teachings made him suspect to Jewish religious leaders. But the upper class of Jewish society were not the primary audience for Jesus' message. From all scriptural indications, Jesus' movement and teachings were directed to the lower, disenfranchised members of Judaism at that historical period, although there were some exceptions.

Just as the message of Jesus must be grasped within its Jewish cultural context, it must also be grasped within the context of eschatological (end of time) expectation. The Jewish eschatological pattern follows three periods: an original age in paradise that is equated with righteousness; the fall from paradise ushers into existence the present historical age; and finally a restored righteousness arrives at an uncertain period in the future. In comparison to the Jewish pattern, New Testament scholars have identified three types of eschatology in the text. Firstly, there is a futuristic eschatology that claims that the Messiah (Anointed One) has already come and will return in the future to usher in the new age. This type of expectation concerning Jesus' return dominated early Christian thinking. The second type is a realized eschatology that begins with Jesus' ministry. Because the new age had begun with Jesus, the Christian already lives in this age. Thus, the Christian does not have to look ahead to the return of Christ but looks back to the time he initially arrived. In the Gospel of John, scholars have identified an existential eschatology, which means that a restoration has occurred in the moment of faith. In this act of faith, the individual Christian has been reborn. In contrast to the three types of eschatology identified in the Gospel literature, there is also a fourth type found in the letters of Paul, who anticipates the return of Jesus and the opening of a new age, although the old age remains. Paul suggests that a Christian lives a dual life within this age and anticipates a coming age when time will be fulfilled as promised.

Within these different types of eschatology anticipation, Jesus' ethical message and eschatology constitute a unity. But the central aspect of his message is love. For Jesus, love is not a virtue that one should cultivate, is not an aid to social well-being, and is not an emotion. Rather, love is a requirement of obedience, which emphatically implies that by loving my neighbor, I prove my obedience to God. Moreover, love is an attitude of the human will because it depends on the commandment of God and is thus an overcoming of self-will. For his followers, Jesus did not advocate love associated with friendship (*philia*) and was not concerned about stressing passion or erotic love (*eros*), but he did stress a self-sacrificial love (*agape*) that he demonstrated by his death on the cross.

The Jewish understanding of the relationship between love and the law was radicalized by Jesus. The law represents the fulfilment of God's will, which is the basic condition for participation in salvation. According to Jesus, God requires radical obedience and commands love. It is through love that a person obeys God's will. This demand of love is threefold: to love God with your entire being, which includes your heart, soul, and mind (Mark 12:28–34). Then Jesus extends the demand of love to love your neighbor as you would yourself, and finally to love your enemies (Matt. 5:44).

Jesus' understanding of love pushes Jewish law further by radicalizing laws against murder, adultery, and perjury. God is concerned with what a person's intention was prior to when she acted. The demand of love surpasses every legal demand, because it knows no limits for Jesus. In fact, the demand of love, which is grounded in obedience, asks for more than ordinary law. It demands, for example, that you love your enemies, because God acts with mercy and compassion to all humans. Jesus' understanding of the demand of love and the law sets the stage for his Golden Rule: "In everything do to others as you would have them do to you; for this is the law and the prophets" (Matt. 7:12). Jesus pushes the demand of love in a more radical direction by asserting: "Be perfect, therefore, as your heavenly Father is perfect" (Matt. 5:48). At first glance, these demands to love one's enemies, treat others as one would want others to treat one, and to strive for perfection are somewhat utopian wishes. The demand to be perfect with God as one's model seems to be an impossible achievement for imperfect and fallible humans. But if the end of time is near, this radical ethic makes perfect sense in the short term.

In the River Jordan, Jesus was baptized by John, and as he walked to the bank of the river he saw the heaven part and the Holy Spirit descend upon him like a dove. A voice from heaven acknowledged that he was a son with whom God was pleased. Thereupon, the Spirit drove him to the wilderness for forty days, where he was tempted by the devil. After the arrest of John, he arrived in Galilee proclaiming God's good news. It is this moment when he chooses to share his message. Moreover, the eschatological content and context of Jesus' message embodies an urgency that asks listeners to immediately commit themselves. Teaching within the tradition of John the Baptist, Jesus is quoted in the Gospel of Mark (1:15) in the following way: "The time is fulfilled, and the kingdom of God has come near; repent, and believe in the good news." Jesus is calling listeners to make a decision in the now moment, which includes those who might be tempted to look back (Luke 9:62) or might make excuses about dropping what they are doing and immediately following him (Matt. 8:22). Jesus is unequivocal when Luke (14:27) reports him to say, "Whoever does not carry the cross and follow me cannot be my disciple." To carry the cross means to behave righteously.

The Apostle Paul's Good News

If there is a single person who is responsible for transforming the Jesus movement from a Jewish sect to a major religious tradition, this figure is the Apostle Paul, a Jew and early persecutor of the movement. While walking on the road to Damascus, Paul is struck down by a sudden overpowering flash of light from heaven. While lying on the ground, Paul is asked by a disembodied voice, identified as Jesus, "Why do you persecute me?" Paul's companions helped him, because he could not see, and took him to Damascus. For three days, Paul was blind and did not drink or eat anything. While Paul is praying, Jesus appears at a different location to Ananias, a Christian disciple, and instructs him to go to Paul to cure him of his blindness by laying his hands on Paul. Ananias is reluctant to go to Paul because of his evil reputation as a persecutor of Christians, but Jesus assured him that Paul has been chosen as an instrument to spread his message to the Gentiles. After Paul's sight is restored by Ananias, he was baptized, regained his strength, and began to preach about Jesus to those in a local synagogue (Acts 9:1–20). The narrative in Acts continues to relate how Jews plotted to kill Paul, his escape with the help of disciples, his journey to Jerusalem, the initial reluctance of the Christian community to accept him because of his previous persecution of them, and how Barnabas told the apostles what happened to Paul and how he converted to their side, his argument with Hellenists and their plot to kill him, his escape to Caesarea with the help of believers, and the continuation of his mission to spread the good news. Paul's life would finally end in Rome, where he was convicted and sentenced to death.

The primary concern of Paul's mission was the preaching about the good news of the death and resurrection of Jesus Christ (1 Cor. 15:3–4). Paul continues to recount the people to whom Jesus appeared after his resurrection on the third day after his death, including himself, even though Paul humbly admits that Jesus appeared to him in spite of his persecution of the church and goes on to say that he is the least worthy of the apostles. For Paul, Jesus is the *Logos* (Word) or *Sophia* (Wisdom). As the Son of God, Jesus exceeds the limits of Jewish messianism. And as the second Adam, Jesus repairs damage done by the first Adam of Genesis.

Paul encountered problems conveying his message to a Jewish audience. The reasons for Paul's difficulty convincing other Jews of the validity of his message was due to several reasons, beginning with the fact that Jesus did not fit the accepted pattern or image of the Messiah, because he was neither a king nor a divine being. From the Jewish perspective, Jesus appeared to undermine their institutions, to acquiesce to the power of the emperor, and to tell his followers to love their enemies. Christian preachers had the audacity to claim that Jews did not understand their own scriptures, although Christians did grasp them. Even though Paul's mission was primarily directed at the Gentiles, he still had problems with the Greek audience, because they found the Christian claim that a recently executed criminal was the savior of the world to be utterly foolish to them. But Paul was well aware of the problem, and referred to the "folly" of what he preached (1 Cor. 1:18–31). In fact, Paul embraces this foolishness by urging members of his audience "to be fools for Christ's sake."

Just as it was for Jesus, Paul thought that his preaching was occurring during the end of time. According to Paul's letter of 1 Thessalonians (4:15–17), the return of Christ is expected with little delay, and Paul admits himself that he will be alive to hear the trumpet call of the archangel, see Christ descend from heaven, experience the living being caught in the clouds, meet the Lord in the air, and remain with him forever. With such a vision, Paul views the return of Jesus opening a new age, but the old age remains for Christians, who thus live a dual life. According to Paul, life in the old age is dominated by sin, a cosmic and ontological power that holds humans in universal bondage. The old age also produces perversity. And the wages of sin are death. The new age represents the act of God in Christ, but the old age persists for Paul. Since the human situation leads to hopelessness, self-despair, and death, God acts in Christ to save humans, because they are unable to save themselves. The primal human represented by the first man, Adam, is the archetype of the sinner. In sharp contrast to Adam, Christ is the new archetype, who replaces the primal sinful human because Christ is without any flaw.

Despite being stuck between the new and old ages, Paul calls the Christian to become actively engaged in the world but with the proviso that a Christian is to act in the world "as if not" (*hōsmē*), which means to act in this world but to act as if they are not important. Instead of offering listeners new virtues, Paul's ethic shares a new power: God's love in Christ. It is this type of power that makes a person responsible to adhere to the will of God and makes a person doubly responsible: for himself and his brother. The second form of responsibility is love. Paul's conception of the Christian's dilemma living between two ages and within the world means that he sees the Christian community living in tension with the world. Because of his mistrust of the world, Paul conceived the Christian community as a self-contained fellowship. Thus he advised Christians to avoid going to Roman courts but to instead settle disputes by means of arbitration within the community. Paul's basic guideline for Christians was for them to act in a way so as to be a credit to their God. In

Romans 13, Paul advises, for example, Christians to obey Roman magistrates, with the exception of demands that belong only to God. Then the Christian should practice passive resistance, which may lead to martyrdom. In general, a Christian should concentrate on service to God and to look forward to the end of this old age.

We have noted that the old age for Paul is dominated by sin, a cosmic and ontological power that holds a person in universal bondage. Sin produces perversity, a dire situation that calls for correction, a process already begun by the righteousness of God. According to Paul's letter to the Romans (3:23–24), God has already taken the initiative to restore humans to their proper relationship by His action in Jesus Christ. The benefits of this divine action are offered as a gift to be received by the faith of a person. By Jesus' offering of himself on the cross, the barrier of guilt, which separated a person from God, has been removed (Rom. 5:19). By receiving Christ in faith, the sinner is justified by her faith and restored to a position of righteousness. In other words, the sinner is both pardoned (justified) and reconciled to God.

The Post-apostolic Age

The period after the deaths of Peter and Paul in 64 CE marks the beginning of the post-apostolic age. The infant Christian community was not only without two of its major leaders but encountered various problems adjusting to the historical changes. The intense expectation concerning the imminent end of time began to diminish and lose its urgency. This meant that the primitive church had to take seriously the realities and demands of an extended intermediate time before the final end of time. The primitive church also encountered a problem with unity that was originally strong, unpremeditated, and spontaneous. Even the early form of unity was not free of variety and tension, as evident by Jewish and Gentile Christians. Leaders of the Jewish branch of the early church were troubled by Paul's mission to the Gentiles. Those claiming to speak for Christ increased, which called into question the unity of the developing church.

Set within Jewish notions of purity and pollution, there evolved a problem concerning holiness. When earlier Christians referred to themselves as saints, this implied that they were elected by God, purified, and made holy in order to fulfill God's mission. There was an expectation that sin would not dominate this group. But in the post-apostolic age, sin is inundating the church both internally and externally. Thus the church needed to redefine the nature of holiness by developing an ethical code. Another problem was centered on apostolicity. When the church was new, it was guided by apostles, who had authority to function as a court of appeal for disputes. Thus the apostles represented a continuation of the authority of Jesus. But with the death of the apostles, Christians did not know where a new apostolic tradition could be discovered. This problem involved the church needing to establish standards to distinguish true teaching from false doctrine.

During the post-apostolic era, a narrative was circulated that portrayed Jesus as the illegitimate son of Mary through a sexual encounter with a Roman soldier. This type of salacious story exposes a tension and conflict between Jews and Christians. Rabbinical sources refer to Christians as heretics. In response, Christians portrayed Jews as responsible for the death of Jesus, as dramatically depicted by the Gospel of Matthew (27:24–26) when Pilate asks the crowd gathered to decide the fate of the prisoner Jesus and whether he should be freed or not, then washes his hands of the blood of an innocent man when the crowd selects a criminal to be set free over Jesus, and the crowd responds that the blood of Jesus would be upon them and future generations. Thus, the Christian polemic against Jews portrays them as having taken full blame for the death of Jesus, a curse on Jews that was stoked during the medieval period with public passion plays that retold the death of Jesus by emphasizing its gruesome details and contributed to enhancing anti-Semitic attitudes common in Europe. The counter-polemic between Jews and Christians was played out earlier than the Middle Ages by Josephus (first century CE), a Jewish historian, and Eusebius (c. 260–c. 340), a Christian historian. The conflict between Christians and Jews reached a climax with the destruction of the Jewish temple in Jerusalem in 70 CE by the Romans. After this event, the Jewish branch of Christianity slowly died out. The destruction of the temple was interpreted by Christians as a divine judgment on Judaism for killing and rejecting Jesus.

An important feature of the post-apostolic age was the development and acceptance of pseudonymous writings. The genuine authors of these works, such as the Pastoral Epistles 1 and 2 Timothy and the three works of Titus, the so-called Catholic Epistles 1 and 2 James and the three volumes of Peter, along with the Gospels of John and the work titled Jude, are unknown. Using a commonly accepted literary device, the authors of these texts adopted the name of an apostle, but they did not necessarily intend to deceive readers. Their intention was rather to preserve the true apostolic tradition and to probably extend it. During this period of time, the early church had to counter and fight against false doctrine.

In tension with the Jewish community and Greco-Roman culture, the book of Acts, which is attributed to the authorship of Luke, argues that the primitive church is an indispensable antecedent of the coming end of the age. Luke places Jesus' ministry and the work of the church in the context of the universal purpose of God for the world and its inhabitants. God's plan for the world is divided into three major epochs. The first epoch includes ancient Israel to John the Baptist, who marks the end of the period of the law and the prophets (Luke 16:16). The next epoch is represented by the ministry of Jesus, at which time Jerusalem plays a central role in the whole redemptive purpose of God, as evident by the facts that Jesus is rejected in the city and it is later destroyed. According to Luke's perspective (24:47), the world mission of the church begins in Jerusalem. The final epoch extends from the Ascension to the return of Christ. Luke depicts Jesus as seated at God's right hand (Acts 2:33), where he must remain until the restoration announced previously by God (3:20–21).

Luke's religious interpretation of history emphatically indicates that history is meaningful because of the actions of God for the benefit of sinful humans.

Church Doctrine and Heresy

As the primitive church evolved, its members were exposed to a variety of opinions that represented a challenge to members' belief systems. Within the Christian context, doctrine defines what the church believes, teaches, and confesses, which is based on the word of God preserved in sacred scripture. Doctrine is thus a way for the church to define itself. The early church had to often respond to internal and external heretical teachings and attacks by utilizing polemics, creeds, apologetics, and dogma. Protecting the church from going astray, clearly defined doctrine represents the saving knowledge of the church that is derived from the word of God. By developing and agreeing on matters of doctrine, the church defined orthodoxy, set boundaries for the community of the faithful, and avoided inciting heresy or dissent. The problems associated with Christology and the Trinity are two excellent examples of church doctrine that were responses to heretical opinions about these subjects.

The doctrine of Christology is concerned about the problem of defining the relationship between the divine and human nature in Christ. The primitive church regarded Jesus as God from an early date (Rom. 10:9; Phil. 2:11). The New Testament also regarded Christ as pre-existent (Rom. 1:3, 8:9; Gal. 4:4; 2 Cor. 3:17). The Gospel of John (1:14) asserts that Jesus is the word (*logos*) become flesh. But not everyone agreed with the scriptures' interpretation of Jesus being man (flesh) and divine (spirit). The Ebionites ("poor ones") rejected the implications of the virgin birth and claimed that Jesus was simply the human son of Mary and Joseph, who was destined to become the Messiah and return to establish God's kingdom. Although Jesus had been given special gifts by God, he was a mere man. Another challenge to the depiction of Jesus in the scriptures was offered by Marcion, a member of the Gnostic movement, in which knowledge was a key factor, with his Docetism (a Greek term meaning "to seem"). Marcion argued that Christ was a man only in appearance because he united himself with the man Jesus but left before the crucifixion. These two opinions about the nature of Christ were deemed heretical by the orthodox community at the Council of Chalcedon in 451 CE. The council ruled that Jesus Christ was truly God and truly man, meaning that both natures are united in one person. Possessing a rational soul and body, Christ's two natures are unchangeable, indivisible, and inseparable.

The doctrine of the Trinity had an equally interesting history before an orthodox agreement was reached by the church. There is no indisputable or systematic doctrine of the Trinity found in the New Testament. It is possible to find references to Jesus Christ and his likeness of God (2 Cor. 4:4; Col. 1:15). In the Gospel of John (1:1–18), the pre-existence of Christ is affirmed with reference to the divine *Logos* (Word), which was with God in the beginning and became flesh. The Holy Spirit is somewhat ambivalent in the New Testament, when Romans (8:9) refers to the spirit of God and the spirit of Christ. It is also possible to find triadic formulas in the early Christian scriptures (2 Cor. 13:13; Eph. 4:4–6). In the Gospel of Matthew (28:19), it states that baptism should be performed in the name of the Father, Son, and Holy Spirit.

We find unorthodox opinions voiced by the Monarchist thinkers and a Gnostic thinker such as Valentinus. The Dynamistic Monarchist argues that Christ was a man filled with the impersonal power of God. Because Jesus was adopted as the Son of God, the divinity of the Son was merely derived and not actual. Sabellius (c. third century), a Modalistic Monarchist, asserted that God is active in various modes. Thus, the Son and the Spirit represent modes of the appearance of the Father. Valentinus argues from the basis of his Docetism that Christ only had a phantom body, which he abandoned before his crucifixion. This means that it was not Christ, Son of God, who died on the cross but only the man Jesus.

Another heretical position was promulgated by Arius (d. 336) by his desire to emphasize the uniqueness and transcendence of God. Arius rejected the notion that the Son came forth from the Father, because this notion applies physical categories to God, which implies that God is divisible and subject to change. Arius admitted that the Son is a perfect creature, but there is no unity between the Father and Son. It is permissible to call the Son God, but his divinity is not an attribute of his being, which suggests that the Son is neither able to communicate with nor have direct knowledge of the Father. This implication rests on the fact that the essence of the Father is distinct from the Son. This implies that the Son is liable to change and even sin. Finally, the divinity of Jesus is bestowed upon him by God's grace. Arius' position turns Jesus into a mere demi-god.

These heretical formulations of the doctrine of the Trinity were challenged by more orthodox thinkers. Tertullian (c. 160–c. 225) was the first Christian thinker to use the term "Trinity" and to affirm that God is one substance in three related persons. Because the Father is one substance, the Son is a derivation from and a portion of the whole, whereas the Spirit issues from the Father by way of the Son. Because they are identical in substance, they are one, although not one person. Tertullian's position subordinates the Son to the Father, and the Spirit is subordinated to the Son. A major problem with Tertullian's position is that Jesus is given a secondary position as an agent to execute the commands of the Father. A person could conclude that it is better to direct prayers to only the Father and not the Son.

Tertullian's flawed position was corrected by the three Cappadocians: Basil the Great (d. 379), bishop of Caesarea; Gregory of Nyssa (d. 394), a younger brother of Basil; and Gregory of Nazianzus (d. c. 390). These thinkers used the Greek term *ousia* (essence or substance) as a technical expression for the Godhead. They also employed the term *hypostasis* to refer to person rather than nature. Thus, *ousia* refers to the common substance of God, while *hypostasis* indicates the special forms which the divine substance assumes in the three persons. They account for the differences between the three persons as ascribing to the Father "fatherhood," to the Son "sonship," and to the Holy Spirit "sanctifying power." From a slightly different perspective, they expressed the relationship of the three persons of the Trinity as saying that the Father is unbegotten, the Son is begotten, and the Holy Spirit proceeds. The Trinitarian controversy was settled at the Council of Constantinople in 381 by adopting the *homoousia* (of one substance) of the Son and of the Holy Spirit with God the Father.

In addition to Christology and the Trinity, the early church preached the doctrine of original sin, which was challenged by Pelagius (c. 360), who was concerned about the omnipresence and righteousness of God. Pelagius claimed that God cannot demand of a human what she cannot give. He continued to assert that a human cannot help sinning. Moreover, a human had free will, allowing one to choose good or evil. It is obvious that Adam's sin had disastrous consequences for his descendants, but Adam's sin is not propagated by physical descent but by custom and example. Thus, there is no congenital fault in a human being as one is born. In fact, God cannot hold a person responsible for the sins of another. Moreover, a person can live a sinless life, depending on how that person uses her will for good or evil and follows the instructions given by Christ. By rejecting original sin, Pelagius stresses the absolute freedom of the human will against God.

During his career, St. Augustine argued against Arius and Pelagius and exerted a profound influence on the subsequent Christian tradition. According to Augustine, sin has a dual nature: pride and concupiscence. Augustine resorts to telling a narrative to illustrate what he means in which Adam could have remained sinless if he had been willing to accept the aid of divine grace. Because of his pride, Adam wanted to cling to God and to follow the desires of his own heart, which resulted in the fall. Thus, through pride, Adam destroyed the natural and proper constitution of his will. As the ancestor of humankind, Adam passes on his sinful condition to his descendants via sexual lust. Sin is thus a matter of will, which is the locus of sin. If sin is a matter of will, does this not mean that infants are exempt from original sin? Augustine answers that the original sin of infants is voluntary by being derived from the free act of their first parents. The results of original sin can be grasped as inflicting evil and guilt on our natures and also leads to scarring and corrupting human nature. Another consequence of sin is the loss of human liberty, which influences one's ability to avoid sin and do what is right. Augustine does not assert the total depravity of human nature, because there is something noble about a fallen person, who embodies a spark of reason and is made in God's likeness. For Augustine, a human cannot avoid sin without God's grace, a gift of His love that is the only way to be saved.

A Christian Historical Narrative

Augustine (354–430), bishop of the city of Hippo in northern Africa, wrote the first really personal autobiography, aptly titled *Confessions*, in which he shares with his reader the problem of his troubled soul, his sinfulness, his relationship with his mother, his guilt, and his struggle to find God and his true self. In addition to the magisterial *Confessions*, Augustine also composed the influential *The City of God*, which represents the first attempt to write a philosophy of history. In this book, Augustine distinguishes between two cities: *Civitas Terrena* (City of Man) and *Civitas Dei* (City of God), which both began as one community under God. As Augustine tells the story, some angels turned away from God, dividing the single, unified community into two communities: the one community representing God and His angels and the other being of Satan or the fallen angels. According to this narrative, the archetypes of the cities of God and man are to be found in heaven.

In Augustine's narrative, history begins with the expulsion from paradise, which actually represents a pre-history. In actual history, the first act is fratricide, represented by Cain's murder of Abel, which led to the creation of the city of man, to which Cain belongs, while Abel is a member of the city of God. These two cities were formed by two loves: the earthly city formed by love of self, even to the extent of having contempt for God, and a heavenly city formed by the love of God, even to the contempt of self. The former glories in itself, while the latter glories in the Lord. With this basic distinction established, Augustine elaborates on the differences between the two cities. The city of man is ruled by expediency, pride, and ambition, whereas the city of God is governed by self-sacrifice, obedience, and humility. The city of man is temporal and mortal and is predestined to suffer eternal punishment, whereas the city of God is eternal and immortal and will reign eternally with its Maker. In summary, the two cities stand in opposition and conflict with each other, a conflict that represents the substance of human history.

Having established the differences between the two cities, Augustine continues by conceiving of them mystically, which means that the city of God is identified as the mystic Jerusalem as a vision of peace. This is the city of God's elect or those who will be saved. This mystic Jerusalem, ruled by Christ, is being developed and perfected in the church, which contains some who have been chosen and others who have not been selected for salvation. The city of man symbolizes the mystic Babylon, which means a place of confusion; it symbolizes the conquest of nature, acquisition of power, and accumulation of knowledge and is ruled by Satan. These two cities are entangled and intermingled. It is possible that during a person's life one might pass from one city to another, but only God knows in which a person shall reside in the end.

Augustine looks at the two cities within the course of history and says that the city of man represents no true historical progress because empires will always rise and fall. In contrast to the city of man, there is progress in the city of God, because there is a gradual revelation of the divine truth. Thus, the city of God represents the history of salvation. From Augustine's perspective, there is progress in history in the sense that in each generation, there are those who are entering into the heavenly city.

Having established the fundamental distinctions between his two cities, Augustine identifies the six epochs of history, which are parallel to the six days of creation and the six ages of humankind: infancy, childhood, youth, early adulthood, later adulthood, and old age. The initial epoch extends from Adam to the great flood, the second from Noah to Abraham, the third from Abraham to David, the fourth from David to the Babylonian exile, the fifth from the exile to the birth of Jesus, and the sixth epoch from the first to the second coming of Christ at the end of time. With this pattern of history relying on the Judeo-Christian scriptures, Augustine refrained from any apocalyptic calculation of the duration of the last epoch. The initial five epochs prefigure the sixth epoch of the Christ event, which suggests that Augustine is narrating a Christo-centric view and interpretation of history. In the first epoch, Abel and Seth represent, respectively, grief and resurrection, which foreshadows, for example, the death and resurrection of Christ. If the Christ narrative is the central event of world history, this means that the beginning and end of history are not meaningful by themselves but only with reference to this central narrative.

This position makes history significant and meaningful at the present moment because it represents salvation history—God's sending of his Son to earth—in which we can recognize the workings of God. In summary, God created the world and set an end to the historical process that will culminate in the last judgment. Augustine's narrative interpretation of history is a limited Christian view of time because it does not include a cross-cultural, all-encompassing narrative. Nonetheless, it can serve as an imperfect metaphor for the interrelationship between the Christian church and the state over the centuries. Over the course of Christian history, there have been periods when the state sparked church development; at other times, the church was the dominant player; and in many cases, there were those who were dissatisfied with the church and broke away to create their own religious organizations. Overall, Christian history is a narrative of conflict, triumph, heroism, creativity, and sinister happenings.

The Two Cities in Historical Narrative

Historical developments after the time of Augustine can be informed by his basic distinction between the two cities, even though it is certainly not a perfect metaphor, but the two cities can operate to enhance understanding. There are periods in Christian history during which the city of God is subordinate to the city of man, and times when the city of God dominates the city of man, such as during the medieval period. And there have been times when those within the city of God have been critical of it and sought to reform it, such as during the time of the Protestant Reformation. In the post-Reformation era, other inspired Christians have attempted to create their own version of the city of God.

From the second to the fourth centuries, the church was persecuted by the Roman authorities. The fortunes of the church changed dramatically after Emperor Constantine converted to Christianity and took an active interest in the development of the new religion, such as calling the Council of Nicaea to condemn the Arian heresy over the divinity of Christ, which represented an embracing of the city of God to improve the city of man. The reign of Constantine contributed to the strengthening of the church from both spiritual and temporal perspectives. The reign of Charlemagne in the ninth century revived the pretensions of the temporal power over the spiritual power when he imposed his will on popes and bishops. During the period of Charlemagne, church and state formed a single unity, although they had different tasks, with the pope praying for the welfare of the kingdom and the emperor providing protection. Pope Leo III reasserted the superiority of the papacy by crowning Charlemagne, which meant that the title of emperor was given by the church, making the emperor protector of the papacy. Pope Nicholas I (r. 858–67) was the first to assert that the pope was the supreme regulator of kingdoms and kings, a development that blurred the distinction between the two cities. Pope Leo IX supported his position by citing *The Donation of Constantine*, a document that alleged that the Emperor Constantine had recognized the pope as Christ's vicar on earth, making all bishops subject to him. In the tenth century, Pope Otto I saw no essential division between church and state and obscured the distinction between the two cities by allowing the king to appoint clergy. In the following century, Pope Gregory VII saw the need for urgent reform of the church because the lay domination over the church was introducing into it unworthy people, placing the salvation of Christians in jeopardy. Among his reforms, Gregory VII introduced the theory that the secular power was dependent on the church, a state founded by God to rule humanity. The head of this church-state was Christ, and as the representative of Christ on earth, the pope is the head of the church and all humankind.

Protestant efforts attempted to reform the church from the inside before starting to develop their own version of the church. Martin Luther (1483–1546) was a Catholic priest when he nailed his 95 theses to a church door concerning abuses of the church that needed to be changed. In 1521, Luther was excommunicated by Pope Leo X for criticizing the church over issues such as the practice of indulgences, sacraments, and doctrine. Luther's writings are theocentric because he wants to "let God be God," which suggests viewing everything from God's perspective. He emphasized returning to the plain sense of the Scriptures, a measure for what is permissible and valid. Inspired by the Apostle Paul, Luther preached justification by faith alone, with repentance serving as the medium between unrighteousness and righteousness. If Luther led the German Reformation, John Calvin (1509–64) would be a leader of the Swiss reform, along with men such as Ulrich Zwingli (1484–1531), a strong critic of Lutheran views about the Eucharist. Calvin, for instance, did not think that the church and state are at variance because they are both subject to the rule of God.

The English Reformation had its roots in a love affair involving King Henry VIII and his desire to divorce his wife so that he could wed his lover and beget a male heir. After the Church refused his request, Henry VIII gradually gained control over the Church in England by a series of political maneuvers.

In 1532, the king extracted two major concessions from bishops and clergy: (1) They agreed not to make any new canons unless approved and licensed by the king; (2) They agreed to submit the entire corpus of canon law to the judgment of a commission. Henry maneuvered to cut off funds going to Rome and won for the Church of England, which was to become the Anglican Church, the right to settle its own cases without appeals to Rome. The Pope had called Henry VIII a great defender of the faith for his criticism of European reformers, but Henry was now given an imperial title and authority. With The Supremacy Act of 1534, Henry is described as the head of the Church of England, making him ruler of the two cities of St. Augustine.

When Edward VI ascended the throne, the major marks of the medieval cult were abolished, such as the veneration of images, the doctrine of purgatory, and the invocation of saints. The other major accomplishment of this time was the *Edwardian Prayer Book*, a work of compromise. With the reign of Mary Tudor, a resurgence of Catholicism and bloody strife annulled most of the religious legislation of Edward's reign. The Church of England was restored to the position that it held in 1543, the final year of Henry VIII's rule. The Elizabethan era restored royal supremacy and returned to the *Book of Common Prayer* of 1552 because the *Edwardian Prayer Book* was too ambiguous. The so-called Elizabethan settlement was attacked by the Puritans, a group of nonconformists.

The Roman Catholic Church responded to the Reformation at the Council of Trent, 1545–1563. It focused on three major problems: the relationship between scripture and tradition; the doctrine of justification; and the certainty of salvation. The council placed the apostolic tradition on par with scripture, which they based on divine inspiration and authority of the Church, to counter the call to rely on only scripture made by Luther. The council took a compromise position on justification by ascribing everything to divine grace and permitting humans to gain justification by their own merits earned by good works. Justification consisted in the forgiveness of sins, sanctification, and renewal of the inner person. The council insisted that a person can receive this justification through the seven sacraments recognized by the church.

An earlier split began after the Council of Chalcedon in 451, when the Greek and Latin branches of the Church began to drift apart because of different languages, culture, and doctrinal issues of two types. The doctrinal controversy focused initially on the problem of whether or not the Holy Spirit issued from God the father or from the Latin position of both the father and son. The original Nicene Creed supported the Greek position. But neither side could come to any consensus. The other major issue was a disagreement over papal authority, because the Eastern Orthodox branch of Christianity envisioned a major role for all five equal patriarchates, whereas Rome claimed to be the head of the church because it represented the authentic lineage dating back to St. Peter, the rock on which the church was built in the early Jesus movement. The Roman and Eastern Orthodox officially split apart in 1054 and have coexisted this way ever since that time.

In later centuries, Christianity would be spread around the globe by Catholic and Protestant missionaries, adhering to Jesus' command to spread the good news of the Gospels. The Catholic Church would attempt to further define itself during the period of 1869–70, with Vatican I, a council, called by Pope Pius IX. The leadership defined the monarchical role of the Pope and defined papal infallibility, which means that when the Pope speaks *ex-cathedra*, that is, when fulfilling his official duties while in office, he does so according to apostolic authority. The Pope does this with issues concerning faith and morals. In response to this doctrine of papal infallibility and authority, there were European Catholics who broke away and became known as Old Catholics. During 1962–65, Vatican II was called by Pope John XXIII with the intention of modernizing the Church. This council instituted changes in worship and language, with the use of vernacular language instead of the traditional Latin. During worship, the officiating priest must face the congregation. In the wake of this council, Catholics reached out to Protestants, Eastern Orthodox Christians, and Jews in an ecumenical spirit.

Popular Christianity in the Medieval Latin Church

The medieval period of the church has been chosen for extra scrutiny because the church was at the height of its power and influence, and many of the cults are typical of this historical period. In order to better grasp these cults, it is useful to review the worldview of those Christians living in the Middle Ages. Medieval thinkers viewed the universe as a whole that was pervaded by a divinely instituted harmony in which everyone has an assigned place within the whole. Individual humans represent a microcosm in which the macrocosm is mirrored. Thus, the constitutive principle of the universe is unity, with the absolute unity represented by God, who is the source and goal of everything. God's will is forever active in the uniform government of the world, which suggests that God directs every existing thing to its end. In this perspective, the many originate in the One and return to the One.

Christians of the Middle Ages viewed humankind as one community under God. In fact, humankind is identical with Christendom and a single purpose, which means that it is one law and one government identified with the law and rule of God. Within this theocentric worldview, there is also a dualism between the temporal and the spiritual realms, a division that is due to the will of God. But this dualism is not final, because a reconciliation can be found in a higher unity.

Within the context of this medieval worldview, there was the popular religious perspective of the peasants who farmed the land or earned a living doing some type of craft skill. Their popular religion was a mixture of Christian, heathen, and folk traditions. From the perspective of the peasant view of life, there was a cosmic battle occurring between the evil spirits of Satan and the army of Christ, whose standard-bearer was St. Michael. In fact, Catholic mass was interpreted as a battle with the devil, and a priest's vestments represented the armor of salvation. The mass was also viewed by peasants as a judicial tribunal where God judged the sinners, with the devil playing the prosecutor and the priest acting as the defense counsel. Ultimately, it was believed that demons were powerless before the sign of the cross, which prevailed against all magic and sorcery.

Because of the frequency of warfare, popular religion was militant and concerned with justice. Ordinary medieval people had a single faith: God, the saints, and the priesthood all worked together toward a person's protection, healing, and redemption. But there was also a conviction among the people that it was impossible to live in the world and be wholly a Christian. And yet peasants believed that there must be people capable of leading a perfect Christian life. Monks and nuns were expected to represent these people of perfection because they could model their life on that of Jesus. The expectation that monks and nuns could be perfect by imitating the perfection of Jesus is evident in a cloister that was called "the gate of Paradise" or "Paradise" itself.

Because of the violence and feelings of helplessness in their lives, peasants sought refuge in sacred power from violent forces threatening their existence. A source of such power was the relics of martyrs and saints that were collected to enhance the wonder-working power of a particular sanctuary and to attract pilgrims and money to their towns. Sacred relics consist of bodily parts or items associated with a holy person, such as a martyr or saint. The cult of martyrs played a key role influencing the veneration of relics. The cult of relics altered notions about who is or is not dead. This means that martyrs, witnesses to their faith, are not dead, because they continue to live in their relics.

Sacred relics had economic and political importance in the Middle Ages, as evident, for instance, with Charlemagne (742–814), who wore a necklace with two crystal amulets containing pieces of the true cross on which Jesus died and strands of hair of the Virgin Mary. Charlemagne also used relics as gifts to powerful people and as a means of binding senior courtiers to him. Towns and cities often competed with each other over relics because the sacred relics attracted pilgrims and their money. In addition to its economic impact, the cult of relics helped to legitimate rulers who protected the relics. Moreover, relics were also symbols of prestige. The relics were so ardently sought by Christians that when apparent saints died, their bodies often had to be protected from being cut up and their parts divided among seekers. If a town or city was bereft of sacred relics, leaders of some locations were known to steal them from other locations. The cult of relics could and did reach heights of absurdity, as evident by all the locations claiming to have the foreskin of Jesus from his circumcision and the multitude of places with pieces or entire replicas of the original cross or breast milk of the Virgin Mary.

The power of the relics was proven by miracles associated with them. The relics of holy persons usually were housed under church altars. A sacred relic could reach larger numbers of people when it was housed in a portable reliquary, enabling it to be easily carried in containers elaborately decorated and expensively encrusted with jewels. These reliquaries were often made in the shape of the bone or body part they housed, such as an arm or leg. When this popular practice proliferated between the fifth and ninth centuries, the relics symbolized the presence of saints throughout the Christian world and subsequently symbolized a community of saints. In summary, relics had a dual power: They were a means to communicate with the saint in order to ask the saint to intercede for the salvation of helpless sinners, and they functioned as a means to spark miracles for the benefit of Christians on earth.

In addition to the power of relics, peasants also resorted to the usage of images and icons. Initially in early Christian history, members were hesitant to use images and icons. But by the second century CE, paintings appeared as funeral decorations in the Roman catacombs. Icons were later conceived as things through which supernatural power was conveyed to ordinary mortals. It was believed that God's grace and power abided in icons. The divine power inherent in sacred icons was prefigured in the Hebrew Scriptures, when Elisha's staff was believed to have miraculous power, and his bones could restore a person to life. In the New Testament, the shadow of Peter was believed to heal sick people. After handkerchiefs and aprons had contact with the body of Paul (Acts 19.12), they were able to effect cures and dispel evil spirits from the afflicted. The context for the veneration of relics, images, and icons is grounded in the incarnate nature of Jesus, which enables people to grasp the divine in a material form. This religious context favorable to sacred objects was historically endorsed by Pope Gregory the Great (c. 540–604), who ruled that homage directed to images was only veneration, while St. Thomas Aquinas (c. 1225–74) agreed with Gregory, saying that gestures of homage directed to an image of Christ was simply adoration. But genuine worship is addressed to Christ.

Christian images took many symbolic forms, as evident by a figure hanging on a cross, a simple or jeweled engraved cross, a simple cross attached to a chain to be worn around the neck, a metal of someone such as St. Christopher that can be worn around the neck or attached to the interior of a vehicle, statues of the Virgin Mary painted blue and white standing on a globe, images of Mary and her son represented in stone carvings or paintings, statues of saints, and other items.

In addition to the cross, a popular image and symbol venerated was the fish, which was symbolic of baptism, the resurrection, Eucharist, and the kingdom of God. Within the ritual context of baptism, Jesus is the sacred fish and baptized Christians are the little fish. St. Augustine refers to the fish which is eaten, which refers to Christ who suffered and serves as the food of the Eucharist. In Christian literature, the consecration of the bread and wine is often depicted by the consecration of the sacred fish. Moreover, the food of the future heavenly banquet is symbolic of the final consummation of the kingdom of God. In Jewish apocalyptic literature, the sacred fish is the Leviathan, which is also the main course at the heavenly banquet. The fish is often depicted as a dolphin, which is a friend of humans, savior of the shipwrecked, and guide for the soul to the underworld and the island of the blessed. The symbolic associations of the fish are summarized by the Greek letters for fish (*ichthys*), which form the initial letters of Jesus' full title—Jesus Christ Son of God, Savior.

A figure depicted praying is often female and called an *orante*, although it sometimes appears as masculine. The figure stands with arms extended upward and bent at the elbows. It represents the soul of a dead person, which is regarded as feminine. The *orante* represents victory over death, suggesting that the day of death was really a day of birth. *Orante* also stands for the kingdom of God, the holy church, communion of saints, and a form of the cross. It is possible to find early pictures of the crucifixion showing Christ in this attitude of prayer.

Popular Christian life was periodically punctuated by religious holidays (e.g., Christmas and Easter) and festivals. During the Middle Ages, the Feast of Fools was very popular and celebrated around January 1. Townsfolk and priests wore bawdy masks, sang outrageous songs, and enjoyed revelry and satire of the upper classes. During this festival, ordinary rules were reversed, as when minor clerics painted their faces and strutted about the town in the robes of their superiors. Moreover, the stately rituals of the church were mocked. It was common for local people to elect a Lord of Misrule, a mock king. Or they might elect a boy bishop, who presided over the festival or even a parody mass. The Feast of Fools is scripturally grounded in Paul's injunction to be "fools for Christ's sake," which actually represented a new type of wisdom. Festivals such as the Feast of Fools represented a break from ordinary life and work, when people took a break to celebrate life and overturn common social distinctions. Festivals are repetitive and form a basis for both stability and change despite their excessive nature with overeating and excessive drinking, dancing, and singing. In short, a festival is a joyous time of pure revelry. In addition to festivals, common people also participated in the cults of the Virgin Mary and saints and believed in the existence of angels and the devil, which deserve and are given separate attention later.

Ritual Action and Sacraments

The term sacrament comes from the Greek word *mystērion* (mystery), which became *sacramentum* in Latin translation. The number of sacraments recognized as orthodox by the Latin Church and Protestant Reformation leaders has been debated over a long time. Peter Damian (1007–72), cardinal and theologian, argued for twelve sacraments, whereas Peter Lombard (c. 1100–60), theologian, bishop of Paris, and author of a theological textbook the *Sentences*, fixed the number at seven for the Latin Church: baptism, Eucharist, confirmation, penance, extreme unction, ordination, and marriage. According to the accepted wisdom of the Latin Church, the sacraments confer grace by the force of the action itself and represent words and actions that are instruments of God. They are a means of grace in the sense that God produces a change in the soul. The effect of the sacraments is not dependent on the worth of either the minister or recipient. At a basic minimum, the recipient must be receptive and place no impediment, which could take the form of a lack of faith in the working of the sacrament. In contrast to the recipient, the minister must intend what the church does for the rite and what it means. In the end, the validity of the sacrament does not depend on the faith or moral character of the minister. Overall, sacraments are remedies for human weakness caused by sin.

Baptism, confirmation, and ordination are unique and cannot be repeated. Not only do these sacraments consecrate one to God, but they also enable one to participate in the priestly power of Christ. The character of the sacraments means that they have a distinctive mark that separates unbelievers from believers. Their character implies a certain likeness to God. In addition to their character, sacraments have a symbolic reality, which refers to its effect, which is distinct from grace. The Eucharist is, for example, such a reality because the real body of Christ is present, which is its validity measured by some type of result. Marriage is valid, for example, because it results in an indissoluble bond.

The Latin Church understands baptism as a restoration to paradise from which Adam was driven by God. The baptistery is often octagonal in shape because the number eight was symbolic of the resurrection. The candidate for baptism imitates Christ's nakedness on the cross, which involves a return to primitive innocence. The initiate is healed with oil, which is intended to strengthen one for future struggles. Immersion into the baptismal pool is symbolic of purification from sin and Christ's death. The triple immersion of a candidate imitates the burial of Jesus for three days and nights. The baptismal waters are both a tomb and mother in a sequence of symbolically experiencing death and rebirth. The traditional ceremony concluded with the initiate donning a white garment, which is interpreted as the clothing of innocence, the purity of the soul, a symbol of the resurrection of the body, and putting on Christ (Gal. 3:27). And the white garment is given an eschatological meaning because the victors over the devil are clothed in white. Often at the conclusion of the rite, the sign of the cross is imposed on the forehead of the initiate, which is symbolic of being marked and thus belonging to Christ. Besides being a sign of ownership, the sign of the cross offers protection from demons and imprints the image of God on the soul.

After a person is baptized, one is considered a child, but when one is confirmed, one becomes an adult. The Latin Church traces the sacrament of confirmation back to the Hebrew Scriptures, where anointing was a rite by which priests and kings were consecrated, back to the Apostle Peter's laying his hands on the ill, and it recalls the anointing of Christ by the Holy Spirit after his baptism. Confirmation represents an additional outpouring of the Spirit after baptism that stands for developing one's faith and strengthening one's spiritual life.

The Eucharist rite involves preparation of the offerings, washing of hands, the kiss of peace, transforming the bread and wine into the body and blood of Christ, the sacrifice, and the distribution of the consecrated elements during communion. The sacred altar on which this occurs represents the body of Christ. St. Cyril of Alexandria (d. 444) states "Christ is the altar, the offering, and the priest." Again, St. Cyril says that the kiss of peace represents the union of souls, whereas Augustine stresses that it is a sign of peace within our hearts. The rite also symbolically transports the faithful to heaven. The sacrificial aspect of the rite recalls the Cross event, which enables the faithful to participate in the heavenly liturgy.

The sacrament of penance differentiates the Latin Church from Reformation churches. In the early church, penance involved the readmission into the church of those who had fallen into sin after baptism; it was a public event. The Celtic Church did not use a public form of penance, but it did use a private method that consisted of a confession to a priest, who levied satisfaction on the sinner that could consist of fasting, prayer, giving alms, or living a life of abstinence. This Celtic type of penance gradually became the basis of the Latin Church, where contrition and confession before a priest was instituted along with satisfaction before a sinner could be reconciled to the community by being given private priestly absolution.

A major focus of disagreement between the Latin Church and a Protestant reformer such as Luther was that not all seven sacraments are based in scripture, which implies that they are divinely instituted. Thus, Luther rejects confirmation, marriage, ordination, and extreme unction, because ordination and extreme unction are inventions of the church and thus fictitious. In an essay devoted to the subject written in 1519, Luther says that a sacrament is an outward sign that consists of the appearance of bread and wine in the Eucharist rite, but it serves internally as a sign of the fellowship of all saints. The sacrament is also a working act of faith. Luther also accepts baptism as a legitimate sacrament grounded in scripture because it serves as a sign for the people of Christ and signifies dying to sin and being resurrected in the grace of God. Luther also accepted infant baptism because it had been practiced since the beginning of the church. Luther finds hints of this practice in Acts and the letters of Paul, which report the baptism of all inhabitants within a home, it being rationally assumed that some members of a home must have been children. Luther also thought that private confession was necessary, even though he could find no scriptural basis for it, but he affirmed that penance has been abused by the church. Although Luther thought that penance was useful, it is, strictly speaking, not a genuine sacrament.

In contrast to Luther, other radical reformist groups were even more critical of certain sacraments. The Anabaptists, who were nicknamed re-baptizers and viewed the Reformation as only half-complete, believed that there was no valid baptism distinct from faith, which also calls for maturity of the believer. They rejected infant baptism because it lacked scriptural basis and because of their conviction that faith precedes baptism. For the Anabaptists, the Eucharist is an expression of communion and a rite of fellowship. They did not believe that Christ was present in the elements of bread and wine. The Anabaptists wanted to model their community on the voluntary association typical of the New Testament community, in which there was no distinction between clergy and laity and members could lead a simple and holy life. They espoused that the church must be separate from the state. At least three important implications resulted from this position: No Anabaptist can be a magistrate, no one was allowed to participate in war, and a believer must refuse to swear oaths. The Anabaptist emphasized a new life in Christ and not justification of faith, as did Luther. The basis of the Anabaptist conception of the church was an experience of Christ's presence.

Christian Monasticism

Monasticism became an important component of the Latin Church beginning in the fourth century. The term comes from the Greek *monachos* (alone, solitary). The term referred to individuals who withdrew from society to devote their full attention to their spiritual life by spending their time in a condition of celibacy, praying, and following an ascetic lifestyle of various degrees of rigor. When considering such a way of life, a person could choose to become an anchorite and live alone or could decide to adopt a cenobitic lifestyle (living in a community of similar people).

There are some attitudes and comments made in the New Testament that reveal monastic inclinations. Jesus challenges disciples, for example, to take up their cross and follow him (Mark 8.34). In the Gospel of Matthew (19:12), there is a reference to those who have renounced marriage for the sake of the Kingdom of Heaven. In the Gospel of Luke (9:23), Jesus says those who follow him must leave their self behind and take up the cross. In other passages in Luke, Jesus refers to himself as someone without a home (9:58) and says that a potential disciple must hate his relatives and carry his cross (14:26–27). The theme of hatred of the self is also evident in the Gospel of John (12:25). These types of passages reflect becoming detached from others, the self, and the world. And Paul writes about mastering the body (1 Cor. 9:26–27) and being crucified with Christ (Gal. 2:20).

Even with such passages in the New Testament, the historical beginning of monasticism begins with the Desert Fathers in Egypt. St. Anthony is credited with organizing hermits. But the first founder of Christian monasticism was St. Pachomius (d. 346), who established monasteries in southern Egypt. St. Basil (c. 330–79), bishop of Caesarea from 330–379 CE, devised monastic rules that were named after him. According to St. Basil, a monk must lead a life of prayer, work, poverty, celibacy, and obedience. The injunction to work often took the form of running hospitals, orphanages, and schools. The ascetic regimen of monastic life was intended to restore the soul to its original condition of purity in preparation for salvation.

The spirit of monastic life is captured in a narrative written by Athanasius, a controversial bishop of Alexandria from 328 to 373, titled *The Life of Anthony*, a hagiographical account of the monk's life. Anthony was Egyptian and born into a prosperous family, but tragedy struck when his parents died when he was around 18 years old, making him the guardian of his younger sister. Attending church six months later with a troubled mind, he heard the priest refer to a Gospel passage from Matthew (19:21) that challenged others to give what they have to the poor, which is precisely what Anthony did. After securing a safe situation for his sister, he turned to a life of prayer and asceticism, which included sleepless nights, eating once a day, eating only bread and salt, and drinking only water. A constant theme in the narrative is his battles with demons, who torture him physically and mentally. Anthony endured considerable pain but remained resolute in his struggles with demonic beings. Anthony healed the sick who journeyed to him and purged others of demons. His positive actions to help others were always interpreted by Athanasius as God working through him. A tall demon appears to Anthony claiming, for instance, to be the power of God. By Anthony uttering name of Christ, the giant figure disappeared into a puff of smoke. Another episode recounts a man possessed by a demon who forces the possessed person to eat his own excrement. After staying awake with this man all night, Anthony was attacked by the young man, which he interpreted as the withdrawal of the demon; this was confirmed when the man regained his senses. Another narrative relates the plight of a young woman afflicted with a strange disease, which manifested itself when she issued forth tears and mucus from her eyes and mouth. When these fluids reached the ground, they became worms. She was also paralyzed and suffered eye problems. When her parents took her to visit Anthony he cured her but insisted that the cure came from the power of God and not him. Later in his life, Anthony increased his ascetic regimen by fasting, wearing a hair shirt, not bathing his body, and not washing his feet. Toward the end of his life, he intuitively realized that his death was near and announced this coming event to his monks. When he became ill, he instructed two monks to bury him in the earth in an unmarked grave. Athanasius' hagiographical account of Anthony's life became a model for other ascetically inclined Christians to copy, although other figures shaped the monastic life in accord with their personal vision of the religious life spent in service and devotion to God.

St. Benedict of Nursia (480–543) envisioned, for instance, a simple, rustic, and largely uneducated community with the purpose of leading a quiet Christian life. St. Benedict thought that it was not the job of a monk to reform the world because his first duty was to reform himself, which is very difficult to achieve when living in a town. The Benedictine Rule included obedience to superiors, which involved relinquishing one's will both to God and to the monastic community. A Benedictine monk also took a vow of stability, which meant that a monk was to remain in a particular monastery until death. In addition, a monk must not own anything, because all property must be shared in common. Humility functioned as a guiding idea for the life of the monk, which could be learned, for example, by working in the fields like slaves of God. Later Benedictines worked from within the scholarly and artistic life of the church. The passage of time witnessed the birth of new monastic movements.

Using the Apostle Paul as his model, St. Dominic (1170–1221) was interested in winning converts by preaching. He adopted the rules of St. Augustine for his movement and obtained approval for his order in 1216. His order embraced mendicancy, which involved begging for one's daily food. The Order of Preachers established by St. Dominic adhered to a structure led by a master-general chosen by the general chapter; next came the provincial prior, elected for a four-year term; and each monastery elected a prior for four years. This system was a combination of authority and representative government, which was revolutionary for its historical time.

The Franciscans were inspired by the humble model of St. Francis and his insistence on absolute poverty, wearing of simple clothing, and acting like Christ, a paradigm of love. St. Francis sent his monks in pairs to preach about the necessity to repent, to sing, to help farmers, to care for lepers and social outcasts, and to beg for food. After the death of St. Francis, others organized his order and established the *Rule of St. Francis*, which made three spiritual demands on monks: absolute poverty, a refusal to solicit or accept any ecclesiastical privileges, and renunciation of all human learning. The opposites of these rules were viewed as sources of spiritual corruption. In later English religious history, Dominicans were known as Black Friars, whereas Franciscans were known as Gray Friars because of their contrasting clothing.

The Dominicans and Franciscans were followed by other orders, such as the Cistercian Benedictines, who wanted to reform the Church by renewing the practice of rigorous asceticism. St. Ignatius of Loyola (d. 1556) founded the Society of Jesus, or Jesuit order, in 1540. He wrote *Spiritual Exercises*, a thirty-day series of retreat meditations required of monks twice during their training. Ignatius convinced St. Francis Xavier (1506–52), a missionary to India, to join him. The Jesuit order was established to promote teaching at many levels and to propagate the faith by becoming global missionaries. Less outwardly focused, the Cistercians were founded in 1098 at Citeaux in Burgundy and promoted an austere monastic style that was devoted to a life of silent piety and prayer. St. Bernard of Clairvaux was among the order's most famous members. The seventeenth century witnessed the rise of the so-called strict observance, which was more rigorous. A. de Rancé (d. 1700), abbot of La Trappe, played a leading role in this reform. These Cistercians of the strict observance became the Trappists in the nineteenth century. The order withdrew the vow of silence on Thomas Merton (1915–68), who became the face and voice of the order, a participant in interreligious dialogue, and author of the renowned autobiography *The Seven Storey Mountain*.

Christian Mysticism

The history of Christian monasticism is intertwined with mysticism, which is related to profound religious experiences by an individual. The origin of the term derives from ancient Greco-Roman mystery cults discussed in chapter 2. These cults were called *muein* (literally, to close the eyes), which implies something secret and hidden from the visual perspective of outsiders but revealed to initiates. Christian writers adopted the Greek term *muein* and applied it to the mystery of Christ. As the term evolves in the Christian tradition, it comes to mean an experience that is deep, profound, personal, and spiritual. In the sixth century, Pseudo-Dionysius, author of *The Mystical Theology*, uses the term *muein* to stress what he calls a *via mystica* (mystical path). This type of extraordinary subjective experience is so profound that mystics constantly tell readers of their personal accounts that they cannot truly verbally or orally convey to an outsider its ineffable nature because of the inexplicable experience and the inadequacy of language to express it. The mystical path involves different types of ascetic practice as preparation for the overpowering experience. The mystic follows a path that may differ from one figure to another, but it involves following a path that represents a journey from multiplicity, conflict, ignorance, and change to a position of unity, cohesion, certainty, and stability. The mystic path is often characterized as a death to the world and a rebirth in the divine when the mystic achieves the unitive experience, which is defined differently depending on the mystic.

St. John of the Cross (1542–91), a founder of the Discalced Carmelites and spiritual mentor of St. Teresa of Avila, was born into a family of the lower nobility, being the youngest of three sons, but his father died when he was 2 years old, leaving the family without basic necessities of life. After his mother moved the family to another town in the quest for a better life, John failed to settle into an apprenticeship with any of the four that he attempted. John was sent to school, where he flourished, and continued his education at a Jesuit college. However, in 1563, he became a Carmelite novice of the Mitigated Rule and later studied at the University of Salamanca in 1565, where he was ordained in 1567. It was during this period of time that he met St. Teresa, who asked John to become the confessor and spiritual director to nuns of her convent despite John's youthfulness. During December 1577, John was seized by Carmelites of the Mitigated Observance and taken to Toledo as their prisoner when he refused to renounce the reform of the order. While in prison, St. John composed the initial thirty stanzas of the *Spiritual Canticle*, a poem and commentary on the entire spiritual life. He would escape his captors to later be named Prior of the Carmelite monastery in Segovia, where his contemplative life reached its greatest heights, and was expressed in *The Ascent of Mount Carmel* and the *Dark Night of the Soul*. Both works were intended to be commentaries on the same poem, although the interpretations were very different. In these works, St. John makes creative use of light metaphors.

The dark night represents the emptying of the soul of everything not God. The night has three phases, with the middle one being the darkest, although there is really only one night. It is just that the mystic subjectively perceives the second phase of the dark night as the darkest of all because natural light has been withdrawn and supernatural light is not yet tolerable by the soul. The dark night of the soul is analogous to mystic death, when the soul loses the presence of God and feels abandoned by God. During the dark night, God plays a game of hide and seek with the soul. Feeling hopeless, imperfect, and sinful, the soul experiences a relapse to lower spiritual levels, but this represents the final purification of the soul, which now totally surrenders itself and loses its individuality and will. But the true goal for the mystic is the unitive experience.

According to St. John, union is characterized by a peaceful joy, enhanced powers, and intense certitude as the soul is transformed in God, which is a state of conformity to the will of God. St. John often describes this as a union of love, a principle that begets likeness between the one who loves and the object of one's love. It follows from this that perfect love must issue in perfect likeness, which St. John illustrates with the metaphor of the sun shining on a window. God is comparable to the sun, and the human soul is represented by the window. When the window is completely covered with dirt, the sun cannot illume it as it can when the window is clean. To the extent that the window is clean, the sun illumines it. When the window is entirely clean, sunlight so illumines it that it makes it appear to be the light. Nonetheless, no matter how it resembles the light, the nature of the window remains distinct from the nature of the sunlight. Therefore, St. John denies any transmutation of the substance of the soul into the substance of God, suggesting that their union consists of love and likeness but not substance.

Some Christian mystics got themselves into trouble with church officials by speaking and writing in provocative ways that seemed to suggest that the unitive experience is akin to the mystic becoming God or a part of God. An example of this type of Christian mysticism is evident in the works of Meister Eckhart (c. 1260–1327), who was accused of heresy by officials but died before his trial could be adjudicated. Eckhart writes about being coated with God, suggesting that no creature can touch him without first touching God. Eckhart implied that a flea united with God ranks higher than an angel. Eckhart also refers to the spark of the soul, which is pre-existent, originally free, and connected to divine reason, which enables the soul to penetrate the hidden ground of God. This line of thinking implies that the soul has the same properties as God, and the image of God is in the soul and forms its ground. Thus the soul can directly know God. Needless to say, the church was suspicious of any suggestion that a human being is divine in any way. In Eckhart's case, his preaching to other monks was radical because his audience could understand and appreciate his teachings, although his remarks could easily be construed as heretical by those with less advanced spiritual development.

The Role of Christian Saints and Martyrs

Before he became known as St. Francis of Assisi (1182–1266), Francis was born into an economically successful family and lived a life of vanity and pleasure. While attending church, he heard words from the Gospel of Matthew (10:7–19) related to Jesus' commission to go forth and preach, which sparked a religious wake-up call. According to one version of his life, he renounced worldly things and his father's wealth and stripped naked in front of Santa Maria Maggiore, site of the episcopal palace. He took an absolute vow of poverty and patterned his life on that of Jesus. St. Francis gave alms to the poor and tended to the needs of lepers, who were commonly considered the dregs of society and avoided by nearly everyone. When traveling and preaching, Francis spoke about the need for penance, peace, and mercy. His absolute vow of poverty suggested that he was a poor person among the poor and imitating the behavior of Jesus. True to his emphasis on peace, Francis rejected power and its concomitant violence.

Francis eventually won permission from the pope to establish the order that was later named after him. Besides taking a vow of poverty, members of the order were encouraged to travel in pairs to preach the Gospel. Francis inspired Clare, a nun, to establish a Second Order of St. Francis for women, commonly known as the Poor Clares, in 1212. During the period of the Crusades, Francis traveled to Egypt, where he argued his case for Christ before the Sultan. In 1221, he established the Tertiaries, a third order that was a compromise for those inspired by his ideals but continuing to live in the world. There are hagiographical narratives about him preaching to birds and having relations with other creatures of nature. Narratives tell readers about a falcon that woke him at dawn each morning and a pheasant that did not want to leave his cell. Although he did not like mice and flies, Francis took care not to step on worms because they reminded him of humility. His selective nonviolence applied equally to sheep, which he saved from going to slaughter, and wolves. Many of the creatures and elements of nature evoked religious connotations for him. Birds were symbols of the soul, water was a symbol of the purification of the soul, the sun represented God, a tree suggested the cross event, and fish were an image of an active life. Migratory birds reminded Francis of souls that wander far away but return to their nesting areas later in the year, which implied souls returning to God. If Francis's biographers are correct, he looked at nature through the lens of Christianity and spiritualized God's creation. All creatures are part of a universal fraternity, within which all are brothers and sisters.

Two years before his death, Francis received the stigmata, marks on his body resembling those that Jesus received at His crucifixion to his hands, feet, and side. According to his hagiographers, Francis received them in a vision from a figure in the sky with six wings suspended from a cross. Francis fell to the ground in joy, not grasping the significance of his vision until he stood and saw the marks on his body. By receiving the stigmata of Christ, Francis was allowed to participate in the passion of Christ. Although the stigmata were conceived as receiving the grace of God, St. Francis was embarrassed by them and tried to hide them. But many saw them during his life and after his death. According to hagiographical narratives, the stigmata of St. Francis were confirmed by many miracles, often in the form of healings. Many other types of miracles were attributed to him, such as changing water to wine, and bread that he blessed had healing powers. In his biography of the saint, St. Bonaventure (1221–74), becoming a member of the Friars Minor because he credited St. Francis with saving his life from an illness, interpreted the stigmata as a divine seal given to St. Francis by God to authenticate Francis' teachings and monastic order. It is ironical that a saint who preached peace would receive the stigmata, a symbol of a violent act. Nonetheless, the stigmata allowed St. Francis to become a martyr, a role that he embraced during his life.

Similar to St. Francis, many Christian saints were also martyrs. The phenomenon of martyrdom began with St. Stephen (d. c. 35), according to Acts (6–8: 2). St. Stephen, a member of the early Christian community, was selected by his community leaders to distribute food to the poor along with six other men. He was falsely accused of blasphemy, convicted by Jewish authorities, and condemned to death despite his angelic face. The concept of martyrdom is derived from a Greek term for witness (*martus*). Martyrs are witnesses to their faith, suffering death for their convictions, and venerated as saints. From the second century, it has been a common understanding that martyrs are imitators of Christ. Popular belief conceives of the martyr's death as Jesus appearing to the martyr and enduring all the suffering in place of the martyr, who must not actively seek death. But a martyr is expected to submit passively to it. During the Middle Ages, martyrs could expect to receive visions and dreams that foretold the martyr's future destiny in this life and the next.

The Feminine Dimension of Christianity

Because Christian/Jewish women lived under the same patriarchal social system, it does not seem necessary to repeat the role of women discussed previously about Jewish women. However, it seems useful to discuss the feminine thread or influence in Christianity, because it enhances our portrait of the religion. The female who has proven to be the most influential feminine figure in Christianity is Mary because she was the mother of the Messiah and has proven to be a very popular figure among the church hierarchy and ordinary believers. Mary Magdalene and female martyrs, saints, and mystics have played special roles in Christian religious history, although a discussion of them will have to be selective, with the exception of Mary, mother of Jesus.

The angel Gabriel was sent by God to announce to the maiden Mary, who was engaged to Joseph, that she will bear a son who will become great. She was perplexed by such a greeting, but the angel assured her that she had won favor with God. Mary did not think that becoming pregnant was a realistic option because she was a virgin, but the angelic messenger told her that the Holy Spirit will come over her (Luke 1:26–35). This event was later celebrated as the Feast of the Annunciation (March 25) by the church. The next important pre-birth episode has Mary visiting her relative Elizabeth, who was pregnant with John the Baptist. When the two women encounter each other, the fetus in Elizabeth's womb leaps for joy. Elizabeth says to Mary, "Blessed are you among women, and blessed is the fruit of your womb" (Luke 1:42). In later church history, the words of Elizabeth and Gabriel were combined to create the "Hail Mary" prayer. After giving birth to Jesus, Mary fades into the New Testament narrative background, with the exception of the wedding at Cana (John 2:1–11), where wine ran out, and Mary tells the servants to do whatever Jesus says, even though he brushes her aside because it is not his time to reveal himself. This narrative shows Mary's maternal influence on her son and becomes the basis for the later belief in Marian intercession.

Revelation (12:1–6) describes a woman clothed by the sun with the moon under her feet and a crown of twelve stars on her head. The unnamed woman is pregnant and cries out in pain, while a seven-headed, ten-horned, seven-crowned dragon threatens to devour the child. People of the middle ages interpreted the subjects of this episode to be Mary and infant Jesus. Carved medallions of this scene adorn churches in northern Europe, depicting a dragon or snake curling around Mary's feet, suggesting the defeat of evil. With imagery from the book of Revelation forming the artistic context, Mary is portrayed as the queen of heaven. This type of literary and artistic expression by the time of the medieval period, which was a high point of Marian piety, seems to suggest that Mary has assumed the role of a goddess figure, but this impression is not the position of the Latin Church because it separates devotion to Mary and worship of God. Medieval art has produced many works depicting Mary and her infant, which evokes Mary's role as *Theotokos* (the God-bearer).

Since Mary did not have a fully developed biography in the New Testament, a body of pseudo-epigraphical (undetermined authorship) writings evolved later to fill in her biography, especially her miraculous birth to aged parents and her Assumption to heaven with her body and soul, which the Latin Church celebrates on August 15. The popularity of Mary is also evident with the celebration of the Immaculate Conception, observed on December 8. These writings and feasts are examples of the force of popular opinion and acceptance by average people.

Lay devotion directed to Mary was related to the common belief that she had the power of intercession, which was supported by her being the mother of Jesus, having influence over her son, and being queen of heaven. The popular Christian tradition believed that she had the power to work miracles, as did her relics. In the popular tradition, her breast milk was believed to cure blindness, cancer, and other illnesses. The popular tradition was partly responsible for the creation of grand cathedrals dedicated to her, such as those located at Notre Dame in Chartres and Paris with their soaring Gothic towers.

The popular devotion to Mary continues into modern times in part because of Marian apparitions at places such as Guadalupe, Lourdes, and Fatima. These places became sacred because Mary appeared at these locations to others and have become important centers of pilgrimage, especially for those afflicted with some handicap or illness. These modern locations represent a continuation of Mary's devotional cult, with its promise of cures and healings to the faithful.

Mary Magdalene is an especially interesting female figure in the history of the Latin Church. It is suggested in the Gospels that she was a woman with financial resources because she could provide for Jesus and his followers. In fact, she was a permanent member of the Jesus movement, as evident by her presence at the crucifixion and a witness to the resurrection, which made her an apostle and witness to extraordinary events. In the non-canonical literature of the *Gospel of Thomas* (c. second century), a gnostic text, the apostle Peter is depicted attempting to undermine her authority, but he is rebuked by a resurrected Jesus when he declares that he will transform her into a male to enable her to enter heaven. Other gnostic texts depict her receiving teachings directly and privately from Jesus and being a leader within the primitive Christian community. The *Gospel of Philip*, another gnostic text, refers to Mary Magdalene as Jesus' most beloved disciple and follower and says that he often kissed her. As the Latin Church developed over the centuries, Mary Magdalene's prominent place during the early Jesus movement declined within the Church as the institution became dominated by male authority. Pope Gregory I (c. 540–604) transformed Mary Magdalene into a redeemed prostitute. Nonetheless, Mary would subsequently become the paradigm for the repentant sinner in the teachings of the Church and a popular figure in Christian inspired art.

The accounts of Mary Magdalene in the Gospels are very suggestive with respect to her importance to the early Jesus movement. According to Mark (14:50), Jesus' male disciples disappeared around the time of his passion, but there were four women present including Mary Magdalene, who sees where Jesus is laid to rest by Joseph of Arimathea, a wealthy man and disciple of Jesus. The Gospel of Mark (16:9–11) narrates that Jesus appears first to Mary Magdalene after his resurrection, but others did not believe her. According to the account in Matthew (28:1–3), when the women arrive at the sepulcher, there is an earthquake and an angel, who rolls back the stone, sits on the stone, and tells the women not to be afraid and that Jesus would meet them in Galilee. Before reaching Jesus' disciples, the women encounter Jesus. An interesting addition to the portrayal of Mary Magdalene appears in the Gospel of Luke (18:2–3) where she is referred to as a person exorcised of seven demons. Overall, the narratives concerning Mary Magdalene from the synoptic texts are in general agreement.

In the Gospel of John, Mary Magdalene is identified with three other women at the cross (19:25). In the following chapter of the text, Mary Magdalene finds the sepulcher empty and runs to Peter and the other disciples, fearing that the body of Jesus has been stolen. The disciples deliberately proceed to the sepulcher to verify her story. In medieval Christianity, this race to the tomb of Jesus is reenacted as part of the Easter observance and medieval mystery plays. In the Gospel of John, Mary Magdalene maintains a lonely vigil weeping at the tomb. When she looks into the sepulcher, she sees two angels. After responding to the angels' question about her motivation for weeping, she turns back to see Jesus standing there, who also asks her why she weeps, before she then recognizes him and exclaims "Teacher" (John 20:14–16). She attempts to embrace Jesus, and he tells her not to touch him because he has not yet ascended to God, the Father. Mary Magdalene then informs the disciples of her encounter with Jesus.

The account of Mary Magdalene in the four Gospels confirms her status as an expert witness, a person of faith, and a figure of unequivocal conviction, and she assumes the position of first among the apostles. Mary Magdalene is a female witness of the first rank and a paradigm of service. The sketchy portrait of Mary Magdalene in the four Gospels was enhanced by the later Christian tradition, when she would become a model for female mystics, conversion, penitence, a symbol of the contemplative life, an exemplar for prostitutes, and a paradigm of fidelity and love and was associated with miracles. These themes were recounted by European painters and creators of sculptures.

During a historical period when there were few employment options for women, church history records women joining monastic institutions during the Middle Ages, which freed them from a life of marriage, housework, and the dangers associated with childbirth. Some monastic women became leaders of their institutions. And some leaders injected a feminine spirit into their monastic institutions. Hildegard of Bingen (1098–1179), a mystic and visionary, allowed her nuns to dress as brides of Christ, a practice that was considered provocative and gave rise to rumors about possible salacious behavior occurring behind the monastic walls. These celibate, virgin nuns appeared in church with long flowing and unbound hair, wearing long, white, silk veils that touched the floor. The nuns wore golden crowns with crosses inserted into them, which were adorned with a lamb on the front of the crown. On their fingers, they wore golden rings. Nuns could also don white bridal gowns. This scenario suggests a symbolic marriage or betrothal to Christ. In order to counter her critics, Hildegard argued that the nuns under her care were virgins, which implied that they were freed of social restrictions imposed on married women. Hildegard made it clear that her nuns were married in sacredness to the Holy Spirit, which also gave them an opportunity to celebrate their beauty.

Some female mystics wrote autobiographically of their profound experiences in often erotic ways. In the thirteenth century, Hadewijch of Antwerp and St. Teresa of Avila (1515–1582) used erotic language to convey their experiences, and Julian of Norwich (c. 1342–c. 1413) had a series of visions that included God as a female figure. Hadewijch confessed to having an ecstatic experience after receiving the Eucharist communion wafer. After ingesting Christ's body, she confessed that it was Christ giving himself to her in the form of the sacrament. Hadewijch imagined that Christ took her in his arms and pressed her to himself like a lover. She confessed that she felt his felicity with all the parts of her body. She continued to describe an experience of erotic intensity.

Formerly a Jew whose parents were pressured into converting to Catholicism, St. Teresa became an important female figure in Spain during the Inquisition by writing about her religious experiences without framing her mystical experiences in Christian theology, which raised suspicions among church authorities, and she renovated her Carmelite nuns by having them express their poverty by wearing no shoes (resulting in the Discalced Carmelites). When discussing rapture, St. Teresa imagined her soul being ravished by Christ, the Bridegroom, leaving her speechless, unable to collect her thoughts, and feeling her body raising upwards. She experienced being pierced in her heart by the arrows of love and having an experience akin to a sexual orgasm.

After St. Teresa's death, nuns observed strange phenomena associated with the saint, such as the barren tree outside her window becoming filled with blossoms in winter, objects that she touched emitting a sweet fragrance, and visions of Teresa in heaven. St. Teresa's body was transformed after her death, as evident when her face became beautiful and free of wrinkles, her skin became very white and comparable to alabaster, her flesh became very soft, and her body exuded a sweet fragrance. Nine months after she died, her body was exhumed and still found to be uncorrupted and giving off a strong smell of sanctity, which further confirmed her virginity and saintliness.

Living as an anchoress near a church in Norwich, England, Julian lay, gravely ill, on May 13, 1373, a time at which she experienced sixteen visions after asking for them and received the last rites of the church, experiencing death as a paralysis of her lower body. As she presumably lay dying, a priest placed a cross before her, and she received her first vision, which consisted of seeing blood flowing from the crown of thrones on Christ's head. She saw, for example, God reigning as a king (sixth vision), the passion of Christ (eight vision), a formless body from which a beautiful child sprang forth and ascended to heaven (fifteenth vision), and a final vision that confirmed the previous visions, which validated as genuine all the visions for her. In her autobiography, Julian conceived of God as equally father and mother.

Julian's comments about the motherly nature of God are tame in comparison to the erotic language of Mechthild of Madgeburg, bride of the Trinity, with Jesus specifically identified as her lover. She even depicted God uttering erotic language as when, for example, God spoke about her giving herself to Him, lying naked in His arms, playing with her, and admitting to surrendering Himself to her alluring powers. Mechthild envisioned a mutual desire and game of love, during which each party was embracing and kissing each other as they lay together on a bed of love.

This erotic type of religious experience from the perspective of a female is only one aspect of the importance attached to the female gender. The side wound that Jesus received from the spear of a Roman soldier at the crucifixion began to be revered in iconography and devotional texts around the fifteenth century. It appears in some manuscripts, on woodcuts, and in prayers, appearing as a large, isolated oval shape. When arranged horizontally it gave the appearance of a mouth, while at other times it was arranged vertically and resembled a vagina. In addition, there existed textual identifications that explicitly associated the side wound with a vagina, symbolizing it as a source of and receptacle of life. The wound/vagina of Jesus was used as an amulet to protect a woman wearing it against a difficult labor and dangerous childbirth. In some medieval texts, Jesus' body was depicted with feminine features, such as lactating, conceiving, and giving birth. These developments were indicative of the feminine influence on Christianity despite male dominance of the power structure.

The Role of Angels

In Hebrew Scriptures, three angels appear to Abraham as men, to whom he graciously extends hospitality. They announce to the aged patriarch and his wife, Sarah, that she will give birth to a child, and she responds with laughter because the prospect seems so impossible due to the couple's advanced years (Gen. 18:1–19). These angels have no names, wings, or halos. The angels simply deliver messages and have no personal identity. In another example, Micah, a prophet, describes a vision of God that reveals God sitting on a throne surrounded by angels—soldiers of God's army (1 Kings 22:19). The book of Genesis (3:24) refers to a distinct kind of angelic being—the cherubim—given the task of guarding paradise to prevent Adam and Eve from returning. Another type of angel, a six-winged seraph, is identified in Isaiah (6:2). The book of Daniel marks an important development for angels, with its different ranks of them, having the duty to protect cities and nations. The post-exile period of Jewish history marks a shift reflected by concerns with hierarchies, ranks, and numbers of angels. Another important change is the belief that there is a guardian angel assigned to each person.

Christian Scriptures continue the connection between Abraham and angels. This is evident when Jesus tells a story about a poor man who dies and is carried by angels to Abraham's bosom (Luke 16:22). The angel Gabriel ("mighty man of God") announces to Mary that she will bear a son (Luke 1:26–38). The Hebrew word for angel (*malach*) means messenger, but this is not the only role that angels play in Christian Scriptures. The angel Michael battles the Devil in Revelation (12:17). Michael's name means "who is like God." In later Christian art, Michael is portrayed with a sword or a lance in his hand. The fact that he drove the Devil out of heaven connected him to the military. The angel Raphael ("God heals") is the patron healer of the sick, those with eye problems, and those with mental illness; he is also the patron of lovers.

Around the fourth century, angels begin to appear in art with halos and wings. It is possible that Christian artists borrowed the halo from pagan culture from figures such as the goddess Nike and the deity Eros. Artists were probably attempting to link the angels with Jesus. Within a Christian context, a halo is related to the power and glory of God. Musical instruments also became connected to angels, a feature that goes back to the book of Revelation (8:2), where seven angels are given trumpets to blow in the presence of God. Revelation (15:2) also portrays saints in heaven playing harps that they receive when they die. Angels are also associated with harps, which might be a reflection of a popular confusion between saints and angels in heaven. According to words of Jesus, angels do not marry (Matt. 22:30). They are neither made male nor female, although they are portrayed in early Christian iconography as exclusively male. Renaissance artists depicted angels as little children, and there was a tendency to portray them as androgynous or effeminate.

During his preaching career, Jesus supported the notion of people having guardian angels (Matt. 18:10). These guardian angels are conceived to be small of stature, with the duty to look after a single person. The smaller size of the angels parallels their lower rank within the hierarchy of angels. They also become associated with death. In the Gospel of Luke (16:24), Jesus refers to Lazarus dying and being carried by angels to Abraham's bosom. In Revelation (14:19–20), angels represented with sharp sickles reap a harvest of wicked souls, a description that prefigures the grim reaper of later religious imagination. Ordinary people offered devotion to angels because they believed that they could protect and help citizens with everyday problems beyond their ability to remedy.

Material Christianity

Early Christians gathered to worship in homes of the faithful. Eventually, the worship in homes became more open after an edict was passed in 313 by Constantine giving Christians the freedom to practice their religion in public places. Early sanctuaries included the Church of the Nativity and the Church of the Holy Sepulcher in the Holy Land. Christian artists rejected the structure of the Roman temple, a pagan building. Instead, Christians modeled their church structures after the civil law courts, which were called *basilica* (a Greek term meaning "royal"). These basilicas included a dais at the end of a hall farthest from the entrance, with widows set on a row of columns. The dais end of the church was called the apse and had a semi-circular half-dome. The sides were extended at the center of the building, which provided a cruciform floor plan that gave the floor the shape of a cross. Other types of floor plans included the circle or octagon, with the shrine object at the center under a dome that rested on a polygon or a circle of columns and arches.

A new style of church developed during the medieval period in northern Europe in the eleventh century that was called Gothic, a term that is an Italian slur originating with Renaissance writers because it gave the impression of being another invasion of barbarians. Two excellent examples in France are the cathedral of Notre-Dame in Paris and the Chartres Cathedral, about 100 miles southwest of Paris. This architectural style consisted of two curved sides rising to a point at the top, a style that gave the church a sense of height. Christian writers explained that high structures directed thoughts and prayers of worshippers toward heaven. The interior of the church included carvings in stone and wood, while the exterior spires pointed directly toward heaven. During this historical period, stained glass windows came into use made of colored glass and strips of lead. These windows embodied scenes from biblical narratives, which gave illiterate, faithful people a way of reading the stories with their eyes. A unique feature of Roman Catholic churches was the Stations of the Cross located along the side walls of the edifice, which represented a sequence of fourteen scenes in the form of paintings or plaques. The sequence of events recall occurrences from the time of Jesus' trial to his tomb. A parishioner moved from one station to the next reciting prayers and meditating on the scenes, especially during the season of Lent.

In addition to churches, Christians slowly developed works of sculpting and painting. Early Christian art resembled that of Judaism and its adherence to the second commandment about prohibiting the making of images of divine beings. Around the second century, a nascent Christian material culture begins to take shape, with representations of the cross and the representation of sacred names in manuscripts. Early Christian art included wall and ceiling paintings in the Roman catacombs, sarcophagi, and symbolic images depicting biblical scenes and symbols such as the fish and dove. Nonetheless, a distinctive Christian style developed around 500. An important historical moment inspired the use of the cross when Constantine wore it on his person in 315. After 420, depiction of a crucified Christ began to appear.

Before the fifth century, portraits of individuals were rare. But a generic representation of piety began to appear depicting people standing erect with their arms extended (*orantes*). From these modest beginnings, Christian artists would distinguish themselves and their religion with impressive paintings and sculptures with biblical themes. Giotto di Bondone (1266/7–1337) was commissioned, for example, to paint frescoes in the Arena Chapel in Padua narrating the lives of the Virgin Mary and Jesus. The term *fresco* means "fresh," using water-based colors painted onto a wet plaster wall. The so-called "dry fresco" is painted on top of dry plaster, whereas a true fresco is painted on a thin layer of wet plaster laid onto a dry wall, which is a more permanent technique. To avoid dripping paint on finished work, the artist starts at the top and works downward. Another great Italian painter was Duccio di Buoninsegna (d. 1315/18), who completed a work called the *Maestà* (majesty). In this masterpiece, Duccio painted *Madonna and Child* enthroned and surrounded by angels. The theme of mother and child has been a favorite subject of artists over the centuries.

A different perspective on a religious theme was provided by Sandro Botticelli (d. 1510) with his *Coronation of the Virgin* depicting Mary in the sky, with Jesus crowning his mother Queen of Heaven. Another example provides a scene from the life of Jesus that was captured by Leonardo da Vinci (d. 1519) with his rendition of *The Last Supper*, depicting Jesus with his arms outstretched touching the table, which forms a triangle. The twelve apostles are divided into two groups and into subgroups of three and appear agitated, possibly at Jesus telling them that one of them would betray him. Saints were also a subject that inspired artists, such as the sublime sculpture of St. Teresa of Avila (1515–82) by Giovanni Bernini (d. 1680). The sculpture depicts St. Theresa, a mystic, being pierced through her heart by an angel with a spear. *The Ecstasy of Saint Teresa* was inspired by her mystical writings and captures the emotional and erotic nature of her experience. The sculpture also reflects the style of Baroque art, which tends to be more ornate, emotional, and passionate.

Arguably, the greatest achievement of Christian art was the painting of the Sistine Chapel in St. Peter's Cathedral at the Vatican by Michelangelo (1475–1564), who combines in his masterpiece the themes of creation, death, resurrection, and salvation by the sacrifice of Christ. Michelangelo was also responsible for two of the most famous marble statues: *David* and *The Pietà*. The latter was unique and controversial because the subject had not been expressed in art before, and some thought that it was blasphemous because it did not have scriptural support. The Virgin Mary is portrayed as youthful and beautiful, seated and accepting the dead body of her son on her lap. Additional great artists could be mentioned, but the important point is to acknowledge the inspirational role that the Christian narrative has played in Western culture, leading to some beautiful works of art.

Apocalyptic Speculation

Derived from the Greek term *apokalypsis*, meaning "to uncover, unveil, or reveal," the apocalypse is associated with revelations concerning the end of time, which is expressed in bizarre visions, inexplicable symbolism, and supernatural events. The apocalypse represents a secret knowledge that reveals hidden events concerning the world, humans, and the supernatural realm. Christian apocalyptic speculation was deeply influenced by Jewish texts, such as parts of the book of Isaiah (24–27) and the book of Daniel. This type of revelatory speculation represents an important theme that runs from the early Jesus movement to contemporary expressions of Christianity. Certainly, John the Baptist, Jesus, the Apostle Paul, and the disciples expected the end of time at any moment. But the most fascinating expression of the Christian apocalypse appears in the book of Revelation, a book attributed to the Apostle John and composed approximately sixty years after the death of Jesus. During this time, Christians were being persecuted by Romans for not worshipping the emperor, creating an environment of violence, uncertainty, and anxiety.

After opening with Jesus declaring his victory over death, other highlights of the book of Revelation include the symbolism of the number seven, as evident in the seven messages, seals, trumpets, bowls, and visions. Apparently, the number seven was selected by the author because it had cosmic significance and represented reality. The text mentions a millennium that signifies a thousand-year rule by Christ on earth. This is predicted to be a time of peace and plenty because the Devil will be bound and unable to interfere with this period. The beginning of the millennium is marked by the resurrection of the righteous. This thousand-year reign of peace ends with Satan being released for a final battle between the forces of evil and good. Once Satan is defeated in this cosmic war, a second resurrection occurs, with all the dead being revived for the final judgment before God.

As recorded in Revelation (4:1–8), John's vision reveals a throne in heaven framed by a rainbow and twenty-four additional thrones with elders seated on them. Flashes of lightning and thunder issue from the central throne, with seven flaming torches and seven spirits of God before the throne. At the center of the throne are four living creatures with multiple eyes, appearing as a lion, an ox, a human face, and an eagle with six wings. John also sees a scroll that is sealed with seven seals. He also sees a lamb with seven horns and seven eyes. After taking the scroll and breaking its first seal, John sees a rider with a bow on a white horse. John proceeds to break the remaining seals and successively sees the following: (2) a creature on a red horse holding a sword; (3) a black horse whose rider is holding a pair of scales; (4) a creature on a sickly pale horse whose name was death; (5) souls of the martyrs; (6) a violent earthquake, the sun turned black, and a red moon; (7) the seal of God on the foreheads of the saved (Rev. 7:2). The initial four seals, once broken, represent the Four Horsemen of the Apocalypse, signifying in succession war, civil strife, famine, and death from plagues mounted on a pale green horse. The revelation continues with John seeing seven angels being given seven trumpets. When the trumpets are played, parts of the world are destroyed. Moreover, John reports seeing a woman clothed by the sun; under her feet was the moon, and on her head a crown of twelve stars. She was pregnant and trying to deliver her infant. And a dragon appeared with seven heads and ten horns, and on his head were seven diadems. He stood before the woman ready to devour her child once delivered, but the infant is taken up to God and saved (12: 1–5). Reflecting the historical period in which the text was written, John refers to the number 666, the mark of the beast who threatens to kill anyone who does not worship him. This number probably refers to the Roman emperor, because the letters of Nero Caesar add up to 666 if spelled in Hebrew. John shared his vision not to frighten people but to comfort them during a period of persecution. Apocalyptic visions and expectation of the imminent end of time have influenced Christianity throughout its history.

Intertwined with the apocalyptic speculation is the Antichrist, a human agent who represents a false messiah, a great deceiver, a false prophet, and a hypocrite. The historical roots of this figure date back to late Second Temple Judaism (from the third century BCE to 70 CE). For Christians, the Antichrist legends are located in the views about Jesus emerging during the early church period. The *parousia* of Jesus refers to his triumphant return at the end of time as the Messiah. But Jesus had already come, and yet he would still come again at the end of time, which thereby creates a middle time period that will be filled by the Antichrist. It is possible to find evidence for the possibility of an Antichrist in the little apocalypse in Mark (13:5–8) where Jesus warns listeners about someone who comes to lead people astray from the path of righteousness. This fake person will imitate Jesus but will ultimately be exposed and defeated.

In early Christian history, there developed speculation about the identity of the Antichrist, who was expected initially to be born a Jew to initiate a revival of Judaism. But throughout Christian history, the Antichrist has been identified with the Roman Emperor Nero, Muhammad and Islam, and various popes. The Protestant reformer John Wycliffe is credited with being the first to identify the papacy with the Antichrist, which implied that it was not necessary to speculate any further because the Antichrist already existed in the papacy. In contrast to Wycliffe, Martin Luther identified Muslim Turks as the Antichrist.

For recent Christian believers, the Antichrist has become anyone who represents evil from one's perspective, including the president of the United States, and plays a role in right-wing political conspiracies in America.

Death and Afterlife

The early Christian community accepted Jewish notions pertaining to death, which were often intertwined with apocalyptic speculation and beliefs about the afterlife. The certainty of death is recognized by everyone. The Judeo-Christian tradition acknowledges that it is the wage that must be paid for sin (Rom 6:7, 23). A common Christian way of conceiving of death is that it is a sleep, and the grave is a resting place (John 11:13; 1 Thess. 4:13).

In contrast to ordinary people, Jesus' death represents a unique historical event. His victory over death combined with his resurrection promise eternal life (1 Cor. 15:21–22). Thus the death and resurrection represent a sole unified salvation event, according to the Apostle Paul (2 Cor. 5:15). The early community interpreted Jesus' death as a propitiatory sacrifice that functioned to forgive sins and cancel the guilt associated with sin. Another interpretive strategy was to view the death as a vicarious sacrifice, implying that Jesus died for humanity. In his letters, Paul (2 Cor. 5:14) merged these two types of sacrifice. If the sins of humanity necessitate punishment by death, the death on the cross redeems or ransoms humanity, bestowing on them freedom from punishment, freedom from the guilt of sin, and freedom from sin and death.

Christians' beliefs about the afterlife include their conceptions of hell, heaven, and purgatory. Before being sent to one of these locations, a judgment is necessary to determine one's fate in the afterlife. According to some evidence, the final judgment is preceded by a particular judgment that is rendered immediately after death. In a parable told by Jesus, a rich man lives a life of luxury compared to the poor man with sores on his body, lying hungry at the gate of the rich man. The poor man dies and is carried away by angels to the bosom of Abraham. When the rich man dies, he finds himself in hell, where he suffers from the flames, and sees from his place in hell the poor man existing in comfort; he cries for relief, but Abraham tells him that he received his benefits during life, while the poor did not receive any good things (Luke 16:19–26). This narrative can be read as implying that some will receive compensation in their afterlife while others will suffer for ignoring the needy. In Roman Catholicism, at the end of a person's life, Christians can expect to face a final judgment that determines their fate, with hell a place of punishment, heaven a place of comfort, and purgatory functioning as an intermediate place for the sinful to atone for their transgression during life.

In early Christianity, heaven is not discussed in great detail, although we learn that it is a place of mercy and like a wedding banquet (Matt. 22:1–10). But heaven is not extensively described in the early Christian writings, which is probably because early writers expected the imminent return of Christ and the end of the world, making speculation about the precise nature of heaven rather superfluous. Because Christ's saving action is eternal, Paul emphasizes the present nature of heaven. In general, heaven was conceived as a theoretically universal place, but it could also be a place of exclusion because not everyone gets to enter heaven.

During the course of Christian history, the conception of heaven has changed in response to historical and cultural developments. Irenaeus (c. 140–200), bishop of Lyons in Gaul, conceives of heaven as a continuation and completion of a person's current life, suggesting a glorified material world similar to life on earth but devoid of need. Earlier in his career, St. Augustine, bishop of Hippo in North Africa, conceived of heaven ascetically as an immaterial place similar to an ecclesiastical community, where souls exist without flesh in a theocentric place in the company of God. During the Middle Ages, heaven was conceived by scholastic theologians to be a place of light, harmony, contemplation, love, and knowledge of God. Along with this intellectual conception of heaven, it was also imagined to be an eternal city, a new Jerusalem, consisting of streets of gold, jeweled buildings, and richly dressed residents. Later in Western history, heaven is envisioned as an empyrean, a place of light where the saved and angels live with God, which is also characterized by a lack of active life, where one contemplates God, a subjective activity that leads to a beatific vision of the divine.

In the New Testament, hell is depicted as being thrown into darkness accompanied by weeping and gnashing of teeth (Matt. 25:30). The Gospel of Mark (9:43) refers to hell as an unquenchable fire, while Revelation (21:8) describes it as a burning lake of fire and sulfur. These types of descriptions suggest a place of punishment. In addition to this place of punishment, hell is also a metaphor for being excluded from God's fellowship, which is for those remaining in a state of sin and excluded from God's grace, according to Hebrews (10:27). Satan, a fallen angel, rules hell. Satan's name comes from a verb meaning "to oppose." Later in Christian history, Dante's *Divine Comedy* and John Milton's *Paradise Lost* influenced the popular imagination and church teachings.

In the conception of the afterlife in the Latin Church, there was room for a notion such as purgatory, an intermediate place between heaven and hell and the death of a person and the final judgment. Purgatory represents a place for individuals tainted by sin at the end of their lives who are not yet worthy of being admitted to heaven. The concept of purgatory is related to the notions of free will and responsibility for one's actions. It is not until the period of 1150–1200 in European history that the notion of purgatory becomes firmly established in Latin Christianity.

The presumptive founders of purgatory were Clement of Alexandria (c. 150-c. 215) and Origen (d. 254–254), who were influenced by the use of fire as a divine instrument in Hebrew Scriptures, the New Testament idea of baptism by fire, and the notion of purification. Clement conceived of two types of sinners: incorrigible ones and those who can be corrected. The incorrigible sinner needs punishment, whereas the latter type of sinner can benefit from learning. Clement imagined an afterlife where the incorrigible was destroyed by fire, while the correctable sinner experienced a fire that sanctifies and does not consume. The controversial Origen conceived of the soul as capable of being purified in the next life. Origen also drew a distinction between mortal and venial sins. Later Christian thinkers would consider it possible for venial sins to be purified from the soul, and purgatory was the place where this could occur.

By means of his *Divine Comedy*, Dante (1265–1321) did more than anyone to shape the notion of purgatory by weaving together many fragmentary themes. Dante created a narrative about a journey that he takes accompanied by three guides: Beatrice, Virgil, and St. Bernard, a renowned mystic. Not only does the symbolism of the Trinity shape the text, but Dante's journey is similar to that of Jesus while on earth: traveling to hell, purgatory, and heaven, and then returning to earth, which will presumably occur at the end of time. Dante's personal account assumes the form of a vision that he has during the holy week, stretching from Maundy Thursday to Easter Sunday.

Dante's conception of purgatory is represented as a mountain rising to heaven comprised of seven circles arranged on top of each other, with circumferences that diminish as a sinner moves upwards toward the summit. Besides this symbolic emphasis on ascent and wholeness with the number seven, Dante's purgatory is a place for the purification of the soul of seven deadly sins, represented by each of the seven circles: pride, envy, wrath, sloth, avarice, gluttony, and lust. As they progress on their journeys of purification, the sinners are purged of their sins by three means: punishment, meditation on each sin to be purged and its correlative virtue, and prayer. Within each of the seven circles of purgatory, love, which functions as the guiding principle, is combined with hope for the sinful soul. A sinner enters purgatory by passing through a narrow gate— standing in sharp contrast to the wide gate of hell—where one encounters three differently colored steps that symbolize the three acts of a sacrament: contrition (white), confession (causing the penitent to become purple with shame), and satisfaction (imagined to resemble the flaming red of love). Dante envisages a length of time for the soul to complete its journey of purification that extends from the death of the sinful soul to the Last Judgment.

During the Middle Ages, it became common for people to believe that they could assist a soul in purgatory by the practice of indulgences, a practice that enriched the church by its acceptance of money and contributed to abuse by officials and corruption of church leaders. Protestant reformers opposed the use of indulgences. The criticism of the practice of indulgences appeared as the fourth of the ninety-five theses that Luther nailed to the church door at Wittenberg because they evaded the theology of the cross, and the true treasure of the church was the Gospel message. Luther calls attention with theses 71 to 86 to the evil practices of the sale of indulgences. At this point in his career, Luther still considered himself a Roman Catholic and did not intend to abolish indulgences, because he thought that he represented the pope's view on them. He was simply concerned about how preachers selling indulgences abused the practice.

Christianity in America

Early Christian groups coming to America often did so to escape religious persecution in their European homelands, and the Puritans are a prime example of such a group. Later, Catholics came from Ireland and Italy to join the Protestant denominations already in the country. These Protestants consisted of Congregationalists, Baptists, and Quakers. For these various groups, America represented a new beginning, along with God's promise of a new land, assured in the books of Isaiah and Revelation, in order to start anew. Moreover, colonists interpreted what was happening as the will of God. Other Protestant groups included the Quakers, a group that was instrumental in the founding of the state of Pennsylvania in 1681. They were led by the efforts of William Penn, who wanted to conduct a holy experiment by building a society based on Quaker ideals. The Quakers, also known as the Society of Friends, were brought together by George Fox. The Quakers were plain people with respect to their style of dress, speech, and behavior. Quaker leaders preached that Christ had already returned to earth. The group would gather in silence for worship, and the service would remain quiet until someone was motivated by the Holy Spirit to speak. Anglicans, Congregationalists, Presbyterians, Baptists, Dutch Reform, Mennonites, Dunkers (Church of the Brethren), and Moravians also made their spiritual contributions to the cultural fabric of America.

American Protestants experienced a couple of Great Awakenings that appealed to people's emotions. The preaching of Jonathan Edwards (1703–58), a Yale University graduate at 17 years of age and future president of Princeton University, is credited with igniting the Great Awakening, a revival in New England from 1740–43, by sparking fear and trembling in his listeners with allusions to the fires of hell and having to suffer punishment for one's sins. This new type of preaching was intended by Edwards to counteract Arminian, optimistic convictions about the human ability to act to help achieve salvation, because they subverted divine grace. Edwards thought that members should recognize themselves as sinners and estranged from God. The Second Great Awakening occurred in the 1790s, and Charles G. Finney represented a Northern phase of this awakening by asking church members to give up sin and accept Christ, an appeal to a believer's heart. A typical service involved having sinners move forward, publically accept Christ, and become the center of attention for a short time. The Second Great Awakening also featured camp meetings in tents in the frontier areas. These meetings were characterized by people falling to the floor and begging for mercy for their sins. These types of camp meetings would be used extensively by the Methodists.

In the early eighteenth century, England was a spiritual wasteland, with the lower classes spiritually destitute. John Wesley (1703–91) filled this spiritual void with his teaching about perfection, a belief that a person could be perfected in love during this life, and his concern for social issues, such as poverty, education, slavery, and alcoholism. Wesley shared his conversion experience at Aldersgate Street in a personal way by telling his readers that he heard someone reading Luther's preface to the reformer's *Epistle to the Romans* and talking about the change that God works in the heart through faith in Christ. Wesley confessed that he felt his heart become strangely warmed and was given assurance that his sins had been removed and that he was saved from sin and death. This autobiographical statement stands in sharp contrast to John Calvin's doctrine of double predestination, which gave Puritans nightmares. Wesley's notion of assurance rejected the doctrine of predestination because we can have assurance of present salvation while waiting in hope for our final salvation. Assurance of faith is a gift available to all believers. Wesley conceptualized sanctification as a gradual process, but a person cannot achieve total perfection because of sin.

Wesley's notion of the possibility of sanctification influenced the development of holiness churches in America: Church of the Nazarene, Church of God, Pentecostal, and Methodist. These holiness churches invited people to let their emotions flow and to be open to the Holy Spirit. Parishioners would respond by rolling in the aisles of the church and speaking out ecstatically in tongues, or glossolalia. Taking seriously Jesus' urging of followers to be perfect, even as God is perfect, these holiness churches rejected sinful behavior such as drinking alcohol, smoking tobacco, and taking illicit drugs. They also prohibited swearing, blasphemy, gambling, motion pictures, dancing, and swimming in mixed-gender groups. In addition to holiness churches, there were indigenous examples of Christianity that originated in America, such as Pentecostals, Seventh-day Adventists, Jehovah's Witnesses, Mormons, and Christian Science. The last three movements will be discussed in the final chapter, but the initial two will be considered next.

Evolving from nineteenth century holiness revivals, Pentecostal movements believe in the baptism of the Holy Spirit and post-baptismal gifts, such as speaking in tongues and healing by the laying on of hands, phenomena that have a base in the early Jesus movement as recorded in Acts 2:3, described as tongues like flames of fire. Speaking in tongues (glossolalia) represents a visit of the Holy Spirit to a believer, prefigures the return of Christ, and anticipates the end of time. Pentecostal denominations, whose members are also called Holy Rollers for their emotional outbursts and falling to the floor, tend to be represented by lower-income groups, rural inhabitants, and racial minorities and are characterized by small independent congregations. Many of these churches are populated by black followers, such as the Church of God in Christ, while whites join denominations such as the Assemblies of God. Some of these churches located in the Appalachia region of North America engage in handling poisonous snakes, expecting their faith to protect them in a test and public exhibition of their faith. This type of religion represents the dispossessed and alienated within society.

Two key early figures in the movement were Charles Fox Parham, who founded a Bible school called the College of Bethel in Topeka, Kansas, and William Joseph Seymour, a former slave and student of Parham. Seymour is well-known for establishing the Azuza Street Mission in Los Angeles in the spring of 1906. Seymour wanted to restore practices associated with primitive Christianity. In addition to speaking in tongues, the church included experiences connected to healing, prophecy, expectation of the end of time, and miracles. A famous healer of the church was Aimee Semple McPherson, founder of the Church of the Four Square Gospel. Several of the early Pentecostal churches still exist around the country, with the largest being the Assemblies of God.

The Seventh-day Adventists are a good example of apocalyptic Christianity that looks forward to the return of Christ to earth, when the righteous will be resurrected, judged, and taken to heaven. William Miller, a farmer, predicted an advent would occur around 1843. The key scriptural passage for Miller was Daniel 8:14, which refers to an evil ruler who will suppress the Holy Place for 2,800 days. What Miller started became an organized movement in 1840, led by Joshua V. Himes. When the year came without anything happening, followers were disappointed, and Miller confessed that he had made a mistake in his calculations but remained assured about the coming end of time. Followers accepted that the advent would arrive at an unknown time. Among the Ten Commandments, the Sabbath held a special place for the Adventists, who celebrated it on Saturday. The group promotes good health practices by urging people to get exercise and eat a nutritional diet and avoid alcohol, tobacco, and illicit drugs.

Overall, the American religious landscape is shaped by two religious aspects guaranteed by the United States Constitution: freedom to practice religion for everyone and the separation of church and state. Another central feature of American religion is denominationalism, which is the primary characteristic of Protestantism in America. Although denominationalism was originally associated with religious tolerance and freedom, it now manifests separate and competing bodies of Protestantism. From Jonathan Edwards' sparking of the Great Awakening, there runs an attitude that America is a special place because it is where God's redemptive work begins, which implies that God has a special destiny for America that has been foretold in ancient scripture. In short, America is God's country.

For a movement that began with the heroic efforts of Martin Luther in Germany by breaking with the Latin Church, Protestantism has never ceased splitting apart over issues about the nature of church governance and worship. Although co-existing with other denominations, Protestants share a common faith but are divided by other issues and often embody different political ideologies, socio-economic status, and types of religious experience sought by members.

Some Protestant groups have coalesced around fundamentalist (a belief that the Bible is literally the true Word of God) preachers, who have created mega-churches that have become wealthy and politically influential. Some of these ministers have also created television empires by which to reach the faithful and solicit money. These fundamentalist pastors have used their celebrity status to push their conservative brand of politics, which culminated with Pat Robertson unsuccessfully trying to win the 1988 Republican presidential nomination. After his political defeat, he returned to his Family Network station and his hosting of "700 Club." Along with getting rich, some television pastors—such as Jim Bakker and Jimmy Swaggart—were victims of their own hubris and fell from grace after being convicted of various ethical and moral transgressions that they preached against on a regular basis.

With its numerous Protestant denominations, Roman Catholics, Jews, Muslims, and Eastern forms of religion, America is now truly a pluralistic religious culture, although some conservative people maintain that America is still a Christian nation founded on Christian principles. According to some scholars, there is even a civil religion within which a vast majority of Americans participate. The sacred scripture of this civil religion is the Constitution; its gods are the Founding Fathers, while its martyrs are Abraham Lincoln, John F. Kennedy, Robert Kennedy, and Martin Luther King. The Washington, D.C., Mall provides the temples for some of these figures. The Washington Monument represents an Egyptian pyramid, a huge statue of Lincoln sits in a Greek temple, a huge statue of King suggests something beyond a mere human being, and John Kennedy's remains rest under an eternal flame in Arlington National Cemetery. For those who are skeptical about the existence of a civil religion, as I have been, the viability of the civil religion was manifested to me one Sunday morning many years ago. After attending a conference in the capital at one of its universities, I decided to go sight-seeing at the mall before going home. While standing in Lincoln's temple before his large image, I overheard a woman tell her husband how she feels awestruck when seeing Lincoln's statue. Hearing this conversation and the sincerity expressed by this emotionally moved American housewife, I became a convert to the acceptance of the possibility of a civil religion that provides the glue that binds the country together because we share its values.

Christian Religious Experience

As the preceding pages make clear, Christian religious experience is very diverse. It is more than a faith type of experience. On the one hand, because of the overwhelming, profound nature of their experiences, Christian mystics were reduced to silence, and telling others that what they experienced was too overpowering for mere words to capture it. The rapturous experience of St. Teresa of Avila was, however, expressed rather dramatically in her autobiographical account. She describes being transfixed by Christ himself and tells her reader that the experience was like a sharp instrument being driven into her heart, a representation of the pain of love. She described how God sent a cherubim, an angelic figure with its face aflame, holding a golden dart in its hand, who plunges the dart several times into her chest and draws it out. Teresa moans from the spiritual pain and describes how she was on fire with the love of God. What a reader can recognize about her profound experience is that she experiences feelings of *eros* (physical erotic love) and spiritual love (*agape* or a self-surrendering love). St. Teresa's rapturous experience involves a temporary paralysis of her body. But in her imaginative marriage with Jesus, she experiences a fusion of *eros* (sexual passion) and *agape* (self-negating love).

On the other hand, other Christians are inspired by the Holy Spirit to speak in strange languages, fall to the ground, cry overtly, and shout out for joy as a way to praise and glorify God. These types of experience were proof to those having the experiences and others witnessing them that God was present among them. Those having the joyful experiences were imitating members of primitive Christianity. Afro-American experience was, for instance, associated with rhythmic interaction between the preacher and church members and bodily movement. In these African denominations, preachers use a call-and-response method to reach believers. Words, melodies, and hand-clapping to introduce percussion are improvised during services.

Reaching back to the Puritan period of American history, believers internalized the Calvinist message that humans were sinful and depraved and are thus incapable of saving themselves. This situation resulted in emotions related to fear of damnation and despair that one could be destined for hell. From the Puritan perspective, it was necessary for believers to give themselves completely to the will of God and leave their fate in the hands of an angry but merciful deity. Puritan Christian religious enthusiasm manifested itself with acts of swooning, falling, becoming speechless and motionless, and uttering shrieks and screams.

Overall, Christian religious experiences evoke all types of emotions and states of mind, from unity with God to alienation from God, from boredom to high levels of enthusiasm, from tears to laughter, from being humiliated to exaltation, from irrationality to rationality, from not having a clue to complete awareness, from sorrow to happiness, from kneeling silently in prayer to shouting out aloud, from inertness to shaking or rolling on the floor, or from sadness to joy.

Suggestions for Further Reading

Brown, Peter. *The Body and Society: Men, Women, and Sexual Renunciation in Early Christianity*. New York: Columbia University, 1988.

———. *The Cult of the Saints: Its Rise and Function in Latin Christianity*. Chicago: University of Chicago Press, 1981.

Bynum, Caroline Walker. *Christian Materiality: An Essay on Religion in Late Medieval Europe*. New York: Zone Books, 2011.

Castelli, Elizabeth A. *Martyrdom and Memory: Early Christian Culture Making*. New York: Columbia University Press, 2004.

Freeman, Charles. *A History of Early Christianity*. New Haven: Yale University Press, 2009.

————. *Holy Bones, Holy Dust: How Relics Shaped the History of Medieval Europe.* New Haven: Yale University Press, 2011.

Frend, W.H.C. *The Rise of Christianity.* Philadelphia: Fortress Press, 1984.

Kee, Howard Clark. *Miracle in the Early Christian World: A Study in Sociohistorical Method.* New Haven: Yale University Press, 1983.

Lang, Bernhard. *Sacred Games: A History of Christian Worship.* New Haven: Yale University Press, 1997.

Le Goff, Jacques. *The Birth of Purgatory.* Trans. Arthur Goldhammer. Chicago: University of Chicago Press, 1984.

Marty, Martin E. *Pilgrims in Their Own Land: 500 Years of Religion in America.* Boston: Little Brown and Company, 1984.

McDannell, Colleen and Bernhard Lang. *Heaven: A History.* New Haven: Yale University Press, 1988.

McGinn, Bernard. *Antichrist: Two Thousand Years of the Human Fascination with Evil.* New York: Harper Collins Publishers, 1994.

Meeks, Wayne A. *The Moral World of the First Christians.* Philadelphia: Westminster Press, 1986.

Oberman, Heiko A. *Luther: Man between God and the Devil.* New Haven: Yale University Press, 1989.

Pagels, Elaine. *The Gnostic Gospels.* New York: Vintage Books, 1989.

————. *Revelations: Visions, Prophecy, and Politics in the Book of Revelation.* New York: Viking, 2012.

Pelikan, Jaroslav. *Jesus through the Centuries: His Place in the History of Culture.* New Haven: Yale University Press, 1985.

————. *Mary through the Centuries: Her Place in the History of Culture.* New Haven: Yale University Press, 1996

Sanders, E. P. *The Historical Figure of Jesus.* London: Penguin Press, 1993.

Stark, Rodney. *The Rise of Christianity: A Sociologist Reconsiders History.* Princeton: Princeton University Press, 1996.

Theissen, Gerd. *The New Testament: A Literary History,* trans. Minneapolis: Fortress Press, 2012.

Wilken, Robert Louis. *The Spirit of Early Christian Thought: Seeking the Face of God.* New Haven: Yale University Press, 2003.

14 Islam

From a cross-cultural perspective, religious leaders have suffered from prejudice, fictional accounts, and stereotypical portraits by opponents that are often
vicious personal attacks on a particular figure that have little basis in history.
An excellent example of such a figure is Muhammad, prophet of Islam. Some
of these attacks can be attributed to incidents of warfare, political machinations, interreligious rivalry, revenge, and hatred of others unlike us. For many
hundreds of years, Muslims and their prophet had been poorly understood in
the West because of ignorance, misunderstanding, and prejudice, while similar types of problems prevail on the side of Muslims' views of the West. If
we attempt a brief historical overview of Western portrayals of Islam and its

prophet, we can illustrate these assertions from the Western perspective. John of Damascus (d. c. 748), for example, treated Islam as a Christian heresy and spoke about the false prophet who arose among the Arabs. Theophanes Confessor (d. 817), a Byzantine historian, wrote a biography of Muhammad in which he called the prophet the "false prophet of the Saracens," who contracted epilepsy. A more scurrilous attack upon Muhammad was made by Eulogius of Cordova (d. 859), reporting that Muhammad's soul descended into hell upon his death. While his followers waited for his body to be resuscitated by angels on the third day after his death, dogs came and began to devour the prophet's body, which exuded the odor of corruption. This story was altered by Guibert of Nogent (d. 1124), who had Muhammad's body devoured by pigs while unconscious in one of his epileptic attacks. In the thirteenth century, Bartholomew of Eddessa summarized the medieval view of Muhammad by asserting that the prophet was defiled to the core of his being, a brigand, a profligate, a murderer, and a robber. During the same historical period, the name of the prophet was corrupted to Mahound, which was regarded as a name of the devil. Western medieval literature also cherished the concept of Muhammad as a god and portraying Muslims as praying to him. In the minds of many contemporary Westerners, Muslims are equated with terrorism.

Needless to say, Muslims have viewed their religion very differently; for them, Islam is the primordial religion in two senses: (1) It is a reassertion of the original religion of humankind, which is equated with monotheism; (2) it comes at the end of the human cycle to reassert the essential, hidden truth. In a sense, Islam, from the Muslim perspective, represents a rediscovery of what was present from the beginning of time. In fact, Islam is based on the conception of the universality of revelation. Thus the existence of other religions is presupposed by it.

Pre-Islamic Background

Before attempting to understand Islam, it seems prudent to briefly review the cultural situation before its advent. A folk narrative illustrates the difference before and after Islam by calling attention to al-A'sha, a famous Arab poet, who set out to convert to Islam. Along the way, he met a pagan friend who told him that the prophet prohibits fornication, but he declared that such a restriction did not matter to him. The friend also told him that the prophet prohibits wine. The poet replied that this is a rule that he could not easily relinquish. The poet decided to return home and drink heavily for an entire year and then to accept Islam. He died, however, before the end of the year. This story hints at the cultural spirit of pre-Islamic Arabia, because the poet's addiction to wine reflects the love of drinking and hedonistic attitude among the inhabitants of Arabia. This hedonistic spirit was embedded within a this-worldly attitude in the sense that their world was the only one that existed and any hope of eternal life was remote. The hope for a long life was tempered by a pessimistic view of life. Pre-Islamic poets cried in despair of the emptiness of human life, its vanity, its ephemeral nature, and a lack of anything beyond it. The only alternative was to enjoy life to the utmost in the present.

Pre-Islamic Arabia was inhabited by nomadic Bedouins and settled town dwellers who both were motivated by self-interest and self-preservation. Between these two groups, there occurred a peaceful exchange of goods and raids by Bedouins to acquire resources that they lacked. The nomadic Bedouin often played two roles: land pirate and broker. In spite of the fact that raids were a cultural institution, there was an emphasis on not shedding blood except in cases of absolute necessity; it could lead to retaliation by the offended side because any shedding of blood called for vengeance and more blood. Non-avenged shedding of blood is akin to dew on the grass, expressing the idea that a person died in vain. The primary responsibility for revenge falls on the nearest of kin. When normally employed, a male might be involved in sheep and camel raising, horse breeding, and hunting, which were the only occupations worthy of a man, whereas agriculture, trades, and crafts were beneath one's dignity. Living in a desert environment made survival difficult, but it also isolated Arabs from intruders and made it easier to preserve their cultural tradition and purity of their speech and blood.

In the Arabian dessert, the clan formed the basis of society, with each tent representing a family unit. An encampment of tents formed a *hayy*, with the members of one *hayy* constituting a clan. The tribe consisted of a number of kindred clans together, and members of the same clan were considered to be of one blood line. The titular head of the clan was a sheikh, who was chosen based on his seniority and personal qualities, such as wisdom, generosity, and courage. Within this social context, the worst calamity for an individual would be to lose his tribal affiliation, because such a person is beyond the pale of tribal protection and safety. Being without a tribe also implies that one has attained the status of an outlaw.

The Arabian tribes practiced little religion, and what religion they did practice was animistic, such as believing in the beneficent spirits of arable land, water wells, and caves, which were associated with underground deities and forces. They also revered the moon and the principal deity of the city of Mecca called Allah (God), who was associated with three daughters, including al-Lāt (meaning "goddess"), al'Uzza, the morning star, and Manāh, goddess of destiny, worshipped as a black stone. The overall religious impression was a weak or not fully developed polytheism. The deities associated with this polytheism were honored at local shrines called *harams*, which were often centered on a sacred tree, rock, or spring that the deity inhabited. Within the defined boundaries of a *haram*, there was a prohibition against members of a cult engaging in violence.

The religion established by Muhammad challenged and undermined many of the beliefs of Arabian tribalism. To the worldliness of the pre-Islamic Arabs, Muhammad offered the hope of meaningful existence and eternal life in the afterworld. The tribal sense of honor based on blood relations was undermined by Muhammad's declaration of the superiority of religious relationships instead of biological bonds. In contrast to blood relations, the brotherhood of Islam was based on faith. Instead of a sense of honor based on heroism and valor, which caused a prideful person to refuse to bow before any human or divine authority, Islam introduced humility and fear of God. In place of the tribal need for revenge for an act of shedding blood of a member, Muhammad changed the direction of vengeance from a horizontal—person to person—to a vertical direction, from God to human beings. These types of changes simply magnify Muhammad's religious and culturally altering achievements.

The Prophet of Islam

At the time of his birth, Muhammad ibn Abdallah, future prophet of a new religion, was born into a noble family of the city of Mecca associated with the Quraysh tribe of the Hashim clan around 570 CE, which was identified as the year of the elephant because an Abyssinian prince marched to Mecca with a large army that included an elephant. Muhammad's father died before the boy was born, making 'Abd-al Muttalib, head of the Hashim clan, his guardian. Muhammad lived with his mother, who sent him for a year or more to live in the desert. His mother entrusted his care to Halima, a nurse, for a period of time. When Muhammad was 6 years old, his mother died, and two years later his grandfather died, making the new leader of the Hashim clan and his protector his uncle, Abu-Talib.

Prior to 590 CE, there occurred two significant events: the Meccan military victory in the Wicked War and the establishment of the League of the Virtuous. The first event extended the commercial enterprises of the Meccans, while the second event created an alliance of the various competing clans, which reflected the political and social fragmentation of the period. The creation of the league was witnessed by Muhammad. These events had little consequence for the major political structures of the time period: the Byzantines with their capital in Constantinople and the Persian Empire under the Sasanian dynasty. Within the Arabian Peninsula, these two powers supported competing groups, with the purpose of preventing nomads from raiding settled lands. The Persians supported the Lakmids, while the Byzantines supported the Ghassanids.

The city of Mecca in Arabia functioned as a commercial and financial center for the region, which was an adaptation to its barren, rocky land, which made agriculture very difficult. Prior to its growth as a commercial center, Mecca was an ancient religious sanctuary (*haram*) to the pagan god Hubal, focusing on the Ka'ba, a large black rock contained in a cubical structure. The Quraysh tribe served as custodians of the shrine. Mecca was governed by chiefs and leaders of the various clans. Since the clans were theoretically independent, the most effective decisions were those that were unanimous. This situation served as the socio-political context for a continuous struggle among the competing commercial interests. This situation enhanced the development of individualism, undermined the nomadic moral code, led to a deterioration of religious life, and contributed to the weakening of tribal solidarity, in which weaker community members were oppressed.

When Muhammad was 25 years old, he married Khadijah, an older wealthy merchant's widow, and they had six children, with the two sons dying as infants. This marriage enabled Muhammad to engage in commerce, where he could develop his business acumen and negotiating skills. Muhammad took time from his business tasks to spend long periods of time in solitude on the mountain of Hira in Mecca, where he began to have strange experiences, often in the forms of vivid dreams and visions. In other instances, he found words in his heart without imagining that he had heard anything. Some verses of the Qur'an refer to God speaking to him behind a veil. An early vision took the form of a glorious being standing erect in the sky, whereas a second vision was of the same figure beside a tree. Muhammad originally identified this being as God, but later thought that it was a spirit of some kind. Finally, he identified it with the angel Gabriel. Muhammad experienced physical consequences from his encounters, such as a ringing in his ears, trembling, or sweating on his forehead.

The initial revelation to Muhammad occurred in 610 CE, when he heard a heavenly messenger ordering him to speak, but Muhammad refused, whereas a second command prompted him to ask what he should recite. At the third command, Muhammad was ordered to recite the verses of the ninety-sixth *sūra* (chapter) of the Qur'an. The command to recite verses implied that public worship was to be instituted. When the visitations ceased Muhammad felt abandoned, and a painful period of emptiness followed. Nonetheless, his wife sustained him with her faith and encouragement. Beyond his wife, Muhammad informed an intimate circle of friends of his experiences. In 613, Muhammad began to preach publicly to small groups of people in Mecca by presenting himself as a messenger of God. His early preaching encountered opposition from some quarters, although he was able to win some adherents to his message, beginning with his wife. The initial male convert was open to dispute, with three leading candidates: Ali, Muhammad's cousin; Zayd ibn-Hairthah, a slave freed and adopted by the prophet; or Abu-Bakr, a long-time friend who became Muhammad's chief lieutenant and advisor.

Muhammad's early message embodied a sense of urgency, because he spoke about the coming last judgment that was to occur on the last day. He referred to his vocation as the prophet of God. He also spoke of God's goodness and power, his creatorship, and his role as a judge at the final hour. Muhammad's original message was not intended as a criticism of the prevailing paganism of his time and locale because he was speaking to people with at least a vague belief in God, although his message was critically directed to the materialism of Meccan merchants. Muhammad urged listeners to respond to God's message with gratitude, generosity, and worship.

Many Meccans opposed Muhammad and his message on both politico-economic and intellectual grounds. Because of Muhammad's claim about receiving revelations from God, a higher authority, Meccan merchants reasoned that these messages would undermine their power. As a result of Muhammad's received revelations, the pre-existing shrines and deities associated with them were no longer recognized, which resulted in a loss of trade for merchants. Opposition to Muhammad intensified when Muhammad was asked about whether or not his deceased grandfather was in hell, and he responded positively. This was interpreted as an insult to the entire clan, and Abu-Lahab, its new leader, withdrew the clan's protection of Muhammad, which meant that the prophet had to find a safe place to live, leading to his emigration to Medina, an oasis town that lent itself to agriculture. This event was called the *Hijrah*.

Muhammad was invited to Medina to settle some disputes among rival clans. In return, the Medinans promised to accept him as prophet, obey him, and avoid committing transgressions, which was called the First Pledge of al-'Aqabah (621). The next pledge, or Pledge of War, in 622 involved the Medinan Muslims when they added the injunction to fight on behalf of God and His messenger. Before the actual Hijrah of 622, Muhammad sent followers to Medina before him. Muhammad and Abu-Bakr left Mecca and initially hid in a cave to protect themselves against enemies. On September 24, 622, the two men reached the settlement of Qubā, an event that marks the beginning of the Islamic era. The Islamic tradition refers to the Meccans as the Emigrants, whereas the Medinans became known as the Helpers.

While living in Medina, Muhammad married A'ishah, a young daughter of Abu-Bakr, while Muhammad's daughter, Fatimah, was married to Muhammad's cousin Ali. In addition to these domestic developments, Muhammad challenged Meccan caravans by raiding them. These raids took place within a religious context, pitting the believers against the unbelievers, a practice that was gradually transformed into a holy war (*jihād*, literally meaning "striving in the way of God"). These raids would develop into battles and finally culminated with Muhammad's victory over the Meccans and nomadic tribes in 630, making the city of Mecca the center of the Islamic world and ultimate destination of Muslim pilgrimage. On June 8, 632, Muhammad died of a fever, and Abu-Bakr assumed leadership of the developing community of believers.

During his prophetic career, Muhammad had hoped to reconcile his message with Judaism by originally adopting Friday worship, facing toward Jerusalem while praying, fasting on the Jewish Day of Atonement, and institution of midday worship. Jews did not accept his claim of prophethood, and thus Muhammad won few Jewish converts. Breaking with the Jews, Muhammad received a revelation commanding him to face Mecca while praying instead of Jerusalem on February 11, 624. Later that year, he changed the fast day to the month of Ramadan. He also intellectually attacked the Jews by adopting the religion of Abraham over the Jewish religion of Moses. Abraham was neither a Jew nor a Christian, representing the true religion of God, which was called *hanīf* (a monotheist who is neither a Jew nor a Christian). At a later date, Muhammad used the term "muslim" (one who submits to God) to replace *hanīf* and believed that Abraham founded the sacred Ka'ba. By the time of his death, Muhammad found himself the undisputed head of an economic, social, and political system with a basis in religion. Membership in this society was grounded in a profession of faith, while its peace and security were guaranteed by God and His messenger.

The Qur'an and Prophethood

When Muhammad received his first revelation (96.1–5) he was commanded to speak, but he initially refused, and finally recited after a third command the ninety-sixth *sūra* (chapter) of the Qur'an, which was destined to become the holy book of Islam. The term Qur'an and the verb "to recite" share a common Arabic root, implying a verbal revelation that is closely associated with inspiration. According to the holy text, the purpose of the revelation (6.19) is to be a warning to hearers, and what is revealed is the order or command of God. The preferred way for a person to receive the message is to memorize it, which keeps the revelation ever present in a person's mind. The sacredness and authoritative nature of the revelation preserved within the book sets it apart from other books. Because of its very nature, the Qur'an, a sacred book, represents for the faithful something with order, unity, and perfection and has the ability to inspire a reader or hearer of its message. From a historical perspective, the Qur'an has had the ability to affect people by motivating them to behave in a certain way, reflecting its dynamic nature to transform people and events and a compulsive aspect to coerce or prohibit actions and thoughts. The Qur'an has these types of powers because it is grounded in the ultimate authoritative source, which is identified with the word of God. Muslims also believe that the text was revealed in Arabic in order to facilitate understanding of God's message by hearers.

Since the origin of the Qur'an is the eternal word of God in book form, the prophet Muhammad is certainly not its author but was simply the recipient of it. The Qur'an was not revealed at a single moment but was revealed periodically over a period of about twenty years. The words were given to Muhammad by the angel Gabriel, suggesting that the prophet did not compose the words himself, although he did orally share the revelation with others, who wrote the words on available materials such as stones, bones, parchment, leather, palm leafs, and the hearts of humans. The collection of the verses of the Qur'an owes its origin to the deaths of many reciters after the battle of Yamanah, occurring many years after the death of the prophet. The Muslim tradition credits Umar ibn al-Khattab, a later second caliph, with preserving the oral traditions of the verses from Abu-Bakr, the first caliph, who commissioned Zaid ibn Thabit to collect the different versions and to transform them into a more permanent written form. The four early collections of the verses currently in separate locations have not survived to the present. The different versions of the text motivated the third caliph, Uthman, to end disputes by commissioning a revised text, a process that gave preference to the version of the Quraysh tribe of the prophet when some verses disputed each other.

The Qur'an is divided into 114 *sūras* (chapters, originally a Syrian term that means "writing" or "text of scripture"). Muslims have also separated the text into thirty ritual divisions that consist of approximately equal portions. In general, the title of a chapter of the text has no reference to the subject matter of the chapter but is adopted from some prominent or universal term in the chapter, such as "The Bees" (16) or "The Cave" (18). The individual chapters are dated either from the Meccan or Medinan periods depending on the location of the prophet at the time of the revelation. All chapters of the Qur'an begin with the following *bismillah* phrase: "In the name of God, the Merciful, the Compassionate." The lone exception to this feature is the eleventh chapter. In twenty-nine chapters, the *bismillah* is followed by mysterious letters or a letter of the alphabet. Individual chapters are divided into verses (*āyāt*, "sign"), and are written in rhymed prose in verses without meter or definitely fixed length, and they end with a rhyme or assonance. Within the body of the chapters, Allah speaks in the first-person singular (51.56), sometimes God is referred to in the third person, and some passages are clearly spoken by angels (19.65). Overall, Muhammad speaks in only a few passages (27.93). The traditional orthodox position is that the sacred text represents the literal word of Allah because it is believed that God is speaking through the angels and the prophet. The Qur'an is based on a heavenly version that is preserved in the presence of God, which stresses the eternal nature of the book.

During the life time of Muhammad, there was a generally accepted belief that demonic spirits exercised influence over people and events. This belief implies that they could delude a person and compromise that person's message. In order to protect the contents of the Qur'an, there evolved the doctrine of abrogation, which stipulates that a later verse of the Qur'an might nullify an earlier revelation. Therefore, any false message could be corrected by a later revelation. But after the death of Muhammad, the revelations ceased and the book was closed, although the sacred text did invite commentary by pious scholars on problematic passages.

An early non-revelatory body of literature distinct from the Qur'an is the *hadīth* (a term that embodies something new, coming to pass, or an occurrence such as a report). During the evolving of the Islamic tradition, the term came to mean "tradition," assuming the form of a brief report about something said, done, approved, or disapproved by the prophet, a source that gave it authority. A typical *hadīth* consisted of two aspects: textual, and a chain of transmission that alerted a person to the identity of the originator of the report and the line of those that passed it to others. Although of a secondary nature to the primacy of the Qur'an, these reports were considered authoritative sources of Islam by the middle of the ninth century, by which time six collections were considered authoritative. The authenticity of a particular report depended on its line of transmission by considering whether the line was broken, the alleged character of the transmitter, and reliability of the transmitters' memories. The *hadīth* is accepted as coeval and consubstantial with the *sunnah* (literally "traveled path") of the prophet, which embodies his exemplary conduct. This literature reflects everyday problems that arose for which there was uncertainty about the proper course of action. In such a case, people could consult with the prophet about a resolution of a problem, and he would make a ruling that was considered genuine. If the *hadīth* represents a report and something theoretical, it can be differentiated from the *sunnah*, a report that has acquired a normative quality and becomes a practical principle as the non-verbal transmission of tradition. This means that the *sunnah* represents the exemplary conduct of the prophet, which can serve as a standard for the behavior of ordinary people in the sense of agreed-upon practice and social consensus.

Prophethood of Muhammad

According to the Qur'an, God has sent prophets to all peoples to proclaim His unity, to urge people to act righteously, and to warn about the Last Judgment. The Qur'an refers to numerous prophets that it accepts from the Jewish tradition, such as Noah, Moses, David, Solomon, and Jonah. Abraham holds a special place in the text because he was a destroyer of idols, builder of the Ka'ba, and ancestor of the Arabs. The Qur'an also accepts Jesus as a prophetic figure, calls him Christos, accepts his virgin birth, refers to him as a spirit of Allah, and acknowledges that he performed miracles. The text does not, however, accept Jesus as the son of God, because this claim is incompatible with God's unity. This also means that the text rejects the doctrine of the Trinity and considers Mary the third person of the Trinity instead of the Holy Spirit (5.76–79; 116). The Qur'an also denies the crucifixion event (4.155) because God took Jesus immediately to heaven and someone resembling him died on the cross (4.156). The text does assert that Jesus will return shortly before the final day (43.16). In Islam, there is no need for a redeeming death, because Islam does not accept the doctrine of original sin.

In the long line of Jewish and Christian prophets, Muhammad represents the last or seal of the prophets. The Qur'an perceives a unity in the preaching of all prophets and a gradual evolution in their messages toward a final and perfect revelation, culminating with Muhammad. In the Qur'an (33.40), Muhammad is called simultaneously an apostle of God and a seal of the prophets, terms that are sometimes used interchangeably (7.157). Besides truthfulness, fidelity, ability to propagate God's message, and intelligence, the Qur'an insists that a prophet is endowed with immunity from error and sin. Since Judaism and Christianity had prophets whose messages were preserved in writing, they are people of the book, much like Muslims. The Qur'an traces the Jewish and Christian prophetic heritage to Abraham's son Isaac, while Islam derives from Abraham's son Ishmael, making Islam part of the Abrahamic tradition.

If the Exodus event and the cross/resurrection event are the primary events for Judaism and Christianity, Muhammad's prophecy (*rasuliyyah*) is the paradigmatic event for Muslims. Since Muhammad was chosen by God to be His communicative instrument, it was his duty to proclaim and to vindicate the message of God, which is preserved in the Qur'an. Thus, for Muslims, the only true miracle of their religion is the Qur'an. This was not a miracle performed by Muhammad, because the orthodox interpretation of his status insists that he was only a man; he was not divine, not a mediator, and had no superhuman status. He was simply God's prophet of flesh and blood.

Similar to other prophets in Jewish and Christian scriptures, Muhammad was a bearer of *charisma* (a Greek term meaning favor, gift), understood as a personal talent of leadership. As an instrument of God, the prophet is called to do something. When the prophet proclaims a religious message, he is conscious of being the organ, instrument, or mouthpiece of the divine will and accepts the tremendous burden given to him. Since a prophet's authority comes from God, it is a secondary or derived authority. Prophetic revelations tend to arise spontaneously and are received passively; they are not induced. The work of the prophet does not provide any monetary rewards because he propagates God's message for its own sake and not for economic rewards.

The Qur'an and Its Worldview

The worldview reflected by the Qur'an represents a system based on conceptual opposition concerning an ontological, communicative, Lord-servant distinction, an ethical feature, two divisions of community, and a twofold view of the world. The ontological relation between God and humans suggests that Allah stands at the center of the world of being. Other beings are His creatures, implying that they are infinitely inferior to God because humans owe their existence to Allah. Thus the ontological world is theocentric. There are two kinds of communicative relations: verbal and non-verbal. The verbal relationship is vertical from God to humans in the form of revelation and from humans to God in the form of prayer; it is non-verbal in the sense that God sends signs to humans, whereas humans respond with ritual worship. The Lord-servant relationship emphasizes God's majesty, sovereignty, and absolute power, while the servant aspect implies human humbleness, modesty, and absolute obedience. The ethical side of the divine-human relation stresses two different aspects of Allah: infinite goodness, mercy, and forgiveness countered by God's wrath and strict justice. Human ethical responsibility includes such responses as thankfulness for God's merciful side and fear of His wrath. The community is divided into two parts: people of the book versus those without the book (revealed scripture). In short, these are distinctions based on the dichotomy between believers and unbelievers.

The twofold view of the world is divided into the unseen and the visible. Allah reigns over both of them, while humans reign only over the visible. The world is further divided into the present, a lower place where humans live, and the afterworld, which is the world to come in the near future. The afterworld stands in sharp contrast to the present world. The present and afterworld are connected by the Last Day, Day of Judgment, and resurrection, although the afterworld is divided into two very distinct parts: the Garden (Paradise) and Hell fire.

Compared to some religious traditions, the Qur'an does not go into great detail about the origin of the world, which came into existence by God's command along with everything within it (6.73), being completed within six days (10.3). With respect to human creation, the Qur'an (40.68) states, "It is He who created you of dust, then of a sperm-drop, then of a blood-clot, then He delivers you as infants." Even if Qur'anic cosmogony is minimal, it emphasizes Allah's absolute nature and His role as the unquestioned commander and sustainer of the universe. The Qur'an makes it clear that nature, a result of God's creative efforts, obeys God automatically. In comparison to nature, humans are an exception, because they have an opportunity for either obedience or disobedience. Unlike humans, the universe is Muslim, because it has surrendered itself to God's will (3.83). The Qur'an depicts Allah sitting on a throne, from where He manages the affairs of the world through His angelic and spiritual messengers who report back to God.

The Qur'an states that Allah measures out. This means that he places within things their power or the laws whereby they fit into the rest of the universe (20.50; 87.2–3). Consequently, all things have their potentialities, such as an acorn that can become an oak tree. If something is measured out, this suggests that it is finite and dependent on God. By measuring out the universe, Allah gave it laws that order it. If the laws are broken, there is a danger of chaos. Moreover, the universe is a natural sign or proof of God's existence and power, which implies that compared to God, the universe is nothing. But why is there something rather than nothing? The Qur'an replies to this question by affirming that the universe is due to the mercy of Allah. In comparison to classical Hinduism, the Islamic universe is not a product of divine play, because it was created for a purpose: to enable people to reflect on its signs (41.12–14). Nature also exists for humans to exploit and to improve their lives. Although humans are invited to use nature for their needs, they are, however, commanded not to corrupt the earth.

Qur'anic Understanding of the Ethos of Islam

The closest notion that we find in the Qur'an to the Western idea of religion is the term *din*, which carries the sense of a personal religion; it is equivalent to piety. *Din* can also refer to a particular religious system. During the seventh century in Arabia, *din* had three major meanings: a systematic religion, a verbal noun meaning "judging" or "passing sentence," and a verb that means to conduct oneself, to conform to traditional usage, or to observe certain practices.

In contrast to the term *din* and its usages, the term Islam is the name of a religion given by Allah to a specific people at a particular time and location: "This day I have perfected your religion for you, and completed my favor unto you; and have chosen for you as a religion Islam" (5.3). This term occurs eight times in the Qur'an, where it tends to refer to an action rather than an institution.

Islam represents a personal decision by a person to accept the responsibility of living according to God's law. In short, Islam thus means submission to God, which entails obedience, commitment, and awareness of one's insignificance and worthlessness before Allah. The Qur'an also refers to your personal Islam, suggesting a personal commitment to heed God's word. This implies that Islam is something vivid and dynamic. A Muslim is someone who has submitted to God and is a committed monotheist like the patriarch Abraham, although the earliest uses of the term were applied more inclusively rather than its later confessional connotations.

This religion chosen by God and bestowed on humans is a way or path ordained by Allah (6.154). It is called a straight path because following it leads a person directly to salvation. It is implied that other paths will lead one astray because they are crooked. This image of a straight path does not mean that Islam is a unified religion, because a major division is evident among the Sunnīs and Shī'ites. The latter follow the tradition of Ali, the cousin of the prophet.

Supernatural Beings and Human Nature

The centrality of God for Muslims in the Qur'an is evident in a copy that a former Arabic student gave to me as a gift, in which all references to Allah are highlighted in red ink. Allah is often called the One, or emphasis is placed on His ninety-nine beautiful names (7.179; 17.11). Allah is also called the Compassionate and the Merciful. These various names of God are not merely attributes but are considered realities by the faithful. Allah is the Creator, Sustainer, and Judge. His creative power is purposeful and not playful (21.16–17), implying that the world has meaning and is not a product of chance. This type of theological position means that the universe is not cyclic, because such a pattern is incompatible with purposefulness. Allah measures out things, which suggests creating the laws by which nature operates and giving each thing its range of potentiality. Allah's wisdom and power are evident in nature and in the course of history. Allah is not a distant or aloof deity, because he is involved in history.

The relationship between Allah and humans is expressed as God being wholly other than humans. This means that God is completely transcendent to such an extent that "sight reaches him not" (6.101). Allah's utter transcendence is mitigated by the fact that he is closer to an individual than that person's jugular vein (50.16). A favorite way to express the God-human relationship is to stress that humans are God's servants or slaves, suggesting their dependent status with respect to God. This means that the only proper relationship to God is that of submission. A Muslim is reminded of this status when she thinks about Allah's creatorship, which indicates that the source of one's being is God. The verbal and non-verbal signs that God sends to humans represents his attempt to communicate with humans. According to the Qur'an, the most significant form of communication is verbal revelation received by a prophet, which is too mysterious and extraordinary for ordinary people. By means of this revelation, God does not reveal his being but rather reveals his will. Thus, instead of knowledge about God, the intention of revelation is obedience by humans.

When God sends verbal or non-verbal signs, humans can either accept or reject them. Acceptance is the initial step toward faith and makes possible understanding, which lies in one's heart (3.114). The acceptance of a sign results in gratitude by humans. Allah's signs can be grasped as manifestations of Divine guidance. Therefore, Allah intends to guide humankind to the right path, leaving humans the responsibility to either accept or reject the signs and guidance. Moreover, to respond either positively or negatively to divine guidance results from God's will. This position of the Qur'an was to lead to later theological debates about free will and predestination among scholars.

Passages reflecting predestination and free will provide a foundation for arguing either position, as with the following verse: "God changes not what is in a people, until they change what is in themselves" (13.12). A different type of verse suggesting predestination appears a few lines from the previous example: "When God desires evil for a people, there is no averting it" (13.18). Other deterministic and free will types of statements can also be found in the text. These apparently contradictory statements and attitudes can be understood by grasping the cultural context of the text. The Qur'an includes a pre-Islamic belief that a person's life is controlled by an external power. Muslims refer to fate as *qismat* or "what has been allotted." This is not a passive acceptance of a blind personal fate but is rather a feeling that God has ordered some event according to eternal wisdom. This belief does not exclude human responsibility, which is assumed in the Qur'an. Those who believe in God's guidance are rewarded, whereas those who disobey are allowed to go astray (2.24). It is unbelief that is the cause of straying rather than a consequence of it because God withdraws his grace from the sinner as a punishment.

Besides the majestic power of Allah, the Qur'an refers to spirits (*jinn*) who were spirits of the desert during the pre-Islamic period in Arabia. The Meccans asserted a kinship between them and Allah, made offerings to them, and sought their assistance. The Qur'an identifies them as having airy or fiery bodies being created from a smokeless flame (55.15). Besides their intelligent and imperceptible nature, these spirits are capable of appearing under different forms and can carry heavy loads. Some of these spirits will be saved at the end of time, while others will be thrown into hell.

The Qur'an also refers to angels who are created from light, endowed with intelligence, and can become visible. In addition to angels being called the army of God, the Qur'an refers to three prominent angelic figures: Gabriel, angel of the revelation; Mīkā'il called the faithful spirit; and Israfil, who will blow the trumpet ushering in the last day. Angels function as messengers in the Qur'an. The individual human is accompanied by two angels who record a person's deeds (82.11; 43.80) and a guardian angel who protects a person (6.61; 13.12).

Predating the creation of Adam, the satanic Iblīs was created by fire. Within the Qur'an, Iblīs (Satan) is numbered among the angels (2.34) and spirits (*jinn*, 18.50). At the creation of Adam, Iblīs acted rebelliously because he refused to obey Allah's command to bow before Adam; it was beneath his dignity to pay homage to a being made of earth. Iblīs was banished and cursed, but he begged postponement of his punishment until the Day of Judgment. Iblīs is credited with tempting Eve to eat the forbidden fruit of the tree of paradise. In this Islamic scenario, Iblīs is more a rival and enemy of humans rather than God, who is far beyond the influence of Iblīs. He can use his limited powers to entice humans, but he cannot force a person to commit an evil deed, even though he is very artful and cunning.

Among the creative acts of Allah, the last being created was Adam, who was formed from clay and water as God breathed his spirit into the first man. Allah created Adam to serve as his vice regent on earth, but the angels protested because the first man would be mischievous, while the angels would sing about the glory of God; but Allah told the angels that he knew something that they did not about the first man. To prove this to the angels, Allah instituted a contest between the angels and Adam to name things. The angels could not name things, whereas Adam could do so because he had been given power over the things of the world by Allah, who taught Adam the names of things (2.31). The cultural context for this ability by the first man reflects the fact that to know the name of something means to possess power over it and to have a capacity for creative knowledge. Then God requested all the angels to prostrate themselves before Adam and honor him for his ability, but one angel (Iblīs) refused and insisted that he was superior to Adam. This narrative demonstrates that Iblīs is an anti-human force and that Adam is unique in the order of creation.

For those who wonder about the divine rationale for creating Adam, the answer is that a human's purpose is to serve God, a service that is not for God's benefit but rather for a human's advantage, since without God, humans would be non-existent; it is God, however, who has complete authority over humans. In turn, humans owe gratitude, praise, and obedience toward God by adhering to his commands.

The Qur'an exhibits a conception of human nature that views beings as consisting of a body and a spiritual element. Humans have an animal soul (*nafs*), which is one's lower spiritual part that incites evil (12.53; 77.2), and a spirit (*rūh*) that originates with Allah and animates the human body (15.29), which is a subtle body located somewhere within the gross body. A person also has reason or intellect, which gives him the ability to know what is right or wrong. The reason is different in kind from the soul. In spite of these aspects, humans are limited creatures who are relatively weak and incapable because their bodies are subject to disease, intellectual weakness, and, finally, death. As a consequence of these limitations, humans fumble about, suffer, and engage meaninglessness. Humans need to learn how to live with their limitations but cannot know this by themselves because of intellectual flaws. Therefore, the basic problem is ignorance, and its solution is guidance provided by divine revelation, which instructs humans to be a servant of Allah. This means to submit to God's will, which functions as the meaning and end of human life. Even though Adam and Eve sinned and were expelled from Paradise, their sin is not contagious, meaning consequently that a redeeming figure is not necessary. A human must repent of wrongful behavior, which involves a feeling of guilt, regret, and a decision not to repeat the transgression. Thus the path to salvation includes following the commandments of God and the example of his prophet.

The corporate body of Muslim believers forms a community (*ummah*) with Allah at the head of it, protecting its security. This community of believers (49.10) is thus a theocratic structure. The community represents the believing, acting, intending, and struggling community of faith. It is a covenant community that begins with Allah's covenant with his messenger and, through him, with the people (33.7; 3.81). The Muslim covenant is a mutual agreement, even though the partners are not equal. The Muslim community is also an eschatological community because it calls everyone to salvation and provides a foretaste of Paradise with God in this world. In the Qur'an, the unity of the community is stressed (43.33; 23.52). In comparison to pre-Islamic Arabia and its tribal/clan structures, the community established by Muhammad is based on religion and not kinship.

Five Pillars of Islam

The Qur'an makes a fundamental distinction between things to be believed (*īmām*) and things to be done in rites (*dīn*). The notion of intention is important to the pillars of Islam in the sense that it must precede confession and other religious acts, which implies that religious acts must not be perfunctory or mechanical. Therefore, intention to engage in an act of faith is used as a defense against inattentive and external performance.

The first pillar of the Islamic faith is the confession of faith (*shahādah*): There is no God but Allah, and Muhammad is his prophet. This simple and profound confession forms the basis of the other pillars. The second pillar is the necessity of prayer: institutional (*salāt*) and spontaneous prayers (*du'ā*). The former type of prayer is derived from an Aramaic word meaning "bowing." Rather than being impulsive, institutional prayer is not spontaneous because it is a religious obligation and a duty rendered to God. Institutional prayer has a legal basis in the sense that it is a performance of what God has established. By neglecting or abandoning this type of divinely prescribed prayer, a Muslim forfeits his Islamic status.

The origin of institutional prayer is related in a narrative from the *hadīth* literature. According to this account, as he ascends to heaven, Muhammad arrives at the seventh heaven, where he is given instructions that his community should say 50 prayers every day. While descending to earth, he meets Moses, who tells him to go back and ask for remission because Muslims are unable to meet such a substantial obligation. This same scenario is repeated three times, until daily prayers are reduced to five times, which are specified as the following: daybreak, noon, mid-afternoon, after sunset, and early part of the evening. The different times for prayer avoid any suggestion that Muslims worship the sun. It is common for the times of institutional prayer to be announced by a *muezzin* calling from the top of a minaret (tower) atop a mosque.

The first prerequisite that must be observed is purification of the believer. There are two types of ablution, which are called lesser and greater ablutions. The former type involves washing both hands with water to the wrists, rinsing the mouth three times, taking water into the nostrils three times, washing the face three times, washing both arms to the elbows, wiping the forehead once with the right hand, wiping the ears, head, and neck once, and washing both feet to the ankles. In contrast, the greater ablution involves washing the entire body, which is usually done after any major pollution. If no water is available, a Muslim may wash with fine clean sand. Since the place of prayer must also remain clean, worshippers leave their shoes outside of a mosque, and a mat is often used for the prostrations.

Muslims are expected to pray no matter where they are located, although the most desirable place is a mosque. Muslim prayer is not merely recited but

Figure 14.1 Blue Mosque in Istanbul, Turkey. Photograph by Jake Boynton.

is also performed by executing a fixed number of bowings (*rak'ah*) that include seven movements with their appropriate recitations. With one's hands raised on each side of the face, a Muslim recites the phrase "Allah akbar" (God is most great). Standing with hands before one's body, a person recites the opening chapter of the Qur'an, which is followed by another Qur'anic passage while standing upright, bowing from the hips while placing hands on the knees, and standing straight upright. The prostration is performed by gliding to the knees, followed by putting nose and forehead on the ground, sitting back on one's haunches, and announcing in a sitting position "God is great," followed by a second prostration. With these steps, a Muslim completes a single bowing. This pious pattern is indicative that Muslim prayer is performed, a sign of submission and an act of homage, and powerfully demonstrates the totality of human surrender to God as a person places one's face in contact with dust, the lowest thing in nature. Institutional prayer is also a way to take refuge in Allah and to place one's trust in him. By performing prayer, a person demonstrates that he is part of a community that is identified as the people of God, and this community directs its prayers toward the direction of Mecca, the holy city and symbolic center of Islam.

In addition to the confession of faith and command to pray five times a day, the third pillar of Islam is almsgiving (*zakāt*), an obligatory contribution of one-fortieth of one's annual income. The term is related to purity in the sense that the given portion of income purifies or legitimatizes what is retained (9.103). The *zakāt* is distinguished from a free-will offering (58.13–14) because it is an obligation for being part of the community, although giving should not be performed grudgingly or disparagingly. A consequence of this pillar is that a society permeated with genuine giving would eliminate usury. Within the context of early Islam, giving is akin to a loan made to Allah that he will repay many fold and can also be interpreted as repentance and atonement for a giver's misdeeds.

The fourth pillar of Islam is fasting (*saum*) during the month of Ramadan, ninth month of the lunar year. This pillar originates during a period before Islam because Arabs practiced fasting and observing holy periods of time. There are, however, three reasons for the Islamic fast: (1) it is commanded by God and thus an obligation for all Muslims; (2) the month of Ramadan is the time during which the Qur'an was first revealed; (3) the notion of the forgiveness of sins also plays an important role. The holy month of Ramadan is a period when divine intercession is appropriate and is referred to as a time when the gates of Heaven are open, which suggests that it is a propitious time for the acceptance of prayer.

The observance of fasting during Ramadan is replete with certain prohibitions, such as abstaining from food and drink during the hours of daylight and other restrictions, although compensation is made for children, pregnant women, sick people, old people, and travelers. Food can only be taken by participants during hours of darkness. The practice of fasting can be grasped as a restraining of the body and soul, during which time the body is subordinated and authority is exercised over the soul. In general, fasting during Ramadan provides a communal atmosphere by reinforcing the collective sense of being a Muslim. This imposed pattern of discipline on everyone is a sacramental sign of oneness.

The last pillar of Islam is pilgrimage (*hajj*) to Mecca, location of the Ka'ba, which was allegedly built by Abraham and his son Isma'il in ancient times. It is a practice that a Muslim—male or female—is obligated to perform once in a person's lifetime, assuming that one can afford it. The guidelines for going on pilgrimage include the following criteria: A person must be old enough, which usually means puberty; be of sound mind; and be able to afford it. Before going on pilgrimage, a person must enter a sacred state by performing the greater ablution and donning an unsewn cloth garment made of two white sheets of cloth. Prohibitions accompany the practice because pilgrim must not cut their hair or nails, must avoid sexual activity, must not shed blood, must not hunt, must refrain from uprooting plants, must avoid cutting wood, must not arrange a marriage, and must not act as a witness, and men must refrain from wearing rings or using perfumes.

A pilgrim makes the lesser pilgrimage to Mecca on the first day by circumambulating the Ka'ba seven times and kissing the black stone. Pilgrims run seven times between the hills named Safā and Marwā. The seventh day marks the proper beginning of the pilgrimage, marked by participants listening to a sermon in a mosque. The eighth day is called "day of moistening" because pilgrims secure water for the following days. After going to Minā, pilgrims listen to a sermon there and throw seven stones three times at a pillar representing Satan, who appeared to Abraham at this location and was driven away by the patriarch. On the tenth day at Minā, sheep and camels are sacrificed before pilgrims journey to Mecca to circumambulate the Ka'ba, an action that is repeated on the thirteenth day. After the second visit to the Ka'ba, pilgrims wash themselves to cleanse themselves of sacredness before observing days of eating and pleasure at Minā. Again, stones are thrown at the Satanic pillars before resuming a sacred condition prior to the final visit to Mecca. Many pilgrims take this opportunity to visit Muhammad's tomb in Medina. Muslims believe that if a person dies on pilgrimage, that individual becomes a martyr and is destined for heaven.

The performance of pilgrimage gives a person an opportunity to present herself before God and imitates actions performed by the prophet. As a visible symbol of unity and brotherhood, pilgrimage binds believers together into an annual mass congregation, and contributes to the solidarity of Islam. Individual pilgrims exhibit a state of liminality, according to some scholars, which represents a place and moment in and out of time and a location between or on the periphery. As a liminal figure, the pilgrim is characterized by ambiguity and paradox and is structurally invisible, eluding normal classification. It is an existential experience of community that is a spontaneously generated relationship stripped of structural attributes, during which everyone is equal, as symbolized by their simple dress.

A feature of early Islam that did not become a pillar of the religion was *jihād*, a notion that literally means striving within a religious context that came to mean holy war at a later time. The Meccan chapters of the Qur'an teach patience when attacked, but the historically later Medinan chapters recognize the right to repel the attackers. In early Islamic history, *jihad* was a voluntary individual commitment to work or strive in the path of God. In the Qur'an (3.187), a believer is enjoined to spread knowledge of God's revelation. Believers are also urged to strive against unbelief (8.65) and to strive against unbelievers and hypocrites (9.73). *Jihād* gradually developed into a duty to fight against and subdue the Meccans persecuting the Medinan community. After the death of Muhammad, *jihād* became a duty, according to the interpretation of it by legal scholars in the eighth century CE. As the notion of *jihād* developed into its meaning of holy war, it incorporated an ideal of surrendering a believer's property and self in the path of Allah. The overall purpose of *jihād* was to establish an Islamic socio-moral order that would encompass the globe. If a believer died fighting for this just cause, this type of person became a martyr and was assured of attaining Paradise. There are some who might view this as a radical ideal, but it is mitigated by ethical attitudes expressed in the Qur'an.

Ethical Teachings of the Qur'an

The ethical system of the Qur'an is built on a threefold belief: belief in Allah, in his Judgment, and in a necessity for virtuous deeds. From this ethical foundation, a believer has a duty to God to be just and to do good deeds. Based on this duty to God, a believer is instructed to be moderate or "not to exceed the limits" (2.190), to forgive others, to repel evil with whatever is better (23.96), and not to obligate someone beyond their capacity (6.153). The believer knows that God rewards good deeds and punishes evil ones (53.31–32). The religious context for these ethical principles is the imminent Day of Judgment, when the true believers and the unbelievers will have their fate decided by Allah.

The genuine believer inwardly manifests piety (8.2–4) and a deep earnestness and stands in awe when hearing the name of God. It is faith that motivates a person to do good deeds; otherwise, faith is not genuine. The faith of the true believer contains four elements: contrition, awe, obedience, and gratitude. But the ground of faith is fear of God. Thus faith is rooted in fear and caution. To believe in God is to fear him as the austere Judge. This fear of God implies fear about the consequences of one's actions, which involves an acute sense of responsibility by a believer, an acceptance of the limits imposed by God, and a willingness not to transgress these limits. Besides fear, a Muslim must be thankful, knowing that God will reciprocate likewise. In addition to thankfulness, God also bestows forgiveness, although God does not pardon unbelief. Divine forgiveness is judiciously dispensed and discriminatively given when a believer contritely asks for it. Moreover, a genuine, ethical believer manifests several virtues: humility, honesty, generosity, kindness, and trustworthiness.

In contrast to the believer stands the unbeliever (*kāfir*), a term with a root meaning of covering and implying knowingly ignoring received benefits because one is unthankful and ungrateful. The unbeliever does not manifest gratitude and even acts rebelliously. The unbeliever is more apt to manifest insolence, haughtiness, and presumptuousness. The heart of the unbeliever is hard like a stone (2.69), or the unbeliever's heart is veiled, a metaphor that suggests a partition exists between such a person's heart and revelation (61.42–44). The Qur'an also describes the unbeliever as blind and deaf to divine signs (66.25–28).

It is possible for unbelief to end in *shirk* (literally forgery); it is forging a lie against God, of which idolatry and polytheism are the prime examples. This forgery is grounded in groundless, unwarranted thinking (30.28). This is a manifestation of the unbeliever going astray from the right path (25.46). The Qur'an describes the unbeliever as haughty and prideful. Such a person loses a sense of his being a creature and disregards God, disobeys God's command-ments, and acts against God's will. This type of person risks becoming a doer of evil (*zalim*), a person who transgresses the proper limit established by Allah, from one perspective, and exceeds the bounds of proper conduct in social life.

Death and Eschatology in the Qur'an

In the Qur'an, the certainty and universal nature of death is emphasized (3.185) and is conceived within the omniscience of Allah (6.58, "Not a leaf falls, but He knows it"). The precise hour of each person's death is ordained (16.61). Death is akin to sleep. When a person is dying, she is turned to face the direction of Mecca, and a relative recites the confession of faith (first pil-lar). When a believer dies, that person is visited by white-faced angels who take the soul to the seventh heaven before being returned to the body in the grave, where it is questioned by Munkar and Nakir. The death of an unbeliever is strikingly different, because that person's soul is visited by angels with black faces who take the soul and present it to other angels, who place this smelly soul into a hair-cloth. The soul is transported to the lowest heaven, but is not admitted; it is rather returned to the body in the grave, where it is questioned by Munkar and Nakir, whose appearances are fearsome with black faces and green eyes, voices like thunder, eyes like lightening, and long fangs. These fig-ures question the deceased concerning his beliefs and deeds during life. If the answers are correct, the deceased is given a view of the Garden of Paradise, or he is given a glimpse of the Fire when the answers are incorrect. This does not mean that a deceased person's fate is determined solely by correct responses to the questions, but they do determine one's intermediate condition while awaiting the day of resurrection.

If heaven is described by sensuous terms, hell is called the Fire, and its seven gates are guarded by nineteen angels (74.30–31). At the bottom of the pit of fire, there is located the *zaqqum* tree (37.62–68), with heads of devils for flowers, which sinners are forced to eat and that burn their stomachs. The tortures of hell are described as flames roaring, water boiling, sighing and wailing by unbelievers, and iron hooks that drag back anyone trying to escape. The enduring of the hell fire is referred to as a second death, which is a state of not dying and yet not living. The notion of a second death expresses two concepts simultaneously: immortality of the soul and eternity of divine retribution.

In sharp contrast to the suffering and pain of hell, heaven is called the Garden or Paradise, with rivers of water, milk, wine, and honey flowing through it. Within this place, the faithful are content, secure, and peaceful, eating and drinking as they desire, reclining on couches, and wearing gold, pearls, and beautiful robes. Awaiting male believers are beautiful, virgin maidens (hūrs), who can be identified by the name of Allah and that of her spouse inscribed on her chest. These maidens are a reward to a male for leading a virtuous life. These heavenly maidens have some desirable attributes: they cannot get pregnant, they never lose their virginity, they do not menstruate, they do not spit or blow their noses, they never get sick, they never get angry, and they are immortal. In contrast to the rewards awaiting faithful males, the Qur'an is unclear about what reward is waiting for female believers in heaven.

The sacred text is not unclear about the end of time because it is coming soon and affirms a bodily resurrection, when bodies will be joined with their souls. Besides a bodily resurrection, there will also be a final judgment, when God determines a person's fate. As with Jewish and Christian speculations about the end of time, there are some signs of the final hour (81.1–14): a disruption of the natural order, a reversal of the process of creation, the destruction of the heavens, the stars falling and becoming extinguished, the sun and moon becoming covered, earth quakes, a mixing of the seas together, creating a primordial chaos, and moral disasters. According to tradition, a false messiah will arrive, who is described as blind in one eye, reddish in color, with the word unbeliever written on his forehead. The powerful giants Gog and Magog will appear (18.92; 21.96). Christ will also appear to cleanse the world one more time.

These various types of signs prefigure the beginning of doomsday announced by the angel Israfil, who will blow his trumpet once (69.13) or twice (39.68). The first blast from the horn signals the disruption of nature, while the second blast represents the dramatic final cataclysm. which includes the death of all living creatures. Then God resurrects deceased bodies and joins them to their spirits. The final judgment is next, when Allah appears with his angels and humankind gathers before Him. The book of deeds is opened, and people's limbs will testify against or for them (17.14–15; 36.65; 34). If it is determined that one is among the righteous, the book is placed into one's right hand, or if one is unrighteous, the book is hung around one's neck. Other passages in the Qur'an utilize the motif of balances, which expresses the possibilities of weighing people, the book of deeds, or just the deeds. Another motif is the bridge (sirāt) to or over Hell (36.66; 37.23–24). The Islamic tradition describes it as sharper than a sword or as thin as a hair. Both the sacred and condemned must pass over this bridge. The faithful will easily pass over to Heaven, whereas the damned will fall into the fire. The Qur'an also refers to a veil, wall, or purgatory (7.44) where certain persons will abide without entering heaven or hell.

Islamic Legal Tradition and Women

At the core of the Islamic way of life, there is the law that supports its ethical theism in which the faithful are guided by the revelation and summoned to submit to Allah, making all life and activity a realm of God's authority. The law (*shari'a*) is a term that originally meant a path leading to water, which is a path to the source of life. The law informs believers that the right path of action is that ordained by God. The *shari'a* is an all-embracing sacred law that includes legal and social transactions and personal behavior. Islamic religion and law are difficult to separate from each other.

Islamic law is based on four foundations: Qur'an, *sunna* of the prophet, consensus (*ijmā*), and analogical reasoning (*qiyās*). The Qur'an is the revelation received by Muhammad and has the highest authority in the legal tradition. The *sunna* of the prophet consist of decisions, sayings, or pronouncements of the prophet. During Muhammad's life, these decisions were authoritative, but after his death they became infallible. The *sunna* comes to a conclusion with the so-called Companions and their generation. This is the time for the beginning of consensus (*ijmā*), reflecting the agreement on legal issues by the Muslim community. It is the instrument by which the nature of the *sunna* and right interpretation of the Qur'an are determined. And it is analogical reasoning that prepares the way for consensus. Analogical reasoning is a means of reaching a decision about a new legal issue by concluding from a given principle to determine a common essential feature, called the reason, and making a decision based on a similar precedent. A good example of its operation is a charge of marital infidelity. Reasoning from the Qur'an's requirement for four witnesses to a violation, legalists concluded that a fourfold confession by the culprit is necessary, or that the recording of commercial transactions is necessary to prevent fraud based on an injunction to register marriages. This type of legal reasoning moves from the known to the unknown. Thus, analogical reasoning represents a way for Islamic law to be extended to cover situations analogous to, but not explicitly stated in, the Qur'an or the tradition of *sunna*.

These four foundations of the law did not allow for independent judgment. Thus, the individual legal mind is subordinated to the consensus of the community, which could not agree on an erroneous point of law, according to a *hadīth* saying attributed directly to Muhammad. Popular legal opinion reflects the attitude that all essential questions have been discussed and settled, and consensus of the community establishes that no one is qualified to render independent legal opinion. Legal activity becomes restricted to explanation, application, and interpretation, with an emphasis on acceptance rather than innovation in the legal sphere. Nonetheless, legal experts are able to devise legal fictions to meet new problems. As Islam developed historically, a number of orthodox legal schools evolved along with legal experts, such as the judge (*qāḍī*) and jurisconsult (*muftī*), who renders a learned opinion called a *fatwā*. Muslim governments appointed official *muftīs*, who were often attached to tribunals. The chief *muftī* of a country is called Shaykh al-Islam.

Over the centuries of the religion, the legal tradition has reflected and shaped cultural attitudes toward women, although the Qur'an forms the basis for later developments. The Qur'an is unequivocal about the status of women, because they are to be managed by men and be obedient (4.38); men are superior to women (2.228), men are protectors of women (4.34), and women are similar to fields to be plowed by men (2.223). Not only are women subordinate to men, but they are also incapable and unfit for public duties. But women are also part of the community and can achieve paradise for their faithfulness.

Muslim women have traditionally married at a young age, within the social context of arranged marriages that are considered contracts and not sacraments. Women are restricted to a single husband who must be Muslim, whereas a male can practice polygamy with a limit of four wives, although the husband must treat each wife equally. A woman is not bereft of rights, because she must consent to a marriage and can dictate the terms of the marriage contract. The Qur'an allows for temporary marriages (4.24–28) that end automatically when the length of the contract expires but does not necessitate a divorce. This arrangement is intended to provide a male with a spouse when he is away from home for extended periods of time. Because this system lent itself to abuses, the Islamic tradition declares that Muhammad made it unlawful.

Generally speaking, women are at a legal disadvantage when it comes to divorce because a husband needs no justification for divorcing his wife, although the same right is denied to a wife unless a husband fails to convert to Islam. After a divorce, custody of the children traditionally reverts to the father. An important innovation of the Qur'an is permission for women to inherit and own property, but a woman is restricted to an inheritance half that of a male. Within the public sphere, women must be modest, although the Qur'an does not refer to face veils or being covered from head to toe. The legal tradition has restricted female attendance at the mosque, where they would encounter men, although tradition demonstrates Muhammad praying with women.

In pre-Islamic Arabia, women living in the desert were unveiled, whereas city dwellers did don the veil. Upper class and urban middle class women did wear the veil as a mark of social rank, a practice that had been sanctioned by Muhammad. The Islamic tradition recognizes different forms of veiling: a veil covering the face from just below the eyes, a *chador* or *burka* that covers the entire body, or a full face mask with small slits through the eyes. The advantage of veiling allows a woman a degree of anonymity. Some modern Muslim women of Egypt interpret the Islamic dress code as liberating in contrast to the immodest dress of many Western women, because the practice is a protection from possible molestation or misunderstanding about female motives. Other Egyptian women reject the veil because it is perceived as backward, a product of patriarchal oppression and slave psychology. In Iran, the wearing of the *chador* was used by women as a political anti-Shah symbol, although women protested when it became mandatory in the post-revolution period in 1979. In Oman, the *burqa* is a visible symbol of a woman's marital status, and Omani woman testify that it makes them beautiful in a spiritual sense and suggests their moral excellence.

Early Theological Tradition

From the orthodox Islamic perspective, the Qur'an is the revealed word of God, but problems arise from it that confound ordinary mortals, related to its meaning. In order to solve these problems, theologically inclined individuals feel called to interpret, defend, and justify the revelation. In fact, numerous Qur'anic verses invite theological reflection on the meaning of aspects of the revelation. Early Islamic theology is called *kalam* in Arabic, a term that means speech or oral discussion, suggesting that theology was dialogical and represented "God talk." Theological speculation took place within the context of influence from Greek philosophy and as a response to Christian theological critics and developed within the context of historical developments affecting Islam. In order to counter external critics and internal disagreements, Muslim thinkers adopted Greek logic and methods of argumentation. In the early Muslim tradition, four schools emerged: Khārijites, Murji'ites, Mu'tazilites, and Ash'arites.

The Khārijites represented a political reaction to the party of Ali, and then the Umayyad dynasty. They advocated "No judgment but God's," which implied that everyone must follow the Qur'an because what God intends for people is already and clearly known. The Khārijites envisioned a righteous community of saints that knows and practices the divine law. Thus, the very structure of society must be based on the revelation. This means that the sinner is excluded from the community and is destined for hell, which implies that salvation is attained through faith, membership in the community, and performance of good deeds.

In contrast to the Khārijites, the Murji'ites are the group that postpones judgment on people until the end of time. In other words, a sinner's fate will be decided by God, suggesting that one should not pass judgment on a sinner. Moreover, a Muslim does not lose faith through sin. The Murji'ites used a Qur'anic passage (9.101–106) to support their position, which recalls a period when Muhammad made a distinction between Medinese who had forsaken him. Some of the Medinese were not penitent and would receive punishment in this and the next life, while those who showed regret were left to Allah's mercy. A third group who did not repent was left in a suspended state. Reflecting on these passages, Murji'ite thinkers argued that where there is faith, sin will do no harm, because faith is indelible. The Murji'ites held a more indulgent and forgiving attitude toward sinners and embraced a hopeful attitude for the future prospect for sinners at the final judgment.

The Mu'tazilites are known as neutralist with respect to the political quarrel between Ali and his opponents. They rejected the deterministic interpretation of Islam, and argued instead for the goodness of God and making humans responsible for their deeds by arguing for free will. If a person did not have free will, it would be unjust for God to hold her responsible for her actions. Thus, an important consequence of a free will position is that God cannot do the unreasonable and the unjust, making God necessarily just. This position leads to the doctrine of promise and threat, which means that God cannot pardon the sinner and violate his threat, and he cannot punish a pious person and violate his promise. Therefore, God must do whatever is best for humankind. But we know that good people endure undeserved pain and suffering in life, which seems unjust. How can this fact be justified? The school introduces the law of compensation, which means that those unfairly treated in this life will be compensated in the next life. A child who dies young, for example, will be given a permanent place in paradise.

In order to grasp the implications of the Mu'tazilites' position on divine justice and power, imagine the parable of the three brothers. The first brother occupies an exulted place in heaven because of his positive deeds while alive during a long life. In comparison to the first brother, the second sibling occupies a lower rung of paradise. He complains to God that he did not live long enough to perform more good deeds than his brother, whereas the third brother, a grave sinner, is being punished in hell. He inquires of God why he did not die before he became an abject sinner. The Mu'tazilites applied logical reasoning to resolve this type of problematic situation by arguing that God foresees that the second brother would have sinned if he lived longer. Thus God stopped him from becoming a grave sinner. The third brother is responsible for his evil actions and is being punished in accord with God's justice. A more conservative position affirms that the punishment of the third brother is simply a matter of God's will, and beyond this assertion, the dire situation of the third brother cannot be explained.

Contrary to the orthodox position, the Mu'tazilites argued that there is no absolute good or evil, which are rational and arbitrary concepts that one can establish through unaided reason. This means that an action is good not because God commands it, but rather God commands it because it is good. This necessarily means that God's way is rational. Accusing the Mu'tazilites of an extreme form of humanism, the orthodox asserted that their opponents' position represents freedom for humans and bondage for God. The orthodox school and the Mu'tazilites also disagreed about the unity of God and his attributes. The Mu'tazilite position is that God's unity demands that one reject the literal grasp of anthropomorphic expressions in the Qur'an. Because God is pure essence, he is without eternal names and qualities. The orthodox claim that this position denudes God of all content and renders him unsatisfactory for religious consciousness. The Mu'tazilite position has important consequence because it denies the eternity of God's word, which is declared to be created by passing through human phases of recitation and writing. Reason is now equal to revelation and is superior to tradition.

The more conservative Ash'arite school counters the Mu'tazilites by arguing that revelation is superior to reason, although reason does support revelation. With respect to free will, the Ash'arites claim that all human acts are created by God by means of acquisition. This position means that acts attach themselves to the will of a person, who thus acquires them. The result of the doctrine of acquisition is that God is all powerful, whereas all responsibility rests with humans. The Ash'arites also argue that God possesses real and eternal attributes and rewards and punishes humans as he wills. Since God is both merciful and graceful, divine justice cannot be defined in human terms. From the Ash'arite perspective, the Mu'tazilite's position does not solve the problem of evil, restricts divine action, and denies God's omnipotence and infinite compassion.

Diversity of Islam

The theological differences and the split within Islam between Sunnis and Shi'ites are indications that Islam is not a monolithic entity. Islam also differs according to its geographical location. Thus, Islam demonstrates a wide diversity of thought and practice, even if different versions of the religion accept the Qur'an as the revelation of Allah. In fact, there is even diversity within a movement such as the Shi'ites, which begins as a series of political failures.

When Muhammad's cousin Ali died in 661 after being assassinated by Umayyad forces over leadership of the Muslim community, he was succeeded by al-Hasan, a son born to Ali and the prophet's daughter Fatima. Lacking political talent and ambition, al-Hasan relinquished all claims to leadership for a substantial sum of money from the Mu'āwiya, leader of the Umayyad forces. The brother of al-Hasan was al-Husayn, and he was encouraged to lead a revolt in Iraq, but he and his band were massacred at Karbala in October of 680. Shi'ites annually commemorate this event with a passion play and public display of self-flagellation during the month of Muharram, the initial month of the year of the Muslim calendar. In 684, the Penitents, a group seeking revenge for al-Husayn's death, were defeated by Umayyad forces. These events gave rise to the term Shi'a, which means the party of Ali. This group believed Ali to be the first *Imām*, a figure chosen by the prophet as his successor and entrusted with secret knowledge not shared with most of the prophet's companions. This secret knowledge has been passed down in Ali's family as a kind of inheritance, rendering them the rightful successors of the prophet. Later Shi'ites interpreted al-Husayn's death as a redemptive martyrdom, which makes salvation a possibility for everyone.

The historical context within which Shi'ites arose allows a person to confess contrary to his true beliefs if his life is threatened. The Shi'ites claim that the Qur'an has double or multiple interpretations because there are hidden levels of meaning located beneath its external meaning. Moreover, the channel of the revelations' grace and the prophet's teachings is the prophet's family.

Although these features differ with the Sunnis' position, both movements agree with the doctrine of divine unity, prophecy, and resurrection.

Two other major differences have to do with the nature of the *Imām* as the successor of the prophet and the notion of divine justice. The *Imām* is chosen by God either directly or through a preceding figure, which is interpreted as a divine act of grace. The *Imām* is defined as sinless and absolutely infallible on matters of dogma, while a prophet can sin. Representing the ultimate human being, the *Imām* represents the apex of the created universe and an epiphany of the primeval light and possesses divine qualities but not divine essence. The *Imām* has three major functions: to act as an intermediary between humans and God, to interpret God's message, and to guard the law. As a result of these functions, the *Imām* replaces the consensus of the Muslim community, resulting in Sunni Islam being the religion of consensus and Shi'a Islam being the religion of authority.

The two branches of Islam also disagree about the workings of divine justice, the role of reason, and predestination. The Shi'a argue that justice is innate to divine nature, which means that God cannot act unjustly, because his nature is to be just. It is human reason that can determine whether an act is just or unjust. Not only does Shi'ite theology place a greater emphasis on reason, but it also rejects the Sunni concept of predestination and accepts freedom of choice. In addition, Shi'a do not believe that independent legal reasoning is closed, which leaves open the possibility for creative rational thinking.

The Shi'ites developed some sub-sects during the course of their history, based often on the number of *Imāms* that a movement accepts. Twelver Shi'a believes in twelve visible *Imāms*, with the last one named Muhammad al-Muntazar (born 873), who mysteriously disappeared and represents the hidden *Imām*, whose reappearance is anticipated at any time. The figure who will appear before the end of time is called the Mahdī, and will bring equity, justice, and peace. In the meantime, he is alive but invisible.

The Isma'ilis are another sub-sect of the Shi'ites, who are called the Seveners. For this group, the rightful *Imām* is identified with Isma'il, a son of the sixth *Imām*, Ja'far, who died in 765, although the majority of Shi'a recognize Ja'far's son Mūsa, the eldest son, as the true successor, because Isma'il was guilty of drinking wine. In its theology, Shi'a recognize a universal intellect that evolves into a triad of Muhammad, Ali, and *Imām*. Their theological thinking revolves around the number seven because there are seven *Imāms*, seven spiritual worlds, seven heavens, seven earths, seven cycles of prophecy, and seven cycles of history identified with Adam, Noah, Abraham, Moses, Jesus, Muhammad, and *Imām*, which is called the series of speakers. From the Sunni perspective, the seven speakers destroy the doctrine of the finality of Muhammad's prophethood. Finally, the messianic Mahdī is identified with the seventh *Imām*, called *Imām* of the resurrection, who instead of bringing a new law reveals the inner meaning of the revelation. The resurrection refers to the reinstatement of humans and their divine prototypes (Adam and Eve) to their original condition in paradise.

Sufism and the Islamic Mystical Tradition

A narrative episode that appears in Ibn Ishaq's biography of Muhammad relates Muhammad's ascension to heaven, called the prophet's night journey (*mi'rāj*). According to the account, the angel Gabriel lifted the prophet onto a heavenly mount called Buraq, whom later poets describe as created from light, with a woman's head, a body of a horse, and the tail of a peacock. In later times, Buraq becomes a talisman for truck drivers in Pakistan, intended to protect their vehicles. On the night journey with the angel, Muhammad is shown the marvels of heaven and earth. Muhammad meets former prophets and leads them in ritual prayer in Jerusalem. Although some writers separate the night journey and the ascent to heaven, Ibn Ishaq combines them. Muhammad gains entry into heaven by giving satisfactory answers to questions pertaining to his identity. He visits various heavens and encounters prior prophets such as Jesus in the fourth heaven and Abraham in the seventh. He is also shown the punishment of sinners before he enters paradise. Orthodox Muslim theologians interpret this journey as something physical and not as something spiritual. Whether it is physical or spiritual, Muhammad's ascent served as a mystical metaphor of transcendence for humans from the earth to God.

A Muslim mystic is called a sufi, and the term "sufi" is derived from a term meaning "wool," much like the undyed garments worn by Christian ascetics. By the ninth century, Sufi refers to those who practice an ascetic lifestyle in order to directly experience God or a mystic having a supra-rational, meta-empirical, intuitive, and profound unitive experience. A Sufi's goal is captured in a narrative about a candle (God) and a moth (soul). The narrative begins with moths meeting to discuss their desire to be united with a burning candle. A moth is selected to approach the candle and report back about its experience. A wise moth concluded that the first moth did not truly understand anything about the nature of the candle because it lacked any experience about the nature of the burning candle. Another moth ventured forth and had the flame of the candle burn the tip of his wings, but his report was no more satisfactory than the first moth. Finally, a third, love-intoxicated moth threw himself on the flame by embracing it with his forelegs and uniting joyously with the flame; his body became as red as fire. Watching from a distance, the wise moth witnessed that the flame and the moth appeared to be one, and concluded that only the third moth truly understood, and nothing more can be said about it.

Any Muslim aspiring to become a Sufi needs a teacher (*shaykh*), who serves as an absolute authority on spiritual matters and is regarded as a mouthpiece of Allah. A disciple owes the teacher total obedience, must not keep secrets from him, and must get the teacher's approval for any ventures. It is the teacher who guides a disciple through the Sufi path. Likewise, the disciple views herself as a traveler who must journey through seven stations and six states. The biggest distinction between the stations and states is that the former are attained by the disciple while the states are conferred by God.

The Sufi traveler journeys through the seven stations by first travers-ing repentance, which means to turn away from sin and worldly concerns. According to a Sufi narrative, Ibrahim ibn Adham heard a strange sound on the roof of his palace and discovered a man looking for his lost camel. Accused of undertaking an impossible task, the man responded that his search for his camel on the roof was no more absurd than attempting to lead a religious life in the midst of luxury. In response to these comments, Ibrahim repented and repudiated his possessions. Subsequent stations include the following: fear of God; renunciation; poverty; patience; trust in God; and contentment. These seven stations constitute the ascetic and ethical discipline of a Sufi. In addition, the stations emphatically assert that the world is a transient trap for humans, much like the fly that got stuck in honey, or the spider that spends lots of time spinning a web to catch a tasty fly only to have a housewife swipe the web away in an instant with a broom. Because of the transient nature of the world, a vow of poverty means to possess nothing and to be possessed by nothing. The Sufi takes poverty to the extreme by forgetting it, along with having surrendered and quitting the world.

The six states of the Sufi path include the following: meditation; nearness to God; love; fear of God; contemplation; and certitude. Considering the human and divine relationship in the Qur'an, where fear of God is emphasized and love of God is not a viable option for a believer, Sufism is a path of love, a feature that arouses suspicions among the orthodox. The Sufi poet Rumi con-tinuously expresses love in his work: "When the angel falls in love, he is the perfect human" or "Who knows love's mazy circling, ever lives in God." These types of poetic verses are indicative of an intense yearning in the soul for God.

The Sufi must purify his soul by self-control and redirecting his thinking by practicing the method of thinking only of God (*dhikr*). A Sufi can either con-centrate on the first words of the Islamic credo: "There is no God but Allah," or he can simply focus on the name Allah. Rigorous practice is often compared to being in a grave and then being reborn. Another Sufi practice is listening (*sama*), within the context of an ecstatic recital or concert that includes dance and music, driving a participant into an ecstatic trance state that is the goal of the whirling dervishes spinning around their teacher (*shaykh*) located at the center of a circle.

The goal of the Sufi path is called passing away (*fanā*) and achieving immor-tal life in God. There are three stages of passing away: (1) becoming annihi-lated in God and assuming His attributes; (2) annihilation of vision because the individual soul is surrounded by the primordial light of God; (3) anni-hilation of one's vision of annihilation because one is now immersed in the existence of God, which is often called finding God. The experience of pass-ing away is symbolized as an experience of the black light. When this divine light appears in the Sufi's consciousness, all things disappear and all that is left is the light of the Absolute. The Sufi is like a piece of iron thrown into a furnace that becomes so hot that it appears as fire. This type of image suggests that passing away (*fanā*) is the complete nullification of ego consciousness and achievement of a moment when only God existed. From the state of passing away, the Sufi reaches a continual abiding (*baqā*) in God, representing eternal life in God.

Sufis often expressed themselves in provocative ways, to the extent of incurring the censure and wrath of orthodox authorities. The famous Sufi al-Hallāj (d. 922) proclaimed, "I am the truth," which is equivalent to saying that he is Allah. Unwilling to recant or admit that he was mad, he was convicted and ordered to be whipped, mutilated, crucified, and decapitated. Finally, his remains were cremated. According to legend, his ashes were thrown into a river, and the ashes floated upstream. As they proceeded against the current of the river, those on the bank could hear the following words: "I am the truth."

Islamic Rites and Festivals

The major life cycle rites observed by Muslims around the globe are marriage, birth, circumcision, and death on the level of popular religion, or religious practices of ordinary people. For marriage, Muslim families arrange these civil unions, although the daughter must give consent in many locations. Families may bargain over the dowry, which is essential for a valid marriage based on Islamic law, although there is no maximum dowry or specific ceremony fixed by law. At the groom's home in Morocco, others apply *henna*, which is a coloring matter, to him. This colored substance is called the "Light of the Prophet;" it has cosmetic uses and medicinal purposes, protects a person from evil influences, is used to purify the body of the groom, and contains holiness. The colored substance is applied to the groom's fingers or right hand, sometimes to both the hands and the feet. An unusual prophylactic practice is beating the groom to rid him of evil influences. Bachelors break a bowl with the same intention of dispelling evil. Other actions are intended to bring good fortune, such as putting a white egg into a bowl, wearing a silver bangle, or giving silver coins. The bride is purified in her home with *henna* and water. With her face covered by a veil, the bride is lifted onto a low table, and others dance around her. Then she is given money, kisses, milk, and a date. The milk is intended to make her life white (happy), and a date represents wealth. The bride is carried to the home of the groom amid loud music, singing, firing of guns, and use of candles and salt to avert evil. After the bride encounters her husband in his home, the couple retires to the nuptial chamber to consummate the marriage. If the bride is not a virgin, the wedding may suddenly cease; or if she is a virgin, the blood-stained sheets can be shown to celebrants. The marriage concludes with a feast. This wedding scenario in Fez, Morocco, is similar to that performed in a Palestinian village, even though there are some differences with respect to specific aspects.

In a Palestinian village, Islam and folk ways are intertwined when God's name is called before a married couple engages in sexual relations. This folk practice dispels Satan and evil spirits and makes God present. It is believed that conception occurs if God allows it, and the child's gender depends on

God. Other villagers say that a woman is blessed when she does not menstruate and claim that she is not blessed if she does menstruate because she is
not pregnant. The birth of a child is possible with the help of a midwife. The
mother-to-be is believed to be in God's hands because she hovers between
life and death. The midwife calls on others present to pray because angels are
recording the event, and heaven's gate is believed to be open to accept pleas
of participants for the successful birth of the child and to protect the life of the
mother. There is a folk belief that the mother's grave is open for forty days, a
saying that reflects the danger that she faces for that time period. At the end of
the forty-day period, mother and child are bathed, because the danger comes
to an end. On the seventh or eighth day after birth, a child is given a name,
which is marked by a sacrifice and feast.

Circumcision is a major male rite of passage in Fez, Morocco. The boy, whose
age can vary, is prepared by washing him and applying a red dye (*henna*) to his
hands and feet. A blue spot is painted on the boy's forehead to protect him
from the evil eye. Family members and friends celebrate the evening before
the actual rite by dancing. Before the actual circumcision, males form a circle
around the circumciser, and the boy is lifted over the men's heads into the
ring. During the rite, people clap their hands and sing, which tends to drown
out the painful cries of the boy. After it is cut off, the foreskin is put into a little
bag and buried. The rite concludes with a feast. At the successful conclusion
of the rite, the boy is now clean, which means that he can perform religious
duties, such as praying in a mosque. Those males that are uncircumcised incur
great shame and cannot enter paradise. The uncircumcised are derogatorily
called "foreskin" in Arabic. For some males who are uncircumcised during
their lifetime, the rite is performed after they die to enable them to enter
paradise, if God wills it.

Muslim festival observances are sometimes marked by prayer and fasting,
while some are more festive. Not all Muslim days of observance are obligatory
for everyone and not all holidays are universally celebrated. New Year's Day
is, for instance, a festive celebration similar to that in the West but devoid
of alcohol for the pious. This holiday occurs in the lunar month of Muharram, which is considered a dangerous time because of evil influences spread
by active spirits (*jinn*) and a folk belief that what happens during this month
shapes what happens the remainder of the year. Folk beliefs of Fez and Tangier
encourage a person to buy a new garment so that a person would have something to wear later in the year, or a married couple will have sexual intercourse to strengthen their sexual capacity for the entire year. At Marrakesh,
Morocco, there is a tug of war between males and females, predicting what
gender will rule over the other during the year. In Tangier, a person must
not buy a broom and bring it into a home on the first ten days of the month,
because good things will be swept from the house for an entire year, according
to Moroccan folk beliefs.

A major observance during this month of Muharram on the tenth day
is observed by Shi'a Muslims, commemorating the assassination of the

prophet's grandson Husayn and son of Ali. Shi'ites interpret his death as a self-sacrificial martyrdom. The narrative of Husayn's tragedy is recited from mosque pulpits, which often causes many to cry and groan with pain. Rows of men parade through the streets naked from the waist up, pull out their hair, and inflict sword or chain wounds upon themselves as they reenact and share in the suffering of Husayn. On the tenth day, the festival culminates with a large funeral procession that includes Husayn's coffin, with more self-inflicted wounds to make blood flow. Husayn's horse also participates in the procession, amidst singing of a martial tune. This festival marking a historical tragedy enables the faithful to vicariously participate in the martyrdom of their spiritual hero. The Shi'a Muharram observance culminates with theatrical reenactments of the martyrdom. This passion play includes a boys' choir that chants a lamentation, and another male choir dressed as women utter the wailing of females. Consisting of a loose sequence of 40 to 50 scenes, the play's final scenes depict the agonizing progression of the martyr's severed head to the court of the caliph.

Other Muslim festivals include the birthday of the prophet in the third month, believed to be an especially blessed month, which people believe has a positive effect on any child born during this time. During this week-long celebration, it is typical for mosques to be decorated with lights, fasting until sunset occurs, gifts are exchanged with children, and the prophet is eulogized. The night journey of the prophet is observed during the seventh month, which commemorates Muhammad's night journey from Mecca to the al-Aqsa Mosque in Jerusalem and his ascent to heaven and return the same night. The observance is marked by fasting, prayers, and reading of passages from the Qur'an.

The observance of the Night of Repentance on the 14th of Sha'ban marks the time when God is believed to approach the earth to call humans and to grant them forgiveness for their sins. People believe that on the 15th day, angels make an account of everyone's life (which is the reason for calling this time "the day of the copy") in a book given to the angels by God that records those destined to die during the ensuing year. An Egyptian folk belief describes a lotus tree at the boundary of paradise containing as many leaves as there are humans, which are each inscribed with the name of a single person. It is believed that the tree is shaken that night, and the leaves that fall represent those who will die that year. Besides the reciting of a special prayer, chapter 36 of the Qur'an is recited.

The festival of Ramadan represents a month of fasting during the ninth lunar month, which includes a commemoration of the time at which the revelation was first given to Muhammad. It is a common folk belief that prayers recited during the night of the 27th will be answered. Ramadan is followed on the first of the following month with the Feast of Breaking the Fast, which is a joyous festival when family and friends visit each other, people exchange gifts, and businesses and government offices are closed. The Muslim folk tradition associates this time with the festival of the dead, when families visit the tombs and graves of their relatives. A common feature of this festival is placing broken palm branches on graves.

The Feast of the Sacrifice occurs at the end of the annual pilgrimage (*hajj*) to Mecca. The sacrifice of animals and the distribution of meat are the chief features of this festival, although it is accompanied by donning new clothing, offering prayers, giving gifts, visiting relatives, and visiting cemeteries. In Fez, the blood of sacrificed animals is smeared on the hands and feet of children to protect them from swelling or chapping of their skin. Some Moroccan tribes smear blood on their stomachs to prevent indigestion or on the eyes to prevent soreness. Members of some tribes hang the animal's gall bladder inside their homes because it is considered holy. A Moroccan may dress in the skins of sacrificed animals with his face covered by a mask and beat people with the flap of the skin with the purpose of expelling illness. The strangely dressed figure is teased, mocked, and pushed about by observers. In retrospect, these festivals represent a synthesizing of Islamic elements with folk beliefs, customs, and superstitions.

Islamic Art and Material Culture

Islamic art and faith are traditionally intertwined throughout the Islamic world, just as there is no distinction between art and craft. It is believed that God can be praised and served by artistic creations. It is possible to see this expressed in religious buildings that point to divine unity upon a plane of worldly multiplicity and the dependence of this multiplicity on the one. Art originates with inspiration and wisdom that comes from God, which suggests that art is another sign of God. Providing a witness to divine unity, Islamic art expresses this unity as beauty. The stalactite (*muqarnas*) structures, decorative elements often used over doorways typical of Muslim art, suggest descent of the heavenly abode to the earth.

This more positive view of artistic creation exists alongside a more conservative and suspicious view of art in the Islamic world. Artistic expression is in tension with the revelation because art deflects attention away from revealed scripture, rendering artistic creations potential forms of idolatry. By means of their work, artists and sculptors give to the conservative mind the impression that they are imitating God. From a historical perspective, Muslim artists have circumvented the iconic or representational prohibition by portraying images as usually two-dimensional and unrealistic. And artists have also utilized abstract designs to adapt to religious attitudes.

Islamic art tends to be abstract and geometric because naturalism is avoided. This tendency is used to avoid confusing an imaginary world with the reality of God's world. The Islamic preference for abstract art is believed to free the human spirit. An artistic consequence of this thrust of Islamic art is the relatively minor role of paintings and portraitures. Paintings of human figures and animals tend to be confined to miniatures or as illustrations in manuscripts. The subjects of these miniatures are often kings and queens and scenes of their court life. The most important influence on Islamic artistic expression is the veto of representational art because there is a danger of idolatry. The Qur'an is absolutely clear that only God is a proper object of devotion (4.48). Within the context of the *hadīth* tradition, the prophet says that angels will refrain from entering a house in which there is either a picture or a dog, and another saying promises severe torment on judgment day for image makers.

With this injunction against representational forms of artistic expression, Muslim artists were pressured by the religious culture to use line and angle to create geometric designs when creating buildings to resemble crystals, associated with ice and, hence, coolness in arid climates, which tends to give a person a sense of relief from the heat. This sense of relief is increased by the use of cool colors such as various shades of blue and green. Geometric patterns are also combined with depictions of flowers, leaves, and vines. These floral and vegetation motifs also contribute to the refreshment of human senses. The weaving together of geometric designs and plant motifs suggests the rhythm of the Arabesque style.

The Qur'an emphasizes the unity and otherness of God and the transient and insubstantial nature of everything that is not divine. Since God is totally beyond the human mind and senses, this invites the artistic use of emptiness to express both the transcendence of God and His presence in all things. The veil of matter is removed by emptiness, which enables the divine light to shine through a structure like a mosque. The light that shines through structures is indicative of the certainty of divine unity and the fact that God is the light of heaven and earth. According to a prophetic saying, God initially created light, which is identical to the word of God, making light the spiritual principle that creates, orders, and liberates. To the extent that things share in the light of God, they are real, indivisible, and dependent. The interior richness of light is revealed by colors, though the light is not altered by its refraction into colors.

The noblest art form is calligraphy because it can visibly reveal and glorify the word of God. This exquisite art form also functions as the external covering for the word of God. The Muslim attitude toward writing is shaped by the Qur'an, where writing is important because it distinguishes humans from other creatures of God. The act of writing is stressed throughout the Qur'an. Two angels, for instance, sit on a person's shoulders and write down that person's misdeeds and thoughts, which are recorded in writing and used to testify for or against a person in the Book of Reckoning (69.18–19).

Calligraphy is a result of a disciplined mind, a sign of the soul, and a mark of a cultured person that helps one to recollect God. Calligraphy is an art form that is sanctioned by the Qur'an (96.3–4) and thus a human imitation of a divine act. Each letter of Arabic is believed to possess its own personality and serves as a symbol of a specific divine quality because the letters correspond to divine archetypes, based on the notion these letters are related to God as the divine scribe. The letter *alif* (1) is, for example, a vertical symbol for God's transcendence and the origin of all things because it represents the first letter of the alphabet; it is also the first letter of God's name, Allah. Arabic script is both vertical and horizontal, with the former signifying the unalterable nature of each letter and its correspondence to the permanent essence of things, whereas the latter links the letters together into a continuous flow of letters that suggests becoming. Arabic is written from right to left, which means that it flows toward the heart of the writer.

These remarks about Islamic art are indicative of artistic expression being put into service to teach fundamentals of the religion and to remind the faithful of basic theological truths. The geometric designs represent, for instance, order, whereas vegetal depictions represent vibrant growth. Geometric and vegetal designs combine to symbolically suggest a dynamic relation between certainty and development. Islamic culture has left impressive structures using these artistic motifs, such as the Dome of the Rock in Jerusalem, the Alhambra Palace in Spain, the Selimiye Mosque in Turkey, and the Taj Mahal in India.

Folk Expressions of Religion

Folk religion throughout the Islamic world is the piety of ordinary people, which is combined with local traditional forms of superstition. This popular form of faith often manifests a gap between its faith and expressions with the beliefs and practices of the official or orthodox religion. This folk form of Islam often finds more room for the expression of emotions than the orthodox tradition. The folk appropriation of Islam enables one to see that the religion is not a homogenous or unified entity because the social and religious practices are very different depending on location, even though the character of daily life proceeds from Islam. This grounding in the religion provides ordinary people stability and motivates them to conservatively hold on to long-cherished religious beliefs and practices and to resist change, because they already possess what is true and certain as guaranteed by the revelation, making Islam the best way of life because it reflects a divinely ordained pattern. Ordinary folk are also assured that they are part of a sacred history. Nonetheless, many folk beliefs and practices are not sanctioned by the revelation. This is evident by a common belief in spirits, a veneration of saints, magical uses of the Qur'an, the role of Muhammad, the mosque as a center of religious life, and folk beliefs concerning the evil eye, cursing, and dreams.

Within the popular worldview, the world is inhabited by many supra-human and normally invisible beings. With hooved feet and an ugly appearance, *shaytāns* are a class of malevolent spirits that whisper into the ears of humans to lead them astray. They oppose the will of God and use disease as a weapon to harm people. Another group of spirits that populate the folk world are *jinn*, who are normally invisible but can assume human shape and can attain paradise by following the straight path of Islam. In Morocco, *jinn* are believed to live underground but like to visit the surface of the earth, are fond of darkness, are terrified by light, and are especially active after mid-afternoon prayer. *Jinn* normally lack individual identity, although there are exceptions such as Aisha Quandisha, a woman with a beautiful face, long pendant breasts, and the legs of a goat. She enjoys seducing handsome young men. People can take prophy-lactic measures to counter *jinn* by burning candles, using salt, sacrificing, utter-ing passages from the Qur'an, and using steel and gun powder to dispel them.

The veneration of Muslim saints is a widespread phenomenon among ordi-nary members of the faithful. Saints are called friends of God. They are holders of *baraka* (blessing, holiness, power), a mysterious force that can work wonders such as miracles, which are considered blessings from God. Within Islamic his-tory, no human possessed more of it, however, than Muhammad. A particular saint has the ability to transfer *baraka* to another person by several means, such as spitting into another's mouth, having a person eat the leftover food of a saint, or drinking water in which a saint has washed his hands. Saints are distinguished from other people because they typically think only about God and are depicted as mediators of divine powers in the world. Popular narra-tives recount the supernatural powers of saints, such as being able to travel swiftly, walk on water or air, communicate with animals, disappear from sight, and perform miracles. A saint also has the ability to appear simultaneously at several places. The Sufi poet Rumi, for example, attended seventeen parties at one time and composed a different poem at each one. Barren women are espe-cially attracted to the veneration of saints because of their perceived ability to perform fertility miracles.

The Muslim folk religion exhibits some unusual ways of using the Qur'an. This holy text is generally treated with great respect, as evident when pick-ing it up and kissing it. The holy text is also not allowed to be touched by an unclean person, to be taken to an unclean place such as a bathroom, or to be taken to a place at which there is wine drinking or gambling taking place. In addition to respecting and protecting the text, there is a folk practice called "cutting the Qur'an" to determine whether or not it is expedient to make a journey, make a business transaction, accept an offer of employment, or have a surgical procedure. There is a pattern of sayings and actions to be performed before one opens the text and reads the sentence on which one's fingers stop. Based on the character of the words, the expert gives a person an answer about what that person should decide. This type of practice amounts to using the holy text in a magical and divinatory way. In addition, prayers or written portions of the Qur'an are used as talismans intended to protect people or cure them of an illness. This type of usage of the text can also be utilized maliciously. Verses 122 to 124 of the third chapter can cause an opponent's house and property to be destroyed, or verses (2.256–260) will cause the death of a victim.

In the Qur'an, the prophet Muhammad never claimed to have superhuman qualities, because he was just a mortal man, although there are passages that point to his exceptional role, such as God teaching him the Qur'an (96.3), being sent as a mercy on the world (21.107), having God's blessings on him (33.56), having a noble nature (68.4), and several verses urging people to obey God and his messenger. It is these types of references that form the bases for later veneration of Muhammad and development of legends about him.

In the popular imagination, Muhammad is depicted as the most handsome man. According to one poem, when Muhammad walked into a garden, a flower blushed in reaction to his physical beauty, a flower that is identified as a rose. Flies would not land on him because he was so pure and fragrant, and because of his purity, he did not cast a shadow. Muhammad had a special mark called the "seal of prophethood," which is identified as a fleshy protuberance or a mole the size of a pigeon's egg located between his shoulders. The popular imagination matched his exterior beauty with an equally exquisite interior by stressing his moral qualities, such as humility and kindness. He loved animals and promised paradise to a sinful woman who saved a dog from starvation. Muhammad was especially fond of cats. Because he petted the backs of cats, they never fall on their backs. Unlike ordinary men, he was free of moral depravity or any human faults.

Acts of generosity and curing illness are included in his biography. His sandals were special because they had *baraka* (holy force) and could protect a person from the evil eye. The prophet's sandals represented holy relics during the Middle Ages because it was a common folk belief that they had touched the divine throne on his night journey to heaven. In addition to pictures of his sandals, hairs of his beard became revered relics, which are reflected by the practice of taking an oath by saying "by the prophet's beard."

During his life, Muhammad did not claim to have produced any miracles, because the only necessary miracle was the Qur'an. But this did not stop the faithful from attributing miracles to him, such as creating a bird from a stone, making rain fall, performing food miracles, and healing the afflicted. Beyond his role as a producer of miracles, the folk tradition depicts him as a merciful intercessor, a gift of God's love to His servants. A powerful way for a person to ask for intercession is to implore God to bless Muhammad and his family. Finally, in the popular imagination, Muhammad is associated with light symbolism and called "light of all lights," which is connected to the legend that he did not cast a shadow. The prophet's relation to light symbolism evolved into a folk belief that he was the original light of creation, suggesting a pre-existence of his essence.

For many Muslims, the mosque is central to their religious life, and on a daily basis brings together a cross-section of social classes, with few exceptions. Worshippers attend a mosque because of its proximity to home or place of employment, or it is selected because of the reputation of its Friday sermon preacher. Since it is essential to keep the holy interior of the mosque free of pollution, certain actions and people are prohibited to attend a mosque. Because of the polluting nature of blood, menstruating women, unclean individuals, murderers, those having sexual intercourse, or those passing gas are excluded from a mosque. There is a folk belief that passing intestinal gas kills angels in the mosque. Whistling is also prohibited in a mosque because the Qur'an relates it to an idolatrous practice in Mecca before the arrival of Islam. It is a folk belief that whistling makes a mosque empty. Moreover, when outside of a mosque, a Muslim should not urinate or defecate toward the direction of Mecca.

Figure 14.2 Interior of the Blue Mosque in Istanbul. Photograph by Jake Boynton.

A common folk feature throughout the Muslim world is the role of the evil eye, which can be used to harm another either intentionally or unintentionally. In order to protect himself, a person can stretch out the five fingers of his right hand toward another person and say "Five in your eye" or "Five on your eye." This gesture is followed by a similar action using the left hand, which is intended to throw back the evil influence coming from the eye of an antagonist. It is not unusual to see large eyes painted on the sides of trucks in Pakistan to protect the driver and vehicle.

Another example of folk practice in the Muslim world is the curse, which is an intentional form of injury. It is common to curse the mother or father of the object of one's anger. The folk tradition holds that curses uttered by parents are very powerful. As a general rule, the efficacy of a curse is influenced by the guilt or innocence of the person on whom it is pronounced. A categorical type of curse represents people calling down on themselves some evil in the event that what they say is not true, whereas a conditional curse is directed against someone else, which is called "a shame upon you" because misfortune befalls people who do not do what is asked of them within the context of popular hospitality and certain social anticipations associated with it.

In addition to the popular role of cursing, dreams also play an important part in ordinary life. In Morocco, there is a common belief that the soul leaves the body during sleep, and what is seen and heard is real and not illusory. It is believed that an unpleasant dream is a punishment for some transgression, such as neglecting one's prayers. A dream can also be an admonition that something should be done, an indication of a present fact, or an indication of a future event. Thus, dreams can be omens of good or bad fortune. Folk beliefs regarding dreams often involve the opposite outcome in everyday life. If you dream that someone dies, it means that you will have a long life. Or to dream of sorrow or weeping is an augur of happiness. In order to avert an evil dream, a person can say, for example, to a stone, the following: "O God, bestow upon us its goodness and free us from its evil," which diverts the evil into the stone. The fact that some of these features contradict aspects of the Qur'anic tradition does not seem to puzzle ordinary Muslims because this is the faith that has been practiced for as long as anyone can recall. However, these beliefs and practices did not find favor with modern Islamic reformers of the modern period beginning in the eighteenth century.

Modern Islamic Reformers

By the eighteenth century, the Islamic world experienced a collective loss of power, expansion, and prosperity. These types of loss were accompanied by economic decline, undermining of a strong central authority, and military revolts and reversals. The conservatively religious minded believed that these failures could be traced to a departure from genuine Islam. Therefore, any revitalization of Islamic civilization would only come by a return to the straight path of Islam and thus needed to be based on the Qur'an.

The arguably best-known revivalist movement was the Wahhabi movement, founded by Muhammad ibn Abd al-Wahhab (1702–1792), who was appalled by many popular religious practices, such as the veneration of saints and pilgrimages to their tombs. He denounced such practices as pagan superstitions and idolatry (*shirk*) because they compromise the unity of Allah, whereas political weakness of the community was traced to moral decline. The answer to these problems was a return to Islamic practice that is based on the Qur'an. The movement combined ultra-conservative religious zeal with military action centered on a holy war on unbelievers and enemies of God. The Wahhabi forces destroyed Sufi shrines and tombs and even sacred tombs in Mecca and Medina. They also destroyed the tomb of Husayn at Karbala, a major Shi'a holy place.

The Islamic world also saw other jihadist revivalist movements such as the Sanusi movement, founded by Muhammad Ali ibn al-Sanusi (1787–1859). The so-called Grand Sanusi initiated a neo-Sufi movement that rejected tribalism because it led to political fragmentation and called for Islamic unity and solidarity. He founded the Sanusiyyah Brotherhood in Libya as a reformist and missionary movement that embraced a path of militant activism. The movement established centers or Sufi lodges that served as places of prayer and instruction and preached a message of equality, brotherhood, and peace.

In the Sudan, Muhammad Ahmad (1848–1885) founded the Mahdiyyah Movement and proclaimed himself the Mahdī (divinely guided one) in 1881. The intention of this movement was to free the Muslim community from oppression, restore true Islam, and create a just society. As the divinely appointed and inspired representative of Allah, the Mahdī represented a reenactment of the establishment of God's rule on earth as occurred in the seventh century with Muhammad and thereby created an Islamic community/state. The early victories of his forces were attributed to divine approval, guidance, and the validation of his mission. The Mahdī called for Muslim unity and purification of Islam as evident by denouncing alcohol, gambling, music, and prostitution as foreign forms of corruption introduced into the culture.

During the latter nineteenth century, movements developed in response to the external political and religio-cultural threat of colonialism, which was interpreted by Muslim leaders as evidence of a decline of Muslim power and a loss of divine favor and guidance. The leaders proclaimed a need for Islamic reform by focusing on the religious law and family because of their importance to the religion. The reformers blamed internal decline on a blind and unquestioned clinging to the past, pressed for change through a process of reinterpretation and selective adaptation of Western ideas, science, and technology, and engaged in a process of internal self-criticism.

A major nineteenth century reformer was Jamal al-Din al-Afghani (1838–1897), who advocated reclaiming reason, science, and technology, although he rejected Western secularism and the otherworldliness of popular Sufism. In turn, he preached a this-worldly Islam that utilized Western science and learning, which should not be perceived as threats to Islam. He also depicted Islam as a comprehensive way of life that included worship, law, government, and society. From al-Afghani's perspective, a true Muslim struggles to enact God's will in history to ensure success in this life and in the next life. There is also a need to reopen the door of interpretation to make Islam a relevant force in intellectual and political life.

Another renowned reformer was Muhammad Abduh (1849–1905), a disciple of al-Afghani and founder of the Salafiyya Movement, who attempted to synthesize modern Islam. He saw no inherent contradiction between religion and science, which he claimed to be complementary. He traced the reasons for Muslim decline to un-Islamic popular religious beliefs and practices, such as saint worship, belief in miracles, Sufi passivity and fatalism, and rigid legal scholasticism. In following this line of criticism, he made a distinction between Islam's inner core of unchanging truths and outer layers that were added later to the core. Abduh, who became rector of al-Azhar University, was critical of educational opportunities for women and argued that polygamy had deleterious effects on Muslim society.

The initial half of the twentieth century gave rise to neo-revivalist movements that were critical of capitalism and Marxism because they were perceived to be humanly constructed secular paths, which is alien to the divinely ordained straight path of Islam. In order to remain faithful to Allah, Muslims must reject secularism and materialism. These types of criticism were espoused by Hasan al-Banna (1906–1949), with his founding of the Muslim Brotherhood in Egypt, and the Islamic Society in India, by Mawlana Abul Ala Mawdudi (1903–1979). Like the prophet Muhammad, they wanted to establish a community of true believers by transforming society from within. These men traced Muslim social decay to political disunity, social dislocation, moral laxity, and an indifferent attitude toward religion. The atheism of Marxism and materialism of capitalism, along with its secularism and separation of church and state, were responsible for Muslim impotence. In response to these threats, these reformers called for a return to the Qur'an and the tradition (*sunna*) of the prophet, which would give them an Islamic form of government through legal reform. Mawdudi called for a theo-democracy, although he rejected a theocracy (a clergy-run state). In the later 1970s, Shi'a leaders in Iran led a revolt against the Shah and established a theocracy with some democratic elements, although the clergy retained control over the apparatus of government.

The latter part of the twentieth century witnessed the rise of jihadist movements around the Islamic world and a more violent response to Western domination. The holy war advocates use an ancient practice to justify the slaughter of innocent people to spread terror, which culminated with the destruction of the twin towers of the World Trade Center by two hijacked passenger jets on September 11, 2001. The attack resulted in the deaths of approximately 3,000 people, bringing al-Qaeda international infamy, and an American response that has resulted in the destruction of many of its leaders. Terrorism is arguably a military/political strategy of the weak, disaffected, and disenchanted members of the Muslim world. Its goal is to punish Western nations for rendering Muslim countries impotent and to eventually establish a worldwide Islamic dominance. The appropriation of the strategic use of holy war also represents the highjacking of a pious and peaceful religion for malevolent purposes. The life of Muhammad and the revelation that he received from Allah make it clear that violence merely begets more violence in a never-ending cycle of destruction. In short, terrorism is non-Qur'anic.

Religious Experience

The Islamic narrative from the time of the prophet stresses the awe and fear evoked by an all-powerful God, leaving the individual trembling and quaking in his sandals because the individual Muslim is nothing compared to almighty God, and the threat of his wrath is very real. Nonetheless, the Muslim is offered a measure of comfort because God's wrath is counter-balanced by his mercy and compassion. Allah is a radically singular and transcendent God who is wholly other than humans. But these features are counter-balanced by his felt presence, expressed in the Qur'an as God being closer to a person than his jugular vein. His presence and mercy suggests that Allah is a caring God, even though he is wholly other and is involved in historical time and space.

In addition to these types of experience, the biography of Muhammad recalls the prophet's visions, dreams, auditory experiences, and more subtle types of experiences, such as receiving a message in his heart. These various types of experience occurred within a context of urgency because the end of time was imminent along with its promise of a final judgment. It is incumbent on humans to hear the word of God from his messenger and to respond to it. Responding to God's message involves more than just listening to it, because it is essential that an individual submit to God by becoming his abject, submissive slave. From this submissive position, a person offers gratitude, obedience, generosity, and worship to God and other members of the believing community. The submissiveness of the faithful Muslim is beautifully expressed in the act of prayer, with its humble series of bowings.

If the classical tradition of Islam is based on an experience of faith and submission to God, the Sufi tradition stresses a more intense, immediate, loving, and self-negating experience of God. Although Sufis do not neglect fear of God, they experience a more loving God and existentially passing away in God, which is described as being annihilated in God in a total nullification of one's ego. From the Sufis' radical perspective, the mystic assumes the attributes of God, a position that orthodox Muslims view with suspicion and even alarm. But from the Sufi perspective, the mystic experiences abiding in God. Along with the celebration of Muslim rites and festivals, Sufism celebrates life and softens the wrathful side of God's nature, emphasizing God's mercy and compassion.

The complete surrender to God is illustrated by a Sufi literary anecdote. A whirling dervish fell into the Tigris River. He was asked if he wanted to be saved and replied no. When he was asked if he would prefer to die, he replied that he had nothing to do with willing. His responses to these questions imply complete surrender to God and trust that he will do what is best for the believer.

The Sufi tradition makes a distinction between two types of Sufis: sober and intoxicated. On the one hand, the sober figure is in control, fulfills all obligations, and completes the path. On the other hand, the intoxicated Sufi is in a state of ecstasy, during which the wine of love plays a metaphorical role for his ecstatic condition. Within the state of ecstasy, it is possible to lose consciousness for an extended length of time. But before the human soul reaches an ecstatic state, it goes through a maturing process by means of suffering. A Sufi narrative way to express the importance of suffering is to affirm that just as grape juice is purified by the process of fermenting, it eventually becomes wine.

The whirling dance of the dervishes is closely associated with ecstasy. The dance not only sets the soul free but also allows it to enter the eternal source of all movement. Sufis interpret the whirling dancing metaphorically, as a ladder to heaven and as a way to a unitive experience. The Sufi dances his way into a trance condition and loss of consciousness as the dancer exceeds himself. The dancing Sufi is a cultural cipher pointing beyond himself to something greater and whole.

As noted earlier, Islamic art and material culture serve as signs pointing to God, who inspired these cultural creations with his wisdom, whereas the folk tradition injects popular practices that often border on the unorthodox. Certainly, Sunni orthodox Muslims look askew at Shi'ite festival participants when they experience vicarious martyrdom by publically flagellating and cutting themselves with whips, knives, or swords in a reenactment of the death of Husayn.

Suggestions for Further Reading

Cragg, Kenneth and B. Marston Speight. *The House of Islam*. Third Edition. Belmont. CA: Wadsworth Publishing Company, 1988.

Denny, Frederick Mathewson. *An Introduction to Islam*. New York: Macmillan Publishing, 1985.

Donner, Fred M. *Muhammad and the Believers: At the Origins of Islam*. Cambridge: Harvard University Press, 2010.

Esposito, John L. *Islam: The Straight Path*. Third Edition. New York: Oxford University Press, 1998.

Firestone, Reuven. *Jihad: The Origin of Holy War in Islam*. New York: Oxford University Press, 1999.

Mernissi, Fatima. *Beyond the Veil: Male-Female Dynamics in Modern Muslim Society*. Bloomington: Indiana University Press, 1987.

Momen, Moojan. *An Introduction to Shi'i Islam: The History and Doctrines of Twelver Shi'ism*. New Haven: Yale University Press, 1985.

Nasr, Seyed Hossein. *Islamic Art and Spirituality*. Albany: State University of New York Press, 1987.

Peters, F.E. *The Hajj: The Muslim Pilgrimage to Mecca and the Holy Places*. Princeton: Princeton University Press, 1994.

Rahman, Fazlur. *Islam*. New York: Holt, Rinehart and Winston, 1966.

Richard, Yann. *Shi'ite Islam: Polity, Ideology, and Creed*. Trans. Antonia Nevill. Oxford: Blackwell, 1995.

Savory, M. Ed. *Introduction to Islamic Civilisation*. Cambridge: Cambridge University Press, 1976.

Schimmel, Annemarie. *And Muhammad Is His Messenger: The Veneration of the Prophet in Islamic Piety*. Chapel Hill: University of North Carolina Press, 1985.

———. *Deciphering the Signs of God: A Phenomenological Approach to Islam*. Albany: State University of New York Press, 1994.

———. *Mystical Dimensions of Islam*. Chapel Hill: University of North Carolina Press, 1973.

Smith, Jane I. *Islam in America*. New York: Columbia University Press, 1999.

Smith, Jane Edelman and Yvonne Yazbeck Haddad. *The Islamic Understanding of Death and Resurrection*. New York: Oxford University Press, 2002.

Walther, Wiebke. *Women in Islam*. Princeton: Markus Wiener Publishers, 1995.

Wikan, Unni. *Behind the Veil in Arabia: Women in Oman*. Chicago: University of Chicago Press, 1982.

15 New Age and New Religious Movements

According to the anti-Vietnam War musical *Hair* of the 1960s, the New Age is the Age of Aquarius: "When the moon is in the seventh house, and Jupiter aligns with Mars/Then peace will guide the plants, and love will steer the stars/This is the dawning of the Age of Aquarius." These utopian, romantic lyrics anticipate a soon-arriving period when the planets are favorably aligned, peace and love will reign and direct the cosmos, and a new age will succeed the old socio-political order, which is outdated and gives us nothing but suffering and pain. As the lyrics of the song suggest, the "Age of Aquarius" takes a holistic perspective, emphasizes harmony, and is counter-cultural, especially against the military-industrial complex and its basis in capitalistic economics. Before the performance of the musical *Hair*, the New Age had already arrived in America in the form of various religious movements. But before these New Age movements in America can be considered, it seems wise to place the dawning of the New Age movement into a historical context, which prompts us to consider Western esotericism and how it prepared the ground for the New Age movement and developments of other new religions.

A Brief Review of Western Esotericism

During the eighteenth and nineteenth centuries, Western esotericism was also called occultism, a term that conveys a sense of something strange, mysterious, and secret that recalls the ancient Greco-Roman mystery cults, with their secret initiation rites and restricted knowledge that was only available to members. The development of Western esotericism was influenced by thinkers such as Jacob Boehme (1575–1624), a cobbler by trade, a mystic, and theosopher, who composed books such as *The Aurora* that provoked opposition and *Mysterium Magnum*, a commentary on the book of Genesis for which he claimed divine inspiration, although most of his works were published posthumously. In his books, he referred to the *Ungrund* (abyss) as the origin of everything and as being beyond the distinction between good and evil. The *Ungrund* was identified with the Son of God, who represents light and wisdom. Boehme viewed redemption as coming by means of Christ, representing symbolically the victory of good.

Another source of influence on esotericism was Hermeticism, which traced its origin back to *Corpus Hermeticism*, a body of initiatory and revelatory texts allegedly dating back to the Greek god Hermes Trismegistus (the Greek rendition of the Egyptian god Thoth). These texts were rediscovered in the fifteenth century and originally dated sometime around the second and third centuries CE. Believers attempted to link esoteric beliefs of the Hellenistic period with the European Renaissance. The hermetic texts promoted a correspondence between the material and spiritual realms. The hermetic maxim can be summarized as: "As above, so below." This core belief helped to shape practitioners' alchemical theory and its attempt to transform base metals into something precious. Within the belief system of Hermeticism, God was associated with light. There was a unity between humans and God because humans represented a mortal God, while the heavenly God was an immortal being. Moreover, humans occupied a central place in a cosmic creative process. In addition to Hermetic speculation, esotericism was also shaped by Jewish Kabbalism, discussed in chapter 12.

In addition to the Hermetic tradition, esotericism was also influenced by Rosicrucian alchemical notions and Rosicrucians' emphasis on finding the inner meaning of a text, which they thought came in the form of pictorial symbols, numbers, and initiatory rites. The origin of the movement was associated with the appearance of a new star, which was hailed by Johannes Kepler, a famous astronomer, as foretelling the appearance of a prophet coming to establish religious unity. This unity, totality, and perfection was symbolized by the Rose and Cross, a harmony of opposites. The Rose was a symbol and synonym of the soul being drawn down to matter, a process that conferred life on the body, whereas the Cross was a symbol of totality.

Among the secret techniques that the Rosicrucians used in their spiritual arsenal, there was a kind of spiritual alchemy and theurgy (invocation of angels). According to the narrative in their text the *Fama Fraternitatis* (1614), a legendary hero named Christian Rosenkreuz, born in 1378, learned science and passed on his knowledge to others before he died in 1448. The book related that Rosicrucian doctrine rests on the notion of perfect harmony between the microcosm and macrocosm. Moreover, nature is a book about God's marvels.

Western esotericism went through a secularized phase under the influence of Emmanuel Swedenborg (1688–1772) and Franz Anton Mesmer (1734–1815). Swedenborg, an assessor in the Swedish royal mines, became a visionary reformer. From 1743 to 1745, he went through a religious crisis that triggered a series of dreams and visions, turning him away from science to religious matters. His crisis was finally resolved by a vision of Jesus, which motivated him to work on a new version of Christianity that he expressed using Neoplatonic language. Swedenborg composed the eight-volume *Heavenly Secrets*, which recounted his experiences. Moreover, he wanted to convert others to this revised Christianity and its truth and not to establish a new religion or church.

Mesmer began his career as a physician in Vienna and moved to Paris in 1778, where he became famous for his new method of treatment called "animal magnetism." Mesmer's simple discovery involved his identification of an invisible fluid that connects all parts and everything within the universe, regardless of whether it be spiritual or material. This fluid represents the universal key to health and harmony, implying that the fluid is an animated nature permeated by an occult force. This subtle physical force that permeates and connects the entire universe helps to explain illness. When the fluid is unequal in the human body, disease occurs, and recovery involves restoration of one's equilibrium. Mesmer teaches that the fluid can be channeled, stored, and conveyed by an expert to others by particular techniques. This theory implies that there is a single illness, and the mode of healing entails techniques for inducing trance states.

Mesmer and Swedenborg were important because they gave spiritualism a theoretical framework to enhance efforts to communicate with the spirits of the other world. The theories of these men were alluring for spiritualism because they promised scientific proof for the supernatural. Their theories functioned like a non-elitist folk science that could be practiced by anyone.

Swedenborg and Mesmer were followed by other occultist types of teachings by Alice Bailey (1880–1949), who was influenced by Rudolf Steiner (1861–1925), an Austro-Hungarian citizen. In order to promote a new study of humanity, Steiner established the Anthroposophical Society. Anthroposophy represented a path of knowledge with the purpose of guiding spiritual life. This knowing is individual, objective, active, loving, spiritual, and free. When he was 39 years old, he began to publically demonstrate his occult and clairvoyant abilities. During this period, he experienced Christian redemption. He believed that it was necessary for spirit to descend into matter, otherwise it could not ascend and acquire a specific form. This scenario represented an evolution of the spirit. In his thought, Christ, whose second coming will free the spirit from matter, represented a paradigm for spiritual development.

Another esoteric thinker of influence was G. I. Gurdjieff (c. 1877–1949), a native Russian, who founded the Institute for the Harmonious Development of Man in Paris in 1922. He taught that anyone could become enlightened, although unfortunately humans are unaware of this possibility, making them more akin to machines and being prisoners of their own ignorance. By using transformational methods, his institute attempted to awaken clients. In his posthumously published *All and Everything, or Beelzebub's Tales to His Grandson*, he traced the development of the universe from its origin. This project reflected his interest in the significance of human life. He saw people transforming themselves by means of self-study and experience, which he argued led to changes in human consciousness and eventually becoming liberated and immortal souls.

Edgar Cayce (1877–1945), an itinerant American psychic healer and clairvoyant, also embraced the influence of theosophy by becoming a clairvoyant giving readings to clients about their health and reincarnational status. By entering a state of sleep, Cayce could operate in the spiritual world by means of his mental powers. For those suffering from physical and/or psychological problems, he could diagnose a client's problem and prescribe a treatment. It is very natural to view this type of healing procedure as a modern form of shamanism, discussed in chapter 3.

These types of thinkers developed an occultist metaphysics, stressed millenarian expectations, taught the importance of altruistic love, and advocated service to humanity, values, and morality. Western esoteric adherents advocated the acquisition of a knowledge that saves the individual, which gives esotericism a strong experiential dimension. But if there was a single movement that strategically and decisively paved the way for the New Age movement, it was the Theosophical Society founded by Madame Helena Petrovna Blavatsky (1831–1891) and Henry Steel Olcott (1832–1907).

The Theosophical Society

Dedicated to the investigation of spiritual phenomena, the society was founded in 1875 in New York after the two main figures met at a home in the New England area characterized by supernatural phenomena. The term "theosophy" means divine wisdom, whose roots can be traced back to Neo-Platonist and gnostic traditions in the thought of the fourth-century philosopher Porphyry. Theosophy represents a revival of the *philosophia perennis* (perennial philosophy), a belief that everything was derived from an eternal, unitary principle that was essentially spiritual. This principle was manifested most dramatically by individual enlightened beings.

Olcott was an American army colonel who fought in the American Civil War and worked on a commission investigating the assassination of Abraham Lincoln. As a young man, Olcott became interested in spiritualism and investigated psychic phenomena and wrote about his findings. While working as a journalist, he met Blavatsky, a Russian émigré and spiritualist, in a farmhouse located in Vermont where he was investigating some supernatural events. He became the first president of the organization.

Arriving in America in 1873 after a divorce, Blavatsky published two major esoteric works: *Isis Unveiled* (1877), a work concerned with the occult, and *The Secret Doctrine* (1888), a work that presented a vision of the universe evolving from its original spiritual form to its present material status. The spiritual evolution included souls that were identical to the universal soul and those that were reborn, depending on their karmic condition. This book rested on three major principles: existence of one absolute reality, the appearance and disappearance of cycles of the universe, and the identity of all souls with the single universal soul. Referring to her work as "Esoteric Buddhism," she also published *The Voice of Silence* (1889), which was alleged to have been originally written in an ancient language that has never been identified. She claimed to have studied with spiritual masters in Tibet and claimed that she could communicate with these masters telepathically during her life. While in central Asia, she allegedly discovered the *Stanzas of Dzyan*, a secret text that was a product of her imagination.

Blavatsky and Olcott traveled together to India, where they established a headquarters in 1879 on the outskirts of Madras (now called Chennai), and they also went to Sri Lanka and other Asian countries. While in Sri Lanka, Olcott immersed himself in Buddhism before becoming a promoter of the religion during colonialism, and he defended the island's Buddhists from Christian missionaries. Because he was appalled by the Sinhalese ignorance of their own religion, Olcott's efforts on behalf of Buddhism culminated with his creation of a Buddhist catechism consisting of fourteen principles, a work that went through many editions, printings, and languages and was used in many Buddhist countries for the purpose of instruction.

Even though Olcott was a strong advocate for Buddhism, the major principles of the society consisted of an attempt to synthesize Buddhist and Hindu notions in a quest for core beliefs that govern all religions. Olcott and Blavatsky accepted the doctrine of karma and rebirth, the existence of astral bodies, and other types of spiritual ideas without rejecting nineteenth century science, which results in an eclectic blend of religious and occult elements. From this heterogeneous combination of ideas, Blavatsky and Olcott gave the Theosophical Society some objectives, which included the following: (1) promotion of universal brotherhood, in which there would be no distinction made between race, creed, sex, or caste; (2) investigation of inexplicable laws of nature and possibilities of human potential; (3) and encouragement of efforts to study the lessons of comparative religion, philosophy, and science. In addition to their work promoting the Theosophical Society, Blavatsky and Olcott also got involved with the Ārya Samāj, a Hindu reform movement, although they never merged their society into a single entity with it. The Theosophical Society was also involved with the Indian National Congress, a political movement that played a major role in the drive for independence.

A couple of additional important figures of the society were Annie Besant (d. 1933) and C. W. Leadbetter. Besant led the Adyar theosophists in India, adopted the cause of Indian nationalism, and played an instrumental role in establishing Central Hindu College, which later became Benares Hindu University. Leadbetter, an Englishman born in 1847, became a convert to Buddhism and was considered a gifted clairvoyant, but he fell from grace when it was discovered that he was a pedophile. His forced resignation eventually led to a schism in the organization after he was readmitted. Leadbetter discovered Jiddu Krishnamurti, a young boy and the son of an associate of the movement, and he was proclaimed to be the next World Teacher, which was equivalent to acclaiming him a messiah. This eventually led to the creation of the Order of the Star, an organization created to promote this new messiah. Krishnamurti later resigned from the society and began a lecturing and writing career.

New Age in America

Emerging from the Western esoteric movement, the New Age was not precisely an organized movement but was rather a loose affiliation of different ideas, values, lifestyles, experimentation, seeking, and personal experience. From this perspective, it represented a popular, counter-cultural reaction to two world wars, the impersonal nature of capitalism and industrialization, where people were perceived as numbers to be exploited and manipulated, the growth of bureaucracy, a general disenchantment with Western culture, static forms of religion, the influence of the scientific method and worldview, modernization, rationalization, and secularism. There was a sense that change was occurring that would lead to something positive, which was captured by the spirit of Bob Dylan's song "The times they are a-changin'." After Dylan composed the lyrics to this song and recorded the number, it became a kind of youthful anthem associated with the advent of 1960s America and the rise of the beatniks and their emphasis on freedom, expanding the boundaries of consciousness and participating with other like-minded people in happenings, be-ins, love-ins, or tribal gatherings. Many of these young people experimented with various forms of drugs, such as LSD or mescaline, in an attempt to expand their consciousness.

The New Age or "Age of Aquarius" was embraced by many as a potential spiritual and religious renewal and re-enchantment of life in America. Thus, the New Age represents the dawning of something better, contrary to the conditioning and indoctrination of the prevailing culture, which takes away one's individuality and uniqueness. There is an outer and interior spirituality at work that will spiritualize nature and the inner self, which will guide a person on her life journey to a state of liberation devoid of formal organizations. New agers are to be guided by an inner ethical voice, which makes a person responsible for what she does and becomes. The principle virtue of the New Age is freedom, along with a conviction that unity is better than diversity, although new agers embraced religious pluralism. These features of new agers give impetus to a celebratory optimism, a utopian ideal, and spiritual humanism. The New Age emphasis on individualism results in the rejection of authority and a stress on personal experience because it is important to experience the truth for oneself and not to simply learn it from a book. This enables one to verify the truth for oneself and to not have to trust what others are promoting. The individualism of new agers gives rise to a stress on self-healing of various types of diseases, which can assume economic, political, bodily, or mental forms.

The notion of the New Age is fraught with ambiguity because of its plurality of beliefs and practices and the fact that it does not fit into scholarly constructs such as a cult, sect, denomination, or church. But this ambiguity did not stop its critics and the media from labeling it a cult and as something dangerous for young people. Therefore, religious movements that were called New Age often denied this connection. Nonetheless, the term "cult" became associated with something negative and harmful. The emerging New Age religious movements did, however, have a positive attitude toward Western science, even while simultaneously stressing the pervasive presence of the divine throughout the world. New agers tended to believe that science could help explain how the spiritual operates within the world, which would help to provide a scientific basis for religion.

Even if many movements that grew out of the soil of the New Age denied such a label, these movements shared many attitudes with new agers. The New Age stress on healing and personal development provided a sympathetic audience for the Human Potential Movement, which was associated with and experimented with transpersonal psychology in an attempt to strip away the outer layers of experience and to reach a person's inner unity. While attempting to synthesize Eastern religions with Western psychology, the Human Potential Movement held that healing promotes harmony after illness causes an imbalance of the human organism. With the human mind playing an essential role, healing makes a sick person physically, mentally, and emotionally unified.

Embracing holism, the mysterious nature of the earth, and magic, the New Age gave rise to Neo-paganism, and its use of magic was intended to affirm the mystery of the earth. Neo-paganism was an effort to capture a time before the arrival of the theistic religions, during which mother earth was predominate. Neo-pagans saw the revival of ancient magic rites as a path to re-enchant the world, in which life is again meaningful. Neo-paganism adopted the New Age emphasis on this-worldliness, the unified nature of reality, and the optimistic conviction that humans can change reality.

The goddess movement and Wicca were good examples of Neo-paganism. Many dissatisfied feminists sought in the goddess movement a greater role, usually predominant, for feminine divine figures, because the prevailing major religions in America were primarily structured along patriarchal lines and denigration of the feminine gender. Wicca (which is a term derived from an Old English root meaning "to bend" or "to shape") was founded in 1939 by Gerald Gardner, a retired British civil servant, who received initiation into witchcraft by a secret coven, creating a new religion. Wiccan beliefs and rituals were based on the goddess and her male partner, the Horned God, creating binary powers of male and female deities, although the goddess permeates the cosmos because of her immanent nature. A more recent leader was Starhawk (Miriam Simos), who found her inspiration in pre-Christian sources and European folklore and myth and composed *The Spiral Dance: A Rebirth of the Ancient Religion of the Great Goddess* (1979). Wiccans worship the goddess in her three aspects as maiden, mother, and crone, with the ultimate goal of using powers to change existing circumstances.

Besides Neo-pagan types of movements, the New Age witnessed the rise of UFO (unidentified flying objects) cults and their sightings of such objects. The intelligent beings inhabiting these spaceships from distant planets represented an advanced culture that was functioning to announce the arrival of the New Age, with its promised spiritual consciousness, and to teach humans advanced forms of culture, technology, and spirituality. The movement called Heaven's Gate ended in tragedy when many members died, a group that will be discussed more fully later.

The so-called est (Erhard Seminar Training) was founded by Werner Erhard in 1971 after he achieved an enlightenment experience. His seminars were intended to enable participants to overcome their old ego by becoming detached from it and to experience what lies within the mysterious recesses of their consciousness. The influence of Eastern religions is evident with Erhard's emphasis on world rejection.

Another New Age development was the evolution of the Esalen Institute, located in Big Sur, California, which was founded by Michael Murphy (president) and Richard Price (vice-president), two psychology majors who graduated from Stanford University. The founders envisioned Esalen as a place for experimentation with respect to drugs that alter one's consciousness, meditation, and health therapies. It was important that no single solution, method, or religiosity should gain the upper hand and be singled out as the absolute correct way. It was also important to the founders that diversity rule the institute. They rejected the label of a New Age religion, although it was part of the countercultural shift that was more open to Eastern religions. From its founding, Esalen embraced human potential and valued human existence.

Esalen has been called the religion of "no religion." This astute characterization suggests that it was not part of any historical religious tradition. The institute ran seminars, weekend or longer retreats, and outreach programs in places such as San Francisco. The place was characterized by various kinds of experiments, which included nude bathing, messages, various kinds of drugs, sexual techniques with roots in the Hindu Tantric tradition, with the purpose of arousing energy within the human body, parapsychology, and Gestalt thoughts and techniques. It was important to the founders that no single idea or method should dominate and become their unique approach and message. Because of the influence of Sri Aurobindo, Hindu mystic and philosopher, on Murphy, the theory of evolution was embedded into its message. Esalen attracted many famous people over the years, such as Abraham Maslow, Wilhelm Reich, sitar musician Ravi Shankar, George Harrison of the Beatles, Joseph Campbell, author Henry Miller, and numerous Hollywood movie stars. In the 1970s, hippies used the grounds as a safe place to smoke pot and openly use different types of drugs without fear of being arrested.

New Religious Movements in America

Over the past two hundred years or more, America has given birth to numerous new religious movements, which have even included movements grounded in pre-Christian paganism, such as Wicca, Rosicrucianism, Satanism, I AM, Solar Temple, and Astartes. When discussing New Age movements, I made reference to groups related to UFO sightings and alleged teachings of space aliens, representing more advanced type of creatures who have much to teach earthlings. These groups include Heaven's Gate, Orantiax, Raelians, and the Aetherius Society. Attention has also been focused on the American Potential Movement that helped to shape movements such as Scientology, est, Silva

Mind Control, and Synaron. Some of these movements have been based on Jewish, Christian, and Muslim beliefs, such as Jews for Jesus, the Children of God, the Church of Jesus Christ of the Latter Day Saints, the Nation of Islam, Scientology, the Unification Church, and Baha'i. Jews for Jesus was, for example, a movement intended to convert Jews to Christianity, which drew the ire of the Jewish community and many Christians. The Children of God was founded, for instance, by David Brandt Berg (1919–1994) after receiving a revelation warning that California would sink into the sea because of a catastrophic earthquake. Berg and his followers wandered for eight months, with Berg becoming known as Moses David. The movement dispersed around the country, with members following a disciplined lifestyle, before it scattered around the globe because it predicted the impending collapse of America.

The Unification Church was led by the Rev. Sun Myung Moon, a South Korean minister, whose followers were called Moonies. He taught that the world was a fallen place because of Satan's seduction of Eve in paradise. And since Adam failed to achieve his divine potential, the world is being controlled by Satan. In order for world restoration and salvation to be achieved, it is absolutely necessary that a messiah lead the way. But what about Jesus? According to Moon, Jesus failed to achieve his destiny because he did not take a female consort. If Jesus failed, this can be rectified by turning to Rev. Moon, the true messiah of this age. This reasoning turns this movement into a cult centered on a single charismatic person.

In contrast to the Christian overtones of the Unification Church, the Baha'i movement represented something more inspired by Muslim faith, beginning in Iran in the nineteenth century within a Shi'ite Islamic context. The movement was founded by a man called the Bab (Arabic for "gate"), born in 1819 in Shiraz, Iran, and called the Baha'ullah (Arabic for "Glory of God"). He claimed to be the messenger/prophet for this age, following other figures such as Abraham, Moses, Zoroaster, Buddha, Jesus, and Muhammad. He angered religious authorities by claiming to be a prophet within the Muslim tradition, which represented blasphemy to orthodox Muslims, motivating them to execute him in 1850. But the termination of his life neither stopped the movement that he initiated nor the persecution by the state, although the claims of the Bab transcend Islam to include all world religions, a position that makes all religions really one. The singularity of religion is also true of God and humanity, which are basic tenets of the faith, reflecting a progressive series of revelations of the truth.

The Bab's message taught that every soul was created to know God, not only in the next, but also in this world. He envisioned a process that included manifestations of God, obedience to God's commands, and doing good deeds. The Bab's vision involved the union of all people on the earth along with their religions. He preached that everyone should work for world peace, a single world government, a single language, and the abolition of racial, national, and religious bias. His message also taught that there should be an end to slavery and to extremes of social and economic disparity and no sexual inequality.

Without intending to slight any of these new religious movements, black religious movements, Jehovah's Witnesses, Scientology, and the Mormon Church seem to deserve a more detailed treatment for their unique roles in American religious culture. Moreover, these movements represent new indigenous American religious movements.

Black Movements

In 1909, the National Association for the Advancement for Colored People (NAACP) was founded amidst a rise of racial consciousness and conflict with a revival of the practice of lynching blacks to keep them in their socially inferior status. This was also a time of the rise of Black Nationalism, inspired by the message of Marcus Garvey and his Universal Negro Improvement Association, with its message that there was a home for blacks in Ethiopia by appealing for them to return to Africa.

Unlike Garvey's message, George Baker, who was inspired by the message that all humans are divine, moved into Harlem on the island of Manhattan and changed his name to Father Divine, a flamboyant figure teaching that he was God, in 1915. In his dress and mannerisms, he flaunted his exalted status and drove around in a Rolls-Royce, an automobile symbolic of high socioeconomic status. His cult attracted both black and white followers. He was arrested and jailed in 1932 for allegedly being a public nuisance. The judge presiding over his case suddenly died, sparking speculation that the judge died for committing blasphemy against Father Divine, while even more unusual punishments awaited his critics. The Father Divine cult began to assume the appearance of a sect or church with his creation of the Peace Mission, which was intended to promote not only peace but also racial equality. He also published a newspaper that functioned as the cult's sacred scripture. Father Divine endeared himself to local people in Harlem by establishing social programs that provided free food for the homeless and other services.

In contrast to the cult surrounding Father Divine, the Black Muslim Movement arose with the work of Timothy Drew (Noble Drew Ali), who claimed to be the final prophet of his version of a heterodox Islam. Drew was influenced by the Muslim tradition and Freemasonry, which prompted him to reject white Western culture. In 1913, he established the Moorish Science Temple (MST) in Newark, New Jersey. Drew's work proved to be the herald of an even wider religious turning to Islam for inspiration by other black leaders.

During the 1930s in Detroit, Wallace Ford, who would reject his prior slave name for Wallace Ford Muhammad, used the Bible to help blacks raised and shaped by this book to make the transition to the Qur'an. Claiming to be a representative from the holy city of Mecca, Ford used his charismatic skills to teach that his black version of Islam was intended to liberate blacks from white oppression. His anti-white message struck a chord with some blacks and enabled them to find a new identity by adopting new names to replace their former slave names. Ford preached a message of liberation from oppression, giving his religious message a strong political, anti-white racial, and anti-cultural impetus.

In 1934, Ford was followed by Elijah Muhammad, who was influenced by elements from the Jehovah's Witness, Freemasonry, and Baptist apocalyptic notions that he incorporated into his message. He would later be accused of sexual improprieties and financial malfeasance by those led by Malcolm X, who was killed while preaching at a mosque by those following Elijah Muhammad. Before his life was terminated, Malcolm X was moving away from his anti-white message to a more tolerant and inclusive message shaped by his pilgrimage to Mecca, where he witnessed Muslims with blue eyes, blond hair, and white skin intermingling comfortably with people from the Middle East and Africa within a single brotherhood of faith.

In past centuries, white slave traders forcibly transported captured black African natives to places such as the Caribbean, the Americas, and Europe to meet the demand for cheap labor. As their days of enslavement grew long, enslaved Africans developed a nostalgia for their homeland. In the mind of these slaves, Africa evolved from a wishful nostalgia into a sacred, promised land characterized by peace and goodness. These types of sentiments lead to the emergence of back-to-Africa movements. This wish to return to Africa and to be free again was influenced by black thinkers such as Edward Wilmer Blyden (1832–1912), who attempted to instill pride in being black and also stressed returning to Africa. This message was echoed by Marcus Garvey (1889–1940). In addition to stressing black pride and a return to Africa, Garvey espoused an even more prophetic message by preaching about the coming of a black king and redeemer.

During November of 1930, the Negus of Ethiopia crowned a new king, who was named Ras (prince) Tafari (creator) Makomen. This new king declared himself a member of the lineage of King Solomon of ancient Judaism. In addition to his royal name, the king added another name: Haile Selassie I (Might of the Trinity). Many followers of the king accepted him as the messiah.

On the island nation of Jamaica, Leonard Howell, a Jamaican native, called attention to a passage in the book of Revelation that prophesied that Africans would be freed from oppressive white domination and led back to Africa, specifically to the land of Ethiopia, which became a symbol of Africa. During the 1950s in Jamaica, the Rastafarian movement began to spread quickly throughout the island because it captured the imagination of black residents with its message of black superiority, destruction of the white oppressors, and a return to the paradise offered by Africa, a land of peace and justice. The movement also promised the dawn of a new age of peace and love. With more liberal immigration regulations passed in America in the 1960s, Jamaicans transported their ideas to American cities, where the movement became associated with popular culture and the reggae music of entertainers like Bob Marley.

According to Rastafarian thought, the divine is located with oneself, implying that a person must turn inward to known the truth. A follower is assisted in her quest by the sacramental smoking of ganja (marijuana). This practice is grounded in passages from Revelation (22:2) that allude to the leaves of the tree of life that heals nations. Ganja is believed to be able to heal a person both physically and spirituality. Instead of engaging in something illegal, Rastafarians claim that they are living naturally, according to the laws of nature, by smoking ganja. In addition to being their sacrament, ganja is a source of inspiration for a smoker.

Besides smoking ganja, many Rastafarian members are recognized by their long dreadlocks, which are compared to the mane of a lion, a symbol of strength, vitality, superiority, and royalty. This practice is grounded in the Nazirite vow to not cut one's hair. This practice recalls the biblical figure of Samson and his hair being the source of his strength. At the very least, the dreadlocks of Rastas set them apart from the rest of society. Overall, Rastafarianism represents a millennial type of religious movement because it looks forward to an apocalyptic end of the current stage of history. At the end of time, there will occur a divine judgment of white people for their sinful ways and oppression of blacks. There is, however, considerable latitude among Rastafarian groups about doctrine, organization, and ritual. Therefore, it is a religious movement that is devoid of formal practices, symbols, or creeds.

Jehovah's Witnesses

Another indigenous American denomination is the Jehovah's Witnesses, which is officially called the Watchtower Bible and Tract Society. Through the influence of Adventist thought, Charles Taze Russell believed in the imminent end of the world. In 1879, he founded the newspaper *The Watch Tower* for what he established as the Watch Tower Bible Society. According to Russell, God begot two sons, Logos or Christ and Lucifer. Russell rejected the existence of hell and the doctrine of the Trinity, although he taught the reality of the resurrection of the human body at the Last Judgment. Along with some associates, Russell was arrested for his political opinions and convicted of violation of the Espionage Act.

Russell died in 1916 and was succeeded by Judge J. F. Rutherford, who turned his original Bible Student Movement into the Jehovah's Witnesses after 1919. The name for the movement is derived from the four consonants of God's Hebrew name rendered into English from Isaiah 43:12. The church members adopted a pacifist position during World War I, rejected oaths of allegiance, refused to salute the national flag, and decided not to stand for the national anthem. They also published literature advocating resistance to induction into the armed forces and making antiwar statements. Under the Sedition Act of 1918, their leaders were arrested. Jehovah's Witnesses congregate in what they call Kingdom Halls and not churches. They practice an aggressive kind of door-to-door evangelism by dispensing their literature and spreading the good news of the scriptures. They believe that they live during a marginal time, looking forward to the thousand-year reign of Christ on earth. They also envision separating themselves from the remainder of society in order to live in a theocracy, a community being ruled directly by God.

Because of their beliefs, the Jehovah's Witnesses are opposed to blood transfusions because of the biblical prohibition pertaining to eating blood. Being true to its roots, the movement continues its intensive study of the Bible by means of its question-and-answer method. At the same time, Bible study is guided by the *Watch Tower* literature that the church gives free to others as a form of evangelism. In retrospect, the Jehovah's Witnesses have forced American courts and the general public to confront the implications of freedom of religion and the separation of church and state in the Constitution.

The Mormon Church

The largest apocalyptic denomination in America is the Church of Jesus Christ of Latter-day Saints, which was founded by Joseph Smith (1805–44), a Vermont farmer who was promised a new revelation from God and Jesus. Smith received a message that other religions had strayed from the truth and none of them represented the truth. In 1827, he received a second vision of the Angel Moroni, who informed Smith about a secret history of early inhabitants of America written on gold plates. This was the *Book of Mormon*, an eclectic combination of Arminian thought that stresses the physicality of Jesus and God, evangelism, Pentecostal spirit, and Adventist aspects of Christianity. Mormons reject the doctrines of the trinity and original sin and hold that salvation comes from a combination of faith and good works. They also believe that there are degrees of heaven, and those who are truly exemplary can attain the status of gods. From the Mormon perspective, there has existed a continuous revelation, which allows the leadership flexibility with issues that do not appear in scripture. The book depicts America as the site of the original Garden of Eden and says that the promised City of Zion will be located on the American continent. The book was written in a secret script, but Smith was given help to assist with the translation.

Early persecution drove the group westward to Illinois, onward to Missouri, and eventually to Salt Lake City in Utah. Smith and his brother were arrested in Carthage, Illinois, and murdered by a mob while in jail. Smith's death led to a split in the movement when his widow and son disagreed with Brigham Young. The mother and son formed the Reorganized Church of Christ of Latter Day Saints and remained in Illinois, while Brigham Young trekked to Utah with others of the movement. A curious aspect of Mormonism is plural marriage. What were called celestial marriages, which implied for an eternity and never to be broken by divorce, were revealed to the membership by Brigham Young, nine years after Smith revealed the doctrine to the council of apostles in 1843. By some estimates, Smith had around 40 wives, and Young had over 50 of them. This social practice was presented as part of a new covenant with God. The practice of polygamy not only set Mormonism apart from other forms of Christianity in America, but it ignited virulent criticism of the religion by other Americans. Because of government pressure, the practice of polygamy was abandoned in 1890 as a condition of statehood for Utah.

Church of Scientology

An American religious phenomenon that has received negative publicity on occasion because of its beliefs about health and faith was founded by Mary Baker Eddy (1821–1910), who was also considered its prophet, after publishing *Science and Health*, a book that has gone through 400 editions. During her life, Eddy would change parts of the book each year. Eddy was inspired and cured of serious back pain while reading about a healing made by Jesus in the Gospel of Matthew (9:1–8). According to her theory in the book, reality is a unified whole, although matter does not exist because it is a product of erroneous belief. The spirit transcends gender distinctions, with each person being a reflection of the divine spirit. This means that humans are immortal and spiritual beings, who are born but do not die. For Eddy, it is essential for people to become aware of this. The path to awareness is combined with the road to health. In conclusion, sickness and death are illusions. When someone does become ill, that person is urged to rely on the power of God to be cured through the power of prayer. Rather than seeking converts through missionary activity, the movement invites people to make use of their reading rooms. The movement is known through its publication of the *Christian Science Monitor* newspaper, a highly respected national publication.

Eddy proved to be a controversial figure after she denied the virgin birth of Jesus, his miracles, the need for the Atonement, and the resurrection of Christ. Since there is no such thing as sin, there is no need for redemption. Moreover, she taught that Jesus' death was nothing more than an illusion. These types of teachings certainly did not endear her to Christians of various kinds. Not only did her church demonstrate rigid intolerance of dissent or criticism, she made two further provocative claims: that her own book surpassed the Bible and that she had divine status. In fact, she told some followers that she was the woman clothed by the sun in the Book of Revelation. Speaking for many Americans, Mark Twain, a famous American author and humorous, portrayed her as a power-hungry religious dictator.

The Coming of Eastern Religions

A final group of new religious movements involved the arrival of Eastern religious traditions to America, a series of movements prepared to be tolerated and accepted because of the work of the Theosophical Society and the occurrence of the World Parliament of Religions in conjunction with the 1890 World's Fair in Chicago, where representatives of many of the world's religions exchanged ideas and shared their perspectives with the audience. Numerous Eastern religions established themselves with various degrees of success, such as Soka Gakkai and Zen Buddhism, along with meditative and devotional versions of Buddhism from Sri Lanka, India, and Tibet. With its numerous missionary-inclined religions, India was to contribute the largest number of new religions, including Self-Realization Fellowship, Krishna Consciousness, Brahma Kumaras, Divine Light Mission of Guru Maharaj Ji, Osho Movement of Bhagwan Shree Rajneesh, and Transcendental Meditation.

Guru-centric Hindu Movements

The Self-Realization Fellowship was founded by Yogananda (1890–1952) after his arrival in America. He was born into an upper caste family of eight children in northeastern India. At the age of 8 years old, while suffering from cholera, he had a religious vision of a blinding light that enveloped his entire body as he looked at a photograph of a holy man named Lahiri Mahasaya, which cured him of his disease. He graduated from Serampore College and later traveled to Boston in 1920 to attend a conference sponsored by the Unitarian Church, staying after the conference to teach yoga to interested Americans. He called yoga "the science of religion" because science and religion shared a conviction that all views should be tested for authenticity by an experiment or experience. Thus, he emphasized self-realization rather than god-realization or absorption in some higher reality.

He eventually created the Realization Fellowship in California in 1925, and a couple of decades later published his *Autobiography of a Yogi* in 1946, which continues to be reprinted and sold. In this autobiography, Yogananda recalls some of his powers acquired by practicing yoga, such as defeating a tiger with only his bare hands, receiving telepathic messages from his former teacher, and healing powers. His message implies that anyone can acquire such powers, even though one must move beyond acquired power to one's final goal of self-realization. Yogananda's stress on personal experience found a positive reception from many Americans. His organization later developed a mail-order course consisting of 180 lessons intended for practice at home.

Guru Maharaj Ji was very young when he arrived in America in 1971 and introduced to America his Divine Light Mission. At the age of 8, he succeeded his deceased father in 1966, although early in his career, his mother and eldest brother led the mission, a loosely and flexibly organized religious movement. This organizational arrangement and the level of maturity of Maharaj led to a split in the organization. A factor contributing to the split was Maharaj's rejection of an arranged marriage, and his marriage to an American follower. In the 1980s, the Divine Light Mission changed its name to Elan Vital, an apparent attempt to free itself from any specific religio-cultural accretions. When he initially came to America, he became a media darling because of his boyish playfulness and pranks. He did not seem to be a stereotypical staid Hindu holy man.

Maharaj Ji's message to followers was to turn within themselves to discover the truth, along with contentment and joy. The goal was knowledge that can be gained by anyone, although the guru was the central, inspiring figure. This guru-centric movement dispensed with the normal trappings of a religion, such as doctrines, ritual, scriptures, and observance of sacred days or places. Following initiation by a guru or someone appointed by him, followers chanted the praises of God, listened to religious discourses, and sought knowledge that led to God realization. Within the movement, adherents are called "premies" (lovers of God). There is a stress on the necessity for a vegetarian diet, rejecting drugs, and abstaining from alcohol consumption. The movement insisted that previous great religious leaders had basically taught the same message: that knowledge based on meditation techniques was the key to liberation.

The Osho Movement of Bhagwan Shree Rajneesh (Osho) was another guru-centric New Religious Movement. Rajneesh was born Rajneesh Chandra Mohan (1931–1990) in India. He was originally a professor of philosophy at Jabalpur University, but he retired from teaching to become a guru in 1966. His flamboyant rhetorical skills and procreative views about sex and politics gained him attention at first in Bombay (now Mumbai) and eventually the West. At Poona, he established a center (ashram) and changed his name in 1972 to Bhagwan Shree Rajneesh (only later to change it to simply Osho). In 1981, he established a community in a small town in Oregon that was renamed Rajneeshpuram. At this location, followers worked long hours but would take a break and stand by and watch as Osho drove past in one of his cars from a fleet of Rolls-Royces. The work of followers was promoted as a form of meditation with the intention of creating a Buddhafield for the creation of a new human being. His utopian community in Oregon came to an end when he was arrested on charges of tax evasion, embezzlement, wire-tapping, and violation of immigration laws. A few of his primary administrators were arrested, but Osho was deported. On his return to Poona, he changed his name to Osho and continued his movement on a more modest scale. Osho was believed to be an enlightened master by his followers, and he also personally admitted to having attained enlightenment.

Before an adherent could enter the path to enlightenment, it was necessary to be initiated. The path was open to everyone regardless of gender, age, or nationality. In addition to initiation, followers had to change their names, don orange robes, wear a locket containing Osho's picture around their necks, and meditate at least once a day. The garb and lifestyle of followers evoked images of ascetic figures to external observers. Contrary to the traditional Indian ascetic's renunciation of the world and material life, Osho's ascetics were life-affirming. Osho summarized his attitude by advocating the three L's: life, love, and laughter. His basic religious perspective was formed by Tantra and its teaching about sexuality, which he taught was to be enjoyed and used as an element on the path to enlightenment.

Osho's guru-centric movement embraced the traditional Hindu practice of *darshan*, an opportunity for an adherent to see god, which became a time for celebration, using live music, singing, and dancing. This was practiced to create ecstatic states among followers, with the purpose of giving them a glimpse of enlightenment. In retrospect, the promotion of Tantric teachings has important consequences for females of the group because they are spiritually superior to males, because it is easier for women to surrender to a guru due to their possession of intuition, receptivity, and devotion. To many outsiders, the use of sexual techniques seemed scandalous. Nonetheless, Osho combined yogic meditation, Hindu devotional practices, and sexual techniques to create his own religious synthesis. Not all religious imports from India were strictly guru-centric, because there were some Hindu religious missions that represented other styles of Hinduism, such as devotionalism. Krishna Consciousness and the Brahma Kumaris are a couple of good examples of these types of Hinduism.

Krishna Consciousness Movement

Popularly known as the Hare Krishna Movement and publically visible in towns, city streets, college campuses, and airports, capturing public attention by their distinctive Indian dress, shaved male heads, singing, chanting, and musical instruments, the movement is also known as The International Society for Krishna Consciousness (ISKCON), with its roots deeply in medieval Hindu devotional religion directed to the deity Krishna, a key figure as the companion and chariot driver for the warrior Arjuna in the *Bhagavad Gita* and the later ninth century *Bhagavada Purāṇa*, which relates the incarnated life of the deity in book ten.

As a follower of Chaitanya in Bengal, Bhaktisiddhanta Saraswati established the Gaudiya Math, a missionary organization intended to spread the teachings of Chaitanya and the chanting of the Hare Krishna mantra. Before Saraswati died, he directed his disciple A. C. Bhaktivedānta Swami Prabupada (1896–1977) to take the movement to the West. Arriving in New York City in 1965 without any money, he sat in Tompkins Square Park and began to chant. Becoming a fixture in the hippie culture of the East Village, the 70-year-old guru began to attract a small following, which eventually expanded into a major international movement. With the death of Prabupada in 1977, disaffection and disillusionment arose among his followers, which gave rise to disputes and power grabs among the eleven surviving gurus. The 1980s marked a reorganization of its leadership. But the 1990s witnessed a scandal over physical and sexual abuse of children of members by their teachers, including its deceased leader, which led to further polarization among different factions. Diaspora Hindus have more recently injected support for the movement because they view the movement as a representative of genuine Hinduism, as in India.

The ISKCON movement, with its roots in ancient India and more precisely the sixteenth-century Indian saint/incarnation named Chaitanya, who inspired what became Gaudiya Vaishnavism, was a monotheistic organization focusing on Krishna as the sole, true divine figure within the overall religio-cultural context of polytheism. In the *Bhagavad Gītā*, Krishna instructed the warrior Arjuna that a person could defeat the binding effects of karma by thinking only of God at the point of death, a practice that would beneficially alter a dying person's chances for a better rebirth or birth in paradise. ISKCON teaches that the human soul gains Krishna consciousness by returning to the Godhead, Krishna. The path requires faith and physical commitments that entail chanting the name of Krishna daily, which is called the great mantra, rendering a chanter ideally full of Krishna consciousness.

This apparently simple and easy form of practice is a bit deceptive because it presupposes an austere lifestyle for adherents. All devotees must renounce all possessions and enter a temple complex. Members must daily apply sectarian markings on their foreheads in order to identify them as devotees of Krishna. Males must shave their heads, whereas women grow long hair, tie it together in long braids, and wear saris like women in India. A typical member's day begins at 4:00 a.m. with devotional chanting, dancing, and mantra meditation. A member lives his life according to four principles: nonviolence, no gambling, no intoxicants, and no illicit sex. In addition, members are instructed to avoid alcohol, tobacco, coffee, and tea. Thus, the movement synthesizes moral, devotional, meditative, and ascetic elements from the Hindu religious tradition.

Brahma Kumaris Movement

In 1936 in the city of Hyderabad, Lekraj Khubchand, a wealthy diamond dealer, began to have visions that he interpreted as gifts from God urging him to create a new world and serve as God's instrument to bring this goal into being. These visions of Vishnu were blissful experiences and taught Khubchand, for instance, about the death of his uncle by enabling him to witness the life energies and soul leaving the deceased's body, serving as a lesson that the soul is immortal, while the body is not. From these personal visions, Khubchand (also known as Dada and Brahman Baba) developed a small community of family, friends, and neighbors that held its regular meetings (*satsangs*) at his home, where he shared his visions in the form of pious messages in the form of songs, which functioned in part as the sacred literature of the community, along with the *Bhagavad Gītā*. From this modest origin, the community developed into a world-wide movement. As the community evolved and its message was spread in India, it encountered local opposition, which caused it to move to other locations.

Besides its devotional nature and emphasis on meditation, the movement embodied two unique features from the perspective of the author: the assumption of a leadership role by various capable women and the necessity of celibacy for everyone, although it is possible for a couple to be married within a celibate arrangement. Another feature already mentioned is the *murli*, a term meaning "flute," especially identified with the musical instrument of Krishna, forming daily messages of the founder read publicly at centers every day. If the daily *murlis* were the internal aspect of the movement, the external and visible aspects were expressed by establishing a high school, university, and hospital.

The movement was opposed and persecuted by other Indians because of three factors: (1) its sudden appearance; (2) a rift that developed because of its different interpretation of the end of the world and coming golden age on earth, necessitating a movement from body-consciousness to soul-consciousness, and insisting that all souls were of the Brahmin caste, even though all embodied humans became Shudras (members of the fourth caste) in the final age; (3) a perception by outsiders that the leadership roles played by women within the movement and its injunction about celibacy, an embracing of purity from the perspective of the members, were threats to the orthodox religious culture.

The Brahma Kumaris affirm a faith-based movement, with yoga added to the devotional core nature of the religion. Because of his importance for the origin of the movement and his manifest holiness during his life, Brahma Baba receives devotional attention. As a general rule, the rituals of the religion are borrowed from the prevailing Hindu tradition, while its ethics stress peace and nonviolence. This scenario suggests that normative theological beliefs are not germane to the religion, although the soul and its role are crucial for a follower. And the overall purpose of yoga is to cultivate God consciousness, whereas the donning of white clothing in public signifies purity.

Transcendental Meditation

Beginning as a method discovered by Maharishi Mahesh Yogi, Transcendental Meditation (acronym: TM) became an international movement that was presented as a scientific response and practical remedy to the various problems of modern life. This impetus was stressed even more when its founder and teachers denied that the movement was a religion. Instead, they argued that it was an easy technique that could be mastered by anyone. By using this method, a person could overcome ordinary problems like alleviating mental and emotional stress and reducing high blood pressure and could produce relaxation, gain greater physical energy and mental clarity, and help achieve more advanced stages of consciousness. In spite of its many modern benefits, this new method of yoga claimed to be part of an ancient Hindu spiritual lineage.

Maharishi Mahesh Yogi, who was born Mahesh Prasad Varma on October 18, 1911, in Uttar Kashi, traced his spiritual heritage to the great Advaita Vedānta thinker Sankara (c. 788–820) and beyond him to ancient Vedic literature. Maharishi studied for fourteen years with Swami Brahmananda Saraswati at the Jyotimath, located high in the Himalayan mountain range of India, although he was never appointed successor to his own teacher. Before his student apprenticeship, Maharishi earned a college-level degree in physics and mathematics at Allahabad University. His educational background helps to partially explain his tendency to wrap his message in scientific jargon and to stress the scientific advantages of his method. The Science of Creative Intelligence (SCI) is, for instance, the official name of his belief system, which is conceived as dynamic due to its ever-expanding and increasing nature.

The use of scientific language to convey a religious message accomplishes at least two objectives: (1) It gives the belief system legitimacy; (2) it forms a cognitive connection to the contemporary Western worldview, which is dominated by science. Transcendental Meditation operates from the basic presupposition that there is a compatibility between Advaita Vedānta, the Vedas, and Western science. Since 1988, Transcendental Meditation has, for instance, intensively worked to demonstrate the parallels between quantum physics and transcendental meditation.

Maharishi arrived in America in 1959 and lectured on yoga in San Francisco, with additional trips to Los Angeles, New York, London, and Germany. When Maharishi initially arrived, he stated at a press conference his rationale for coming to America. He confessed that he had learned a secret, swift, deep form of meditation that he was motivated to share now with the world for the spiritual regeneration of its inhabitants. A few years later, he established the Spiritual Regeneration Movement of Great Britain, located in northern London. In 1975, Maharishi announced the "Dawn of the Age of Enlightenment." This bold and optimistic pronouncement suggested the realization of the commencement of a period during which humans can reach their fullest potential, which will be characterized by boundless happiness, harmony, peace, and personal fulfillment. This new dawn will also represent a period when science will verify and validate the teachings of the Maharishi. Moreover, even those who did not mediate would enjoy the benefits of this new age. The Maharishi took this message on tour to various countries. The impetus for such millennial hope continued in July 1985, when he created the Taste of Utopia Assembly, which was staged in several nations. The purpose of this organization was to unite Vedic wisdom and the practice of the TM-Sidhi program. Their fusion would usher into existence a utopian age of peace and prosperity. This vision represented a fuller expression of a utopian hope embodied within the movement from its earliest moments.

His initial movement began as the Spiritual Regeneration Movement, which was later to become the adult branch of the movement. The other wing of the movement was named the Students International Meditation Society (SIMS), which was established in 1964 in Germany. An early emphasis of the movement focused on its mission to college campuses, which was given a huge impetus in the mid-1960s when the British rock group the Beatles studied with the Maharishi in India. This event generated worldwide publicity for his movement. After his estrangement from the Beatles, the Maharishi initiated, instructed, and toured with the Beach Boys. Maharishi used his celebrity status with members of popular culture to endear himself with the youth culture. By the 1970s, student centers could be found at over a thousand campuses. The movement estimated that 1.5 million people had practiced transcendental meditation with a teacher. The college campus focus of the movement culminated with the establishment of Maharishi International University in Fairfield, Iowa, in 1974 on the campus of the bankrupted Parsons College.

Pushing the margins of science, Maharishi established the Maharishi European Research University in 1975 at two lakeside hotels on Lake Lucerne in Switzerland. The purpose of the university was to research the effects of transcendental meditation and to determine the existence of higher states of consciousness. During the following year, Maharishi envisioned his own world government, with the ancient Indian Vedas as the basis of its constitution. He appointed ministers to various positions with titles like the Development of Consciousness, Prosperity and Fulfillment, and Health and Immortality. During the 1980s, Maharishi began a program called TM-Sidhi, with the purpose of teaching students to achieve yogic powers like the ability to fly or levitate. There was a public demonstration before 120 journalists in Washington, DC, on July 9, 1986, which did not correspond with the media hype for the event and resulted in media ridicule of the movement.

The meditative technique of the Maharishi is grounded in a neo-Vedānta metaphysical philosophy, in which an unchanging reality is opposed to an ever-changing phenomenal world, in a book titled *Science of Being and Art of Living: Transcendental Meditation*, which expresses his basic philosophical position. This reality is equated with Being, which represents a state of pure existence that is omnipresent, unmanifested, and transcendental. Not only is Being beyond time, space, causation and ever-changing phenomena, it remains unrecognized by human beings because their minds do not realize their essential identity with Being, because minds are captive to the outward-projecting senses. The essential nature of Being is further identified with absolute blissful consciousness, which radiates from Being. Maharishi compares Being to the ocean, upon which are many waves, likened to the field of continually changing phenomena. What is really important for Maharishi is for human beings to realize Being, because without this realization a person's life is without foundation, meaningless, and fruitless. However, a person is capable of having a direct experience of Being, which is possible by means of transcendental meditation.

This form of meditation is intimately connected to a person's breath (*prāna*), which is an expression of Being in the sense that it represents a tendency of the unmanifested to reveal itself. The breath represents the latent power of Being within a person. As the nature of Being, breath plays a role as the motivating force of creation and evolution. The breath can be harnessed and used to help the mind of a person realize Being directly. This is accomplished by transcendental meditation, which enables a person to extricate himself from a state of relative experience, transcend ordinary thinking, and gain the permanent state of Being. This means that a particular mind loses its individuality and becomes a cosmic mind, omnipresent, and attains a pure and eternal mode of existence.

Before achieving this cosmic state of mind, the human mind is compared to a seed that produces a tree. What this analogy attempts to show is the interdependent nature of the mind and karma (action). It is impossible for action to occur without a mind. In turn, it is karma that produces the mind, which in turn creates more karma. This suggests that karma owes its existence to the mind and, in turn, creates the mind. By means of karma, the original pure consciousness of Being is transformed into a conscious mind. If karma represents what is temporary and perishable, Being is the exact opposite of it

516 New Age and New Religious Movements

because it represents eternal unity, whereas karma creates diversity within the unity of Being.

Within the context of this metaphysical edifice, the technique of transcendental meditation involves saturating the mind with Being by harnessing one's breath and making it harmonious with the rhythm of nature and cosmic life. Maharishi emphasizes the naturalness of his technique. Moreover, the technique is a simple, easy, and direct way to develop one's mental capabilities and latent potentialities. Unlike ancient ascetic traditions of India, it is not necessary to renounce the world or withdraw from one's family. Maharishi's ascetic practice can be performed within the context of the ordinary activities of the world. It is even unnecessary to believe in the effectiveness of the technique. What is important is the correct practice of the technique.

Instruction in the technique of meditation stresses that it is an easy and natural process. Students are instructed to devote twenty minutes each day to practice that is ideally performed in the morning and early evening. At the beginning stage, a student does not have to be convinced that the method will work. What is important is the correct practice. If a student performs the technique properly, positive results will follow automatically. The proper technique involves seven steps. The initial step involves attending an introductory lecture that is intended to prepare a person for what is to follow. The theory of transcendental meditation is given in the second step, with a preparatory talk. The third step involves an interview with the teacher, at which time a student is given a scared mantra (repetitive formula) that is personally fitted to a person, which one is not to reveal to others. By focusing on the mantra, a person is able to concentrate one's attention on it. The final steps involve periodic verification and validation of a person's experiences by returning to and checking with a teacher. Maharishi identifies seven levels of consciousness, with the final state culminating in a state of unity. The fifth state represents cosmic consciousness, which represents an awareness of Being even after the cessation of meditation, whereas the fourth stage stands for the transcendental state, which is a state of pure consciousness described as beyond the previous state of waking, dream, and deep sleep consciousness. The sixth state is called God consciousness. Traditional yogic postures are unnecessary. A person can simply sit upright and comfortably on a chair with eyes closed. The movement stresses that anyone can learn this simple, effortless, and easy mental technique.

This yogic technique and neo-Vedānta metaphysical edifice does not represent a form of Hinduism from the perspective of the founder. In fact, Transcendental Meditation is not a religion at all, according to leaders. By de-emphasizing its Hindu roots, stressing its non-religious nature, and focusing on the scientifically demonstrable value of the technique, Transcendental Meditation created a successful message that was embraced by many spiritual seekers and a scientifically minded audience. The movement used scientific means to demonstrate how the technique calmed the mind, increased awareness, relaxed the body, and lowered metabolism.

As Transcendental Meditation grew in the awareness of ordinary citizens, there was a tendency to associate it with New Age religion. During the 1960s and 1970s, people were experimenting with drugs like LSD in order to induce altered states of consciousness and bliss. Within the context of the drug culture and New Age religions, Transcendental Meditation appeared to ordinary people to be offering similar results. Thus, numerous practitioners of various forms of New Age religion and former drug experimenters were attracted to the Transcendental Meditation movement because of its apparent kinship with these other forms of spiritual experimentation. Besides such perceived forms of kinship among TM, drug culture, and New Age spirituality, Transcendental Meditation shared with New Age movements a holistic view of life. This was a form of thinking and living that attempted to extricate itself from all forms of dualism, like that of the dichotomy between body and mind. The Transcendental Meditation movement also intersected with New Age spiritualties with respect to organic and vegetarian dietary practices and alternative forms of medicine. In 1985, Maharishi launched, for instance, the "World Plan for Perfect Health" along with a World Center for Ayurveda medicine.

The Transcendental Meditation movement promised both a transformation of the individual and society by means of an expansion of consciousness to unimagined states. In short, Transcendental Meditation aimed to create a perfect society inhabited by perfect individuals. The movement offered a realized eschatology for a transformed mode of living in the present moment that promised a horizon of material economic well-being, psychological and somatic healing, good health, peace, and mental comfort.

In retrospect, the Transcendental Meditation movement has attracted disenfranchised, disaffected, and disenchanted seekers looking for spiritual experience, healing, community, a general sense of well-being, and happiness because of the decline of community, the rise of impersonal organizations, alienation, fragmentation of life, secularism, competing multicultural messages, and religious pluralism. Transcendental Meditation offered a personal and private form of spirituality for many disenchanted seekers. After 1970, it was introduced to business people and educators after making gains among college students and countercultural youth.

Reaction to New Religious Movements and Violence

During the historical period from 1976 to 1981, there was an anti-cult reaction in America. Critics leveled charges of mind control and brainwashing against the cults and the new religious movements that seemed to be cults. Desperate parents had their sons and daughters kidnapped from the cults and had them deprogramed by so-called experts charging fees for their expertise and services. The basic assumption was that the children were either sick or being mentally controlled and manipulated. After this initial emotional storm, so-called cults and new religious movements began to lose their appeal and started stagnating, and some began to actually disband or disintegrate. Some of the new religious movements succumbed to violence, which attracted widespread media attention. The rise of violence further tainted all cults and new religious movements. The violence associated with new religious movements can be illustrated by reviewing the following five cases: the Peoples Temple; Branch Davidians; the Solar Temple; Heaven's Gate; and Aum Shinrikyō.

The Peoples Temple was founded by Jim Jones (1931–1978), a native of central Indiana attracted to Marxist teachings and associated with the Methodist Church, which he left because of its alleged anti-black racial practices, from his perspective. In 1955, Jones founded a new church that was named the Peoples Temple. An affiliation with the Disciples of Christ helped Jones get ordained despite no theological education. Within his new church, Jones assumed a prophetic role as he preached racial equality and harmony. It was internal and external conflicts that motivated Jones to move with his church followers to Guyana, South America. Due to pressure from concerned relatives about followers of Jones now in Guyana and unable to contact family in the U.S., an investigation was started by Leo Ryan, a U.S. congressman. After traveling to Guyana, Ryan and three companions were killed by someone within the church on November 18, 1978.

Anticipating a negative response from the U.S. government, Jones called for a revolutionary suicide, an event that the church members practiced in the past in preparation for such a crisis moment. Members drank a concoction of poison, tranquilizers, and Kool-Aid, resulting in the tragic mass suicide and murder of over 900 people, whereas Jones shot himself. The horrific scene of dead church members decomposing in the hot and humid South American climate captured by news crews for broadcast on television sent shock waves and feelings of disgust through viewers and raised questions about how such an event could arise from a religious community apparently committed to social harmony and the well-being of everyone. Outside observers characterized Jones as suffering from paranoia, megalomania, irrationality, and being a psychopath.

A different type of scenario unfolded with the Branch Davidians, although the end result was another tragedy. With its original roots in the Seventh-day Adventist Church, the history of the Branch Davidians was marked by the death of its leaders and continual splitting apart. Victor Houteff (d. 1955) founded the group, and after his death his wife, Florence, assumed leadership of the church. She prophesied God's coming on April 22, 1959. When the event did not occur, followers became disillusioned. Some members left her to join the Branch Davidian Seventh-day Adventists, following Benjamin Roden, whose wife began to have spiritual visions in 1977, which informed her that the Holy Spirit was female, the Messiah would assume a female guise, and that God is actually androgynous. Lois Roden became the leader of her husband's movement after he died in 1978. After another split occurred, mother and son became locked in a political struggle for control of the group.

The 67-year-old Lois Roden came to favor Vernon Howell, a handyman working for her, a situation that raised his status, while the battle with her son, George Roden, continued. In a dramatic attempt to counter her son, Lois named Howell her successor. Howell apparently attracted followers by his keen knowledge of the Bible. After Lois Roden's death, the struggle for leadership between Howell and the son continued, with Howell eventually emerging victorious. In 1987, Howell began to take spiritual wives from among the unmarried women members and later included those women married to followers, an action that called some to leave the movement. Howell concocted a rationale for his behavior a couple of years later, when he claimed that he was the Messiah and the rightful husband for all followers. He further explained he was establishing a new family lineage from his own reproductive powers. The children of this new lineage would eventually rule the world.

Howell changed his name to David Koresh in 1990. The surname recalled a Hebrew word for Cyrus, the ancient Persian King and conquer of the Babylonians. The personal name—David—recalled King David of Jewish history. Koresh explained that he was unlike Jesus because he was a sinful Messiah, whose death could only save humans who died previous to the crucifixion, meaning that Koresh had become the Messiah to save humans who had died after the death of the sinless Jesus. Koresh prophesized that the final age would occur in America. The group prepared for this momentous event by assuming a survivalist perspective and storing large quantities of food, weapons, and fuel. The end time was associated with an attack on the group by the U.S. government. In the meantime, members led an austere lifestyle by avoiding meat, alcohol, caffeine, and tobacco. Members wore simple clothing, did not observe birthdays, and did not watch television.

The Branch Davidians were located near Waco, Texas. Charges of child abuse within the compound led to an investigation by the local child welfare agency. On February 28, 1993, the U.S. Bureau of Alcohol, Tobacco, and Firearms raided the group's compound, leading to the death of four federal agents and five Davidians. After a protracted standoff, FBI agents assaulted the compound, which led to a conflagration and subsequent destruction of the buildings and the death of seventy-four members of the group. This story also captured the attention of the American public because of television coverage and confirmed further the public's negative perception of cults and new religious movements. The tragic end to the Branch Davidians became known simply as "Waco" to the general public.

In contrast to the Branch Davidians and their tragic end, the Order of the Solar Temple represented a wider number of groups led by Jo Di Mambro (1924–1994), who led a movement shaped by esoteric ideas as preparation to entering the Age of Aquarius. Another leader was Luc Jouret (1947–1994), a Belgian homeopathic physician and charismatic speaker. The 1990s witnessed various internal crises and defections that led to legal problems and destabilization of the group. Di Mambro and some followers decided to leave this world for another planet. Over fifty people either committed suicide or were killed in Switzerland in 1994, and other deaths followed in France and in the Canadian province of Quebec.

Similar to Solar Temple, another cult that ended in violence was Heaven's Gate, founded by Marshall H. Applewhite (1931–1997) and Bonnie Lu Nettles (1955–1997), who claimed to be the two witnesses mentioned in the book of Revelation (11). Combining occult and UFO speculation in their message, the founders promised that members would be transported to a new location via a flying saucer. Meanwhile, members should work to perfect themselves. Once taken aboard the spacecraft, perfected members were instructed that they would enter a cocoon-like state. Afterwards, they would be reborn in new bodies. Applewhite altered his thinking from ascending physically to a spiritual exit of the earth. The appearance of the Hale-Bopp comet was interpreted by the leadership of the cult as a sign that the moment had arrived for an exit to the next level of life on another planet. Having seen the sign in the form of the comet, the cult members engaged in a collective suicidal act in 1997, with the expectation that they would be leaving the earth in a spiritual form. The remains of the thirty-nine members were found in a mansion on March 26, 1997, on the periphery of San Diego.

Another example of a cult associated with violence developed in Japan among members of Aum Shinrikyō, founded by Matsumoto Chizuo, a nearly blind person, who adopted the name Shoko Asahara. Before becoming the leader of a cult, he was an ordinary businessman selling Chinese medicines. In addition to practicing yoga to attain powers, he confessed that the Hindu deity Shiva told him to create a perfect society, which motivated him to establish Aum Shinrikyō. His thinking synthesized aspects of Tibetan Buddhism, Hinduism, Christianity, and the prophecies of Nostradamus (1503–1566), a French seer who published a collection of renowned prophecies. Ashara viewed himself as a messianic figure and warned others about a coming Armageddon unless others followed his teachings. Moreover, Asahara justified the use of violence by stating that murder of a protagonist prevents that person from acquiring negative karma. Thus, murder was an act of mercy for both the victim and the perpetrator. Cult members manufactured nerve gas in order to attack the Tokyo subways on March 20, 1995. The attack killed five people and injured over 5,000, leading to the arrest of the culprits and their leader. In the case of Aum Shinrikyō, violence was used to hasten the end of time.

Academic scholars of cults and new religious movements have attempted to make sense of the violence advocated and used by various cults. Looking for common characteristics among the violent cults, the scholars have pointed toward the existence of apocalyptic beliefs. Scholars of these movements have also stressed other similar features, calling attention to the gravitation around a charismatic leader by members, a strong commitment to this leader, an acceptance of such a leader's authority without challenging it, intense internal control of members, and a strong sense of group solidarity. And, finally, the leader and members isolate themselves from other members of the broader society in response to the group's paranoia and subsequent siege mentality, and the movement toward and feeling of isolation is enhanced by perceived persecution.

Religious Experience

Many of the members of these new religious movements and cults were seeking new religious experiences that would give their lives meaning and purpose. And these experiences assumed a variety of modes of experience devoid of doctrine and formal structure. The types of experience include trance, automatisms (e.g., automatic writing), and spontaneous or intentional challenging, which are articulate visions or revelations, whereas articulated revelations assume the form of intuitions, sudden insights into the nature of something, enhanced imagination, and heightened inspirations. These types of experiences tend to pass by the rational ego/self. The self, soul, or mind represents the microcosm that reflects the greater macrocosmic universe, a complex within which supernatural realities are inscribed, rendering nature a symbolic image of the divine.

For many of the New Age movements, the individual self is divine within its essence; it possesses a vast consciousness that it is limited by space and time. The empirical self is metaphorically akin to a transient shadow and is thus not one's genuine self. Humans live alienated from their true identity, which has a spiritual nature. Since God is the universal energy that permeates the universe, humans and all created things participate in God. Whether or not God is a personal deity is not all that important. What is important is to directly experience God oneself. Thus, God is not a reality in which one believes, but rather God is a being that one can experience.

Humans are also evolving spiritually, which represents a process that began before one's birth and will continue after one's death. As humans evolve, they also anticipate a coming New Age, a utopian vision that can take a variety of forms depending on the powers of one's imagination. At the very least, it will be a time and place superior to what humans have now. When the New Age arrives, humans will directly experience it. This expectation suggests the union of occult, gnostic, theosophical, esoteric, romantic, and utopian elements into a grand unity in which evil is an illusion. Once this happens, humans will be self-empowered and spiritual. And they will be able to verify the union themselves because they will be able to personally experience it. This event will be the end of the experience of religion as it has been previously known and practiced for centuries.

Suggestions for Further Reading

Bryant, Edwin F. and Ekstrand L. Eds. *The Hare Krishna Movement: The Postcharismatic Fate of a Religious Transplant.* New York: Columbia University Press, 2004.

Campbell, Bruce F. *Ancient Wisdom Revised: A History of the Theosophical Movement.* Berkeley: University of California Press, 1980.

Faivre, Antonie and Jacob Needleman. Eds. *Modern Esoteric Spirituality.* World Spirituality: An Encyclopedic History of the Religious Quest Volume 21. New York: Crossroad, 1992.

Hanegraaff, Wouter J. *New Age Religion and Western Culture: Esotericism in the Mirror of Secular Thought.* Albany: State University of New York Press, 1998.

Hanegraaff, Wouter J. and Jeffrey J. Kripal. Eds. *Hidden Intercourse: Eros and Sexuality in the History of Western Esotericism*. New York: Fordham University Press, 2014.

Heelas, Paul. *The New Age Movement: The Celebration of the Self and the Sacralization of Modernity*. Oxford: Blackwell Publishing, 1996.

Jenkins, Philip. *Mystics and Messiahs: Cults and New Religions in American History*. New York: Oxford University Press, 2000.

Kripal, Jeffrey J. *Esalen: America and the Religion of No Religion*. Chicago: University of Chicago Press, 2007.

Lewis, James R. Ed. *The Oxford Handbook of New Religious Movements*. New York: Oxford University Press, 2004.

Partridge, Christopher. Ed. *New Religions: A Guide: New Religious Movements, Sects and Alternative Spiritualities*. New York: Oxford University Press, 2004.

Whaling, Frank. *Understanding the Brahma Kumaris*. Edinburgh: Dunedin Academic Press, Inc., 2012.

York, Michael. *The Emerging Network: A Sociology of the New Age and Neo-Pagan Movements*. Lanham, MD: Rowman and Littlefield, 1995.

Persons, Divine Beings, and Texts Index

Subject Index